Human Resources Management for the Hospitality Industry

Second Edition

Human Resources Management for the Hospitality Industry

Second Edition

Mary L. Tanke, Ph.D.
Florida International University

Africa • Australia • Canada • Denmark • Japan • Mexico • New Zealand • Philippines
Puerto Rico • Singapore • Spain • United Kingdom • United States

NOTICE TO THE READER

Publisher does not warrant or guarantee any of the products described herein or perform any independent analysis in connection with any of the product information contained herein. Publisher does not assume, and expressly disclaims, any obligation to obtain and include information other than that provided to it by the manufacturer.

The reader is expressly warned to consider and adopt all safety precautions that might be indicated by the activities herein and to avoid all potential hazards. By following the instructions contained herein, the reader willingly assumes all risks in connection with such instructions.

The Publisher makes no representation or warranties of any kind, including but not limited to, the warranties of fitness for particular purpose or merchantability, nor are any such representations implied with respect to the material set forth herein, and the publisher takes no responsibility with respect to such material. The publisher shall not be liable for any special, consequential, or exemplary damages resulting, in whole or part, from the readers' use of, or reliance upon, this material.

Delmar Staff
Business Unit Director: Susan Simpfenderfer
Executive Editor: Marlene McHugh Pratt
Acquisitions Editor: Erin O'Connor Traylor
Editorial Assistant: Alexis Ferraro
Executive Production Manager: Wendy A. Troeger
Production Editor: Elaine Scull
Executive Marketing Manager: Donna J. Lewis
Channel Managers: Nigar Hale, Eleanor J. Murphy
Cover Design: Elaine Scull

Printed in the United States of America
2 3 4 5 6 7 8 9 10 XXX 06 05 04 03 02 01

For more information, contact Delmar, 3 Columbia Circle, PO Box 15015, Albany, NY 12212-0515; or find us on the World Wide Web at http://www.delmar.com

Library of Congress Cataloging-in-Publication Data
Tanke, Mary L.
Human resources management for the hospitality industry / Mary L.
Tanke. — 2nd ed.
p. cm.
Includes bibliographical references and index.
ISBN 0-8273-7321-X
1. Hospitality industry—personnel management. I. Title.
TX911.3.P4 T36 2000
647.94'068'3—dc21 00-030680

CONTENTS

SECTION 5

SECTION 6

Dedication

With love to Andrew and Michele,
who are my reminders of
what really matters in life.

PREFACE

Human resources management has had a profound impact on the success of hospitality organizations in the past decade. As the service sector continues to grow, traditional work forces continue to shrink, and expectations regarding work continue to change, new human resources skills and practices are required. Human resources management in the hospitality industry is no longer limited to the traditional service functions such as recruitment and selection. To be competitive, managers with human resources responsibilities must be adept at developing an increasingly diverse work force skilled in the new technologies. New work attitudes, employee rights, and other employee concerns must be managed with care and sensitivity. Counseling and interpersonal relations skills, motivational techniques, and major legislative changes have all become increasingly important for successful hospitality managers.

While marketing, operations, and finance have historically dominated the high-level executive positions, human resources expertise became equal in organizational stature during the 1990s. Understanding sound human resources theory and practice will be a requirement for frontline hospitality managers, regardless of the sector of the hospitality industry they choose or the job function they are hired to perform and practice. Human resources practices and principles must be an integral part of a strategic plan that line managers can use in their day-to-day interactions with employees. It is these individuals who seek to accomplish the goals of the hospitality organization through the employees who actually provide the service. Your company's greatest asset *is* its people!

Human Resources Management for the Hospitality Industry was written ten years ago to fill a void and meet a need for a book that specifically addressed human resources issues in the context of the hospitality work environment. When I was asked to teach a course in human resources management in the mid-1980s, I realized that not one textbook existed that was hospitality-industry specific! In the years I have been teaching, I have always found that hospitality students have a greater difficulty assimilating material that is not industry specific. Although there are literally dozens of generic personnel and human resources management textbooks on the market, few deal specifically with the issues of importance to the hospitality industry.

Hospitality and other service-related industries **are** unique and do deserve a book that addresses the entire spectrum of human resources management activities from the perspective of the service sector. The very nature of hospitality and service is people, people, people! The quality of service our guests receive is how our hospitality operations are judged. Our employees are the critical link between the hospitality operation and the guest. It's service that keeps guests returning. Take care of your **people** and they will take care of the guests and everything else takes care of itself.

As service industries continue to grow, there is increasingly more competition for employees. Restaurants and hotels are not only competing among themselves for people to fill their job vacancies, but we also are competing against the local grocery and retail stores. This has been compounded by the reduction of the 16- to 24-year-old age group that has historically been where the hospitality industry has obtained a large proportion of its work force. With a serious labor shortage upon us, a renewed emphasis has been directed towards the recruitment function. Today it is more important than ever that the **right** people are hired into your hospitality organization.

The management of our employees affects the lives, dreams, goals, and ambitions of the individuals we employ and their families. Once quality people have been recruited and hired, the functions of training, development, counseling, discipline, and evaluating performance come into play. These functions revolve around retention and make retaining the right people just as important as hiring the right people. Employee concerns are just as important today as competitive concerns for the manager with human resources responsibilities. Adapting to a diverse work force, being sensitive to employees' needs outside of the workplace, and adjusting to new work attitudes are critical HR skills.

Each chapter of this book focuses on human resources processes and procedures presented as an integrated picture that will assist the reader in both attracting and retaining a quality hospitality work force. Innovative approaches to such human resources functions as development, counseling, team building, coaching, corrective actions, compensation, benefits, and motivational techniques in the hospitality industry have been included. The chapter on employee assistance programs contains a detailed section on AIDS to assist the reader in becoming better educated on this critical issue that is of concern to all management.

The change in demographics has placed a new burden on the hospitality manager with human resources responsibilities in "the next chapter." "The next chapter" will be a reference point throughout the content of this book that was written to alert you to the human resources challenges you face in the new century. Whenever you see the phrase "the next chapter" used, it should serve as a signal that this is an idea or concept that deserves your careful attention. My suggestion is that, as you read through this book, you make a list of these ideas, challenges, and trends. At the book's conclusion you will have a list covering all facets of human resources management that will require your watchful eyes as the new century ages.

WHAT'S NEW IN THE SECOND EDITION?

At the suggestion of readers and reviewers the organization of the text was slightly modified to improve readability and flow of content. Whereas the chapter on Multiculturalism originally was found in the early section of the first edition, it is now Chapter 12. The material and information in Chapter 4 on the labor market and recruitment was almost totally rewritten due to the large impact of this information on human resources management practices today.

The myriad legal changes since the first edition have been added and include the Civil Rights Act of 1991, the Family and Medical Leave Act, the Americans with Disabilities Act, and negligent retention. Current issues critical to human resources management such as literacy, welfare-to-work and school-to-work initiatives, web-based training systems, distance learning, 360-degree performance appraisals, alternative dispute resolution, workplace violence, corrective action, and work-family were added in the appropriate chapters.

The chapter on computer applications was greatly expanded to include the Intranet, Internet, Extranet, and Virtual HR. Internet references and addresses, including a recommended web site section at the end of each chapter, are found throughout the text. These references direct students to the latest on-line resources available. *Please note that Internet resources are of a time-sensitive nature and URL sites and addresses may often be modified or deleted.*

INDUSTRY CONTRIBUTIONS

My years of teaching in hospitality administration programs were preceded by twelve years in operations, primarily in the food service sector, and although I make a conscious effort to stay current on what is happening in the industry, I am not naive enough to believe that the world of hospitality management has not changed in the years since teaching has been my primary occupation. The last thing that I wanted to write was an esoteric, highly theoretical text that had little purpose beyond the classroom lecture, discussions, and testing. To me, the most serious criticism that student can make of a text is that it has no "real world" application or value beyond the classroom. To ensure that this was not a deficit in *Human Resources Management for the Hospitality Industry, Second Edition,* and that this book would emphasize the pragmatic, I went to the hospitality industry for assistance.

Thirteen of the sixteen chapters in this book have specific input from some of today's leading human resources management experts. From presidents, vice presidents, and senior vice presidents of human resources of hospitality companies to representatives of the National Restaurant Association to the Vice President of Employee Development for Burlington Northern Santa Fe, thirteen human resources management representatives served as my advisors on the matter you are about to read. Upon being revised, each chapter was sent to one industry advisor for his or her critique and review. They helped me to identify inaccuracies and clarify theory by providing specific industry-related examples, practical common-sense guides, and hands-on help based upon their own human resources experiences. In the **Industry Experts Speak** portions of each chapter, some of their advice has been highlighted for special consideration. These industry leaders are identified in a special section following this preface. Please take a few minutes to read the abbreviated backgrounds of these industry experts who advised me on the following chapters.

FEATURES OF THE TEXT

To assist the reader in exploring human resources management, each chapter has been preceded by a general discussion of the human resources topic under discussion followed by a list of objectives that you will have accomplished by reading the chapter. At the chapter conclusion, Case Problems have also been included so that the reader may apply the concepts of each chapter to hypothetical industry situations, followed by a list of Key Words. Next, you will find a list of selected Recommended Reading and Recommended Web Sites chosen for those readers who wish to expand upon the human resources management areas broached by this book. Finally, a series of Discussion Questions has been provided to test your understanding of the chapter material.

ACKNOWLEDGMENTS

This text could not have been completed without the friendship, assistance, and support of numerous individuals. Foremost, my deepest gratitude goes to Dr. Lendal Kotschevar whose patience during the first edition endured endless questions pertaining to the writing and preparation of a book manuscript. An author writing her first book could not ask for a better mentor, friend, and colleague.

I am especially thankful for the support and help of my industry advisors, who not only made writing this book an enjoyable experience, but an educational one as well. I know you spent time reading chapter drafts between meetings, early mornings and late nights, while commuting and traveling on business, between opening new restaurants, and at home on weekends when you undoubtedly had more pleasurable things to do. I am indebted to your kindness and willingness to assist me in the preparation of a useful tool for future and present hospitality managers.

And, finally, to all of my students, whose words of encouragement, genuine concern about the progress I was making, and supportive notes slipped under my office door: Thank you, you helped me make what follows a reality.

Welcome to *Human Resources Management for the Hospitality Industry, Second Edition!*

Mary L. Tanke
Miami, Florida
March 2000

About the Author

Mary L. Tanke, PhD is a professor of human resources management in the School of Hospitality Management, Florida International University, Miami, Florida. After receiving her bachelor's degree from Florida International, she later went on to complete her master's and PhD degrees from Purdue University. This is Dr. Tanke's twentieth year of teaching Hospitality Management, which includes two semesters in Switzerland at the Centre International de Glion. She holds an FMP designation from the Educational Foundation of the National Restaurant Association and a CFBE designation from AH&MA's Educational Institute and has been an active participant in the Council on Hotel, Restaurant, and Institution Education where she cochaired the Accreditation Committee. Her work on this committee led to the formation of the Accreditation Commission for Programs in Hospitality Management (ACPHA), which is the specialized accrediting body for programs granting baccalaureate degrees in hospitality management. Dr. Tanke was the founding chair of this committee serving for two consecutive terms. In 1987 she received the Ryder System, Inc., Award of Excellence in Research/Scholarship for her work on accreditation and Multicultural Management, and in 1991 she received the CHRIE Achievement Award for her work in the areas of accreditation and managing diversity in the work force. In addition to this textbook, Dr. Tanke has coauthored a text in bar and beverage management with Dr. Lendal Kotschevar.

In addition to Dr. Tanke's educational background are twelve years of food service industry experience. Starting at Strongbow Turkey Inn in Valparaiso, Indiana, as a busgirl, she worked for several different companies, primarily in the back-of-the-house. Her experience includes working chef at the Alabama Hotel, Winter Park, Florida; cook at Valparaiso University; manager of the student lab-cafeteria at Purdue University; banquet chef at Holiday Inn and assistant to the chef at the Depot, Miami, Florida; and as a food specialist aboard Amtrak.

INDUSTRY ADVISOR BIOGRAPHIES

Mike Hurst . . . Professor, Restaurant Owner, Speaker, Industry Leader . . . enough jobs to keep anyone busy. Currently he serves as Chairman of the National Restaurant Association's Educational Foundation. He is a past Chairman of the National Restaurant Association. Mike currently serves on the Boards of HSI and Bill Knapps, Inc. and as a trustee of The Culinary Institute of America. He was given the first Champion of Education Award by CHRIE in recognition of his services to education.

Ed Evans has spent thirty years in various aspects of the hospitality industry. He has had both general management and staff responsibilities and has been involved in restaurants, lodging, and managed services. His career to date has included significant roles with Saga Food Services, Marriott Corporation, and ARAMARK. Ed earned both his BS in Hotel Administration and his MBA in Organizational Behavior from Cornell University. He is a founding member of ACPHA (The Accreditation Commission for Programs in Hospitality Administration) and a current member of the Cornell University Council. Ed is currently the Senior Vice President of Human Resources for ARAMARK Uniform & Career apparel headquartered in Burbank, California.

Jan Barr began her hospitality career at age 17 as a Hostess with Steak & Ale Restaurant in Knoxville, Tennessee. She worked there to pay for college, graduating from the University of Tennessee with a B.A. degree in communications in 1979. Jan worked for Steak & Ale in Tennessee for three years as a Manager and General Manager, then moved to the corporate headquarters where she founded the training department. She then advanced to Director of Training for New Concepts for Steak & Ale Restaurant Corporation. Jan joined Chili's Grill & Bar in 1989 as a Regional Recruiter. She was promoted to the Director of Recruiting for Chili's in 1992 and Human Resources Director in 1996. Jan is a member of the Society of Human Resources and received her "Senior Human Resource Professional" certification in 1997.

Charles Robert Morrison (Bob) founded Quetico Corporation in 1993 after fifteen years' experience in human resource management. Quetico is a retained executive search firm that focuses on the placement of human resource and finance professionals in all industries and of retail/restaurant professionals in all functions. Before establishing his own firm, Mr. Morrison was Vice President—Human Resources for the international business of Burger King Corporation, and subsequently for the franchise sales & service and real estate organizations. Earlier he served in various capacities, primarily in human resources, with Eckerd Drug, J.C. Penney, and McDonald's. Prior to beginning his business career, Mr. Morrison did a stint as a minor league baseball player. Mr. Morrison is a graduate of St. Olaf College in Northfield, Minnesota. In addition to his international experience at Burger King corporation, Mr. Morrison spent most of his youth as an expatriate in Turkey, Thailand, the Philippines, and Belgium, completing his high school at the International School of Brussels. Mr. Morrison is a member of the Society of Human Resource Management, the American Compensation Association (ACA), the Organization Development Network, and the Human Resource Planning Society (HRPS).

Loret Carbone, Senior Vice President of Human Resources at *Left At Albuquerque*, has more than twenty-five years' experience working with people as a psychologist, human resource specialist, and speaker. She was the first woman partner at *Lettuce Entertain You* and has been a nationally acclaimed consultant and speaker to the restaurant and hospitality industry. Her clients have included: PepsiCo, IHOP, KFC, Hyatt Hotels, and Michael Jordan's Restaurant. Loret was the 1994 National President of the Roundtable for Women in Foodservice and has served on industry boards including Women Foodservice Forum, Women Chefs and Restauranteurs, Purdue University's and San Francisco State's hospitality program boards. She received the Elliot Hospitality Motivator of the Year Award in 1990 and the RWF Pacesetter Award in 1993. Loret has appeared on the Oprah Winfrey Show and on several national radio programs as an expert on restaurant human resources. She has also appeared frequently on Hospitality Television. She writes and contributes to articles for *Restaurant Hospitality, Nation's Restaurant News,* and *Restaurant Business*. Loret received both her undergraduate and master's degrees in psychology from San Jose State University. She is a licensed psychologist in the State of California.

Pam Farr is Senior Vice President, Marriott Lodging for Marriott International Corporation in Washington, D.C. She most recently held the position of Senior Vice President of Human Resources, Marriott Lodging, responsible for the human resources management for 1,500 hotels in fifty-three countries that employ more than 150,000 associates worldwide. She joined the company in 1979 and has previously held the positions of Vice President of Human Resources, Courtyard/Fairfield Inn; Vice President of Human Resources Planning and Development; Director of EEO/Affirmative Action; and Manager of Compensation Systems. Prior to joining Marriott, Ms. Farr worked in the public sector as a Human Resources specialist for a large public school system, handling human relations and organizational development. Ms. Farr is a member of the Board of Trustees of the American Foundation for the Blind and Chairperson for the Executive Education Advisory Council for the University of Maryland School of Business. She holds a B.A. and an M.A. from Barry University and has completed additional studies in human resources management at Cornell University. Ms. Farr resides in Chevy Chase, Maryland, with her two children.

Jeanne Michalski has her PhD in Industrial Organizational Psychology from the University of South Florida in Tampa, Florida. She is currently the Assistant Vice President of Employee Development for the Burlington Northern Santa Fe Railway Company based in Fort Worth, Texas. Her responsibilities include a broad range of human resources programs that support business goals and strategies including recruitment/selection strategies, work force reduction efforts, performance management, training, and organizational development programs. Most recently she held a similar position for the Burlington Northern Railroad. Before joining the railroad industry, Jeanne spent over ten years in the telecommunications industry working with a number of GTE business units, progressing through increasingly responsible human resources positions. She was responsible for a number of employee development efforts that were recognized as "Best Practice" by HR Effectiveness, Inc. and highlighted as "Best in Class" by *HR Executive Magazine* in June 1994 and in 1996 by the Business Roundtable Best Practice research in *How to Build Employee Capability*.

Ronald H. Meliker grew up in the food business with his family's catering business in Baltimore, Maryland. His nonhospitality career included human resources work for Westinghouse and Emery Air Freight Corporation. Ron has over twenty-five years of work experience, exclusively in the human resources arena. He worked for G. Heileman Brewing Company and is currently the Vice President of Human Resources for Sunbelt Beverage Corporation, a national leader of wholesale distribution of wine and spirits to the hospitality industry.

Kathy Roadarmel is a native Nashvillian with undergraduate degrees in social work and psychology from Middle Tennessee State University. After holding several positions within the social work and sociology fields, Kathy began her career in hospitality human resources in 1984. She joined Opryland in 1987 as the Manager of Employee Relations, and since then has held the positions of Human Resources Manager and Director of Human Resources. Kathy is currently serving as Vice President of Human Resources for the Hotels and Attractions Group, which includes the 3,000-room convention hotel, the Springhouse Golf Club, the Inn at Opryland, the General Jackson Showboat, the KOA Campground, the River Taxi's, and the Grand Ole Opry Tours. In this role, Kathy is responsible for Recruiting, Employment, Benefits, Compensation, Employee Relations, Employee Events and Programs, Human Resources Administration, Employee Assistance and Wellness Program, and the Opryland Child Development Center (on-site day care).

Regynald G. Washington is General Manager, Food & Beverage for Epcot at Walt Disney World in Orlando, Florida. His responsibility is to oversee a $168 million food and beverage operation. The operation consists of twelve internationally themed table service restaurants, ten quick service restaurants, twenty-one outdoor food locations, and a multi-million dollar special events and catering organization. He also serves as President and Chief Executive Officer for Washington Enterprises, Inc. Prior to joining the management team at WDW, Regynald was the Corporate Executive Vice President for Concessions International, Inc. in Atlanta, Georgia. Regynald began his professional career in the food services business in 1974, after receiving a B.S. degree in International Hotel and Restaurant Administration at Florida International University. He currently is a member of the Board of Directors of the National Restaurant Association and a member of the Board of Trustees of the Education Foundation of the National Restaurant Association.

Andrew J. Juska has spent over twenty-eight years working in food and beverage operations in the hospitality industry. He has over twenty-two years of operational experience in management. A 1978 graduate of the School of Hospitality Management at Florida International University (FIU), his career has primarily been in the special events and catering arena. In 1990 he was certified by the American Culinary Federation as a Certified Executive Chef (CEC). Andrew now holds the position of Vice President of Operations for the Signature Companies, a large on-premises catering organization with properties in South Florida. He is a frequent guest lecturer and an active alumnus at FIU where he serves as the President of the South Florida Hospitality Alumni Association.

Section 1

Human Resources Planning and Organization

CHAPTER 1

Introduction to Contemporary Human Resources Management

INDUSTRY ADVISOR

MICHAEL HURST, *Chairman, National Restaurant Association's Educational Foundation and Owner 15th Street Fisheries*

"Good timber does not grow with ease; the stronger the wind, the stronger the trees."

—J. WILLARD MARRIOTT

"If you're working in a company that is NOT enthusiastic, energetic, creative, clever, curious, and just plain fun, you've got troubles, serious troubles."

—TOM PETERS

INTRODUCTION

How do you get your **employees**, your people, your **human resources**, to be the best they can be? The best dishwasher, the best front desk clerk, the best bartender, the best bell person, the best prep cook, the best housekeeper? Human resources skills have always been important for the hospitality industry; since the late 1980s human resources has been the single most important set of skills for a manager to have—and will continue to be as far beyond the year 2000 as we can see. You will have to have these skills to stay competitive and survive. That's what this book is about: surviving the enormous new challenges of today's workplace so that you, and your hospitality organization, can stay competitive and be successful. This challenge means that your people skills must be far greater than those of the people competing against you and certainly better than those of the era of the 1970s, 1980s, and 1990s.

How important are human resources management skills to you as you graduate and enter the hospitality work force as a manager? Managing people will be something that you will do every workday. Regardless of the segment of the hospitality industry you choose, the company you plan to work for or start on your own, the job title you are assigned, or the size of the operation you will work in, human resources will affect you and be affected by your actions. We welcome the opportunity to show you, through our own personal experiences in the hospitality industry, how you can be recognized as a great people manager who is both enthusiastic and clever while creating a work environment that is just plain fun!

At the conclusion of this chapter you will be able to:

1. Describe the important historical influences that led to the emphasis on the human resources aspect of management as we know it today.
2. Define human resources management and the functions associated with its actions.
3. Distinguish between personnel skills and human resource skills.
4. Discuss the importance of the role of the manager with human resources responsibilities in the hospitality industry.
5. Explain the people challenges faced by human resources managers in today's hospitality workplace.
6. Explain how certain terminology will be used in the remainder of this text.

DEFINING HUMAN RESOURCES MANAGEMENT

In the hospitality industry all managers are human resources managers, or more appropriately, all managers have responsibilities that include their human resources. Dealing with people is what our business is all about: whether it's our employees or those guests who walk in the front door. When providing services to our guests, our primary resource is our people, our workers, our employees. Being such a labor-intensive industry, you would think that it would be hard to neglect these valuable resources, but oftentimes we do.

Successful hospitality managers need the ability to work with people. We need to develop a people orientation in our management approach. This text is not about management per se but rather about a singularly important skill of management: human resources management. What's the difference, you ask? A manager with human resources responsibilities is first and foremost a manager of people. As a manager with human resources responsibilities, your concern is those people and how their needs, wants, and desires fit into the needs and desires (or rather the organizational goals and objectives) of the hospitality enterprise. We are not talking about your management style or how specifically you manage your people but rather the knowledge and skills it takes to effectively work with, develop, utilize, and coordinate your people resources. It is through effective human resources management skills that your hospitality organization can gain a competitive advantage in today's marketplace. Gaining this advantage is very challenging. It is indeed the challenge YOU face as a manager with human resources responsibilities in today's hospitality industry.

We define **human resources management** as the implementation of the strategies, plans, and programs required to attract, motivate, develop, reward, and retain the best people to meet the organizational goals and operational objectives of the hospitality enterprise.

INDUSTRY EXPERTS SPEAK

Mike Hurst further emphasizes, "The role of management is changing–overmanagement in the past and underled. Hospitality is based on the gift of friendship–nice people who care. With competition intensifying, capital requirements accelerating, and the dilemmas imposed by an expanding industry and shrinking labor force, it has become imperative in a service society for management to shift its focus–*from profit to people* and its style–***from the back door (office) to the front door***."

The activities or ***functions*** required by human resources management are what make up the job duties of the manager with human resources responsibilities. These functions serve to assist the hospitality organization in improving its bottom-line results as well as adapting to the changing workplace (Figure 1-1).

Before reading any further, take out a pencil and piece of paper and write down a list of what you believe are the job duties of a hospitality manager with human resources responsibilities. In other words, just what does a manager with human resources responsibilities do in the course of his or her workday? What does your list look like? Does it include hiring? interviewing? job placement? and what about performance appraisals, discipline, termination, development, orientation, and training? If these are some of the items on your list, you already have a good idea of the job duties that you, as a manager with human resources responsibilities, will need to be able to perform. Table 1-1 lists the numerous functions of human resources management. The best way to view the **human resources functions** is as the job duties of the manager with human resources responsibilities.

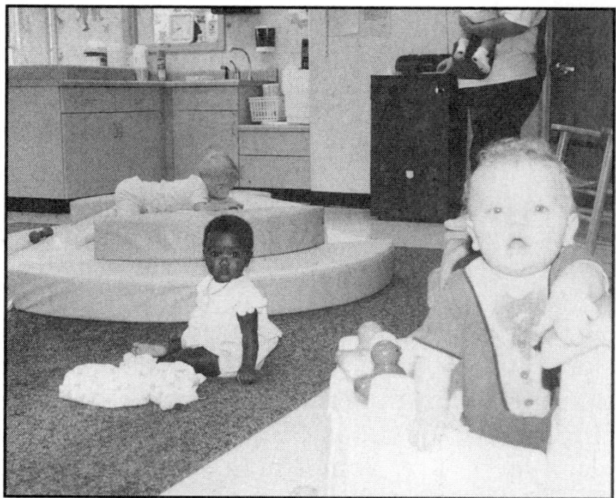

FIGURE 1-1 Providing on-site childcare as a benefit for employees is an example of how human resources functions assist the company in adapting to the changing workplace. *(Courtesy of Opryland Hotels & Attractions)*

TABLE 1-1 Human Resources Management Functions

Planning	Compensation administration
Analysis	Benefits planning and administration
Recruitment	Discipline
Selection	Counseling
Hiring	Termination
Placement	Labor relations
Orientation	Managing diversity
Training	Retention
Development	Information systems
Coaching	Employment law
Teambuilding	Improving work environments
Performance evaluation	
Performance improvement	

You might have noticed that the listing in Table 1-1 corresponds closely to the table of contents for this text. That is not by accident. This book was carefully designed, with the assistance of several industry advisors, to give you a comprehensive overview of the types of activities and programs that make up the field of human resources management in the hospitality industry (Figure 1-2). You will have the opportunity to actually assume, through role-playing, the job of a manager with human resources responsibilities as you read through the following pages.

The human resources department (whether it formally exists or not) plays a critical and increasingly involved role in assisting the hospitality organization in meeting its goals and objectives. Without the presence, involvement, and cooperation of a human resources department (even in an informal structure), the goals and objectives of the hospitality organization are becoming increasingly difficult to reach.

FIGURE 1-2 The hospitality industry provides job opportunities for numerous skill levels. *(Photo A courtesy of Marriott Corporation; Photo B courtesy of Michael Upright; Photo C courtesy of Strongbow Inn, Valparaiso, IN; Photo D courtesy of Stouffer Hotels and Resorts)*

Each chapter discusses one or more human resources function where you will learn about the specific duties of the manager with human resources responsibilities in the implementation of that function. "How to's" and the actual forms being used in the hospitality industry today have been generously supplied by a number of industry advisors. It is our hope that this book will not only be useful during your academic endeavors but also serve as a beneficial guide when you enter the hospitality work force.

Human resources management is a term for what historically was referred to as personnel administration or **personnel management**. In today's arena, human resources managers are sometimes called "people managers," and employees are referred to as "our people" or "our associates." Let us review the major historical contributions to human resources management that have led us to these important changes in terminology.

INDUSTRY EXPERTS SPEAK

Mike Hurst believes "Leaner/flatter organizations are in a position to react faster to change, the very drive towards globalization if not simply multiple level expansion of small units requires a simpler structure than the centralized administration/control behemoth of yesterday. Marketing, accounting, human resource management, purchasing, recipe development—done with limitations on a local basis by a more knowledgeable manager complemented by local specialists give quicker, faster solutions better suited to the dynamic needs of an individual unit in a diverse marketplace. Polling point-of-sale equipment and high-speed data transmission will keep headquarters advised of pertinent data."

HISTORIC CHANGES IN HUMAN RESOURCES MANAGEMENT

The human resources managers of today have earned a place of respect for their contribution to organizational effectiveness. The contemporary role of managers with human resources responsibilities is a critical one to any hospitality organization. Most people spend more than one-third of their waking hours at their jobs, and as a manager of human resources you will make decisions that affect and influence the lives, dreams, goals, and ambitions of these individuals and their families. A look at the historical development of the human resources profession shows that this was not always the situation.

Early Employer-Employee Relationships

Practices related to human resources management can be traced back to the Babylonian Code of Hammurabi around 1800 B.C., which provided for an incentive type of compensation plan as well as a minimum wage. From high school history you recall the institution of slavery, one of the earliest forms of structured employment. When you read the chapter on discipline and learn about "corrective actions," you might recall that one of the reasons for the failure of slavery was the precept of punishment as a motivator. Slaves had no incentive to work harder, and their major achievement was to avoid the whip.

Serfdom followed slavery. This was still an oppressed form of labor since serfs were forced to work for their landowners; however, they fared better than slaves since their income was tied to their productivity. This provided for some of the early forms of incentives.

The guild system, composed of apprentices, journeymen, and master craftsmen, is still used, in part, in the hospitality industry in Europe, and to a lesser degree in the United States. This formed the basis for early training and development systems. Since the guild system also required careful selection of apprentices along with a reward system built on retention, you might say that this was the true beginning of human resources management.

The Early Contributions

Though not specifically concerned with the management of people in the workplace, some of the earlier philosophers, such as Machiavelli, did exhibit a good understanding of how people should be treated. It was in *The Prince* that Machiavelli pointed out that a leader cannot make people love him, but that he can make people respect him. The conclusion, therefore, was that leaders should concentrate on those aspects of human behavior over which they had control and get their people to respect them.

By the mid-1850s, the United States was experiencing its **industrial revolution**, which had already occurred in Europe. Robert Owen, a British businessman, was probably the first individual to study the effects of the work environment on productivity. He implemented his ideas in model villages located next to his cotton mills in Scotland. Some of his ideas included the installation of toilets in his factories, shortening the work day to ten hours, and eventually abolishing child labor from all his operations. Mr. Owen's ideas were quite revolutionary for his day!

Scientific Management

Toward the end of the nineteenth century, **Frederick W. Taylor** began his experiments leading to the birth of **scientific management**. Taylor believed that workers could receive high wages and that management could keep labor costs down by improving productivity.[1] His arguments to treat workers fairly resulted in the elimination of dismissal without cause and the institution of "just cause" as a standard for termination. Though scholars are still not sure of Taylor's motives, the principles of scientific management did take into consideration the welfare of the worker.[2]

It is important for you to keep in mind that working conditions were very bad during the Industrial Revolution. There was no protection from employers who expected their workers to live and work in unsanitary conditions, suffer long work hours, perform their jobs in unsafe environments, and endure great physical fatigue.

Many others picked up Taylor's teachings, and the study of employee productivity became popular. Frank and Lillian Gilbreth, Henry Gantt, Carl Barth, and others spent their lives studying how to maximize output while minimizing input (Figure 1-3). This was the wave of efficiency experts who studied division-of-labor techniques and conducted time-and-motion studies to reduce expending any unnecessary energy when performing a job task. The efforts of these individuals did result in improved training methods, the development of a more appropriate wage system, and pointed out the importance of proper selection procedures. These studies also pointed management towards a more humanistic approach to managing. The idea of making work easier for the worker was instituted as long as it was tied directly to increased productivity and profitability.

FIGURE 1-3 In creating a more productive workplace, efficiency experts also helped make repetitive tasks less physically demanding for employees. *(Courtesy of ARAMARK Corporation)*

It was during this time, preceding World War I, that individuals started to specialize in personnel management. In 1900, for example, the B.F. Goodrich Company started an employment department.[3] Welfare secretaries or social secretaries were hired to deal with matters involving housing, wages, medical, and recreational concerns. The National Cash Register Company, in 1902, established a Labor Department that handled compensation administration, employee grievances, working conditions (one of the first companies to institute a safety function in human resources management), and recordkeeping.[4]

World War I

In 1913, two books were published, first by Hugo Munsterberg and then by Lillian Gilbreth, that dealt specifically with management behavior.[5,6] Munsterberg's work in accident reduction led to the development of the first preemployment selection tests. It was Munsterberg's idea that some people are better suited to certain job positions than are other people, an idea that is still used today to improve the quality of selection and placement decisions. Lillian Gilbreth continued the work of her late husband, which discussed the importance of human factors in the work environment. Taking considerable care in matching the right people to the right jobs has led to vast improvement in job satisfaction and performance, and continued the idea that a more humanistic work environment for employees might be a beneficial concept for any organization.

The need to improve selection and placement decisions during World War I led to further research and test development. Much of this work was conducted by the U.S. Army under the leadership of Robert Yerkes. The committee he headed developed an intelligence test for recruits known as Army Alpha. Later, Army Beta was developed for use in testing illiterate recruits. Army Beta became even more useful after the war in the psychological testing of immigrants who could not speak English.

During the 1920s, companies continued to add personnel departments, and several colleges and universities began to offer courses in personnel management. The areas of specialization at that time emphasized selection and training needs along with employee welfare. Of special concern was employee health and safety. To this day, health and safety concerns continue to fall under the auspices of the human resources department.

The Hawthorne Experiments

The original intent of the Hawthorne studies was to examine the effect of lighting and ventilation on productivity. The results of these historic experiments, however, indicated that the most important factors affecting productivity levels were the concern and interest of management in their workers.[7] These findings have become the basis for the human relations movement. People finally recognized that the individual workers were really important and needed to be treated with a certain amount of consideration.

After World War I, the United States experienced a period of great prosperity during the Roaring Twenties. Personnel policies and departments that were established during the war continued to grow, although personnel management was still not fully accepted by all managers.

The 1930s ushered in the Great Depression. What had been so good in the 1920s was now reversed. It was during this period that the Roosevelt administration passed several pieces of legislation to regulate personnel management practices. The **Social Security Act of 1935** provided for retirement packages, disability and unemployment insurance. The **Fair Labor Standards Act of 1938** established a policy for minimum wage and a maximum length for the workweek. Managers with human resources responsibilities in hospitality organizations today continue to deal with this legislation. (As this book went to press, Congress was again revisiting the issue of raising the minimum wage.) Personnel departments were seen as an unnecessary cost of doing business during this period, and the human resources management function suffered a setback.

World War II

The setback encountered during the Depression was soon to change with the serious labor shortage that resulted during World War II. It is unfortunate, but historically true, that the greatest advances in human resources management were made in the United States during periods of war.

The greatest influx of labor into the workplace was that of women as men were called upon to serve in the armed forces (Figure 1-4). New and more-advanced technologies generated the need for specialized training programs and better methods of using the limited work force that was available. The principles of human engineering were applied to design work spaces and equipment. More-effective ways of teaching large numbers of unskilled people how to use the new equipment led to great advances in training and development, and a government-imposed wage structure led to the development of fringe benefits to attract people to the workplace.

Training programs for managers at the nation's universities and colleges were encouraged by the government. For the first time, courses were offered in personnel administration and office management. By the end of the

FIGURE 1-4 Since World War II, women have played an increasingly important role in the workplace. *(Courtesy of Strongbow Inn, Valparaiso, IN)*

war, training at all skill and responsibility levels was commonplace. The initial development of the computer in the workplace also occurred during this period.

The Forties and Fifties

After the war, the baby boom began that would lead to the abundance of workers in the 1960s, especially for the rapidly growing hospitality industry. New technologies and occupations had been created because of the war. The government required that businesses hire veterans, a practice that is still regulated today. The role of the business schools at universities expanded, with a number of research centers established specifically to study personnel and manpower problems. The interstate highway system was built, which, along with the growth of the automobile industry and the shift from industrial production to service industries, contributed to the rapid expansion of hospitality businesses throughout the United States.

Mike Hurst points out that an increase in leisure time and more disposable income lead to a greater demand for food away from home, and no supply to service it. This was a period of expansion for fast food and the limited menu.

The Sixties and Seventies

The personnel manager came of age during the 1960s and 1970s. The government passed a series of legislative actions that continue to affect human resources management today. These include the Civil Rights Act of 1960, the Work Hours Act of 1962, the Equal Pay Act of 1963, Title VI of the Civil Rights Act of 1964, the Age Discrimination Act of 1967, the Occupational Safety and Health Act of 1970, and the Equal Employment Opportunity Act and Commission.

The **behavioral sciences** influenced training and development with the introduction of sensitivity training and programmed learning. The evolution of the computer assisted the personnel manager with an increasing variety of tasks. Technology began to allow managers to be managers of information as opposed to the oftentimes perceived paper shufflers. With their increasing ability to assist employees in a variety of different areas within the workplace the status of personnel managers within hospitality organizations began to rise.

Personnel functions during the 1960s generally consisted of staffing, training and development, wage and salary administration, labor relations and collective bargaining, and employee benefits and services. The work of the personnel manager was still not widely respected by other managers in the organization. A similar situation was found in the hospitality industry.

The personnel department was seen as a staff function, one that supported the other departments whenever they were in need. Personnel was viewed as an advisory role. The personnel managers could make suggestions and recommendations, but they did not have the authority or power to implement their ideas.

> *The hotel personnel director commonly is responsible for recruiting and screening new employees, checking unemployment insurance claims and doing a variety of odd jobs that just don't seem to fit any other department's domain. As a result, he tends to have a clerical status rather than the professional standing enjoyed by his counterparts in other industries.*[8]

The 1970s expanded the personnel function to include motivational techniques, organizational development, and policy development. Legal issues centered around equal opportunity and affirmative action. For the first time, the role of personnel managers was seen as affecting the outcomes of the organization as a whole, in particular with an impact on the bottom line. Personnel management was now being referred to, upon occasion, as human resources management. This reflected the broadening perspective of this area.

The Eighties

It was during the 1980s that the disparities between the line managers and the human resources managers disappeared as both came to the realization that they shared a commonality of purpose. The human resources department was more than just a place where employees went to be hired or fired. Human resources managers became aware of the needs of their work force and that the satisfaction of those needs was a critical function of their jobs. Human resources responsibilities were seen as a job duty of all frontline managers.

The needs of the hospitality organization also entered into the picture. Selecting human resources that fit into an organization's corporate culture became important. Managers with human resources responsibilities also recognized that it was up to them to make sure that the people they selected had all the tools and knowledge necessary to be successful in their job positions. It was now believed that employees needed work that they found challenging and in keeping with their skills and abilities. Career development was seen not just as a path for management but as a strong retention tool for the hourly employees as well. Job enrichment programs came into the hospitality workplace.

INDUSTRY EXPERTS SPEAK

Mike Hurst, owner of 15th Street Fisheries adds, "The perfect labor cost is zero. Just leave your doors locked and get rid of your customers. That will get it for you instantly! On a more serious note, remember that the greatest compliment we can get in this business is, 'Where do you get the nice people who work here?'"

The Nineties

Human resources managers truly began to see the people in the work force as human resources and not as mere employees. An employee is, after all, a human being first!

This attitude also reflected company acknowledgment that its employees were indeed corporate assets—and valuable ones at that. Although this sounds obvious and matter-of-fact to many of you reading this today, during the late 1980s and early 1990s this idea was considered quite revolutionary! Because employees were now recognized as resources (assets), they were seen as having a value to the organization.

As the 1990s marched on, the labor market tightened. In March 1999 the U.S. unemployment rate was at an astonishing 4.2 percent, its lowest level in twenty-nine years. In ten years, companies went from having as many as 200 applicants for every job to a dozen job opportunities for each job candidate. It became impossible for hospitality companies to find the right people to fill their job openings. Keeping the valuable people they had became a priority, and "retention" was the buzzword of the late 1990s. Employees were offered more benefits than ever before in an effort to recruit and retain them. Everything from stock options to company-provided childcare to job sharing to longer vacations were offered. Signing bonuses, some as high as $500, were the norm in some job markets for servers.

The Americans with Disabilities Act of 1990 required the workplace to "reasonably accommodate" the disabled, both as customers and as employees. The Welfare-Work movement initiated by a 1996 welfare reform measure shifted a large number of former welfare recipients into the work force. The long trend to early retirement ended. Wage increases, the first since the 1970s, spread out among all income levels. The trend to tap into underutilized segments of the population was not unlike the employment period during World War II. When companies did not have enough men to fill their job positions, they hired women. Likewise, the 1990s was a time of labor shortages, so companies looked to hiring more ethnic minorities, the older worker, the disabled, and former welfare recipients.

The 1990s was also a period of globalization and an expansion of technology that had never been seen before. As the composition of the workplace changed, so did the needs and demands. Work-family issues became a priority, benefits were seen as a way to build employee loyalty. Employers struggled with the need to be flexible and with workplace accommodations. "Change" was the word of this decade.

THE ROLE OF THE HUMAN RESOURCES MANAGER

The manager with human resources responsibilities in today's hospitality organization participates in strategic planning sessions, understands financial documents, and can relate the job to the bottom line. In many hospitality organizations the human resources manager is part of the senior management team (Figure 1-5). The reactive stance of fire fighting has been replaced with the proactive stance of anticipating the future needs of the hospitality organization.

The recognition has occurred that the human resources professional role is social as well. The new needs of our work force have required some new responses. The changing

FIGURE 1-5 The human resources manager is often part of the senior management team. *(Courtesy of ARAMARK Corporation)*

demographics of our society have created the need for new programs such as flextime, job sharing, childcare, flexible benefits, and employee counseling. The effects of relocation are being more carefully considered than they have been in the past. The enormous strain that relocation places on the family is sometimes not worth the benefits for either the employee or the hospitality organization.

INDUSTRY EXPERTS SPEAK

Mike Hurst tells us that even with the changing demographics, "Common sense tells us that everyone is different—always have been. Management focused on control treated them as a mass and as long as people conformed, there was not much problem. Enlightened management started to change things and people realized other values could be in the workplace. These values would enhance the guest experience through friendly, sincere performance over time.

"If we can make our work serve the interests of our employees (as opposed to making the employees serve the interest of the workplace), there is no doubt that as they gain some freedoms, accomplish their goals progressively, retain job security while developing skills and knowledge on the job, an enhanced performance results."

The role of the human resources manager is more complex and more important than ever before in the hospitality industry. It is up to us to keep management informed of what their people need and want to be happy, to be productive, and to be loyal. In a study on employee loyalty conducted in 1999 it was found that people were pretty loyal to their employers. The participants pointed out things that companies could do to keep them loyal:

- A recognition by management about the importance of balancing work and personal life
- An opportunity to grow within the organization
- A better explanation of employee benefits
- A feeling that their coworkers have the necessary skills to do their jobs
- A feeling that the company's customers are satisfied[9]

This list is certainly a good place for human resources managers to start in their efforts to improve employee loyalty.

Another critical issue for human resources managers in the hospitality industry is a reduction of turnover and improved retention rates. As you will see in Chapter 4, this begins by recruiting and then hiring the right people for the jobs we have identified as necessary. The cost of replacing a worker is, on average, 1.5 times that person's salary and benefits. Companies are using all sorts of innovative tools to assist them in the selection process. The trend in the 1990s was to job hop. In a study conducted in 1998 a field poll estimated that nearly half of all workers had held their current job less than two years![10] Federal labor statistics indicated in 1999 that 25- to 34-year-olds have held their current jobs for a median of 2.7 years, whereas in 1983 the median was 3 years. With such a tight labor market, many people feel that if a job doesn't work out, they can always find something else—and they probably can.

An added challenge for human resources managers in the twenty-first century is the issue of workplace literacy. The National Alliance of Business and the National Institute for Literacy estimate that employees' lack of basic skills costs American companies $60 billion dollars each year in lost productivity. People who can't read operating instructions can damage costly equipment or, worse, seriously injure themselves or cause workplace accidents. Despite this outrageous figure, in a 1994 survey by the Bureau of Labor Statistics

INDUSTRY EXPERTS SPEAK

Mike Hurst looks at turnover and training in the following way: "When the guest really is at the top of the organizational chart, it would seem that approaching training as a fixed cost—teaching people new things and reminding them of old things as well as teaching new people the basics—puts an organization in the position of hiring superstars at every level, some of which grow beyond you. That growth affords an opportunity to secure the services of someone with even more potential. Thus turnover is not a cost but an investment in an enhanced guest experience.

"Training, retraining, and coaching are a continuing and fixed responsibility of management. Raising the bar in terms of higher expectations stimulates the staff and enhances the guest experience. Mismanagement creating unnecessary turnover is a management problem—to be resolved or eliminated. Leadership is about bringing out the best in people, not abusing them."

only 2.2 percent of U.S. employers provided basic skills training.[11] In this century, there is no excuse for an illiterate work force.

YOUR DUTIES AS A MANAGER WITH HUMAN RESOURCES RESPONSIBILITIES

Having now entered the twenty-first century, hospitality leaders in both academia and the industry face numerous challenges and opportunities in the arena of human resources management. Within the context of this text, as we examine these issues, we ask you to put yourself in the role of a manager with human resources responsibilities. It does not matter what segment of the hospitality industry you select, the size of the operation or its location (Figure 1-6). Envision yourself where you would like to be when you graduate, whether it's with a major hospitality corporation or back in your home town in your family's hospitality enterprise.

We will refer to you, the manager with human resources responsibilities, in an applied context. We recognize that most of you will not actually hold a title of human resources manager when you graduate. In fact most of you, throughout your entire hospitality career, will not hold that title. But as we have stated before, as a manager with human resources responsibilities, human resources management will need to be part of your skills and knowledge base. The human resources manager is an adjunct to all departments.

Perhaps as assistant food and beverage director the only human resources function you perform will be that of training. Or, as a front desk manager you will select, hire, train, evaluate, and be responsible for initiating disciplinary (corrective) actions. As a recruiter for a major hospitality company your human resources function might be limited to recruitment and maybe selection, with someone else in your organization doing the actual hiring and placement functions. If you go back to your family's operation or elect to work for an individual proprietor, then your job will likely include every human resources function that we discuss in this text, along with the job of accountant, marketing director, designer, menu planner, purchaser, to name a few. So no matter if the duties and responsibilities of the human resources manager are a portion of your job or your entire job, it is important for you to begin to think like a manager with human resources responsibilities, and not just as a manager of human resources.

The role of the manager with human resources responsibilities in the hospitality industry is no longer a simple one of filling out paperwork and making sure that the food and

FIGURE 1-6 Service in the hospitality industry is viewed as a positive experience that can lead to a great career. *(Courtesy of Chili's Grill & Bar, Brinker International)*

INDUSTRY EXPERTS SPEAK

The hospitality industry is recognizing the need to emphasize people and human resources functions as vital to the success of their organizations. Mr. Hurst emphasizes, "In our service society, the customer is the focal point of the organization. How to insure that 100% of your guests are made salesmen by your staff is critical. The ten year value of a customer who spends $50.00 a year, sends two friends to your operation who do likewise and repeats this pattern every year is in excess of $1,476,200! A single party of four may be worth more than your whole restaurant. ***Think customers, not dollars!***"

beverage director has a dishwasher for the evening shift. The world of today's hospitality manager is filled with complexities, largely due to changing demographics and increasing legal constraints. These will be pointed out to you throughout this text.

CONCLUSION

You might have noticed that the last chapter of this text is titled "The Next Chapter . . .". In it you will find some ideas about where the industry advisors to this text believe human resources management will be in the year 2010. They have also been kind enough to give you some advice that you can use in your own career development. This advice is based upon their years of industry experience.

In the development of the chapters that follow, it becomes increasingly apparent that "the next chapter" of human resources management must be planned for today (more of that proactive stance mentioned earlier). Therefore, you will find those areas pointed out to you. Even though the specific direction is yet unknown, it is already clear that preparations for "the next chapter" need to be happening now.

Human resources functions such as recruitment, hiring, training, and development used to be considered as solely costs that somehow had to be written off. These programs were often deemed unnecessary expenses in times of financial need. Understaffing, terminations, and minimal training were commonplace. While saving the hospitality operation money in the short run, these practices destroyed morale and motivation. Career development was unheard of.

The attitude we hold about our human resources has changed. In the twenty-first century we no longer consider employee programs as unnecessary expenses. Instead we view these programs, such as training and development, as a necessity to both attract and retain the hospitality enterprise's most costly and valuable assets.

Employees add a unique value to our hospitality organizations because they are *human* beings. Our orientation in human resources management is on those people. The change in terminology from *personnel* to *human resources* is more than mere semantics. It is a significant attempt to recognize human needs and their importance in the organizational structure of the hospitality enterprise. It is with this focus that hospitality can overcome the labor crisis in America.

> *"The young men and women entering business organizations have plenty of skill to do their work, but they fail because they do not know how to get along with people."*
>
> —John B. Watson[12]

Case Problem 1

You have just been hired by a hospitality organization as a manager with human resources responsibilities. Because you want to be sure to make a good impression upon arrival at your new job, you have decided that it would be a good idea to prepare a list of the duties and responsibilities you might be asked to assume in your new position.

To bring some realism to the situation you are about to put yourself into, ***you*** decide which segment of the hospitality industry (either food service or lodging) your new job position is in. It can be either. A suggestion would be to place yourself in the "ideal" hospitality manager's job—one in which you see yourself in the future.

In one or two paragraphs describe the operation in which you will be employed. You should provide enough of a description so that the reader has a feel for the type of operation in which you envision yourself. Next, continue to prepare yourself for your new job position by identifying the human resources functions for which you might be responsible. (During the job interview process, this information was vague and not spelled out specifically.) Now you can prepare the list of job duties and responsibilities.

Next identify four or five challenges that you will have to face in your job as a hospitality manager with human resources responsibilities. Which of these challenges do you personally feel will be the greatest? Why do you think so? Defend your position. Which of the duties and responsibilities that you identified will you enjoy the most? the least? Which of these duties and responsibilities are you most familiar with at the present time?

Key Terms

behavioral sciences
employees
Fair Labor Standards Act of 1938
Hawthorne Experiments
human resources
human resources functions
human resources management
industrial revolution
people management
personnel management
scientific management
Social Security Act of 1935
Taylor, Frederick W.

Recommended Reading

Avery, M. J. "Rising Salaries: Reflect HR's New Role." *HR Magazine.* 1997. www.shrm.org/hrmagazine/articles/1197sal.htm (4 Oct. 1998).

Branch, S., M. Borden, and N. Tarpley. "The 100 Best Companies to Work For in America." *Fortune,* January 11, 1999, p. 118.

Dingman, B. "Four- and Five-Star Hotel GM Survey." *Lodging Magazine.* 1999. www.lodgingmagazine.com/9902/human.htm (7 May 1999).

Epstein, M. Z. and D. G. Epstein. "Hiring Veterans: A Cost-Effective Staffing Solution." *HR Magazine.* 1998. www.shrm.org/hrmagazine/articles/1198epstein.htm (2 May 1999).

Halcrow, A. "We've Listened and Learned." *Workforce Magazine.* 1998. www.workforcemag.com/workforce/listen/index.html (2 May 1999).

———. "Survey Shows HR in Transition." *Workforce Magazine.* 77, 6 (1998): 73–80.

Hayes, J. "Labor Retention Panel: Workers Growing Clout Altering Personnel Strategies." *National Restaurant News* 32, 40 (1998): 76.

Joinson, C. "Moving at the Speed of Dell." *HR Magazine.* 1999. www.shrm.org/hrmagazine/articles/0499dell.htm (2 May 1999).

Judy, R. W. and C. D'Amico. *Workforce 2020.* Indianapolis: Hudson Institute, 1997.

Linnell, L. P. "What's the Price Tag?" *The Richmond Times.* 1999.

Miller, A. "The Millennial Mind Set." *American Demographics.* 1999. www.demographics.com/publications/ad/99_ad/9901_ad/ad990102a.htm (15 Feb. 1999).

National Restaurant Association. "Restaurant Industry: Pocket Factbook." 1999. www.restaurant.org/research/pocket/index.htm (7 May 1999).

Peters, L. H., S. A. Youngblood, and C. R. Greer (eds.). *Human Resources Management.* Blackwell Publishers, Malden, MA, 1997.

Prezioso Linnell, L. "What's the Price Tag?: Cost of Good Employees Varies from Job to Job, Industry to Industry." *The Richmond Times Dispatch.* 1999. www.lexis-nexis.com/more/shrm/19214/4568463/3 (4 May 1999).

Sheridan, M. "Top 400: Difficult Labor." *Restaurant and Institutions,* July 15, 1998.

Recommended Web Sites

1. American Hotel & Motel Association: www.ahma.com/main.htm
2. Educational Foundation: www.edfound.org/home.asp
3. Educational Institute: www.ei-ahma.org
4. *Cornell Hotel & Restaurant Administration Quarterly:* www.hotelschool.cornell.edu/publications/hraq
5. *Restaurant Business:* www.restaurantbiz.com
6. *Restaurants & Institutions:* www.rimag.com
7. Restaurants USAA: www.restaurant.org/RUSA
8. Employment Management Association: www.shrm.org/ema
9. Families and Work Institute: www.familiesandwork.org
10. *Nation's Restaurant News:* www.nrn.com
11. National Organization on Disability: www.nod.org
12. National Restaurant Association: www.restaurant.org
13. U.S. POPClock Projection: www.census.gov/cgi-bin/popclock
14. Work & Family Connection: www.workfamily.com
15. The International Association for Human Resource Management: www.ihrim.org
16. Associations of HR Management: www.ahrm.org

Endnotes

1. Frederick W. Taylor, *The Principles of Scientific Management* (New York: Harper and Brothers, 1911).
2. Sudhir Kakar, *Frederick Taylor: A Study in Personality and Innovation* (Cambridge, MA: The MIT Press, 1970).
3. Henry Eilbirt, "The Development of Personnel Management in the United States," *Business History Review* 33 (Autumn 1959): 345–364.
4. Ibid.
5. Hugo Munsterberg, *Psychology and Industrial Efficiency* (Boston: Houghton Mifflin Co., 1913).
6. Lillian Gilbreth, *The Psychology of Management* (1913 Reprint, Easton, PA: Hive Publishing Company, 1973).
7. Daniel A. Wren, *The Evolution of Management Thought* (New York: The Ronald Press Company, 1972).
8. Gerald W. Lattin, *Modern Hotel Management* (San Francisco: W.H. Freeman and Company, 1966), 98–99.
9. Timothy Burn, "Most U.S. Workers Are Loyal to Their Employers—Up to a Point," *The Washington Times,* 1999. web.lexis-nexis.com/more/shrm/19216/4531537/3 (2 May 1999).
10. Ilana DeBare, "Keeping a Packed Bag at Work; Employees Today Are More Apt to Job Hop Than Ever Before," *The San Francisco Chronicle,* April 30, 1999. web.lexis-nexis.com/more/shrm/19213/4562928/2 (2 May 1999).
11. Scott Hays, "The ABCs of Workplace Literacy," *Workforce* 78 (April, 1999): 70–74.
12. John B. Watson (1878–1958) was both a psychologist and an exponent of behaviorism.

DISCUSSION QUESTIONS

1. Over the past century numerous social, political, and economic factors have changed *personnel* management to *human resources* management. Trace these changes from the Industrial Revolution through the 1990s.
2. Identify the major human resources management functions. Are these common to all hospitality organizations regardless of size? Please explain.
3. Compare the functions of human resources management at the beginning of the twenty-first century with those of the traditional personnel management models.
4. How does the role of the human resources manager change in relationship to the size of the hospitality organization? in relationship to the segment of the hospitality industry you might find yourself working in (lodging or food services)?
5. Describe the current challenges facing you as a manager with human resources responsibilities in the hospitality industry.

CHAPTER 2

Human Resources Planning

INDUSTRY ADVISOR

ED EVANS, *Senior Vice President for Human Resources, ARAMARK Uniform Services*

"All this will not be finished in the first one hundred days. Nor will it be finished in the first one thousand days, nor in the life of this administration, nor even perhaps in our lifetime on this planet. But let us begin."

—JOHN F. KENNEDY

"There is nothing more difficult to take in hand, more perilous to conduct, or more uncertain in its success than to take the lead in the introduction of a new order of things."

—NICCOLO MACHIAVELLI

INTRODUCTION

Planning is a topic that is addressed from many perspectives in hospitality management programs. Nevertheless, the subject of planning and its relationship to human resources management is frequently overlooked. And how can this be? As you will soon learn, it is the planning process that sets the stage for all functions in the human resources arena. It is the purpose of this chapter to assist you, the manager with human resources responsibilities, in integrating the various components of planning and management that you are already familiar with into a logical framework. The sequence of the material in this chapter has been carefully planned to lead you through the stages of planning necessary for effective human resources management. The activities appear in the order you would perform them if you were working in a hospitality operation today.

At the conclusion of this chapter you will be able to:

1. Present a conceptual framework that sequences the stages in the human resources planning process.
2. Define planning within the context of human resources management and the changing environment.
3. Describe why planning is necessary for effective human resources management.
4. Interrelate the various components that make up the human resources planning process.
5. Develop a systematic approach to human resources planning and implementation that can be applied in the hospitality industry.
6. Distinguish between planning, forecasting, and determining objectives.
7. Discuss the role of forecasting in the human resources planning process.
8. Determine operational objectives for human resources management.

WHY PLAN?

Imagine that this is your first day as a manager with human resources responsibilities in the hospitality industry. Perhaps the operation you are in is a fast food restaurant, or a table service restaurant with a high check average. Maybe the operation you are working in is part of the lodging sector of the industry, a property owned and managed by a multinational hotel company, or a single operation owned by your family. The operation you are now a part of might serve 1,000 covers a day or 100, it might have 1,000 rooms or 100 rooms. The size of the operation and scope of services offered are limited only by your imagination.

No matter what the size and scope, you are responsible for the human resource functions of this operation. If your title is manager or director of human resources, your entire job depends upon the people side of the business. If your title is a little more generic, say assistant manager, partner or owner, then your job involves both the production and the people aspects of the business.

Knowing that you are responsible for the people of your hospitality operation, where should you begin? What is the starting place in human resources management? We have already discussed the numerous functions that occur in human resources management. Which one would you pick to begin? What do you do first? If you are like many managers when asked this question you will respond with "hiring." After all, there is very little you can do with respect to orientation, training, development, and compensation until you have hired! Right? Wrong!

If the first thing you do as a manager of human resources is hire, you are just like the production kitchen manager who starts with the designing and construction of the kitchen and then determines the menu. It is not long before the work flow in the kitchen and types of equipment it contains dictate what the production kitchen manager can include on the menu. Courses in production management teach you that the starting place is with the menu. What is a menu? It is a *plan* that provides guidelines for decision making with respect to work flow and equipment needs (Figure 2-1).

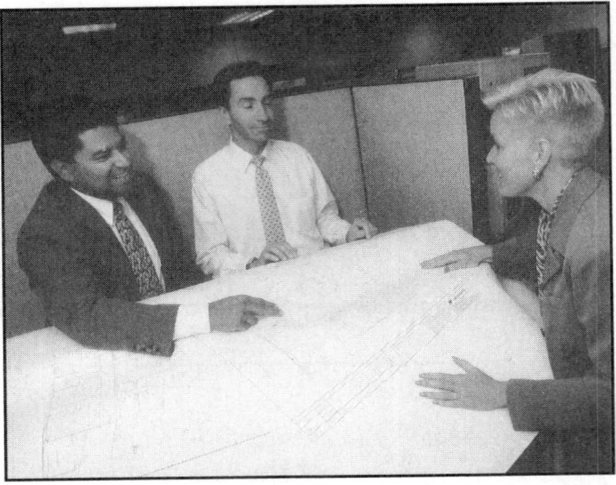

FIGURE 2-1 A plan provides information needed to determine work flow and equipment needs. *(Courtesy of ARAMARK Corporation)*

Just as a good production kitchen manager begins with a plan, so should a good manager with responsibilities for the operation's human

INDUSTRY EXPERTS SPEAK 

"Even the best run operation experiences unexpected events (problems) every day," states Ed Evans. "Without a well thought out, well articulated plan—you and the people who work for you will react rather than respond to these problems. With a plan some of the work has already been done, thus you and your team can focus on the tactics to carry out the PLAN rather than scrambling to develop one. If you don't have a plan at the point you encounter a problem—by the time you come up with one, it probably will be ***too late!***"

resources. The way planning is carried out is largely determined by the way an organization is structured. The types of planning required depend heavily on the situation in which that organization finds itself, and on its particular needs. The need for planning, for example, changes and may be affected by the age of the operation. A new operation may call for more flexibility and centralization in planning, whereas a more established operation may be more formally structured and have a tendency to be increasingly decentralized. As the operation evolves, so does planning. Though planning must always be conducted in light of the situation in which it is going to be used, there are many important reasons why you should begin human resources management with planning.

The Importance of Planning

To begin with, planning increases both effectiveness and efficiency. **Effectiveness** refers to an operation's ability, via its human resources, to accomplish its goals and objectives. **Efficiency** refers to the ability of the systems that are in place to achieve maximum results with minimum input. Planning helps keep an operation on track and moving forward. Without something to guide us, how do we know where we are going, or if we have arrived? Do you remember traveling as a small child in the car on a long trip and asking your parents, "When will we get there?" A frequent response was, "When we get there!" Without planning, managers are like small children in a car: never sure of when they will get there. A plan forces you, the manager with human resources responsibilities, to think about where you want your hospitality operation to go and how you are going to get there (Figure 2-2).

Planning, or more specifically the results of planing—plans—guide the actions of everyone in the operation. From the dishwasher to bell captain to maître d' to front desk clerk, plans

FIGURE 2-2 Without a plan, our people will not have a clear picture of what we want them to do. *(Courtesy of ARAMARK Corporation)*

define both employee and employer expectations. Imagine what chaos would occur if our employees, upon reporting for work each day, did not know what was expected of them! A plan becomes a road map for you and all your human resources to follow as your business develops and grows. Planning can improve productivity and increase human satisfaction.

INDUSTRY EXPERTS SPEAK

"Planning has a profound effect on employee morale–even on retention," states Industry Advisor Ed Evans. "As I mentioned before, even in the best managed operations unexpected things happen. When the unexpected happens in a hospitality operation it usually falls to the hourly employee (or associate) to 'handle it.' If these people that you depend upon cannot depend upon you, their manager, for **LEADERSHIP** they will lose confidence in the professionalism and eventually the viability of your operation.

"If you can show them that the unexpected is nothing more than a chance to utilize the plans you have developed–instead of morale falling it will rise because your staff will see that they can master sudden changes in the operation. You see, with the right plans **NOTHING** is unexpected, it just wasn't expected right now."

Employee morale is also influenced by planning. Morale is extremely important in an environment where people work closely together in a team effort. By the nature of the work in the hospitality industry, our employees work together in decentralized, informal work groups. The dishwashers share a common bond, as do the bellhops, the front desk personnel, the housekeeping staff, the dining room staff in the restaurant, and so on. Being a member of these informal groups means that people share ideas and concerns about the operation they work in and the managers they work for. Have you ever worked for a manager who seems disorganized, who was constantly running around "putting out fires?" The informal work groups in an operation, quick to rally around a manager they have faith in, will rapidly become disillusioned and unmotivated when they begin to wonder: "How did she or he ever get to be a manager? I could do a better job than that." Planning leads to an improved common understanding of operational objectives, which leads to greater cooperation among departmental work groups. Even managers work better together when they know what to expect.

Planning impacts every function in human resources management. For example, planning leads to goal setting, and without goal setting, performance appraisals are not effective. How can managers evaluate how their people contribute to the organization's growth? How do you know whom to hire, or how many people to hire? What should their skill levels be? How much should you pay them?

Planning is the *most* important factor in the continuing success of any hospitality operation. All aspects of management—finance, marketing, sales, production—are planned. Planning is a management function, and to be a good manager of human resources, you need to know how to plan for your accountability in this area.

Human Resources Planning for Hospitality Enterprises

The hospitality industry has been one of the fastest growing segments of the global economy. Throughout the world increasing numbers of dollars are being spent annually for food, beverage, and lodging away from home. In the United States, hospitality is the largest consumer industry. An industry originally comprised of small chains and independent operators has grown into an industry of multiunit, multiconcept, and multinational conglomerates.

With such rapid growth, you may be asking yourself, "How can I afford *not* to plan?" You are absolutely correct in your conclusion: You *cannot* afford not to. Unfortunately, though, many of you can probably think of places where you worked where management failed to plan. What were the common denominators of these operations? Managers who overworked their good employees because they knew they could depend on them in a pinch. Managers always seemed to be in a crisis mode of operation: either overstaffed or understaffed, never having time to train or evaluate your performance. If raises were given, it was because the manager knew who you were. This is what happens in an operation that does not plan, but instead chooses to simply respond to events as they occur (Figure 2-3). Managers seemingly averse to planning choose to rely on intuition, experience, and chance to get them through their day-to-day operating challenges.

> **INDUSTRY EXPERTS SPEAK**
>
> "It is an understatement to say 'you can't afford not to plan.' . . . A more accurate statement is that 'you will ***not*** be allowed ***not*** to plan.'
>
> "Unless you have the financial means to totally self fund your enterprise someone will ask you for your ***PLAN***. Afford is the operative word–anyone who has provided you capital (money, product, people) will want to know how you plan to put them to work generating ***REVENUES, PROFITS***, Return to the Investor(s). . . . If you don't have a plan why would someone risk investing in you? That includes employees, who have more choices than ever of where to invest their time and energies," states Ed Evans.

The human resources plan should be based upon the hospitality organization's strategic business plan. In some organization's the human resources plan will be a separate document; in others it as a component of the business plan. Because hospitality organizations run their business through and with people, each objective of the business plan contains a human element. **Human resources planning** is responsible for determining the human resource contributions as well as the processes and activities required to achieve the goals and objectives of the business plan. Evaluating current human resources policies and practices in light of the business goals and determining which new human resources initiatives are necessary are all part of the human resources planning process. In "the next chapter," one of

FIGURE 2-3 Without a plan, many operations and organizations fail.

the most important aspects of human resources planning will be determining and monitoring the legal requirements for all human resources policies and practices.

Efficient and effective management of human resources requires planning. Achieving the coordination of human resources in a hospitality enterprise is not an easy task. Yet as a manager, your success depends on your ability to achieve results through your people. For your human resources planning to be effective, it must meet the needs of the individuals you hire, the groups they become members of, and the needs of the formal organization. Which of these three needs is *most* important? To sacrifice any one of these needs is to sacrifice all three.

Consider an additional perspective of the hospitality industry. In a service business such as hospitality, the relationships established between employees and customers (your guests) are of supreme importance. More than 50 percent of the people you hire will come into *direct* contact with your customers! Do these employees know what to expect in the performance of their jobs? Without planning, probably not.

The human resources planning process drives what all the people in your operation do. You have to know what positions you need to hire for. If you cannot find individuals with the necessary skills, you will have to train to develop the skills you need in your personnel. Without long-range planning, you would not know whom you needed or what skills were available. You would live day-to-day, fighting fires, working many extra hours, and becoming very frustrated.

Planning human behavior is a skill each of us must master to succeed as a manager. The operations side of hospitality management is certainly easier to plan for than the attitudes, behaviors, temperaments, and whims of our human resources. But this does not mean that planning has no place on the people side of management. Figure 2-4 sketches this perspective of a **hospitality enterprise** for you.

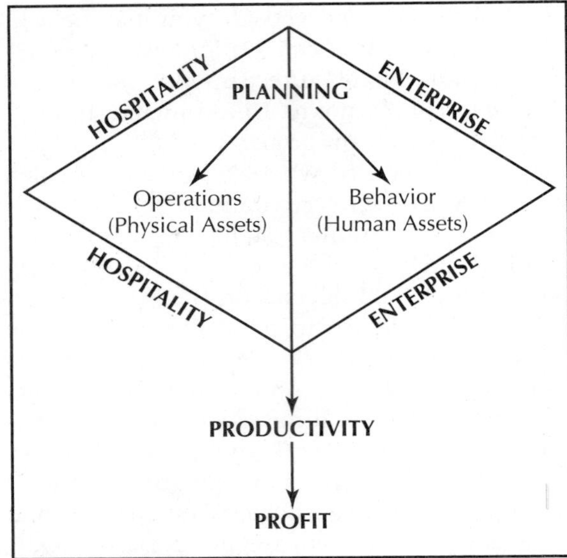

FIGURE 2-4 Conceptual diagram of a hospitality enterprise.

Operations-oriented planning, as shown on the left side of the diamond in Figure 2-4, determines the physical assets. In a food service operation those assets would include, but certainly not be limited to, the menu items to be served; equipment requirements; physical layout of the facility; the china, tableware, glassware, and linens to be used; as well as the purveyors who provide you with the products your plans determined you need.

Behavior-oriented planning, as shown on the right side of the diamond, determines the human assets or resources. This includes influencing what people do, what skills they must have, how long they will perform those skills, upon what basis their performance will be evaluated, and how they will be compensated for their performance in terms of both money and benefits.

Effective human resources planning is a process that can give your operation the competitive advantage over another operation.

INDUSTRY EXPERTS SPEAK

"The difference between good and great operations can often be traced back to the planning process. Obviously, a strong operations based plan must be in place. What we find is that more often than not, a behaviorally based plan is in place.

"For instance, many times when we take over the operation of an existing F & B operation we find good people, a good facility, even good procedures. What we don't always find are assessments of and plans to resolve behavioral issues impacting customer service and satisfaction."

Ed Evans continues with a concrete example, "Style of service changes from back of the house preparation to front of the house (display and cooking). All of a sudden technical (operational) skills are only part of the equation. The interpersonal skills of the employee (the entertainment factor) now play a significant, even primary role.

"Failing to plan for these behavioral interpersonal needs is sure disaster."

Planning takes a good idea (vision) and transforms it into a process with predictable results. Without productivity from our human assets, the physical assets have little chance of achieving profitability. As the available labor pool shrinks, management needs to plan increases, as other operations within the hospitality industry compete for the same people. Human resources planning provides the framework for accomplishing all this and, as you will learn, much more!

WHAT IS PLANNING?

As a manager with human resources responsibilities, you can already see many reasons for becoming more proficient in planning. To do so allows us to direct our future instead of letting the future direct us. So before we do human resources planning, let us first more clearly define what planning is.

Planning has been defined in a variety of ways. D. W. Ewing offers this definition:

> *"A method of guiding managers so that their decisions and actions affect the future of the organization in a consistent and rational manner, and in a way desired by top management."*[1]

J. E. Miller and M. Porter state simply:

> *"Planning means looking ahead to chart the best courses of future action."*[2]

What these definitions indicate is that planning is foremost a process, or series of actions or behaviors. Actions, such as forecasting and decision making require planning to be a continual process because change is continual. Behaviors such as communication and motivation are necessary to produce the desired outcomes.

During the 1990s the term "planning" from a human resources perspective took on a different and more significant meaning. It was no longer enough to think of planning merely as a process of matching supply to demand. The labor supply was dwindling, and the business demand was growing in many markets. In the past, plans were developed and implemented that guaranteed that the right number of people would be available in the right numbers at the right time. Business needs were fairly predictable based upon historical data. Therefore if business increased by 14 percent during the busy season, you would plan a work-force increase of 14 percent.

The drastically changing environment in the 1990s made the planning process much more dynamic than in previous decades. The hospitality industry experiences acquisitions, mergers, new and increasing amounts of employment legislation, diversity, downsizing, and other issues. Look, for a moment, at just some of the facts about the U.S. labor force:

- By the year 2005, 23 million people will have left the work force, and 39 million new employees will have joined.
- By the year 2005, the average age of the work force will be nearly 40.
- The fastest growing work group population will be Asian workers, followed by Hispanics, largely due to immigration and an increase in birth rates of these two groups.
- By the year 2005, women will make up roughly 48 percent of the work force.
- Service work is expected to be one of the fastest growing occupations.
- Two and a half million functionally illiterate Americans enter the work force each year.[3]

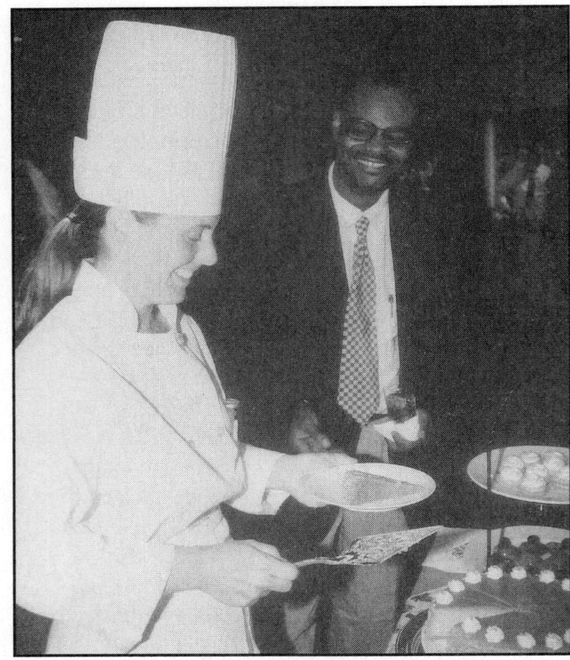

FIGURE 2-5 Every person you hire could have direct contact with your customers. *(Courtesy of ARAMARK Corporation)*

For this book we continue to define **planning** as a process of collecting information that allows hospitality managers to make decisions in order to formulate objectives and determine which actions are most appropriate in achieving those objectives. This definition views planning as a process. It allows managers of human resources to remain flexible, a necessity in a changing environment. The result of planning, the plan itself, is a product of the process. The framework for human resources planning that we now begin to build answers the following questions:

- How many people do you need?
- What kind of people, with respect to skills and abilities, do you need? (Figure 2-5)
- Where will you find the type of people you need?
- How will you keep the people you need and prevent them from being hired away by other companies?

Hospitality managers typically have technical competence, but the exceptional managers who want to grow in both ability and achievement possess planning skills. No longer will you have to operate by hunches and intuition. To plan, you must step back, know the key business issues in your company, understand the impact of the changing external environment surrounding you, consider the long- and short-term human resources implications of change within your organization, forecast the future, anticipate what will be the desired outcomes, and determine how they should be accomplished.

At the beginning of this chapter you were asked to think of a hospitality operation that you might like to work in as a manager with human resources responsibilities. We said that the size and scope of the operation did not matter because the principles of planning we discussed are applicable in any of the situations in which you imagined yourself. There is no one best system that applies in all situations. Hospitality operations differ in their objectives, their complexities, the types and number of services they offer, the external and internal environments they operate in, and the resources they have available to them. Therefore, the degree to which you can implement the approaches and techniques discussed must be evaluated in light of the situation in which you are operating. There is, however, a *systematic process* of human resources planning that is appropriate to all situations in the hospitality industry. If you understand the process by which a human resources system is developed, you can then modify the system to fit your particular situation.

The systematic process we are referring to begins with forecasting, discussed next.

FORECASTING

Planning is not forecasting; however, forecasting is one of the activities that make up the planning process. As Ewing points out,

> *"Equating the two is probably the oldest trap that managers and teachers in business . . . have fallen into."*[4]

It is possible for planning to occur without being involved in forecasting. In human resources planning, forecasting is where the process begins. It is important for you to recognize the distinction between the terms *planning* and *forecasting*.

What Is Forecasting?

Forecasting involves an analysis of the environment to determine what future needs will exist, and what opportunities there will be for us to fill them. On the basis of estimates and predictions, forecasting makes assumptions about the future. Forecasts about the future environment enable you, as a manager with human resources responsibilities, to reach assumptions that provide guidelines for all of your planning activities. Forecasting is concerned with the events that occur in a changing world. It does not matter what size your hospitality operation is because forecasting will continue to play an important role in the effectiveness of management's decision making and ability to perform. The hospitality industry is a volatile enterprise and, as such, we must learn to make forecasts and use them in our planning process.

Forecasting is defined as the task of making educated predictions about the future of the hospitality industry formulated on the basis of data and estimates that better enable us to plan for a changing business environment.

Depending upon your hierarchical position within the company, the scope of your forecasts will vary. As an example, the chief executive officer (CEO) of a corporation may have a mission for the corporation. That mission may be to become the premier hospitality corporation in North America with an annualized x% return to shareholders and an x% annualized growth rate. The vice president of an operating division may have a goal of being the market leader in his or her business(es) with sales growth of x% and an operating profit of y%. The staff members supporting this vice president then put together functional plans to support the mission and organizational goals. If you were a director of human resources, your forecasts would focus on management and hourly people needs and supplies for specific operations and/or geographies. If, on the other hand, you were manager of a specific operation or department, you would focus on forecasting to determine what your unit human resources

INDUSTRY EXPERTS SPEAK

ARAMARK Food and Support Services uses human resources planning in a variety of ways according to Ed Evans. "One of the best examples is through our Bandwidth Gap Analysis form [see Figure 2-6]. Due to the estimated growth and matriculation at ARAMARK, we will need one manager every eight hours, 24-hours a day, to fill our management needs. A forecast of our future management needs becomes extremely important.

"Every region develops a forecast for the amount of managers needed in their region for the end of the current fiscal year and the next fiscal year (Column A). The current number of managers is indicated (Column B), in addition to the candidates who are in line for a promotion (Column C) and managers we hired specifically as benchstrength (Column D). Once the region projects their turnover, whether through termination or promotion (Column E), an amount of currently available managers can be calculated (Column F). Our management need, or Bandwidth Gap Analysis (Columns G and H), can be forecasted, by taking the delta of the number of managers needed (Column A) and the number of currently available managers (Column F).

"By utilizing this as a resource in human resources planning, ARAMARK is able to strategically devise a realistic number of management needs throughout our organization. In doing this, we can better plan our recruitment efforts to meet our needs."

Business Services
BANDWIDTH GAP ANALYSIS
April 1, 1997

Region:

	A		B	C	D	E		F		G	H
	Number of Managers Needed		Number of Current Managers	Number of Candidates for Promotion in Next Lower Bandwidth	Number of Benchstrength (Reserve) Managers	Number of Projected Terminations/ Promotions from Bandwidth		Number of Currently Available Managers (B+C+D - E)		6 MON GAP (A - F)	18 MON GAP (B - F)
Management Bandwidth	END OF FY 1998	END OF FY 1999				(1) NOW - END FY 1998	(2) NOW - END FY 1998	(1) NOW - END FY 1998	(2) NOW - END FY 1999		
2 Multi-Unit Management/ Functional Staff AE 11-14								0	0	0	0
3 Front Line Management AE 09-11								0	0	0	0
4 Front Line Management AE 07-08								0	0	0	0
5 Assistant Front Line Management AE 06 and Below				0				0	0	0	0
TOTALS =	0	0	0	0	0	0	0	0	0	0	0

FIGURE 2-6 Business Services, Bandwidth Gap Analysis. *(Courtesy of ARAMARK Corporation)*

TABLE 2-1 Forecasting Considerations

- Competition
- Demographic Shifts (both customer and work force)
- Economic Environment
- Governmental Policies and Regulations
- Technological Advancements/Changes
- Trend Analysis
- Societal and Cultural Differences
- Services/Products Demand
- Financial Resources
- Turnover
- Management Philosophy/Corporate Culture
- Education of the Work Force
- Unemployment Rate

needs were and then work toward meeting those needs.

There is no one way in which forecasting is applied. The method you select is the one that best meets your needs and your assumptions about the environment in which your unit must operate. In other words, concentrate on the areas of greatest importance by asking yourself, "Which areas will influence our future success in this market?" Table 2-1 is a list of some considerations you must take into account when forecasting. As we will see next, forecasting involves both the forecasting of human resources demands and the forecasting of human resources supplies.

Determining Human Resources Requirements

Human resources forecasts stem from the operational plans of finance, sales, marketing, and production. Predicting the number of employees that you will need to recruit, hire, train, develop, transfer, and promote is based upon operational objectives. These predictions are made for a specific period of time, generally on an annual basis. The methodology for determining your human resources requirements depends on whether you are forecasting management or hourly employee needs.

Demand for employees is based upon a combination of variables that are common to all operations. These variables would include the expected productivity levels, the demand factor for your products and services, projected turnover, and projected growth rates. Entwined with these variables are the financial performance objectives of your organization. In the hospitality industry the process is further complicated by the fact that the variables differ by job category. Turnover rates, for example, change depending on whether you are forecasting management or hourly needs. And among hourly employees, the turnover rate can further vary between dishwashers and waitpersons, between bellpersons and front desk personnel, or between any two other job categories you might like to compare.

Forecasting in the hospitality industry has been handled typically on a qualitative or intuitive, nonstatistical basis. This is predominantly the case when forecasting hourly human resources needs. To quantify this approach, you need to identify the number of employees by job category for a specific period of time. Table 2-2 shows a simplified example of this forecasting approach done on an annual basis. For the purpose of this example, we will assume that the operation is currently fully staffed.

Once the number of employees per job category is identified (through human resources inventories), the percentage of hourly work force per category is calculated. Forecasts made for the upcoming year would use the same percentage breakdowns as a proportion of human resources needed by each job category. Thus, if sales were projected to increase, the proportion of buspersons needed would still represent 10% of the total work force. ***Caution:*** You must be conscious of the fact that these increases

TABLE 2-2 Forecasting Hourly Human Resources Needs

Job Category	Current Year Number of Employees	Percentage of Total Workforce	Projected Year Number of Employees
Waitpersons	48	40%	64
Hostesses	6	5%	8
Buspersons	12	10%	16
Cashiers	6	5%	8
Dishwashers	12	10%	16
Cooks	20	17%	27
Production	16	13%	21
TOTAL	120	100%	160

may not always follow a simple geometric progression based upon volume. In many businesses, thresholds exist that have some absolute range where a set number of employees can handle a set range of customers (e.g., if the minimum number of wait staff is two, they can handle 0–40 customers, as opposed to an absolute number).

Management needs can also be forecasted on both a qualitative and a quantitative basis. Qualitatively, you could estimate your management requirements as a measure of sales volume and company goals. For example, based upon what corporate management feel needs to be accomplished with respect to quality of service, they want to raise the number of managers per operational unit from two to three. Quantitatively then, with a goal of three managers per unit, it is easy to calculate projected management needs for the next several years. Taking into account planned growth, length of training programs, and turnover ratios, you know exactly how many management trainees to hire and when to hire them.

The methods used in forecasting have become more sophisticated in the past decade with respect to objectivity and reliability. The quantitative techniques available do help to increase the accuracy and reliability of predicting human resources requirements.

Forecasting Variables

Forecasting deals with a common set of variables that follow operational lines within an organization. Specifically related to human resources management, manpower planning variables to be forecasted include the following:

- Changing customer's demands
- Product demand
- Labor cost trends
- Availability of labor (unemployment rates)
- Number of employees needed per job category
- Need for additional training
- Turnover per job category
- Absenteeism trends
- Government regulations affecting
  - — labor costs
  - — changes in working hours
  - — changes in retirement age
  - — social security benefits
- Legal conditions of employment
- Unions

Each of these **forecasting variables** must be considered and addressed for the particular environment you are working in to identify the skills and people required at both hourly and management levels (Figure 2-7). Forecasting should be viewed as a tool to improve decision making surrounding human resources requirements, and as the key to achieving organizational objectives in a well-planned hospitality enterprise. Good decision making requires having as much information as possible to make rate predictions about the future.

FIGURE 2-7 Forecasting variables include availability of labor and number of employees needed. *(Courtesy of ARAMARK Corporation)*

The Forecasting Function

The techniques we are discussing are largely necessitated due to increasing competitiveness within the hospitality industry and the shortage of employees. Regardless of the operation size, forecasts play an increasingly important role in the effectiveness of management decision making and performance ability.

Uncertainty is part of forecasting. Your forecasts are only as good as the data and information that goes into their formulation. In hospitality organizations, historical data is typically the basis for forecasting. When historical data is not available, as when you open a new operation, forecasts must rely more on qualitative, rather than quantitative data. Qualitative data includes managerial judgment and good sense, or what may be referred to as subjective estimates. According to Ed Evans, "The secret or trick here is NOT to be bound by your paradigm. Einstein is credited for having said that 'NO problem is ever solved at the same level of understanding that it was created on.' This certainly applies to the HR planning paradigm."

We have identified the following questions as important to ask when forecasting human resources. But remember, the questions *you* must ask are determined by the areas that are critical to your success. What information must you absolutely have in order to continue the planning process? The answer to that question will lead you to developing the appropriate questions for your particular situation.

Here are some suggestions to get you started:

- What is the prevailing hourly wage in your market?
- What is the unemployment rate? In other words, how discriminating can you be?
- Will you have to train employees to achieve the skill levels you require or will you hire them from other organizations?
- What has been the nature of your labor pool in the past?
- What influences will cause the labor pool to change?
- What will the skill levels of the labor pool be in the future?
- How successful have you been at attracting the skill levels you need?
- What effect will new competition in your market area have on the availability of labor?

Forecasts can serve as a valuable management tool when targeted to fit the particular needs of your hospitality operation. Again, there is no one correct approach to forecasting human resources requirements. Approaches differ from company to company, just as demographic considerations vary widely from location to location.

In general, human resources forecasting in the hospitality industry is both **qualitative** and **quantitative**. Many organizations conduct labor productivity studies, and there are numerous, tested quantitative models available to you to assist in forecasting human resources requirements. Examples of statistical procedures used include time-series analysis, regression, and correlation techniques. Just because these quantitative models are not used frequently does not mean they have no value to you; they do. Mastering quantitative forecasting techniques will make you better prepared to face human resources planning. As the hospitality industry continues to grow in sophistication, and computer technology is now found in even the smallest mom-and-pop operations, the use of these quantitative methods has increased. The handling of mass quantities of historical data is as easy as turning on your computer. Hospitality managers in "the next chapter" must be as comfortable with analysis as today's managers are with intuition.

INDUSTRY EXPERTS SPEAK

Ed Evans states, "We have mentioned behavior vs. operations orientated planning earlier in this chapter. We must quantify as many variables as we can in order to effectively plan. There is a point at which the numbers just don't get you there. Have you ever had an experience at a restaurant, or hotel that you knew according to 'the documented procedures and policies' was perfect but you as a guest/customer left feeling less than satisfied? Conversely have you had an experience when you knew things didn't go 'according to the plan' but you had a terrific experience—one that you recommended to others or caused you to return again and again?

"Herein lies the difference between the hospitality industry and the manufacturing or consumer products industries—in hospitality once you have done all the quantitative planning and analysis you have an additional dimension—'the how does it feel' dimension. Too often the mistake we make in hospitality is that we think it is an either/or decision. It's ***not***—it's both.

"To use an over-simplified analogy, quantitatively we must know HAACP/Food sanitation to be sure that in a F & B environment we serve a safe product—that being said we still may lose customers if they don't like it or the environment created for consumption or vice versa if they like the environment but it makes them ill . . ."

THE HUMAN RESOURCES PROCESS

Effective human resources planning refers to identifying and selecting the right person for the right job at the right time. The right person refers to the appropriate qualifications in terms of skills and experience. The right job implies that a careful analysis has been done to determine what the work requires in both mental and physical energies. The right time would indicate some knowledge of projected needs.

Figure 2-8 presents an overall view of the needs-versus-supply analysis through which the human resources process evolves. The human resources process begins with organizational goals and objectives and adds those to the data gathered through your trend forecasts. This determines the human resources requirements for your operation. Next, you need to identify the status of your current work force while also taking into consideration your employees' career goals, and compare that with an inventory of your current human resources skills and numbers. This comparison gives you an analysis of your human resources supply. A gap between your needs and supply, either as a shortage or surplus, indicates that corrective action needs to be initiated by management. As is true with all human resources planning activities, the entire process is governed by budgetary considerations.

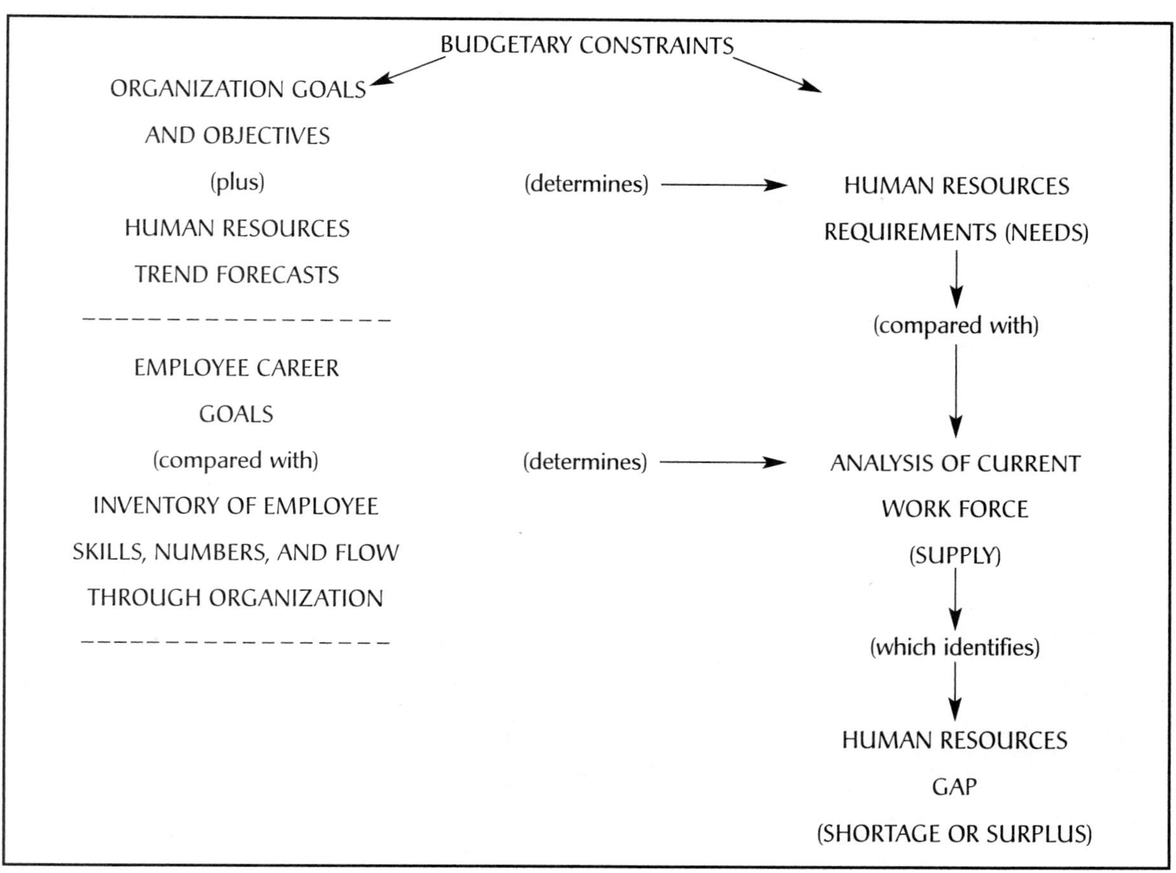

FIGURE 2-8 The human resources process: needs versus supply analysis.

Many of the functions in human resources planning occur simultaneously. When you assume human resources responsibilities in an existing operation, the planning process must occur while products and services are being offered to your customers. You will not have the advantage of having your system planned and in place before the doors open for business. How quickly you will be able to develop your plan will depend largely on how much information about the employees has been kept on a historical basis.

The remainder of this chapter is spent on determining goals and objectives. Chapter 3 studies job analysis and job descriptions along with conducting human resources inventories to identify the gaps between the overall job category requirements (demand) and current supply. Plans developed to close these gaps become the decision-making basis for recruitment, placement, training, and the development of human resources.

Goals and Objectives

Planning stems from both long-range (possibilities of diversification in products and services) and short-range (How many covers do we want to be able to serve tonight?) goals. Long-range goals provide growth, viability, and development; short-range goals keep the operation running day-to-day.

What will our customers' perceived needs be? This is one of the first questions we must ask. We can then, based upon these needs, make decisions that will determine how we can best achieve customer satisfaction, or even better, exceed expectations. And that is why we are in the services business: to make a profit by satisfying customer perceived needs (Figure 2-9).

To begin with, you must keep in mind that the appropriateness of any objective is contingent on the particular situation in which it must be used. Simply stated, objectives specify what an organization or operation desires to accomplish. Much literature has been devoted to the topic of goals and objectives, and each author has selected his or her own interpretation of how to define goals and objectives. For our purposes in this text, **operational objectives** stem from **organizational goals**, which are determined by the **corporate mission** (Figure 2-10). Furthermore, in human resources management we are primarily concerned with the operational objectives of our specific arena. Again, because managers with human resources responsibilities do not operate in a vacuum, all other operational objectives both affect and are affected by what we do.

The corporation's mission statement is fundamental to the business plan. A mission statement sets the overall direction for the corporation. Some companies, such as ARAMARK, develop vision statements (Figure 2-11). The

FIGURE 2-9 Customer satisfaction comes from meeting their needs and exceeding their expectations. *(Courtesy of ARAMARK Corporation)*

FIGURE 2-10 Establishing goals and objectives.

OUR VISION

A company where the best people want to work.

Customers who recommend us to others because we constantly exceed their expectations.

Success measured in the growth of our company, its earnings and ourselves.

The world leader in managed services.

FIGURE 2-11 Our Vision. *(Courtesy of ARAMARK Corporation)*

organization's goals then follow directly from the mission statement. Typically, goals are developed for each of the business areas such as sales and marketing, development and physical plant. ARAMARK uses *Guiding Principles* (Figure 2-12) that each employee is expected to know and follow. Corporations are increasingly integrating their human resources strategies into their overall business strategies. Hence, "in the next chapter" the human resources goals are linked horizontally to the business goals of the entire organization. This more closely connects the human resources plan with the rest of the organization's business plan. What are the organizational goals and how does human resources management fit into those goals? What are the implications for human resources? This then determines the organizational goals for human resources.

Remember that the lower your position in the organizational structure, the more narrow and focused (micro) your objectives become. The higher your position in the organization, the broader your objectives (macro). Each level in the organization must take into account the objectives of its superiors when developing

OUR GUIDING PRINCIPLES

Because we value our relationships,
we treat customers as long-term partners,
and each other with candor and respect.

Because we succeed through performance,
we encourage the entrepreneur in each of us,
and work always to improve our service.

Because we thrive on growth,
we seek new markets and new opportunities,
and we innovate to get and keep customers.

And because we're ARAMARK, we do everything with integrity.

FIGURE 2-12 Our Guilding Principles. *(Courtesy of ARAMARK Corporation)*

objectives for a unit. Though incorporation of the corporate mission follows a top-down path, generally human resources objectives must follow a bottom-up path in planning to effectively support the mission statement.

Do you forecast first or set objectives first? They are related. To say that one must follow the other should not imply some greater importance to one than the other. The operation's success is dependent upon each function in the planning process being effectively carried out, but it is helpful to first set your operational and human resources objectives in order to effectively forecast human resources needs.

Determining Objectives

Objectives are stated in terms of actions or activities. Notice the objectives at the beginning of each chapter in this book. The manner in which they are written always states an action that will occur as the result of your participation in the reading material.

A second characteristic of the operational objectives is that they are specific, meaning that they can assist the hospitality manager in his or her decision-making process (Figure 2-13). Objectives should also state a time frame in which they are to be accomplished. Without a time frame it is up to the hospitality manager responsible for carrying out the objective to determine if it is to be accomplished within this week, this month, this year, or perhaps five years from now. In other words, is this a short-range or long-range objective?

Objectives must also be consistent with each other as well as with organizational goals. This is of particular importance in the hospitality industry where you have several decentralized departments all operating under common organizational goals. The operational objectives of the housekeeping department must complement the operational objectives of the front desk; the operational objectives of the food and beverage department must complement the operational objectives of the sales department; and so on and so forth.

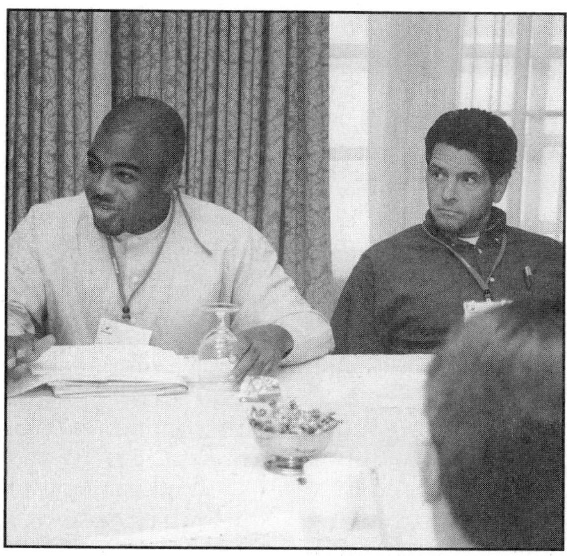

FIGURE 2-13 Sound planning is a critical human resources function in a hospitality organization. *(Courtesy of ARAMARK Corporation)*

Even within departmental units, objectives must be consistent and complementary. If one objective for the food and beverage department is to increase service quality and another is to lower labor costs, they may well be in conflict. Is it possible to increase quality and at the same time lower costs? Can the manager achieve only one of these objectives at the expense of the other? If objectives do not support a common goal but rather create a conflict and a sense of frustration, no matter what objective the manager chooses, he or she is doomed to failure.

Objectives for Human Resources Management

Objectives, for managers with human resources responsibilities, state desired outcomes that provide guidance in attracting personnel within a specific time frame. Objectives can be thought of as expectations with respect to evaluating not only operational performance but human performance (productivity) as well. Objectives for managers with human resources responsibilities are used for defining acceptable performance, determining what kinds of recruitment activities are necessary, reducing turnover (employee satisfaction), and individual development plans for both hourly staff and management.

Remember the earlier example about menu planning? The menu should dictate everything required on the operations side of the hospitality enterprise. Does it? Not always. Should it? Yes. The same analogy can be used in thinking about human resources objectives. The objectives we develop should dictate our human requirements. The number of people currently on the payroll should not form the basis for dictating our human resources needs.

EMPLOYEE HANDBOOKS

The **employee handbook** is a manual that contains information that is useful to the employee. This may include historical information on the company, corporate mission statement, organizational goals, commitment to customer service, along with work rules, procedures, and policies that the employee must follow. The purpose of the handbook is to communicate information that is important and relevant to the employees while at the same time educating them about the hospitality organization. Some hospitality companies have very strong corporate philosophies about certain policies. Often times they will place statements such as these at the front of the handbook:

- We are an equal opportunity employer.
- We enforce a drug free workplace.
- We promote from within when and where possible.
- We provide our customers with the highest service possible.

The purpose of an employee handbook is to pass on valuable information to your employees. You can identify your expectations of them along with what they can expect of you. Identification of your service policy and philosophy is an important component of an employee handbook for a hospitality organization. Tell your employees about your place in the hospitality industry as well as in the local community. Tell them what makes your operation a good place to work. When viewed from this perspective, handbooks can be a helpful positive tool for your valuable human resources, a source of information presented in a consistent way for all who work in your hospitality organization.

However, employee handbooks also carry with them certain obligations and risks. There is a danger that you have created an employment contract with your handbook that could make it difficult to terminate employees. And if you want to change any of the workplace rules or benefit offerings, you may find yourself liable to your employees. With the increase in employment litigation, some employers have found themselves being legally bound in a court of law based on what they wrote in the employee handbook. At other times employers have found that their employee handbook has kept them *out* of court. Because most employee handbooks are intended solely as a useful resource for information, disclaimers are often found as part of the content. At a minimum, make sure that your lawyer reviews your handbook before you give it to your employees. Not all situations can be anticipated, therefore be prepared to modify and revise your handbook when necessary.

Handbooks should be written in a friendly and positive manner, clearly written and well organized. At the same time a certain amount of legal language will be necessary in our litigious society. Disclaimers need to be stated clearly if they are to be effective. At their best the employee manual can and should be a valuable communication tool between employer and employee. It can serve as a excellent guide for the orientation (Chapter 6) of your employees. If care is not taken to have the information reviewed carefully by a lawyer, employee handbooks can backfire on you. Remember to review them regularly and make updates as needed.

INDUSTRY EXPERTS SPEAK

Ed Evans feels that "the impact of the employee handbook is underestimated by many hospitality industry managers. You absolutely must have your handbook reviewed by a legal expert, but not just any legal expert. Select one who is knowledgeable in personnel law and not only in personnel law but federal, state and local since there are inconsistencies among them.

"There is also a double standard to watch out for here. Although you as an employer may be held liable for items contained within your handbook, your employee will not be held liable for following it unless it can be shown that the employee actually received the current version of the handbook (e.g., a dated signature page for the employee file).

"Employee handbooks can range from one page, even one statement (e.g., Nordstrom) to hundreds of pages. Whatever it looks like, make sure that it is accurate in its depiction of your organization and current with regard to your policies, practices and procedures.

"And, oh by the way . . . if you have a diverse workplace, you may want to have it in multiple languages and have made accommodation for functionally illiterate employees."

CONCLUSION

Human resources management objectives identify the continuing results that must be obtained to meet the human resources goals of your organization. Objectives are what you will accomplish through an effective utilization of human resources. Remember that these objectives are based, in part, upon the information you gathered in forecasting, pertaining to costs and availability of labor in the geographic area you will be operating in. Once the goals and objectives are established, action plans are then developed that identify the decisions and activities that must be taken to meet your objectives through implementation. Human resources planning establishes goals and objectives based on the corporation's mission statement. The planning process then outlines the procedures and assigns responsibilities in order to achieve the desired results.

Human resources planning has proven to be one of the most important determinants for an organization to succeed. It is integrally linked to the business plan. When things don't work out the way you expect, then it is time to revisit your original assumptions and if necessary revise the plan.

All human resources functions develop from planning. Planning therefore should not be viewed as a single exercise for analyzing staffing needs but rather as a continuous process. People are the key element in any hospitality enterprise. Planning efforts to better capitalize upon the operation's human resources are critical. The human resources planning function requires that both operational and personnel objectives be combined to meet the goals of the organization. Although human resources functions usually do not include the development of operational objectives, this is one of the numerous occasions where the human resources arena interacts directly with other departments within the organization.

Human resources management cannot and does not act independently of the rest of a successful organization.

As the number of the people available becomes increasingly limited, we need to become better planners, committed to the efficient utilization of those human resources we have. Established objectives, developed through our forecasts, become the focal point for planning all other human resources functions. It is important, then, that the objectives clearly state the results we need the achieve. The results allow us to determine the jobs necessary to achieve the objectives. Hence, the objectives become the basis of our **job analysis** and determine the job categories that are necessary to accomplish the work activities of our organization.

CASE PROBLEM 2-1

Welcome to your new job as the manager with human resources responsibilities for the La Cesta Resort. This beautiful property is located on the west coast of the state of Florida and borders both the Gulf and the Bay. It is a full amenity resort that caters predominantly to upper-middle-class families. The property is halfway through a five-year renovation plan to update the rooms. The two restaurants (one open air casual and the other fine dining) have already been renovated along with the bar/nightclub.

La Cesta Resort has a good name in the state of Florida. It provides nice amenities for its guests. The problem? Other similar properties are doing quite well (with respect to revenue and profit) and you are ***not!*** You have been hired specifically because of your expertise in the area of human resources planning. Develop an HR plan to analyze and address the problem.

The General Manager of La Cesta Resort has asked you to submit a detailed three-page outline of your initial plan by next Tuesday. In addition to providing any other information you feel you should include (based on your HR planning expertise), she has specifically requested you to do the following:

- Develop a mission statement for this property.
- Include a minimum of two organizational goals specific to human resources management.
- Prepare one operational objective for each goal.
- Present a list of six observations you have made about the property based on your initial analysis of the situation.
- Prepare a two paragraph statement defending how your human resources plan will specifically address the problems with respect to revenue and profitability.

Just a reminder that your task is to develop an HR plan to analyze and address the reasons why La Cesta Resort is not doing as well as other similar resorts. Be sure to include any additional information in your initial three-page report that you feel would be appropriate.

Case Problem 2-2

You have decided to become an entrepreneur in the hospitality industry and open your own food service operation or lodging property. Use the hospitality operation that you described in Case Problem 1 to draft an abbreviated three-page human resources plan.

Begin by deciding what items should be included in the framework of your plan. How do you plan for style of service? How do you plan for level of service? What top three variables in human resources management would you have to consider? How many people do you need? What kind of people, with respect to skills and abilities, do you need? Where will you find the type of people you need? Include answers to any other questions you feel would be appropriate as part of this abbreviated HR plan.

Case Problem 2-3

You have inherited the human resources responsibilities for a 200-seat family style restaurant in New Orleans. There is no employee handbook. Would you implement one and why? Develop a three-page outline for the sections that this handbook would contain. Whom would you involve in the development of this handbook? What review steps would you go through?

Key Words

behavior-oriented planning
corporate mission
effectiveness
efficiency
employee handbook
forecasting
forecasting variables
hospitality enterprise
human resources planning
job analysis
operational objectives
operations-oriented planning
organizational goals
planning
qualitative forecasting
quantitative forecasting

Recommended Reading

"Population Demographics." 1998. www.cch.telebase.com/cgi-bin/scribe/mpop.htm/BAOL (26 July 1998).

"Encyclopedia of Associations." 1998. www.secure.telebase.com/cgi-bin/scribe/cch/p/poll4ae.htm/BAOL (26 July 1998).

Bailey, A. D. 1992. "The Quick Way to Produce an Employee Manual." *Restaurant USA* 12(8): 16–18.

The Conference Board. 1996. *HR Executive Review—HR Challenges in Mergers & Acquisitions.* New York: The Conference Board.

de Geus, A. 1994. *The Living Company: Habits for Survival in a Turbulent Business Environment.* Boston: Harvard Business School Publishing.

Galpin, T. 1993. *Making Strategy Work.* San Francisco: Jossey-Bass Publishers.

Harkins, P. J., S. M. Brown, and R. Sullivan. 1995. *Outsourcing and Human Resources: Trends, Models, and Guidelines.* Lexington: LER Press.

Inman, C. and C. Enz, 1996. "Shattering the Myths of the Part-Time Worker." *The Cornell Quarterly* 36(5): 46–54.

Smith, B. J., J. W. Boroski, and G. E. Davis. 1992. "Human Resource Planning." *Human Resource Management* (Spring/Summer): 81–93.

Tulgan, B. 1996. "Common Misconceptions about Generation X." *The Cornell Quarterly* 37(5): 46–54.

Walker, J. W. 1996. "Integrating the Human Resource Function with Business." *Human Resource Planning* 14(2): 59–77.

Walkup, C. 1995. "Companies Vie for Workers as Labor Pool Evaporates." *Nation's Restaurant News* 29(8): 1,4.

Recommended Web Sites

1. Court TV Legal Help: Model Employee Handbook Online: www.courttv.com/legalhelp/business/forms/936.html
2. HR Strategies & Tactics: www.hrstrategy.com/main.htm
3. HR Tools: www.knowledgepoint.com/hr/tool-home.html
4. Policy Handbooks on the Web: www.shrm.org/hrlinks/policy.html
5. EEO/Affirmative Action Policy: www.usm.maine.edu/~hrs/policy/1221.html
6. HR Policy Manual: www.system.missouri.edu/hrs/manual/301.htm
7. Emory University Employee Handbook: www.cc.emory.edu/ITD/HANDBOOK
8. Loyola University Policy and Procedures on Sexual Harrassment: www.luc.edu/infotech/sae/sexual.html
9. HRM Manuals and Handbooks Online: www.nbs.ntu.ac.uk/staff/lyerj/list/hrmh.htm

Endnotes

1. D. W. Ewing, *The Practice of Planning* (New York: Harper and Row, 1968), 17–18.
2. J. E. Miller and M. Porter, *Supervision in the Hospitality Industry* (New York: John Wiley & Sons, 1985): 301.
3. "Charting the Projections: 1992–2005," *Occupational Outlook Quarterly* (Fall 1995): 1–27.
4. Ewing, *The Practice of Planning,* 16.

Discussion Questions

1. Where does the human resources process begin? Why?
2. Describe the importance of planning and the changing environment within the context of human resources management.

3. Why don't we do a better job of human resources planning in the hospitality industry?
4. Human resources planning controls what all people do in your operation. Comment on this statement.
5. What is forecasting? How does it differ from planning?
6. Are hourly and management needs forecasted in the same way? Explain.
7. Identify seven considerations you must take into account when forecasting.
8. Forecasting in hospitality is largely based on historical data kept by the property or operation. What does this historical data consist of?
9. Describe the needs-versus-supply analysis in the human resources process.
10. Discuss the top-down and bottom-up approaches in determining objectives.
11. Explain why operational objectives must be consistent with each other.
12. Describe the importance of goals and objectives in the human resources planning process.

CHAPTER 3

Analysis of the Workplace

"The difference between the right word and a similar word is the difference between lightning and a lightning bug."

—MARK TWAIN

"Making allowances for human imperfections, I do feel that in America the most valuable thing in life is possible; the development of the individual and his creative powers."

—ALBERT EINSTEIN

INTRODUCTION

Planning, forecasting, and the determination of objectives can be thought of as broad or general human resources activities. As we begin our discussion of job analysis, we begin to narrow the scope to the more specific human resources functions. Our interests in this chapter now turn to the nature of the jobs that we need to successfully run our hospitality operations. A careful analysis of these jobs is essential at this stage in the human resources planning process. All other human resources functions that we will be examining in the future depend upon effectively defining jobs. Can you imagine selection, performance appraisals, promotions, training, or even terminations taking place without taking into consideration the jobs that we expect our employees to perform?

The analysis activities that we discuss in this chapter will further help you, the manager with human resources responsibilities, to use your knowledge of organizational goals, operational objectives, and forecasting to close the human resources gap that is created by an imbalance of human resources need and supply. It is the purpose of this chapter to assist you in understanding the procedures involved in analyzing both human resources needs and supply according to job category.

At the conclusion of the chapter you will be able to:

1. Distinguish between job analysis, job description, and job specifications.
2. Use the job inventory approach to determine job tasks.
3. Identify how the results of the job analysis process are used.
4. Determine the job-related information necessary to perform a job analysis.
5. Prepare a job description and job specification.
6. Understand the impact of the Americans with Disabilities Act on the development of job descriptions.
7. Identify the uses of a job description.
8. Describe the importance of job redesign to human resources managers.
9. Conduct a skills inventory assessment.
10. Define succession planning and explain its importance to the strategic human resources planning process.

JOB-RELATED TERMINOLOGY

When we discussed planning in Chapter 2, we identified it as a process. In the same way, we now look at the job analysis process that will assist us in turning the operational objectives we have developed into specific human actions. It is these actions that need to be taken by our employees in order to satisfy the needs and desires of our customers. Even the most creative planning and analysis processes are of no value unless the needs and desires of our customers are satisfied. Contemporary management thought suggests that the sole reason for the existence of a business is to *satisfy the needs of customers*. Some say it is to make a profit, but you can't do that unless you are meeting customer needs. Effectiveness and efficiency are measured not in terms of creativity, but in terms of guest satisfaction. Before we begin to examine the processes involved in job analysis, we must first reach a common understanding of what work is.

Work is the exertion of mental and physical energy to accomplish results. It comes from the Greek word *erchon*, meaning "to do." It is important to note that not all energy accomplishes results that contribute to the goals of the hospitality organization. For our purposes only work leading to results that contribute to the goals of our hospitality organization is considered in the discussions in this chapter. What we are interested in is work that relates to performance. Individuals in the workplace can accomplish results through their own efforts (hourly personnel) or through the efforts of others (supervisory or management). The study of human work involves an improved understanding of how to effectively and efficiently get work done. As such, human work is a legitimate area of study unto itself and has made numerous contributions leading to better solutions in dealing with the human problems in human resources management.

Jobs, in the hospitality industry, are designed for the purpose of either producing products or creating services to meet the needs and desires of our customers. In human work terminology, a **job** is a group of positions that have common tasks and responsibilities. A job revolves around a type of work that needs to be accomplished to meet the operational objectives. A position is the place or slot that is to be occupied by an individual. A **position** exists whether it is vacant or filled, and thereby determines your human resources needs or supply. For example, in most food service operations a job that has common tasks and responsibilities is that of a dishwasher. Depending, however, on the size of the operation, the type of service provided, the amount of chinaware used, and other related factors, the number of dishwasher positions required will vary. Although each dishwasher, once hired, will perform the same job, he or she will each hold a different position within your hospitality enterprise.

In the performance of their work, your dishwashers will have **duties** and **tasks**. A duty refers to a major activity or action required by the job, which may be composed of many tasks. A task may be thought of as a subset of a duty, or more specifically a piece of the work that the duty requires. A duty that your dishwashers might have would be to clean the dish machine at the end of their shift. One task that would be involved in completing this duty would be to drain the water from the machine, another task would be to clean out all the food particles from the machine drains. When studying tasks, the work activities are broken into **elements** that are motions or movement required to complete the task. In draining the water from the dish machine, the employee must bend to open the drain. The bending motion would be one element, the movement of turning the drain valve would be a second element, and standing back up again would be the third element required in just this one task.

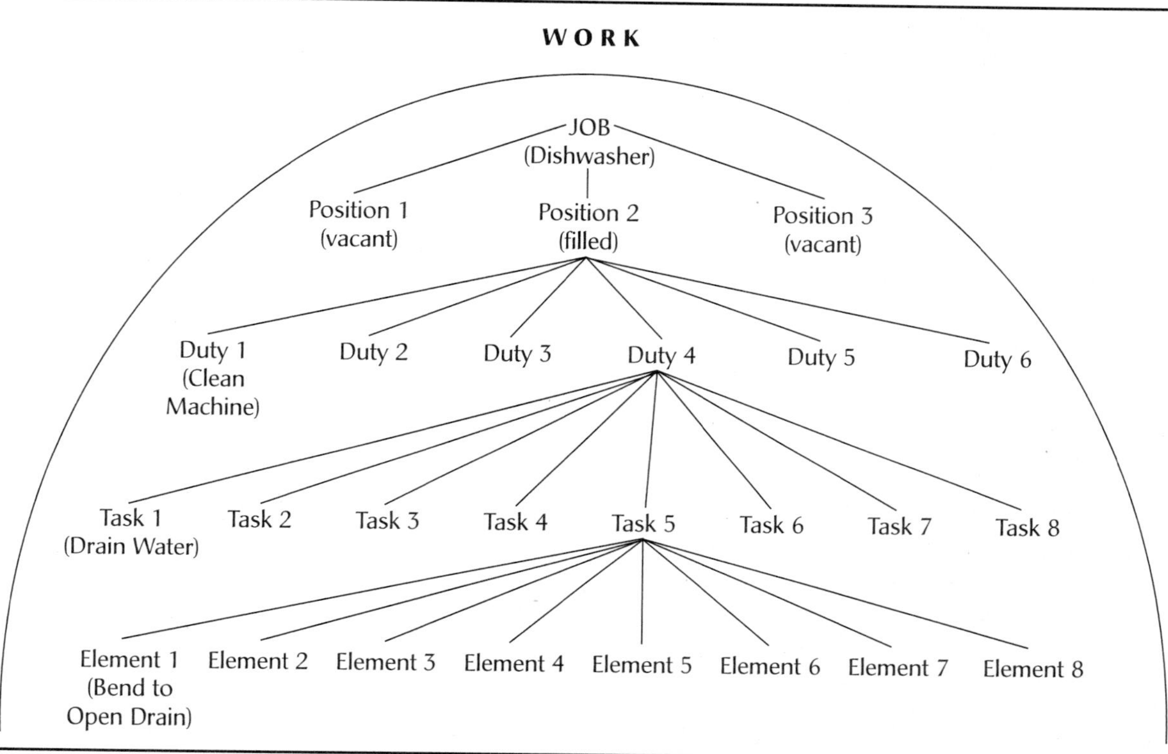

FIGURE 3-1 Diagram of the relationships between job-related terminology.

To clarify the work terminology for you, Figure 3-1 schematically shows these relationships. Elements combined together make up tasks; series of tasks are a duty; a position involves all the tasks and duties required of one individual. A job includes all positions that perform similar work activities. The **occupation** to which your dishwashers and all other employees belong is that of food service workers.

Why It Is Necessary to Describe Jobs

Before developing a job description and specification through the job analysis process, it is important to determine what you are going to use the information for. This determines what information you need to include in the document and, therefore, the data you need to collect during the job analysis. Job descriptions and specifications can be used for many purposes in a hospitality operation. Some of these purposes are:

- recruiting
- selecting
- communicating expectations
- doing performance appraisals
- identifying training needs
- making promotional decisions
- identifying development needs
- determining compensation
- human resources planning

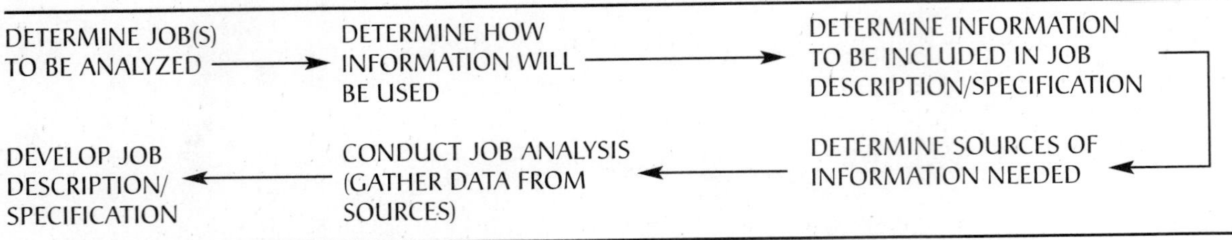

FIGURE 3-2 The job analysis process. *(Courtesy of ARAMARK Corporation)*

Figure 3-2 shows what the analysis process looks like.

THE JOB ANALYSIS

The **job analysis** predicts or indicates the job activities of the people who will eventually be hired to achieve the operational objectives of the hospitality enterprise. There are two different approaches in conducting a job analysis. The one you use will depend on whether you find yourself responsible for the employees in an existing operation or if the operation you will be working for is still in the conceptual or preoperational phase.

The **bottom-up approach** is used most frequently when the organization exists and the basis for your analysis becomes incumbent employee behaviors and the job activities they perform. A bottom-up approach may also be used for a start-up organization by analyzing similar jobs in other organizations. If you are analyzing new and future jobs, the **top-down approach** is used. Because you don't have employees to study and observe, you must analyze the corporate mission statement, organizational goals, and operational objectives to determine what tasks must be performed to achieve the planned objectives. Sometimes you might want to take a top-down approach even when your employees are in place. This will help ensure that people are performing the appropriate tasks and that you are organized and staffed adequately, without making any assumptions. This fresh-start approach—the human resources equivalent to zero-based budgeting—is often used when organization restructuring is being considered.

Where does the job analysis process begin? Before the employees are hired, and before the jobs themselves actually exist. When the job analysis is used before the operation opens its doors to the first guest, the designing of the job is done to maximize its benefit, not only to the hospitality enterprise but also to the future employee.

When employees were plentiful in the 1970s and 1980s, very few owners and operators of hospitality organizations took time to think about how the job would impact or affect the employees they would be hiring. It was not uncommon, for example, to have food service operations that would close between the lunch rush and the dinner hour. Servers were expected to punch out during that period of time, go home, and report back to the operation in time to prepare for the evening customers. Although the designing of a job that includes the idea of a split shift maximizes the benefit to the hospitality operation, we think that you will agree that this does not typically reflect the best interests of your employees. In some situations in some operational locations, this practice might be highly acceptable to both the operation and the employee. But in "the next chapter" you will continue to face a serious shortage of hourly personnel in many geographic locations. In situations where people are difficult to find, jobs will have to be designed to take into consideration the needs of your future employees. This is where you will use the information you gathered previously in your forecasting.

Job analysis determines the content for each job that is needed to meet the operational objectives. Job analysis in the top-down approach defines the nature of the work activities by determining the appropriate tasks that are required by the job rather than by what the people in the job are doing. It asks what tasks need to be accomplished in order that the objectives are met. It does not look at what work the **job incumbent** is (or is not) capable of performing.

In addition to determining the tasks, job analysis also defines the skills necessary to do the work and identifies the time in which the job needs to be completed. Table 3-1 lists the essential job tasks identified through a job analysis. Knowing the work to be done, the skills necessary, and the time frame required, you can outline the employee needs for the future hospitality enterprise. The recruitment program can then be developed based on a solid knowledge base of how many people are needed, what the skill levels will have to be, and a good indication of the training requirements (Figure 3-3). At this point you have identified the number and types of jobs that are needed.

TABLE 3-1 Essential Job Tasks Identified in a Job Analysis

BRINKER INTERNATIONAL
6820 LBJ Freeway
Dallas, TX 75240

Chili's

Products Manufactured or Services Rendered: Chili's is a restaurant that prepares and serves traditional American and Southwestern cuisine. Table service is provided via a food server.

JOB ANALYSIS

Job Title:	Food Server
D.O.T. Number:	906.688-010
Person Contacted:	Debbie Shuey
Title:	Manager
Prepared By:	General Rehabilitation Services, Inc.
Date Prepared:	8/98

Purpose and Nature of Job: The primary purpose of the position of Food Server is to courteously take customer food and beverage orders and serve food order in a timely manner. Also, observes customers to ensure satisfaction with food and service, and recognizes and responds to customer requests promptly. Totals customer bill and handles payment correctly. Maintains assigned food service area and coordinates with other employees to ensure a pleasant and efficient dining experience for customers.

(continued)

TABLE 3-1 Essential Job Tasks Identified in a Job Analysis *(concluded)*

Description of Tasks Performed:

Essential Job Tasks:

1. Courteously greets customers and informs of current food promotions and specials, answers questions and makes suggestions regarding food.
2. Accurately writes food and beverage order (using abbreviations learned in training) on ticket and promptly submits to cook. Uses computer system to ring up food and beverage orders.
3. Retrieves food orders from kitchen and places on food service tray. Places food service tray on "jack" and delivers to customers in a timely manner.
4. Accurately assesses the need for customer assistance.
5. Visually inspects all products in order to ensure all garnishes are added appropriately and all food products are eye appealing as designated.
6. Removes dirty dishes as needed between courses and at end of meal and returns them to the dishwashing area.
7. Utilizes runner/helpers as needed to expedite serving of food orders.
8. Accurately handles payment of food/beverage bill by ensuring charges reflect items ordered and the financial transaction is correct. Operates credit card machine correctly by placing customer card in correct slot and making imprint on sales receipt. Accurately calculates change due to the customer and returns appropriate amount of change in a timely manner.
9. Reports all food and service complaints to manager.
10. Sets up assigned food service area for anticipated business by placing menus, silverware, and beverage coasters on assigned tables.
11. Completes daily side work as assigned by the Manager and outlined on daily side work board. Tasks include:
    a. Wiping off specific counter areas in restaurant, food product accessories, and specific furniture items.
    b. Stocks dinnerware, small ice containers, food products/garnishes, condiments, and various business forms.
    c. Retrieves various food products and dinnerware from appropriate storage area.
12. Identifies vacated tables and promptly informs Host/Hostess.
13. Incorporates all aspects of "sizzle service" training program when serving customers.
14. Performs additional duties as needed or requested by other employees.

JOB RESTRUCTURING OR OTHER REASONABLE ACCOMMODATION IN ORDER TO FULFILL THE ESSENTIAL JOB DUTIES WILL BE MADE ON A CASE BY CASE BASIS AS APPROVED BY MANAGEMENT.

Non-essential Job Tasks: None

Describe Machines, Tools, Work Aids Used:

Tickets for orders, menus, soft drink machines, iced tea container, coffee maker, plastic Lexan tubs, metal containers, utensils for ladeling, microwave oven, plastic pitchers, coffee pots, writing utensils (pen), 10-key calculator, unicard or credit card reader and pad, taco press, shake machines, computer point-of-sale system.

Describe Materials and/or Products Handled:

Food products, glassware, dinnerware, silverware, 36" and 24" round serving trays, small plastic food baskets.

(Courtesy of Chili's Grill & Bar, Brinker International)

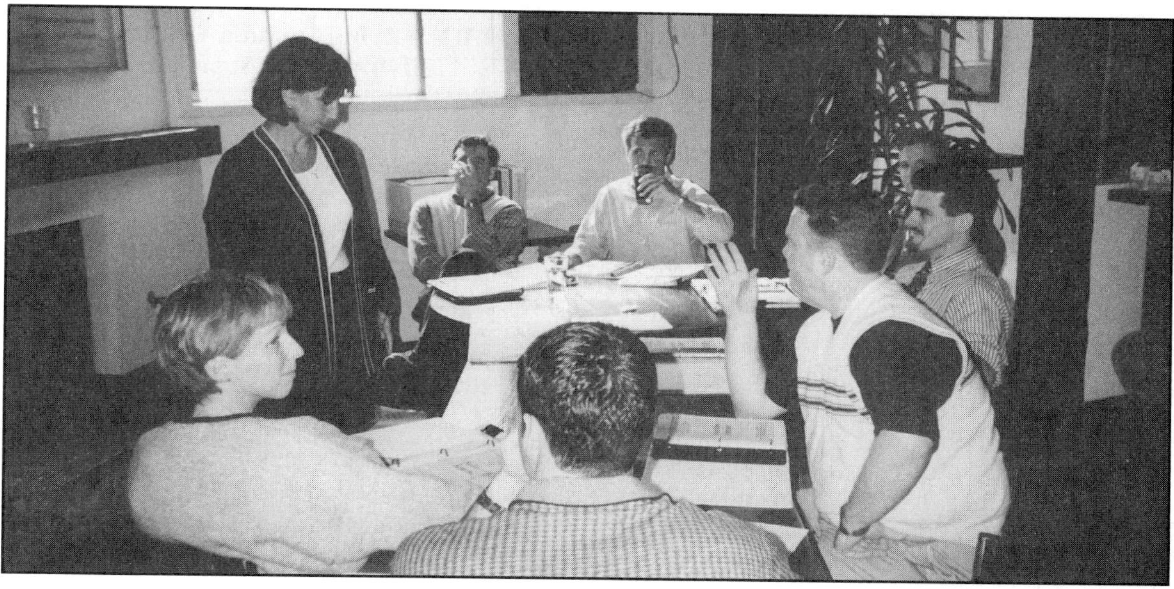

FIGURE 3-3 Job requirements will be matched with applicant qualifications during the employment process. *(Courtesy of Left At Albuquerque, Palo Alto, CA)*

Job analysis can be performed for any job, hourly or management. The top-down approach to job analysis uses the objectives and goals of the hospitality operation to predetermine the jobs that are necessary. Once the jobs are identified, the job duties (along with acceptable performance standards), job tasks, and sequence in which the job activities should be completed are defined.

Now that we have discussed what job analysis is and how the process works when applied to a new hospitality operation, we can more clearly present to you a definition. Job analysis is the process by which job information is obtained so that the job duties and tasks can be determined. It is the job duties and tasks that then define the abilities, knowledge, skills, and responsibilities that are required for successful job performance.

From our earlier example of the dishwasher used in Figure 3-1, we can apply this definition. A job analysis of the job "dishwasher" indicates to us that one of the duties of this job is to clean the dish machine. Furthermore, the job analysis tells us that for the duty of "clean the dish machine" one of the tasks is to drain the water. The next question you must ask yourself is what abilities, knowledge, skills, and responsibilities does a person need to have to "clean the dish machine," the duty, and to "drain the water," the task. You can probably already see how useful this job information is to us in the writing of job descriptions and job specifications.

Job Inventory Approach

The **job inventory** approach is one method of conducting job analysis in hospitality organizations that are doing business. Because you have job incumbents in all, or most, of your job positions, an inventory or audit of all the tasks that comprise their jobs can be collected and organized. This would be an example of the bottom-up approach to job analysis. Job inventories are conducted on-site providing a first-hand account of tasks, the knowledge and skills required for the performance of each task, the time requirements of each task, as well as an identification of where the knowledge and skills were obtained. Did the job incumbent have specialized training or education? Was the training conducted on-the-job or in a classroom setting? What types and how much education does the job incumbent have? One area of particular concern for managers with human resources responsibilities in the hospitality industry is the past experience requirements of the job incumbents. For the majority of hourly personnel in hospitality, it is job experience, rather than the educational background, that qualifies them for and makes them proficient at their jobs.

The job inventory approach is referred to by many different names, including task analysis, task inventories, task identification, and task and skill analysis. Generally, these terms are synonymous in the job analysis literature, but it is always a good idea to compare definitions just to make sure the author is using the terms in a manner consistent with how you want to use them in your own operations. We define job inventory as a method of obtaining **job-related information** through an audit of tasks performed by job incumbents.

The job inventory approach focuses on the performance requirements of the job by listing the relevant job tasks. Care must be taken not to look solely at job titles that can oftentimes be misleading. Although job content is an important component of any job analysis, the job inventory provides detailed objective information about a job or sets of jobs through a study of jobs and work. Table 3-2 is provided to present you with information that is commonly obtained from a job inventory. To get the most use from a job inventory, you should modify this table so that it reflects the specific needs of your operation. Can you think of any other information, based on your past work experiences, that we should have included?

TABLE 3-2 Information Obtained in Job Inventory Approach

The job inventory approach provides an audit of:

- Essential Job Content
  basis for recruitment, training, development
- Basic Educational Qualifications
  basis for selection, placement, development
- Experience Requirements
  basis for selection, placement, training, development
- Required Training
  basis for content and length of training
- Development Patterns
  basis for internal career paths, individual development

Deriving Task Statements

There is no set number of tasks that appear on a job inventory. The number of tasks is completely dependent on the job or set of jobs being inventoried. The first step in conducting a job inventory is to determine the tasks. A **task description** or **statement** of job requirements (what must be accomplished) is a descriptor of the work that is performed in target jobs.

Where does the task statement come from? To write a job task statement, you need a job information base that may be derived in one of several ways, or through a combination of different approaches. One approach is to have either the job incumbent or the supervisor or both identify what they feel is relevant in completion of the job being inventoried. Another method of deriving task statements might involve a content analysis of written job-related documents such as job descriptions, hiring guides, work flow charts, policy manuals, and the like. Oftentimes a job analyst will be hired as a consultant to make observations of job incumbents and supervisors while they work. This observational information is then frequently supplemented with data acquired through individual and group interviews.

A job observation form used to gather job information through the observation method is shown in Figure 3-4. The job analyst would begin by recording the first task in the left-hand column, the second task would be recorded on the same row in the right-hand

Job Incumbent's Title ____________________ Date ____________

Job Title ____________________ Observer's Name ____________

Department ____________________ Page Number ____________

TASK	AMT. OF TIME	TASK	AMT. OF TIME
Align box springs & mattress		Center bed pad so it is flush w/head of mattress	
Spread bottom sheet over bed		Tuck sheet across top of bed	
Miter corners (top)		Place top sheet over bed	
Smooth sheet		Place blanket over bed	
Fold top & cover sheet over top of blanket		Go to opposite site of bed	
Straighten top sheet & blanket		Miter bottom corners	
Tuck sheets & blanket together		Place spread on bed	
Fold top of spread across top sheet		Flip pillows	
Lay pillows on bed		Slide pillowcases over pillow	
Place up spread		Lay pillows beneath spread	
Re-check bed for smoothness		Check telephone	
Wipe clean		Check pad & dialing instructions	

FIGURE 3-4 Job observation form.

column, the third task is recorded in the second row in the left-hand column, the fourth task in the second row in the right-hand column, and so forth. In some jobs, tasks may have a specific sequence, such as cleaning a slicer; in other jobs, sequence may be irrelevant. This form provides the analyst with a detailed flow of the tasks as the job incumbent proceeds from one task to another. Remember that a task is a specific unit of work with a beginning and an end. The analyst can indicate when a duty has been completed by drawing a heavy line at the end of the last task as indicated by the example shown in Figure 3-4. The amount of time required to complete each task can be recorded simultaneously by the job analyst. Job observation forms may be modified to include additional information that you, as the manager with human resources responsibilities, might be interested in for purposes of your specific job analysis (Figure 3-5). One word of caution when using observational methods: Care must be taken to study not the characteristics of the job incumbent but rather the requirements of the job itself.

FIGURE 3-5 The observation method can be used to gather job-related information for your job analysis. *(Photo by Michael Upright)*

TABLE 3-3 Task Statements for Housekeeper (Evening Turndown Job)

- Knock on the door and identify yourself.
- Open door.
- Turn on lights.
- Position cart in front of door.
- Remove dirty ashtrays and dishes.
- Remove loose trash.
- Tidy newspapers.
- Replace used matches.
- Move into bathroom.
- Remove soiled linen to linen bag.
- Wipe down sink, mirrors, and tub.
- Replace used soap.
- Replace soiled linen with fresh linen.
- Remove bedspread and turn down bed.
- Place mint and card on pillow.
- Close drapes.
- Turn on lamp by bed.
- Turn out light by door and close door.

The job information that you have gathered is then used to develop a list of task statements. The actual job task statements are important because the job descriptions that are derived from these statements directly reflect their accuracy and thoroughness. The task should be written in a clear and unambiguous manner, brief, and to the point. Examples of task statements for a housekeeper, evening turndown job, are found in Table 3-3.

The Job Inventory Questionnaire

The list of job tasks that you have identified for each job or set of jobs is then cast in the form of a questionnaire similar to the one shown in Figure 3-6. The job incumbent rates each listed task in terms of how significant, or important, it is in relationship to all the other tasks that need to be performed for that job. The amount of time spent to complete the task is also given.

(1) Task List	(2) Task Performed?	(3) Time Spent	(4) Significance to Job?	Skills Required	(5) Difficulty Level	(6) Supervision Required?

(1) Task List–what is done in job-oriented terms
(2) If task is performed
(3) 5 = Great amount; 4 = Above average; 3 = About average; 2 = Below average; 1 = Small amount
(4) 5 = Most significant aspect; 4 = Major part; 3 = Substantial part; 2 = Minor part; 1 = No part of job
(5) 3 = Hard; 2 = Medium; 1 = Easy
(6) Y = Yes; N = No

FIGURE 3-6 Job inventory questionnaire.

A variety of judgmental responses can also be included on the job inventory questionnaire that will assist us in the development of job descriptions. Such responses might include the skills required, where the job incumbent learned the skills (on-the-job training, brought to the job, trade school, etc.), the level of difficulty of the task, or if supervision or if both of them is required. The answers are coded so that they may be analyzed either manually or by the computer. An interview might have to be done to obtain this information for incumbents in lower-level jobs.

The job inventory method is based on the idea that the basic source of job information is contained in the on-the-job tasks that are performed. The questionnaire is often used as a way to validate what the job analyst has found out in interviews or through observations. The job inventory method of job analysis is used mostly to analyze existing jobs, but it can also be applied to future jobs by using an operation similar to yours, relying on consultants or upon your own experiences to guide you. To assist you with the job analysis process, a listing of job-related information that might be of interest for your hospitality operation is presented in Table 3-4. Job inventories as we have discussed them are limited to manual activities. Tasks pertaining to mental activities and thought processes are much more difficult to identify. As a manager with human resources responsibilities you will find the job inventory approach to job analysis to be an effective way to obtain job-related information from job incumbents.

TABLE 3-4 Job-Related Information

Job analysis should conform to the needs of your operation. The job information listed here is identified to assist you in focusing your job analysis to the area(s) that will help you most.

- Work activities (process and activities)
- Skills involved
- Worker-oriented activities (human behaviors)
- Job demands
- Working conditions (physical and social)
- Equipment, tools, and work aids
- Work performance standards (error rate and time per task)
- Materials used
- Services rendered
- Products made
- Work schedule
- Accountability
- Personal attributes (personality)
- Education and/or training requirements
- Work experience background

Once you have decided what information is most beneficial to you, the items are placed together on the job analysis form.

Other Types of Job Analysis Methods

There are many variations on the specific job analysis methods described so far in this chapter. Safety implications, job satisfaction levels, demographic factors, or all of these may be included on the job inventory questionnaire, depending on the specific needs of your operation, thereby maximizing the amount of information obtained for time spent. Any job analysis method is time-consuming; however, the value of the information, and even the process itself, is worth the investment.

Though job analysis forms and procedures vary, the process itself is common in all job analysis methods. The **critical incident technique** is a method of job analysis that identifies job-related behaviors of incumbents by examining successful (effective) types of behavior or unsuccessful (ineffective) behavior. This can be done through an interview or by observations. The recording of the incident can be made by observers, supervisors, or by the employees themselves. One of the greatest values of the critical incident method is as a performance appraisal tool. For job description purposes, this method provides valuable insight to the human qualities necessary for successful performance in a particular job.

Other sources for information for job analysis include the following:

- Incumbent observations
- Structured or critical incident interviews with job content experts (incumbents, supervisors, those who interact with the job, those who have been in the job previously)
- Work-related documents

- Strategic and business plans, mission statements
- Individuals in similar jobs in other companies
- Questionnaires completed by job content experts and incumbents

The information we have presented on job analysis provides you with a systematic approach to the processes of gathering and analyzing job data. For the job analysis to be of most benefit to you, that is, applicable to your situation, the first determination you must make is what types of job-related information you need in order to achieve your operation's objectives. Then you can select the best method of collecting the necessary job information for your particular work environment.

Job analysis involves collecting and interpreting relevant job data. Although the study and analysis of human work has become more systematic and scientific than a decade ago, the basic outcome of the conventional job analysis has been, and is, the **job description** and **job specification**. The advantages of work simplification, however, can be among the side benefits of a thorough job analysis.

Job analysis is not a complicated procedure, but it is detailed and time-consuming. The importance of the analysis justifies the time. Job analysis can be used for designing new jobs or redesigning existing ones that have been found through job evaluation to be less efficient than what is desired by management, or where tasks have been found to overlap between jobs, creating conflict in the workplace. We predict that in "the next chapter" your role as a manager with human resources responsibilities will highly rely on the information obtained in an accurate job analysis. Especially with the labor shortages, we will have to make jobs more efficient and simplify them so that they can be performed by less skilled or disabled workers.

JOB DESCRIPTIONS

The results of the job analysis are used to develop job descriptions. Job descriptions are in turn used as the basis for preparing job evaluations, recruitment procedures, training requirements, and performance appraisals. Job analysis gives management information about the work that needs to be accomplished to meet operational objectives. Job descriptions tell the employee what job duties need to be accomplished to ensure progressive individual development within the hospitality organization. It is the job description that ultimately becomes the basis for the training plan, as training needs are one of the outcomes. Job descriptions are also called **position descriptions**.

In order to write a good job description, both quantitative and qualitative job-related information is necessary. This is where the task data collected through your job inventories are analyzed. The task inventories have provided you with an indication of how many job incumbents in the same job perform various tasks and how much time they spend on the tasks. The quality of the job description that you develop is very much a direct reflection of the quality of job analysis performed.

Preparing Job Descriptions

It is indeed difficult to run an efficient, profitable operation unless every employee knows what his or her job is. In order for this to occur, management needs to first determine what every employee's job consists of. This sounds like common sense, but think of some of the jobs you might have held in the hospitality industry where you were hired, given a job title (such as bellperson, server, or bartender), and told to perform. As you probably learned in a situation like this, titles rarely are sufficient explanations of the roles and tasks that you and other employees like you actually performed. In some cases, job titles can even be misleading—for example, a dishwasher whose job title is "sanitary engineer."

Once you have collected complete and accurate information about the job, you are ready to prepare the job description. This will include a job summary, detailed duties of the job, and specific job requirements (skills, mental and physical requirements, responsibilities, and job conditions). It is of utmost importance that these be both clear and detailed in order to effectively communicate the standards for good performance (Figure 3-7). A prerequisite to satisfactory performance is a clear understanding by employees of what they are supposed to do, how and when they are suppose to do it, and the results that are expected of them. The hospitality industry is full of people—our human resources—who want to achieve results for themselves and the organizations of which they are a part. Job descriptions better enable them to meet these objectives.

FIGURE 3-7 Job descriptions must be clear and specific. *(Courtesy of Strongbow Inn, Valparaiso, IN)*

We can now define a job description as an accurate, complete statement of the duties and responsibilities required of a specific job. In a very real sense a job description represents a written contract between the employer and the employee. Employees want, and have the right to know, what is expected of them when they report to work each day, and employers have a need and right to know what tasks they can expect will be performed. A written agreement of expectations is likely to lead to a greater understanding and better relationship between management and employees.

At this point you know that job descriptions are derived from the information obtained and analyzed in the job analysis process. You also know that job descriptions are written for the job incumbent as well as for use by management. More examples of how management uses job descriptions are presented later in this chapter.

By identifying the "what," the "how," and the "why" of each job, within the composition of each job description, you will be sure to include all relevant job-related information. The "what" is both the physical and mental activities required to do the job. Physical tasks in a hospitality operation might include such activities as transporting material, cutting, cleaning, delivering, kneading, portioning, folding, wiping, sanitizing, and measuring. Mental activities might include planning, judging, directing, and organizing. The "what" can be taken from your job inventory, although tasks may need to be rewritten so that the description reads clearly and smoothly. Table 3-5 identifies sample questions that will assist you in developing job descriptions for your own operation.

The "how" includes all the procedures, processes, and methods used to do the "what," and again can be divided into both physical and mental actions. Operating machinery, following standardized recipe procedures, and using

TABLE 3-5 Questions to Ask When Developing Job Descriptions

WHAT the employee does:

- What are the tasks performed by the job incumbent?
- What is the frequency with which the tasks are done?
- What is the difficulty of the task as compared with all the tasks done?
- What tasks exist that have not been identified?

HOW the employee performs the job:

- Which tools and equipment are required to perform the job?
- Which materials will the job incumbent need?
- Which processes and procedures are required?

WHY the employee does the job:

- Why does this job exist?

work simplification methods in routine activities are physical in nature, whereas a mental action would be making calculations to increase or decrease recipe amounts. The "why" is simply the basic purpose of the job. It can be found in the job summary, sometimes stated in the form of a job objective.

The actual job description can be very detailed or very brief, depending on the size and the needs of the organization in which it is used. The writing style should be direct and terse, not wordy, and written in the present tense. Typically, the language is easily understandable. The listing of job duties is behaviorally based with each sentence beginning with an action verb. The arrangement of job descriptions is not entirely rigid. With relatively simple jobs a chronological order can be used. For a job such as that of a busperson or bellperson, the description can be arranged according to the general order in which the tasks occur. Job descriptions prepared for supervisory and management employees require more planning and generalizing with fewer specifics and mechanics.

Whichever format you decide to use, there are certain items essential for a good job description. To start with, there must be an accurate title, one that is descriptive of the work. The title of the immediate supervisor is included, along with a job summary. The job summary is a brief statement that sets forth the purpose of the job. Next comes a list of not only the duties but also the responsibilities of the job. These can be determined by referring to the job inventory analysis. It is often wise at the conclusion of job duties and responsibilities to state "may be called upon at times to perform other related tasks not specifically included in this description." Proper relationships with others in the organization is an important component so that the job incumbent understands the position his or her job plays in the success of day-to-day operations. Table 3-6 is an example of a position description used by Left At Albuquerque.

ADA Considerations

The Americans with Disabilities Act (ADA), under Title I, protects both job applicants and employees who have disabilities from discrimination provided that they are able to perform the essential job functions either with or without reasonable accommodation. We discuss the ADA at length in Chapter 4, but at this time we need to be aware of its effect on the job analysis process as well as in the design of our job descriptions and job specifications.

The Americans with Disabilities Act does not require job analysis nor does it require formal job descriptions. However, for a hospitality organization to comply with this standard, it is critical that they accurately define the essential functions of each job position. If you have been following the guidelines and process we have discussed so far in this chapter, you have

TABLE 3-6 ***Left At Albuquerque*** **Job Description: Line Cook (Grill)**

I. Reporting Relationships
Reports to: Executive Chef and Sous Chefs
Subordinates: None

II. Basic Function
To produce food items from the grill station that maintain the quality standards of *Left At Albuquerque*.

III. Essential Duties	IV. Measures of Effectiveness
1. Set mise en place of all grilled and sautéed menu items according to par	1. Prior to the beginning of service, the grill station is prepared and stocked according to the standards set forth in the training programs & the pars set by the executive chef
2. Prepare all grill menu items in a sanitary, timely, efficient and correct manner	2. All grill menu items are prepared in the sanitary, timely, efficient and correct manner set forth in the training programs
3. Communicate with expediter and pantry station before plating an item, in an effort to coordinate both hot and cold food	3. Grill menu items are placed in the window at the same time as cold items and they are at their optimal temperature
4. Restock and maintain the back up of all mise en place	4. Grill station does not run out of mise en place or back up items during the shift
5. Lunch grill cook is responsible for preparing uncooked food product for both lunch and dinner shifts	5. Grill station does not run out of uncooked food product for neither the lunch nor the dinner shift
6. Dinner grill cook is responsible for checking and stocking back up for the dinner shift	6. Grill station does not run out of back up stock during the dinner shift
7. Dinner grill cook is responsible for breaking down all remaining mise en place into small containers, to transfer the containers to sheet pans and properly store in the walk-in	7. All mise en place is placed into small containers and transferred to sheet pans before being properly stored in the walk-in at the end of the dinner shift
8. Dinner grill cook is responsible for proper storage of all meat, poultry and seafood items in the walk-in	8. At the end of the dinner shift, meat, poultry and seafood items are stored in the walk-in as explained in the training programs
9. Dinner grill cook is responsible for the cleaning of the grill and surrounding area	9. At the end of the dinner shift, the grill and the area surrounding it are clean according to the standards in the training program

TABLE 3-6 ***Left At Albuquerque* Job Description: Line Cook (Grill)** *(concluded)*

10. Any additional duties or special projects related to the overall operation of the kitchen or the restaurant as requested by management	10. A sense of urgency and follow-through is demonstrated in a timely manner regarding any assignment, task or special project assigned by management

V. Qualifications

Knowledge

1. Knowledge of proper knife handling
2. Basic cooking methods
3. The ability to determine temperature doneness by touch
4. Basic sanitation knowledge
5. Basic hot line operational knowledge

Skills/Aptitudes

1. Proven ability with oral interpersonal communication skills
2. Proven ability with written interpersonal communication skills
3. Demonstration of a high energy level
4. Ability to take direction
5. Strong sense of urgency
6. Strict attention to detail
7. Highly developed organizational skills
8. Ability to work cooperatively in a team environment
9. Ability to work calmly and effectively under pressure
10. Self motivation
11. Common sense and good judgment
12. Ability to work on multiple tasks at the same time

Working Conditions

1. Must be able to report to work when scheduled and work the entire shift assigned
2. Arrive for work in a clean, crisp uniform which complies with prescribed company standards
3. This position will spend 100% of the time standing
4. Regular contact with other employees and management is required
5. Must be flexible and have the maturity to respond positively to change
6. Must be able to transport up to 50 pounds regularly and 100 pounds upon occasion
7. Must be able to communicate in English
8. Must be able to hear with 100% accuracy with correction
9. Must be able to see with 20/20 vision with correction

Level

1. This individual will work under a moderate to high degree of supervision
2. This individual must exercise a high degree of common sense

(Courtesy of Left At Albuquerque, Palo Alto, CA)

already identified the essential functions of each job during your job analysis. Your written job descriptions can also serve as supportive evidence according to the Equal Employment Opportunity Commission (EEOC), which states, "If written job descriptions have been prepared in advance of advertising or interviewing applicants for a job, they will be considered as evidence, although not necessarily conclusive evidence, of the essential functions of the job."

This means that as a manager with human resources responsibilities it will be very helpful to maintain updated job descriptions that clearly identify the essential functions of each job. A job function is considered essential if it constitutes the primary reason the job exists, such as in the job description of a room service attendant. For example, the carrying of trays or pushing room service carts would be considered the primary reason the job exists. If a job function is so highly specialized that employees would be hired primarily for their expertise in performing that function, it can also be considered essential.

Based upon recent court rulings, it is critical that your job descriptions be reality based. They must identify and clearly describe the physical and mental demands of the job based on a job analysis that has conducted interviews with previous job incumbents.[1] These job requirements can then be developed into interview questions and used in the selection process to determine whether job applicants are able to perform the essential functions of the job. A more in-depth discussion of this aspect of ADA requirements can be found in Chapter 4.

Uses of Job Descriptions

The importance of the job description to the hospitality industry is often understated (Table 3-7). The information is useful to every area of

TABLE 3-7 What to Include in a Job Description/Specification

Purpose	Information Needed
Recruiting	Competencies Education/Experience Working conditions
Selection	Competencies Education/Experience Working conditions Tasks/Behaviors
Communicating expectations	Results Tasks/Behaviors Reporting relationships Individuals/Groups job interacts with Tools/Materials/Work facilities Working conditions
Performance appraisal	Results Tasks/Behaviors
Identifying training & development needs	Tasks/Behaviors Competencies Education/Experience Individuals/Groups jobs interact with
Making promotion decisions	Competencies Education/Experience Working conditions Tasks/Behaviors
Determining compensation	Results Competencies Education/Experience Individuals/Groups job interacts with Working conditions Tasks/Behaviors Degree of autonomy Managerial responsiblity for others Consequence of errors
Determining the HR Gap	Competencies Education/Experience

(Courtesy of ARAMARK Corporation)

supervisor-subordinate relationships as it maintains a more closely organized work group based on job duties and responsibilities. Job descriptions that identify job entry requirements are used to aid the interviewer in the selection process. By knowing the necessary job qualifications and skills, training can be more effective.

In addition, job descriptions can be used as a basis for compensation administration, as well as in the creation of development, transfer, and promotion programs. Supervisory control, performance appraisals, placement activities, work load evaluations, and incentive program planning: The job description provides a source of basic job information that can assist each of these human resources functions. Job descriptions can even help establish organizational charts in their identification of who reports to whom. Using job descriptions to set standards and assign responsibilities can help you eliminate the "but it's not my job" attitude. These are basics. You and your organization are free to use job descriptions to the extent that you want, depending upon your particular needs.

Redesigning Jobs

One last aspect of job descriptions is their ability to be modified for the purpose of employing the mentally or physically disabled, the senior citizen, or members of the new immigrant populace. As hiring employees becomes more difficult, the idea of redesigning jobs to meet people's needs becomes a very real possibility. In some job markets, knowing what your labor supply consists of (forecasting) can influence how a job is structured.

Job entry requirements tend to be reduced when employees are hard to find and then increase in periods of unemployment. The theory behind job redesign is that profits will not be sacrificed and job performance will not be affected if you are selective in the altering of the job content. The manager with human resources responsibilities plays a large role in this process as you attempt to locate the most-qualified persons available for employment. Relaxing job requirements means that the jobs are redesigned to fit the abilities of the people available to fill them (Figure 3-8). Reading, writing, and arithmetic requirements may need to be designed out of the job. In many cases, complex tasks cannot be expected to be completed, so the complex parts of the jobs must be eliminated by reorganizing the tasks in some jobs to be simpler and more routine in order that satisfactory performance can be accomplished.

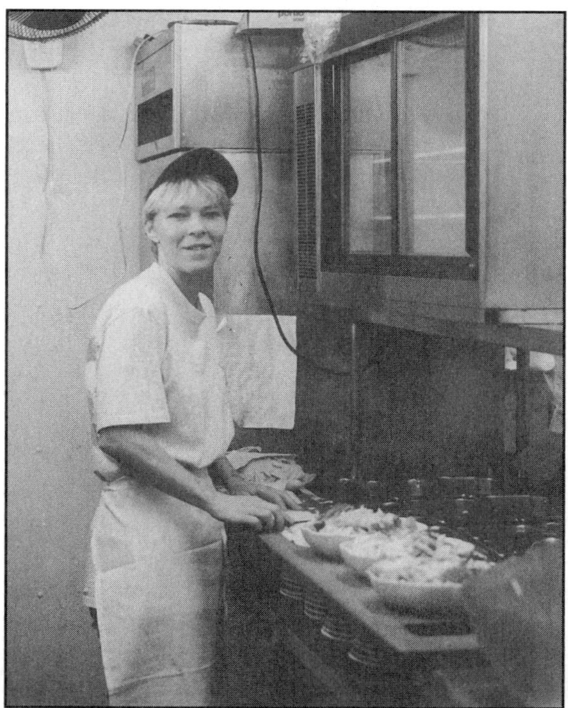

FIGURE 3-8 Job redesign takes into account human considerations that allow employees to be more efficient and improves employee job satisfaction. *(Courtesy of Strongbow Inn, Valparaiso, IN)*

TABLE 3-8 Attitudes for Job Redesign

Redesigning jobs to meet people's needs

- Flexibility in management.
- Employees do not always need to do the adapting.
- Be creative in your approach to employee-job relationships.
- Can prospective employees develop the qualifications while on the job?
- Be goal- rather than task-oriented.

Thus, not every job in every organization possesses the ability to be redesigned in such a manner (Table 3-8). A relatively high percentage of the jobs in the hospitality industry, however, could be changed to make the job less demanding and less psychologically frustrating for the many nontraditional pools of labor that are available to us in certain markets. A certain amount of redesigning may even be beneficial to the operation. Accomplishing work more efficiently always contains the possibility of resulting in higher profits for the organization.

JOB SPECIFICATIONS

Whereas job descriptions concentrate on what the job itself consists of, job specifications are concerned with the qualifications needed to perform the job. Specifications include such things as education, physical characteristics, experience, training, personality, skills, and the degree to which each is needed by the employee for every job. We can define job specifications as the human requirements and qualifications needed by someone filling the job. Job requirements are translated into employee requirements. Job specifications provide guidelines for hiring, frequently forming the basis of interview questions. We discuss this in further detail in the chapter on recruitment and selection.

Caution needs to be exercised so that employee requirements do not become overly specific or request too much background. Outside of legal ramifications, which can be costly, unnecessary requirements (for example, in the amount of work experience) can inflate the wages that your operations must pay. In addition, inflated requirements can give the employee unrealistic expectations of what the job actually contains, causing frustration and eventual job turnover.

Remember also that many of the jobs in the hospitality industry require direct guest contact. Obviously, in our industry, personality characteristics and communication skills become extremely important for both guest satisfaction with our products and services and for employee satisfaction. And almost all jobs in hospitality operations require that our people work closely and effectively with their peers. Here, skills in interpersonal relations are equally important.

As we have seen, the concept of developing and using job descriptions is easy to understand. Job descriptions must be flexible enough to encourage growth and change. Once job descriptions are established, it does not mean that they will remain stable forever. Organizations in the hospitality industry are under constant change and revision. For this reason job descriptions and job specifications should be reviewed at least once, if not twice, a year to update them. It must be kept in mind also that job descriptions are used as positive tools and as such should encourage greater contributions to the operation by the employee. They should not be used as tools for disciplinary actions or they will quickly lose their usefulness.

In summary, remember that your basic objective in developing job descriptions and specifications is to relate specifically, simply, clearly, and understandably to the employee just what his or her job is and what qualifications are needed to perform the job effectively.

To be of value, they must be accurate, complete, current, and used. The hospitality industry is full of employees from dishwasher to manager who want to achieve results for themselves and for the organization of which they are a part. These human resources tools better enable them to succeed.

HUMAN RESOURCES INVENTORIES

When the hospitality industry was comprised of mostly family owned and operated businesses, little concern was given to who their employees were. It was generally assumed that family members would all pitch in whenever business was better than usual. In the early 1980s the situation was quite different. The hospitality industry had grown and was composed of companies that had numerous operations or companies made up of several individuals who had selected the hospitality business as an investment and really knew nothing about the business. Today, although the family operations still exist along with many successful small chains and entrepreneurs who find hospitality both exciting and challenging, the multinational corporations have changed the size and scope of the hospitality business. The size and diversity in locations make it difficult for the manager with human resources responsibilities, sitting in a corporate office, to know what talents and skills his or her employees have. With no knowledge of the in-house skills available, it becomes difficult for that manager to replace his or her employees when they retire, quit, or are fired.

Skills or human resources inventories, computerized when company size demands, list all the employees by name along with their respective skills, training, and educational backgrounds, providing necessary data when changes occur in the hospitality organization. Skills inventories, as we will discuss, can and probably should be developed for both hourly and salaried employees.

In addition to providing an inventory of your current employees with respect to size and skill distribution, the skills inventories also can be used as indicators of turnover rates, productivity levels, and wage scales. They present you with an idea of how the people are currently progressing within and through your organization. Replacement charts, succession charts, and manning tables are all derived from skills inventory data.

Human Resources Supply Analysis

In order to plan for both the present and the future, you, as a manager with human resources responsibilities, need to analyze the abilities, skills, talents, and growth potential of the people in your operation and organization. This involves the need for both an inventory of internal labor supplies and a forecast of external labor supplies that we discussed earlier in Chapter 2.

We define **skills inventory** as a data system that describes the employees working for the hospitality organization by name, skills, and important characteristics. The skills inventory is a management tool used for assessing the supply and available skills of your employees. It is an ongoing system, which means that it will provide you with a procedure for monitoring the capabilities and performance levels of your work force. Because skills inventories provide a useful way of recordkeeping when retrieving a vast amount of data, they have become a true human resources planning tool. Through **succession planning,** they permit a strategy and technique for rationalizing the essential process of filling position vacancies. In addition they assist with structuring career paths for present and future human resources.

Designing a Skills Inventory System

The primary, and most difficult, decision in designing a skills inventory system for your particular situation is to determine what information the inventory should contain. Remember that you can only access the information you have placed into the system in the way that you designed the system to retrieve the information. Care should be taken to identify the types of information *essential* to your operation. This provides you with a list of items that your skills inventory must contain. Next, you will want to identify the information that is *useful* to your operation, and make a decision item by item as to its value in the skills inventory system. You should design your skills inventory system to include the information that is necessary for human resources planning as this is an integral component of the overall process. Table 3-9 is a list of potential items that might be included on a skills inventory. The information you decide to contain in a skills inventory in your operation is dependent upon the specific needs of your operation. That is why no two skills inventory formats will be identical.

TABLE 3-9 Skills Inventory Checklist

- Incumbent's name
- Date of birth
- Sex
- Current job
- Present location
- Date of employment
- Prior work experience
- History of work experience in organization
- Current and past wage levels; dates of raises
- Membership in professional groups
- Test scores
- Retirement information
- Geographic location preferences
- Education (special courses, e.g., cake decorating)
- Health information
- Specific skills and knowledge
- Foreign languages
- Supervisor's evaluation of job incumbent capabilities
- Job incumbent's own stated career goals
- Potential for promotion
- Amount of training necessary for promotion

Much of what is contained in a skills inventory is determined by how you plan to use the inventory system. When skills inventory systems contain information regarding employees' desires and career goals, promotions or transfers can be planned that satisfy both organizational and individual development plans. For training purposes, skills inventories are used not only to identify the skills that exist, but simultaneously to indicate the skills that need to be present in your work force and are not. For recruitment, these inventories identify the strengths, weaknesses, and imbalances in your current work force. Individual development programs (identifying employees for promotion, transfer, or training), long-range human resources planning (projection of work force capabilities), turnover reports (present and projected), and EEO compliance updates are some of the potential ways skills inventory data can be used in hospitality operations and organizations. Skills inventories can also be a motivational device, helping employees to reach their full potential. You should recognize at this point that for skills inventories to be effective for any of these intended purposes, an accurate job analysis is essential. If the job tasks, work load requirements, productivity levels, and skill needs have not been adequately identified, the procedures involved in inventorying skills are worthless.

The initial information for a skills inventory database is collected through a questionnaire or interview. Though much of this information is probably available in the personnel files in most hospitality organizations, it might not be easily and readily available, or it may not be current. Once the information is obtained, the challenge arises of maintaining and updating data. For many operations this is the most difficult aspect of the skills inventory system. Maintaining the information must be part of the human resources planning process, for the data serves no purpose if it is outdated and inaccurate. The frequency with which the inventory should be updated is a function of the size and growth rate of the organization to which you belong. Some operations place update forms in their payroll envelopes on a periodic basis. In a stable operation with very low turnover, once a year might be adequate; in a dynamic high-growth operation, updates may be necessary every quarter.

Remember also that skills inventories cannot select your people. They provide the basis for a list of qualified individuals. Because specific skills may belong to a number of persons, it is impossible solely through this process to select only the one best person for the position. This inventory is only a tool that must be coupled with proper interviewing, evaluating, and selecting. It cannot replace good human resources decision making, but may supplement sound human resources practices.

MANAGEMENT INVENTORIES AND SUCCESSION PLANNING

Skills inventories for your salaried employees are generally called **management inventories**. Frequently it is desirable to keep different information about your salaried employees than for your hourly employees.

When skills inventories are used to identify individuals for promotions and advancement, they become a key tool in the process of succession planning. We define succession planning as a formal process in which plans are developed to ensure that replacements can be readily identified to fill the key positions in your organization. As part of the overall planning process, succession planning supports the strategic goals and mission of the organization and is supported by the training and development programs. In succession planning, through the use of replacement or succession charts the future supply of management can be forecasted by analyzing the current supply in relationship to the patterns of progression in your organization. Used in this way, skills inventories identify, at any one period in time, the types of individuals with specific skills who are or will be available.

Succession planning begins with the first level of supervision and operates on a continuing basis. It requires a broad perspective when looking at the organization and not just an up-the-ladder approach to advancement. By tracking the development and preparedness of potential job candidates within your organization, succession planning assists in ensuring the availability of the employees needed to staff your organization. Staffing tables, manning tables, staffing guides, and manning charts are all formats for presenting a census of the employees found within your organization. When determining replacement needs, consideration is given to the effect of expected attrition whether through death, retirement, or promotion. Such an analysis of management skills and progression permits a projection of future internal supply.

Succession planning assures that development activities are ongoing and relevant for job incumbents as well as provides input to specific training programs. An organization that is known for investing in and developing its own people is an organization people want to work for. Succession planning makes obvious the need for effective initial selection of management personnel. In "the next chapter" of human resources management, succession planning ensures the optimum use of a scarce pool of employees by helping to show current employees that your organization has an interest in their planned development and growth. New meaning can be given to the term human resources planning as identifying qualified individuals, not on a one-time basis, but on a continuing basis.

CLOSING THE GAP

At the beginning of this chapter you learned through job analysis the types and numbers of people you need for your particular work environment. The information from your job analysis must now be compared with information obtained through a skills inventory of the employees presently employed. Recall in Chapter 2 the needs-versus-supply analysis (Figure 2-8). We said that the human resources process began by matching organizational goals and operational objectives with the human resources needs developed through your forecasts. An analysis of the current work force would then be conducted to identify the supply of human resources available to you. Any gap between the two would indicate a corrective action that you, as the human resources manager, would need to take. Figure 3-9 shows how to continue that process in order to close the gap.

A gap, or the difference between the future state of affairs and the organizational goals, is what will happen if no new action is taken. **Human resources gaps** take the form of either a surplus or shortage of personnel or specific skills. It is not enough in the hospitality industry to just have the people, our people must also possess the skills necessary for the operation to meet its objectives. The human resources decisions that you need to make are all action oriented, meaning that you need to have a plan developed for each potential decision before you can implement it.

From the information you have already learned to obtain, you can now prepare an esti-

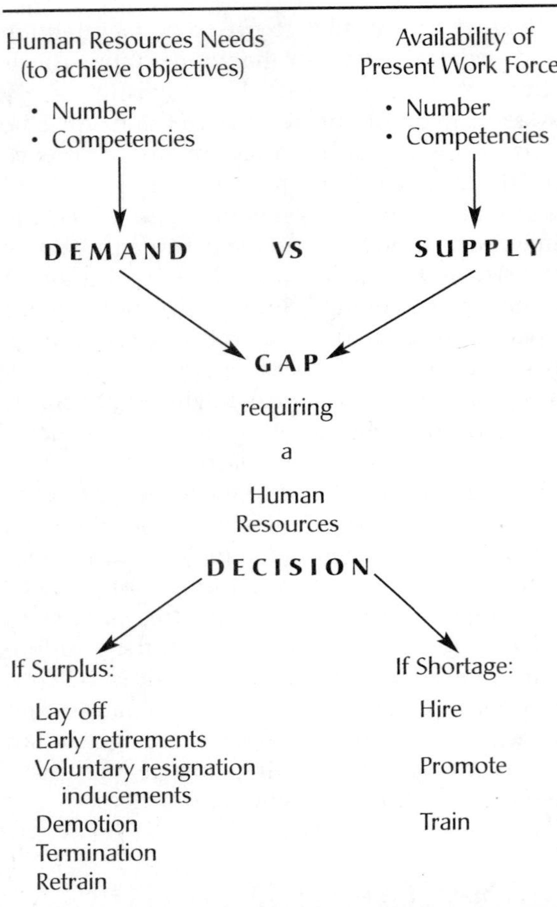

FIGURE 3-9 Closing the gap between human resources needs-versus-supply.

mate of the total human resources needs from external sources. The plans for fulfilling these needs become the basis for recruitment and selection, which we discuss in Chapters 4 and 5. You now know how many jobs need to be filled; you will learn how to fill them as we initiate our discussions of the employment process. Promotion and training are involved when the human resources needs are to be filled from within the organization.

CONCLUSION

One of the most beneficial outcomes of the skills inventory is the ability to effectively match individuals with jobs and in so doing increase both productivity and job satisfaction. As with job analysis, job descriptions, and job specifications, the skills inventory is one of the tools in human resources planning that assists both you and your employees in using and developing their skills to their fullest abilities.

Unless each employee knows what his or her job is, there is a high probability for work left undone, arguments over responsibilities, indifference, and a high turnover. In order to avoid this confusion, you must plan your human resources activities. The human resources planning system as we have explained it determines the activities to be done, the method of completion, the employees involved in the activity, and when the activity should be performed.

The tools discussed in this chapter assist you in answering the following questions:

- What work has to be done?
- What tasks comprise the work?
- What skills do the employees need to perform the tasks?
- How many employees will it take to accomplish the work?
- Who will perform the tasks?
- When will the work be performed?
- How much time and effort are required for each task?
- What skill levels do your present employees have?
- How many employees are available to accomplish the work?
- What are the shortages or surplus of employees for each job?
- Who will be available in the future within your organization to fulfill job needs?

Job analysis identified the essential tasks and who should do them based upon the organizational goals and operational objectives. Job descriptions were then structured to delegate the tasks, responsibilities, and relationship of one particular job to all other jobs. All activities in the human resources system indicate that they are dependent upon the job description document and would be ineffective without it. The ineffectiveness of the human resources function would have definite repercussions throughout the entire organization. The human resources manager or department is responsible for the functions of obtaining, maintaining, and retaining the employees of the organization, with the job description serving as a connecting thread. This thread is the key to each activity we discuss in upcoming chapters. Along with the job description are the job specifications that indicate the qualifications necessary to perform the job.

The skills inventory provides you with information on the skills, knowledge, and background of your current employees. The difference between what you have and what you need indicates the gap that must be filled to effectively meet your operational objectives. This indicator of strengths and weaknesses focuses not only on individuals in their present positions, but, through succession planning, on future positions as well.

The job analysis process as discussed in this chapter determines much of the content for future human resources decisions. Training program content, individual development and organizational development content, recruitment, selection, placement, and even compensation and benefits are based upon the data you have obtained so far. Throughout this chapter we have tried to emphasize that the human resources analysis process must be designed to fit the circumstances of the environment in which you are currently working in or will be working in in the future. The larger the organization you work for, the more formal each of these procedures and formats must be to maximize efficiency. The bottom line for this chapter is to maximize *your* effectiveness in matching people to jobs with respect to skills, abilities, and performance levels thus creating organizational human resources efficiency.

CASE PROBLEM 3

Background

As a manager with human resources responsibilities in a large multinational hospitality corporation, you are aware that one of your organizational goals is to achieve maximum productivity through the efficient use of your employees. To achieve efficiency, you must have a solid organizational structure for each of the required job tasks necessary, identified, and then assigned to the appropriate job position. Unless each person knows exactly what his or her job entails, there will be work left unfinished, arguments over responsibilities, indifference, and eventually a larger than desired turnover. Thus, the very heart of human resources management is the ***job***.

The company that you work for has hotels, resorts, freestanding food service operations, and catering facilities. The company is headquartered in the United States, where it maintains over 450 individual hospitality establishments as well as a dozen hotel properties located throughout Europe.

The senior vice president for development has shown you the following organizational goals: "To expand lodging operations into the economy hotel market within two years, with expansion into a five-state region in the Midwest within a period of five years after entering the marketplace."

3-1 The vice president of development is under pressure to prepare a prospectus for the company president in two weeks. Because of your previous experience with job analysis procedures and techniques you have been asked to provide information from which a projected payroll budget could be determined. What will you need to do in order to prepare this information for the senior vice president of development? (***Hint:*** Remember that it has been stressed that job analysis procedures follow a logical sequence.) The information that the vice president is requesting from you will become the basis for the long-range plans for the human resources functions of orientation, training, and development for this newly proposed chain of lodging properties. In this particular situation, would it be best to use a top-down approach or bottom-up approach for your job analysis? Would the job inventory approach be a suitable method of job analysis in this particular situation? Defend your response.

3-2 After you completed the job analysis, you determined that one of the job positions that needs to be filled is that of laundry room attendant. Develop a job specification for this job description. What are the skill levels and educational background that will be required of the individual filling this job position? Could this job position for laundry room attendant be redesigned to accommodate the skill levels and educational background of some nontraditional sources of labor (such as the physically or mentally challenged)? How would you go about redesigning this particular job?

CASE PROBLEM 3 *(concluded)*

**JOB DESCRIPTION:
LAUNDRY ATTENDANT**

JOB DUTIES:

1. Make sure all linen for rooms is washed and ironed.
2. Make sure all linen for restaurants (including country club) is washed and ironed.
3. Help to sort out all soiled linen.
4. Help to make up the laundry carts when needed.
5. Keep the laundry area cleaned and organized.
6. Keep the machines cleaned.
7. To inform the laundry supervisor when there is any problem with the machines.
8. To separate all stained linen.
9. To do the side work assigned every day.

JOB LIST:

1. Sign in.
2. Sort linen.
3. Wash linen.
4. Dry linen.
5. Fold guestroom linen.
6. Run restaurant linen through mangle.
7. Restock all laundry carts and replenish laundry room shelves with guest linen.
8. Clean all machines.

KEY WORDS

bottom-up approach
critical incident technique
duty
element
human resources "gap"
job
job analysis
job description
job incumbent
job inventory
job-related information
job specification
management inventory
occupation
position
position description
skills inventory
succession planning
task
task description (statement)
top-down approach
work

RECOMMENDED READING

"Writing and Managing Job Descriptions Just Got Easier: Top Selling Job Description Writer Enhanced with Internet Updates and Employment Ad Editor." *Business Wire*, October 12, 1997.

Chipkin, H. "Masters of the Hotel Universe." *Lodging*. www.ei-ahma.org/webs/lodging/9807/coverstory.htm (10 August 1998).

Frost, M. "HR Cyberspace." *HR Magazine*. www.shrm.org/hrmagazine/articles/0897cybr.htm (9 July 1998).

Harvey, R. J. *The Americans with Disabilities Act: Using Job Analysis to Meet New Challenges*. Presentation at 1992 IPMAAC/Conference, Baltimore, MD.

Navaratnam, P. "Job Description Minus Job Analysis. *The New Straits Times*, September 2, 1998.

Pritchard, K. "What's in a Job Description?" *SHRM White Papers.* www.public.wsj.com/careers/resources/documents/19990125-pritchard.htm (28 February 1999).

U.S. Department of Labor. *Occupational Outlook Handbook (1998–1999).* Washington, D.C.

Woods, R. H., and M. P. Sciarini. "Diversity Programs in Chain Restaurants." *The Cornell Quarterly* 35, no. 3 (1998).

Recommended Web Sites

1. Job Analysis & Personality Research: www.harvey.psyc.vt.edu
2. The Occupational Information Network: www.doleta.gov/programs/onet
3. Public Sector Jobs: www.publicsectorjobs.com
4. KnowledgePoint: www.knowledgepoint.com/home.html
5. Job Descriptions: www.jobdescription.coom/dnppv/index.asp

Endnote

1. Teresa C. Fariss, "Carefully Draft Job Descriptions," *Delaware Employment Law Letter* (July, 1998). web.lexis-nexis.com/more/shrm/19213/3524092/9 (28 July 1998).

Discussion Questions

1. Distinguish between job analysis and task identification. Why are they performed?
2. Describe the relationship between job analysis and all other human resources functions.
3. Identify and define the techniques for collecting job-related information.
4. Describe the key elements of a job inventory. What information is obtained?
5. What items are typically contained in a job description?
6. Discuss the importance of, and uses for, a job description.
7. Discuss the idea of redesigning jobs to meet employees abilities. How do you respond to this idea?
8. Define a job specification.
9. What is a skills inventory? How would you use it in a hospitality operation? for hourly employees? for salaried?
10. What is the major difficulty in using a skills inventory? Identify the various uses of skills inventory data.
11. Describe the process of succession planning and its importance to the hospitality enterprise.
12. What possible decisions do you have to make as a human resources manager when the gap shows a surplus? when the gap shows a shortage?

SECTION 2

The Employment Process

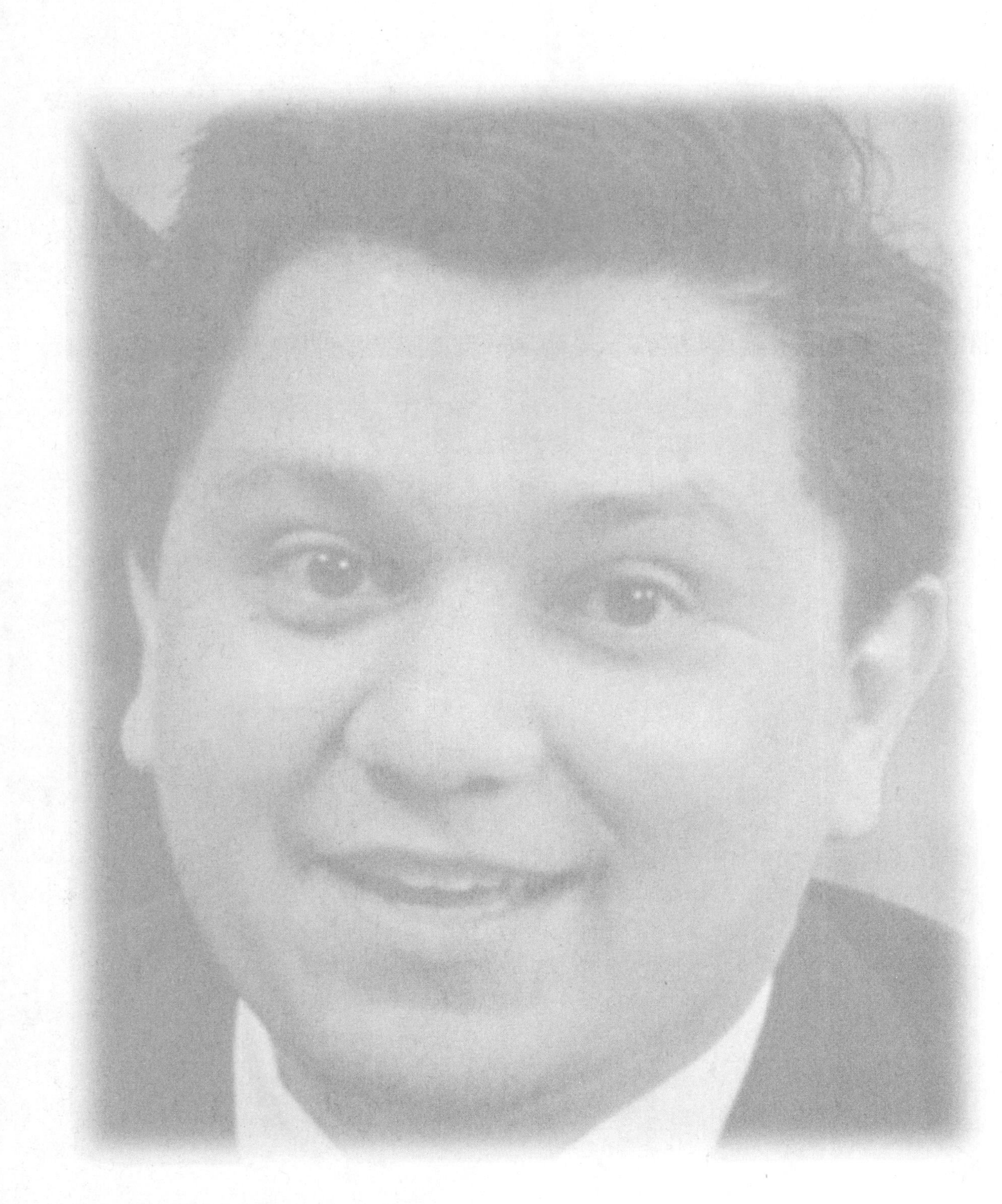

CHAPTER 4

The Labor Market and Hospitality Recruitment

 **INDUSTRY ADVISOR**

JAN BARR, *Human Resource Director, Chili's Grill & Bar*

"Choose a job you love, and you will never have to work a day in your life."

—CONFUCIUS

"You can dream, create, design, and build the best, the most wonderful place on earth, but it requires people to make that dream a reality."

—WALT DISNEY

INTRODUCTION

In the introductory chapter of this text we stated that one of your greatest challenges as a manager with human resources responsibilities in "the next chapter" will be to find quality people to fill your vacant job positions. As you will soon read, the demographic changes that occurred in the United States during the past ten years have created the greatest labor shortage of the century. In the past decade our human resources became increasingly scarce. And there is no indication that the extremely tight labor market that hospitality organizations find today, worldwide, is going to loosen in the near future. According to the National Restaurant Association most operators identified finding qualified and motivated employees as their most significant challenge for 1998. Knowing this, you should continue to plan creative approaches for the recruitment efforts of your hospitality organization. With the census data available from the Bureau of Labor Statistics we know exactly how many people will be available in labor pools five years from now, ten years from now, twenty years from now. Competition for the limited human resources available to us will continue to be incredible! For those hospitality managers who wait, labor will not be available to staff their hospitality operations.

Recruitment needs to be innovative, from the sources of available labor to the methods used, to find the people you need. Hospitality operators no longer have the luxury of having a desk drawer full of applications from eager applicants. Young people no longer stop by our operations every day after school to see if there is a possible opening. The next time you are out running errands, notice the number of Help Wanted signs hanging in fast food operations, pizza delivery chains, and grocery stores. These employers have always relied on large numbers of people ages 16–24 to supply the majority of their work force. And in the year 2000 and beyond they simply can't find enough of those people. Look to what these operators are doing to recruit human resources, and you will find the most innovative approaches today.

At the conclusion of this chapter you will be able to:

1. Relate the demographic changes occurring in the United States to your role as a manager with human resources responsibilities in the hospitality industry.
2. Distinguish between internal and external recruitment methods in relation to hourly and full-time salaried employees.
3. Identify several different alternative pools of labor.
4. Develop a plan for incorporating the elderly worker and disabled worker into your work force with the assistance of state and federal programs.
5. Incorporate the requirements of the Americans with Disabilities Act (ADA) into your recruitment plan for both hourly and full-time salaried employees.
6. Develop a plan for utilizing Welfare-to-Work initiatives.
7. Understand where recruitment fits into the human resources planning process.
8. Describe a variety of recruitment methods that will assist you in locating human resources that match your business needs and requirements.
9. Develop an understanding of the different types of external recruitment methods.
10. Gain a basic understanding of the importance and achievements of online/high-tech recruiting.
11. Discuss the legal issues surrounding the recruitment of human resources.
12. Understand the importance of being able to make changes in job structures that will enable you to accommodate the needs of today's work force.

THE LABOR MARKET

Whether you are planning on entering the lodging or food service sector of the hospitality industry, labor shortages have become a predominant factor in human resources planning. "The number of U.S. jobs is projected to increase 12.7 percent between 1998 and 2010, to almost 172 million,"[1] with the population growth slightly behind at 10.2 percent. "The result would be 19.6 million additional jobs by 2010, for 27.7 million new residents of all ages."[2] In industries throughout the United States, Canada, and Europe the decline in the work force labor pool is one of management's worst problems.

Labor shortages, especially for entry-level positions, have recruiters for the hospitality industry frantically searching for enough labor to fill job vacancies. The Hyatt Orlando has hired new employees from other countries, such as Bosnia and Poland. The Hyatt in Key West employs workers from Poland and Russia.[3] Other operators, such as The Carriage House Restaurant in East Boothbay, Maine, stopped offering lunch service because they couldn't find enough labor.[4] To understand why these labor shortages exist, we must turn to information about the changing demographic patterns of the United States.

Age Factors

The hospitality industry has historically relied on human resources between the ages of 15–24 to supply the largest percentage of workers. For teenagers, the hospitality industry has offered numerous types of entry-level jobs. Finding these jobs in hospitality in the 1960s and mid-1970s was not all that easy. Hopeful teens needed to be persistent, filling out job applications at several restaurants and/or motels if they truly wanted to work. And want to work they did. The jobs in hospitality, especially those that received tips as part of their compensation, were considered excellent opportunities to make money for that car or stereo you had your eye on. With the baby boom peaking (born between 1946–1964), hospitality operators had more applicants than jobs to fill. What a comfortable position for a human resources manager to be in! We could afford to be highly selective in the applicants we chose, and if they did not work out or "tow the line," we could let them go, knowing another eager applicant would take their place.

This is no longer the case. And because of this fact, we are running our operations differently. For the twelve-year period 1980–1992 there was a steady decline in the total number of teens in the 15- to 19-year-old age group. Since 1993 there has been a slight increase (Table 4-1). Hospitality companies must compete with other service industries, such as grocery stores and retail outlets, for this same pool of human resources. More often than not, these companies offer working hours that are more desirable than our industry presently offers. Our more affluent lifestyle makes hands-on food jobs less desirable. Fewer teens are walking into our hospitality operations looking for jobs. The drawer full of teenage applications is empty (Figure 4-1).

TABLE 4-1 Population of the United States by Age

Age Group	July 1, 1992	1994	1996	1998	2000*
15 to 19	17,170	17,707	18,644	19,391	19,820
20 to 24	19,085	18,451	17,562	17,643	18,257
25 to 29	20,152	19,142	18,993	18,674	17,722
30 to 34	22,237	22,141	21,328	20,241	19,511
35 to 39	21,092	21,973	22,550	22,604	22,180
40 to 44	18,806	19,714	20,809	21,800	22,479
45 to 49	15,362	16,685	18,438	18,752	10,806
50 to 54	12,059	13,199	13,931	15,768	17,224
55 to 59	10,487	10,937	11,362	12,217	13,307

* projection; numbers in thousands

(*Source:* U.S. Bureau of the Census)

FIGURE 4-1 The hospitality workplace will continue to have more employees from alternative labor pools in the future. *(Courtesy of Chili's Grill & Bar, Brinker International)*

What other changes have occurred in age group patterns? Traditionally, the 20- to 24-year-old age group has been the second largest in the food service industry. By 1986, that group switched places with the 25- to 34-year-old age group. As the **baby boomers** grow up, the age patterns change to reflect their position in society. As can be seen in Table 4-1, the 24- to 34-year-old age groups are projected to decline quite drastically. These decreases reflect not only the aging baby boomers, but the decreases in the birthrates in the late 1960s and early 1970s. In 1992 the 35- to 44-year-old groups started to swell. By the year 2000, these age groups are projected to account for the largest percent of the total work force. Currently the 45- to 54-year-old age groups have started to increase in size. These age groups will continue to grow faster than the labor force of any other age group during the next decade. America's baby boomers are beginning to gray, and as they age, so does the age of the work force in the hospitality industry. This aging brings with it new human resources management challenges.

The age differential is magnified by the fewer number of teens who will be entering the work force. The baby boomers, unlike their parents, chose to have smaller (and in some case, no) families. This translates into a smaller group of people available for the entry-level positions that our industry has historically filled with the teenage group. As we enter the new century, we also need to be prepared for an increasing number of human resources who will be approaching retirement age (60 and over) (Figure 4-2).

Ethnicity

The **ethnic composition** in our work force has become increasingly diverse. As you learn in Chapter 12, your ability to manage a multicultural workplace will be one of the most important factors in your success as a manager with human resources responsibilities in the hospitality industry. According to the Census Bureau the United States is projected to become a nation of minorities by the middle of the twenty-first century. Projections indicate that Asian and other labor forces will increase faster (41.0 percent change) than either Blacks (13.8 percent change) or Hispanics (36.2 percent change) between 1996 and 2006. This is due both to an increase in the net immigration of these groups and the higher-than-average birthrate. The White labor force, for this same period, is only projected a 9.3 percent change (Table 4-2). By the year 2006, the Black and Hispanic labor forces will be nearly equal in size as more members of these groups are projected to enter the labor force during the 1996–2006 period. The total ethnic minority share of the work force is expected to grow to 28 percent, up from 18 percent in 1980 and 22 percent in 1990. Certain geographic regions of the country will be more heavily affected than others, but ethnic diversity is no longer confined just to the large metropolitan areas. As a result of these demographic changes, the ability to attract and recruit a qualified work force from diverse populations will become critical for the survival of all hospitality organizations.

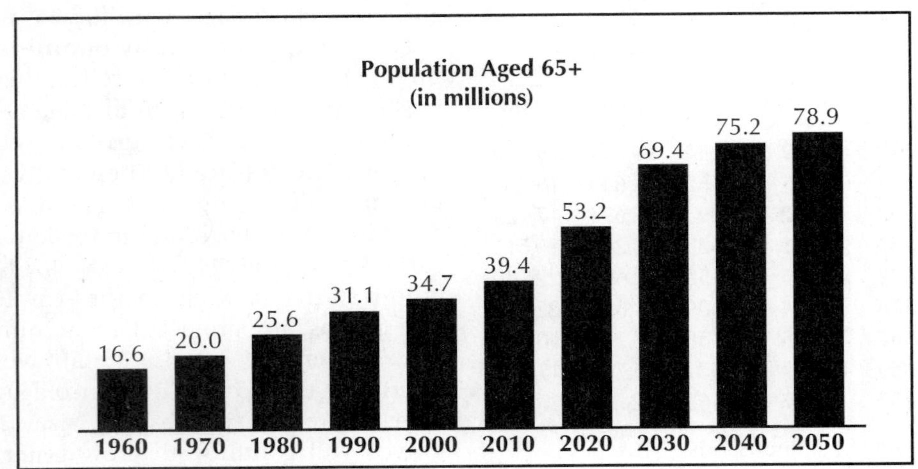

FIGURE 4-2 Aging-related statistics. (*Source:* U.S. Bureau of the Census)

TABLE 4-2 Ethnic Group Labor Force Projections for 2006

Ethnic Group	Work Force* 1986	1996	2006
Asian and other	3,371	5,703	8,041
Black	12,654	15,134	17,225
Hispanic	8,076	12,774	17,401
White	101,801	13,108	123,581

*numbers in thousands

(*Source:* U.S. Bureau of Labor Statistics)

The Effect of Women

Women are making up a larger proportion of the work force than ever before. In the hospitality industry, this means that we will continue to hire women in job positions traditionally held by men. Today there are more women in upper-level management positions, which has a direct impact throughout the hospitality organization.

According to the Bureau of Labor Statistics the labor force participation rates of women will increase in nearly all age groups. Men's labor force participation rates are projected to decline for all age groups under 45 years of age. With the women's labor force now growing faster than the men's, the women's share of the labor force is projected to increase from 46 to 47 percent. "Employment rate among women in the 25 to 44 age group increased from 71% in 1985 to 76% in 1996. Employment rate among women in the 45 to 54 age group increased from 55% in 1985 to 75% in 1996. Employment among mothers in this age group increased from 49% in 1975 to 60% in 1985 to 76% in 1996."[5] As we discuss in upcoming chapters, this has direct implications for benefit planning, which seeks to assist women with childcare, parental leave, and flexible working hours. The hospitality industry continues to be well suited to accommodate the needs of more women in our work force, making women a very viable pool of candidates.

Other Demographic Considerations

The U.S. unemployment rate hit a low of 5.3 percent in 1988, and in New England the rate dropped to an amazing 3.3 percent. In May 1998 there were 5.9 million unemployed persons in the United States with the unemployment rate holding at 4.3 percent. These figures are and continue to remain extremely low. Taking into account that a certain percentage of that group is unemployable, those figures are extremely low. And even as that may be good news for the economic health of our country, it also means that the pool of available labor for vacant hospitality jobs is lower than ever before.

The hospitality industry is not the only industry suffering from these changes in demographics. All service industries from health care to grocery store chains are feeling the labor shortage in nurses and checkout clerks. The need for human resources in the hospitality industry continues to be enormous. In 1996 the lodging industry employed 1.1 million people full- and part-time, paying $17.6 billion in wages and salaries.[6] "Employment in the restaurant industry is expected to reach a record 12.0 million workers by 2006—up from 10.2 million in 1996."[7] Service-producing industries will account for virtually all of the job growth. It is expected that the highest growth rate of any occupation in our industry will be food service and lodging managers gaining 35 percent between 1996 and 2006.[8] The Bureau of Labor Statistics also indicates that hourly job occupations in the food service industry will see growth as well as their annual growth rate for employment exceed that of the annual growth rate for employment in all industries.

Competition is not only more intense for customers, but equally intense for human resources to meet our work force requirements. And all service industries will be competing for the same people. The greatest shortages will be felt in the unskilled, lower-paying job positions, in particular the evening part-time shifts that traditionally have been held by our teenage workers. They are often the people who have the first contact with our guests.

Turnover has continued to increase in unskilled and semiskilled job positions. Workers filling these jobs no longer have to tolerate the poor working conditions, long hours, autocratic treatment, and low pay that has accompanied these positions. Nor do workers have to accept positions with no advancement opportunities, poor management, or little training. Why? Because if you don't satisfy their basic needs, the operation down the street will. Curbing turnover is the major answer to solving the staffing needs of the future.

INDUSTRY EXPERTS SPEAK

According to Jan Barr, Human Resources Director for Chili's Grill & Bar, "Keeping turnover down is a reflection of how well you take care of the people who work with you. Taking care of your people means that you satisfy their needs, which also helps you ***attract*** the good employees. If you build a reputation as a great place to work, word will spread among the local market. Low turnover is a powerful recruiting tool."

THE LABOR SHORTAGE: SOLUTIONS

Throughout the remainder of this text we focus on how each of the human resources function areas can contribute to either the attraction or retention of your human resources. *Attract* and *retain* are the two words that are repeatedly seen in these pages, for as a manager with human resources responsibilities in the hospitality industry, your focus must be directed towards these two goals.

To attract more job applicants, here are just some of the methods being used in the hospitality industry today:

- Raising wages. With an unemployment rate of 4.3 percent employees will not work for minimum wage.
- Using alternative sources of labor. A smaller number of available teens means we have to look for **alternative labor pools** to replace them.
- Implementing innovative methods of recruitment. An **advertisement** in the Help Wanted section of the daily newspaper is no longer sufficient.
- Gaining expertise and familiarity with **online recruiting**. This is a very powerful tool, but the effectiveness of the ad's written message and placement is crucial. Job applicants who look for jobs online do so differently than applicants who read a trade magazine or local newspaper advertisement.
- Bussing employees to the work location. If there is no labor in your geographic area, you will need to look beyond and provide transportation to work (and frequently pay the employees for their transportation time as well).
- Improving benefit offerings. Part-time employees have not always been entitled to health and other benefit plans that our full-time employees have been receiving. With a trend towards part-time employment, this restriction may need to be reconsidered.
- Offering flexible scheduling. According to Jan Barr, Chili's Grill & Bar, this is the *key* issue. It is not only attractive to the teens and college students of all ages who are out

there, but it is attractive to single parents and the mature worker.

- Making work fun. The best managers we have ever worked for are those who made the work environment enjoyable. Create a place where your human resources want to be, not have to be.
- Putting the "human" back into your management philosophy. People want to work in an environment where others care and are concerned about their welfare. Treat them like the valuable assets they are to your success.
- Improving orientation and training programs. We simply can't throw people into the work force and expect them to survive, let alone succeed. Too often employees are considered a high cost of doing business. They should be considered an asset to increasing sales, *human* resources.
- Offering internal paths of advancement and added responsibility within the food service operation or lodging property. Show our human resources that they can have a career in hospitality, not merely a job to help them with expenses while in college or until they find a "real" job.

All of these solutions are aimed at either attracting or retaining quality human resources. In today's labor market these methods for attracting quality job applicants are not a choice. You must institute these ideas as a way of doing business. Nor can you just use a select few of these methods. Hospitality operations must use *all* of these to be effective. Treating your human resources as an investment is really what human resources management is all about. Just as you protect your physical assets, you should be equally concerned about the protection and care of your human assets.

INDUSTRY EXPERTS SPEAK

"Bill Serra was an experienced manager with Boston Chicken who had been looking to return to his first love, casual dining. After going through the interview process, we hired him to train in our Parsipanny, New Jersey, Chili's. Bill and I maintained communication through training and he mentioned his wife Deb was also in the business. As Bill progressed through training, Deb became more interested in Chili's. I honored her request with an interview and we hired her soon after. Bill and Deb continue to live and compete with each other in separate Chili's in New Jersey." Had Jan Barr not kept in touch with Bill after he was hired and during his training, she might never have learned about Deb.

INDUSTRY EXPERTS SPEAK

"While working out at Gold's Gym, one of our Recruiters frequently wears Chili's or Brinker t-shirts. One day the desk clerk was talking about pursuing a full-time management position with Don Pablo's (one of our competitors). The clerk was almost ready to make a career change when she noticed the Chili's t-shirt on our Recruiter. The more she found out about us, the more she liked. The desk clerk is currently managing a Chili's."

The **demographic information** we have shared with you is intended to raise your awareness of a critical situation that continues to plague the hospitality industry. A better understanding of the labor market will enable you to maximize your efforts in attracting and retention. We begin with a look at recruitment in "the next chapter."

HOSPITALITY RECRUITMENT

Recruitment can be defined as the process by which the best qualified applicant for a specified job vacancy is found in compliance with all federal, state, and local regulations pertaining to employment. We will identify several methods for conducting the recruitment activity that will include both internal and external searches for potential job candidates. The laws regarding employment are strict, particularly those for hiring non–U.S. citizens. The responsibility for the recruitment of job applicants for employment varies depending on the size of the hospitality organization. In some companies you will be responsible for the recruitment of all nonmanagement positions at the unit level. Other organizations use their human resources department for the recruitment of all job applicants. Regardless of the level at which recruitment is conducted, the methods and legal issues remain unchanged. However, before we can discuss how to recruit, let's first identify several different alternative sources of labor.

Sources of Alternative Labor Pools

You have just been given the responsibility for recruitment in your hospitality operation. You are aware that most of the operation's human resources are working on overload because of a lack of staff—a dangerous situation that, according to industry advisor Jan Barr, leads to high management and employee turnover. In order for you to become successful given your new responsibility, you need to fill these vacant positions as quickly as you can but, at the same time, with the right people. How can you do this effectively without falling into the **"warm body" syndrome**. The warm body syndrome strikes a hospitality operation when the manager simply hires the first warm body that walks in the door and can fill out a job application. According to Jan Barr the "warm body syndrome" is a vicious cycle, actually increasing turnover by causing your quality employees to look elsewhere. Great employees want to work with other great employees, not those whose work performance is inferior. With fewer bodies walking in the door, this style of hiring should, thankfully, become the exception in hospitality employment practices.

The key word in our previous definition of recruitment is *qualified*. The job applicants we seek in the recruitment process should be qualified if we ever hope to reduce the high turnover rates we experience in this industry. So if job applications aren't walking in the front doors of our operations, where are you and I going to find them? (See Table 4-3.)

Just because the sources of labor in Table 4-3 have been identified as "alternative" does not mean that they are unqualified or of a lesser quality than the labor markets we have historically tapped. It makes sense to examine the demographic shifts to see where there will be sources of labor for us to draw upon. With the aging of America the employment of the elderly becomes a natural alternative and most talented resource.

TABLE 4-3 Alternative Sources of Labor

- Contingency work force
  - Free-lancers
  - Independent professionals
  - Leased employees
  - Part-timers
  - Subcontractors
  - Temporary staffing
- Disabled
- Elderly
- Generation X'ers
- Immigrants/Ethnic populations
- Internationals
- Retirees
- School-to-Work programs
- Single parents
- Welfare-to-Work participants

INDUSTRY EXPERTS SPEAK

"Having a Chili's tag on the front of a car is a great attention getter. One day our Regional Recruiter was stopped at the car wash by another patron inquiring if she worked at Chili's. Our Regional Recruiter handed the person a business card and a month later the other patron at the car wash became a Manager in our Orlando market."

The Older Worker

According to labor statistics, the median age of workers in 1994 had increased to 37.6. In 2005, when baby-boom employees are aged 41 to 59, it will reach 40.6. The number of people over the age of 50 in the United States is increasing and will continue to do so as the baby-boom generation ages. While some of our employees are seeking early retirement, others are not and would like very much to remain contributing members of the hospitality work force. We cannot afford to overlook this valuable, knowledgeable pool of potential workers.

What kinds of attitudes and adjustments do we need to make to become attractive work environments for the mature worker? One thing that we can do as managers is to continue to provide opportunities for career development. Just because our employees are older does not mean that they have lost their incentive, initiative, or motivation for advancement. Most people at the age of 60 still have ten to fifteen years of productivity. And wouldn't you be eager to hire an individual who you knew would remain in your hospitality organization for ten years? We think you would.

Providing the opportunity to reduce the number of work hours from full-time to part-time can be an incentive to retain our mature human resources. Frequently, the number of hours an older worker desires is dependent on Social Security restrictions. This is why recruiters should emphasize total compensation, not just pay, to older **job candidates**. Frequently, fringe benefits such as health insurance opportunities, free or reduced meals, and other noncash offerings may be recruitment tools. Many job positions in the hospitality industry are highly conducive to part-time employment, providing opportunities for more mature workers to stay or join the hospitality work force.

The mature individual can also be enticed to continue working by providing him or her with health insurance that supplements Medicare. Though possibly an expensive benefit to offer, the expense needs to be weighed against the costs of hiring an inexperienced worker who will require training and still not be as productive. The older worker has a willingness to work and has an already acquired set of skills, which should be taken into consideration (Figure 4-3). This makes offering a benefit which may appear at first to be costly, more cost-effective.

FIGURE 4-3 The older worker is a viable, hard-working alternative source of labor.

How else can we attract and retain the older worker as a hiring resource? By providing more flexibility in schedules, permitting weekends off (when you can supplement your staffing needs with school-age workers), and allowing for extended vacations. Part of the advantage to being retired is that you have the free time to participate in the leisure activities that you previously could not work into your schedule.

In recruiting older workers we need to be sensitive to their needs, knowing that in turn we will have a work force of knowledgeable, loyal human resources. They can be a tremendous networking source to recruit other older workers. Many older individuals do not look at the employment ads in the classified sections of the newspaper, as they consider themselves to be "retired" not "unemployed." Therefore you are better off attracting their attention by contacting retirement centers, the Office on Aging, local chapters of AARP (American Association of Retired Persons), senior citizen centers, and organizations that serve the needs of the mature citizens in your local community. Both AARP and C.A.R.P. (Canadian Association of Retired Persons) have **web sites** set up to assist their members in exploring work options available to their set of unique needs and skills. "Canada's fast food industry is increasingly hiring older workers instead of younger workers who have become more expensive because of government regulations and higher payroll taxes."[9] The National Council on Aging (NCOA) is the world's largest organization representing agencies and individuals committed to the well being of our increasing older population. They can be found on the Web at www.ncoa.org.

What then are the advantages to recruiting the mature employee? A study of food service managers reported in 1988 found mature workers to be rated highly in the areas of attitude, dependability, emotional maturity, guest relations, and quality of work produced.[10] This study certainly dispels some of the myths about recruiting a mature worker. Advantages include:

- an employee who is more likely to take his or her job seriously. These human resources are not using their job as a stepping stone to bigger and better positions. Rather, they are quite content to do a good job within the scope of their job description.
- an employee who is less likely to have behavior problems that might interfere with the quality of work performed. Recreational drugs, young children, and night life are not likely to be part of the mature employee's lifestyle.
- an employee whose pattern of sick leave and unexplained absences has already been determined. Sick leave is not more common among the mature workers, but is rather dependent upon the lifetime health of an individual. Thus, while benefit needs may differ from those of the younger human resources, they are no more expense to retain.
- positive impact on coworkers.
- an employee with higher productivity rates. Remember these are an experienced pool of human resources. Their life experiences give them an advantage over younger workers.

The next time you question the quality of a mature work force, remember our industry's success story. Colonel Harlan Sanders, penniless at retirement at age 65, went on to found Kentucky Fried Chicken with his first Social Security check of $105. At age 73 he became a millionaire by selling his rights for the recipe!

The Disabled

There are many job positions in the hospitality industry that have been satisfactorily filled with **disabled**, or challenged persons. Though similar to hiring the elderly, these potential employees have special needs. The results of hiring the disabled have generally been favorable. Table 4-4 provides an explanation of the award winning TeamWorks Program for Disabled Persons used at Chili's. Many other companies such as Marriott and Burger King have similar programs. These hospitality organizations have recognized the benefit of recruiting this alternative source of labor.

TABLE 4-4 Chili's TeamWorks Program

TeamWorks is Brinker's national program to employ persons with disabilities. The program is administered by Integrated Resources Institute, a nonprofit organization, which piloted TeamWorks with California Chili's units in 1991.

The TeamWorks success in California has led to a gradual expansion of the program to other major Brinker markets. To date, TeamWorks has been implemented successfully with restaurants in California, Colorado, Florida, Georgia, Illinois, Dallas/Ft. Worth and Houston. In addition, the annual turnover rate of the 600 employees hired through the program is less than 25%, while the eligibility rate for TJTC exceeded 90% while it was in effect.

TeamWorks is now a national employment program offering people with mental, physical and sensory disabilities the chance to work and enjoy life with dignity and respect. By providing challenged individuals with consistent work routines, compensation, possibilities for social interaction and skill development, TeamWorks promotes independence and increased self-confidence.

Prospective employees for the program are recruited at the community level through nonprofit rehabilitation agencies and placed in positions that best utilize their skills. Interacting with restaurant managers, these agencies also assist with interviews, on-the-job training, and follow-up supervision. Job responsibilities have included assisting with opening duties, dishwashing, food preparation, readying tables for customers and supporting food servers.

Brinker International is positioned to create additional positions at all levels of the corporation. The initial goal of Brinker International is to employ at least one TeamWorker in every restaurant—and several at corporate headquarters.

(Courtesy of Chili's Grill & Bar, Brinker International)

One of the biggest advantages of recruiting the disabled is their availability. At the end of 1994, 20.6 percent of the population, about 54 million people, had some level of disability. Those individuals with a severe disability accounted for 9.9 percent of the population or about 26 million people. Disability rates vary by race and ethnicity (see Figure 4-4).[11]

With the hospitality industry booming, unemployment at record lows, and recruiters competing to find workers here sits a pool of available labor that can, and want to work. In the age group of people between 21 and 64 years of age, the employment rate was only 76.9 percent for those with a non-severe disability and 26.1 percent for people with severe disabilities. And yet advancements in health care and technology make it increasingly possible for people with even severe disabilities to work. The disabled, once given an opportunity, have proven to be some of the most hardworking, highly motivated and productive employees. Companies, like Brinker International, that incorporate some type of disability hiring program have had exceptional employees as a result.

What should you keep in mind when developing and implementing such a program in the hospitality organization you work for? Disabilities may be of either a mental or physical nature. In most areas, there will be a government or nonprofit **rehabilitation agency** that can assist you in planning a specific program for the needs of your operation in conjuction with the needs of the disabled in your area. You will need to prepare a very detailed list of the job tasks that you need the employee to perform. This assists the agency in matching your organization with a suitable employee. Your state's unemployment office can refer

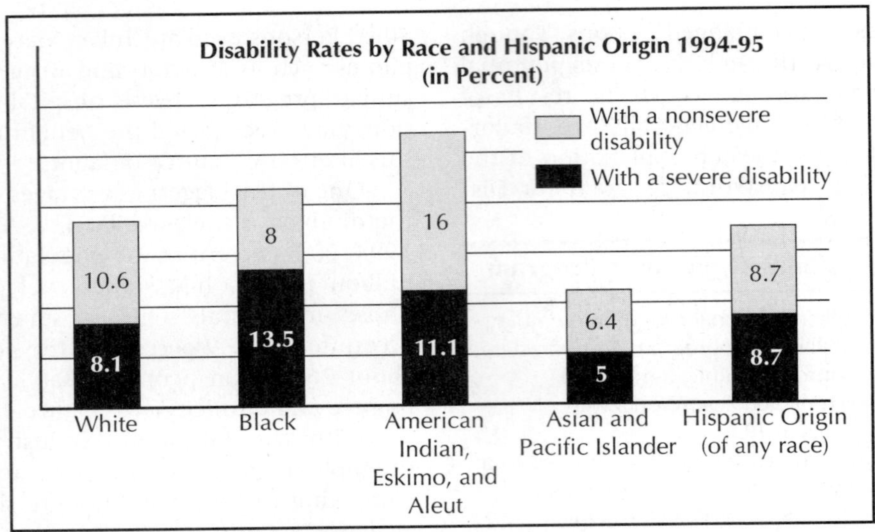

FIGURE 4-4 Disability Rates by Race and Hispanic Origin 1994–1995. (*Source:* U.S. Census Bureau)

you to an appropriate agency. The National Restaurant Association also assists its members in locating agencies that help in the recruitment and placement of the disabled. Jan Barr suggests that in your areas contact some well-known agencies such as Easter Seals and United Way and ask them for their recommendations. Begin to establish a positive working relationship with local agencies and show them you are serious about hiring the disabled for your hospitality organization.

In addition to recruitment assistance, the federal government provides reimbursement dollars to employers who establish on-the-job training programs for disabled employees. This is to assist employers with the extra expenses incurred in training employees with special needs. Different states have set aside special funds in addition to that provided by the federal government. It pays to investigate what reimbursements you might be entitled to when implementing recruitment programs for the challenged. Agencies will often send in job coaches to help you design training tools and work areas to better accommodate the special needs of the disabled worker. The Arc is the country's largest voluntary organization committed to the welfare of individuals with mental retardation. They were a leader in helping to get the **Americans with Disabilities Act (ADA)** passed into law and continue to remain very active in issues dealing with the ADA and employment. Another organization you should become acquainted with is JAN, the Job Accommodation Network. JAN is a federally funded national organization whose mission is to assist employers in the hiring, retention, and advancement of persons with disabilities through job accommodation. Many of these organizations have established well-maintained web sites that are easy to use and contain a wealth of information to assist you in your journey to recruit the disabled worker. Take advantage of all the agency services.

Legal requirements such as the **Rehabilitation Act of 1973** prohibit discrimination on the basis of handicap by the federal government, federal contractors, and by recipients of federal financial assistance. The veterans from the Vietnam War have been protected by the **Veterans Readjustment Assistant Act**, 1974. **The Education of All Handicapped Children Act** guarantees education for every disabled child, meaning that the disabled population in "the next chapter" will be better educated than ever before. The National Council on Disability (appointed by the President of the United States) reviews and makes recommendations on federal laws that affect the disabled. In 1986 they released a study entitled *Toward Independence,* which recommended that comprehensive civil rights legislation was needed to define and protect the rights of the disabled in American society. Attempts to integrate the disabled into American society were, at best, minimal. There were many doors, both figuratively and literally, that the disabled were unable to open. That changed significantly on July 26, 1990, when the Americans with Disabilities Act (ADA) was signed into law by President George Bush. Quite simply, the ADA prohibits discrimination in employment, programs, and services provided by state and local governments, goods and services that are provided by private companies and in all commercial facilities on the basis of disability. This law is so significant for managers with human resources responsibilities in the hospitality industry that we have devoted an entire section to ADA later in this chapter. All of this translates to a larger proportion of disabled employees in the labor force. And with the predicted labor shortages, this potential labor pool is being used in hospitality organizations throughout the United States.

The Immigrant Populace

Even though we discuss the importance of managing cultural, ethnic, and racial diversity later in Chapter 12 in this text, it is essential that we don't lose sight of this growing segment of potential labor. This is especially true for hospitality organizations that have made Multicultural Management part of their companywide philosophy and corporate culture. Ethnic groups are not just found in border states or metropolitan areas any longer. Throughout the country, rural and urban regions are experiencing a diversity of cultures and ethnic composition.

The United States, indeed the world, will never be less culturally diverse than it is at this moment, right now, as you are reading these words. The racial and ethnic composition of today's newborns tells us the composition of our hospitality work force of the future. According to the Census Bureau, by the time the children born in the late 1990s reach their late fifties, non-Hispanic whites will no longer be a majority of Americans. The way we think about the term "minority" is already starting to change as non-Hispanic whites are the minority population in some of our major cities, such as Miami, today. We already see the awkward term "majority minority" being used to describe the population mix in certain geographic locations. In 1995, for the first time in U.S. history, the number of births to Blacks was surpassed by the number of births to Hispanics. It is anticipated that the proportion of births to Hispanic and Asian women will increase to the number of non-Hispanic white births. This is due to the women of the baby boom generation moving out of their childbearing years and the increase in the number of young immigrants anxious to start their families in America (see Figure 4-5).

Though the labor force of the past was dominated by white men, the labor force of the late 1990s was equal parts women and men, and still mostly white. But in the entry-level positions, a multicultural, multiracial, and multiethnic work force was born as our country approached the millennium. Because so many

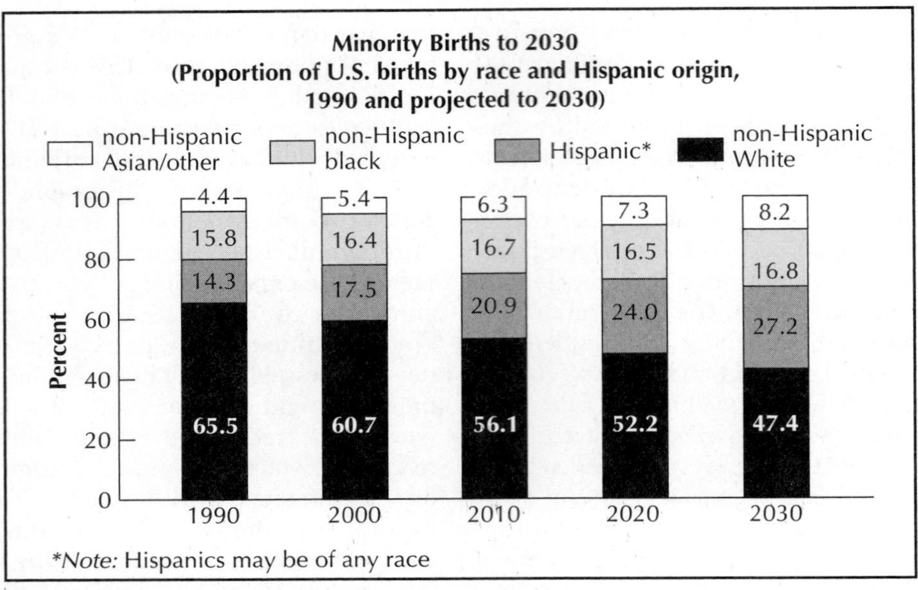

FIGURE 4-5 Minority Births to 2030. (*Source:* U.S. Census Bureau)

white men are retiring, the non-Hispanic white labor force will show very little growth between now and the year 2005.

The hospitality industry is already taking advantage of the talent found within the large populations of ethnic groups in the United States. In 1996 seven out of ten supervisors in food preparation and service occupations were women, 11 percent were African American, and 11 percent were Hispanic. Of the 1.4 million managers found in lodging and food service organizations, 46 percent were women, 9 percent were African American, and 7 percent were Hispanic. Eating-and-drinking establishments are increasingly being owned by African Americans and women.[12] Yes, the hospitality industry has much to offer members of all ethnic groups found within the United States.

So, how does this increasing ethnic diversity impact you as you assume responsibilities for recruitment for your hospitality organization? You need to perform a mini-demographic study on the work force within your own organization. Then compare your findings to the demographics already found within your geographic region. How do they compare? Next, compare your findings with the projected demographics in the geographic areas you recruit within. If certain ethnic groups are projected to increase in your recruiting areas, then you should plan on having a higher percentage of those ethnic groups in your future work force. This is where the forecasting plans, discussed in Chapter 2, come into play in human resources management.

The Immigration and Naturalization Service provides assistance in locating legal **immigrants** through its **Legally Authorized Worker's (LAW) program**. This program was in response to the **Immigration Reform and Control Act** that was signed into law in 1986. In 1990 the **Immigration Act of 1990** (IMMACT90) was passed in an effort to reform the immigration laws to better benefit the U.S.

businesses. This Act increased the number of employer-sponsored permanent immigrants who can come to the United States each year, from 54,000 to 140,000. Additionally, it eased the admission process for some of the temporary ("nonimmigrant") categories used by business. Immigration procedures, however, are not simple. Much work on immigration legislation still needs to be done to encourage the immigration of skilled aliens. There are numerous immigrant and nonimmigrant categories, a discussion of which goes beyond the scope of this text. Exploring the immigration categories with the advice of legal counsel might turn up recruiting options that have not been explored by your hospitality organization.

As with other alternative sources of labor, the immigrants you recruit may require special assistance. One of the most obvious concerns is the ability to speak English. There are several alternatives to this problem. One is to place non–English-speaking human resources in work groups with others who are bilingual. We feel that this should be a short-term solution to a long-term problem. An interim step is to provide training material, signage, and information in several different languages. Many hospitality organizations are finding that the best solution is to provide instructional classes in the English language for these valuable human resources. The structure to these programs varies. Some companies provide the instruction at no cost, others pay employee wages while they attend class. Some companies make the instruction part of their shift hours, others require the employees to take the classes at times that do not interfere with the work schedule.

Speaking English is a skill, one that native Americans take for granted. If any of you have visited abroad in a country where you did not speak the language, you know firsthand how frustrating the experience can be. No matter how intelligent, capable, or skilled you are, without the ability to communicate, you feel like the most ignorant person in the world. If we can teach human resources to perform job tasks that they are not skilled at, then why can we not also educate our human resources to effectively communicate?

Women

Women have become an increasingly important component of the hospitality work force. In the early 1970s, rarely did you see a female working in the back of the house; that environment consisted solely of men. Today, there are more women working both the front and the back of the house in hospitality operations than ever before. As stated earlier, there are also more women in upper management now.

The demographic data supports the increase of women in the work force. As of 1995, 77 percent of women aged 30 to 49 were in the labor force. The rate shows no sign of reversing, or even stabilizing, in the near future. Baby boomer women who have time and money in careers and education are quite unlikely to quit their jobs in middle age. Work could become increasingly important to them as they, and their children, age. And as more and more families depend on two-paycheck incomes, as women become better educated and trained, and as the childcare service providers in the country improve, it is easier to attract women to your labor force. With women predicted to make up 48 percent of the work force by the year 2005, this is a significant alternative source of labor for your hospitality organization.

Women make up the greatest percent of part-time employees in the hospitality industry. Accommodating part-time schedules for young mothers who want to spend time with both work and family is relatively easy due to the natural peaks and valleys of our business day. Oftentimes, our operations become more labor efficient when work schedules are supplemented with part-time human resources.

Welfare-to-Work Reform

In August of 1996, President Clinton signed the Personal Responsibility and Welfare Reconciliation Act of 1996. This required that 25 percent of the people receiving welfare assistance be either working or involved in some type of a work/training program by September 1997. Each year, until September 30, 2002, the percentage rises by 50 percent. The Welfare Reform Law, as it is known, is an attempt to significantly change the welfare system of the United States. Quite simply, it requires work in exchange for welfare. Industry leaders throughout the country have been challenged to do what they can to hire welfare recipients. The challenge for managers with human resources responsibilities in the hospitality industry is to discover a way of tapping this relatively new work force.

The **Balanced Budget Act of 1997** assists these efforts by authorizing the U.S. Department of Labor to provide **Welfare-to-Work** Grants to states and local communities to create job opportunities for the hardest-to-employ recipients of Temporary Assistance for Needy Families (TANF). Prior to August 22, 1996, this was known as Aid to Families with Dependent Children (AFDC). As of June 15, 1998, twenty states already had approved grants.

During the early 1990s there were about one million adults, ages 18–64, who received welfare benefits. This was approximately 3 percent of the U.S. work force. There are many myths about what the welfare population actually looks like. Reality, in many cases, is quite different than the myths. According to a report from The Urban Institute based on data from the 1995 AFDC Quality Control Survey, over 90 percent of the welfare parents are single parents. Most welfare mothers are in their twenties and thirties, 37 percent are white, 36 percent African American, 20 percent Hispanic, and 6 percent fall into the other category. Over half have received at least a high school education, with some who have attended college. Most welfare recipients have only one or two children. The majority have work experience.

Marriott Corporation's "Pathway to Independence Program" is considered a model program for other companies to follow. It has required time, effort, and resources to make it successful. It takes a serious commitment on the part of the employer to keep a former welfare recipient on the job. Self-esteem training, work ethic, preparation for every-day work are just some of the training and counseling activities that are required to make the program a success. Not only do the welfare recipients need to be trained on what to expect, so do the managers who will be supervising these employees.

Moving people from welfare-to-work is now one of the primary goals of the U.S. federal welfare policy. Information about Welfare-to-work activities can be found on the **Internet** at www.doleta.gov. Regional U.S. Department of Labor offices can also provide you with information and assistance. While these requirements apply directly to federal employers, in today's tight labor market it makes good business sense to look at ways to recruit, hire, and retain this valuable alternative source of labor.

Other Alternative Sources

Part-time employees include more than just women. Flextime and job sharing (where two employees share the same full-time job position) serve to attract moonlighters, single parents, individuals seeking supplemental income, and students in both high schools and colleges.

Other viable alternative sources of labor include:

- Employees in transition:
  - retirees
  - retired military (veterans)
  - ex-offenders
- On-call human resources
- Relatives of present human resources
- Work-release programs

THE ROLE OF RECRUITMENT IN THE PLANNING PROCESS

If we are to attract the individuals who possess the education, skills, and experience to perform the job tasks that our vacant job positions require, we must rely on our job descriptions and job specifications. Figure 4-6 shows you where recruitment falls in the human resources planning process that we initiated in Chapter 2.

The specific procedures for recruitment should be developed into a written policy. A written policy can often save you when it comes to employee-filed discrimination suits. Your selection is largely dependent upon the size of the hospitality operation. In some organizations the department that has a job vacancy issues a **hiring requisition** to the human resources department indicating that position needs to be filled (Figure 4-7). The job descriptions and specifications for that job position are reviewed with the human resources manager to ensure accuracy. After gaining a full knowledge and understanding of what the job position entails, recruitment takes place. The specifics of this process vary slightly from organization to organization. In some cases, you as a manager with human resources responsibilities determine the job vacancy description and begin recruiting. In some segments of the industry, more commonly in lodging, departments with vacancies submit a job requisition to the Human Resources Department, who then initiate and coordinate the selection process. It is more typical in food service and for hourly positions for the manager to be closely involved in recruitment. In today's marketplace most hospitality organizations are always recruiting, always hiring.

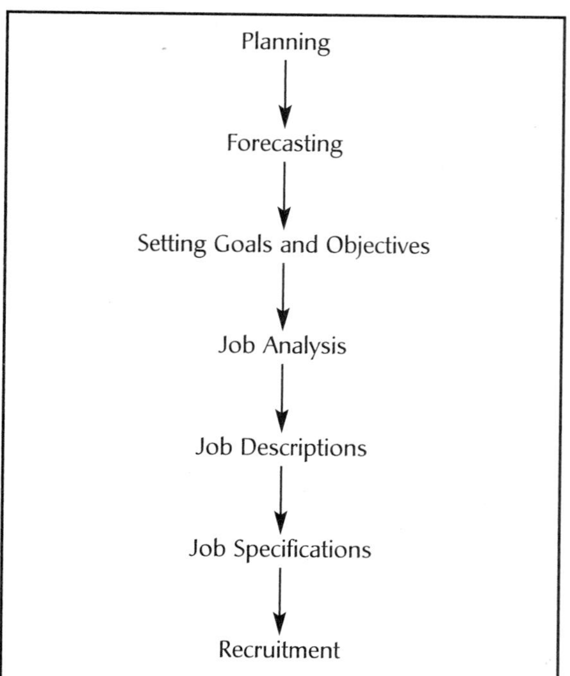

FIGURE 4-6 Recruitment's role in the planning process.

There are two different methods of recruitment that may be used, internal or external. Internal sources include those found within your own hospitality organization. External sources of labor are those from outside your organization. Most hospitality organizations use a creative combination of both methods. The types of internal and external methods that you choose to use are dependent upon a specific recruitment strategy that you develop. Jan Barr highly recommends the use of a recruitment strategy. Where do your candidates come from? This question can be asked during the first interview. "How did you hear about us? What brought you in to see us today?" Based upon that information, outline a specific recruitment strategy and keep it updated. Your recruitment strategy should be ongoing but not job-position specific.

Methods of internal recruitment are covered next, followed by a discussion of external recruitment methods.

REQUISITION FOR PERSONNEL FORM

JOB TITLE ____________
SUPERVISOR ____________
BUDGETED ☐ Yes ☐ No If yes, which quarter ____________

TODAY'S DATE ____________
DEPARTMENT ____________
DATE NEEDED ____________
ESTIMATED STARTING SALARY $ ____________
JOB CODE ____________ GRADE ____________

REASON FOR HIRE

☐ New Position
☐ Replacement For ____________ (name)
Date Vacated ____________
Position Need Re-Evaluation ☐ Yes ☐ No

TYPE OF EMPLOYMENT

☐ Permanent Full Time ☐ Exempt ☐ Consulting
☐ Permanent Part Time ☐ Non-Exempt

SPECIFIC EDUCATIONAL QUALIFICATIONS

REQUIRED: ____________
DESIRED: ____________

SPECIFIC WORK EXPERIENCE

REQUIRED: ____________
DESIRED: ____________

PRIMARY RESPONSIBILITY OF POSITION

____

Internal Move: ________ Yes ________ No
If Yes: From Position: ____________ (Present Job Title) / To Position: ____________ (New Job Title)
From Department: ____________ (Present Department) / To Department: ____________ (New Department)

1. Requisition must be completed in full with approvals before search can begin.
2. Please attach *current* job description.
3. If requisition is for a new position, please attach supporting documentation as needed.
4. Replacement positions will take approximately 6 weeks to fill.
5. Positions requiring evaluation will take approximately 3 months to fill.

APPROVALS

SUBMITTED BY: ____________ (First Level Supervisor) TITLE: ____________ DATE: ____________
APPROVED: ____________ (Vice President of Department) TITLE: ____________ DATE: ____________
REVIEWED BY: ____________ (PRC) TITLE: ____________ DATE: ____________
APPROVED BY: ____________ (Human Resources) TITLE: ____________ DATE: ____________

THIS SECTION TO BE COMPLETED BY HUMAN RESOURCES

Requisition # ____________ Date Received ____________
SOURCES CONTACTED:
____
DATE COMPLETED ____________
NAME OF CANDIDATE SELECTED ____________

APPLICANTS APPLIED ____________
APPLICANTS INTERVIEWED ____________
SOURCE ____________
HIRED BY ____________
STARTING DATE ____________

FIGURE 4-7 Requisition for Personnel Form. *(Courtesy of Chili's Grill & Bar, Brinker International)*

Internal Methods of Recruitment

Promotion from within your own organization has numerous advantages over bringing in people from external sources. The most significant advantage is that these human resources are completely familiar with the hospitality operation and organizational culture. Corporate culture is a topic we discuss at length later in this text, but it is an important consideration in the recruitment of qualified job applicants. An understanding of the hospitality operation, its procedures, its layout and design, along with a knowledge of operating policies, is a great advantage for a job applicant to have. If you have conducted a planned process for crosstraining or if you have been specifically grooming an employee for your job vacancy, the decision to promote or transfer from within is quite obvious. According to Jan Barr most companies have a set goal for internal hires. A key is keeping the pipeline full of internal candidates in various stages of development.

In most situations, however, salaried vacancies do not occur on such a timely, planned basis, and a decision needs to be made on whether to hire someone from within. If your hospitality organization has a succession plan for management positions, you have some direction in which to look. If it does not, then careful consideration needs to be given to each of the human resources already in your employ. The following are examples of the types of questions you should ask to help you determine if your hourly employees are ready to advance to salaried positions:

- Is the individual, or can the individual, become qualified for the job vacancy? A trade-off for job knowledge versus company experience often results in a positive match. This person does not need all the skills and knowledge base of the new job if he or she can be trained into it. You might not find someone with 100 percent of the qualities that you are looking for. The qualities that are lacking should be weighed against the advantages of knowing what kind of person he or she is, an awareness and understanding on the person's part of the corporate culture and the support of peers in making the job transfer.
- Is the individual available? What is the nature of the job position he or she will be vacating? How critical is it to the success of your hospitality organization? How difficult will that job position be to fill? Much of this depends upon your long-range employment goals. If your hiring is done to maximize flexibility and you offer ongoing training programs to prepare your human resources for job vacancies, then availability should not be a problem with **internal recruitment**.
- Is the climate of the hospitality operation such that other human resources will not feel threatened or jealous by job transfers or promotions? If you have established an individual development program that fosters the growth of all human resources in your operation, then internal recruitment should not have a negative effect on your work force. In fact, in the right climate, internal recruitment can raise employee morale by indicating to your staff that you are loyal to them. Sometimes bringing in an employee from the outside can send the message that no one in your employ is worth your consideration. The underlying message that could be seen is that the job the person presently holds is a dead-end position with no opportunity for advancement or change.

If there are no viable job candidates within your hospitality organization, then you will need to turn to external labor sources. When this occurs, it is critical that you keep the lines of communication open with your current work force. It will be important that they understand the necessity to look outside the organization for job applicants. If they do not understand your reasons, you are likely to bring a new job candidate into a hostile work environment, thereby minimizing his or her chance to succeed. With all the dollars you have invested into the recruitment process, this can be a costly lesson to learn. Jan Barr feels that in today's marketplace if you find a good person, you hire that person. In a progressive hospitality organization, there is always a place for a good employee.

External Recruitment Methods

So far in the recruitment process we have verified the accuracy of our job descriptions and specifications and discovered that none of our human resources is qualified or interested in the job vacancy. We now turn to the variety of **external recruitment** sources we need to examine. One of the things we will be looking for is the relevancy of the method we select to the type of job position that is vacant. Geographically, academically, and from the standpoint of experience level and pay structure, we need to determine the best approach for attracting candidates with the job specifications that our vacant job requires. Jan Barr says to remember that people work for people, not companies. The personal touch is critical to success. You *are* the company to the people you recruit.

Advertisement

The oldest, but not necessarily the most effective recruitment method, is advertising. The key to advertising is knowing when and where to run an ad that will be viewed by the greatest number of qualified readers. This is not an easy task. Most hospitality organizations rely on experts in the field of advertising to help them design an ad that will appeal to the ideal job candidate. Recruitment advertising agencies are not a cost to the employer. They receive their commission from the newspaper. Most hospitality managers do not have the expertise required to target an ad to the intended audience, nor the time to conduct all the follow-up with the newspapers. Even if you have to pay an advertising agency to be creative, it is still worth it to use them. And when hiring an advertising agency, look for one that provides a maximum number of services such as market research, art design, and employee referral, and has a good track record attracting the type of candidates you need for your hospitality organization.

Effective advertising requires creativity and market research. The goal for recruitment advertising is to provide your hospitality organization with a competitive edge over other hospitality organizations in attracting the right caliber of human resources, whether the job vacancy is for a dishwasher or unit manager. Advertising objectives might include capturing the image your company wants to portray, establishing an identity with the products and services you offer within a geographic region, letting people know what kind of an employer you are with respect to benefits, promoting career opportunities, or attempting to overcome a negative public image of the hospitality industry. Advertising also must conform to government regulations regarding discrimination, which is another good reason to use an agency.

In developing recruitment advertising always keep in mind what the ideal job candidate would look like and write all copy to attract that person. Position your copy in sources that the ideal candidate is likely to read. Be creative with your advertising strategy and experiment with sandwich signs, brochures, posters, banners, radio, and events, as well as newspapers. Examples of advertising used by Chili's to attract hourly employees to work for the company are seen in Figure 4-8 and Figure 4-9. Recruitment advertising is much more aggressive and proactive than it

FIGURE 4-8 Chili's Management Recruitment Advertisement. *(Courtesy of Chili's Grill & Bar, Brinker International)*

FIGURE 4-9 Chili's Hourly Recruitment Advertisements. *(Courtesy of Chili's Grill & Bar, Brinker International)*

was in the 1980s and early 1990s. At that time, recruitment was more of a retroactive process. Today recruitment is an ongoing process.

Though newspapers are still the most popular vehicle for recruitment advertising, **electronic recruiting systems** are rapidly taking over as the choice media for advertising job openings. So much so we have devoted the next section to this "new" method of recruiting.

ONLINE RECRUITING

We know that unemployment rates remain low, and will continue to remain low for the next decade. As a manager with human resources responsibilities it becomes even more important for you to use every tool at your disposal when recruiting qualified job applicants. This is where the use of online recruiting resources comes into play. Whether we like it or not, the Internet has changed our world. Some people believe that within the next decade the paper résumé will be phased out almost completely in favor of the electronic version available today. There is much to learn about recruiting on the Internet. Entire books have been written about it, entire websites are devoted to it. We cover more in-depth information, specifically about the Internet, in Chapter 15. This section is intended as a brief overview so that you can get a feel for this very new, yet very important resource available to you as you seek to recruit the best for your hospitality organization.

New? New indeed. "The number of online job sites has exploded from 500 in 1995 to a predicted 100,000 in 1998 . . . and the number of resumes found online grew from about 10,000 in 1994 to 1.2 million by the end of 1997."[13] If you execute an Internet search using the word "job," you will get over 1 million responses. Online recruiting is being used across all industries.

Even retailers who create their catalogs online to sell products, have established "help wanted" pages on their sites to sell themselves as an employer. Hospitality organizations, like Chili's, are also finding this a successful way to find job applicants (see Figures 4-10a and b). In a way, using advertising on your company's web site prequalifies candidates that are needed with technical skills. If they are familiar with your company and found your web site, then they are comfortable with surfing online and the new media. A number of job candidates can simply use your company's homepage to learn more about you and develop an interest in your company. But wait; this resource is so new that first let's explain alittle about what we mean by "online."

Exactly What Is "Online"?

Going "online" generally requires the use of a modem and phone line which connects your computer to a computer that is located in a remote, usually distant, location. You can go "online" directly to the Internet, or you can subscribe to a private, commercial online network service such as America Online, CompuServe, or Prodigy. When you subscribe to one of these services and sign on, you are not connecting to the Internet, but only to a part of the Internet. As a subscriber you have access to that private network's online services. The services offered by each of the online services vary, but one of those services is always a connection, or access, to the Internet. Users of the Internet are not, however, able to connect to a private network service without becoming a subscriber.

INDUSTRY EXPERTS SPEAK

Ken Meyers, the General Manager of the Chili's in Tucker, Georgia, has created a personal web site with America Online (AOL). He included Chili's as one of his interests and restaurant management as his profession in his personal profile. Jim Fink of Charleston, West Virginia, happened to be looking through the Internet and searched AOL for Restaurant Managers. He located Ken's site and e-mailed him asking about Chili's. Ken contacted Jan Barr who interviewed and hired Jim about two weeks later. Just another way web sites can find job candidates for your hospitality organization.

Working at Chili's is just as much fun as dining at Chili's! The friendly, flavorful dining experience is consistently rewarding - no matter which side of the table you choose. Guest, manager, food server, host, kitchen staff - ***Chili's is always fun!***

Fortune magazine named us ***"One of America's Most Admired Companies"*** in the casual dining food service category in 1999. Our #1 rated product quality, #1 rated management quality, #1 rated innovation, and #1 rated talent places Brinker International at the top of the industry. These prestigious attributes and the integrity found at Chili's create a thriving "ChiliHead" culture.

Because we value our ChiliHeads, Chili's Grill & Bar offers you rewarding opportunities from entry-level positions to management. As a member of our team, you will have fun, have a life outside of work, and be challenged to realize your potential. We are building 40+ units per year and have positions available nationwide.

Chili's managers are winners!

They are decision makers. They are coaches and they are leaders. They know the meaning of empowerment and sense of ownership.

Chili's managers enjoy:

- A five day work week
- An attainable monthly bonus
- A great base salary
- Two weeks of vacation each year, starting after six months and more after five and ten years
- Unlimited growth potential based on your abilities, not tenure
- Competitive benefits including a variety of insurance options, a 401K plan, stock options, paid maternity and paternity leave

Chili's has great opportunities at all levels.
Hourly employees enjoy:

- Excellent compensation
- Paid vacations
- Tuition assistance
- Health insurance
- Free or discounted meals
- Flexible scheduling
- 401K plan

To send a Resume or locate a Recruiting office near you, click on the map below for information.

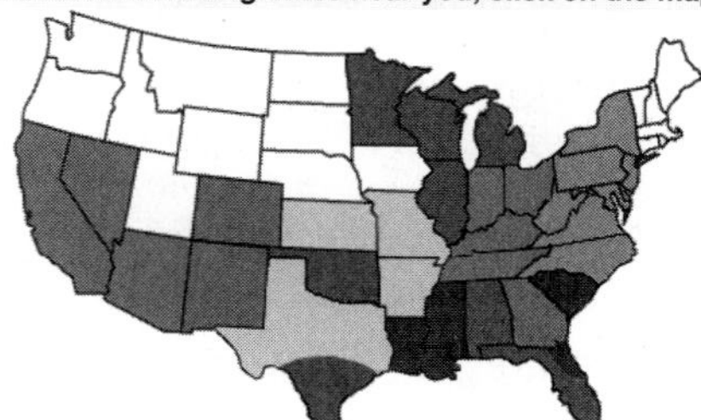

FIGURE 4-10a Join the ChiliHead Team Employment Web Site. *(Courtesy of Chili's Grill & Bar, Brinker International)*

Chili's Recruiting

Lisa Kent
5510 West LaSalle Street, Suite 200
Tampa, FL 33607
Fax: 813-282-3499
E-Mail: Lisa.Kent@brinker.com

To send a brief online resume, click here.

FIGURE 4-10b After clicking on the map, the next screen shows recruitment office information for that area. *(Courtesy of Chili's Grill & Bar, Brinker International)*

Options Available for Online Recruiting

The number of resources on the Internet available for recruitment is vast. As the number of resources increases, so does your ability to acquire more résumés. Therefore getting enough résumés is not going to be your problem with online recruiting; getting résumés from people who are truly interested in your hospitality organization and who are qualified for your job openings is going to be the issue. Online recruiting enables you to instantly inform interested people about the job openings that you have available right at this moment. Here are just a few of your options:

- ***Company Internet Web Sites.*** As we discussed earlier, this is a great way for you to identify the employment opportunities that are available in your organization. Table 4-5 is an example of an advertisement found on Chili's web site (www.chilis.com).
- ***Online Résumé Databases.*** There are numerous databases available where job candidates post their résumés and employees can search for candidates that meet their needs. Examples of two are Career Magazine (www.careermag.com) and Monster Board (www.monster.com).
- ***Online Résumé Forwarding Service.*** Hospitality companies can contract with these services to forward them résumés of job applicants that meet your qualifications. The service acts as a pre-screen so you only spend your time reviewing résumés that have the minimum qualifications that you determine.
- ***Employment Classified Ads.*** These are ads that are posted by you, the employer. The concept is analogous to the classified print ads you find in newspapers and trade magazines. The advantage is that you can literally have access to individuals all over the country, and world, without having to place ads in newspapers in major cities. There are many of these databases available online. Examples would include Yahoo Classifieds (classifieds.yahoo.com/employment.html) and E-span (espan.com).
- ***Chat Rooms on Network Services.*** People like to chat and this option is one of the most popular on the network service providers.

TABLE 4-5 Chili's Web Site Employment Opportunity

Restaurant Management with Chili's Grill and Bar

What does it feel like to run a restaurant that averages 2.5 million dollars in sales?
What does it feel like to drive home from work knowing that you have contributed to a winning operation?
What is it like to receive a bonus that directly reflects your commitment to quality?

It's like management no place else.

No Place Else But Chili's.

At Chili's our Managers are Winners.

- They are Decision Makers.
- They are Coaches and they are Leaders.
- They know the meaning of Empowerment and Sense of Ownership.

Fortune Magazine calls us "one of America's Most Admired Companies" because we foster these qualities and consider the personal and professional growth of our team members an integral part of our culture.

Chilli's Managers Enjoy:

- An Easily Obtainable Monthly Bonus
- A Great Base Salary
- A Five-Day Work Week
- Two Weeks of Vacation Each Year, Starting after Six Months and More after Five and Ten Years.
- Unlimited Growth Potential Based on Abilities, Not Tenure.
- Competitive Benefits Including a Variety of Insurance Options, a 401K Plan, Stock Options, Paid Maternity and Paternity Leave.

As a Member of Our Team, You Will Have Fun, Have a Life Outside of Work, and be Challenged to Realize Your Potential.

We are building 25+ units per year and have Positions Available Nationwide.

Hourly Positions with Benefits Available at a Chili's Near You!

Send a resume to: Hal Pyke, Chili's Grill & Bar,
PO Box 362 Warwick, NY 10990
Fax us at 914-988-9302,
E-Mail HAL.PYKE@Brinker.Com
SEE US AT: www.chilis.com

(Courtesy of Chili's Grill & Bar, Brinker International)

INDUSTRY EXPERTS SPEAK

"Using the Chat room on AOL has drummed up interest in Chili's. You never know who you are chatting with and what their background is. One day, one of our Recruiters was in casual conversation and someone looked up her profile which identified that she worked for Chili's. The conversation took more of a business tone. His restaurant was closing down in the next couple of weeks and was on an active job search. His search ended with Chili's where he is a Manager in the Jacksonville, Florida, market."

Links to general classifieds, recruiting agencies, company web sites, newsgroups, résumé banks, and more are all available for the manager with human resources responsibility for recruitment in "the next chapter."

Referrals

Referrals are oftentimes the best source for locating potential job applicants. Referrals come from a number of sources. Employee referrals are individuals recommended to you by an employee. In most cases, employees will only recommend a person if they feel he or she would like to work with them. Some hospitality organizations have instituted an employee referral system that rewards employees with cash bonuses for recommending a person who is hired and stays with the organization for a specified period of time (generally ninety days). Some companies offer cash incentives, others offer gifts and prizes. For these systems to be most effective they need to be publicized by posters and flyers enclosed in paycheck envelopes. Some companies present the awards at a luncheon, again communicating the advantages of the referral system to all employees. Jan Barr tells us that at Brinker International they rely on managers and employees as a key recruitment tool. She emphasizes that you have to really work at referral programs to make them successful—talk about them and be aggressive (Figure 4-11).

Referrals may also stem from personal friends, suppliers, or other industry professionals; even guests can help! If you work in a large hospitality organization, check with other local managers to see if they have some good applications on file. Your suppliers visit numerous accounts and may know of individuals who are looking for a position like the one you have vacant. Think about other organizations in your location that might be able to refer people to you such as the Boy's or Girl's Clubs, YMCA or YWCA, clergy or youth organizations such as 4-H clubs. Though it takes time and effort to create effective work-

FIGURE 4-11 Chili's Referral Campaign. *(Courtesy of Chili's Grill & Bar, Brinker International)*

INDUSTRY EXPERTS SPEAK

"In our Baton Rouge market, one of our General Managers was talking to our beer purveyor about how much she enjoyed working at Chili's, along with what a great manager referral bonus plan we have. The "Bud man" was so impressed that while he was on his route he proceeded to mention Chili's to some other managers at some other restaurants. One manager that he talked to was having a bad day, contacted Chili's and is now a manager. A recommendation from our local beer purveyor goes a long way!"

ing relationships with community organizations, they can be of enormous assistance when they understand the type of individuals your hospitality organization is looking for. Participate in community events, even help sponsor them when possible.

Schools

Schools include more than universities and high schools. Vocational and two-year programs should also be considered. Many high schools hold job fairs, which are excellent opportunities not only to attract the workers you need to fulfill your immediate needs but also to promote the hospitality industry as a viable career choice. Many colleges and universities will provide you with an opportunity to recruit on their campuses. Mailings could also be sent to these programs in an effort to attract their students. Contact should be maintained with program heads and faculty members. Opportunities to speak in class might also be available. If you have employees who attend these schools, make sure the other students you talk to know who they are. They can serve as excellent representatives of your company. To maximize your results from schools, you will have to invest time and effort according to Jan Barr.

Employment Agencies

The U.S. Department of Employment Security supervises a national computer network of job openings. Its major goal is to assist individuals drawing unemployment compensation in finding jobs. The federal government also sponsors training programs for youth, veterans, and women. The **Job Service Center** is the state agency that assists unemployed individuals in locating job openings. Job vacancies that you have may be listed with these agencies. Some offer assistance in screening potential job candidates. You should also investigate the services provided by local government agencies. A phone call to the county court house and/or city hall will direct you to the appropriate departments.

In addition to government agencies, there are professional **employment agencies** who will locate potential job applicants for a fee. Individuals seeking employment list their names with these services. You, as an employer, pay a fee to obtain names of qualified candidates. All of these agencies operate a little differently. Some only charge a fee if you actually hire someone they have referred to you. Frequently, these agencies act as middlemen and conduct the interview. Sometimes even wage negotiations between you and the potential job candidate are handled. Others simply refer individuals to you who meet job specification qualifications, and they charge a fee for the potential candidates they refer to you. Many of these firms sponsor career nights that attract many job candidates.

You must be sure to do a careful screening of the agency under consideration to make sure that it can provide you with the type of individuals you will need. Don't hesitate to conduct reference checks on the agency and make sure that it fully understands the nature of your specific operation. Some hospitality organizations have specific policies pertaining to the use of private employment firms. Make sure that your actions conform to your organization's policy.

Executive search firms specialize in locating professional and management job candidates. These firms typically have a minimum salary base that they will recruit for. The services they provide are extensive, leaving you only with the tasks of final interview and the hiring decision. Often a financial commitment is made up front. Because their job is to fill an executive position, it is critical that the search firm you select thoroughly understands your hospitality operation as well as the job qualifications.

ALTERNATIVES TO RECRUITMENT

There are many considerations that you need to take into account before the decision can be made to hire human resources for your hospitality organization. The growth and career advancement of your human resources is one of the most important influences on recruiting. If you have established a good program for individual development, then you expect your human resources to progress through the career ladder. This means that the entry-level positions are the ones that need to be filled most frequently. When recruiting, you are looking for people who have the capability to be promoted, and must take that into consideration when planning your recruitment efforts. You must not, however, expect all your human resources to want to move up the corporate ladder. Some individuals might be perfectly content simply being the best dishwashers they can be. Value those people. As the manager with human resources responsibilities, you must be aware of the potential advancement capabilities and desires of your work force.

Employee turnover also affects recruitment planning. As you have already learned, forecasting assists you in estimating the number of job vacancies you will have so that you can be better prepared.

The projected growth of your hospitality organization also affects the need for recruitment. Acquisitions, mergers, expansions, and new product and service offerings all equate to a need for more employees. Plans for recruitment must take organizational growth into consideration.

Recruiting individuals either externally or internally is not your only alternative for filling vacant job positions. Some hospitality organizations are relying on companies that provide **temp-help**. Temporary help is advantageous to companies that have short-term staffing needs. Caterers and seasonal operations are two examples of organizations that can maximize the advantages of temp-help services.

These companies will lease trained human resources for a day, a week, or even for several months. The advantage for you is that you can keep your permanent staff down to a minimum, while filling positions that you cannot afford to staff on a continual basis. Bookkeeping advantages abound. The temporary-help company writes all the paychecks. You write one check in place of several. **Leasing companies** can frequently afford to offer better benefit packages than can small hospitality operations. Benefit plans such as medical are proportionally cheaper per person and decrease in cost when you have a large number of employees. The more individuals who ascribe to the plan, the less the cost per individual.

When you consider a leasing company, you must carefully check its financial stability, as well as the quality of human resources it will be leasing to you. The training that it provides must match the standards of your hospitality organization, as your reputation, not the leasing company's, is at stake. There are professional organizations that monitor their members for financial stability and accountability. It is a good idea to make sure that the leasing company you deal with belongs to such a certifying organization.

RECRUITMENT AND THE LAW

We have already mentioned some of the federal legislation: The Veterans Readjustment Assistance Act, 1974, requires government contractors to take **affirmative action** in the hiring and promotion of the disabled and Vietnam-era veterans. The Rehabilitation Act of 1973 requires government contractors to take affirmative action to prevent discrimination in the employment of mentally and physically disabled persons. Just what exactly is meant by the words "affirmative action"?

Affirmative action programs and requirements are a result of past difficulties in enforcing the civil rights policies. **Executive Order 11246** (1965, amended in 1968 to include sex) states that any employer signing a government contract agrees it will not discriminate on the basis of race, creed, national origin, or sex. **Revised Order No. 4** (1971) requires employers receiving government contracts of $50,000 or more with a work force of at least fifty employees to develop and maintain a written affirmative action program to ensure that minorities and women are hired at a rate that their availability in the work force would suggest.

Thus, Executive Order 11246 encompasses two concepts, nondiscrimination and affirmative action. Nondiscrimination requires the elimination of all existing discriminatory conditions. Affirmative action requires that you as the employer move to ensure employment neutrality with regard to race, color, religion, sex, and national origin. Affirmative action requires that you make additional efforts to recruit, employ, and promote qualified members of groups covered under the order that you have formerly excluded, even if that exclusion was not due to discriminatory action on your part.

Revised Order No. 4 requires you to determine if minorities and women are being underutilized in your hospitality organization and, if that is the case, that you develop specific goals and timetables designed to overcome the underutilization. This then becomes part of your affirmative action program. These goals and timetables are at the heart of the effort to monitor the affirmative action procedures. Critics have argued that goals are simply another name for quotas. Supporters argue that goals and timetables are merely management tools to monitor the progress of affirmative action. Affirmative action continues to be a controversial issue as we enter the new millennium. There are no easy answers, no easy solutions. Managers in hospitality organizations with human resources responsibilities should pay close attention to the future of affirmative action.

The Carnegie Report issued in 1975 identified several features of a formal recruitment effort. Included in these recommendations was the idea that all recruitment announcements should state that the company is an equal opportunity or affirmative action employer. It also suggested that interviewers include women and minority group members whenever possible.

The Immigration Reform and Control Act of 1986 makes the hiring of undocumented employees illegal. The act further specifies that it is the employer's responsibility to verify the legal immigration status of all employees hired since November 7, 1986. You are not required, however, to verify the authenticity of the documents. We suggest that you retain copies of all documents that you check as part of the employee's personnel file. This will serve as proof that you have inspected all immigration documents. The now famous **I-9 form** (Figure 4-12) that you must sign states that these hiring documents have been seen by you. Documents that serve to verify citizenship

(continued on page 109)

U.S. Department of Justice
Immigration and Naturalization Service

OMB No. 1115-0136
Employment Eligibility Verification

INSTRUCTIONS

PLEASE READ ALL INSTRUCTIONS CAREFULLY BEFORE COMPLETING THIS FORM.

Anti-Discrimination Notice. It is illegal to discriminate against any individual (other than an alien not authorized to work in the U.S.) in hiring, discharging, or recruiting or referring for a fee because of that individual's national origin or citizenship status. It is illegal to discriminate against work eligible individuals. Employers **CANNOT** specify which document(s) they will accept from an employee. The refusal to hire an individual because of a future expiration date may also constitute illegal discrimination.

Section 1 - Employee. All employees, citizens noncitizens, hired after November 6, 1986, must complete Section 1 of this form at the time of hire, which is the actual beginning of employment. **The employer is responsible for ensuring that Section 1 is timely and properly completed.**

Preparer/Translator Certification. The Preparer/Translator Certification must be completed if Section 1 is prepared by a person other than the employee. A preparer/translator may be used only when the employee is unable to complete Section 1 on his/her own. However, the employee must still sign Section 1 personally.

Section 2 - Employer. For the purpose of completing this form, the term "employer" includes those recruiters and referrers for a fee who are agricultural associations, agricultural employers, or farm labor contractors.

Employers must complete Section 2 by examining evidence of identity and employment eligibility within three (3) business days of the date employment begins. If employees are authorized to work, but are unable to present the required document(s) within three business days, they must present a receipt for the application of the document(s) within three business days and the actual document(s) within ninety (90) days. However, if employers hire individuals for a duration of less than three business days, Section 2 must be completed at the time employment begins. **Employers must record**: **1)** document title; **2)** issuing authority; **3)** document number, **4)** expiration date, if any; and **5)** the date employment begins. Employers must sign and date the certification. Employees must present original documents. Employers may, but are not required to, photocopy the document(s) presented. These photocopies may only be used for the verification process and must be retained with the I-9. **However, employers are still responsible for completing the I-9.**

Section 3 - Updating and Reverification. Employers must complete Section 3 when updating and/or reverifying the I-9. Employers must reverify employment eligibility of their employees on or before the expiration date recorded in Section 1. Employers **CANNOT** specify which document(s) they will accept from an employee.

- If an employee's name has changed at the time this form is being updated/ reverified, complete Block A.
- If an employee is rehired within three (3) years of the date this form was originally completed and the employee is still eligible to be employed on the same basis as previously indicated on this form (updating), complete Block B and the signature block.

and • If an employee is rehired within three (3) years of the date this form was originally completed and the employee's work authorization has expired **or** if a current employee's work authorization is about to expire (reverification), complete Block B and:
  - examine any document that reflects that the employee is authorized to work in the U.S. (see List A **or** C),
  - record the document title, document number and expiration date (if any) in Block C. and
  - complete the signature block.

Photocopying and Retaining Form I-9. A blank I-9 may be reproduced provided both sides are copied. The Instructions must be available to all employees completing this form. Employers must retain completed I-9s for three (3) years after the date of hire **or** one (1) year after the date employment ends, whichever is later.

For more detailed information, you may refer to the INS <u>Handbook for Employers</u>, (Form M-274). You may obtain the handbook at your local INS office.

Privacy Act Notice. The authority for collecting this information is the Immigration Reform and Control Act of 1986, Pub. L. 99-603 (8 U.S.C. 1324a).

This information is for employers to verify the eligibility of individuals for employment to preclude the unlawful hiring, or recruiting or referring for a fee, of aliens who are not authorized to work in the United States.

This information will be used by employers as a record of their basis for determining eligibility of an employee to work in the United States. The form will be kept by the employer and made available for inspection by officials of the U.S. Immigration and Naturalization Service, the Department of Labor, and the Office of Special Counsel for Immigration Related Unfair Employment Practices.

Submission of the information required in this form is voluntary. However, an individual may not begin employment unless this form is completed since employers are subject to civil or criminal penalties if they do not comply with the Immigration Reform and Control Act of 1986.

Reporting Burden. We try to create forms and instructions that are accurate, can be easily understood, and which impose the least possible burden on you to provide us with information. Often this is difficult because some immigration laws are very complex. Accordingly, the reporting burden for this collection of information is computed as follows: **1)** learning about this form, 5 minutes; **2)** completing the form, 5 minutes; and **3)** assembling and filing (recordkeeping) the form, 5 minutes, for an average of 15 minutes per response. If you have comments regarding the accuracy of this burden estimate, or suggestions for making this form simpler, you can write to both the Immigration and Naturalization Service, 425 I Street, N.W., Room 5304, Washington, D. C. 20536; and the Office of Management and Budget, Paperwork Reduction Project, OMB No. 1115-0136, Washington, D.C. 20503.

Form I-9 (Rev. 11-21-91) N

EMPLOYERS MUST RETAIN COMPLETED I-9
PLEASE DO NOT MAIL COMPLETED I-9 TO INS

FIGURE 4-12 Example of I-9 Form (*Source:* U.S. Department of Justice, Immigration, and Naturalization Services)

U.S. Department of Justice
Immigration and Naturalization Service

OMB No. 1115-0136
Employment Eligibility Verification

Please read instructions carefully before completing this form. The instructions must be available during completion of this form. ANTI-DISCRIMINATION NOTICE. It is illegal to discriminate against work eligible individuals. Employers CANNOT specify which document(s) they will accept from an employee. The refusal to hire an individual because of a future expiration date may also constitute illegal discrimination.

Section 1. Employee Information and Verification. To be completed and signed by employee at the time employment begins

Print Name: Last	First	Middle Initial	Maiden Name
Address *(Street Name and Number)*		Apt. #	Date of Birth *(month/day/year)*
City	State	Zip Code	Social Security #

I am aware that federal law provides for imprisonment and/or fines for false statements or use of false documents in connection with the completion of this form.

I attest, under penalty of perjury, that I am (check one of the following):
A citizen or national of the United States
A Lawful Permanent Resident (Alien # A____________
An alien authorized to work until__/___/___
(Alien # or Admission #____________________

Employee's Signature	Date *(month/day/year)*

Preparer and/or Translator Certification. *(To be completed and signed if Section 1 is prepared by a person other than the employee.) I attest, under penalty of perjury, that I have assisted in the completion of this form and that to the best of my knowledge the information is true and correct.*

Preparer's/Translator's Signature	Print Name
Address *(Street Name and Number, City, State, Zip Code)*	Date *(month/day/year)*

Section 2. Employer Review and Verification. To be completed and signed by employer. **Examine one document from List A OR examine one document from List B** __and__ **one from List C** as listed on the reverse of this form and record the title, number and expiration date, if any, of the document(s)

	List A	OR	List B	AND	List C
Document title:	_____________		__________________		__________________
Issuing authority:	____________		__________________		__________________
Document #:	_____________		__________________		__________________
Expiration Date *(if any)*:	__/__/__		__/__/__		__/__/__
Document #:	_____________				
Expiration Date *(if any)*:	__/__/__				

CERTIFICATION - I attest, under penalty of perjury, that I have examined the document(s) presented by the above-named employee, that the above-listed document(s) appear to be genuine and to relate to the employee named, that the employee began employment on *(month/day/year)* **___/___/___and that to the best of my knowledge the employee is eligible to work in the United States. (State employment agencies may omit the date the employee began employment).**

Signature of Employer or Authorized Representative	Print Name	Title
Business or Organization Name	Address *(Street Name and Number, City, State, Zip Code)*	Date *(month/day/year)*

Section 3. Updating and Reverification. To be completed and signed by employer

A. New Name *(if applicable)*	B. Date of rehire *(month/day/year) (if applicable)*

C. If employee's previous grant of work authorization has expired, provide the information below for the document that establishes current employment eligibility.

Document Title:____________Document #:____________Expiration Date (if any):__/__/__

I attest, under penalty of perjury, that to the best of my knowledge, this employee is eligible to work in the United States, and if the employee presented document(s), the document(s) I have examined appear to be genuine and to relate to the individual.

Signature of Employer or Authorized Representative	Date *(month/day/year)*

Form I-9 (Rev. 11-21-91) N

FIGURE 4–12 Example of I-9 Form *(continued)*

LISTS OF ACCEPTABLE DOCUMENTS

LIST A		LIST B		LIST C
Documents that Establish Both Identity and Employment Eligibility	**OR**	**Documents that Establish Identity**	**AND**	**Documents that Establish Employment Eligibility**
1. U.S. Passport (unexpired or expired)		1. Driver's license or ID card issued by a state or outlying possession of the United States provided it contains a photograph or information such as name, date of birth, sex, height, eye color, and address		1. U.S. social security card issued by the Social Security Administration *(other than a card stating it is not valid for employment)*
2. Certificate of U.S. Citizenship *(INS Form N-560 or N-561)*		2. ID card issued by federal, state, or local government agencies or entities provided it contains a photograph or information such as name, date of birth, sex, height, eye color, and address		2. Certification of Birth Abroad issued by the Department of State *(Form FS-545 or Form DS-1350)*
3. Certificate of Naturalization *(INS Form N-550 or N-570)*		3. School ID card with a photograph		3. Original or certified copy of a birth certificate issued by a state, county, municipal authority or outlying possession of the United States bearing an official seal
4. Unexpired foreign passport, with *I-551 stamp or* attached *INS Form I-94* indicating unexpired employment authorization		4. Voter's registration card		4. Native American tribal document
5. Alien Registration Receipt Card with photograph *(INS Form I-151 or I-551)*		5. U.S. Military card or draft record		5. U.S. Citizen ID Card *(INS Form I-197)*
6. Unexpired Temporary Resident Card *(INS Form I-688)*		6. Military dependent's ID card		6. ID Card for use of Resident Citizen in the United States *(INS Form I-179)*
7. Unexpired Employment Authorization Card *(INS Form I-688A)*		7. U.S. Coast Guard Merchant Mariner Card		7. Unexpired employment authorization document issued by the INS *(other than those listed under List A)*
8. Unexpired Reentry Permit *(INS Form I-327)*		8. Native American tribal document		
9. Unexpired Refugee Travel Document *(INS Form I-571)*		9. Driver's license issued by a Canadian government authority		
10. Unexpired Employment Authorization Document issued by the INS which contains a photograph *(INS Form I-688B)*		**For persons under age 18 who are unable to present a document listed above:**		
		10. School record or report card		
		11. Clinic, doctor, or hospital record		
		12. Day-care or nursery school record		

Illustrations of many of these documents appear in Part 8 of the Handbook for Employers (M-274)

Form I-9 (Rev. 11-21-91) N

FIGURE 4–12 Example of I-9 Form *(concluded)*

include a U.S. passport, certificate of U.S. citizenship, green card, foreign passport with the Immigration and Naturalization Service (INS) stamp authorizing the individual to work, certificate of naturalization, U.S. birth certificate with picture ID, or social security number with picture ID. A *Handbook for Employers: Instructions for Completing Form I-9* is available from the U.S. Department of Justice that details the appropriateness of documents and the verification of documents.

Americans with Disabilities Act

The Americans with Disabilities Act (ADA) has been called the most significant civil rights legislation to pass Congress since the Civil Rights Act of 1964. Since becoming law on July 26, 1990, with President George Bush's signature, the ADA outlaws discrimination based on disability in employment, public accommodations, government services, transportation, and telecommunications. This antidiscrimination legislation is intended to assure the civil rights of disabled persons. Nondiscrimination is prohibited by the ADA in all employment practices. This includes all aspects of the employment process, including recruitment, advertising methods, job application procedures, hiring, and placement. It also applies to all other employment-related activities such as training, advancement, compensation, benefits, tenure, leave, termination, and other terms, conditions, and privileges of employment. It is critical that managers with human resources responsibilities in the hospitality industry become aware of their legal obligations under this legislation.

The ADA is divided into five major components, called titles. Title I requires that businesses provide reasonable accommodation to protect the rights of persons with disabilities in the areas of employment we just discussed. A reasonable accommodation is "a modification or adjustment to a job, employment practice, or work environment that enables a *qualified individual with a disability* to participate in and enjoy equal employment opportunity."[14] If an employee's job or disability changes, the reasonable accommodation requirement still applies as long as it does not cause undue hardship for the employer. An undue hardship means that the adjustment does not require significant difficulty or expense "in relation to the size of the company, available resources, or the nature of the business."[15] Accommodation refers to any modifications or adjustments to the job process, work environment, or conditions under which the job is performed that enables a qualified disabled person to do the job. One of management's challenges in working with the ADA in the area of reasonable accommodation is to seek available funding from other sources (such as a state vocational rehabilitation agency) if shown that the cost of the accommodation would impose an undue hardship. The employer should also give the disabled person the option of paying for, or providing the accommodation when undue hardship is proven.

The ADA gives the Department of Justice (DOJ) the authority to issue regulations for Title II, which deals with Public Services, and Title III, which deals with Public Accommodations (including food service and lodging establishments). The DOJ also provides technical assistance and enforcement. Title IV applies to companies offering telecommunication services, and Title V prohibits threats or retaliation against those who assert the rights of the disabled under the ADA (see Table 4-6).

TABLE 4-6 Titles Under ADA

- Employment (Title I)
- Public Services (Title II)
- Public Accommodations (Title III)
- Telecommunications (Title IV)
- Miscellaneous (Title V)

A *disabled person* is defined as:

- anyone with a physical or mental impairment that substantially limits a major life activity
- anyone who has a record of such an impairment
- anyone perceived as having such an impairment

Major life activities include caring for oneself, walking, seeing, hearing, speaking, breathing, learning, working, and performing manual tasks. Thus the ADA applies to persons with substantial, not minor impairments. The ADA does not give a list of specific disabilities; what would be a disability in one person might not be in another. For example, the ADA does not specifically name arthritis as a disability. Whether a person with arthritis would be covered under the ADA would depend upon the severity of the arthritis and the effect it has on the person in specific situations.

The second part of the definition of a disabled person would include, for example, a person who had a history of mental illness or a person who had cancer that is currently in remission. And the third part of the definition would cover an individual who, though not really disabled, is treated as though he or she were by others. This would include a person who is disfigured or deformed and may be refused employment because of the perceived negative reactions that disfigurement might have on other people.

A *qualified individual with a disability* is one who meets the skill, education, experience, and other requirements of the job description and job specification for a particular job position and can perform the *"essential functions"* of the job position with or without reasonable accommodation. This means that if there are certain functions of the job that are merely incidental, an individual cannot be considered unqualified simply because of an inability to perform them. If the person is unable to perform an essential function, the issue of reasonable accommodation is raised. Table 4-7 identifies some examples of reasonable accommodation used by Brinker International, parent company of Chili's.

TABLE 4-7 Examples of Reasonable Accommodation Used by Brinker International

1. Job restricting. Reassigning some secondary job duties, or allowing employees to swap these duties to accommodate a disability.
2. Changing the work schedule. Shifting the schedule to allow an employee with epilepsy to use local public transit.
3. Changing test and training materials. Verbally reading a test to a visually impaired employee.
4. Acquiring and/or modifying equipment. A special phone amplifier for a hearing impaired employee working at the hostess stand.

(Reprinted with permission from "Title 1: Employment All You Need to Know," *Brinker International.)*

Although the ADA does not provide a list of named disabilities, we know that it does cover all impairments including vision, hearing impairments, speech impediments, neuromuscular, emotional, mental retardation, AIDS, persons with HIV infection, cancers, heart disease, epilepsy, cerebral palsy, multiple sclerosis, diabetes, and persons who have successfully completed or are currently enrolled in a drug rehabilitation program and are no longer illegally using drugs. Individuals who currently use illegal drugs are specifically excluded from ADA coverage. The ADA does not authorize, encourage, or prohibit drug tests. Testing for illegal drug use is not considered a medical exam under the ADA.

Providing reasonable accommodations is not always as expensive as you might, at first, think. Brinker International has found that most accommodations cost relatively little and that half of all accommodations cost less than $50.00. They also point out that oftentimes the cost of special equipment is covered by the state rehabilitation department or local agencies who assist in helping employers and potential employees who are disabled make successful partnerships.

Please remember that at all times you are free to select the most qualified job applicant for a job vacancy. The ADA does not require you to hire unqualified employees. The ADA does not require you to replace an incumbent employee with a disabled person. The ADA does not require you to change essential job functions to enable a disabled person to perform the job. Nor does the ADA require you to lower your service or production standards to accommodate a person with a disability. As managers with human resources responsibilities, you should exercise caution in the employment process. It is more important than ever that you follow good human resources practice and determine job qualifications and "essential functions" before starting the recruitment process. Remember that properly prepared job descriptions are critical in complying with the regulations. Thoroughly review your employment policies, processes, and procedures, including your application forms and selection criteria. Don't rush to make a judgment about whether a job applicant has a disability, what the job applicant is capable of doing, or what type of accommodation might be necessary to enable the job applicant to perform the job.

One of the most helpful things that you can do as a manager with human resources responsibilities in the hospitality industry is to immerse yourself in ADA literature. And luckily that is not hard to do. There is an increasing wealth of information available on the ADA. Much of this information can be found on the **World Wide Web (www)**. Government resources, general resources, resources on specific disabilities, news resources as well as a multitude of other Internet resources are readily available and very user friendly. Some of these are identified in Table 4-8 and Table 4-9. The more basic background information you have learned, the easier it will be to make good, defendable human resources management decisions. You should always check with legal counsel as you develop your policies, processes, and procedures in the areas we have discussed.

There are many hospitality organizations that have traditionally and voluntarily offered employment opportunities to people with disabilities. Today, hiring disabled employees is the law. In the area of recruitment, you must make sure that you thoroughly review the job-application forms. Make sure that you limit questions to only those that concern the applicant's ability to perform the job. The EEOC recommends avoiding questions that pertain to disabilities such as:

- history of mental-health treatment
- listing of diseases or major illnesses
- disabilities, impairments, or impediments
- hospitalization history
- days absent from work in prior years or jobs because of illness
- worker's compensation history
- list of prescription medications
- history of treatment for drug abuse or alcoholism

Though not all of these questions are in violation of ADA regulations, they are not job related and, as such, serve no job-related purpose. Although some answers to these questions might be needed by the hospitality organization, you are better off waiting until the job candidate is hired. When in doubt talk to your hospitality organization's legal counsel. And remember that you *can* ask whether an applicant can perform specific job functions or would need a specific accommodation if hired.

TABLE 4-8 Internet Sites and Resources on ADA

ADA Home Page
This site is operated by the U.S. Department of Justice. There you can find information about the ADA Information line, the Department's ADA enforcement activities, the ADA Technical Assistance Program, proposed changes in ADA regulations and requirements among other helpful items.
(www.usdoj.gov/crt/ada/adahom1.htm)

ADA Technical Assistance Program
This is a federally funded network of grantees that provide information, training, and technical assistance to businesses and agencies with duties and responsibilities under the ADA and to people with disabilities with rights under the ADA.
(www.icdi/wvu.edu/tech/ADA.HTM)

American Association of People with Disabilities (AAPD)
A non-profit, non-partisan, cross-disability organization whose goals are unity, leadership, and impact. Anyone can join this organization.
(www.aapd-dc.org)

American with Disabilities Act Document Center
This website contains copies of the Americans with Disabilities Act of 1990, ADA regulations, technical assistance manuals, and links to disability-related web sites.
(janweb.icdi.wvu.edu/kinder)

JAN (Job Accommodation Network)
Provides free consulting on the American with Disabilities Act, job accommodations, and the employability of people with disabilities.
(janweb.icdi.wvu.edu)

Job Links
The President's Committee on Employment of People with Disabilities provides direct Internet links to the employment pages of employers seeking qualified job applicants with disabilities.
(www.pcepd.gov/joblinks.htm)

National Association of Protection and Advocacy Systems (NAPAS)
This association represents federally mandated programs that protect the rights of persons with disabilities.
(protectionandadvocacy.com)

TABLE 4-9 For More Information on ADA Concerns and Issues

For information about ADA requirements affecting employment (Title I issues), contact:
Equal Employment Opportunity Commission
1801 L Street NW
Washington, DC 20507
800-669-4000 (Voice) 800-669-6820 (TDD)

For information about ADA requirements affecting Public Services (Title II) and Public Accommodations (Title IV), contact:
Office on the Americans with Disabilities Act
Civil Rights Division
U.S. Department of Justice
P.O. Box 66118
Washington, DC 20035-6118
202-514-0301 (Voice) 202-514-0383 (TDD)

For information about ADA requirements affecting transportation (Title II), contact:
Department of Transportation
400 Seventh Street SW
Washington, DC 20590
202-366-9305(Voice) 202-755-7687(TDD)

For information about requirements for accessible design in new construction and alterations, contact:
Architectural and Transportation Barriers Compliance Board
1111 18th Street NW
Suite 501
Washington, DC 20036
800-USA-ABLE (Voice) 800-USA-ABLE (TDD)

For information about ADA requirements affecting telecommunications (Title IV), contact:
Federal Communications Commission
1919 M Street NW
Washington, DC 20554
202-632-7260 (Voice) 202-632-6999 (TDD)

Executive Order 13078

On March 13, 1998, President Clinton signed into law **Executive Order 13078**, establishing the Presidential Task Force on the Employment of Adults with Disabilities. "By the authority vested in me as President by the Constitution and the laws of the United States of America, and in order to increase the employment of adults with disabilities to a rate that is as close as possible to the employment rate of the general adult population and to support the goals articulated in the findings and purpose section of the Americans with Disabilities Act of 1990, it is hereby ordered the establishment of the Presidential Task Force on the Employment of Adults with Disabilities."[16] The task force has been mandated to evaluate existing Federal programs and identify what modifications and changes may be necessary to remove some of the barriers faced by disabled persons when seeking employment. Some of the areas they will look at will include childcare, vocational rehabilitation, training services, employment retention, on-the-job support and promotion opportunities, or lack thereof. The Task Force issued its initial report to the President by November 15, 1998, with a final report due on July 26, 2002, the 10th anniversary date of the American with Disabilities Act of 1990. While the scope of the investigation is limited to existing federal programs, there is the potential that recommendations might reach the private sector through further legislation in the years to come. With so many of the areas being looked at by the Task Force overlapping our human resources functions, the outcomes of this Executive Order will be something for us to watch.

CONCLUSION

Hospitality organizations were once accustomed to selecting their human resources from piles of applications, but the baby boomers and the changing demographic patterns in the United States have forced us to become more aggressive and more innovative in our recruitment methods. Recruiting the labor we need has become very competitive, not only among other hospitality organizations but among all service industries. That means that we need to become more flexible in our recruitment practices.

Recruitment is a necessary function in every hospitality organization. If you can't staff your operations, you can't open your doors for business. The human resources hiring process begins with recruiting. As a manager with human resources responsibilities it will be necessary for you to develop a plan for your recruitment strategy. Though there is no one best strategy for all hospitality operations, with proper identification of viable labor pools and effective utilization of recruitment methods, you can accomplish your goal of locating qualified job applicants when you need them.

The employment process for your hospitality organization begins with recruitment. We now turn to a discussion on selection, hiring, and placement to complete the employment function of human resources management.

INDUSTRY EXPERTS SPEAK

"The bottom line is that we need people. Our customer base is as diverse as our employee base. The most successful recruitment programs are those that find people who are as diverse as the community. The diversity of our employees should be a direct reflection of the diversity in the communities where they work.

"In recruiting today you have to be willing to take chances on good people who may not have the exact background you are looking for, but possess great interpersonal skills. When you recruit you are paid to make decisions on people and that includes making some mistakes. If you never take risks you will never be fully staffed.

"You must use ***all*** the recruiting methods and tools discussed in this chapter. No one source will fill your needs. You must have consistent on-going recruitment efforts. No longer can you start recruiting when you need the people. Recruitment must be a daily focus."

Jan Barr, Human Resource Director, Chili's

Case Problem 4-1

You are the manager of a full-service restaurant located in a suburban location of Jacksonville, Florida. Sales in this operation run about $48,000 a week at the present time, but sales have been increasing steadily week by week. As a result, you need to begin adding staff to replace some turnover and to accommodate the building sales. Your total staff presently is forty front-of-the-house and twenty-six back-of-the-house employees.

Your completed human resources personnel plan shows that you need the following:

- 6 servers
- 1 host(ess)
- 2 bussers
- 1 cook
- 2 dishwashers

In your geographical location there are several community publications and organizations, and one community college very near to you. You have traditionally had a very stable team of employees with very little turnover. Your restaurant and your employees are very involved in community events and have positive name recognition and image in the community.

You have not had to do any recruiting in the last nine months. The unemployment in your area hasn't changed in the last two years, holding steady at 5 percent. Your competition includes four restaurants similar to yours and twelve fast-food restaurants, plus the retail stores at the mall down the street.

Prepare a three-page recruiting game plan for your General Manager. Be sure to be specific as you address how you are going to fill your human resources personnel plan.

Case Problem 4-2

You are the General Manager of an economy lodging property located in the Northwest at an interstate exchange outside a major city. You have been with this company for four years and the General Manager at this particular location for six months. The property has 155 rooms with a complimentary breakfast only food service facility. This property is part of a national chain providing you with some name recognition.

Historically, you have been able to depend on the teenage labor force to supplement your full-time staff during weekends, summer, and busy peak periods. Because your property is located on a major interchange, which is a major travel route, the business is somewhat seasonal with a heavier traffic flow during the summer months. As of late, you have not been able to depend upon the teenage labor force to supplement your full-time staff during these critical peak periods.

Why do you think that you are having trouble hiring the teenage labor force in your area? What are some of the things that you might do to stimulate their interest, not only in a part-time job in your property while they are going to school but as a potential career opportunity?

Additionally, you recognize that you must develop an action plan of alternative sources of labor that you could seek through your recruitment efforts. Develop a list of alternative sources of labor that might be available to you to supplement your full-time staff. List the advantages and disadvantages of each source identified. Of the alternative labor sources you have identified, which do you feel will work out best for your particular property? Explain why.

Case Problem 4-3

You are the General Manager of a full-service restaurant with a huge turnover problem since four new restaurants, a high-paying factory, and a new mall opened in the last six months. You are located in a small town in the Midwest. All this growth has been great for your town, but it has been terrible on your turnover!

You have lost eight employees in the last month because they think they have better benefits where they are going. Your benefits are just as good, but your managers and employees don't understand what is available to them.

You must stop the turnover and add twelve new employees to be staffed as quickly as possible. Everyone in your town has a "Now Hiring" banner displayed because turnover in the area is at an all-time low of 2.8 percent.

You also suspect that one of your key managers is looking for a job that pays more at the factory.

Develop a three-page game plan to (a) stop the turnover and (b) hire the needed employees.

Key Words

advertisement
affirmative action
alternative labor pools
Americans with Disabilities Act (ADA)
baby boomers
Balanced Budget Act of 1997
demographic information
disabled
electronic recruiting systems
employment agencies
ethnic composition
Executive Order 11246
Executive Order 13078
executive search firms
external recruitment
hiring requisition
I-9 form
immigrants
Immigration Act of 1990
Immigration Reform and Control Act
internal recruitment
Internet
job candidate
Job Service Center
labor shortage
leasing company
Legally Authorized Worker's (LAW) program
online recruiting
recruitment
referrals
Rehabilitation Act of 1973
rehabilitation agency
Revised Order No. 4
temp-help
The Education of Handicapped Children Act
Veteran's Readjustment Assistance Act
warm body syndrome
web sites
Welfare-to-Work
World Wide Web (www)

Recommended Reading

Belman, D. 1995. "The Graying of America: Implications of an Aging Labor Pool." *Restaurant USA* 15(4): 14–18.

Bond, J., E. Galinsky, and J. Swanberg. 1998. *The 1997 National Study of the Changing Workforce.* New York: Families and Work Institute.

Bruns, R. "When the Biggest Barrier Falls." *Lodging Magazine.* www.ei-ahma.org/webs/ lodging/ 9802/coverstory.htm (13 July 1998).

Crispin, G. and M. Mehler. 1999. *CAREERXROADS.* Kendall Park, NJ: MMC Publishing.

Grossman, R. "Short-Term Workers Raise Long-Term Issues." *HR Magazine.* www.shrm.org/hrmagazine/articles/0498cov.htm (4 October 1998).

Heubusch, K. and J. Galper. "Jobs at Play and Jobs That Pay." *America Demographics Magazine.* www.demographics.com/publications/ad/98_ad/9805_d/ad980527.htm (23 August 1998).

Magill, B. G. "ADA Accomodations: Don't Have to Break the Bank." *HR Magazine.* www.shrm.org/hrmagazine/articles/0797ada.htm (16 September 1998).

Overman, S. 1997. "People To-Work Initiatives: Nurturing the American Dream." *Restaurant USA* 17(3): 22–26.

Rousseau, R. "Feeding the New America." *Restaurant & Institutions.* www.rimag.com/04/feed.htm (15 July 1998).

Rubis, L. "Show and Tell." *HR Magazine.* www.shrm.org/hrmagazine/articles/0498dish.htm (5 August 1998).

The U.S. Equal Employment Opportunity Commission. 1997. *The ADA: Your Employment Rights as an Individual with a Disability.* Washington, DC: U.S.E.E.O.C.

The U.S. Equal Employment Opportunity Commission. 1997. *The ADA: Your Responsibilities as an Employer.* Washington, DC: U.S.E.E.O.C.

Recommended Web Sites

1. Americans with Disabilities Act Document Center: janweb.icdi.wvu.edu/kinder
2. ADA Disability Information: www.public.iastate.edu/~sbilling/ada.html
3. American Association of Retired Persons: ww.aarp.org
4. American Civil Liberties Union: www.aclu.org
5. Seniors On-Line (Canada): www.ageofreason.com/sol.htm
6. Census Bureau's Disability Site: www.census.gov/hhes/www/disable.html
7. National Council on Aging: www.ncoa.org
8. Statistics Canada: www.statcan.ca/sta
9. Disabled American Veterans: www.dav.org
10. Career-Related Web Sites:
    www.bestrecruit.com
    www.careerlinx.com
    www.careermosaic.com
    www.careerpath.com
    www.classifieds2000.com
    www.hotjobs.com
    www.jobnet.com
    www.jobtrak.com
    www.monster.com

11. U.S. Department of Labor: www.dol.gov
12. Ocupational Safety and Health Administration: www.osha.gov
13. Social Security Administration: www.ssa.gov
14. Welfare To Work Partnership: www.welfaretowork.org

Endnotes

1. Kevin Heubusch, "Jobs At Play and Jobs That Pay," *American Demographics* 20, no. 5 (1998): 50.
2. Ibid.
3. Kathy Seal, "Recruiters Find Labor Worldwide," *Hotel & Motel Management*, 213, no. 4 (1998): 8.
4. Stephanie Armour, "Frantic Employers Search High, Low for Summer Help," *USA Today*, June 17, 1998, p. 5B.
5. Unknown, "Age Often Shapes Worker Paths." *Chicago Tribune*, April 21, 1998, p. 5.
6. American Hotel & Motel Association, *1996 Lodging Industry Profile*. Washington, DC: American Hotel & Motel Association, 1996.
7. Unknown, "Restaurant Employment to Reach 12 Million by 2006," *Restaurants USA* 18, no. 2 (1998): 45.
8. Ibid.
9. Frederick J. DeMicco and Robert Reid, "Older Workers Are New Flavor in Fast Food," *Globe & Mail*, June 17, 1997, p. B9.
10. Ibid.
11. John M. McNeil, *Americans with Disabilities: 1994–95* (Washington, DC: U.S. Census Bureau, 1997).
12. National Restaurant Association, *1998 Restaurant Industry Pocket Factbook* (Washington, DC: National Restaurant Association, 1998).
13. Barbara Grady, "As Job Market Surges, So Do Job Sites," *Internet World*, April 13, 1998. www. internetworld.com/print/1998/04/13/intcareers/19980413-surges.html (15 May 1998).
14. Dale S. Brown, Susan M. Bruyere, and David Mank, "The ADA and Total Quality Management." janweb.icdi.wvu.edu/kinder/pages/TQM.html (4 April 1998).
15. Ibid.
16. Department of Labor, *Fact Sheet Executive Order 13078*. www.dol.gov/dol/-sec/public/programs/ptfead/factsht.htm (30 March 1998).

Discussion Questions

1. What is recruitment? Explain recruitment's relationship to human resources planning and analysis functions.
2. Describe the effect of demographic changes in American society on the recruitment of human resources for the hospitality industry. What actions can you take in a tight labor market?
3. Identify four viable labor pools that might be tapped for recruitment purposes. Discuss the advantages and the disadvantages of recruiting each of the four groups you identified.
4. List several advantages of recruiting internal sources. List several advantages of recruiting from external labor sources. Which do you prefer? Why?

5. Identify and describe at least six methods of recruiting.
6. Explain how the Internet has changed recruitment.
7. Explain affirmative action and how it affects your job of recruiting qualified candidates for job vacancies.
8. Describe the use of temporary help agencies. When might you use their services as a manager with human resources responsibilities in the hospitality industry?
9. How do you feel about recruiting former employees and job applicants? Defend your position.
10. Discuss the effects of the Americans with Disabilities Act on recruitment.
11. Describe who meets the requirements of a disabled person under the Americans with Disabilities Act.

CHAPTER 5

Selection, Hiring, and Placement

 **INDUSTRY ADVISOR**

BOB MORRISON, *President, Quetico Corporation*

"The closest to perfection a person ever comes is when he fills out a job application form."

— STANLEY J. RANDALL

"It's a funny thing about life; if you refuse to accept anything but the best, you very often get it."

—W. SOMERSET MAUGHAM

INTRODUCTION

Employment policies are designed to meet the needs of the hospitality organization and the people who are affected by them. The organization's policies provide answers to employment questions, so it is important that the content be communicated to all members of the hospitality organization to whom they apply. Policies must be developed that pertain to proper selection, hiring, and placement. Individuals in your organization who will take part in the employment process need to be identified. It is not uncommon for the operational managers to shoulder the responsibilities for selection, hiring, and placement. In the course of your already very busy day, you are likely to find yourself needing to conduct an interview or make some calls regarding a reference check. Much of what we are about to discuss presents the ideal situation or environment for undertaking the employment process. We are aware, however, that operational managers with human resources responsibilities do not always find themselves with enough time for the "ideal." These final steps in the employment process are critical in ensuring that the right people are selected, hired, and placed appropriately in your organization. Every attempt should be made to take this process seriously and to find the time you need to do a good job in this area of human resources management.

The employment process varies from hospitality organization to hospitality organization. Each establishment must decide the policies and procedures that best serve the mission statement of the enterprise. Due to the very high turnover ratios in the hospitality industry (quick service operations have reported ratios as high as 400 percent), the proper screening of job applicants has taken on a new importance. Oftentimes, the individuals who leave our operations should never have been hired in the first place. Choosing the wrong individual for a job vacancy can be both time-consuming and a waste of money. In this chapter, we provide you with insight on selecting, hiring, and placing the right job applicant.

At the conclusion of this chapter you will be able to:

1. Describe the importance and effects of employment law in the employment process.
2. Understand the implications of Equal Employment Opportunity (EEO), the ADA, and other employment laws regarding the discrimination of job applicants.
3. Identify the items that should be included on an employment application.
4. Describe what you should do to prepare for conducting a job interview.
5. Develop interview questions pertinent to the job vacancy.
6. Identify questions that are illegal to ask during a job interview.
7. Prepare the necessary forms used for documentation during the employment process.
8. Conduct a reference check for a job applicant.
9. Identify some of the preemployment tests that you might want to use as a screening tool.
10. Discuss the proper maintenance of personnel records and files.
11. Understand the objectives involved in making a hiring decision.
12. Define negligent hiring and it's implications.
13. Identify the benefits of instituting a probationary hiring period.

SELECTION

The **selection** process involves several different screening methods. **Screening** can be defined as a method that allows you to make the best selection from the pool of available **job applicants** while at the same time maintaining compliance with the legal restrictions and requirements at federal, state, and local levels. The organizational level at which the screening of hourly employees occurs varies among hospitality organizations, depending upon their departmental structure. The objective remains the same at each level: to identify the job applicant who will develop into a valuable employee and a good representative of your hospitality organization. A person is only an asset when he or she performs his or her job efficiently and in accordance with job standards.

It is evident in the hospitality industry that poor selection methods are a major factor in high employee turnover. The selection methods used for your hospitality organization should be developed with great care. Proper and legal tools for selection need to be in place. These include **employment application** forms, interviewing procedures, **reference checks**, and even **preemployment testing**. Each tool must be designed so that only information pertinent to that particular job is obtained. Otherwise you may violate legal requirements. You are looking for information that will predict the behavior and performance of each job applicant. Sound easy?

The administration of these selection tools requires qualified, experienced, and trained individuals. Interviewers and other selection personnel must understand the job position, the hospitality organization and how to draw as much information as possible form the job applicant. If selection is the responsibility of the human resources division, then open channels of communication must be maintained with the operations division. Both divisions should play a major role in the selection process.

Before we look at the tools you need to ensure that your selection decision is the best one for your hospitality organization, we need to discuss the legalities of the employment process. These restrictions need to be kept in mind in many of our future discussions of human resources functions, methods, and policies.

Employment Law

Employment law is a broad area of law that covers all areas of the employer/employee relationship except the negotiation process, which is covered by collective bargaining and labor legislation. There are literally thousands of federal and state statutes, administrative regulations, and judicial decisions that make up employment law. Many of the laws, such as minimum wage regulations discussed in Chapter 10, were enacted as protective legislation. Other laws, such as unemployment insurance, were enacted as public policies. Laws such as **Title VII of the Civil Rights Act**, Age Discrimination in Employment Act, and the Americans with Disabilities Act take effect during the employment process and continue through the termination of the employment relationship.

As a general rule, federal labor laws apply to employers who have a defined number of employees. For example, you must adhere to the requirements of the ADA and Title VII if you have fifteen or more employees. Determination of number of employees is done by counting all employees who are on your payroll during a week for each week in the year. If you have fifteen or more employees on your payroll for at least twenty weeks in a year, you would be covered by ADA and Title VII for the entire year. And yes, this means that you must count each of your part-time people as well as temporary and leased workers. You do not count independent contractors. State laws, as you would expect, vary greatly from state to state. Many state laws are much tougher than federal laws especially in the area of **employment discrimination**. Some states require that an employer need have only one employee to become subject to their coverage. Therefore just because you are exempt from federal coverage does not mean necessarily that you are exempt from state civil rights laws. Be sure to check the state you are working in to ensure that you are in compliance. A number of Internet sites contain state information that can be helpful to you. But always, when in doubt consult with a lawyer. Employment discrimination is one of the main areas of employment law that must concern us as we now turn our attention to selection, hiring, and placement.

Employment Discrimination Law

The purpose of employment discrimination laws is to attempt to prevent discrimination on the basis of race, sex, religion, national origin, physical disability, and age by employers. There was an increase in legislation during the mid- to late 1990s that seeks to prevent employment discrimination based on sexual orientation. Throughout the 1990s there was an increase in the number of federal and state statutes in this area. Many states protect groups that are not covered by federal acts.

In the summer of 1999 the Supreme Court ruled that victims of workplace discrimination may be entitled to punitive damages if company officials could be found responsible. That means that if a company, rather than a supervisor, is responsible for the discrimination, then the company would have to pay punitive damages. If, however, a supervisor does not follow company policies and the supervisor is to blame for the discrimination, then it would not be fair to make the company pay punitive damages. This was seen as a huge victory for employers.[1] It emphasizes even more the importance of a strongly worded policy against workplace discrimination.

The Civil Rights Act of 1964

A civil right is an enforceable right or privilege that if interfered with by another gives rise to an action for injury. Discrimination of a person's civil rights occurs when those rights are denied or interfered with because of their membership in a certain group or class. The

Civil Rights Act of 1964 contains Titles I through VII. Title VII deals with a number of discrimination-related elements. It makes it unlawful for an employer to discriminate with respect to hiring, termination, compensation, conditions, privileges, or terms of employment on the basis of race, color, religion, sex, or national origin.

Equal Employment Opportunity Commission

The U.S. Equal Employment Opportunity Commission (EEOC) was established by Title VII and began operations on July 2, 1965. Operating out of its Washington, D.C. headquarters and in fifty field offices throughout the United States, it enforces the major federal statutes that prohibit employment discrimination. **Equal Employment Opportunity (EEO)** is the legal right of all individuals to be considered for employment and promotion solely on the basis of their ability, merit, and potential. EEO is mandated by law and prohibits the intentional or unintentional discrimination of employees because of race, color, sex, religion, age, non–job-related mental or physical disability, national origin, or veteran status. To discriminate means that you have treated an employee unfairly because of one or more of these conditions. When selection and advancement decisions are made, they must be done solely on the basis of ability, merit, and potential.

To provide Equal Employment Opportunity in your hospitality organization, management and nonmanagement employees must act fairly and without bias in all employment matters. This is true for the handling of applications, the conduct of the job interview, the questions that are asked of job candidates, the manner in which references are checked, and the administration of any preemployment tests. Employment decisions must be based on job-related elements, or they may be considered to be discriminatory.

Your position regarding EEO must be proactive, as good intentions are not enough. Any one of your employees or job applicants may go to the Equal Employment Opportunity Commission (EEOC) and file charges of discrimination against your hospitality organization. If that occurs and the EEOC finds that they have jurisdiction in the charges filed against you, the burden of proof is on you to prove that your actions were not discriminatory. Again, it does not matter if you did not intend to discriminate, the EEO law holds you accountable for compliance. If EEOC finds that you did take discriminatory actions in the employment process, then you will have to eliminate the cause of this discrimination and pay monetary compensation to the victims. Violation of EEO law can be very costly to your hospitality organization.

Many hospitality organizations have developed an Equal Employment Opportunity policy that specifies the intent of the organization with respect to discrimination. Procedures are developed for communicating this policy both externally and internally. Responsibilities for implementation of EEO policy are clearly defined. Periodic surveys are conducted to measure the effectiveness of the hospitality organization's EEO program. These surveys include monitoring the employment practices with respect to the racial-gender mix of the work force, the number of disabled in the work force, the place of residence of the work force, and promotion and termination activity.

The key to avoiding EEO complaints is to ensure that all procedures in the employment process are job related, applied uniformly to every job applicant, and objective. Promotions, transfers, and terminations also should be viewed from this perspective. Ask yourself these questions about the procedures you use:

- Is it related to job performance?
- Do you apply it in the same way to all job candidates?

- Will it have the same effect on all job candidates?
- Is it stated in objective terms that do not require subjective judgment?

The EEOC Best Practices Task Force was formed to study the "best" equal employment opportunity policies, programs, and practices of private sector employers. One of their findings is that the companies who responded to the Task Force adopted what they called a "SPLENDID" approach to their obligations under civil rights and EEO laws (Table 5-1). These serve as things that we can do as managers with human resources responsibilities to ensure that we protect the civil rights of each of our employees.

Of all the charges being filed with the EEOC, more than 20 percent involve Title VII of the Civil Rights Act of 1964. The next most common complaints are with the Americans with Disabilities Act (ADA) and the Age Discrimination in Employment Act, which we look at next.

TABLE 5-1 The "SPLENDID" Approach

STUDY–Know the law, the standard's that define your obligations and the various barriers to EEO and diversity. Seek assistance from the EEOC, professional consultants, or associations.

PLAN–Know your own situation with respect to your work force and demographics. Define your problems, propose solutions, and develop strategies for achieving them.

LEAD–Senior, middle, and lower management must champion the diversity as a business imperative. They must provide the leadership for successful attainment of a diverse work force.

ENCOURAGE–Companies should encourage the attainment of diversity by all managers and employees. Business practices and reward systems should be developed to reinforce those corporate objectives.

NOTICE–Take notice of the impact of your practices. Self-analysis is a key part of this process.

DISCUSSION–Communicate and reinforce the message that diversity is a business asset and a key element of business success.

INCLUSION–Bring everyone into this process, including white males. Everyone needs to be included in the analysis, planning, and implementation.

DEDICATION–Stay persistent. Long-term gains may cost in the short term. Invest in the needed human and capital resources.

(Equal Employment Opportunity Commission, "Best Practices of Private Sector Employers")

Age Discrimination

The Age Discrimination in Employment Act of 1967 (ADEA, amended) prohibits employment discrimination against individuals forty years of age and older. The prohibited employment practices outlined in this law are almost identical to those in Title VII. In addition an employer is prohibited from limiting, segregating, or classifying an employee in any way that would deprive that employee of opportunities or adversely affect his or her status because of age. There are explicit guidelines for benefits, pension, and retirement plans to which an employer must adhere. It is designed to promote the employment of older persons on the basis of ability rather than age and help both employers and employees find ways to meet problems that occur due to the impact of age on employment.

The law is enforced by the EEOC, which handles charges of age discrimination in just about the same way as they handle discrimination charges under Title VII. Many states have their own age discrimination laws. Be sure that you are aware of the laws in the state in which you work. EEOC requires that employers covered by the ADEA post notices explaining the coverage. These are available at your regional EEOC office.

The employment process in the hospitality industry must take care that references to age are omitted throughout the process. Although the ADEA does not specifically prohibit an employer from asking an applicant's age, request for age information will be closely examined to make sure the inquiry was lawful if a complaint is filed with the EEOC. Make sure that your recruitment campaigns are not looking for "young energetic types" or "June graduates." Review your applications to make sure it does not include birth date, dates of graduation from high school or dates of degrees received. When a person graduated is not job relevant, although the fact that they are a graduate could be job related information. Care has to be taken that interviewers are trained not to have any discussions related to age. As a general rule this legislation is easy to follow as long as your staff is educated so that they clearly understand that age does not have any place in an employment decision.

Laws Protecting Veterans

There are two pieces of legislation that protect against discrimination of our country's veterans. The first is the **Veterans Readjustment Assistance Act of 1974**. This requires the affirmative hiring practices of Vietnam and disabled veterans. The more recent is the **Veterans Reemployment Rights (VRR) Act** law of 1994. This expands the rights of service personnel who return to the work force after military service. Employers now have a greater responsibility to their employees who leave the workplace to engage in military service. Rights to reemployment are maintained, the time in which people can be away from their job has been expanded, and the employer has a responsibility to provide COBRA coverage (Chapter 11). This law was passed as some 270,000 individuals who had served as part of Operation Desert Storm returned to their civilian jobs.

The Civil Rights Act of 1991

President George Bush signed into law the **Civil Rights Act of 1991 (CRA)** on November 21 of that year. Amended in 1990 this act seeks to ensure all persons equal rights under the law. Under CRA, an employer violates the law if race, sex, religion, or national origin was a "motivating" factor in an employment decision. This law is very important to hospitality managers with human resources responsibilities as CRA places the burden of proof in **disparate impact** cases on the plaintiff. Disparate impact cases are those where an employment practice, while neutral in appearance, has a disparate (different) impact on a protected group, such as minorities or women.

In addition, the CRA created a twenty-one-member body known as the **Glass Ceiling Commission** to identify the barriers and promote advancement policies and practices for the promotion of women and minorities in the private sector. The term ***glass ceiling*** refers to the invisible barriers that prevent qualified people from advancing in their organization. The commission completed their study in 1996 and is now nonexistent. As a result of the commission, there is much literature available (see *Recommended Reading*) that helps identify the differences and similarities in barriers confronting men and women of historically underrepresented minority groups. It is important that the manager with human resources responsibilities make every effort to ensure that no one group is treated differently in the employment process. "If America's businesses fully utilized the nation's human capital, they would be making a solid investment."[2]

Discrimination and the Disabled

Title I of the Americans with Disabilities Act of 1990 (ADA) prohibits employment discrimination on the basis of disability as we discussed in Chapter 4. The type of discrimination prohibited in ADA is broader than that outlined in Title VII. Under ADA the job application is considered a preemployment inquiry. It can gather information on the skills, abilities, and credentials of the applicant, but it cannot be used to gather information about whether an applicant is an individual with a disability or as to the nature or severity of a disability. That means that questions regarding an applicant's prior or current illnesses are prohibited. The same restrictions carry over to the job interview. As the potential employer, your questions are limited to whether a job applicant can perform particular job functions. If the applicant has a disability known to the employer, the employer may ask if an accommodation would be needed to perform any of the job functions. The only time a medical exam can be required as a condition of a job offer is if medical exams are required of all new hires in that job category regardless of disability. Testing for drug use is not considered a medical exam. The ADA does not encourage, prohibit, or authorize drug tests as part of the preemployment process. You should ensure that any tests you use are designed to test the essential functions of the job and that they are accurate predictors of success on the job.

The ADA is intended to protect persons with AIDS and HIV from discrimination as well as those persons with physical or mental disabilities. Remember that this Act requires that as a manager with human resources responsibilities in the hospitality industry you focus on the abilities of your job applicants not their disabilities. The **Rehabilitation Act of 1973**, amended, prohibits employment discrimination against federal employees with disabilities and is enforced by the EEOC. There are many state statutes that provide extension protection from employment discrimination. Be sure that you are familiar with the state laws where your hospitality organization is located.

The Employment Application

Applications for employment are generally filled out by all individuals who express an interest in working for your hospitality organization. Applications make sure that you get all the information you need from your job applicants and enable you to tell the applicant some things about your company. They can be as simple or as complex as you design them. The key question when deciding what to include on an application is "Is this information required for business necessity?". Information requested on an application is used to make an employment decision. Previously in this chapter we reviewed some of the large number of antidiscriminatory laws that exist. It is always a good idea to have your attorney review your job application before you start using it.

On this form the applicant lists skills, work experience, and educational background along with job-relevant personal information. Relevant personal information might include the job applicant's name, address, social security number, and contact number. In the hospitality industry, information on the availability of the job applicant will also be important. For example, can the applicant work nights, weekends, and holidays if the job requires? Relevant information does not include race, national origin, religion, sexual preference, or age on an application. If age issues need to be clarified due to compliance with liquor laws or child labor laws, this should be done during the interview.

The employment application is one of the most common screening tools used today. It can screen out individuals who do not meet the basic job requirements as identified in the job specification. This prevents taking time to interview job applicants who are unsuitable for a particular job vacancy. As such, the application provides a quick and systematic approach to obtaining information about the applicant.

Employment applications (Figure 5-1) should be carefully designed to obtain enough information so that job applicants can be screened for a possible match with a job vacancy. At the same time, they should not invade the privacy of the applicant. Again, we repeat, if the information is not job related, then it probably should not be included on the application form. Many hospitality organizations have had to modify their employment applications in order to comply with constantly changing legislation such as the ADA. EEOC will act on complaints by job applicants who feel that the information asked on the employment application discriminates against them.

The only time questions can be asked pertaining to race, marital status, height, or weight is when they can be proven to be a **Bona Fide Occupational Qualification (BFOQ)**. BFOQ permits hiring practices normally prohibited by the EEOC, if the employer can prove that the violation is necessary to meet the duties and responsibilities of the job position. For example, you would be permitted to recruit and interview only males if the job opening was for a male locker room attendant. Historically, guest preference has not been accepted as a BFOQ defense, though sex and age have in some specific instances. The law basically believes that an applicant has a right to prove his or her ability to perform the job tasks. The law does not permit religion-based, gender-based, or national origin-based differences in pay to those holding the same job.

It is well worth the time to design an employment application that allows you to glean as much information as possible. Interviews are time-consuming and a waste of time when the applicant is clearly not qualified or suitable. The information you ask is based upon the qualities that are important to you and your hospitality organization. For example, short lengths of residence might indicate that the applicant is a drifter. Gaps in employment history might indicate a behavior problem or a period of incarceration.

Some hospitality organizations establish a point system for various job positions. Each item on the employment application such as education, work experience, and number of jobs held is assigned a specific number of points. For recruiting campaigns that stimulate many employment applications, each application is scored to determine how many points the applicant has. Then only those applicants with the most number of points are called in for interviews. It is good company policy to acknowledge every person who fills out a job application. Not only does it maintain good will, it keeps you from receiving numerous phone calls from applicants who want to know if you have their application on file. It is also good practice to let a job applicant know if they are not going to receive any further consideration

(continued on page 131)

INDUSTRY EXPERTS SPEAK

Bob Morrison, President of Quetico, points out that an application is a legal document. "Care should be taken not to write or make notes about the applicant on this document." Years ago when he was a District Manager it was his practice to review the application files whenever he visited one of the operations in his territory. One day he was going through some applications from candidates that had not been hired and noticed the letters U/G on several of them. Bob questioned the Assistant Manager as to the meaning of those letters and was told they meant "unattractive/glasses." Here was evidence of discrimination in hiring, in the Assistant Manager's own handwriting on applications. The manager's behavior was corrected immediately as it was not the company's policy to discriminate against unattractive people who wore glasses! Don't write ***anything*** on the employment application.

APPLICATION FOR EMPLOYMENT

As an EQUAL EMPLOYMENT OPPORTUNITY/AFFIRMATIVE ACTION EMPLOYER, ARAMARK Uniform Services, Inc., does not discriminate against applicants or employees because of their age, race, color, religion, national origin, sex (except where sex is a bona-fide occupational qualification) or on any other basis prohibited by law. Furthermore, ARAMARK will not discriminate against any applicant or employee because he or she is mentally or physically disabled, a disabled veteran, a veteran of the Vietnam era or has a non-job related medical condition, provided he or she is qualified and meets the requirements established by ARAMARK for the job.

PLEASE TYPE OR PRINT IN INK					Date
Name (Last)	(First)	(Middle)			Social security number
Current address (Street)	(City)	(State)	(Zip Code)		Phone number Area Code ( )
Person to contact in case of emergency					
Address (Street)	(City)	(State)	(Zip Code)		Phone number Area Code ( )

TYPE OF POSITION DESIRED		
Position applied for:		
☐ Full time ☐ Part time ☐ Summer ☐ Temporary ☐ Other		Salary expected
Will you relocate? ☐ Yes ☐ No Location preference:	Will you travel? (If applicable) ☐ Yes ☐ No	Date available to work with ARAMARK
Have you ever worked for ARAMARK? ☐ Yes ☐ No	If yes, when and where?	
Have you ever applied to ARAMARK? ☐ Yes ☐ No	If yes, when and where?	
How were you referred to ARAMARK?		

To comply with the Immigration Reform and Control Act of 1986, if you are hired you will be required to provide documents to establish your identity and your authorization to be employed in the United States. Such documents will be required within the first three (3) business days following your hire, or upon your first work day if your employment period will be less than three (3) days.

Are you willing to take a physical exam at our expense if the nature of the job requires one? ☐ Yes No ☐

Have you ever been convicted of a crime (misdemeanor or felony)?		☐ Yes No ☐	
If yes, explain: (Where)	(When)	(Charge)	(Sentence)

(Disclosure of a criminal record will not necessarily disqualify you for employment. Each conviction will be evaluated on its own merits with respect to time, circumstances and seriousness, in relation to the job for which you are applying.)

GO-112L (10/94)

FIGURE 5-1 ARAMARK Employment Application. *(Courtesy of ARAMARK Corporation)*

RECORD OF EDUCATION							
Name and Address of School		Dates Attended From Mo./Yr.	To Mo./Yr.	Graduated Yes	No	Type of degree/ diploma received or expected	Major/Minor Fields of Study
High School (Last Attended)							
Colleges/ Universities							
Graduate School							
Other (Business, Technical, Secretarial, etc.							

Have you ever belonged to a club, organization, society, or professional group which has a direct bearing upon your qualifications for the job which you are seeking? If Yes, Indicate by name.

Do you have any hobbies or interests which have a direct bearing on the job for which you are applying?

Do you have any special skills or abilities which directly relate to the job for which you are applying?

Do you possess a valid current driver's license (only for jobs requiring driving a vehicle)? ☐ Yes ☐ No
Driver's license number and state ____________

MILITARY SERVICE RECORD

Have you ever been a member of the armed forces of the United States? ☐ Yes ☐ No
Branch ____________ Rank upon exit ____________
If yes, did you develop any special skills or abilities which directly relate to the job for which you are applying?

FIGURE 5-1 ARAMARK Employment Application *(continued)*.

EXPERIENCE
(Most Recent Experience First)

1 Name and Address of Employer	Starting position		Job Duties
From Mo____Yr_____ to Mo____ Yr___ Phone Number Area Code ( )	Ending Position		Name and title of supervisor
	Salary (Beginning / Ending)	Reason for Leaving	
2 Name and Address of Employer	Starting Position		Job duties
From Mo____Yr_____ to Mo____Yr___ Phone Number Area Code ( )	Ending position		Name and title of supervisor
	Salary (Beginning / Ending)	Reason for leaving	
3 Name and Address of Employer	Starting position		Job duties
From Mo____Yr_____ to Mo____Yr___ Phone Number Area Code ( )	Ending position		Name and title of supervisor
	Salary (Beginning / Ending)	Reason for leaving	

May we contact the employers listed above? ☐ Yes ☐ No
If no, indicate by number which one(s) you do not wish us to contact ______

Use this space to describe any previous work history and/or to detail particular job responsiblities listed above. Include any additional information which you feel may be relevant to the job for which you are applying.

FIGURE 5-1 ARAMARK Employment Application *(continued)*.

I hereby certify that all statements made in this application are true and correct to the best of my knowledge and belief. I understand and agree that any misrepresentation or omission of facts in my application may be justification for refusal to hire, or termination of employment.

I further understand that an investigative report may be made as to my character and general reputation. I authorize all past employers, schools, persons and organizations having relevant information or knowledge to provide it to ARAMARK or its duly authorized representative for its use in deciding whether or not to offer me employment and specifically waive any required written notification. I hereby release employers, schools, persons and organizations from all liability in responding to inquiries in connection with my application. Upon written request by me, within a reasonable period of time, ARAMARK will make available to me the nature and scope of all reports of every type obtained to the extent required by applicable law.

This application is not a contract and cannot create a contract. I understand that if accepted by the Company, any employment of me will be on a 3 month introductory basis. If employed by the Company, I agree to abide by its rules and regulations. Further, I understand that my employment is "at will" and can be terminated at any time by either party, with or without cause and with or without notice.

In signing this form, I certify that I understand all the questions and statements in this application.

Further, if granted a position with ARAMARK Uniform Services, Inc., or any of its subsidiaries, I will comply with ARAMARK's Business Conduct Policy, a summary of which is printed below.

Signature of Applicant ____________________ Date __________

Business Conduct Policy

ARAMARK
Uniform Services

THIS POLICY APPLIES WORLDWIDE

Compliance with Laws
It is ARAMARK's policy to comply with the laws in each country in which ARAMARK conducts business.

Employment/Equal Opportunity
ARAMARK's policy is to hire, promote, discipline and make all other personnel decisions without regard to race, color, religion, national origin, age, sex, disability, disabled veteran or Vietnam-era veteran status except where bona fide affirmative action programs allow for such considerations.

Sexual Harassment
Sexual harassment in any form will not be tolerated in the workplace. Any employee who feels that he or she has been subjected to sexual harassment is required to report the incident immediately.

Illegal Substances
It is ARAMARK'S policy to maintain an environment free of drug and alcohol abuse.

Environmental
ARAMARK's policy is to comply with environmental laws in all countries in which ARAMARK conducts business.

Collusion
It is fundamental that ARAMARK independently determine the pricing, commissions and other contractual terms offered to clients or prospective clients.

Copyright Infringement
It is ARAMARK's policy to respect copyrights owned by others.

Political Contributions
Any political contribution or expenditure by a component is against ARAMARK policy. Also, any reimbursement of an employee for any such contribution or expenditure is against ARAMARK policy.

Gifts and Entertainment
It is ARAMARK's policy not to make any gift (other than a nominal holiday remembrance) or provide entertainment (except routine lunches or dinners during the conduct of regular business) to any government or union employee (except as provided in the Business Conduct Policy). Gifts given to non-government or non-union employees are restricted to a value of up to $200 (U.S.) per year; where entertainment is involved, lavish expenditures are to be avoided.

Gifts from any supplier or client to an ARAMARK employee may not total more than $200 (U.S.) per year.

Accurate Books and Reporting
All transactions must be accurately recorded. No unrecorded fund, asset or other improper account of ARAMARK shall be established or maintained for any reason.

Conflicts of Interest/Related Party Transactions
It is essential that all ARAMARK employees avoid any situation or interest which might interfere with his/her judgment concerning responsibilities to ARAMARK.

Outside Employment
An ARAMARK employee's outside employment should not conflict with his/her responsibilities to ARAMARK.

Finder's Fee
Payment of finder's fees is prohibited without the written approval of the General Counsel's office.

Disclosure
If you are aware of possible violations of the BUSINESS CONDUCT POLICY, you must report them to the BUSINESS CONDUCT POLICY SECRETARY c/o the Office of General Counsel, at Corporate Headquarters in writing or by telephoning 1-800-999-8989, extension 3246 or 215-238-3246 or to others listed in the policy booklet.

SIGNATURE OF APPLICANT ____________________ DATE __________

FOR COMPLETION BY PERSONNEL DEPT. ONLY
(AFTER EMPLOYMENT)

PAYROLL INFORMATION

Date Application Received	Referral Source	Interviewed By	Department
Results of Reference Check			
Reference Check Completed By			Date
Salary Review Date	Starting Date		Starting Salary
Results of Physical Check			

Date of Physical	Race or Ethnic Group	Date of Birth	Male	Female
Handicapped ☐ Yes ☐ No	Veteran Status			

Job Title	Dept. and Sub.	Title Code
Salary Grade	Exempt	Non Exmpt
Replacement For		
Status: ☐ Permanent ☐ Full Time ☐ Temporary ☐ Part Time		Hrs. Per Week
Remarks:		

FIGURE 5-1 ARAMARK Employment application *(concluded)*.

TABLE 5-2 Sample Rejection Letter

Your company name and address
Date
Applicant's name and address

Dear Applicant,

Thank you for taking the time to fill out an application for job vacancy at (your operation's name). After reviewing your qualifications, we have determined that they do not meet our job needs at this time. OR If your qualifications match our needs, you will hear from us by phone within 10 days.

Thank you for your interest in (your company's name).

Sincerely,

Your name and title

for a job with your hospitality organization. A simple form letter like the one in Table 5-2 is all that is needed. Remember, even if you don't hire this person, he or she is still a potential customer. You don't want to offend someone by not acknowledging his or her application.

THE PREINTERVIEW PROCESS

After reviewing the completed application forms, we hopefully have some viable **job candidates** whom we now would like to interview. **Interviewing** can be defined as a two-way communication process that is designed to predict both a job candidate's ability to perform the job tasks required and the ability to adapt to the hospitality organization's social environment.

If you have held a job, chances are you have experienced the interview firsthand. There is no one right way to interview a job candidate. As a manager with human resources responsibilities you have to select an approach that is the most comfortable for you. However, to keep the job interview on track so that you accomplish your purpose in a minimum amount of time, a plan must be developed before you call in the job candidate.

Preparing for the Selection Interview

The interview, above everything else, must be relevant. What do we mean by relevant? Remember that you are conducting an interview to select a candidate for a specific job position. And, because you have already conducted an analysis of the hospitality workplace, that job position has a job description and a job specification. Preparation for the interview means that you have carefully reviewed the job profile for this position so that you know what the job requirements are. By knowing what the job requirements are, questions can be prepared that focus on specific content that is relevant to the **job vacancy** (see Figure 5-2).

The structure of the selection interview must now be determined. The **structured interview** consists of a series of carefully

FIGURE 5-2 The interview process can be a positive experience when the interviewer is well prepared.

designed questions that are asked by the interviewer of each job candidate. The interviewer asks only what is on the prepared list of questions and does not deviate from the list. This interview structure has two advantages. First, when the same list of questions is asked of every job candidate, you have optimized your ability to make comparisons among the candidates. The second advantage relates to Equal Employment Opportunity. The structured interview maximizes the amount of consistent documentation that you acquire for each candidate. When you ask the same questions of all job applicants, it is more difficult for rejected job applicants to claim that the questions they were asked discriminated against them. The disadvantage is that it does not permit you to react to the interviewee's responses.

Another type of interview is the **unstructured interview**. This requires the least amount of preparation on the part of interviewer. Though it is essential that the interviewer have a complete understanding of the job requirements and skill levels, only general questions are formulated prior to the actual interview. The advantage is that the interviewer can respond to the job candidate's responses to formulate additional questions. For example, if you ask "What has been your success?" The interviewee responds that he or she had received a promotion at their most recent position. You, as interviewer, could follow up with "What qualities do you possess that made you the best choice for this promotion?"

The disadvantage here is the amount of time this interview takes. If you are fortunate to have a large pool of applicants to interview, then you will probably not have time for the unstructured interview. Caution must also be exercised that you, as the interviewer, do not lose sight of the job position for which you are interviewing. It takes a lot of skill in the interview situation to conduct an unstructured interview that also provides you with the necessary information to make your selection decision.

A mixture of these two interview types can be developed into what is known as the **semi-structured interview**. Here a preplanned list of interview questions is developed and asked of all job candidates. You can think of this list as the minimal amount of information you will be looking for during the interview. You can then ask additional questions stemming from the job candidate's responses during the interview session.

Question Development

The questions that you develop must address the types of information you need to elicit from the job candidate. In order to find the most qualified candidate from your applicant pool, the questions must assist you in learning about each applicant. Some information will already be available from the employment application. It is during the interview, however, that you have the opportunity to obtain additional information to assist you with your selection decision.

It is generally agreed that open-ended questions, those that can't be answered with a simple "yes" or "no" response, yield the greatest amount of information from the job applicant. Whereas open-ended questions represent information gathering, close-ended questions tend to give the job applicant information that might alter or affect his or her response. In other words, applicants pick up cues from the question and answer the way they think they should as opposed to how or what they really feel.

What information should the questions you develop attempt to obtain? Your questions should elicit information about what the job applicant has done in the past. The employment application will provide you with the direction for this line of questions. What information does the job applicant know? This would include questions about skills, education, and any special training the applicant has. What are the applicant's potential capabilities? A job applicant's past performance is generally a good indication of future success in your organization. Hospitality companies generally prefer to promote from within. If this is part of your organization's mission statement, then you need to consider the future career opportunities for this applicant.

INDUSTRY EXPERTS SPEAK

When designing interview questions, Bob Morrison points out that your focus should be on abilities, competencies, and skills. "Since so many of our employees come into direct contact with our guests interpersonal and socialization skills should be a high priority. The movement in designing interview questions is towards specifics. Develop questions that can identify the specific behaviors you are looking for in hiring someone for a particular job position. For example, asking an applicant to tell you about their major accomplishments in school would give you a broad, general range of responses. But asking them what extra-curricular activities they participated in would specifically give you information about socialization. Were they members of the chess and reading clubs or members of the debate team?" Bob says that what you want is for your job applicants to talk! "The more they talk and give you information about themselves the better assessment you can make with respect to their qualifications for the job vacancy."

In the hospitality industry it is essential that we also determine the job applicant's attitudes and interpersonal skills. Over 75 percent of the employees in a typical hospitality operation come into direct contact with our guests. Our employees represent our company to those guests, so it is important that the individuals we select have the ability to relate positively to other people. If they don't make a positive impression on you in the interview situation, when people are generally at their best, then you will not want them representing you and your hospitality organization to your guests. Table 5-3 presents some sample interview questions that are designed to obtain specific information from the job applicant.

When designing interview questions, you must take into consideration the employment discrimination laws we discussed earlier. Remember that under the ADA an employer may not ask disability-related questions and require medical examinations of a job applicant until after the applicant has been given a conditional **job offer**. In the past, some employment applications and interview questions requested information about an applicant's mental and/or physical condition. Oftentimes this information was used to exclude applicants from further job consideration.

An employer still can, however, ask questions about an applicant's ability to perform specific job functions. For example, a bellperson's job would require the ability to lift luggage, perhaps up to sixty pounds. You may design an interview question that specifically addresses the applicant's ability to satisfy this job requirement. You can ask the person if he or she fully understands the job and its requirements. You should describe the physical location of the job and be honest about the working conditions. If it would be helpful, include a tour of the job site during the interview process. You might also want to give them the opportunity to see the lunch-/break room and rest room facilities. You also can clearly state your policy regarding regular and reliable attendance.

As a manager with human resources responsibilities in the hospitality industry it is up to you to ensure that disparate treatment does not occur in the interview process. Make sure that all job applicants are treated the

TABLE 5-3 Sample Interview Questions

Work Experience
- Tell me about your current responsibilities at work.
- What were the toughest parts of the recent job you held?
- What did you like about your last job position?
- What did you dislike about your last job position?
- What would your last two employers say about your job performance?

Education
- What extra-curricular activities did you participate in during high school?
- What did you like most about school?
- What did you like least about school?

Job Perspective
- Why did you choose to apply for this job with our hospitality company?
- Why are you interested in working for our company?
- How do you think this job will be different from your last job?
- What other job opportunities have you sought?

Motivation
- What motivates you to put forth your best effort?
- What are your future plans?

Personal
- Are you bilingual?
- What are your greatest assets?
- How would your coworkers at your present job describe you?
- What special interests do you have?

In Closing
- Why should we consider you for this job position?
- What else should I know about you in making the selection decision?

same. Consistent use of questions with each applicant will help guarantee this equality of treatment. And remember, it is challenging to engage strangers in meaningful conversation. After all, having just met, how do you begin this process? With well-thought-out and prepared interview questions.

Let's recap the steps that we have taken so far in the development of interview questions:

1. Based upon the job description and the job specification, we have analyzed the skills, attributes, and characteristics that an individual must have in order to successfully fill our job vacancy.
2. Based upon our job analysis, we list the qualities that our job applicant must have. Some interviewers like to group the qualities they are looking for into three categories: "must have," "desirables," and "undesirables."
3. Based upon the qualities we have identified, we then develop questions that will elicit information about the job applicant in each of those areas.

CONDUCTING THE INTERVIEW

Remember that making the right hiring decision now can save you much time and trouble and minimize problems down the road. The employment process is complex, and interviewing is just one aspect, but an important aspect. So far we have spent considerable time preparing well-written job descriptions so that we knew what type of person we were looking for. Our recruitment efforts resulted in a pool of viable applicants. Next we have to match the applications with our job descriptions and do an initial screening of those applicants who do not meet minimal qualifications (Figure 5-3). And still, before we actually call in our first job applicant, we must do the following:

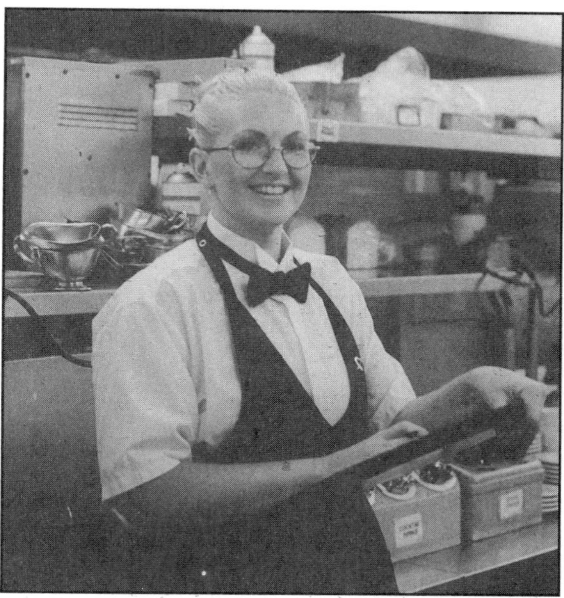

FIGURE 5-3 Job applications need to be matched with job descriptions to make sure that applicants meet minimal qualifications. *(Courtesy of Strongbow Inn, Valparaiso, IN)*

TABLE 5-4 Interview Icebreakers

I see you're from NY. How do you like living in Florida instead?
Did you have any trouble getting here today?
Do you know anyone who works here?
Are you familiar with our company? Or this property?

- Review the job requirements so that we are familiar with the job position.
- Review the employment application so that we are familiar with the applicant.
- Decide on the structure of the interview.
- Decide on the questions we will ask.
- Decide on the right answers to these questions.
- Understand the hospitality organization's mission statement, goals, objectives, and corporate culture.
- Find a comfortable, distraction-free environment in which to conduct the interview.

Interview Structure

The interview contains primarily four different phases. The first is the **opening** where you attempt to establish rapport with the job applicant. A nervous applicant is not going to interview well, and you are going to have great difficulty in judging his or her true capabilities. A relaxed applicant is much more likely to provide you with the information you need to make a selection decision. Icebreakers, such as those nonthreatening questions listed in Table 5-4, will often assist you in calming the applicant. You also want to ask some basic questions that need to be asked to avoid wasting time—for example, the hours the interviewee is available for work and the wage he or she requires.

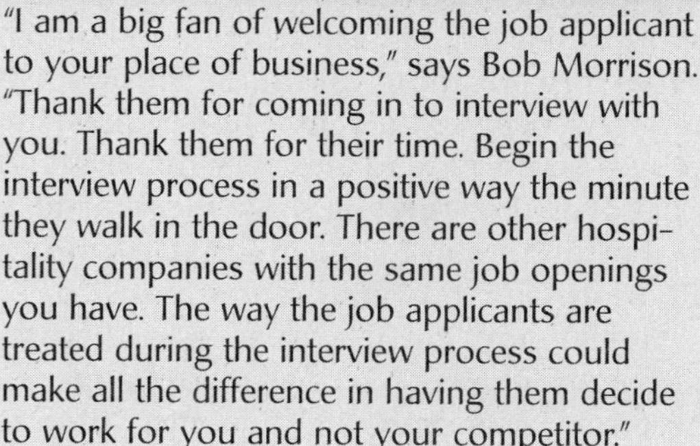

INDUSTRY EXPERTS SPEAK

"I am a big fan of welcoming the job applicant to your place of business," says Bob Morrison. "Thank them for coming in to interview with you. Thank them for their time. Begin the interview process in a positive way the minute they walk in the door. There are other hospitality companies with the same job openings you have. The way the job applicants are treated during the interview process could make all the difference in having them decide to work for you and not your competitor."

You now shift into the **information gathering** phase of the interview. This is *not* the time to discuss either the job, the hospitality organization, or what a great company this is to work for. Interviewers who are great at gathering information know that 95 percent of their time is spent listening in this phase of the interview. The focus should be on the job applicant's experiences, skills, and personal qualities. You should also be noting the applicant's behavior and mannerisms while you are listening to his or her responses. Body language and speech patterns can be indicators of personality traits that may or may not be desirable for the position or company for which you are interviewing. Remember that the way a person looks in the interview is the best they are going to look!

If the information the job applicant provides to you raises other questions, be sure to follow up on them. At the conclusion of the interview, you should not have any unanswered questions. An interview is a chance for the job applicant to sell himself or herself, and you are giving him or her the opportunity.

The third phase of the interview is **providing information** about both the job and the hospitality organization to the job applicant.

Information that you should provide would include the specific job duties and responsibilities, working hours and conditions, opportunities for advancement, and departmental organization. Both the positive and negative aspects of the job should be presented. It serves no purpose to hire a job applicant only to discover that there is some element of the job that he or she is uncomfortable with that will eventually force him or her to resign.

Remember that in many cases the applicant's only perception of the company is the impression that you are making. An interview's purpose is not only to elicit information from the applicant but also to provide an excellent opportunity for you to sell both the job and the hospitality organization you represent. It's up to you to create a positive picture of both in the applicant's mind.

Industry Experts Speak

Let's listen in to a part of a well-conducted, productive interview for an evening waitstaff position in your 200 seat, family dining operation. After each question and response, an explanation will be presented of why the question was asked:

Question: Why do you want to be a server?
Poor response: I like people.
Good response: I like serving people and helping them have a good time.
Intent: To discover the real motivation behind the person's desire for the position. Why they like the job.

Question: Why did you leave your prior job as a server at XYZ restaurant?
Poor response: I disliked doing so much sidework.
Good response: I didn't get enough hours, or, it's too far from where I live.
Intent: To make sure the applicant won't have the same problem at your restaurant.

Question: What would you look for if you were the manager here and you were hiring a new server?
Poor response: I don't know; I never hired someone before.
Good response: Good communication skills, stamina, outgoing, and the like.
Intent: To see if they identify the same characteristics that you have determined to be essential to a good performer in this position.

As you can see, each of the open-ended questions was asked to elicit specific information that is useful when making your final selection decision.

The final phase is **closing** the interview. Indicate to the applicant that the interview is coming to a close so that he or she has an opportunity to provide you with any additional information that may be useful. Putting down your pen is a good way to signal that you're finished. Always end the interview positively. Even though this applicant might not be suitable for the job position, his or her best friend might be, and you don't want to offend him or her. And even if this applicant will not become one of your valued employees, he or she might become one of your valued guests.

You should also let the applicant know when he or she can expect to learn the outcome of the interview. And please don't forget the follow-up within the time frame you have given. For many people, the job interview is a critical part of their life. They are likely to be anxiously waiting to learn of your decision. If you are not interested in the job applicant, you should tell him or her the reasons why. Most interviewers, when interviewing hourly job candidates, let the person know at the end of the interview. If you are interested in hiring the applicant, be careful not to make any commitments to him or her until you have checked his or her references. Always make sure that you contact all job applicants you have interviewed about your decision.

Once the interviewee has left, give yourself some quiet time to collect your thoughts and rate the applicant. Now is the time to expand upon the notes that you took during the interview. Again, be sure your notes concern how the applicant answered job-related questions. Focus on the interviewee's skills, abilities, and background. Do they match the essential duties and requirements found in the job description? Do you feel that the applicant is able to do the job? Do you feel that the applicant is willing to do the job? Be prepared to justify any statements that you write down with respect to job-relatedness.

Questions You Can't Ask

Even though we discussed the implications of EEO earlier in this chapter, we now want to take this opportunity to provide you with specific information regarding the types of questions that you cannot ask during the interview. As you begin the interview, it is essential that you are thoroughly familiar with EEO, ADA, and affirmative action's implications for the selection process. And, in addition to the federal regulations, don't forget state and local discrimination and employment laws also may regulate the employment process.

Questions should never be asked in the areas of age, race, marital status, national origin, religion, physical or mental disabilities, sex, transportation, children, height or weight, type of discharge from the military, credit history or references, or arrest record. Questions may not be asked of citizenship as they may be discriminatory on the basis of national origin. *After* you have decided to hire the interviewee, the Immigration Reform and Control Act requires that you inquire about authorization to work in the United States and fill out a Form I-9, and if the job candidate is an alien, you may request an Alien Registration Number.

Hospitality recruiters recommend that you not ask a question unless you can prove that it is job related. Some applicants upon not receiving a job offer will allege that the reason they were denied employment was due to a discriminatory cause. The number of discrimination lawsuits has risen dramatically in recent years. Even if you win, these cases can be quite costly both in real dollars and in public goodwill. Let's see how well you can identify interview questions that are discriminatory in nature.

Indicate if each of the questions listed below is legal or illegal to ask during a job interview. You will find the answers along with a brief explanation following the discussion questions at the end of this chapter.

1. Where were you born?
2. What clubs, organizations, societies, or lodges do you belong to?
3. How would you describe yourself?
4. What is more important, the wage we can pay you or the type of job position we can offer you?
5. How many children do you have?
6. Could you provide me with the name of a pastor or priest who would provide me with a recommendation?
7. Why should I hire you for this job?
8. How much time have you lost from work or school in the past year due to illness?
9. Will you include a photograph with your employment application?
10. Will you provide names of relatives?

Qualified versus Not Qualified

How will you interpret the answers to the questions that you ask in the interview so that you know you will make the correct selection decision? How do you know if the job applicant is an individual that will succeed once on the job? The question that you need to constantly ask yourself during the interview is "Can the person do the job?"

To be able to honestly answer that question for yourself, you have to learn how to get beyond the person's neat, clean appearance and further get beyond the person's friendly, nice attitude. Though these behaviors are important, they should not cloud an interviewer's judgment pertaining to the job applicant's ability to perform the job. And that ability is what you hope to be hiring them to do. You can't simply like them or the way they look or dress.

The best way to select qualified over nonqualified job applicants is to stick to the interview plan you have established. Determine what are the skills and abilities necessary to do the job, develop questions and answers that indicate to you whether applicants have these skills and abilities, and evaluate their performance in the interview based upon the extent of their skills and abilities. In order to keep track of where a job applicant stands in the interview, we recommend use of an interview evaluation worksheet similar to the one shown in Table 5-5. This form permits you to summarize the applicant on each characteristic required by the vacant job position.

Common Interviewing Mistakes

Interviews are a subjective selection tool. To keep them as objective as possible, we suggest that you take notes during the actual interview. Some people argue that this makes the job applicant nervous. We believe that if you give the job applicant an explanation of why you are writing items down, their anxiety can be reduced. Furthermore, the importance of having written comments can be invaluable when interviewing a number of job applicants. We also recommend that after the interview is over, and the job applicant has left the interview area, that you take time to make a written evaluation of the job applicant. This should be done before beginning another interview session. As we discussed earlier, care must be taken to keep all written comments job related.

As an interviewer you are representing the hospitality organization to the job applicant. Interviews should be kept professional with a business atmosphere. During the interview, you must remain open-minded and objective about the applicant sitting across from you. Do not make comparisons during the interview with other job applicants or former or present employees.

Let the interviewee do the talking; avoid interrupting and agreeing or disagreeing with what they are telling you. Use active listening

TABLE 5-5 Interview Evaluation Worksheet

	Weak	Marginal	Meets Minimum Standards	Strong
Appearance/grooming				
Self-expression/communication skills				
Friendliness				
Relevant job experience				
Job stability				
Enthusiasm				
Positive outlook				
Level of interest in position				
Flexibility in schedule				
Working hours				
Willingness to learn				
High energy level				
Public impression				

techniques that would include nodding your head, saying "uh huh" or using the "echo back." An example of an echo back is when the interviewee responds "I did several creative projects while I was at my last job." You, as interviewer, respond "creative projects?" It forces the interviewee to expand upon his or her background providing you with more information. This is an information gathering-and-giving session, not a debate. At the same time, do not let the interviewee wander into topics that have no relevancy to the job position. Stick to your interview plan and avoid asking irrelevant questions.

Be sensitive to the educational level of the interviewee. Do not use terminology that they might not be familiar with unless it relates to a skill or knowledge required by the job. Avoid talking down to the interviewee. No matter what the individual's job history or experience level, he or she is still a person who deserves to be treated with respect and dignity. The nicer you are, the more the individual will want to tell you. Avoid any indication of being judgmental. If you seem to have heard it all and nothing fazes you, chances are they'll "come clean."

Whatever particular interviewing style you select, it has to be one that is comfortable to you. Don't attempt to duplicate the style or questions that might have been used on you during an interview!

Secondary Interviews

Depending upon the job position that you are interviewing for and the policies of the hospitality organization for which you are hiring, more than one interview might be required of the job applicant. Some companies use the initial interview as a prescreening tool. Job candidates that do not meet the basic job requirements or skill levels are eliminated from the selection process. Initial interviews can also be used to determine the applicant's interests or as a method of disseminating information about your company.

Secondary interviews are used to gain more specific information about the job applicant's suitability to the job position opening. Company philosophies also vary as to who should conduct the second interview. In most hospitality companies the manager or supervisor of the vacant job position conducts this interview. An **applicant flow log** similar to the one shown in Figure 5-4 should be maintained so that you can track each job applicant through the selection process.

Conducting an interview can be a very awkward and uncomfortable activity unless you have developed a good interview plan. Your objective in the interview process is to gather as much information as possible about the job candidate so that an intelligent hiring decision can be made. You must constantly be aware of the legal restrictions imposed upon the employment process by federal, state, and local laws, yet develop questions that entice the applicant to tell all. Remember that although in the course of your day an interview might be viewed as an interruption, it is likely to be one of the most important events that day for the job candidate. And when you think about the costs and headaches of a poor hiring decision, it just might be the most important human resources activity that you perform that day.

Reference Checking

If a job applicant appears to be qualified for the job vacancy, a reference check should be made before a job offer is extended. A reference check can be conducted by phone or mail. Due to recent litigation involving slander and defamation of character, many businesses are careful not to release any information other than dates of employment and salary. In many cases, written permission by the job candidate is required.

Even though reference checks may not be good predictors of job performance, they do provide you with an evaluation of the applicant's attributes and qualifications. If valuative comments can be obtained during a reference check, the referees are likely to give more favorable information than negative. In the hospitality industry, however, information that gives us an indication of the applicant's personality can be useful in the screening process. Certain personality traits are critical if the applicant is to be successful in many hospitality jobs. You might use a preemployment check sheet like the one seen in Figure 5-5. Many employers do not take the time to do a reference check, and oftentimes they regret that decision. The applicant may have misrepresented his or her background and credentials on the application. Taking the time to simply verify dates and places of employment, if nothing else, might serve to save you some problems later.

During the 1990s, litigation surrounding reference checking increased due to defamation claims. Defamation is when one person knowingly and maliciously gives damaging, false statements to a third person about a second person. For example, if you give a former employee a less than glowing reference for another job and that former employee is not offered the job, there is the possibility that you could be sued for defamation. This is why many managers when giving references on former employees will do little more than verify dates of employment. When giving reference check information, you should be sure that

SIGNATURE GRAND
APPLICANT FLOW CHART

DATE OF APPLICATION ______________________

HOW DID APPLICANT HEAR OF JOB OPENING?

EMPLOYEE REFERREL ______

ADVERTISEMENT ______

WALK-IN ______

JOB SERVICE ______

JOB POSTING—SCHOOL ______

OTHER ______

ABLE TO PROVIDE TUXEDO ______ YES ______ NO

EXPLAINED PART-TIME SHIFTS ______ YES ______ NO

AVAILABLE ON WEEKENDS ______ YES ______ NO

PHONE NUMBER VERIFIED ______ YES ______ NO

INFORMATION ENTERED IN APPLICATION DATABASE

ON ____________________

BY: ____________________

SUBMITTED TO DEPARTMENT SUPERVISOR—

__________________ ON ____________________

BY: ____________________

CALLED FOR FIRST INTERVIEW ______ YES ______ NO

INTERVIEW SCHEDULED ON ____________________

OR APPLICANT NO LONGER INTERESTED ______

SECOND INTERVIEW RECOMMENDED ______ YES ______ NO

PLEASE REMEMBER TO PLACE A COPY IN THE GENERAL APPLICATION FILE.

FIGURE 5-4 Applicant Flow Chart. *(Courtesy of Signature Grand, Davie, FL)*

SIGNATURE GRAND
PREEMPLOYMENT
REFERENCE CHECK SHEET

NAME ______________________________

1. IF APPLICANT IS STILL EMPLOYED AND IS APPLYING FOR PART-TIME AT SIGNATURE GRAND PLEASE DOUBLE-CHECK TO MAKE SURE APPLICANT CHECKED ON APPLICATION THAT WE MAY CONTACT CURRENT EMPLOYER.

COMPANY: ______________________________

COMPANY REPRESENTATIVE ____________________ TITLE ____________

A. DOES INFORMATION ON APPLICATION AS TO JOB TITLE AND DATES EMPLOYED MATCH APPLICATION?

   ______ YES   IF NO, WHAT DIFFERS? ____________________

B. IS FORMER EMPLOYEE ELIGIBLE FOR RE-HIRE? ______ YES

   IF NO, WHY? ______________________________

PLEASE HAVE THE APPLICANT RATED USING THE FOLLOWING GUIDELINES: E=EXCELLENT, G=GOOD, F=FAIR, P=POOR, NC=NO COMMENT

ATTENDANCE: ________

ATTITUDE: ________

RELATIONSHIP WITH PEERS: ________

OVERALL JOB PERFORMANCE: ________

ANY ADDITIONAL COMMENTS: ______________________________

REFERENCE CHECKED BY: ____________________
ON ____________

FIGURE 5-5 Preemployment Reference Check Sheet. *(Courtesy of Signature Grand, Davie, FL)*

you only give factual information that can be verified.

At a minimum a reference check should seek to obtain prior dates of employment, positions, duties, and performance quality (Figure 5-6). Questions such as "Why did the employee leave?", "Is he eligible for rehire?", and "Did he have a high absenteeism?" are useful for verifying information on the employment application. Remember that it is not illegal to ask anything of a reference, it is up to them to tell you or refuse you the information. If you get a negative reference, protect your source. Do not tell the applicant that the reference was the reason for not hiring him or her.

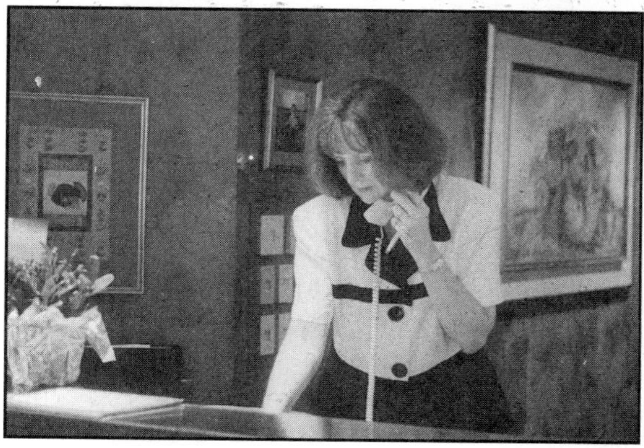

FIGURE 5-6 Reference checks are an important part of the selection process. *(Courtesy of Strongbow Inn, Valparaiso, IN)*

INDUSTRY EXPERTS SPEAK

Jan Barr points out another way reference checks were a benefit to their company. While checking references on a candidate, one Recruiter found out that the person giving the referral had always wanted to work for Chili's. They met, had an interview, and became the next Chili's Manager in the market. It pays to do reference checks!

PREEMPLOYMENT TESTING

There is strong evidence that suggests that the use of standardized tests, which assess abilities, personality, and integrity, are a valuable screening tool. Though initially many companies and selection experts were hesitant about the use of these tools, many hospitality organizations now use testing as a regular component in the selection process. We predict in "the next chapter" that testing will continue to become both more sophisticated and widely used in our industry.

The following list represents just some of the types of tests that you might select from:

- **Skill tests.** These may be conducted to determine if the job candidate meets the qualifications directly related to the job requirements. For example, if a bartender needs to be able to mix drinks with a certain speed, then you could place him or her behind the bar and time his or her performance.
- **Intelligence tests.** These tests measure the job candidate's mental capacity, memory (which might be of importance in hiring a short-order cook), ability to see relationships, and speed of thought.
- **Personality tests.** These tests assist in matching the job candidate with the job position in which he or she is most likely to succeed. This is based upon a measure of that individual's personality characteristics, not his or her experiences and abilities.
- **Integrity tests.** These tests measure a person's honesty. Most of the internal theft that occurs in hospitality operations can be solved by hiring better people. Employers have come to rely more heavily upon written tests that measure an applicant's honesty (Figure 5-7).

Preemployment testing is not meant as a replacement for other screening tools, but

FIGURE 5-7 Integrity tests are used by employers when employees will be handling large sums of cash. *(Courtesy of Chili's Grill & Bar, Brinker International)*

merely as one additional source of information that can help you make the best hiring decision. It is objective information that is consistent from applicant to applicant. Though administering these tests to job candidates is not illegal, it must be shown that the test is job related. Care must be taken in selecting the most appropriate test for your particular needs.

RECORD RETENTION

It is legally necessary to retain all pertinent records on job applicants for employment. As we discussed, an applicant flow record should be maintained on all candidates. A "hold" file is generally maintained for applicants who were qualified for jobs but were not hired. A "reject" file is maintained for all applicants who did not qualify for any job positions. Federal regulations surrounding the EEOC require that employers maintain data on all applicants. The purpose is to determine whether a company's recruitment or hiring practices have a negative or "adverse impact" on women and/or minorities. In addition to the application (and résumé if applicable) the following information should be kept on each employee after he or she has been hired:

- Full name
- Home address
- Employee number (often the social security number)
- Date of birth
- Job title
- Job description
- Reference checks
- Records relating to hiring, promotion, transfer, layoff, rates of pay, education, and training
- Performance evaluations

- Letters of recognition
- Disciplinary documentation
- Exit interviews and termination records

The following information should be kept in separate files:

- Race
- Sex
- Medical records
- Immigration (I-9) forms
- Safety training records

There is no law stating that an employer must maintain personnel files as such. However, there are various federal and state requirements that certain records be kept. As always, it is important that you are aware of the laws that pertain to your location.

Care should be taken that employment applications and other selection data are not left out to be viewed by unauthorized individuals. The confidentiality of employee records must be maintained at all times (Figure 5-8).

FIGURE 5-8 Care must be taken to properly maintain personnel files and records. *(Courtesy of Strongbow Inn, Valparaiso, IN)*

You should also consider adopting a written policy that outlines to whom and under what circumstances access to these files can be granted. Employees do have a right to access and review their files. State if they can copy them. Determine what supervision is required when personnel files are reviewed. This is important to maintain the integrity of the files. It is also a good idea to periodically review the employment records, making sure that you correct or remove outdated or inaccurate information.

SUCCESSFUL SELECTION

Effective employee selection is a process by which you, the manager with human resources responsibilities, seek the best candidate for a specific job vacancy. Your search is aided with a variety of selection tools that you have at your disposal. The particular tools you choose to use in your hospitality organization will depend upon your comfort level with each of them, along with the goals and objectives of the operation for which you are making the selection.

The direct result of a poor selection decision is seen in high turnover that translates into higher costs for recruitment, selection, and training. To calculate the costs, you must add in recruitment where you have the expense of advertising, and then you must add the selection expenses of interviewing and testing, to which you must add the training expenses of management time, effort, and reduced productivity levels plus the salary and benefits that you have compensated the poorly selected human resource.

The process of selection has dramatically improved in the past two decades. Hospitality managers who once hired just to fill a job vacancy have come to realize the importance of developing a comprehensive selection plan for their hospitality organization. A successful selection plan, conducted by trained, skilled professionals can improve the quality and productivity of the hospitality organization.

Now that we have examined the selection process, we are ready to make our hire decision.

HIRING AND PLACEMENT

Through our sophisticated selection plan, we now have a number of individuals who after screening, reference checks, and preemployment testing are still viable candidates for the job vacancy. It is now time to make the hire decision! Again, where and by whom this decision is made will depend upon the structure of your hospitality organization. In some cases it will be made by the human resources department; in other organizations by the departmental manager/supervisor where the job vacancy exists.

If the job analysis, recruitment, and selection processes have been dutifully carried out, the last task of actually making the **hiring** decision becomes a mere formality. If done thoroughly, the first three components of the employment process can lead you to an easy decision. But what happens when you complete these steps and still have more than one job candidate? Other than considering yourself very lucky that you still have a decision to make, what considerations go into making that final determination?

Making the Decision

What are some of the criteria you should keep in mind in making this decision? We suggest the following guidelines:

- You can only hire what you can afford. The candidate's experience and qualifications should equate to the compensation received. If the job vacancy you have pays less then he or she is worth, and if you do not have immediate opportunities for this individual to advance into, the candidate will be looking for a better paying job elsewhere.
- Don't play it safe all the time. Every hospitality organization needs its "stars," regardless of job level. Stars are also those job candidates who come in at high risk. You like everything about them, but there is something in their background or behavior that is unconventional. High-risk hires will either be very successful or very unsuccessful.
- What is the hire objective? Are you looking for someone to improve the current situation in the department in which he or she will be working? Or are you content with an individual who will maintain the current situation?
- Look at the job candidate's temperament. How well is this individual suited for the work that the job vacancy requires? If the job candidate is a very vivacious, gregarious type person, and the job vacancy requires work that is repetitious and done in an area with very little social interaction, this person will not be very happy in the work environment.
- What you see is what you get. Remember the quote at the beginning of this chapter. These job candidates will never look or behave any better than they have throughout the screening process. If you encounter a red flag or negative feeling about the candidate, then carefully consider if you and your hospitality organization can live with this behavior.
- Does the candidate like being around people? Hospitality is a people business. Examine his or her hobbies and interests to determine if this person enjoys being with people in his or her leisure time. If all of the individual's interests center on reading,

needlework, or stamp collecting, this might be a job candidate who prefers not to be around people.

- Have a belief in talent. Don't be afraid of talented people or those more attractive or brighter than yourself (Figure 5-9).
- What is the candidate's energy level? We work in an environment that is full of peaks and valleys. When our hospitality operation is at its maximum productivity level, all of your people need to maximize their own energy levels. We must look for job candidates who we believe to be hard workers.

In making the final hire decision, we suggest that you use a candidate evaluation form similar to the one we discussed previously. This permits you to objectively evaluate each of the final candidates by conducting a comparative analysis. Remember that the only comments that are written on this evaluation sheet or on the interviewer's comment sheet are job related. You must take great care not to write down subjective personal impressions about the job candidate. In the event of a discrimination charge, these selection documents will become part of the evidence used in determining if such a charge is valid.

Negligent Hiring

Negligent hiring occurs when an employer fails to uncover a job applicant's incompetence or unfitness by not checking his or her references, criminal records, or general background.

FIGURE 5-9 Following proper selection procedures can lead to successful hiring. *(Courtesy of Chili's Grill & Bar, Brinker International)*

Under the theory of negligent hiring you can be held accountable for your employee's behavior if you knew, or should have known, that the employee was likely to behave in a certain manner. As a manager with human resources responsibilities in the hospitality industry you must exercise reasonable care when you select your employees. Our industry is one with high guest contact, and it is up to you to protect your guests from a known danger.

Negligent hiring practices are being used increasingly by third parties who have been injured as a result of one of your employees' negligence. Historically, you, as an employer, have always been responsible for the actions of your employees while they were in your employ. Hence, if one of your valet parkers, while parking a guest's car hits a pedestrian, you could be held liable for his or her actions.

Negligent hiring expands the duty an employer has to its guests, and states that your duty is to hire only individuals who can be trusted and are qualified to do the job in which you placed them. Hence, if a bellman whose job is to take guests to their rooms and carry in their baggage assaults one of those guests, you are liable—particularly, if it is found that the bellman you hired had been imprisoned for assault. The negligent hiring actions state that you breached the duty to your guests in your initial hire decision by not conducting a proper screening review. In other words, you acted unreasonably in your hire decision.

Hire decisions must be carefully made on an individual basis. While we have presented general guidelines for you to follow, common sense must be integrated in the process. Some job positions require more careful screening, in that the foreseeable risk to your guests is increased. Unfortunately, the legislation pertaining to discrimination prevents you from directly asking many questions that could assist you in screening out job candidates who are high security risks. This is where your judgment is invaluable. Keep in mind **placement**: Where will these job candidates be working if you hire them? Do you have enough information about them to guarantee the safety of your guests? If not, then you should think twice about making them a job offer.

The Job Offer

At the time of the job offer you should provide the job candidate with the following information:

- Position offered
- Location
- Starting date
- Orientation and training schedule
- Wages and benefits
- Nature of the job
- Work schedule

The job candidate now has a decision to make. Make sure that he or she understands the negatives as well as the positives of this particular job position. The candidate should understand your expectations in the performance of the job duties and responsibilities. The candidate's decision to accept or reject your offer will be based upon the information that you provide the job candidate with at this stage of the employment process. Make sure that there are no misunderstandings, because if there are, you will end up with the same job vacancy to refill.

We recommend that you follow an established procedure for hiring or rejecting the job candidates. The offer, initially made orally, should be placed in writing, again in an attempt to eliminate any misunderstandings. If the candidate is to be rejected, he or she should be notified as soon as possible. If the candidate requests a reason for the rejection, you must be very careful in how you state it. Remember the serious legal consequences of discriminating against a job candidate.

An alternative to making a firm job offer is to offer the job candidate a probationary period of employment. This enables both you and the candidate to better determine if the job vacancy is a good match with the candidate. **Probationary periods** usually last from one to three months. At the end of this time neither party has an obligation to the other. If you elect to use a probationary period, we recommend that you have the employee sign a statement that indicates that the employment period is for a specified period of time, and that no further obligation is extended past that period on the part of either party.

Placement

Once a job candidate is hired, there is additional information that you must obtain that becomes part of the personnel file that we discussed earlier. Much of this information, such as marital status, age, number of children, and ability to work legally in the United States if of another national origin, could not legally be asked before the hire decision was made. It is now necessary to complete the I-9 (Employment Eligibility Verification Form, previously discussed) for immigration purposes. This information is now necessary so that your payroll and benefits divisions can effectively do their jobs. Remember, because this information may not be used for future promotion decisions, you should keep this data separate from the employee's personnel file. Figure 5-10 represents a complete picture of the employment process.

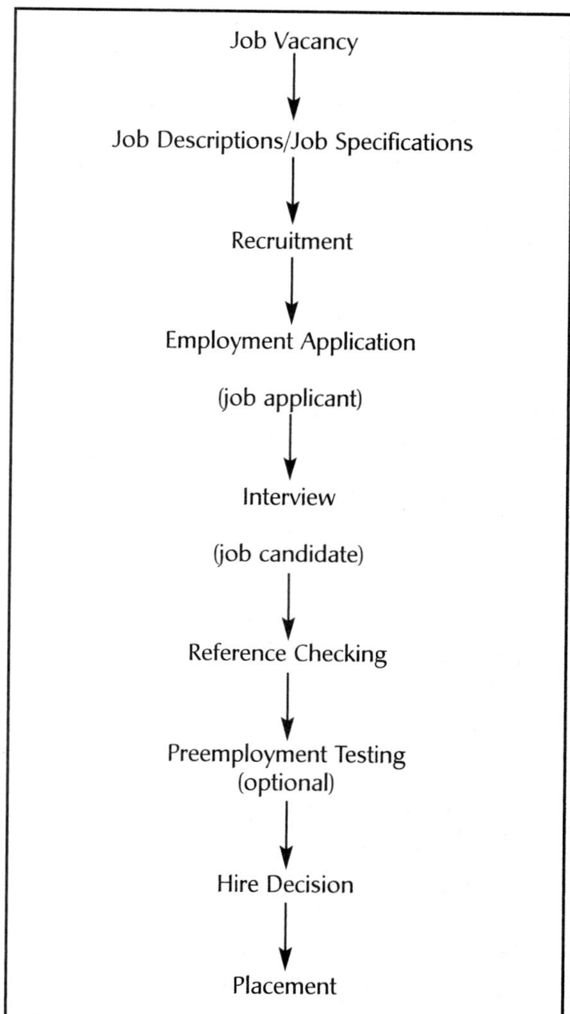

FIGURE 5-10 Planning the employment process.

CONCLUSION

Proper implementation of the selection, hiring, and placement process is crucial to the success of a hospitality organization. These processes require a well-thought-out and well-executed plan, which will require time for effective implementation. The employment process cannot be rushed. Throughout the hospitality industry, professionals are recognizing the great amount of attention that is needed for this human resources process and are taking steps to develop programs or improve upon those already in place. Managers are now being taught to treat the employment process with the same care and respect as in making a capital acquisition.

The selection of your employees is the starting point for building quality into your hospitality organization. In order to become a first-class operation, you must begin by selecting high-quality job candidates to become members of your organization. Each job applicant comes to you with his or her own special skills, talents, and abilities. It is your job to match these individuals to the job positions in your operation.

Over the years, the employment process has become increasingly complicated with legal restrictions and requirements. Lawsuits alleging discrimination are commonplace. The damages, both in monetary losses and in public goodwill, have prompted hospitality managers with human resources responsibilities to become cautious in their screening procedures. We must always be well informed of the legal issues surrounding the employment process.

Today, we view our work force in a different light. We see our employees as valuable resources in the success of our hospitality operations. Employees are not just a bunch of numbers waiting for their paychecks each week for a job that holds no opportunity for growth or advancement. Hiring people is a critical human resources function. Poor employees are the result of poor selection. Only through the development of an outstanding selection process can outstanding people become a part of your hospitality organization.

We now turn our focus to the orientation, training, and development of the human resources we have so carefully selected, hired, and placed in our hospitality organization.

Case Problem 5-1

Congratulations! Your recruitment campaign for servers and prep cooks was a huge success. As the manager with human resources responsibilities at an on-premise catering facility outside of Chicago, you know how much effort has gone into the entire employment process. ***Happy Day Catering*** likes hiring highly motivated students from the local university to fill its job openings. ***Happy Day*** is perceived as an extremely good place to work and generally has a large number of applications after a recruitment campaign.

The applications have been prescreened to ensure that the candidates meet the minimal qualifications (e.g., if a server, old enough to carry alcoholic beverages; if a prep cook, can work the early morning hours required). You are now down to four job applications for each position opening (one server and one prep cook).

Before you call the applicants in for an interview, you must decide what characteristics and factors will weigh into your selection decision. Outline, for each job position opening, what you will be looking for during the interview. Remember you have only the job applications in front of you at this point. Your selection criteria must fit the job responsibilities and demands. For legal reasons, the selection criteria must be reliable and valid. Describe, for each selection criteria chosen, the reason it is important for the particular job. Identify the predictors of successful job performance for each of these jobs. Remember that selection criteria must be both job related and valid.

Case Problem 5-2

You are now ready to call in the four applicants for servers for their interview. Based upon the selection criteria you have identified in Case Problem 5-1, how will you assess each criterion? For example, if being highly motivated is an important selection criterion, what evidence will you be looking for during the interview that would indicate that this person is highly motivated? How can you obtain this evidence? What questions should be asked during the interview to determine each selection criterion? What type of behavior will you be looking for during the interview session?

Key Words

applicant flow log
Bona Fide Occupational Qualification (BFOQ)
Civil Rights Act of 1991 (CRA)
closing
disparate impact
employment application
employment discrimination
employment law
Equal Employment Opportunity (EEO)
Glass Ceiling Commission
hiring
information gathering
integrity tests
intelligence tests
interviewing
job applicant
job candidate
job offer
job vacancy
negligent hiring
opening
personality test
placement
preemployment testing
probationary period
providing information
reference check
Rehabilitation Act of 1973
screening
secondary interviews
selection
semistructured interview
skill tests
structured interview
Title VII of Civil Rights Acts, 1964
unstructured interview
Veterans Reemployment Rights (VRR) Act
Veterans Readjustment Assistance Act of 1974

Recommended Reading

Amack, L. O. "Discriminatory Effects of the Face-to-Face Selection Interview." *Law Info Forum* 1995. lawinfo.com/forum/face-to-face.html (19 July 1998).

Berger, F. and A. Ghei. 1995. "Employment Tests: A Facet of Hospitality Hiring." *The Cornell Quarterly* 36(6): 28–35.

Clay, J. and E. Stephens. 1995. "Liability for Negligent Hiring—The Importance of Background Checks." *The Cornell Quarterly* 36(5): 74–81.

———. 1996. "The Defamation Trap in Employee References." *The Cornell Quarterly* 37(2): 18–24.

Kunde, D. 1999. "Employers Learn to Take Safe Path with References." *The Dallas Morning News*, January 27.

Koss-Feder, L. 1999. "Able to Work: Spurred by The Americans with Disabilities Act." *Time*, January 25, p. 82A.

Leonard, B. "Life at the EEOC." *HR Magazine*. 1998. www.shrm.org/hrmagazine/articles/0198eec.htm (19 August 1998).

Lorenzini, B. 1992. "The Accessible Restaurant." *Restaurant & Institutions* 102(12): 150–151, 154, 158, 162, 166–170.

Losyk, B. 1996. "Mastering the Interviewing Maze." *Restaurant USA* 16(9): 14–16.

Penny, S. "How to Hire Motivated People." *BC Solutions Magazine*. 1997. www.bcsolutionsmag.com/Archives/Nov1997/motivated.html (10 August 1998).

Perry, P. 1998. "A Matter of Privacy." *Restaurant USA* 18(2): 13–17.

Rundquist, K. 1997. "Pre-employment Testing: Making It Work for You." *Occupational Hazards*. 59(12).

Simons, T. 1995. "Interviewing Job Applicants—How to Get beyond First Impressions." *The Cornell Quarterly* 36(6): 21–27.

Thornberg, L. "Computer-Assisted Interviewing Shortens Hiring Cycle." *HR Magazine*. 1998. www.shrm.org/hrmagazine/articles/0298rec.htm (21 August 1998).

Recommended Web Sites

1. U.S. Equal Employment Opportunity Commission: www.eeoc.gov
2. Title I of the Americans with Disabilities Act of 1990: www.eeoc.gov/laws/ada.htm
3. Age Discrimination in Employment Act of 1990: www.eeoc.gov/laws
4. Equal Pay Act of 1963: www.eeoc.gov/laws/epa.htm
5. Section 501 of the Rehabilitation Act of 1973: www.eeoc.gov/laws/rehab.htm
6. Title VII of the Civil Rights Act of 1964: www.eeoc.gov/laws/vii.html
7. Best EEO Practices: www.eeoc.gov/practice.html
8. The Interview Coach: www.interviewcoach.com
9. Online Opportunities: www.jobnet.com
10. Employment Law Materials: www.law.cornell.edu/topics/employment.html
11. Legal Information Institute: www.law.cornell.edu/topics/topic2.html
12. National Organization on Disability: www.nod.org/index.html

Endnotes

1. David Maharaj, "Workplace Bias Damages Expanded; Supreme Court: Ruling Says in Some Cases, Punitive Verdicts May be Allowed," *Los Angeles Times*. web.lexis-nexis.com/more/shrm/19216/4736739/3 (1 July 1999).
2. U.S. Department of Labor. "Press Release." *The Glass Ceiling Commission Unanimously Agrees on 12 Ways to Shatter Barriers*. 1995. www.irl.cornell.edu/lib/e_archive/GlassCeiling/News_Release.html

Discussion Questions

1. What is the objective of the screening process? How can you, as human resources manager, ensure that this objective is met in your hospitality organization?
2. What information do those involved in the selection process need to know before they can begin screening job applicants?
3. Discuss EEO legislation. What does it require? Whom does it cover? What is the role of the EEOC? Who may file a complaint? How can you monitor compliance? How can complaints be avoided?
4. Outline the key points of three pieces of discrimination law.
5. What are the advantages and disadvantages of using the employment application as a screening test?
6. Describe the advantages and disadvantages of the structured, unstructured, and semistructured interviews. Which do you prefer? Why?
7. What must you do before interviewing a job applicant so that the interview is relevant?
8. Describe the four phases of the interview and identify the objective or purpose of each phase.
9. What kind of information is useful to obtain during a reference check? Describe the legal implications of a reference check.
10. Describe the difference between personality tests and integrity tests. Would you use preemployment testing in a hospitality operation? Why or why not?
11. What is negligent hiring? How can it be avoided?
12. What information should you provide the job candidate at the time of the job offer?

Answers to Legality of Interview Questions (page 138)

1. Illegal. Questions may not be asked about an applicant's birthplace, that of his or her parents, nor may you ask to see a birth certificate or a naturalization or baptismal certificate. You may ask about an applicant's place and length of residence or where his or her current employer is located.
2. Illegal. You may not inquire about clubs, societies, fraternities, or other social organizations to which the applicant might belong. These might be of ethnic or religious origin. You may ask about membership in professional or service organizations.
3. Legal.
4. Legal.
5. Illegal. You may not ask questions about the composition of the family, marital status, or sex of the applicant.
6. Illegal. This relates to religious preference. You may ask names of character or professional references. If the applicant supplies the name of a religious leader, you have not violated the law.
7. Legal.
8. Illegal. You cannot discriminate against mental or physical disabilities unless directly related.
9. Illegal. The reasons are obvious!
10. Illegal. You may ask names of relatives you already employ or the name of a relative to notify in case of an emergency.

Section 3

Human Resources Training, Development, and Evaluation

CHAPTER 6

Hospitality Orientation and Training Programs

INDUSTRY ADVISOR

LORET CARBONE, *Senior Vice President of Human Resources/Chief People Officer, Left At Albuquerque*

"There is nothing training cannot do. Nothing is above its reach. It can turn bad morals to good; it can destroy bad principles and recreate good ones; it can lift men to angelship."

—MARK TWAIN

"The classroom should be an entrance into the world, not an escape from it."

—JOHN CIARDI

INTRODUCTION

Orientation and training: familiar words to most students in hospitality administration. Your human resources have been successfully recruited, selected, hired, and placed into vacant job positions. The next step in the human resources process is to properly orient and train your new employees. Unfortunately, too many food service and lodging organizations underestimate the overall value of having a well-planned orientation and training program. Both programs relate directly to the success of the new employees as well as the success of your hospitality organization.

As a manager assuming human resources responsibilities, it will be your job to prepare your employees to perform their jobs. You've both made a commitment to work together. The orientation program will be the new employees' first taste of your role as team leader. It is here that they will begin to develop the sense of teamwork, enthusiasm, and drive that makes your hospitality organization a special place to work. The training program will give you an opportunity to capitalize upon the natural attributes of the new employees, which are, after all, the reason you hired them in the first place!

At the conclusion of the chapter you will be able to:

1. Describe why a good orientation program is a necessity in a hospitality operation.
2. Identify the characteristics of a beneficial orientation program.
3. Explain the importance and goals of a training program.
4. Identify when and what types of training are needed in your hospitality corporation.
5. Understand the importance and role of literacy initiatives in the workplace.

6. Describe some steps you can take to implement a workplace education program in your hospitality organization.
7. Develop a training program.
8. Distinguish among several types of training methods.
9. Explain the importance of the Internet as a training medium.
10. Define distance learning and its role in training.
11. Identify the elements of a successful training program.
12. Explain why the School-to-Work Opportunities Act is important for the hospitality industry.
13. Differentiate between orientation and training.

ORIENTATION

All new employees should be given a well-planned orientation that will help them in getting off to a positive start in their new job. A thorough **orientation program** will acquaint the new employee to the hospitality organization, his or her specific work unit, and job position. In its broadest sense, the orientation process can be thought of as an extension of the recruitment and selection processes.

Just because a person is now an employee, it doesn't mean that they know what they are supposed to do, how they are supposed to behave, or even where they are supposed to be at any given time. Although an orientation should take place every time an employee begins a new position or takes on new responsibilities, we will be discussing new hire orientation in this chapter.

What Do You Do with a New Employee?

What is orientation? A good way to think of orientation is as a way of introducing new employees to the hospitality organization. Can you recall your first day on the job you have now? Even if that job was one you had performed for another hospitality company, such as bartender or room service waitstaff, didn't you feel at least a slight apprehension when going to work on that first day? We can relate to those feelings of anxiety with each of you; the "first day" means that you are entering into the unexpected.

So what can you, as a manager with human resources responsibilities, do to make the "first day" experience a pleasant one for your newly hired human resources? You can begin by making the employees feel at home with each other and their new hospitality work environment.

We define an orientation program as a method of familiarizing or acquainting new employees to the hospitality organization, their work unit or department, and to their job positions. This is done in an effort to minimize problems so that the new employee can make a maximum contribution to the work of the hospitality operation while at the same time realizing personal satisfaction. We want our new employees to fit in with the proper ways of doing business. Those "proper" ways depend upon your hospitality organization's goals, policies, and standard operating procedures.

By defining orientation in this way we begin to see the importance and value of planned programs. In too many situations, hospitality managers are content in turning over the responsibility of orientation to the new employee's coworkers. This unstructured orientation process can, in the long term, be very destructive to the success of the hospitality organization. Not only is this type of orientation unplanned, but it can also be misleading. Because this is the newly hired employee's first impression of how you do things, you want it to be positive, upbeat, and very organized. The worst thing that could happen in an orientation is that the new hire begins to wonder if he or she made a bad decision in accepting your job offer. This could happen if your orientation program comes across as unorganized or haphazard. An effective orientation program is one that is carefully planned and comes across to your new employees as a cooperative effort to make them feel welcome to your company. The more time and effort you invest in helping new employees feel welcome, the more likely they are to become loyal, well-adjusted, and long-term members of your hospitality organization.

Goals of Hospitality Orientation Programs

The purpose of a new hire orientation program is to give new employees an idea of the culture, behavior, facilities, and people skills necessary to make it through their first few months of employment. Orientation programs vary in both length and content based upon the job position for which the employee was hired, but need to be thorough enough to enable the employee to function fully and effectively as a member of the hospitality work team.

Communicating expectations and eliminating preconceptions are perhaps the most important goals of an orientation program. Helping employees to understand what is expected of them is the most valuable message you can communicate. Never assume that people know about your hospitality organization or the job for which they have been hired. These assumptions can seriously hinder employee performance once on the job. Not making any assumptions about what the employees know or don't know can help ensure that their initial progress is successful and prevent problems in the future.

An additional goal of orientation programs is to attempt to provide successful experiences. As you learn in Chapter 7, coaching and team building are part of your job when assuming human resources responsibilities. During the orientation it is important that your new recruits begin to feel like they will be making an important contribution to the team. Not only will your new human resources become contributing members of the team more quickly, many of their anxieties will be relieved when they are guided toward achieving initial successes. Confidence levels also will be boosted along with future productivity. By designing positive experiences into the orientation program, motivation will be fostered that will promote early success.

Hospitality managers are becoming increasingly aware of the fact that orientation programs are beneficial. The more thorough the orientation program, the more quickly the human resources become productive, contributing members of the organization. In addition, you will find a reduction in tardiness and absenteeism. It makes sense that the less job entry anxiety new hires experience, the more positive they are going to feel about your company, their new job, and the people they will be working with. This will translate into a more positive working attitude.

Commitment. This will require a commitment and involvement from unit level managers and senior management to make the new employees feel like they are part of your hospitality organization.

Participation in the orientation program by all levels of management is one way to show the new hires that they are important members of the team. It is also an excellent way for them to meet key people in your hospitality organization, so they can place the names with actual faces. Having all levels of management participating in the orientation allows them to become role models for all those entering your organization. If top management is actively involved in operational functions, the hourly human resources will tend to support them with greater enthusiasm.

INDUSTRY EXPERTS SPEAK

When new employees successfully complete a thorough, well-thought-out, well-executed orientation program, they are positioned for success in their new job. Loret Carbone believes that this process allows new employees to understand what is expected and what they can expect from management. It also teaches employees everything they need to know technically about their job. The goal of orientation is that the new employees know what to expect of you and what you expect of them.

WHAT TO COVER . . .

What are the mission statement, goals, and objectives of the organization? What does it expect of you as an employee? What can you expect the hospitality organization to provide for you? These are all some examples of the types of questions that people entering an organization or operation for the first time might have, and these questions should be covered in an effective orientation program.

For Whom and By Whom

Orientation programs should be developed and implemented for hourly employees as well as for management trainees. Upon graduation, many of you will experience a management training orientation. This chapter focuses primarily on the orientation programs you will be conducting for the hourly employees in your hospitality operation. Though many of the elements are similar to what you will experience, the program for management trainees is likely to be longer and more intensified.

For example, at *Left At Albuquerque*, entry level managers experience an extensive orientation and training program in which they are rotated through each hourly job position. Additionally, they receive training in the culture of the organization, they learn company systems and standards, and they attend seminars on management and leadership. If you are a trainee and wish to become an entry level manager, you are rotated through each of the hourly job positions. You learn how the hotel or restaurant is run, how each department operates, and pick up on a variety of management styles. This type of program is an extensive orientation *and* training program.

Orientation programs are not always just for the new employee, although that is their primary function (Figure 6-1). Orientation programs are also important in hospitality organizations that undergo changes in structure or policies, or following a merger or an acquisition. Acquisitions require a special orientation so that the employees of the acquired company feel a part of the parent organization.

Orientation programs can be conducted by either the human resources department, the individual department manager, or by the supervisor. To maximize effectiveness, there needs to be a great deal of cooperation from all

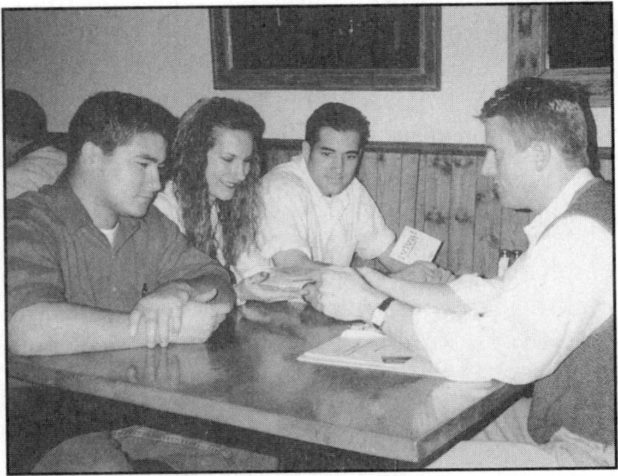

FIGURE 6-1 A solid orientation program is an important human resources function. *(Courtesy of Left At Albuquerque, Palo Alto, CA)*

departmental areas. Typically, the orientation in large, more complex hospitality organizations would be implemented so that the human resources department would describe company-wide policies. The departmental manager or supervisor would then orient the employee to the department he or she will be working in.

The orientation process is so important that care must be taken to make the new employee comfortable and relaxed so that the maximum amount of information can be relayed to him or her. You certainly want to make a favorable first impression upon your new employees, and at the same time you want to create what Loret Carbone calls "a safe learning environment." This environment encourages questions about anything the new employee might need clarified or repeated. Remember that the goal here is for the new employees to learn and to become better informed. If they are afraid or too intimidated to ask questions, this goal will not be achieved. Icebreaker exercises work well in relaxing a group of employees and making them feel more comfortable. Your friendly, open attitude when conducting the orientation will also help abate fears.

Great care must be taken not to load the new employee with too much information at one time or information overload will occur. Taking the time to develop a formalized orientation program specifically for your hospitality organization prevents this from occurring. It also ensures that all the necessary information is contained in the program.

INDUSTRY EXPERTS SPEAK

Loret Carbone suggests the following icebreaker that she uses. "Have the trainees pair up with someone who was born in the same month as they were. (If the months don't exactly match, you can pair them up in a fun way by saying, 'You are June and you are October? That's close enough!') Then have them decide who will be 'A' and who will be 'B'. Have the 'As' spend 60 seconds interviewing the 'Bs' finding out what their name is, where they last worked, what their position is, what their hobbies are (you can be creative in this list.) Then switch and have the 'Bs' interview the 'As'. Finally, have everyone introduce their partner to the group, using the information they just learned about them."

CHARACTERISTICS OF WELL-DESIGNED ORIENTATION PROGRAMS

In the hospitality business, it is important that our human resources have a global view of our hospitality organization. Emphasis should be placed on the culture of the organization, and why it's important. The Disney experience is probably the best example of a company that makes sure that each of its employees knows and understands the corporate culture. Disney World treats their orientation program like a process that they believe is beneficial because ". . . treating it as a single event ignores the development stages that new employees go through."[1] A large part of the orientation program is spent on the traditions, values, language, and culture of Disney.

The employees must be able to see how their specific job relates to other jobs and departments within the hospitality operation. Let's look, for example, at the importance of the relationship between the front office job position and the position of housekeeper. For the new employee who is going to work in housekeeping, an orientation of the front desk should be provided. Showing the human resources working in housekeeping how the front desk operates will give them a better understanding of where their work fits into the total goals of the hotel. It will demonstrate more clearly the awkward position the room clerks are in when they have guests waiting to check in, but do not have enough clean rooms ready. Likewise, showing the room clerks what it takes to clean a room will give them a better appreciation of why all the rooms are not ready for check-in by 10:00 a.m.!

INDUSTRY EXPERTS SPEAK

Loret Carbone points out the importance of the relationship between the host staff and the servers in your dining rooms. "The host staff has to understand the time demands placed on a server when a new table of guests is seated in their assigned work station. Having the host follow a server during their shift would provide them with some empathy when two or even three tables get seated at the same time in one station."

Even though each of the human resources working in a hospitality operation has a specific job position, the nature of our business finds these employees walking around the operation. This means that our employees frequently come into direct contact with our guests in areas outside of their immediate work area. As a service to our guests, our human resources need to be informed about many of the operation's functions and activities so that they can correctly answer questions and inquiries made to them by our guests. Table 6-1 identifies some of the characteristics that a well-designed hospitality orientation program should contain.

TABLE 6-1 Positive Characteristics of Hospitality Orientation Programs

- Presents a complete overview of the hospitality operation/property
- Recognizes the specific problems and needs the new employee might face and addresses those problems and needs
- Orientation procedures are planned, well organized, and effectively administered
- Orientation plans are adapted to the particular department and job position of the new employee
- Keeps the focus on the benefits of the new employee
- Provides a realistic look at the working conditions of the company
- Presents an opportunity for the new employee to meet fellow employees within their department
- Is continually evaluated and improved
- Provides an explanation of the hospitality organization's culture, philosophies, values, vision, and mission
- Presents a historical perspective
- Presents a vision of where the hospitality organization and specific operation is headed

The Specifics

The new employee who is made to feel welcome and immediately a part of the work team is sure to make the guests in your hospitality operation also feel welcome. Hospitality is a service industry, and if we are to excel in service to our guests, then our operations must have employees with what Loret Carbone calls a "high hospitality quotient" meaning a strong, positive service attitude. Don't *tell* them what hospitality is; *show* them! One way might be to give all new hires a certificate for a dinner for two before their first day on the job. Not only is this a warm welcome to your company, it also gives them a familiarity with your operation from the guest's perspective. You can use this during the orientation to describe how you expect them to treat the guests they will be encountering.

Throughout the orientation, then, the importance of good service and your guests is the theme of all discussions. Although orientations (see Table 6-2) vary somewhat depending

TABLE 6-2 Orientation Program—*Left At Albuquerque*

Manager greets trainee and welcomes them.
Manager checks the trainee's uniform.
Manager issues additional uniform items (apron, POS key or card, crumb scraper, etc.).
Manager demonstrates how to punch in on time clock.
Trainee completes all new hire paperwork.
Manager reviews Employee Handbook.
Manager reviews Employee Safety Manual.
Manager reviews company's Sexual Harassment policies.
Manager reviews appropriate job description.
Manager reviews company mission statement and value statement.
Manager reviews rules for personnel (uniform, appearance, attendance, tardiness, scheduling procedures, paydays, meals, breaks, vacation policy, security for personal possessions, personal phone calls, accidents, sidework, lost & found procedures, tip reporting, how walkouts are handled, pre-shift meetings, secret shopper reports, the importance of cleanliness and sanitation, how guest birthdays are handled, discipline and warning notices, emergency procedures, team work, and behavior that will result in immediate termination).
Trainee is given a tour of the restaurant.
Trainee attends pre-shift meeting.
Trainee follows a trainer during the shift.
Trainee eats training meal with manager.
Trainee takes Orientation Test.
Trainee punches out.

(Courtesy of Left At Albuquerque, Palo Alto, CA)

upon the specific job position, they should at a minimum include the following:

The Company

At this point it is appropriate to discuss the operation's history and development. This can lead into a discussion of the hospitality organization's structure and organization chart. A thorough description of the organizational goals and operational objectives should be presented, including the mission statement. The importance of the contribution the new human resources are expected to make to those goals and objectives should be made clear. Loret Carbone explains that what you are looking for is an emotional buy-in and commitment to the company from the new employee. This is the first step to a successful partnership and long-term relationship between the new employee and the hospitality organization.

Survival Information. Though not the most exciting information you share with the new employee, survival information certainly is some of the most important you can share. Care must be taken so that no specifics are overlooked. What may be routine and obvious for present employees can become a major problem area for the new employee who lacks information.

Some of the necessary survival information includes the following:

- Check-in procedures; the use of time cards.
- Issuance of keys, uniforms, and necessary supplies.
- Medical insurance and other benefit forms. Assistance should be provided in filling out these forms, which can be confusing to even the most knowledgeable employee. As you learn in an upcoming chapter on benefits, this area is rapidly changing and becoming more complex. Table 6-3 identifies some of the employment papers that need to be filled out by new employees.

TABLE 6-3 Information Needed from New Hires

- Employee application completely filled out, signed, and dated
- Medical insurance forms
- Life insurance forms
- Federal Withholding form (Form W-4)
- Signatures acknowledging:
  –receipt of keys
  –receipt of company's rules of conduct
  –receipt of policies and procedures manual
  –receipt of employee safety manual
  –receipt of sexual harassment policy
- Proof of age (if required)
- Medical examiners report (if required)
- Health certificate

- ◎ Explanation of how to read the paycheck stub. This includes information on your compensation policy, such as when the employee will be paid and what deductions are taken.
- ◎ Locations of rest rooms, lockers, employee eating facilities/break room, vending machines, parking space, employee entrance, and time clock.
- ◎ Work hours and scheduling procedures; overtime, flextime, and comp-time policies.

This is a good time to distribute the organization's employee handbook, which should contain most of this information:

- ◎ ***Organizational policies.*** Time-off policy, vacation time and scheduling, paid holidays, call-in policy for illness, accrual of sick leave, substitute policy, meal and break policies.
- ◎ ***Operational policies.*** If you have done a good job explaining the hospitality company to the new employee, he or she will already have a good appreciation for why "the way we do things here" is so important. Every operation has values and traditions of which every new employee must be made aware. "We always refer to our customers as 'guests,'" or "we always greet our guests with a smile" are two examples of operational policies that might be part of your hospitality organization's corporate culture (Figure 6-2).
- ◎ Here you would also want to include information on your organization's policies relating to promotion, performance appraisals, career development opportunities, and behaviors that could result in termination.
- ◎ ***A tour.*** Familiarizing the new employee with the hospitality premises is important not only for his or her own knowledge, but just in case a guest asks for directions. The tour should include all areas that will help the new employee to perform his or her job more effectively. The locations of departments that interact with the new hire's department should be given special attention.
- ◎ ***Departmental responsibilities.*** Every employee needs to understand the contribu-

FIGURE 6-2 "We always greet our guests with a smile." *(Courtesy of Left At Albuquerque, Palo Alto, CA)*

tion of his or her work unit to the hospitality operation as well as his or her department's relationship to other departments. Loret Carbone is quick to point out that this translates into teamwork. Introductions to other people the new employee will be working with should be made.

- ***Job responsibilities.*** This is an introduction to what the individual's job will consist of, including how it relates to other jobs in the department. The new employee is shown his or her work area along with any equipment the individual might be working with in his or her job position. An introduction to the employee's immediate supervisor should occur, if it has not been made already.
- ***Sanitation and safety procedures.*** Many hospitality organizations, especially those involved in the preparation and service of food, incorporate a session on sanitation procedures to all food service workers. Many others routinely include information on safety, as many departments in hospitality organizations contain equipment and chemicals that if not handled correctly and with great care could be dangerous to our human resources, and in some cases to our guests. OSHA federal guidelines require all operations to maintain a hazard communication program.

Some hospitality organizations prepare a welcome kit that contains information useful to new employees. This can be given to them when they are hired. They should read the information and bring it to the first orientation session along with a list of questions they may have after reviewing the material. This can be read over at their leisure and can serve as a future reference guide when questions arise. The specific listing you develop for your hospitality organization will depend on its size, mission, and what management considers to be important information for new hires (see Table 6-4). In unionized operations, for example, it would be important to cover the significant provisions in the labor contract. In nonunionized operations, statements about *remaining* nonunionized might be included. A well-thought-out orientation helps new employees feel comfortable and at ease in their new job position.

TABLE 6-4 Sample New Employee Orientation Checklist

- Words of welcome
- History of the company
- Company culture
- Service philosophy of the company
- Organizational structure of the company
- Sexual harassment policy
- Review of job descriptions, hours and days to work, job duties, and responsibilities
- Rate of pay, pay policies, and periods
- Gratuities and tip reporting
- Employee benefits
- Special uniform requirements
- Break periods and meal hours
- Review of rules of conduct and employee handbook
- Unforeseen absences and tardiness
- Review of Equal Employment Opportunity Policy
- Fill out and sign W-4
- Tour of operation and work unit
- Introduction to coworkers
- To whom to report, when, and where
- List of frequently called phone numbers
- Sanitation and safety procedures
- Performance evaluations and salary increases
- Career development and opportunities for promotion
- Progressive discipline
- Grounds for termination
- Emergency situations

FOLLOW-UP AND EVALUATION

Once the hospitality organization has formally established a good orientation program and checklist of items to cover, the responsibility does not end for assuring a successful orientation. It is extremely critical that during the first few weeks of employment some follow-up takes place. This is to ensure that the employee is adjusting to his or her new work environment with the least amount of job anxiety and problems possible.

A follow-up will also clarify any questions that might have arisen as a result of the orientation program. Once your new hire has been on the job for a few days, clarification might be needed on departmental rules or regulations; after he or she receives the first paycheck, another explanation of how to read the paycheck might be needed; another tour might be in order especially if your property is very large and complex. All these measures are taken to assist your new employees in assimilating into the hospitality workplace with as much ease as possible.

Unfortunately, orienting employees to the workplace and their jobs is frequently neglected in many hospitality organizations. All too frequently a newly hired person arrives and is expected to start working with very little guidance or instruction. Not only is this very stressful for the new hire, it translates into low productivity, the probability of mistakes, and poor guest relations. A solid, well-thought-out orientation program can help reduce the anxiety and stress commonly felt by a new employee when entering into a new, unfamiliar situation. It can help ensure that your new employee can go about the job with the assurance and confidence of knowing, not guessing, about what needs to be done. This allows the new employee to become productive more quickly and thereby can often reduce the costs associated learning on the job. In turn, employee turnover is reduced while retention rates improve. You have shown your people that your hospitality organization values their employees and that you want to help them to succeed in their job. Knowing what is expected of them, along with what they can expect of you, can only help your valuable human resources be successful.

Orientation programs, while separate from training, do compose an important part of the human resources planning and employment processes. The more quickly you can reduce the anxieties of your new hire, the more quickly that employee will become a productive member of the team. Orientation programs are about more than just the benefits, rules, and regulations; it is your opportunity to socialize the newest human resources in your hospitality organization and make them team members!

WHY TRAIN?

Training programs need to be distinguished from orientation programs. Whereas orientation programs provide information, training seeks to teach or improve skills and concepts. One of the main objectives of training is to sustain performance at or improve performance to acceptable levels. Orientation aids us in meeting this training objective, for without information about the organization, department, and job, we can hardly expect performance levels to be satisfactory.

In recent years, service—or the seeming lack of it—in American society has been making headlines. The hospitality industry has, along with other industries that provide service, had its share of negative publicity. When you think about it, it is really amazing that individuals who are willing to spend thousands and even millions of dollars building a new restaurant or renovating an old landmark hotel fail to allocate enough dollars for training.

INDUSTRY EXPERTS SPEAK

Loret Carbone relates the following: "People love to tell you about terrible service experiences they have had in restaurants. One that I have heard recently is from a woman who entered a restaurant on a Monday at 2:00 pm and approached the host desk. The hostess, who was obviously talking and laughing with a friend on the phone, ignored the woman to the point where she actually turned her back to the guest to have more privacy on her call. The woman waited patiently. When the hostess hung up the phone she didn't even turn around to the guest, but rather walked away from the desk and went into the kitchen, never even acknowledging the presence of the guest. The woman continued to wait and when the hostess walked back up to the desk, she asked the woman, 'Just one?' From there she silently walked to the smallest table in the restaurant (there was only one other table occupied) and dropped the menu on the table, never pulling out the chair or wishing the woman a pleasant meal. The guest sat at the table patiently waiting for her server. After 10 minutes, the woman was so angry she got up and walked out of the restaurant. On her way out the door, the hostess said, 'Please come again.' "

How much do you think should be allocated per employee for training each year? A hundred dollars? A thousand dollars? Two thousand? Three thousand? Or less? Maybe twenty dollars for a self-study training manual? And how much would you allocate for a redesigned menu for your restaurant, new bed linens for the rooms, or updated software to handle your daily receipts? The last three items are all considered investments: items that improve the quality of the service you offer your guests. Similarly, you cannot afford to consider training any less of an investment. *People* are your most important asset! That is why we refer to them as human *resources.*

What It Is

With the growing emphasis on guest service in the hospitality industry, we must understand how to develop, implement, and maintain effective training programs. We define **training** as a systematic process through which the human resources in the hospitality industry gain knowledge and develop skills by instruction and practical activities that result in improved performance.

Training can be conducted at a number of different levels, making training an on-going activity in your hospitality operation. Upon graduation many of you will be experiencing the management candidate training program. At this level, training provides the management candidate with an overview of every department along with supervisory training experiences.

Training can also be conducted for supervisory human resources. These are individuals such as shift managers and floor supervisors, similar to foremen in other industries. Frequently, these people have been hourly employees who have exhibited great technical skills. The skills they need to develop relate more to interpersonal and leadership skills.

Training programs also need to be established for employees whom you deem to be promotable. These programs work to support the established job and career paths that we discuss at length in Chapter 7. Employees who you believe are promotable are the individuals who excel in their performance levels and are ready to accept more responsibility. Failing to provide this opportunity may result in the loss of some of your best people. These training programs become part of the development opportunities you provide for all of your human resources (Table 6-5). Remember that this is a highly competitive labor market.

Retraining needs might also occur with current employees who display a deficiency or need to be trained in a particular area. This

TABLE 6-5 Server Training Program Outline

Day One	Orientation (Follow server)
Day Two	Philosophy of Service (Follow server)
Day Three	The Details of Service (Follow busser and bartender)
Day Four	POS System (Follow server)
Day Five	Bar & Liquor (Follow server)
Day Six	Food (Follow expediter and runner)
Day Seven	Take Tables

(Courtesy of Left At Albuquerque, Palo Alto, CA)

could be due to a skill deficiency causing substandard performance, the need for new skills due to a change in job positions, or merely a refresher on skills that the employee has mastered but has not had cause to use. It is your responsibility, in human resources management, to pick up on signals that indicate a training need. What are some of those signals? Can you think of any? The following is a list of our ideas:

- ***Low Productivity.*** All hospitality organizations operate according to standards and policies. When you find that an employee is not keeping up with standards, such as a housekeeper who cannot consistently clean his or her assigned number of rooms each day, then you need to look into the reasons why productivity levels are not being maintained.
- ***High Waste.*** Whether it is too many onions being used in your restaurant, too many mixers in your bar, or too much window cleaner in your housekeeping department, high usages can indicate waste. Maybe your cooks don't know the proper way to peel onions, the bartender is using the wrong size glasses, or the housekeepers are using window cleaner to clean everything. Each of these situations could mean that a training need exists.
- ***Grievances and High Turnover of Employees.*** What is the cause of these grievances and high turnover? Though not always related to a lack of training, it could be a plausible reason. If you have ever worked in a job where you were not told what to do or how to do it, you know how frustrated and inadequate you can feel. No one wants to go to work and perform a job he or she really doesn't understand and is uncomfortable with doing for fear of making a mistake. People generally want to be successful, and it is our job to provide them with the proper tools to achieve that success.

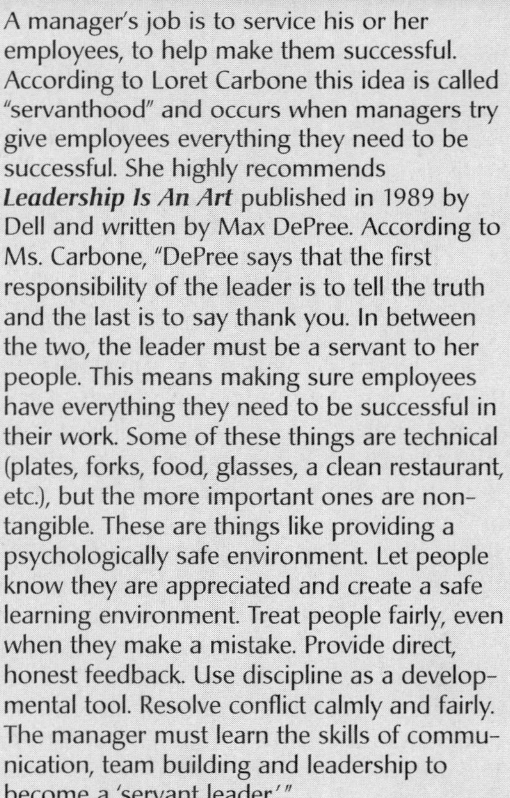

INDUSTRY EXPERTS SPEAK

A manager's job is to service his or her employees, to help make them successful. According to Loret Carbone this idea is called "servanthood" and occurs when managers try give employees everything they need to be successful. She highly recommends ***Leadership Is An Art*** published in 1989 by Dell and written by Max DePree. According to Ms. Carbone, "DePree says that the first responsibility of the leader is to tell the truth and the last is to say thank you. In between the two, the leader must be a servant to her people. This means making sure employees have everything they need to be successful in their work. Some of these things are technical (plates, forks, food, glasses, a clean restaurant, etc.), but the more important ones are non-tangible. These are things like providing a psychologically safe environment. Let people know they are appreciated and create a safe learning environment. Treat people fairly, even when they make a mistake. Provide direct, honest feedback. Use discipline as a developmental tool. Resolve conflict calmly and fairly. The manager must learn the skills of communication, team building and leadership to become a 'servant leader.'"

- ***Guest Complaints.*** Listen to your guests and find out the reasons when they indicating that they are not satisfied. These reasons could spell T-R-A-I-N-I-N-G.

Training should always strive to be responsive to the needs of the hospitality operation (Figure 6-3). This goes back to the human resources planning that we discussed earlier in this text. For the remainder of this chapter we examine training from the perspective of our new hires. Those new employees have successfully completed our well-thought-out orientation program, but have yet to start their job tasks, duties, and responsibilities. These individuals will work more effectively if we provide them with the proper training *before* placing them into their new job position.

FIGURE 6-3 Training should always be responsive to the needs of the hospitality operation. *(Courtesy of Left At Albuquerque, Palo Alto, CA)*

A HISTORICAL PERSPECTIVE

Once upon a time in the hospitality industry, you could tell an employee to do a task, in a specific manner, and he or she would. As we enter the twenty-first century, we find that people don't want to perform a task simply because you have told them to. They want to understand the reason why they are doing that task.

One of the first goals of training, in prehistoric times, was to teach others to use a tool to perform a task. "As man invented tools, weapons, clothing, shelter and language, the need for training became an essential ingredient in the march of civilization."[2] When tools were simple, one training method was sufficient, but as the tools became more complex, different types of training were developed. **On-the-job training (OJT)** is one of the earliest types of training. In ancient times, the type of work that people performed was mostly unskilled or semiskilled work. OJT was used, probably because the people did not have to be able to read or write. Training methods, such as OJT, that involved one person showing another how to do a task was perfect for these situations.

Apprenticeships, although developed earlier, became widespread during the Middle Ages. They were developed to pass down the skills to perform various crafts. A young person would actually be bound to his or her employer by a legal agreement, and in exchange for work the apprentice would learn the craft from the skilled worker. The idea of apprenticeships is still prevalent in the hospitality industry in Europe today, and exists to a lesser degree in the United States, particularly in the area of culinary training.

Classroom training was developed in large part because of the new and unique training needs created by the Industrial Revolution. For the first time in history, the machines in the factories allowed goods to be produced quickly and in large numbers. Because there was a high demand for the goods the factories produced, the factories had a high need for employees who could be trained quickly and in large numbers. This training method required fewer trainers, unlike on-the-job training and apprenticeships.

Numerous training programs resulted from World War II efforts to rapidly train individuals to assist in our nation's defense. Among them are the **job instructor training** program, and the job safety training program. At the same time, the need for management training occurred and was met through the Engineering, Science, and Management War Training program (ESMWT).

Today training can no longer be thought of as a stop-gap activity. We can trace this increasing importance and value of training to the hospitality industry by examining training departments throughout the past several years.

OBJECTIVES OF TRAINING IN "THE NEXT CHAPTER"

The people who work for you have choices. The more frequently they make the right choices, the better off you, the manager, are. The better trained your human resources are, the more likely it is that they will make the right choices. Poorly trained human resources with low morale translate into poor quality service. The more you can maximize the abilities of your staff, the more successful they, and you, will be. We guarantee that you will have a lot more fun. Well-trained employees can assume more responsibility and that makes your job easier.

In the hospitality industry, regardless of job position, what is the most important job responsibility for each of your human resources? We want you to think very carefully about this question. The answer becomes the focus of all training activities. *Maximizing guest satisfaction* is the predominant job responsibility for each person you employ—even the dishwashers, who might never come into direct contact with the guests.

Before training actually takes place, the first thing you must tell your hourly employees is their job responsibilities. The job tasks that you are about to train them to perform are merely the means of achieving maximum guest satisfaction.

The following is a listing of specific training objectives that are commonly found in the hospitality industry. Please note that all can be related directly back to maximizing guest satisfaction.

- *To make the hospitality operation a* ***safe*** *place for both employees and guests.*
  - *—Accident prevention*
  - *—Security measures*
- *To increase* ***worker satisfaction****.*
  - *—Reduction in turnover costs*
- *To* ***provide the knowledge and skill levels*** *necessary to perform assigned job position.*
- *To* ***improve skill levels and performance abilities*** *of our human resources.*
  - *—Increased productivity*
  - *—Improved labor efficiency*
  - *—Improved development and promotional opportunities*

Training is important. Both the guest and the employee benefit from an effective training program. Table 6-6 identifies several of the advantages gained from training human resources in the hospitality industry.

TABLE 6-6 Benefits to Be Gained from the Implementation of a Training Program

- Improved quality of guest services
- Increased comradery and sense of teamwork
- Improved quality
- Reduced work conflicts
- Relief of stress and tension
- Reduced turnover and absenteeism
- Improved performance resulting in cost savings
- Preparation of employees for promotion
- Improved self-esteem of our human resources
- Growing sense of professionalism
- Improved relationships between management and staff
- Reduction in accidents
- Increased productivity
- Improved sanitation and cleanliness
- Decreased fatigue
- Improved sense of job security
- Reduction in amount of supervision required
- Happier work environment
- Reduced waste
- Fun
- Higher morale among all people
- Greater cooperation

A GUIDE TO DEVELOPING YOUR HOSPITALITY TRAINING PROGRAM

As we have seen, there are numerous benefits that can be gained from an effective training program in the hospitality industry. But just what do we mean by "effective"? How do we get our training program to pay off with results? Planning and dedication to the training effort are required. Before you can start training, you must first assess the needs of your hospitality operation and then outline the training program so that it meets current and future needs. Figure 6-4 displays the development process of a training program.

Knowing When Training Is Needed

To initiate a training program, you need an outline of the topics to be covered. The training topics that will be taught are based upon the needs of your human resources. So first you must ask, "What are the needs of my trainees?" Once the needs are identified, the training program can then be designed to specifically address those needs. In order to be efficient and

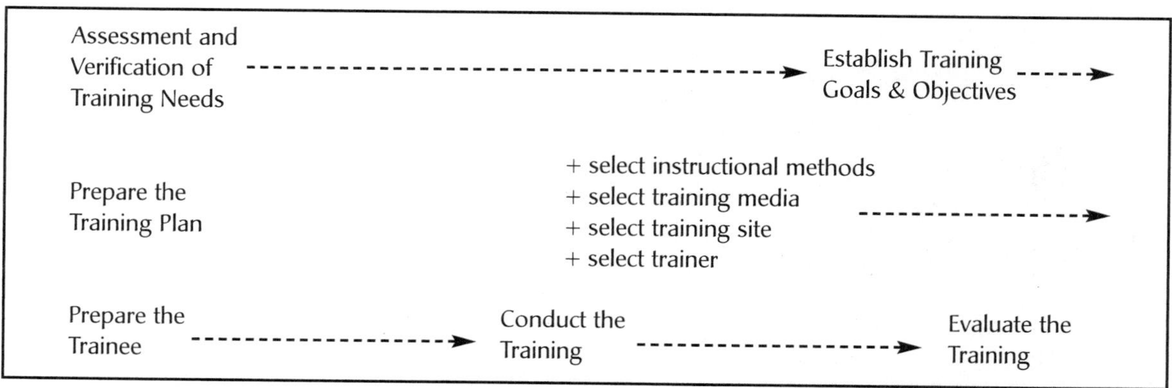

FIGURE 6-4 Development of a training program.

effective, all training programs should start with a **needs assessment**. The assessment seeks to identify "needs" or "gaps" between what is currently in place in the hospitality operation and what is needed. An example of a gap might be a difference between what the company expects to be happening and what is really happening. A gap could relate to a difference in job performance, between what is expected and what is happening. Or a gap could relate to a difference between the skills your human resources need and the ones that they actually have.

There are three areas that require analysis for your needs assessment: the hospitality organization, the job position, and the knowledge and skill level of the trainee. If your training program is going to be effective, it must meet the goals of the hospitality organization, it must be relevant to the particular job duties and tasks required of the job position, and it must satisfy a deficiency in the knowledge or skill level of the trainee.

- ***Organizational assessment.*** The assessment of your hospitality organization was discussed in Chapter 2. It was during the planning phase that we developed the mission statement for our hospitality enterprise, and from it prepared our organizational goals and operational objectives. Now we need to determine the effectiveness of our organization. Are we doing what we planned to be doing? The organizational assessment should identify:
  —The need to address cultural or language barriers based upon the changing demographics in our work force
  —Legislative changes and impacts such as sexual harassment and workplace discrimination
  —New laws such as the Americans with Disabilities Act and the Family Medical Leave Act
  —Social issues that impact the workplace such as Welfare to Work and illiteracy
  —Changing technology and increasing power of the Internet
  —The effectiveness of the hospitality organization in meeting it's goals

INDUSTRY EXPERTS SPEAK

"Effective training begins with a well-thought-out plan," believes Loret Carbone. Once you have developed a thorough outline, it is an easy step to writing the training manual. With the manual in place, the training seminar development and worksheets fall quickly into place. Never underestimate the value of starting with a solid plan (Figure 6-5).

- ***Job analysis.*** Job analysis provides valuable information for a variety of human resources functions. We have already seen the value of job analysis in the recruitment, selection, hiring, and placement functions. Now it serves us again as we attempt to determine the training needs.

  Recall from Chapter 3 that job information was collected by a variety of methods for each job position in the hospitality workplace. A job listing was compiled that contained the specific tasks required in the performance of each job position. A sample task listing for a busperson is found in Table 6-7. From this information, job descriptions and specifications were written.

  The information from the task analysis will give us an indication of the difficulty of learning the task. This will be useful to us in selecting the instructional methods and training media. Information is also obtained relating to the importance of the task in the performance of the job that will help us prioritize our training needs.

FIGURE 6-5 Never underestimate the value of starting with a solid plan. *(Courtesy of Left At Albuquerque, Palo Alto, CA)*

TABLE 6-7 Task Listing for a Busperson

1. Remove all dishes, glasses, and silverware from the table.
2. Wipe down the table with a clean damp cloth.
3. Wipe down chairs with a clean damp cloth.
4. Check to see if the floor surrounding and under the table needs to be swept.
5. Reset table with napkins and silverware.
6. Center condiments on the table.
7. Notify host station that table is reset.

- ***Assessment of our human resources.*** Our recruitment and selection efforts have provided us with the most-qualified individuals for the vacant job positions. Ideally they would walk into the workplace after orientation and have all the knowledge, skills, and abilities to perform the job at a level equal to or higher than our stated performance standards. I cannot think of one case in my operational experience where this situation has occurred. So don't accuse those recruiters or that placement department with bringing you inferior new hires. Your job is now to take those human resources and assess their knowledge, skills, and abilities.

For those of you who work for a hospitality organization that requires preemployment testing, some of this work has already been done by the placement department. From the job analysis you know the knowledge, skills, and abilities needed to perform the job. Whether through preemployment or diagnostic testing, you must now determine the performance levels of your trainees. Training needs are indicated by performance levels that are substandard to those required to successfully perform the duties and responsibilities of the job position.

Another indication of a training need is evidence of a conflict between the needs of the hospitality organization and the needs of the employees. Training is not only necessary when there is a deficiency in skills, it is also necessary to change or improve employee attitudes and behaviors.

This relates directly to our earlier discussion of maximizing guest satisfaction. Our employees have to be trained to maximize satisfaction for every guest who enters our hospitality operation (Figure 6-6). We can do this by reinforcing that message throughout the entire training program by relating everything we teach to the objective of maximum guest satisfaction. That is *why* the dishwashers must be sure to drain the dishmachine on a regular basis. That is *why* the housekeepers must recheck the room they just cleaned before leaving. That is *why* the bartenders must follow drink recipes.

FIGURE 6-6 Employees have to be trained to maximize guest satisfaction. *(Courtesy of Left At Albuquerque, Palo Alto, CA)*

It is clear that completing a needs assessment is a logical first step in the development of a training plan. But if it is so logical, then why don't more hospitality organizations complete this critical step?

Completing needs assessments is a time-consuming process. Unfortunately, in the hospitality industry we need our new hires trained yesterday, and many managers feel that they simply cannot wait for a needs assessment to occur for every new hire. So instead—at best—everyone goes through a general orientation and generic training program with assurances that his or her supervisor will follow up with training in any deficiencies that they see while the employee is on the job. In the worst scenario, no training occurs and the new hire is simply shown his or her workstation and told to feel free to ask any questions. Not wanting to appear stupid, the new hire will either attempt to figure out procedures independently or become so frustrated that the first day at work is also the last. Then management is left wondering what happened. But worst of all, you have neglected your number one objective of maximizing guest satisfaction.

Another reason that needs assessments aren't performed more often is that many people don't have your understanding of what need assessments are and the results that they generate. Hospitality is an action-oriented industry, and if management does not see immediate results, they are likely to question how you are spending your time.

One cautionary note: When making observations for your needs analysis, care must be taken to differentiate between problems and needs that are the result of inadequate training and those that result from inadequate equipment, poor procedures, lack of feedback, or poor supervision. Training needs include only those problems that can be solved through training. Not all problems are training problems, nor are all needs training needs!

Training Goals and Objectives

Your analysis of the organization, the job, and the human resources has provided you with a list of training needs matched with trainees. If your training needs are numerous, you might want to consider prioritizing them into "A," "B," and "C" categories. Your "A" category would be those needs of primary importance for the day-to-day operations of your establishment. For the waitstaff this might consist of learning the proper serving procedures. "B" training needs would be secondary to the functioning of the operation, but critical in maximizing guest satisfaction. For the waitstaff this might include learning how each dish they will be serving is prepared. "C" needs have even a lower immediate priority, but again are necessary to set your hospitality operation above the competition. An example for the waitstaff could include knowing the characteristics of the most recently released wines available on the market.

It is important that your prioritized training needs and broad training goals such as maximizing guest satisfaction, providing basic job knowledge and skills, and providing a means to achieve job satisfaction are translated, in writing, to specific training objectives. The following is an example of a training objective for the busperson's position we identified when we conducted our needs analysis.

Sample Training Objective

Objective: *To clear and reset a table according to XYZ Company standards in sixty seconds.*

You should always specify the behavior or performance desired at the end of the training program. Training objectives must be realistic and should provide for some form of evaluation to determine whether or not they have been obtained. Training objectives must be developed from the perspective of your own hospitality operation; you can't open a book to find a list of training objectives that will be suitable to your situation. The work you have accomplished so far will make the preparation of your training plan much easier.

LITERACY

Before we can train our people, we first need to know if they have the ability to learn. Each of us is born illiterate. Those of us who developed our **literacy** skills early are the most successful learners. Those people who do not develop reading skills at a young age are frequently unable to reach their potential in school, in the world, and in the workplace. The fact that you are able to read these written words means that you have developed literacy skills. However, not all adults can read these words.

The National Institute for Literacy estimates that 20 percent of the adult population read at or below a fifth-grade level. This is way below the level needed to earn a living wage. One result of these alarming statistics is the *National Literacy Act of 1991*. The purpose of the act is "to enhance the literacy and basic skills of adults, to ensure that all adults in the United States acquire the basic skills necessary to function effectively and achieve the greatest possible opportunity in their work and in their lives, and to strengthen and coordinate adult literacy programs."[3] Prior to this time the largest source of federal literacy services was in programs under the *Adult Education Act*.

The act furthered defined literacy as "an individual's ability to read, write, and speak in English, and compute and solve problems at levels of proficiency necessary to function on the job and in society, to achieve one's goals, and develop one's knowledge and potential."[4] In Section 102 this act established the National Institute for Literacy (NIFL), found at website www.nifl.gov, to be the center of national literacy efforts. In addition to serving as a resource for the literacy community, the Institute assists "in addressing urgent national priorities—upgrading the workforce, reducing welfare dependency, raising the standard of living, and creating safer communities."[5]

The United States is not alone in dealing with the problem of literacy. In Canada the literacy issue has become more prominent on the national agenda. The 1994 International Adult Literacy Survey (IALS) studied training issues in Canada, the United States, Switzerland, the Netherlands, Poland, Germany, and Sweden. Canada is using some of the data collected to determine the relationship between literacy and income security.

In the National Literacy Act of 1991, Congress emphasized the need for a "National Literacy Data Base." To that end the National Institute for Literacy has developed LINCS, the NIFL's *Literacy Information and Communication System*. LINCS is a national electronic literacy information retrieval and communication network that seeks to achieve the goals of national information and communication for the literacy community. It provides information about States Literacy Resources, the National Adult Literacy and Learning Disabilities Center, as well as links to other literacy programs and resources. What this means to you is that there are numerous sources of data and information available, at your fingertips, that can assist hospitality managers and others in dealing with literacy-related issues and problems.

There are many different levels of literacy, many of which go beyond the scope of this brief introduction to literacy that we present here. The most recent focus is on "functional literacy," which refers to whether a person's educational level is sufficient to function in today's society. If a person is functionally illiterate, it means that the basic skills of reading, writing, and math are below the fifth-grade level. Below a fifth-grade level could mean that your dishwasher might not be able to read the words "rinse agent" or "soap." Does it matter which chemical they use where when they fill the automatic dispensers on the machine? Below a fifth-grade level could mean that your housekeeper might not be able to read a sign written by a guest requesting "Please do not empty water." That same housekeeper could pour the water glasses complete with contact lenses down the drain. Below a fifth-grade level could mean that your cooks can't read the recipes or measure the ingredients correctly. What is the difference between ¼ tsp. and ¼ cup; the difference between ¼ and ½; the difference between a quart and a gallon? Below a fifth-grade level could mean that your cashier does not know how to count back change. Does this matter? Is this your problem as a manager with human resources responsibilities in the hospitality industry?

Literacy Initiatives in the Hospitality Industry

Fortunately, the hospitality industry has recognized the impact of the answers to those questions. We are an industry that hires a large number of unskilled and semiskilled people. The National Institute for Literacy states that about 20 percent of America's workers have low basic skills. We can assume that the literacy rates for our industry are, at best, the same. In response, a number of hospitality companies have instituted programs to help their human resources with their basic skills.

This is not to be confused with skills training, which we will discuss later in this chapter. This is teaching, or educating, people on the basic skills of reading, writing, and math. Sometimes these programs are referred to as

workplace education. This term tends to be received more positively than does "basic skills program."

The key to these programs is to treat the employee with respect, start with what they know, and build upon the skills and knowledge that they have. These are not children, these are adults and need to be treated differently than you would if you were an elementary school teacher. You also need to differentiate between those employees with language deficiencies and those who cannot read or write. An employee who speaks English as a second language could possibly be mistaken for someone who is functionally illiterate. Being functionally illiterate does not make an employee stupid or mean that the employee has a learning disability or cannot learn English. Most often people who have reading or writing difficulties have not had an opportunity to obtain the skills they need to be successful on the job. And remember that literacy programs are not just for teaching remedial reading and writing. A good literacy program helps people develop the skills necessary to meet the demands of their jobs. With the computer revolution now surrounding each of us, sometimes our people have trouble being able to follow the computer's directions or understand how to process the information it provides them.

Workforce literacy programs have never been easier to start than today. They do not have to be expensive. Oftentimes there are federal and state grants and tax credits available. In 1996 the federal government provided $361 million for adult education and family literacy programs. As the shortage of qualified applicants continues, we need to do whatever we can to help the people who work for us to develop and reach their full potential. This is does not just benefit our hospitality organization and its people, it benefits the whole society in which we live.

THE TRAINING PLAN

The **training plan** could be considered the heart of the training program. It is an outline that takes the training needs, goals, and objectives—or what your operation must do with respect to training—and identifies when, where, by whom, and how the training will be accomplished. *Where* the training takes place is answered by selection of the training site. *By whom* is answered by the selection of the trainer. *How* the training will be accomplished is answered by selecting the instructional methods and the training media. *When* the training should occur is determined by the priority of the training need.

Many job positions in the hospitality industry require a great deal of decision making on the part of our human resources. They just simply cannot be trained for every possible situation that they will experience in the course of performing their job tasks. Part of the assessment of the individual trainee must take into account his or her decision-making abilities, and if deficient, the training plan must meet this critical need.

We are going to initiate our preparation of a training plan by first selecting the training site, then looking at the selection of the trainer, and finally discussing the variety of training methods and media available to assist you in meeting your hospitality organization's training needs.

The Training Location

Selecting the training location will be partially determined by the type of training method that you select, whether it is classroom or on-the-job training or both that you want to provide. The environment is a critical factor in determining the success of your training program (Figure 6-7). The area should be pleasant with a minimum of distractions.

FIGURE 6–7 The proper training environment is important. *(Courtesy of Left At Albuquerque, Palo Alto, CA)*

Think about the type of environment that you learned best in while you were at school. What do you consider distractions to **learning**? The environment temperature, humidity, lighting, your comfort at your desk or chair, the list could go on and on. If something in the environment causes the training experience to be less than it could be, then we bet that those same factors will affect the amount of learning your trainees will do. Without the proper environment and facilities, training will be harder and less effective.

The appropriate training aids also need to be available. Can you imagine your accounting professor giving a lecture without chalk and a chalkboard or an overhead marking pen and transparencies? Can you imagine training your busperson to clean and reset a table without cleaning supplies, cloths, silverware, or napkins? Of course not! Almost every training session will require tools, equipment, supplies, or materials of some type. These should be identified and gathered ahead of time so that they are ready for the training session. This would include any audiovisual equipment or materials that you might need.

Training the Trainer

Many of you who will be assuming human resources responsibilities will also find yourself in the role of trainer. And we also know that for some of you that will be a very uncomfortable position. Getting up in front of a group of people and giving a presentation is not an easy thing for many of us! Those of you who get nervous giving classroom speeches as part of your course work understand exactly what we mean.

Some of you might be planning on having your best employees train your new hires by using the "buddy system." It is generally felt that this is *not* the best training method. You, as manager, lose control over what learning takes place by the trainee. Shortcuts or other procedures that are not up to your performance standards may be taught instead of the correct way to perform a task.

If your hospitality organization is large enough, you might have a staff of trainers employed on your payroll. In most cases, the training will fall on your shoulders, and you should be prepared to assume these human resources responsibilities. The following characteristics are needed in a trainer:

- Knowledge of job skills
- Knowledge of trainee abilities and skill levels
- Knowledge of learning principles
- Ability to communicate effectively
- Ability to motivate
- Patience
- Enthusiasm
- Understanding

Your role as trainer will depend on the philosophy of the hospitality organization. Loret Carbone points out that many organizations place accountability for training with the management team. In smaller organizations the manager will wear the training hat more often than in larger hospitality organizations that might have a ful-time trainer. Very large organizations might have a team of trainers or training department. You can't expect people to train themselves, at least not in accordance with the standards and operating policies that you want to maintain in your hospitality organization. But if you don't train your new hires, they will still learn. Unfortunately, they won't learn what you want them to learn.

Selecting the Training Method

The next decision that you have to make is to determine which method to use in your training program to maximize the amount of learning that occurs for each of your trainees. The training of your human resources can take place in many ways in the hospitality industry. Some of these methods are formal and some are informal. Frequently, multiple methods are used to assist the trainees in developing their skills. Selection of a particular method depends on the training objective (what is to be learned), the number of trainees involved, the skill and ability levels of the trainees, and the training budget.

Although this chapter deals primarily with **in-house training methods**, the following vehicles can be used when in-house methods are not suitable for your particular situation:

- ***College/University courses.*** These frequently extend beyond the management development program that you are enrolled in. Many of the same courses that you take would serve as training vehicles for some job positions.
- ***Correspondence courses.*** The educational arms of both the American Hotel and Motel Association and the National Restaurant Association offer correspondence courses to which your hospitality operation could subscribe. State restaurant and lodging associations can also be quite helpful. There are several other organizations, frequently associated with universities, that also supply correspondence courses.
- ***Educational seminars.*** There are numerous hospitality groups that sponsor seminars throughout the year. Frequently you will find topics that are relevant to the training needs of your hospitality organization.

Each trainee responds differently to training, so as managers with human resources responsibilities, it is up to us to use the right method of training, at the right time for each of our human resources. Let's examine some of the various methods you can choose from when conducting an in-house training program.

The Lecture Method

We know that this is the method that each of you knows best! Its greatest advantage? The **lecture method** is very cost-effective when training large numbers of trainees. Its greatest disadvantage? Unless you're a very clever and witty speaker, it can be very boring and cause you to lose the attention of your audience. Trainee retention is also less than with other methods.

What can you do, then, to overcome the disadvantages of using the lecture method? Think about experiences you have had while in school. Audiovisual materials can be used to supplement the lecturer. Everything from films, slides, videotapes, flipcharts, and overheads to interactions with computer monitors can be incorporated to make the lecture method seem less tedious to the trainees. Another way you can pep up lectures is to encourage questions and feedback from the trainees to get them involved in the training session. This also helps you measure how well your message is coming across.

On-the-Job Training

On-the-job training (OJT) is designed so that learning occurs while the trainee is actually performing the tasks required of his or her job position (Figure 6-8). Those who advocate OJT believe that trainees learn best when faced with the actual job situation. Those who don't use OJT state the following as some of their reasons:

- A good way to pass along bad work habits.
- Can interfere with your objective of maximizing guest satisfaction if OJT takes precedence over, let's say, getting the food to the guest.

FIGURE 6-8 On-the-job training permits learning to occur while the trainee is actually in his or her job position. *(Courtesy of Left At Albuquerque, Palo Alto, CA)*

- Can cause an increase in waste and lost productivity.
- Training can take second place to the job being done and result in a less than satisfactory learning experience.

A good OJT design that is well implemented can overcome these potential problems.

Job Instruction Training

Even though job instruction training is really a form of on-the-job training, we want to discuss it in more detail, because it is the most typical technique used in the training of a new hire.

If you have taken a speech class, you know that the way to present new material to an audience is to tell them what you're going to tell them; tell them; and then tell them what you told them. Job instruction training is where the trainer *tells* the trainee how to do the task; *shows* the trainee how to do the task; *observes* the trainee doing the task; and then provides *feedback* to the trainee on how well he or she did the task.

We would like to incorporate our basic objective of maximizing guest satisfaction into the technique of job instruction training. When the trainee truly understands, without question, the reason *why* he or she is performing a task, the trainee will work with greater efficiency, increasing your chances of achieving maximum guest satisfaction. Furthermore, you should explain *how* the performance of that task affects your operation in relationship to guest satisfaction. For example, if the salad prep person does not rinse the fresh spinach three times using fresh warm water for each rinse, the guest is likely to be chewing sand in his or her fresh spinach salad: a very unpleasant guest experience!

At this point, you should explain to the trainee how his or her job performance can affect the jobs of other employees in your operation. It will probably be the waitstaff person who will incur the effects of the guest having a spinach salad with sand. As a final step in job instruction training it never hurts to ask the trainee to repeat the information back to you in his or her own words. Always use open-ended questions, those that cannot be answered with a "yes" or "no" response. This is your confirmation that the trainee knows what you are talking about. Remember that practice makes perfect. The training cycle is really quite simple: the trainer observes and provides feedback while the trainee practices. Observe — Feedback — Practice — Observe — Feedback — Practice — Observe — Feedback — Practice —

"perfect practice makes perfect"
— Vince Lombardi.

Vestibule

Vestibule training or simulation training methods are those in which the real work environment is duplicated for the purpose of training. This has the advantages of on-the-job training without the potential of interfering, or negatively affecting, the day-to-day operations of your establishment. This experience is similar to the laboratory experience you had in your college program. The simulated approach works best with small groups. Its biggest disadvantage is the high cost of duplicating a work environment that is essentially nonrevenue producing. The long-term training effect should be evaluated to see if it results in a better return on investment (ROI) than other techniques.

Role Playing

Role playing is a training technique that stimulates learning by having the trainees act out real-life situations that they might face in the performance of their jobs. The advantage is that learning results from doing, which usually generates a higher retention than learning from merely observing. Role playing can be used to show trainees how to deal with difficult people, be they guests or other employees, as well as proper serving methods. Skills and behaviors both can be learned through role playing.

Choosing the Training Media

We have already discussed some of the more common training media available to you when we explained the lecture method of training. In "the next chapter" we have available many innovative training aids. Videotapes have replaced the use of filmstrips and slides in training presentations. Videotapes have been found to be an effective training medium. Many hospitality companies are building in-house and audiovisual libraries to use as a supplement with their on-the-job training programs.

Computer-based training programs (CBT) and electronic performance-support systems (EPSS) allow the trainee to advance through the training at his or her own pace. Computer-based training provides instruction via the medium of computers. It works in a fashion similar to the simulation method, only the computer serves as the simulator duplicating real-life industry experiences. Because the trainee can control the pace of the program, the individual can also go back and repeat segments that he or she feels need clarification. Computer-based training provides an opportunity to transfer information to trainees more quickly than in classroom training.

With EPSS the computer program actually guides the trainees through their work—while they are doing it. EPSS software directs the trainee to the appropriate resources, helps them make proper decisions, and helps keep them from making mistakes. These programs work best in jobs that are mental rather than physical and where employees use computers on a regular basis. In "the next chapter" look for an increasing application of these computer programs in the hospitality industry. A disadvantage is the lack of human interaction. Interactive video programs can be used to overcome this disadvantage.

All these methods of training are worthless unless management is behind the programs 100 percent. You can tell if you have management's commitment by their participation in the programs, their role as a trainer of the program, and the focus they give to each manager's performance objectives regarding people development. Understanding these new technologies (Figure 6-9) and how they are being used will be a major challenge for hospitality managers with human resources responsibilities in "the next chapter." After all it just might be up to you to decide which technologies are right for your organization.

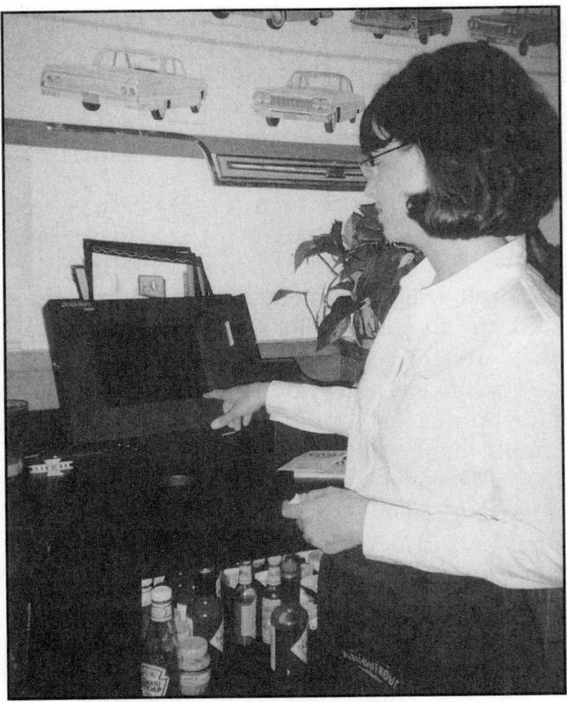

FIGURE 6-9 Understanding new technologies is already an important training initiative. *(Courtesy of Left At Albuquerque, Palo Alto, CA)*

Web-Based Training Systems

Individualized instruction that is delivered over the World Wide Web (www) is a further development of computer-based training. **Web-based training** can be used with any type of computer that can access the Internet and has Web browser software. This gives hospitality companies the ability to economically institute training courses anytime, anywhere in the world, along with the ability to constantly upgrade or modify the training materials. In addition, trainers can provide individual feedback to their employees. Trainees can learn where and when they have the time and trainer interaction can be as easy as an e-mail message.

Several hotel companies have already discovered that "the future is today" and have incorporated aspects of web-based training into their training programs. Sheraton Hotels & Resorts has a CD-ROM–based Sheraton Guest Service Satisfaction 2000 program for their line-level employees. They find that the employees end up learning computer skills along with guest service skills as they undertake the program. Marriott International is currently using its website to prepare their human resources managers for accreditation from the Society for Human Resources Management.[6] The hospitality industry has just barely brushed the surface of the new technology that is and will be available in "the next chapter." Though web-based training is not the solution in all situations, it does provide hospitality organizations with another option to offer.

Distance Learning

Distance learning is the application of technology of electronic means to educate in all areas of learning. The electronic delivery of education and company training can occur by satellite video, one-way and two-way video/audio teleconferencing, video broadcast, audiographic, Internet, or other electronic means. The delivery of electronically mediated learning has opened new retraining opportunities for the hospitality industry.

Distance learning may be delivered in real time or it may be delayed. It has been proven to be as effective as traditional instruction methods in business training situations. Many companies, such as Hewlett-Packard, have saved millions of dollars by using distance learning to train employees more effectively and more efficiently than with traditional methods. As the nature of work has changed, so has training changed to support that work. Advances in technology allow us to look at training as we never have before.

Preparing the Trainee

Remember that for many of our hourly employees training is likely to be a new experience. They probably don't know what to expect, so it will be up to you, as trainer, to make them feel comfortable and at ease. It will help if they understand directly how this training will benefit them. Assure them that your job is to help and support them through the training program and that they will not be punished for their mistakes. They need to have confidence in you, so it is important that you have your act together and come to the training session well organized and prepared.

You might want to begin by giving them a brief overview of their new job position. As they begin to relax with you, they can turn their thoughts towards learning. Although they saw their workstation during orientation, now is the time to take them back to the work area and explain briefly the equipment that is found there. It is important that the trainee understands how each task fits into his or her total job.

During this overview you will also gain a more personal perspective on what the trainee knows, what equipment the trainee may have worked with before, and what kinds of skills he or she has used in pervious jobs. All of this serves to help generate employee interest in the training program.

Industry Experts Speak

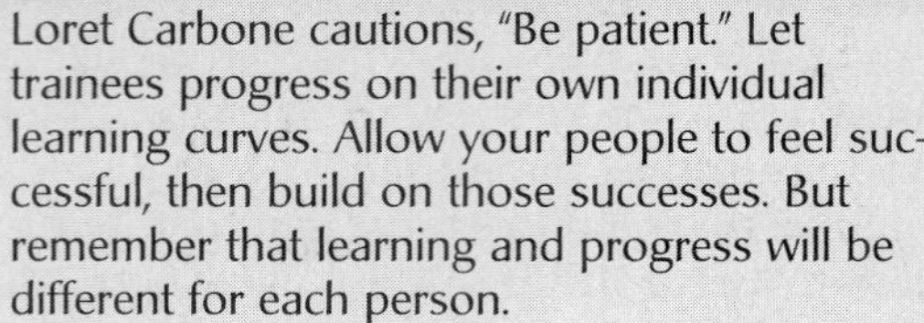

Loret Carbone cautions, "Be patient." Let trainees progress on their own individual learning curves. Allow your people to feel successful, then build on those successes. But remember that learning and progress will be different for each person.

Conduct the Training Session

In your role as trainer you will be facilitating the training of the new hire so that the trainee is able to learn the skills, duties, and responsibilities of his or her new job position as thoroughly and quickly as possible. As we have stated throughout this section, training should always be responsive to the needs of the hospitality organization. While you are aware of the importance of guest satisfaction, you cannot expect the trainee to have this awareness unless you incorporate it into your training program.

Conducting the training program requires the implementation of all elements of the training plan. After you present the job to the employee using the job task listings you developed, have the employee try out each of the tasks while you watch. Yes, we know that operational pressures and responsibilities can be enormous, yet you must keep in mind the importance of a well-conducted training session. It is up to you to instill in the trainee the commitment to persist when left on his or her own in the job.

Evaluate the Training

This step is perhaps the most critical in the training program. Once the transition has been made from training to job, follow-up and evaluation play an important part in maintaining acceptable job performance. Ideally, follow-up never really ends. Even under regular supervision and day-to-day activities, your employees deserve feedback on how well they are doing in their jobs.

Before leaving trainees on their own, they should be told to whom they can go if they have questions. You should make sure that they completely understand the standards of performance for all job tasks that they will be performing. After training is completed, try to be available and encourage questions. Performance should be checked frequently at first, with a gradual tapering off. Evaluating the trainees at the completion of the training program involves measuring the quality of their work based upon the specific performance standards of their job. Let the employees know how they are doing and where they need improvement.

The purpose of evaluating the training program is to determine whether the training has achieved its goals and objectives. Both the training method and the results of the training program should be evaluated. Methods need to be implemented to determine if the training objectives were met. Does trainee performance match organizational performance standards? This in turn measures the success of the training plan.

SCHOOL-TO-WORK

On May 4, the **School-to-Work Opportunities Act** of 1995 was established for the purpose of establishing a national framework for the development of School-to-Work Opportunity systems among all of the states. The Congress of the United States found that 75 percent of high school students in this country enter the work force without baccalaureate degrees and without the necessary entry-level work skills to enable them to succeed in the workplace. They also found that although many students held part-time jobs while in high school, there was no linkage between those jobs and looking at those jobs as possible careers. They found that in 1992 there were approximately 3.4 million persons in the United States between the ages of 16 and 24 who had not completed high school and were not currently enrolled in school. This translated into an alarming 11 percent of all persons in that age group. The passing of the School-to-Work Opportunities Act was a response to those findings.

So, what exactly are school-to-work programs (STW)? The U.S. Department of Education defines a school-to-work program as a partnership between business, education, labor, government, and community organizations that helps to prepare students for high-wage, high-skill careers that are found in an increasingly global world. School-to-work represents a new approach to learning in America. It is based on the proven fact that students learn better when their lessons are applied to real-life, real-work situations as opposed to merely memorizing facts from a textbook.

STW programs are not another form of on-the-job training. Nor are they only for non–college-bound students. These programs aim to better prepare students for college or careers or just plain good citizenship. For the programs to work, a strong relationship between the schools and the workplaces is necessary. There needs to be a clear understanding from both organizations on what the students are expected to do and which organization (school or workplace) is responsible for providing what.

Work-oriented education has the possibility of being a huge asset to the hospitality industry in "the next chapter." It provides us with opportunities to "turn students on" to the idea of a career in the hospitality industry. Allowing students to learn by doing and improving their workplace skills can only serve as a benefit to hospitality managers with human resources responsibilities. The more the youth of tomorrow understand what is required to be successful, the better prepared they will be to make good decisions about their future.

MAXIMIZING YOUR TRAINING INVESTMENT

You have spent a lot of time and effort in the development and implementation of your hospitality training program (Figure 6-10). What are some of the things that you can do to make sure that you are getting the best return on your investment? One way of answering that question is to look at some of the errors made in training:

- Giving too much information at one time. Although the information presented might be common sense to you, none of the tasks is mere routine for the trainee. The trainee is digesting new concepts, and digestion takes time.
- Not tailoring the training to the specific needs of the job. Training cannot be packaged in a generic black-and-white box, put on a shelf, and dusted off when needed. Training needs to be continually updated. If you revise your menu or make other operational changes, you have to make sure that your training reflects those changes.
- Treating the training of hourly employees as less important than management training programs. Hourly employees are the eyes and ears of any hospitality operation. Their importance to our success cannot be overstated, hence training should be treated with great importance. Every employee should be treated as a career employee,

Left At Albuquerque

Server Training Program Outline
Day Two: Passion For Service That Dazzles
Position Training: Busser & Bartender

Time	Activity	Goals	Handouts
9:00am - 9:05	• Trainee punches in • GM greets trainee • GM checks uniform • GM reviews Day One Test	• Insure trainee's uniform is in compliance • To explain answers to missed items from Day One Test	• Sample Lunch Special Menu
9:05 - 9:10	• Trainee completes Map Test • GM corrects Map Test & reviews results with trainee	• Understand table numbers & position numbers before working as busser	• How To Use Squirrel
9:10 - 9:45	• Trainee reads *Server Training Program Day Two Manual ("Passion for Service That Dazzles")*	• Understand company's passion for service	• Promo Categories
9:45 - 9:55	• GM reviews key points of Day Two Manual • GM reviews Busser Priority List	• Understand company's passion for service • Understand busser priorities	• QSA Categories & Reporting
9:55 - 10:45	GM presents *The Responsible Sale of Alcohol* seminar	• Understand how to sell alcohol responsibly	• Gift Certificates
10:45 - 10:55	• GM introduces Certified Busser & Certified Bartender Trainers • GM presents Day Two Goals	• Meet today's Certified Trainers • Understand the goals for the shift	• Home Office Meal Procedures
10:55 - 11:15	• Trainee completes opening sidework with Certified Busser Trainer	• Understand busser opening duties	• Home Office Meal Tickets
11:15 - 11:30	• Trainee attends Line-Up Meeting	• Understand importance of Line-Up Meeting	• Server Sidework
11:30 - 1:30pm	• Trainee follows Certified Busser Trainer completing Day Two Goals	• Understand busser systems & procedures	• Server Sanitation & Hygiene
1:30 - 2:30	• Trainee meets with Certified Bartender Trainer, completing Day Two Goals	• Begin to understand bar systems & products	• The Service Time Line
2:30 - 3:00	• Trainee eats Day Two Training Meal with GM & reviews the day's material & goals • Trainee completes Day Two Test • GM gives trainee Day Two Handouts Trainee punches out	• Continue food training Evaluate trainee's progress • Provide material to study for Day Three	

Total Training Hours: 6

FIGURE 6-10 A page from Left At Albuquerque's training manual. *(Courtesy of Left At Albuquerque, Palo Alto, CA)*

which could result in a stronger development program.

- Trainers who are not qualified to conduct the training sessions. We've already stated the characteristics necessary to be a good trainer. Trainers who do not know the job position or do not have the skills necessary to perform the job tasks can damage your credibility with the new hires.
- Explanations that are too technical or use of terminology that is unfamiliar to the trainees. Always try to explain things in everyday language and define all hospitality terms and slang when used. Never tell when you can show.
- Lack of patience. As a trainer, you must recognize that learning is a slow process. This does not mean that your trainees are slow, but rather that we all learn at different rates of speed. Take care not to lose half of your training class. Each person has a unique, individual learning curve.
- Failure to build in feedback mechanisms. Always make it possible for the trainees to ask questions whenever they feel the need. Without some type of trainee feedback, you don't know whether they have truly learned. Another benefit of feedback mechanisms is that they help to reduce tension.

INDUSTRY EXPERTS SPEAK

Loret Carbone says, "Make sure you check your training program to be sure it communicates your philosophies, policies and rules for employment. Nothing should be left to the imagination. Once the employee completes the training program, it should be very clear to them what they will have to do to be successful. Training sets the parameters for high performance."

BASIC PRINCIPLES OF ADULT LEARNING

When we examine learning from a training perspective, we need to focus our attention specifically on adult learning. The reasons why adult men and women want to learn is a good place to start, as it is hard to improve the learning situation without understanding the motivations for adult learning. Adults want to learn when:

- They find that their work is interesting.
- They can feel important in what they are doing.
- They are challenged.
- They know that their work is recognized and appreciated.
- When they see that the satisfaction of their personal ambition is one of the benefits.
- Their focus is on realistic problems.

Adults learn what they feel is important and contributes to results that they value. This reinforces the need to relate the "whys" of training throughout the implementation of the training plan. Adults need to feel that they are productive contributors to the hospitality organization and its goals.

Barriers to Learning

There are many conditions that can keep our trainees from learning. When we train under these conditions effectiveness is reduced:

- ***Fatigue.*** It can reduce both our physical and mental effectiveness. The more fatigued our trainees are, the longer it takes to learn. This is why training sessions should not be conducted at the end of the work shift. The most beneficial sessions are kept short.
- ***Monotony.*** If you as the trainer find the session boring, it is highly likely that the

trainees will also find it boring. What you are teaching may be routine to you, but it is not to your trainees. Keep the sessions lively and stimulating so that maximum learning can occur. Make the training highly interactive, fun and games.

- ***Distractions.*** Any distractions will inhibit the learning process. This can be a problem in on-the-job training when the daily activities of your operation are going on around you.
- ***Anxiety.*** People are usually tense when they enter into new situations and are with unfamiliar individuals. It is up to you to break the ice and get the trainee to relax, or learning will be inhibited.

There is much information that can be gained from a study of learning theory and methods. Many can be directly applied to training programs in the hospitality industry.

CONCLUSION

Orientation programs and training programs are two of the most valuable tools you have available to you as the human resources manager of a hospitality operation. We need to be the employer of choice, as we are all competing for the best and brightest. As competition increases, we have to look for ways to attract guests to *our* operation as opposed to all the others. Having a staff trained in maximizing guest satisfaction can be the deciding factor for many of our guests. People return to places where they feel at home, and where the staff takes care of their every request.

Successful training does not occur in a vacuum. Many other elements of the system are affected, such as performance appraisals, merit increases, pay-for-performance, and the like. Training impacts the total human resources management system. The more detailed and rigorous, fair but demanding your training program is, the higher the caliber of job applicant you will be able to hire. The interviewer will have to take into consideration whether the job applicant is good enough to pass your training program.

Training is management's responsibility. Training is a skill that takes practice. In too many cases we blame the problems on the poor quality of employees we have, when instead we should be blaming the lack of training. When planning the training program, the manager who assumes human resources responsibilities needs to keep in mind the goals of the organization, the theory of learning, the needs of the job and the trainee, the variety of training methods and media available to them, and a method of follow-up and evaluation.

Our human resources want to be involved in only high-quality training experiences. The quality of the service we provide cannot improve until the quality of our training programs improves. We encourage you to become the most competent trainer you can be. More than just the reputation of your business is at stake. Training is a tool used by management to increase the productivity of all human resources as well as teach them to learn how to react in whatever situation they may find themselves. Good service training can be achieved using the guidelines we've provided for you in this chapter.

Case Problem 6-1

Sara arrives for her first day of training at a restaurant that is part of a small company (six restaurants) located on the West Coast. She is excited about her new job and is looking forward to learning more about the company and its operational systems.

When she arrives at 8:00 a.m. (she was requested to by the person who hired her), she finds the restaurant dark and the front door locked. She knocks on the door, even pounds on the door, but nobody is there. She waits. Finally, at 8:45 a.m. the opening manager, Bill, arrives and is surprised when Sara introduces herself and says she is there for her orientation and training. Bill obviously didn't know that she was coming.

Bill lets Sara into the restaurant and tells her to wait at one of the tables by the door and walks away. He never even turns on the lights for her, so Sara sits in the dark for another twenty minutes before the manager returns. When Bill does, he gives her a menu and the Employee Handbook and says he will come back in "awhile." When Sara has read both of these, she gets up and tries to find Bill. When she does, he tells her that he wants her to work as a hostess today because the scheduled hostess called in sick. So, without any orientation or training, Sara tries her hardest to answer the phone, greet guests, seat guests, and answer their questions. At the end of the day, Sara asks Bill if he could answer some questions. Bill says he doesn't have time today but she should come tomorrow at 8:00 a.m.

Sara doesn't come to work the next day. What happened? What went wrong? Identify some material that you would give Sara ***before*** her first day of orientation and training to prepare her for her first day. Develop a two-page agenda for Sara's first day. Include a time line, goals, and who would work with her.

Case Problem 6-2

You have been rehired by a major lodging chain as an assistant manager and assigned to a property located in the heart of a major city in the Northeast. During your training, you are rotated among the various departments within the hotel property.

Shortly after beginning your training rotation in the housekeeping department, you become aware of irregularities and inconsistencies in the procedures used by the housekeeping staff. When working with Sally, you clean the bathroom and then make the beds. When working with Susie, you make the beds and then clean the bathrooms. Although this did not bother you too much, you also noticed that the amount of cleaning solutions used, the time taken to clean a standard room, and the amount of linens being left in each guest room varied depending upon the housekeeper you were working with.

You discuss the inconsistencies with the executive housekeeper. Upon doing so, you are informed that there have been no guest complaints and that the housekeeping department is ahead of budget with respect to payroll and supplies. "Though I am sure you mean well, the housekeeping department of this hotel has an ***excellent*** reputation! You must be mistaken."

As you continue to work within the property, you suspect that the violations and inconsistencies in procedures are due, not to a lack of interest but to a lack of training. The housekeeping staff simply does not know the correct standards and procedures. Which of your observations could be caused by a lack of training? What are the indicators of a lack of training in each observation you identify? Why have there been no guest complaints? How is it that housekeeping is ahead of budget?

Select one job performed in housekeeping and prepare a training objective for that specific job. Which training method would you select to implement your training? Why did you select this particular training method?

CASE PROBLEM 6-3

During the initial few days of his training period, Ted studied all the written training material, manuals, and guidelines provided. He enjoyed the structure and discipline of the program and was happy that he was receiving such clear information. He couldn't wait to start the practical part of the training where he would actually perform the jobs.

As he rotated through all of the stations in the kitchen, he realized that the standards outlined in the training materials were not being followed. When he asked employees about it, they said things like, "Nobody does it that way. Here is how we really do it." This bothered Ted a lot, but being a new trainee he didn't want to make waves.

If you were in charge of this restaurant, how would you make sure the written training material and the actual work being done was integrated? Develop a two-page training program that ensures that the trainee receives a cohesive message about the systems and standards of the restaurant. How would you structure it so that you were sure that your employees who are training new employees are doing it "by the book"?

KEY WORDS

computer-based training programs (CBT)
distance learning
job instruction training
in-house training methods
learning
lecture method
literacy
needs assessment
on-the-job training (OJT)
orientation program
retraining
School-to-Work Opportunities Act
role playing
training
training plan
training program
vestibule training
web-based training
workplace education

RECOMMENDED READING

Chase, N. "Train, Don't Tell." *Quality Magazine.* www.qualitymag.com/articles/may98/0598++.html (3 July 1998).

Clemmer, J. "Why Most Training Fails." *The Globe & Mail.* www.clemmer-group..com/globe/training.htm (19 July 1998).

"The Evolving Workplace: Findings from the Pilot Workplace and Employee Survey." Ottawa: Statistics Canada for Human Resources Development, 1998.

Frazee, V. 1996. "Workers Learn to Walk So They Can Run." *Personnel Journal* 75(5): 115–120.

Gruner, S. 1998. "Lasting Impressions." *Inc. Magazine* (July): 126.

Kennedy, D. and F. Berger. 1994. "Newcomer Socialization: Oriented to Facts or Feelings." *The Cornell Quarterly* 35(4): 58–71.

Kirsch, I. S., A. Jungeblut, L. Jenkins, and A. Kolstad. 1993. *Adult Literacy in America: A First Look at the Results of the National Adult Literacy Survey*. Washington, DC: National Center for Education Statistics.

Klien, C.S. and J. Taylor. 1994. "Employee Orientation Is an Ongoing Process at The Dupont Merck Pharmaceutical Co." *Personnel Journal* 73(5): 64–67.

Montigny, G., K. Kelly, and S. Jones. 1991. *Adult Literacy in Canada: Results of a National Study*. Ottawa: Statistics Canada.

National School-to-Work Office. 1998. *Managing the Risks of Work-based Learning: A Resource Guide*. Washington, DC: National School-to-Work Office.

Shay, J. and J. B. Tracey. 1997. "Expatriate Managers: Reasons for Failure and Implications for Training." *The Cornell Quarterly* 38(1): 30–35.

Tas, R., S. V. LaBrecque, and H. R. Clayton. 1996. "Property Management Competencies for Management Trainees." *The Cornell Quarterly* 37(4): 90–96.

Tracey, J. B. and M. J. Tews. 1995. "Training Effectiveness: Accounting for Individual Characteristics and the Work Environment." *The Cornell Quarterly* 36(6): 36–42.

VanDerWall, S. "Training Enhances Job Satisfaction, Gallup Survey Finds." *SHRM/HR News Online*. www.shrm.org/hrnews/articles/110398.htm (11 November 1998).

Wilson, W. 1994. "Video Training and Testing Supports Customer Service Goals." *Personnel Journal* 73(6): 47–51.

Young, C. A. and C. C. Lundberg. 1996. "Creating a Good First Day on the Job Allaying Newscomers' Anxiety with Positive Messages." *The Cornell Quarterly* 37(5): 26–33.

Recommended Web Sites

1. Training and Development FAQs: www.workindex.com/workindex/TrainingandDevelopment FAQs.html
2. American Society for Training and Development: www.astd.org
3. Training Supersite: www.trainingsupersite.com
4. National Alliance of Business: www.nab.com
5. Literacy Online: litserver.literacy.upenn.edu
6. National Skills Standards Board: www.nssb.org
7. Training Forum: www.trainingforum.com
8. National Institute for Literacy: www.nifl.gov
9. Teletraining Institute: www.teletrain.com
10. The Interactive Distance Learning Group, Inc.: idl.ncms.org
11. U.S. Department of Labor Employment and Training Administration: www.ttrc.doleta.gov
12. U.S. Distance-Learning Association: www.usdla.org

ENDNOTES

1. Jeff Brechlin, "Orienting New Employees," *Training* 28(April 1991): 45.
2. C. S. Steinmetz, "The History of Training," *Training and Development Handbook* (New York: McGraw-Hill, 1976), 1–3.
3. 102nd Congress—1st Session, *National Institute for Literacy Public Law 102-73* (Washington, DC: 1991), 1.
4. Ibid.
5. National Institute for Literacy, *About NIFL*. www.nifl.gov/nifl/aboutindex.htm (16 June 1998).
6. Robert T. Foley, "Train Smart, Not Hard." *Lodging Magazine* (April 1998). www.ei-ahma.org/webs/lodging/9805/human.htm (5 June 1998).

DISCUSSION QUESTIONS

1. What is orientation? What is training?
2. Compare and contrast company orientation, department orientation, and job orientation.
3. List topics that you feel should be covered during a company orientation program for buspersons in a 200-seat family dining area.
4. What are some of the problems that can occur when we fail to properly orient new employees? What problems occur when training needs are ignored?
5. Discuss how training has changed since the days of apprenticeships.
6. Discuss how the employee, the supervisor, and the hospitality organization each benefit from training.
7. Why is it necessary to conduct an assessment of training needs? Describe in detail each of the three levels at which assessment must occur.
8. Describe the benefits of initiating literacy programs in hospitality organizations.
9. What is a workplace education program?
10. Identify and describe each of the components of a training plan.
11. Why do most hospitality organizations fail to evaluate their training programs?
12. What factors need to be taken into consideration when applying on-the-job-training methods?
13. How can managers with human resources responsibilities in the hospitality industry use the Internet as a training medium?
14. What is distance learning and how could it play an important role in training?
15. Discuss the importance of the School-to-Work Opportunities Act for hospitality companies.
16. Why is training more important in "the next chapter" than it was in the 1980s or 1990s?

CHAPTER 7

Development Programs, Coaching, and Team Building

 **INDUSTRY ADVISOR**

PAM FARR, *Senior Vice President of Human Resources, Marriott Lodging, Marriott International Inc.*

"If you don't have enthusiasm, you don't have anything."

—KEMMONS WILSON, SR.,
Founder of Holiday Inns

"Coming together is a beginning. Keeping together is progress. Working together is a success."

—HENRY FORD

INTRODUCTION

How do you get an employee to be the best he or she can be? How do you get employees to see their work as more than a job? Each human resource working in your hospitality organization is an individual, different and unique from every other human resource. Now that they have been oriented and trained (at least for their current job position), it is time to ensure that we nurture and care for our human resources as individuals.

Development programs are tailored for the individual needs of your human resources. These programs are designed to assist you, the manager with human resources responsibilities, in identifying these needs in an effort to develop improved performance. These programs are designed to assist our human resources in identifying and then meeting their career expectations and aspirations.

Using individual development programs to assist our human resources in becoming the best they can be requires an understanding of motivation. By understanding what motivates people collectively, we will further our understanding of how to meet the needs of individuals. Our goal is to do what is best for the employee and at the same time to do what is best for the hospitality organization. The achievement of this goal requires us to have a knowledge of the techniques of coaching, team building, and mentoring. After all, two of our most important jobs as a manager with human resources responsibilities are to assist in the development of a variety of personal relationships in the workplace and to help others in their careers.

At the conclusion of this chapter you will be able to:

1. Describe the relationship between career development/counseling and performance development/counseling; between career development and succession planning; between development reviews and performance appraisals.
2. Explain how a career development program operates in a hospitality organization.
3. Explain the components of a successful management development program.
4. Prepare for conducting a career development review for each of your employees.
5. Distinguish between the different types of career development programs.
6. Define the relationship between mentor and protégé.
7. Identify the basic theories of motivation.
8. Use motivation theory to assist in the planning of an individual development program.
9. Understand your role as a coach and counselor when assisting your human resources in planning their career development.
10. Explain how career development programs, coaching, and team building assist you with the retention of your human resources.

DEVELOPMENT'S FUNCTION IN HUMAN RESOURCES MANAGEMENT

The goal of a development program is to help our people become better each day. "Better" is a personal desire or aspiration that is defined by the individual employee and supported by the organization. When we assist the individual employee in achieving his or her career aspirations, the hospitality workplace becomes not only a more productive organization but a more desirable environment to work in.

The development of our employees serves to tie together a number of human resources functions. Not only are these programs designed to improve performance and encourage retention, they also impact upon manpower planning at both the organizational and employee levels. To accomplish this, development programs are linked together with performance development, succession planning, and performance appraisal systems.

As we discussed in Chapter 2, succession planning can be implemented at the hourly level as well as at the management level. Succession planning assists you in preparing for the continued growth of your hospitality organization. Career development programs assist succession planning by encouraging the continued growth of talent within that organization. Used in this fashion, succession planning links development to the long-range human resources planning objectives. This helps to ensure that you will have the talent required to meet your current and future human resources needs. In this way, **development programs** link human resources needs to the business plans of the hospitality enterprise.

WorkPower™: Marriott's Guide to Career Success was developed to provide employees with the opportunity to assess their own career progress in a self-paced career-planning process. Part of this process is the ability of each employee to evaluate their own success through the concept of *Career Fit*. "Our theory suggests that the more the PERSON is in sync with the ***Position*** and ***Place***, the more productive and happy the individual will be"[1] (Figure 7-1). A key question that each employee must ask is *"Who am I?"*. This is done by developing answers to five questions (Table 7-1).

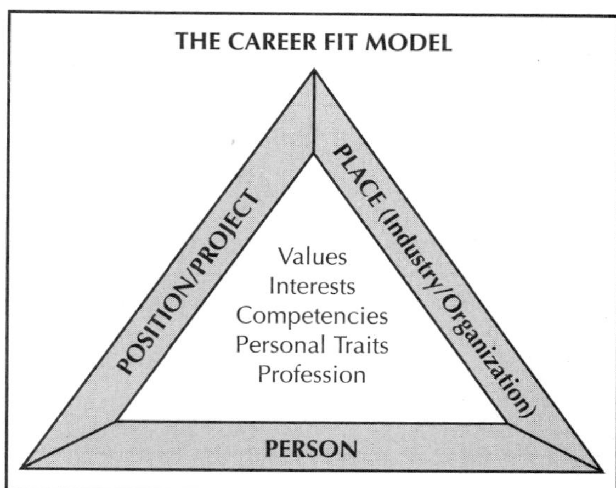

FIGURE 7-1 The Career Fit Model. *(Courtesy of © 1998 Career Systems Int'l.* [Contact 800-577-6916] *and Marriott International Corporation)*

TABLE 7-1 "Who am I?"

- What are my most important **values**?
- What activities really hold my **interest**?
- What are my **competencies**?
- What are my **personal traits**?
- What is my **profession**?

(Courtesy of © 1998 Career Systems Int'l. [Contact 800-577-6916] *and Marriott International Corporation)*

Through career development, opportunities for promotion from within the hospitality organization are increased. Career **development reviews** provide an opportunity for the employee to let management know where the employee would like to go in his or her career. These reviews also give management the opportunity to provide feedback to the employee regarding the individual's progress towards personal career goals. This is quite different from performance appraisals, which we discuss in Chapter 8, where the employee is evaluated on the degree to which his or her performance meets the organization's expectations and standards.

Both development reviews and performance appraisals provide you, the manager with human resources responsibilities, with information on the promotability of each employee. The development reviews are a nonevaluative activity in which management lends support and guidance to each employee's own future job interests and career aspirations. The performance appraisal is an activity in which management evaluates the employee's performance, and sometimes the results become the basis for compensation decisions. Table 7-2 shows you a comparison between performance appraisals and career development. As a general rule the time frame for career development is long range (two years), whereas performance improvement is short range (six months to one year).

Performance development counseling occurs when there is a deficiency in performance standards. Problem-solving techniques are instituted that provide an opportunity for the employee to get his or her performance on the right track. These counseling activities are part of disciplinary actions geared at saving an employee from termination procedures. Performance development counseling involves coaching and team building techniques that assist the employee in achieving his or her own personal career aspirations or just improving the employee as a person.

The terms *development* and *training* have historically been used interchangeably in the workplace. In "the next chapter" these words have very different roles in the hospitality organization. As we saw in the previous chapter, training is a process that teaches our employees the skills necessary to perform the tasks required of their job position. Development activities assume that the basic skill levels already exist and seek to provide a process through which the employees can grow in their personal development within the company.

TABLE 7-2 Comparison between Performance Appraisals and Career Development—Traditional Views

Performance Appraisal *(Realism without Hope)* Managers Ask:	Career Development *(Hope without Realism)* Employees Ask:
• What is the employee contributing? • How is the employee measuring up to expectations? • What do I need to tell the employee about current performance? • How does current performance reflect on compensation? • How does the employee rank against other employees?	• What are my career goals? • What are my options for career movement? • What skills and abilities do I need to acquire? • What plans do I need to make to move toward my goals? • What will be my implementation steps and timetable?

(Reprinted, by permission of publisher, from Personnel, *January, 1986. © 1986. American Management Association, New York. All rights reserved.)*

As you can see, development programs serve to link together a number of human resources functions. In doing so, they can increase the effectiveness of human resources management in your hospitality organization. By improving the promotability of your human resources, you increase your options in the employment process. Your training programs then become tools in developing the talent and potential that already exists.

CAREER DEVELOPMENT PROGRAMS FOR HOSPITALITY MANAGEMENT

Career development, performance development, career management, career guidance, and individual development are analogous terms for programs that seek to assist our human resources in becoming the best that they can be. We define **career development** as a program that seeks to assist employees in their own personal growth and maturity in the hospitality workplace. These programs seek a gradual improvement in the employee's working life by functioning in harmony with the employee's needs so that personal working values are satisfied. Both parties benefit by determining what is good for the employee and at the same time good for the organization. As managers, you should view employee development as a way to improve your own department's performance. It allows you to take ownership of your people's successes (or failures). Accountability for success is shared between manager and employee. Managers are a critical link in the career development of their people.

Career development is a cooperative relationship that works three ways among the employee, the employee's manager, and the hospitality organization. Each of these has specific responsibilities to the planning and development process. The employee's responsibilities include:

- Self-assessment of abilities, interests, and values
- Analyzing career options
- Deciding on development objectives and needs

- Communicating development preferences to manager
- Mapping out mutually agreeable action plans with manager
- Pursuing agreed-upon action plan

Manager's responsibilities include:

- Acting as a catalyst; sensitizing employee to the development planning process
- Assessment of the realism of employee's expressed objectives and perceived development needs
- Counseling the employee and developing a mutually agreeable plan
- Following up and updating employee's plans as appropriate

And finally the organization's responsibilities to the career planning and development process include:

- Providing a career planning model, resources, counseling, and necessary information
- Providing training in career development planning to managers and employees and career counseling to management
- Providing skills training programs and on-the-job development experience opportunities[2]

Development programs are an ongoing process within the hospitality organization. Whereas training is done to prepare your human resources for their present job position, development prepares them to make maximum use of their skills and abilities to achieve both great personal satisfaction and high job performance. The idea is that constant improvement is occurring among both your hourly and salaried staffs. Development programs can lead to career advancement, both horizontally and laterally. Let's look at an example of a lateral advancement for an hourly employee, a dishwasher. Now, although you might think that no one wants to wash dishes as a career, your thinking might be wrong. What you are really thinking is that *you* certainly would not want to wash dishes for a career! Development programs examine what the employee wants, and in the case of our dishwasher, he or she just wants to be a good dishwasher. This individual doesn't want the unfamiliarity of busing tables (a logical career move to get out of the dishroom) nor does he or she want the supervisory headaches of being head dishwasher (a typical management ploy that attempts to recognize outstanding performance).

A development program would permit our great dishwasher to remain a great dishwasher. First, through development reviews you, as the human resources manager, would be made aware of the fact that washing dishes is what this person likes and wants to do. Knowing this, you would not make the erroneous assumption that this person wants to be promoted out of the dishroom. Second, a development program would provide a means for lateral advancement and recognition of a job well done. Perhaps the lateral advancement would be to a day shift as opposed to the night shift. Recognition could be awarded in the form of either monetary or nonmonetary incentives.

What your development program must provide is a means by which your dishwashers can continue to do what they feel is in their best interest, while at the same time serving the hospitality operation's need for reliable dishroom personnel. Your challenge in the implementation of development programs is to keep your human resources challenged, or motivated, to seek continual improvement. This goes beyond merely seeing that the job tasks are performed and that performance standards are maintained. The development programs you establish can be what makes your hospitality organization different from all the others because people want to work in an environment where management cares about their needs and desires. People want to work in an environment that is in harmony with their work values. This is why hospitality organizations should establish values and live by them. Then people can truly decide if their individual values are congruent with the organization's values.

The Purpose of a Development Program

Career development is not something that occurs once or even occasionally, but is a continuous ongoing process that is constantly evolving based upon the needs of the participating individuals. Hospitality organizations that provide development programs offer their human resources the opportunity for maximum job satisfaction. They allow their human resources to become active, not passive, participants in the process. Your employees no longer have to sit back and wait (hopefully) that their company will recognize and promote them. These human resources are given the exciting opportunity to manage their careers. Career development lets each person take responsibility for his or her own professional development, growth, and movement within the organization. It is our job as managers with human resources responsibilities to make sure that opportunities for growth exist both vertically and horizontally in each of our job positions. And don't forget, although career development programs depend on the employee, it *must* be supported by management.

Maintaining productivity and job satisfaction are two outcomes of a successful development program. Even our dishwashers can find meaning in their work when we provide opportunities for lateral promotions, job enrichment, and skill acquisition (Figure 7-2). Development programs translate into a "we care" and "you are important" attitude in the hospitality workplace. By providing career

FIGURE 7-2 Career development opportunities must be provided for all job positions. *(Courtesy of Chili's Grill & Bar, Brinker International)*

counseling, we can make sure that our employee's expectations are both realistic and in harmony with the goals of the hospitality organization.

People, for the most part, want to do well in their work lives. Meaningful work is a goal for most everyone. By linking the growth needs of our human resources with the performance needs of the organization, job satisfaction occurs for both parties. Career development programs are the planned effort that causes this linkage to occur. Numerous advantages can be identified in hospitality organizations that result from career development programs.

For the organization, advantages include the following:

- Facilitation of the succession planning process
- Identification of human resources with promotional potential
- More qualified and skilled pool of human resources
- An increase in the amount of crosstraining
- Improvement in retention and a decreased turnover

- Reduction in recruiting expenses for highly trained personnel
- Minimization of performance problems resulting from job dissatisfaction and frustration
- Teamwork being encouraged
- Improved communications between management and work force
- Preparing people for change
- Releasing the potential of the work force

For the employee, advantages include the following:

- Opportunity to uncover hidden interests and abilities
- Improved attitude about job and the company
- Greater sense of job satisfaction
- Realistic expectations about promotional opportunities, with a clearer sense of direction
- Opportunities to develop talent potential
- Assistance and coaching in the development of his or her careers
- Opportunity to take responsibility for individual growth and development
- Recognition as an individual
- Help in formulating realistic career goals
- Better ability to handle current job responsibilities

Development programs can be a powerful motivation and retention tool for human resources managers. You will read in the section on coaching and team building that the manager plays a very vital role in the development process. Assisting our human resources with personal development is a serious challenge for a hospitality organization and must be conducted with care and concern for all involved participants.

INDUSTRY EXPERTS SPEAK

Pam Farr says, "What I have found intriguing about career management is it's much like solving simultaneous equations. On one side there is the 'company driven' requirements—job openings, locations, competencies, timing. On the other side is the 'employee centered' considerations—hopes, dreams, life goals, etc. In a large, global company each career move is an individual transaction, but multiple transactions must add up to create an entire worldwide workforce of motivated, highly competent people. It's part 'mechanical' because you must plan and forecast but it's 'magical' when you see employees grow and develop and contribute to the Company's success and their own. A company must have managers who can listen, assess and coach people to follow their dreams while at the same time getting the right people in the right job at the opportune time in the required location."

How Does a Career Development Program Work?

A hospitality organization is composed of individuals, and for it to succeed, there must be a commonality of ideas and goals. The design of development programs must take into consideration the mission statement of the enterprise, the organizational goals, and the values. The development paths of our human resources cannot be separate from the development path of our hospitality organization. The individuals in our organization must be able to relate to company goals. Development of competencies is also necessary to achieve business ends as we begin the new century.

Identifying the personal goals of employees requires an atmosphere of trust and open communication. Through communication with our human resources we can identify their interests and concerns that will assist us with their career development. Development programs place you in the role of counselor and coach to help employees identify their goals and career aspirations. Remember that our dishwashers are the only ones in possession of their aspirations. As a manager with human resources responsibilities, our role is to assist the dishwashers in identifying those aspirations and then gear their development program in a direction in which those aspirations can be met. Not all career development must lead to promotional opportunities. When it does, we refer to the activity as **career pathing**, and the information is used by the hospitality organization in succession planning.

Every individual is distinct in their values, interests, and work goals. Hence, successful human resources development stems from communication efforts that accurately identify individual needs and behavior. **Career planning** is the process by which the individual's short- and long-term career goals are identified. Part of this process includes identifying the individual's work values by asking the employee what is important to him or her in the individual's work. No two employees will come up with the same list of work values. **Career counseling** assists your human resources in choosing a career direction. As career counselor, you then analyze the employee's job to see if any of these work values are missing.

A development program begins by assisting the employee in determining individual development goals and needs (Table 7-3). These are based upon the employee's interests, abilities, and attitudes. Next the human resources manager as career counselor obtains information about the employee's job and the organizational goals and needs. This includes data on available job opportunities, skill requirements of jobs, and the employment needs of the hospitality organization. An action plan is then formulated that matches employee needs with organizational needs. The action plan translates into the development plan for that individual human resource.

TABLE 7-3 Steps in a Development Program

1. Identify mission statement and goals of hospitality organization.
2. Assist employee in determination of personal goals and needs.
   - Appraise current skills and knowledge.
   - Define career progress.
3. Obtain information pertaining to organizational needs and priorities.
4. Develop action plan matching employee's needs with organizational needs.
5. Provide feedback and guidance to carry out action plan.

For development programs to be effective, feedback must be continuous. Your employees must understand that participation in this process does not mean automatic promotion. The only individuals who will be promoted are those individuals who are ready to be promoted. This brings us to another point that we wish to emphasize. Participation in the development programs must be optional, not mandatory. The initiative for development must be employee drive to be successful. The desire to grow comes from within each of our human resources with the hospitality organization providing the support and tools for personal growth.

Management Development

The emphasis on personal development, individual abilities, and achieving goals is as important for the members of management as it is for our hourly human resources. Enhancing job satisfaction among managers greatly assists the hospitality organization's efforts to increase retention and reduce turnover. A well-designed management development system can help provide the analysis necessary to help managers identify interests, competencies, life values, activities, and assignments necessary to develop skills for future job opportunities. At the same time, a well-designed management development system assists in achieving a balance between the organization's management requirements and the individual's career needs.

Ours is an industry where managers can move from property to property, operation to operation, and concept to concept and still work for the same company. Managers can easily end up moving back and forth between positions in the front of the house and the back of the house in both food service and lodging. Constant movement, high turnover, mergers, and acquisitions are just some of the reasons why many hospitality organizations have revamped and formalized their management development systems. They recognize that the ongoing development of their managers is an important investment that can pay large rewards for employees, guests, and company alike.

Marriott Lodging's management development system is called the Career Banding System (CBS). This is an integrated system that seeks to support the company's business goals (that we discussed in Chapter 2) with the personal goals and development of their managers. Marriott refers to their managers as "associates." This highly innovative career development system can be seen in Figure 7-3 (taken from Marriott's *Career Banding System*). As you can see, the human resources functions of staffing, career management, performance management, training and development, and compensation are integrated into one human resources strategy.

The two key components are **career bands** and **key competencies**. Career bands place all Marriott Lodging jobs into groups of management positions that have similar roles and responsibilities. Key competencies are the knowledge, skills, and abilities that a manager must demonstrate to be successful within the job position. As you can see, this ties back into the information we gathered from our job analysis and put into job descriptions and job specifications (Chapter 3). Not only do those tools serve us in the staffing functions we have already discussed, they will continue to be important as we look ahead to discussions of performance evaluations, compensation, and benefits.

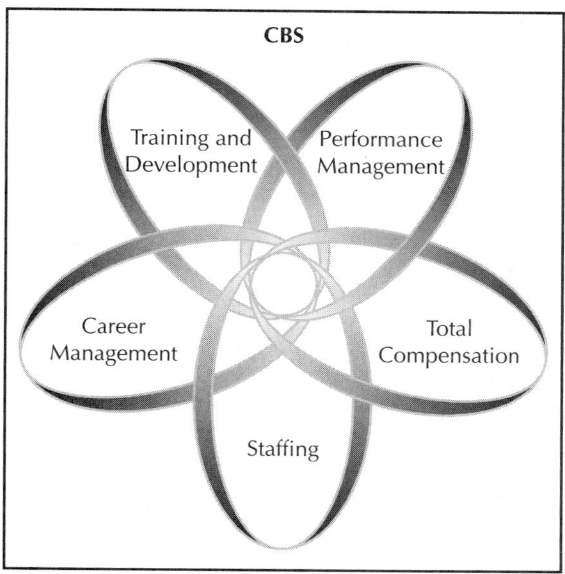

FIGURE 7-3 The Career Banding System Model. *(Courtesy of Marriott International Corporation)*

The uniqueness of the CBS system is that it creates an environment where managers can grow. Managers have the choice under this system of whether they want to grow within their current position, in other positions (either within or outside their career band), or in positions in other brands that the company operates. Managers are permitted to move among jobs, which allows them to gain new skills making them more valuable to both themselves and the organization. "The goal is to ensure that our management associates are equipped to move from brand-to-brand, from discipline-to-discipline, or career band-to-career band for either personal development or business reasons."[3]

INDUSTRY EXPERTS SPEAK

Pam Farr was the executive champion of Marriott Lodging's Career Banding System. Its integrated approach linking staffing, career management, performance management, training and development, and total compensation makes it a powerful human resources management system. According to Pam, "For years, we had strong training and development programs and pay programs, but they were never closely linked to selection and staffing methods or performance management. CBS helps associates chart their career course so they can grow, develop and be rewarded along the way." This system helps managers understand the knowledge, skills, and abilities that must be demonstrated to achieve success in the business.

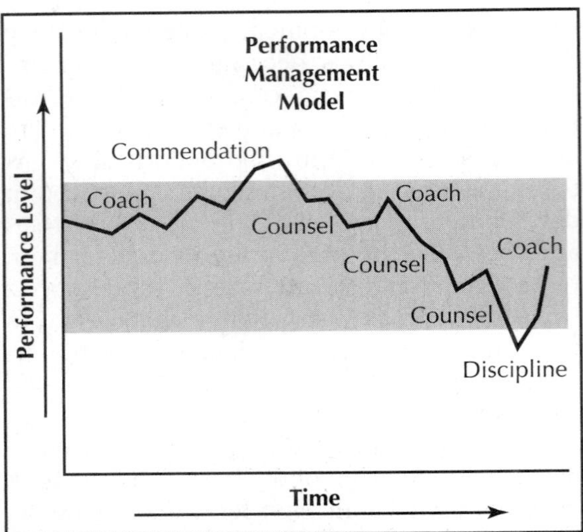

FIGURE 7-4 The Performance Management Model. *(Courtesy of Marriott International Corporation)*

The Development Review

The development review is a tool that will assist you in managing the potential of your work force. We have already stated that feedback should be continuous; the review supplements the feedback program. The development review is a meeting between you and the employee during which the employee's aspirations and potential are assessed in light of the needs of the organization.

To maximize the effectiveness of the development review, it is useful to have each employee fill out a form that provides background information. Personal background information would include work history, education, and training, both external and internal to the current organization. The development review provides an opportunity for each employee to make sure that the information is current.

Your role in the development review is that of coach and career counselor (Figure 7-4). You have the ability to assess the employee's potential for advancement enrichment, need for additional training as well as help the individual keep his or her expectations realistic in terms of the employee's abilities. The review focuses on the needs and career of the individual employee. In development planning, consideration is given to personal interests, strengths, weaknesses, and objectives (Table 7-4). To assist the employee in identifying individual career interests and strengths, a career development form is filled out jointly by the employee and manager (Table 7-5).

The development review involves two-way communication between you, the manager in your role of career counselor and the employee. The discussions should revolve around employee growth and improvement, which might not be the same as employee advance-

Table 7-4 Characteristics of a Good Counselor

A Good Counselor Is:

Consistent
Impartial
Supportive
Open-minded
A good listener
Accepting of success and failure
Patient

AND

- Approaches at a comfortable time
- Greets warmly, sets the climate
- Smiles frequently
- Uses reassuring tone of voice
- Says positive as well as negative
- Nods encouragingly
- Gives undivided attention
- Doesn't allow interruptions
- Doesn't do all the talking
- Pauses, allows associate to talk
- Seeks first to understand then to be understood

(Courtesy of Marriott International Corporation)

ment. The career development form helps guide the direction of the career discussions as well as assists the employee in formulating career goals. Again, we emphasize that career goals are not always vertical in direction.

Action plans are the result of the development review. Action plans provide a timetable for the accomplishment of the employee's goals along with a way of best meeting those goals. The action plans must be driven by the employee's goals and not those of the organization, if career development programs are to be successful. The more self-assessment tools you provide the employees with, the more successful they will be in identifying their interests and skills. This will provide you with the best information possible to assist in the preparation of the action plans.

SELECTING A DEVELOPMENT PROGRAM

As we have seen, development programs provide a type of career path, either lateral or horizontal, for hourly human resources. There are several different approaches to implementing the development process. Each provides a slightly different focus on the intended outcome of the development program. Many hospitality organizations use a combination of the techniques that we discuss next.

Mentoring Programs

According to the Greek mythologist Homer, Mentor was the man whom Odysseus selected to train his son Telemachus while he was away fighting the Trojan war. While Odysseus was gone, his friend and advisor, Mentor served as the boy's guardian, teacher, and father figure to his young **protégé**. Mentor was known for his sensitivity and wisdom, and thus the word **mentor** has come to mean a trusted and wise advisor. Mentors today are influential people who significantly help someone (known as their protégé) reach their own major life goals. Mentors are individuals with the power to promote their protégé's training progress, personal welfare, or career development. The mentor's power comes from whom or what they know as a result of their own life experiences.

In development programs mentors are the individuals who guide the employees in their personal and career development (Figure 7-5). This is accomplished through a deliberate pairing of a more experienced or skilled person with a less experienced or skilled one. The goal that each of them agrees to is to have the lesser experienced person develop and grow in specific areas of their skills and abilities. Mentors can assist their protégés in a variety of ways:

TABLE 7-5 Career Development Form

Name ______________________________ Job Title ______________________________

Employee's Career or Job Goals (Outline each goal.)

____

____

Review Comments: Discuss how consistency, efficiency or accuracy of any of these goals can be improved. Note areas of exceptional performance that has exceeded expectations if applicable.

____

____

Employee's Career Strengths

____

____

____

Employee's Job or Career Development Needs (Identify the experiences the employee needs to achieve the job or career goals.)

____

____

____

Employees Developmental Opportunities are:

____

____

____

Developmental Outline: Discuss how and when training will be accomplished.

____

____

____

FIGURE 7-5 Mentors are individuals who guide the employees in their personal and career development. *(Courtesy of Strongbow Inn, Valparaiso, IN)*

- Giving them constructive feedback and advice on the actions they take and/or the products and services they provide
- Providing informal or formal instruction on both technical information that will help them perform their jobs better and organizational politics
- Providing opportunities for them to demonstrate their skills and abilities
- Making introductions to influential people who can help the protégé

One of the advantages of **mentoring** programs is that the person being mentored receives individualized attention. Mentors know the hospitality organization, its mission and goals, hence, particularly in complex, large organizations, the protégé learns how the system operates from someone who participates in it on a daily basis.

A **facilitated mentoring** program is a structured process which is designed to create effective mentoring relationships. In a facilitated program a process is established to guide desired behavior changes of those involved and to formally evaluate the results for the protégé, the mentor, and the person(s) responsible for supervising the mentoring relationship. A facilitated program is able to better guarantee that the needs of the hospitality organization are being met. In addition, criteria and a process for qualifying mentors, an orientation program for both mentors and protégés, and a strategy for matching mentors and protégés are all part of this structured process.

There are a variety of ways that a hospitality organization can go about establishing a mentoring program and still gain the numerous benefits of mentoring. In 1996 the *Women's Foodservice Forum* established a mentor program that each year successfully pairs professionals in the food service industry in meaningful partnerships. The partnership begins with a one-day workshop where a mentoring expert focuses on how to establish a successful relationship between mentor and protégé. An agreement as to the expectations of the program is finalized on training day, and with effort on the part of both mentor and protégé a successful partnership for mentoring is created. Hospitality organizations can set up their own internal mentoring program. Another option would be to seek the advice of a consulting company that focuses on the implementation of mentoring programs as part of your company's existing development program.

As with all development programs, both the mentors and those mentored will require information and training on how the program operates, what they can expect from each other, problems that they might encounter, and what benefits each will obtain from the mentor program. Mentors are not substitutes for the employee's manager, and these distinctions must be clearly drawn. Whereas there has to be a mutual trust between the mentor and the protégé, the relationship cannot conflict with the authority relationship between the supervisor and subordinate.

INDUSTRY EXPERTS SPEAK

Mike Jannini, Brand Vice President–Marriott Hotels, Resorts, and Suites shares the following on mentoring: "In addition to all the traditional and relevant reasons for mentoring candidates aspiring to meaningful careers in hospitality management, current social trends and emerging industry changes make this activity more important than ever.

"As always, forming a trusted relationship with a leader who is in a position to share personal and professional strategies that have been successful and reflect on ones that haven't in an atmosphere of support and confidentiality provides a precious opportunity to learn and develop important insights that are difficult to come by in any other manner.

"What may not be as evident for a prospective protégé is there is as much value in this activity for the mentor as there is for the protégé. As leaders, we rarely spend adequate time reflecting upon the personal and professional lessons that have brought us to where we are. A well matched mentor/protégé relationship together with the productive discussions that follow forces this activity for the mentor which bears fruit as leadership skills continue to be honed through the reflections and introspection that arise.

"As dual income families become the norm, and our industry evolves from the performance of simpler discrete functional specialties toward complex activities involving the interdependencies of brands, franchising, innovative financial structures for ownership, and the rapid obsolescence of once competitive product/service strategies in an increasingly competitive marketplace spurred on by technology and information, a mentor's current insights on how to flourish in this rapidly changing professional environment without sacrificing a fulfilling and meaningful life can be invaluable."

Management Development Committees

These programs are used primarily for development reviews of managers, such as Marriott Lodging's Career Banding System discussed earlier in this chapter. The committees consist of high-level management personnel who work jointly with individual managers in the achievement of the manager's career goals. The progress reports that stem from these reviews are used in recommending job moves, either lateral or horizontal.

We feel that there is no reason why a committee approach to development would not work for our hourly human resources as well. In the hospitality industry, it is not uncommon for our employees to report to more than one manager. Different managers work different shifts, and shift changes among hourly human resources are common also. All managers to whom the employee has reported should be involved in the development review. Care should be taken that the employee does not feel that he or she is being "ganged up on," but rather that the entire management team is interested in assisting the employee achieve his or her personal and career goals.

We have stated throughout this chapter that development is not always a vertical path. Advancement is in the eye of the beholder, not the eye of management. In the hospitality industry we are always in need of good followers, those human resources who want to do a good job in their hourly job positions. If our entire staff wanted to be managers, we would indeed be in for some serious trouble.

If what your hospitality organization needs is good followers, then your development program should be set up so that good followers are cultivated.[4] In other words, being successful is not only for those who wish to become managers, being successful can occur for employees at all levels in the hospitality organization. Managers and followers can both be a success, the only difference is in the job tasks they perform. In development programs that cultivate followers, employees are counseled on improving their followship skills, not their leadership skills.

Many hospitality organizations use a combination of these themes in their development programs. Job enrichment and positive reinforcement programs are other approaches to employee development. Fundamental techniques that can underlie each of these methods are the motivational concepts of coaching and team building.

FIGURE 7-6 Good coaches, like good hospitality managers, have the ability to motivate their teams to victory. *(Photo by Mike Jula)*

MOTIVATION IN HOSPITALITY ORGANIZATIONS

Let's now turn our attention to the topic of **motivation** and how motivation plays a critical role in the development process.

Motivation as an Element in Development

The ability to motivate is a critical building block in the development process. Just look around you in the world today at all of the motivational speakers who promise to inspire you to greatness by showing you how to motivate your work force. Individuals such as Zig Ziglar (*Born to Win*), Tom Peters (*In Search of Excellence*), and Ken Blanchard (*The One-Minute Manager*) travel around the country as motivational speakers. Since Dale Carnegie wrote his book *How to Win Friends and Influence People* in 1936, managers have sought to increase productivity through the ability to motivate.

Before you can motivate your staff, you must first understand *what* motivates each employee in his or her specific job position (Figure 7-6). As a manager with human resources responsibilities it is easy to realize that differences exist between what motivates hourly and management employees. What makes a job interesting to a group of hourly employees is different from what makes a job interesting to a group of managers. Furthermore, what one employee may find interesting may not be of any interest to another employee. We also know that no matter what we do, there will be some jobs in the hospitality industry that just cannot be made interesting.

Motivation Theory

What do we mean when we say that we are going to motivate someone? We mean that we are attempting to change the individual's behavior, and thereby influence his or her performance through some type of external stimulus. The questions that now arise are: Which types of external stimuli should be used? Which behavior do we wish to modify? How do we want the performance to be influenced? The answers to these questions provide the motivational goals in your development program. Let's briefly examine what the motivation theorists have come up with throughout the years.

The Pygmalion Effect

The **Pygmalion Effect** states that the expectations your human resources have of themselves determine how they perform. If you expect great things, great things will happen. If you expect mediocre performance, mediocre performance is what you will get. Also known as the **self-fulfilling prophecy**, this effect was discovered by Robert Rosenthal of Harvard University.

By emphasizing the positive and what employees *can* do, your employees begin to believe strongly in themselves. This requires vocalizing your belief in their abilities. The more they hear you tell them how successful they can become, the more competent they will be. If you set high performance and quality standards and tell your employees that you believe that they can rise to the occasion, the self-fulfilling prophecy says that they will. Positive expectations equal positive results.

Maslow's Hierarchy of Needs

In the 1950s, Abraham Maslow identified the "whys" of motivation theory. His theory (**Hierarchy of Needs**) states that man is motivated by satisfying a *set of needs* common to all individuals. In ascending order of importance these are:

1. physiological needs (food, clothing, shelter).
2. safety/security needs (freedom from fear of losing job, clothing, shelter).
3. acceptance needs (to belong and be accepted by others).
4. esteem needs (status, prestige, power).
5. self-actualization needs (maximize one's potential).[5]

Maslow believed that until the physiological needs are satisfied, the other needs would not serve as motivators. Furthermore, once a need is met, it no longer acts as a motivator, and another need takes its place. One of the problems with Maslow's theory is that although it works in life situations, it is not applicable to work settings. Clayton Alderfer, in an attempt to apply Maslow's theory to the workplace, reduced the five levels down to three: existence (pay and security), relatedness (social aspects of work), and growth (personal development).

Hertzberg's Two-Factor Theory

Hertzberg's theory identified job satisfaction and job dissatisfaction as separate elements that are not polar opposites of each other. The **two-factor concept** states that job factors generally regarded as motivators should actually be divided into two groups: one consisting of motivation factors (or satisfiers) and one consisting of maintenance factors (dissatisfiers or hygiene).

Because job satisfaction and job dissatisfaction do not balance each other out, the elimination of a dissatisfier does not necessarily lead to job satisfaction. Motivation factors include such conditions as recognition, achievement, advancement, and responsibility. Hygienic factors include working conditions, company policies, and salary. One of Hertzberg's major conclusions was that money was not a motivator.[6]

Hertzberg believes that if motivation factors are present in the workplace, employees will be motivated; if such factors are not present, then motivation will not occur. If hygienic factors are present, then employees will be satisfied with their work; if such factors are not present, then employees will be dissatisfied. Hygienic factors in no way affect motivation, whether they are present or absent.

To relate Hertzberg's theory with Maslow's needs hierarchy, you will note that Maslow's lower-order needs correspond with Hertzberg's hygienic factors, and that the higher-order needs correspond to the motivational factors. For Maslow, a satisfied need does not motivate. Therefore, the need for money is not as effective a motivator in times of financial propserity. For Hertzberg, money was not a motivator but needed to be present for job satisfaction to occur.

Theory X–Theory Y

Douglas McGregor generalized two assumptions about human behavior. **Theory X** assumes that people are generally lazy by nature and must be pushed into productive behavior on the job. **Theory Y** assumes that people can enjoy work and be self-motivating if the right set of conditions exists. McGregor believed that most people's natures conform to Theory Y, whereas most management styles are Theory X. Furthermore, the problem with using Theory X in the workplace is that it is likely to become a self-fulfilling prophecy.[7]

Expectancy Theory

Victor Vroom's **Expectancy Theory** is one of the more implementable motivation theories. The theory states that a person will be motivated when the individual perceives a link between what he or she is doing and the expected reward. The higher the effort, the greater the reward and vice versa. It is important that the reward is attainable and that your human resources will feel rewarded for the effort they produce.[8] Pay-for-performance compensation systems operate on this principle, as you will learn in Chapter 10. Fixed hourly wages or flat salaries do not motivate because there is no link between effort and reward. For the reward to operate as a motivator, the employee must value attainment of the reward, the employee must see a link between his or her work efforts and receiving the reward, and the individual must possess the abilities and skills to do the job.

Money as a Motivator

The motivational value of money may change after a person's basic needs have been reasonably well satisfied. Because human beings have a way of continually redefining their needs, whether money will motivate is to some degree a matter of the amount involved and the amount the employee is already earning. Therefore, while some people will be more motivated to work for money, companies find that for most employees other things are equally, if not more important (Figure 7-7). There is a diminishing law of return for money as a motivator. Do we have to pay a fair base wage? Yes, absolutely, but after that you need to provide "something else." That "something else" is each person's motivator. "How the boss treats me as a human being" is important. Creating an environment where employees are happy is important. Why do your employees come to work every day for you?

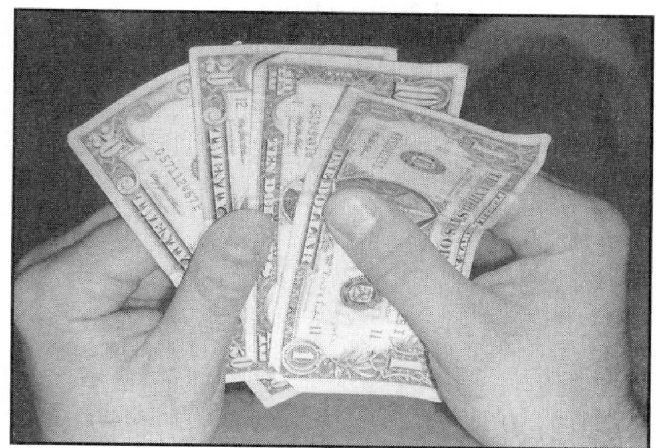

FIGURE 7-7 Just how much of a motivator is money?

In the late 1990s *Fortune* magazine started publishing an annual list of the best companies to work for in the United States. What they continually found was that employees needed to trust the people they work for (the managers), they needed to have pride in their job as well as the products and services they offered to the public, and that they needed to enjoy the people they were working with (fellow employees). In "the next chapter" there will be no one factor that will motivate. It will be a combination of things that will help you retain your people. This again points out the importance of an integrated human resources strategy.

Job Enrichment

In 1968, Hertzberg proposed the idea of **job enrichment** as a reaction to the KITA (kick-in-the-ass) motivational approach that he found most managers practicing. Job enrichment is based on his belief that "The only way to motivate employees is to give them challenging work in which they can assume responsibility."[9] This strategy includes modifying jobs so that they are more meaningful and give the employee an opportunity for recognition and greater responsibility.

Motivational Effectiveness

It should be clear from the preceding discussion that, despite thirty years of study, there is no consensus on how best to motivate your work force. As a human resources manager, consideration needs to be given to several factors that involve human resources functions other than development. Selection procedures need to be effective so that individuals are placed in job positions that they are capable of performing. Training programs must be effective in ensuring that our employees have the necessary skills, and evaluation procedures must be in place to monitor employees' performance. Compensation practices need to be developed that link performance and pay. Furthermore, these practices must all be viewed as fair; that poor performance is not tolerated, high performance is recognized.

If your work force is to be motivated, they must believe that extra effort and superior preformance is of benefit to them. Rewards do not have to be monetary. Flexible work hours, recognized achievement, increased responsibility, and the opportunity to develop personal and career goals work directly toward a motivated work force. The environment of the hospitality workplace has to create desire, commitment, and confidence in your employees. Communciation channels have to be open and organizational goals clearly defined.

Once the environment is conducive to the development of a highly motivated work force, the techniques of coaching and team building can be implemented. Coaching is more than just another type of development approach: It is the strategy used in the development review. Let's now examine coaching and then team building as development strategies that are being used with greater frequency in the hospitality industry.

THE HUMAN RESOURCES MANAGER AS COACH

Development activities require the manager to perform the nonvaluative role of counselor. One of the best techniques in career development counseling is that of coaching. Counseling and coaching are part of a manager's job in a hospitality organization.

Coaching is a method that is used to increase the effectiveness of your development program. The coach is a very powerful motivator in the world of sports. Just as an athletic coach's motivational techniques lead to a greater sense of team spirit, so can a manager as coach motivate his or her work force to perform as a team.

We think that you will agree with us that part of your job as manager is to assist your human resources in the achievement of desired performance standards. We use training to teach basic skills and the techniques of progressive discipline to correct the marginal performer. The focus is on deficiencies in performance levels, where corrective action is taken to improve the job situation.

Coaching is a directive strategy that enhances employee motivation for individual development and improved job performance. The focus is on future performance, in assisting the employee to become the best that he or she can be.

Coaching skills are quite different from counseling skills. Counseling provides advice, assistance, support, and guidance in career development. The counselor listens, clarifies, understands, and helps. Coaching is more forceful, more motivational, more active in its implementation than counseling. The coach prepares, initiates, pushes, and encourages. Coaching is done regularly and consistently.

The athletic coach comes to practice each day with a set of challenging objectives for each player. At the beginning of practice each player is told what is expected of him, and throughout the practice is informed of individual progress. Feedback is immediate! When performance is improved and objectives are met positive reinforcement is used, perhaps a reduced practice period. The outstanding performers are designated as team captains. How is the coach rewarded? Every time his or her team wins a game or match!

As a manager you come to work each day. Do you prepare a list of challenging objectives for your employees? You could, and start each shift with a brief team meeting outlining the objectives. Throughout the shift, you recognize improved performance, frequently letting each employee know how well he or she is doing. If objectives are met during the shift, positive reinforcement is provided, perhaps going home thirty minutes early and getting paid for the time. How are you, as the coach-manager rewarded? Your staff's successful efforts are a reflection on your abilities as manager. In addition, we guarantee you a great deal of personal satisfaction in watching your human resources grow and develop and seeing them accomplish objectives that they didn't think were possible.

Coaches develop commitment in their players, a critical component of the staff in a successful hospitality operation. They do so by clearly indicating the performance expected to all players. Whereas players are selected by coaches because of their skills, the hospitality workplace differs in that we select people that we feel can be trained in the required skills. It is therefore our responsibility to see that the required train-

INDUSTRY EXPERTS SPEAK 

"As the protégé of one of our Senior Executives, I have grown immensely in my leadership style and capability of creating a strong team to accomplish our company's operational game-plan" states Yvette Nowland, Resident Manager Crystal City Marriott, Virginia. "My mentor has provided candid feedback in an environment of trust. It is extremely important as a protégé to accept and receive the feedback on developmental areas and, most important, to demonstrate new behaviors.

"Each month, I telephone my mentor and review my development growth in my leadership style. The candid feedback continues, and as I grow, the conversations move to a higher level. I receive reinforcement on my leadership style.

"Mentoring has been an important part of my development plan for my future, as is the ability to receive feedback in a safe and constructive environment."

ing occurs because without it, we can never expect to have employee commitment.

Coaches also consistently communicate their faith in their players' ability to perform successfully. Perhaps this is the Pygmalion Effect at work. High expectations of player performance yields high performance. Coaches know what motivates each player and what is most important to them individually. Reprimands are not uncommon when a player's performance is poor and can range from extra laps to not being allowed to play in a game. When players cannot meet expected performance standards, they, too, are terminated in the form of being traded to another team or released to fend for themselves.

Coaching assists in the development of your human resources. A great coach can get his people to go beyond their self-imposed limits to do what they never thought possible. Becoming a career coach for your employees can be enormously self-satisfying. Remember that your role is to be supportive, not evaluative, that the atmosphere has to be receptive to open two-way communication, and that the coaching process is done on a day-by-day basis.

BUILDING YOUR HOSPITALITY TEAM

One of the benefits of implementing a coaching strategy into your development process is that it also fosters a sense of teamwork. When you place an emphasis on development and improvement, employees tend to become more comfortable working together, communication is increased, and anxieties are reduced. The common goals become clearer to everyone, and the work force works together to see that they are carried out. Even though it might sound like a contradiction, encouraging independence helps to stimulate teamwork. As a general rule people enjoy being part of a team.

Team building is the process by which people are brought together into teams. A *team* is two or more people with complementary skills and abilities who are united for a common purpose or the achievement of a common goal for which they are held mutually accountable. Team building requires a cooperative effort and dedication among the team members to coordinate their strengths, knowledge, and effort for the common purpose or goal. When effectively developed, team building enables better decisions by fewer people. When effective, the team can accomplish more than the sum of the individual team members combined. To put it quite simply, teams get things done. And that is why you are likely to see more use of teams in "the next chapter."

Team building became a buzzword in the workplace in the mid-1960s, and was considered a very humanistic management approach. Team building advocates say that it:

- reduces conflict among your work force
- acts as a motivator
- improves the quality of decision making
- assists you in managing cultural diversity
- decentralizes the power base
- refocuses management as a development role
- increases involvement, thereby increasing commitment
- improves two-way communication
- encourages discussion and active problem solving
- develops a sense of accountability among your people

Team building is not quick. It takes a long time to create great teams. Team building is not easy. Achieving unified and harmonious groups that successfully achieve goals takes a lot of work and a lot of effort from those involved. Team building is not a cure-all for your organization's business problems. Getting more work out of fewer people is not the purpose of team building, nor should it be the purpose of team building. Teams are not always appropriate in all situations. If a goal or task can better be performed by one person, then it should be assigned to one person. There are tasks best performed by teams and tasks best performed by individuals.

For a team to be effective, the team members must be committed to clearly defined goals. The team needs a strong leader with a flexible leadership style. The members need to be willing to learn from their mistakes as well as their successes. They cannot be afraid of the possibility of failure. Team members need to be comfortable assuming risk, confident to say what they really think, and open-minded to the ideas of others. An effective team both works hard and plays hard while achieving the challenging goals set in front of them. Bottom line is that teams need to be made of highly motivated individuals with common purpose and accountability for results.

Creating a Team Spirit

Motivation, coaching, and team building go hand-in-hand as one strengthens the others. It is impossible to create a team spirit unless you have a highly motivated work force. It is hard to motivate a work force that views itself as a loser. That is where development programs enter the picture. By setting attainable career goals for your human resources, you give them the opportunity to taste winning. Winning teams are always more highly motivated to work hard to repeat their successes (Figure 7-8).

Identify your top performers and work with them in becoming team captains. People improve when they associate with individuals who strive to be their best, not with those who look for the shortest route to completing their jobs.

FIGURE 7-8 A team spirit can create an atmosphere of good feelings. *(Courtesy of Chili's Grill & Bar, Brinker International)*

A lot of team spirit will be generated from your attitude. Before a team can win, they first have to want to win. Second, they have to make the commitment to do what it takes to win. This requires that you believe in them and their abilities. Your positive self-image will transfer to your work force.

Decision-making needs to be delegated. It's hard to get people to work as a team if you retain all the decision-making powers. When employees can make decisions for themselves, they are much more likely to be committed to carrying out the choice they made.

Team building is a process that, when effectively implemented, allows the work force to go beyond what any of its individual employees could accomplish by themselves. Teamwork also stimulates motivation and gives development programs the opportunity to maximize their full potential.

> *"There is no limit to what can be accomplished if it does not matter who gets the credit."*
>
> —Ralph Waldo Emerson

CONCLUSION

Employee development is becoming increasingly important to managers with human resources responsibilities in the hospitality industry. Each day hospitality managers face an increasing labor shortage, shifts in the age distribution of the working population, a slowing of the early retirement trend, more intensive international competition, and accelerated technological change.

Development programs provide you, the human resources manager, with a process by which you can help your employees succceed. Through development activities, you can assess your employees' ambitions, interests, and goals. Career goals and developmental acitivties can then be identified. Progressive hospitality organizations encourage their employees to pursue career development and to take advantage of the opportunities available to them.

Career development programs benefit the hospitality organization as well as the individual employee. Their very structure stimulates communication between management and employees as well as among departmental managers. They force the organization to refocus on its human resources, its most valuable assets.

Development programs stimulate motivation by providing your human resources with opportunities in which they can be successful. Positive work experiences translate into a stimulated work force. Motivation can not only change behavior, it can also improve job performance.

Coaching and team building have been found to be effective motivational strategies. Through coaching, human resources are stimulated to become their best. Through team building, hospitality organizations encourage creativity and innovation. Let's now turn our focus to the evaluation of job performance and improving employee retention.

CASE PROBLEM 7-1

Rebecca Jannis is the human resources manager of ***XYZ Restaurant Corp.***, a family style restaurant with bar, located in six states in the New England area. Rebecca is faced with a problem. She needs three new general managers for the new restaurants the corporation is planning on opening in the next six months. The job specification for General Manager requires five years of management experience. However, a computer check of all assistant manager qualifications came up with only one person currently employed by *XYZ* with the necessary management qualifications. The Vice President of Human Resources has asked Rebecca to present by the end of the week an HR plan for filling the three new positions.

Rebecca now recognizes that the development program at *XYZ* needs some development of its own. First, assist her by coming up with a one-page plan to fill the necessary job vacancies. What kind of information do you need in order to ensure an effective development program? Make, and identify whatever assumptions are necessary. Then outline a development program for ***XYZ Restaurant Corp.*** that will prevent this internal personnel shortage from happening again in the future.

Case Problem 7-2

Now that Rebecca is more attuned to the importance of a development program for management, she wants to improve the program for hourly employees as well. While discussing this idea with some of the employees, she met a seventeen-year-old dishwasher, Ben, who is just entering his senior year in high school. Ben thinks that he would like to become a restaurant manager when he finishes high school.

How realistic do you think Ben is in his career aspirations? Specifically, what guidelines would you suggest to maximize Ben's success in achieving his career goal? Identify several steps (both short-term and long-term) that Rebecca could take to help ensure Ben's success. What if Ben had come to Rebecca with no career aspirations? How might have Rebecca helped him in identifying possible career interests and expectations? What type of lateral career development opportunities might you provide for a dishwasher who came to you with no career aspirations that would maximize his or her potential?

Case Problem 7-3

You are the manager with human resources responsibilities at a busy international airport in a major city in the Midwest. You oversee twelve separate food and beverage venues throughout the airport property and have approximately 120 employees on your payroll. The emphasis on teams and teamwork is critical in the type of environment you work in each day.

What types of team-building strategies and techniques would you suggest? What will be your strategy for motivating your employees and stimulating them to become members of your upbeat team? Relate your strategy to one of the "classic" motivational theories. Will you be able to use pay as a motivator? As the coach of your team, how will you build a commitment in your players?

Key Words

career bands
career counseling
career development
career pathing
career planning
coaching
development programs
development review
Expectancy Theory
facilitated monitoring
Hierarchy of Needs
job enrichment
key competencies
mentor
mentoring
motivation
performance development counseling
protégé
Pygmalion Effect
self-fulfilling prophecy
team building
Theory X—Theory Y
two-factor concept

Recommended Reading

Brooks, J. E. 1995. "Guide to Developing a Successful Career Course." *Journal of Career Planning & Employment* 55(3): 29–32.

Campbell, H. 1996. "Adventures in Teamland." *Personnel Journal* 75(5): 56–62.

Clark, M. 1994. "7 Ways to Build a Better Work Team." *Hotels* 28(7): 24.

"Companies Pay Big Penalties for Poor Employment Practices." *HR Reporter* 16, no. 2 (1999).

Donnellan, L. 1996. "Lessons in Staff Development." *The Cornell Quarterly* 37(5): 42–45.

Ensman, R. 1997. "Morale Audit: How Upbeat Is Your Workplace?" *Restaurant USA* 17(4): 12–13.

Ensman, R., Jr. 1995. "Put Teamwork into Play for Your Restaurant." *Restaurant USA* 15(11): 9–10.

Furman, M. 1997. "Reverse the 80-20 Rule." *Management Review* 86(1): 18–21.

Hedden, J. 1997. "Mentoring: Restauranteurs Help Build Careers." *Restaurant USA* 17(7): 22–26.

Katezenbach, J. R. and D. Smith. 1993. "The Discipline of Teams." *Harvard Business Review* 71(2): 111–120.

Laabs, J. J. 1995. "L.A. Hotel Gives Teens a Career Orientation." *Personnel Journal* 74(11): 50–61.

Matsumoto, J. 1997. "Mentors as Role Models." *Restaurant & Institutions.* www.rimag.com/lo/op-ment.htm (2 June 1998).

Pan-Educational Institute. 1996. *Mentoring Guidebook: Participating as a Mentor in the Pan-Educational Institute NSN Schools Telecommunications Testbed Project.* Independence, MO: Pan-Educational Institute.

Parker, L. B. 1994. "A Program for Planned Professional Development." *Journal of Career Planning & Employment* 54(4): 63–67.

Riell, H. 1993. "Motivating Your Crew." *Restaurant USA* 13(9): 15–17.

Simons, T. and C. Enz. 1995. "Motivating Hotel Employees: Beyond the Carrot and the Stick." *The Cornell Quarterly* 36(1): 20–27.

Sparrowe, R. and P. A. Popielarz. 1995. "Getting Ahead in the Hospitality Industry: An Event History Analysis of Promotions among Hotel and Restaurant Employees." *Hospitality Research Journal* 19(3): 99–114.

Stephenson, S. 1994. "12 Ways to Motivate Employees." *Restaurant & Institutions* 104(24): 112.

Wiley, Carolyn. 1997. "What Motivates Employees according to Over Forty Years of Motivation Surveys." *International Journal of Manpower* 18(3): 263–278.

Waldroop, J. and T. Butler. 1998. "Finding the Job You Should Want." *Fortune* 137(4): 211–214.

Zuber, A. 1997. "People—The Single Point of Difference—Motivating Them." *Nation's Restaurant News* 31(40): 114–115.

Recommended Web Sites

1. The Counseling Web: Career Counseling Resources: seamonkey.ed.asu.edu/~gail/career.htm
2. Academy of Human Resources Development: www.ahrd.org

3. Canadian Youth Business Foundation On-Line: www.cybf.ca/frames/main.htm
4. U.S. Department of Labor Employment and Training Administration: www.doleta.gov
5. Work Force Development: www.doleta.gov/employer/wd.htm
6. Peer Resources: www.islandnet.com/~rcarr/peer/html
7. National Career Development Association: www.ncda.org
8. National School-to-Work Learning Center: http://www.stw.ed.gov
9. National Career Development Association: http://www.workindex.com/workindex/NationalCareerDevelopmentAssociation.html
10. Center for Creative Leadership: www.ccl.org

ENDNOTES

1. Career Systems International, *WorkPower™: Marriott's Guide to Career Success* (Scranton, PA: Career Systems International, 1998), 2.
2. Douglas T. Hall and Associates, *Career Development in Organizations* (San Francisco: Jossey-Bass Inc., 1986), 205.
3. Marriott Lodging, *Career Banding System* (Washington, DC, 1998), 11.
4. Robert E. Kelley, "In Praise of Followers," *Harvard Business Review* 88, no. 6 (1988): 142–148.
5. Abraham H. Maslow, *Motivation and Personality* (New York: Harper and Row Publishers, Inc. 1954).
6. Frederick Hertzberg, *Work and the Nature of Man* (Cleveland: World Publishing Company, 1966).
7. Douglas McGregor, *The Human Side of Enterprise* (New York: McGraw-Hill, 1960).
8. Victor H. Vroom, *Work and Motivation* (New York: John Wiley, 1964).
9. Frederick Hertzberg, "One More Time: How Do You Motivate Employees?" *Harvard Business Review* 46, no. 1 (1968): 53–62.

DISCUSSION QUESTIONS

1. Development programs have recently gained importance as human resources tools in hospitality organizations. What factors and conditions do you think are responsible for their increased popularity?
2. List the steps in the career development process. In your own words, briefly describe each.
3. Identify the benefits of a successful management develpoment program.
4. What do you feel are the two most important ingredients of a successful development review?
5. Discuss two different types of development programs. Which do you feel is most appropriate for a hospitality organization?
6. Describe several different ways that a mentor can assist his or her protégé with career development.
7. Identify and describe three different theories of motivation.
8. What happens when employees don't get satisfaction from their jobs? What do you think is the reason why career development programs improve retention?
9. What can you do as a manager to increase motivation in a work area, such as the dishroom, where motivation is low, despite good pay, benefits, and working conditions?

10. Explain how coaching can assist you in implementing development programs.
11. Discuss how team building could be used as a retention tool.
12. Why would you want to develop coaching and team-building strategies in your hospitality organization?

CHAPTER 8

Evaluating Performance and Employee Retention

INDUSTRY ADVISOR

JEANNE MICHALSKI, *Assistant Vice President of Employee Development, Burlington Northern Santa Fe Railway Company*

"We are what we repeatedly do. Excellence then, is not an act, but a habit."

—ARISTOTLE

"There is something that is much more scarce, something rarer than ability. It is the ability to recognize ability."

—ROBERT HALF

INTRODUCTION

Now that you have recruited, hired, oriented, trained, and initiated a development program for each of your employees, you must evaluate the performance of each. Evaluating the performance of your people is a very powerful tool that serves both the needs of your hospitality organization and the needs of your employees. If properly implemented and performed, the performance evaluation can assist in assuring that each employee is successful in his or her job. This personal success leads to high retention rates that become critical to the success of the hospitality organization. The primary goals of human resources management, to attract and retain, continue in their importance as we discuss evaluating performance.

At the conclusion of this chapter you will be able to:

1. Identify the purpose of performance appraisal as a human resources management tool.
2. Describe where performance appraisal fits into the human resources management process.
3. Discuss how performance appraisal information is used.
4. Describe the conflicting roles of judge and coach in the performance appraisal process.
5. Identify the basics of "how to" appraise an employee's performance.
6. Define the different methods of evaluating performance.
7. Identify the most common mistakes evaluators make when conducting a performance appraisal, and how to avoid them.
8. Increase your effectiveness when appraising the performance of your employees.
9. Understand different ways to improve the longevity of your work force through various retention methods.

EVALUATING PERFORMANCE

Performance reviews, assessments, evaluations, ratings, and appraisals are all terms that refer to the task of assessing the progress of our people. Think of it as a feedback system that provides you with information relating to the successful achievement of your manpower plan. Performance appraisals (the term we have elected to use) tell you how well each of your employees is progressing in his or her individual development as well as how each is progressing in meeting the goals of the business plan. We define **performance appraisal process** as a means for determining how well each of your employees is doing in achieving the criteria considered essential for success in his or her job position. The term *performance appraisal* is generic—that is, it is used to describe a variety of types and methods of evaluating the performance of your human resources. This can be done only after an inventory of human resources skills has been conducted and a plan for improvement developed. Progress can then be assessed.

Think for a moment about a useful analogy that each of you can identify with. In the classroom, professors assess students by testing their performance in a wide variety of subject matters such as accounting, menu planning, food production, and computers (Figure 8-1). This assessment leads them to an appraisal of the student's growth and knowledge levels that eventually translates into a grade given for the student's performance level in a particular subject matter.

FIGURE 8-1 Assessment by your professors provides information for student appraisal.

In the hospitality workplace, as managers, you will assess employees by conducting performance appraisals of their work behaviors and skills. This appraisal will be used to make a number of human resources management decisions regarding wage increases, promotions, and training/development needs for your hospitality operation. Just as in academia, appraisals may be conducted on any type of employee, from hourly wage earners to salaried managers. In all situations, the process of appraising performance is for the purpose of distinguishing among levels of performance.

The Purpose of Performance Appraisals

Performance appraisals let you and your employees know how well they are doing their jobs and what steps should be taken if performance improvement is needed (Figure 8-2). Everyone has a need and desire to know how well they are doing their job. Remember as a student how much better you felt when your professor provided you with frequent feedback so that you knew how you were doing, as opposed to professors who provided minimal feedback so that you didn't know how you performed until you received your grade card in the mail?

FIGURE 8-2 Performance appraisals let employees know how they are doing. *(Courtesy of Strongbow Inn, Valparaiso, IN)*

There are many purposes for the appraisal process:

- To assess the quality of job performance.
- To provide feedback to your employees regarding job performance.
  - —Feedback consists of either recognition of good performance or notification of performance deficiencies.
  - —Feedback could also indicate the need for training.
- To plan future performance goals and objectives.
- To improve job performance through recognition and coaching.
- To establish a better knowledge of the employee so as to understand what motivates him or her.
- To document unsatisfactory performances for possible use in the court systems and arbitration in wrongful termination cases.
- To serve as a basis for compensation distribution in some organizations.

Importance of Appraisal Process

Everyone likes to know where they stand with respect to their performance, even when that information might indicate that improvement is needed. Have you ever worked for a manager who never let you know how you were doing? Did you ever feel unsure of what management's expectations were of you? Fortunately, most hospitality organizations have begun to recognize the importance of letting their employees know where they stand and, as you later learn in our discussions about compensation, rewarding people as performance improves (pay-for-performance).

The appraisal process, when conducted effectively and fairly, yields many benefits to human resources managers. These benefits include the following:

- An open two-way system of communication between management and each employee
- An objective set of criteria to measure job performance
- Improved job performance
- A basis for modifying poor work habits
- A means of gathering employee suggestions for improving performance, methods, or morale
- A more immediate awareness of problems
- A stronger commitment to the organization
- Improved job satisfaction
- An effective motivational tool
- A way of demonstrating concern
- A source of documentation in the event of litigation
- A basis on which to determine promotions and wage increases
- A means to seek alternatives to termination
- Future direction for employee improvement and development
- Focus on continuous improvement
- A means to building a high-performance work force
- Increased productivity

These benefits are based upon the assumptions that your employees have a desire to improve their performance, that feedback regarding job performance can affect performance levels, and that job satisfaction (and a happier work force) stem from improved job performance.

THE ROLE OF PERFORMANCE APPRAISAL

Where does the performance appraisal process fit into the human resources management system? Figure 8-3 illustrates the relationship of performance appraisal to the other human resources function activities. As you can see, the information obtained from performance appraisals serves multiple purpose, for you the manager with human resources responsibilities in the hospitality industry.

Relationship to Performance

We appraise our employees in terms of the results and performance levels we expect them

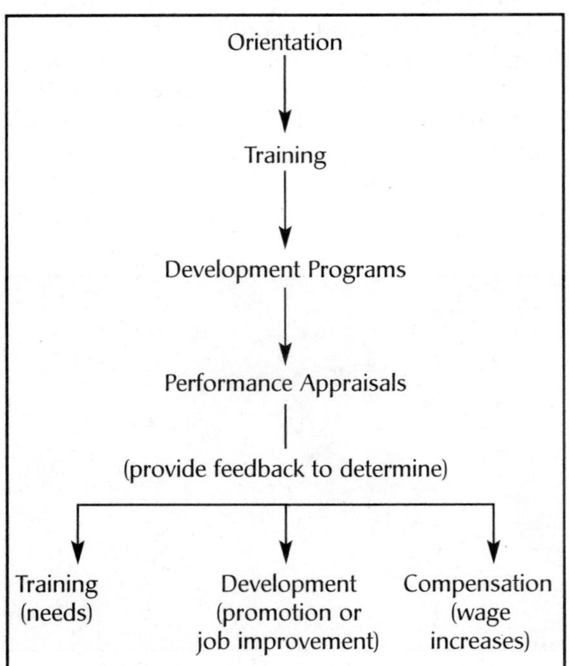

FIGURE 8-3 Role of performance appraisal in human resources management.

to accomplish. Our strategic human resources plans (Chapter 2) become the basis for our appraisal system as they define accountability. We said earlier that our manpower plans could be used as motivators and agreed that all of our operational objectives would need to be supported by performance standards. It is the performance standards that we previously established as an integral component of our human resources plan that become the basis for performance appraisals. The performance standards are what you use to differentiate between good and poor performance, as well as among various levels of performance. Performance levels can range from poor performance to adequate or average performance to good or outstanding performance. It is not always as simple as "good" or "poor."

Relationship to Communication

We also said that our human resources strategic plan would be a communication device. And no where is it more important to communicate clearly than in the process of performance appraisal. Misunderstandings are prevented when the performance standards are clearly communicated to the employees that are accountable for the results defined by your manpower plan. As your hospitality organization grows and your people develop, planning evolves.

Relationship to Development

Your performance appraisal process should emphasize the development of qualified people from within your hospitality organization to fill the opportunities that are constantly generated by a growing organization. A successful development plan integrates the needs and goals of the individual with the needs and goals of the hospitality operation. Just as your development plan provided for lateral and/or vertical career changes, the appraisal process sets behavioral change goals for either improving current job performance or to make career changes. Appraisals assist in linking the individual's goals with the organizational goals.

When appraisals are used for making transfer and promotion decisions, care must be taken that the information on file is only reviewed as it relates to the duties and responsibilities in the new job position (be it vertical or lateral). A person who performs highly in one job position may not necessarily perform at the same level in a different job position that requires different qualifications. Transfer and promotion decisions have to take into account an appraisal of the employees abilities in performing job activities that are part of the new job assignment, not just current job activities.

Relationship to Training

Performance appraisals identify deficiencies in job performance or identify areas of improvement. Identified deficiencies can frequently be traced to the individual's inability to perform the job according to standards. In these situations training needs are identified and training sessions can be scheduled to correct the performance problem. When areas of improvement are identified, it could be for growth opportunities, not just correcting "bad" behavior. The appraisal could identify that the employee wants to improve average, or even good, behavior through the acquisition of new skills or improvement of current skills. Once properly identified and agreed upon, the employee could be sent for the necessary training.

In training, we view appraisal as a needs assessment tool. It can also be used after the training program is completed to assess the level of skill development and learning that has occurred. In other words, what behavior change has occurred as a result of the training?

Relationship to Compensation

Performance appraisals have long been used as a basis for wage determination and wage increases. Unfortunately, some managers view this activity as the sole purpose of performance appraisals. Though the level of performance should certainly have some relationship to the amount of compensation received, you are overlooking a valuable tool if this is the only reason you conduct appraisal activities. The relationship of compensation to performance is of particular concern in the pay-for-performance and merit compensation plans.

When used for compensation decisions, the performance appraisal is used to discriminate between high and low performers based upon established criteria. Compensation scales are established that are commensurate to each performance level. A further discussion of job grading and pay-for-performance can be found in Chapter 10.

When using the performance appraisal for compensation purposes, make sure that the criteria are based on measurable outcomes achieved on the current job. Your employees will be quick to lay blame on management or company weaknesses over which they had no control if they feel that their paycheck is in jeopardy. Measurable work outcomes must be identified that are viewed by your employees as fair and equitable.

When selecting which appraisal process to use in your hospitality organization, it is essential that you have a clear understanding of the mission of the hospitality enterprise. The roles of the performance appraisal will be clearly indicated to you by the organizational goals that stem from the mission statement. You can then develop appropriate operational objectives for appraising performance that are in keeping with the needs of the enterprise.

JUDGE VERSUS COACH

As we have seen, there are numerous roles that performance appraisals assume. One of the major problems with performance appraisals is the inherent conflict among those roles. The primary conflict lies between the appraisal's role as a determinant of compensation decisions, and the appraisal's role in improving job performance and developing employees. In the first situation, the appraiser must act as judge and in the latter as the coach. Even though this dual conflict has been identified for over twenty-five years,[1] the problem still exists. We discuss ways to avoid this problem later in this chapter.

Let's look at how these dual roles can create a conflict in practice. We have an employee, Beth Doolittle, who has been with our 100-room lodging facility for two years. The time is approaching for Beth's performance appraisal meeting, at which time you will discuss with her (1) how she is performing her job, and what needs you mutually see for training and development; (2) what her goals may be and whether they have changed; (3) how you can assist her in satisfying those needs and goals; and (4) what her wage increase, if any, will be.

If you provide Beth with a list of training and development needs and then give her a wage increase, she is likely to be confused. Why must she undergo more training if you are satisfied enough with her present job performance to give her a raise? If, on the other hand, you tell Beth that she will not be receiving an increase because of unsatisfactory job performance, then she is not likely to hear what plans you have for her development and training.

One solution you can institute is a system that provides two different appraisal sessions.

In one, called the **development appraisal**, you wear your coach hat and let your employee know how much you value his or her contributions to the organization. You mutually agree upon training and development needs that assist the employee in achieving the goals that are most important to him or her. The decisions made in this interview become the basis for the retraining that we discussed in Chapter 6 and for the individual development programs we discussed in Chapter 7.

In the second appraisal session, called the **performance evaluation**, you wear your judge hat and provide the employee with information on his or her successes and failures in the hospitality organization. Has the employee met the operational objectives based upon the business plan of the organization? What have been the individual's accomplishments? This information then relates to decisions pertaining to wage adjustments and promotions.

Obviously, these two roles have to be connected to be effective for both the hospitality organization and the employee. Whereas the performance evaluation is controlled primarily by the needs of the organization, the development appraisal is a process controlled by the employee. In a dual review system, the performance evaluation provides the employee with a means of achieving the extrinsic rewards the organization has to offer. The development appraisal then provides the employee with a means of achieving the intrinsic rewards: challenging work, opportunity for growth, and being recognized for a job well done.

Jeanne Michalski points out that although this may be the ideal situation, in reality it is hard to separate out these two roles. In practice, many companies will not want to take the time to sit down with employees twice. Additionally, the reality of heavy workloads and customer counts in the hospitality industry makes it difficult as a practical matter to separate these. It *is* important for you recognize and understand the conflict that can potentially exist for your employees in these dual roles. Dr. Michalski recommends that you use what fits the situation and your organization. You might find yourself working for a hospitality organization that does not even use rating systems of any type. The role of coaching, as we saw in Chapter 7, is taking on an increasingly important role in human resources management. Some hospitality companies, along with other industries, are moving away from appraisals and more to coaching. An effective performance appraisal process provides a method for satisfying the needs of everyone involved in the hospitality organization.

HOW TO APPRAISE PERFORMANCE

Performance appraisal is a term either dreaded or loved by management and employees alike. For each, it can be either a painful or rewarding experience. It is not pleasant to tell or be told that you are not doing a good job and improvements need to be made. On the other hand, many employees look forward to their appraisals, especially if they respect the manager giving it. Have you ever been the recipient of a performance appraisal? If so, we are sure that you can identify with some of these feelings.

The last thing we want the performance appraisal to do is to demotivate our people. When a problem with performance or behavior exists, it is our job as an appraiser to convince that individual that (1) a problem does exist, (2) he or she needs to improve, and (3) that you are available to assist the individual in becoming the best that he or she can be.

We now turn our attention to the elements that make up an effective performance appraisal process.

INDUSTRY EXPERTS SPEAK

Our industry advisor Jeanne Michalski takes this opportunity to relate a performance appraisal strategy to you: "Whenever I have a performance review to give an individual, I always tell him or her a few days in advance that the individual will be receiving it. This allows the employee time to collect his or her thoughts relative to the review and to form well-defined questions if desired. Besides, this permits the employee to become emotionally prepared for the process, if it is anticipated to be strenuous.

"I recall one case in particular with a long service employee who aspired to become a manager. This individual's comfort level with delegation was not strong and had the desire to keep tight control upon all responsibilities. I felt that a promotion into management would 'rob' the company of a very good individual contribution and leave us with a rather poor manager.

"The strategy that I had mapped out was to discuss organizational goals, then the individual's performance as it related to the goals as an introduction to this person's level of performance. I felt that this would, as amicably as possible, illustrate the employees strengths and shortcomings and lead into a discussion of 'Where do we go from here?' My opinion had already been formed based on the employees skills and attitude that this person was not fit for management.

"To my delight and surprise when we came to the point of deciding 'where to go,' the employee suggested continued growth at the individual contribution level. This only served to reinforce in my mind the value of searching for the most appropriate niche for each employee within our company. The challenge to me is to find a job that allows for personal satisfaction by the employee while maximizing the company's productivity."

Goal Setting

The first statement we make about the design of a performance appraisal process is *Keep it simple!* The process we design will be used to both develop and evaluate performance. It logically follows then that the best place to start is by identifying the job standards and responsibilities. If our employees know what is expected of them in the performance of their jobs, they are more likely to be successful.

For an employee to know what is expected of him or her, the employee must understand the functions and responsibilities of the job as well as how he or she should go about achieving those functions and responsibilities. These elements are contained in the goals that are jointly developed by the manager and the employee together (Figure 8-4).

FIGURE 8-4 The goal-setting meeting is an important component of the appraisal process. *(Courtesy of Strongbow Inn, Valparaiso, IN)*

Goal setting occurs for new employees after their orientation and training period, and for current employees at the conclusion of their performance evaluation. The goals become the criteria for determining the acceptable quality and quantity of work levels. They are based on both the business needs, as identified in the business plan, and on the employees' career aspirations, strengths, and weaknesses. Thus, they serve as performance criteria for both the development appraisal and the performance evaluation.

Goals are based upon your job descriptions and are the starting point for an effective performance appraisal process. We recommend that they meet the following criteria for maximum effectiveness:

- Logical. They evolve from an accurate job description and job specification that indicate duties, responsibilities, and accountability.
- Specific. The goals cannot be stated in vague or general terms.
- Realistic. The goals must be clearly achievable. This does not mean that they should not be challenging, but they must be attainable.
- Measurable. The employee must be able to ascertain his or her progress toward the goal and know when the results have been obtained. This keeps the appraisal process objective as opposed to subjective.
- Time sensitive. The employee should clearly understand when this goal is to be achieved.
- Results oriented. This is not the time to discuss the method or activities used to complete the goal, but the time to define the results to be accomplished. The results should be observable by others.
- Mutually committed. The goals should be committed to by every person who has an effect on the employee's performance.

Performance goals include the performance expected of the human resources in your hospitality organization. A **performance planning guide** will provide you with a written record of the performance expectations that you and the employee agreed upon. This record can be used throughout the appraisal process when conducting either development appraisals or performance evaluations.

The Appraisal Instrument

Remember that the performance appraisal should be based on the employee's job performance related to the job description. The **appraisal instrument** should contain certain basic information, such as the employee's name, job position, date of the interview, period covered by the appraisal, and who is conducting the appraisal interview. Table 8-1 is an example of a performance appraisal rating form used in the appraisal of hourly employees.

The specific type of information you include on the appraisal instrument is highly dependent upon the method of performance appraisal used by your hospitality organization. These specific methods are discussed later in this chapter, but there are certain elements that all appraisal instruments must contain, regardless of the particular method.

First, and foremost, you can stay out of costly litigation resulting from discriminatory appraisal methods by using an instrument based upon a job analysis. Management must be trained to use this instrument. The results of the job analysis must then be used to develop an instrument that is both valid and reliable. The appraisal instrument typically contains some type of rating system that permits you to rate each employee with as much objectivity as possible.

Consideration must be given to the number of levels you will use to rate your people. The difficulty in using a limited number of rating

(continued on page 231)

TABLE 8-1 Performance Appraisal Review

Performance Appraisal Review

EMPLOYEE NAME			SOC. SEC. NO.	DATE OF REVIEW
MC or RC-BC	LOCATION CODE	CITY/STATE	REVIEW OF PERFORMANCE From: To:	
DEPARTMENT	POSITION TITLE		CURRENT JOB DATE	SERVICE DATE

INSTRUCTIONS

1. Review employee's work performance for the entire period; refrain from basing judgment on recent events or isolated incidents only. Disregard your general impression of the employee and concentrate on one factor at a time.
2. Consider the employee on the basis of the standards you expect to be met for the job assigned based on the length of time in the job. Place a check in the box which summarizes his/her overall performance on that factor since his/her last appraisal.
3. **REASONS MUST BE GIVEN TO SUBSTANTIATE AND EXPLAIN YOUR EVALUATION!**

PART I - SPECIFIC JOB PERFORMANCE FACTORS

QUALITY OF WORK - Level of accuracy, neatness, and thoroughness of output and production.

- ☐ Excellent
- ☐ Very Good
- ☐ Fully Satisfactory
- ☐ Needs Improvement
- ☐ Unsatisfactory

EXPLAIN: ______________________________

QUANTITY OF WORK - Volume of acceptable work accomplished. Ability to meet schedules. Use of time, and level of results achieved.

- ☐ Excellent
- ☐ Very Good
- ☐ Fully Satisfactory
- ☐ Needs Improvement
- ☐ Unsatisfactory

EXPLAIN: ______________________________

TABLE 8-1 Performance Appraisal Review *(continued)*

JOB KNOWLEDGE & SKILL - Understanding of job assignments and application of job knowledge. Ability to grasp and interpret instructions, methods, and procedures.

☐ Excellent
☐ Very Good
☐ Fully Satisfactory
☐ Needs Improvement
☐ Unsatisfactory

EXPLAIN: ______

JOB RELATED CONTACTS - Level of cooperation and enthusiasm in job-related contacts with customers, employees, and supervisors.

☐ Excellent
☐ Very Good
☐ Fully Satisfactory
☐ Needs Improvement
☐ Unsatisfactory

EXPLAIN: ______

JUDGMENT - Ability to decide on a correct course of action. Ability to size up a problem; obtain and evaluate facts; and reach sound conclusions. Acting within Company policy and conduct guidelines.

☐ Excellent
☐ Very Good
☐ Fully Satisfactory
☐ Needs Improvement
☐ Unsatisfactory

EXPLAIN: ______

PART II - GENERAL JOB PERFORMANCE FACTORS

SAFETY	☐ WORKS SAFELY ☐ NEEDS IMPROVEMENT ☐ DOES NOT MEET STANDARDS	List any preventable personal/vehicular accidents during the review period. ______
ATTENDANCE	☐ PERFECT ATTENDANCE ☐ MEETS STANDARDS ☐ DOES NOT MEET STANDARDS	EXPLAIN: ______
ATTENDANCE CALCULATIONS - Refer to local practice.		

TABLE 8-1 Performance Appraisal Review *(continued)*

OVERALL PERFORMANCE	☐ EXCEPTIONAL ☐ VERY GOOD ☐ FULLY SATISFACTORY ☐ NEEDS IMPROVEMENT ☐ UNSATISFACTORY	EXPLAIN:_______

PART III - EMPLOYEE DEVELOPMENT

1. What particular development activities or guidance will be given to improve the employee's current job performance?

2. What goals has this individual established to improve personal work performance?

3. Comment on the employee's management potential and/or career interests, including training and/or experience needed to develop the employee professionally..

PART IV - COMMENTS - Attach additional sheets if necessary.

COMMENTS BY EMPLOYEE: _______________

COMMENTS BY SUPERVISOR: _______________

COMMENTS BY MANAGER: _______________

PART V - POLICY REVIEW - The following MUST be reviewed with the employee at the time of his/her review.

Code of Business Ethics or Standards of Employee Conduct [ ] Other - _______________ [ ]

TABLE 8-1 Performance Appraisal Review *(concluded)*

PART VI - SIGNATURES

EMPLOYEE (Signature does not necessarily mean concurrence)			DATE
PREPARED BY	TITLE	PHONE NUMBER	DATE
APPROVED BY NEXT LEVEL OF MGMT	TITLE		DATE

Forward ORIGINAL form to the Human Resources Department for review and inclusion in employee's folder.

Human Resources Reviewer: ______________________ Date: ____________

PERMANENT - ***DO NOT DESTROY*** - THIS FORM MUST REMAIN PART OF EMPLOYEE'S FILE DURING ENTIRE TERM OF EMPLOYMENT

(Courtesy of Burlington Northern Santa Fe Railway Company)

categories is that most managers are uncomfortable being forced to distinguish among employees in such a restrictive way and tend to rate most employees as average. How would you like to be told you were *average*? There is no agreement as to the optimum number of rating levels, although most hospitality organizations use between four and seven levels, and most industry advisors concur that three is not enough. The trend towards a more developmental approach in conducting performance appraisals is moving us away from a limited rating approach.

Defining the criteria for each level is the important aspect of the appraisal instrument. Care must be taken to develop performance criteria that allow the appraiser to distinguish between levels of performance. Wording must be clear and unambiguous to be of value. If you are working for a hospitality organization that does not have rating forms already developed, be sure and get plenty of input from the line supervisors. They will be able to tell you if the instrument you develop will assist or hinder their own job performance.

Keep the forms clear, so that the person doing the appraisal does not have a lot of writing to do on the form. Too much written text can be confusing and should be used only to support or clarify the appraisal form. If you have done your homework, you should be able to state the performance standards and objectives precisely. With a well-developed rating scale, the appraiser should not have to do extensive writing on the appraisal instrument. This means that the form will have numbers or letters to insert or boxes to check. And as Dr. Jeanne Michalski points out, once the form is designed, be sure that management is trained to use it properly and consistently.

So far in the appraisal process we have established the employee goals, determined the performance standards against which the goals will be measured, and through the development of a rating scale, we now have our definition of what constitutes superior performance. We are now ready for the appraisal interview. Having discussed the development appraisal in Chapter 7, we focus on the performance evaluation here.

The Appraisal Session

You should give the employee plenty of advance notice before the **appraisal session** so that the individual can prepare a self-evaluation of his or her performance to bring to the session. You, as the appraiser, also have much to do before actually conducting the session.

As the appraiser, you must carefully review the employee's job description and specification so that you are familiar with the individual's job function. A review of the performance standards, employee achievements, and the performance planning guide is also necessary. You should have been keeping a file or journal on the employee's accomplishments during the review period. These files are oftentimes referred to as critical incident files. **Critical incident files** contain a written message for each accomplishment or failure that an employee has had. Before the appraisal session these should be reviewed.

If you are anxious about conducting an appraisal interview, it is important that you work through these feelings before confronting the employee. The person might perceive your anxieties as an indication that the review he or she is about to receive is going to be negative. Care must be taken not to bring into the appraisal session any feelings of anger or hostility that you might have toward a particular individual. This assessment must be kept objective and fair.

At the beginning of the appraisal session you need to establish a positive and comfortable atmosphere that is conducive to honest, two-way communication. Explain to the employee immediately what the procedure is for conducting the appraisal. If this is his or her first appraisal, the employee is likely to be nervous and have no way of knowing what to expect.

Remember that this session is for two-way communication (Figure 8-5), which means that you and the employee should each talk about half of the time. Introverted individuals might have a hard time talking about themselves. The self-appraisal they filled out before the session will be useful in drawing the person into the conversation. The focus of the discussion should be on the goals and results. Pull out

INDUSTRY EXPERTS SPEAK

"I keep a file for every employee. Every time I observe behavior that is either exceptionally good or less than I expected I both recognize the behavior at that time, but I also write it on my file. Later, when I am sitting down to review employee performance, I have my notes on specific behaviors that the employee has performed. These notes help me decide the appropriate rating and ensure that I use the whole rating period in establishing that rating, not just the last few weeks or months. These notes also help me in explaining my rating to the employee. I can remind the employees of the behaviors we have discussed previously and by discussing events as they occur, I ensure that there are no surprises during the appraisal review (performance evaluation)."

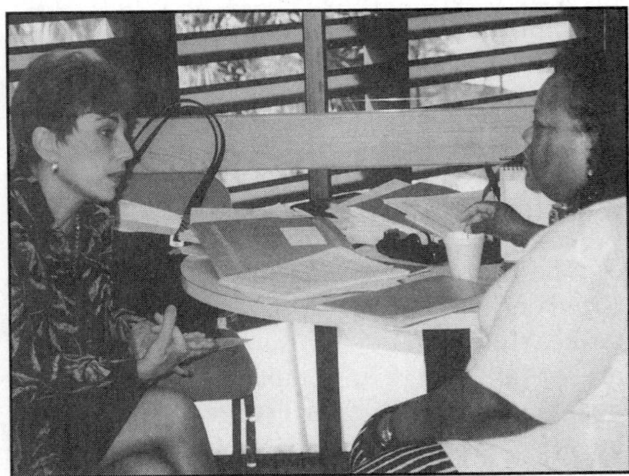

FIGURE 8-5 The appraisal session should be conducted so that two-way communication is encouraged.

the performance planning guide and discuss each goal separately.

Criticisms that need to be made should be specific and performance related. Do not focus on personality or character traits, but on the goals and the reasons why they were not achieved. Give specific examples instead of generalities. Stay calm and do not get into an argument with the employee. Your focus should be on providing feedback to assist the employee in improving his or her performance, not on the actual rating itself.

INDUSTRY EXPERTS SPEAK

Jeanne Michalski says, "I try to approach all appraisal reviews as a coaching opportunity. I do need to evaluate and provide a rating, but that is not my main focus. As I prepare for the appraisal session, I think about each employee and their relative skill strengths and areas for development. For each employee I try to identify two to three things that he or she could improve upon, even if he/she is my top performer. This establishes an environment of continuous improvement. A true coach acknowledges the strengths but also pushes for improvement."

Take as much time as you feel is necessary. Do not plan a tight schedule into which you will attempt to work in an appraisal session. Depending upon the individual, the length of the session will vary. Seek employee feedback especially on projected goals. It is important that the employee feel that he or she is an integral part of the process and can key in to the ideas. Before concluding the session, summarize the employee's strengths and the areas in which improvement is needed. Provide solutions and guidance on how he or she can improve in these areas. Emphasize your commitment to assisting the employee in reaching higher levels of performance. Work with the individual to establish new goals for the next review period. You will continue to use the performance planning guide for this purpose. The focus at the conclusion of the session should be on future performance, not past.

Documentation is an essential part of this process. Feel free to take notes during the session and complete the file shortly after the appraisal session ends, while the discussions you have had are still fresh in your mind. Have the employee sign the appraisal forms and provide him or her with a copy.

METHODS OF APPRAISING PERFORMANCE

There is no one method of appraising performance that is suitable to all organizations. The particular method used in your hospitality organization will be dependent upon the mission statement of the enterprise and the existing corporate culture. We will now discuss some of the more frequently used appraisal methods.

Critical Incident Method

The **critical incident method** focuses on the behavior of the employee that is to be evaluated. As we have discussed, the two of you have already met to mutually agree upon the goals that the employee would work on attaining during this review period. During the course of the review period it will be up to you, the manager with human resources responsibilities, to maintain an incident file. An incident file is an ongoing record of the employee's behaviors, both positive and negative, during a specified review period.

When it is time for the appraisal interview, you have a file of both poor and outstanding performance for each of your employees. For this type of appraisal to be successful, it is important that you give the employee feedback continuously on their critical incidents. That means when an employee does something outstanding, you immediately tell the person verbally to reinforce that behavior, as well as making a note in the employee's file. Additionally, poor performance should be discussed soon after the occurrence so that the employee can immediately correct the behavior. Remember, your role as a coach is more important than your role as judge when you want to reinforce positive behavior and eliminate poor performance. You are not sitting on the sidelines just waiting for your employees to do something wrong. But when they do, they need to know that you are there and are willing to assist them in getting back on the right track.

It is equally important to remember that performance appraisals are not used just to identify "good" and "poor" performance. Even if an employee's performance is not "poor," we want to use the appraisal session as an opportunity to assist the employee in improving his or her performance levels. How does the employee make an average, or standard, performance outstanding?

Behaviorally Anchored Rating Scales

Behaviorally Anchored Rating Scales—BARS, as they are more commonly called—require that a job analysis has been conducted that has identified the types of behavior that are appropriate for various levels of performance. For example, a Level I behavior might be an extremely accurate worker, rarely makes mistakes; a Level II behavior might be consistently accurate, makes few errors that are seldom repeated; a Level III behavior might be work is consistent with job standards, errors are infrequent and so forth.

The BARS method has the advantage of being objective as each human resource is rated against a predetermined specific set of behaviors that have been identified on a job-by-job basis. The BARS instrument is highly reliable, but it is time-consuming to develop. Oftentimes, the expense required to perform a detailed job analysis to determine the behavior criteria is too great for some hospitality organizations. Additionally it is hard to develop behaviors that relate across all jobs. BARS measures performance levels within a job, it does not provide common measures across jobs. What is more effective in performance appraisals is to use a tool that consistently measures performance across all jobs.

Competency Approach

A **competency assessment** focuses on the knowledge and sets of skills an employee needs to know to be successful. In this approach the emphasis shifts from being task-focused to being competency-focused. What competencies are needed for superior performance in this job? This approach works well for jobs that are knowledge-intensive and decision-oriented such as those found in leadership and management positions. The largest advantage to using this approach is that you can identify commonality across jobs. For example, the competencies for superior performance in "leadership" would be the same regardless if you were working in a food and beverage operation or a lodging property. This advantage makes competency assessments particularly useful for large hospitality organizations that have a number of different brands.

360-Degree Appraisals

360-degree appraisals are designed to provide feedback from all sources, including supervisors, peers, subordinates, self, and customers (Figure 8-6). This feedback process can be used not only for performance appraisals but for career development as well. Once

(continued on page 238)

BNSF

Multi-Rater Survey

Please read carefully before completing the survey.

This survey will provide valuable feedback on the leadership style of the person being rated. Your views will help this person learn how he or she is seen as a leader. By answering honestly you will help this person learn about strengths and find opportunities for growth and development.

Directions

1. All of the necessary information should be recorded only on the score sheet provided.
2. Please use a **blue** or **black** ink pen. **Fill in the appropriate circle**. Do **not** use X's or check marks (√).
3. Answer each item on the survey by marking the spaces on the score sheet that correspond to the numbered items on the survey.
4. Respond to each survey item by marking one and **only one** of the choices. The choices are abbreviated as follows:

   SD=Strongly Disagree D=Disagree N=Neutral or Undecided A=Agree SA=Strongly Agree

5. **If you make a mistake** draw an "X" through the mistake and fill in the correct circle.

Your ratings will be grouped with other ratings and not shown by themselves if the person you are rating is your manager, your peer, or anyone who doesn't report to you. For example, if you were the only person to fill out a survey about a supervisor, then your ratings would be mixed into the group results. Managers' ratings of people who report to them will be shown individually.

When completing the survey on your manager, answer all items based on your direct experience with this person. When completing the survey on a "peer" or a "direct report", answer based on your view of this individual as a team member and a manager of others. Even if your experience with the individual is limited, answer as many items as possible. When completing a survey about yourself, be as fair as possible. Your answers will show how you see yourself compared to how others see you.

It is very important that you are honest and thoughtful in your responses. Look carefully at all aspects of the person you are rating so that your responses do not fall into just one category such as "Agree". The more carefully you look at a person's performance, the more helpful your feedback will be. **When you have completed the survey, fax the score sheet to 1-800-763-2660. Do not use a cover sheet.**

Thank you for your cooperation in this important process. Your prompt response will be greatly appreciated.

FIGURE 8-6 Multi-Rater Survey. *(Courtesy of Burlington Northern Santa Fe Railway Company)*

SD=Strongly Disagree D=Disagree N=Neutral or Undecided A=Agree SA=Strongly Agree

This Person...

1. is optimistic.
2. meets customer expectations.
3. listens attentively to the ideas and opinions of others.
4. contributes to a safe work environment.
5. treats people with dignity and respect.
6. understands customer's needs.
7. is open and supportive.
8. strives for continuous improvement.
9. communicates openly and honestly.
10. sets a high personal standard for work.
11. values individual differences.
12. monitors results.
13. makes tough decisions in the face of adversity and uncertainty.
14. works efficiently.
15. demonstrates consistency between words and actions.
16. is action oriented - - takes initiative.
17. confronts prejudice and intolerant behavior displayed by others.
18. manages company resources as if they were their own.
19. balances timely action with complete analysis.
20. celebrates BNSF's rich heritage.
21. shares information in a timely manner.
22. expresses ideas and concerns.
23. works with all people equitably.
24. understands the factors influencing BNSF's earnings growth.

FIGURE 8-6 Multi-Rater Survey *(continued)*.

SD=Strongly Disagree D=Disagree N=Neutral or Undecided A=Agree SA=Strongly Agree

25. anticipates future consequences.
26. listens to customers.
27. performs role and responsibilities effectively.
28. balances work with other aspects of their life.
29. takes initiative for developing oneself.
30. considers the cost impact of decisions before taking action.
31. is confident in the future success of BNSF.
32. embraces change.
33. takes pride in being a part of the BNSF community.
34. by example, fosters a climate where diversity is valued.
35. helps develop business processes that are efficient and effective.
36. Overall, considering all aspects of performance that are important to the job, this person is an effective contributor.

****Items 37 - 56 are to be completed only on individuals who manage people.**

This Person...

37. empowers employees.
38. provides clear direction and priorities.
39. encourages and respects participation in life outside of work.
40. provides all employees equal access to development tools and opportunities.
41. encourages continuous improvement.
42. celebrates successes.
43. recognizes employees for their contributions.
44. encourages the open expression of individualism.
45. gives meaningful feedback on performance.
46. monitors progress of others and redirects efforts when goals are not being met.

Questions continue on the back page.

FIGURE 8-6 Multi-Rater Survey *(continued).*

This Person...

47. shows concern for the well being of employees.
48. clarifies roles and responsibilities.
49. emphasizes safety as a priority in every job.
50. establishes structure and systems for needed change.
51. conveys a clear vision and direction for the future.
52. fosters an environment where employees feel free to communicate openly.
53. inspires others to excel.
54. respects the talents and achievements of employees.
55. fosters pride in the community.
56. Overall, considering all aspects of management and leadership that are important, this person is an effective leader.

Thank you for your cooperation in this important process.

FIGURE 8-6 Multi-Rater Survey *(concluded)*.

employees get used to the process of receiving feedback from all the people with whom they interact, they generally value the feedback. 360-degree feedback does provide the employee with a perspective of how they are seen by others. Supervisors usually like it because it may lessen any feeling of bias or prejudice as the feedback comes from a variety of people and not just themselves. Care does have to be taken to make sure that the person receiving the feedback understands the process and is not made to feel as though everyone is "ganging up" on him or her. It is better to initiate the 360-degree process as a developmental tool first before using it as a performance assessment tool. If performance is tied to compensation, employees may resent that individuals other than their boss is having an effect on their paycheck and possible advancement opportunities.

Management by Objectives

First proposed by Douglas McGregor in the 1950s, **management by objectives** focuses on the results of the behavior, not on the behavior itself. Specific, written goals are developed by the subordinate and supervisor at the beginning of the review period. At the end of the period, the performance is evaluated based on how many of the goals the employee has achieved. This method is more commonly referred to as goal setting in modern day human resources management.

Although this approach is supposedly more objective than some of the other methods of performance appraisal, many people believe that this method can be abused by unfairness, just like any other method. The primary weakness in the process is the ability to establish realistic, yet challenging goals. Many supervisors, upon knowing that their own evaluations will be based upon how well their employees meet their goals, will establish more-obtainable and less-challenging goals for their subordinates. Why establish a difficult goal if you know that your evaluation will suffer if you don't achieve the goal? Management By Objectives (MBOs) or goal setting can usually support other appraisal systems as opposed to being used as a stand-alone system.

Best Approach

There is no one perfect system. The best approach is the one that works for your particular situation. It is much more important that your people receive consistent, objective feedback, that communication channels are open, and that the method is understood by all who will be using it, than it is that you stick with one particular method and not waiver from it. Many hospitality organizations use a combination of approaches. It is important that you find the appraisal process that works for you, your employees, and your company. We now look at some things to avoid in evaluating performance.

MISTAKES TO AVOID IN CONDUCTING PERFORMANCE APPRAISALS

One of the major problems in assessing an individual's performance is the bias of the appraiser. Either negative or positive biases can result in a nonobjective and unfair performance appraisal. A variety of factors can affect even the most well-intentioned appraiser's judgment about the performance of one of his or her employees.

The **halo effect** is one of these conditions that can cloud appraiser judgment. The halo effect results when limited information about an event influences the interpretation of subsequent events. For example, a positive halo may occur if the employee scored very high on a pre-employment skills test. Employees come into the workplace with the manager expecting great things of them because of their high test score. Everything they do in the performance of their job is weighed against these high expectations. If a poor performance is seen by management, the manager might assume that this person is just having a bad day, that this performance is not typical. No consultation about the poor performance is held. This reinforces the idea in the employee's mind that this performance is acceptable. As you can imagine, the longer this occurs, the lower the performance. If this positive halo carries over into the performance appraisal, then the evaluation of this employee's performance will be elevated to meet the high expectations of the appraiser. The opposite result occurs when a negative halo surrounds an employee. This is sometimes referred to as the horn effect or **horn error**. No matter what performance levels the individual achieves, the performance will probably not be good enough. High standards of information gathering before the appraisal can reduce these effects.

Recent behavior bias is a by-product of the time frame that precedes the performance appraisal. All of us tend to remember the most recent behavior of the individuals we know. In the workplace, our employees tend to be evaluated on their behavior in the past several weeks, rather than on their average behavior over the appraisal period. If employees are aware of this, they will strive to improve their performance just before the appraisal session. These biases in appraisal given to an employee are known as **primary bias** and recency bias. This points out the great need for management education and training in the appraisal process.

Another bias to avoid is comparing the employee to yourself and weighing the person's performance against what you would do if you were working in the individual's job position. It is natural for each of us to favor those people who remind us most of ourselves, but to do so in the performance appraisal results in an unfair evaluation. This could also cause a problem from a discrimination perspective.

The development of an appraisal system that none of your people understands can create problems of job dissatisfaction. For the process and method you select to be effective, it must be clearly communicated and understood by all who will be affected by it.

INDUSTRY EXPERTS SPEAK

Jeanne Michalski recalls a negative experience she had with a performance appraisal that was being done on her when she was an hourly employee. "When I first began working, performing an hourly job, the company had a detailed performance evaluation form based on a long list of tasks and duties. The manager used a 5 point rating scale on how well an employee performed these various tasks and duties. These numbers were then totaled to arrive at a point system that had pre-established merit increase amounts tied to them; the higher the total score the higher the increase. The problem, from my perspective, was that because of the hours I was assigned to work, I was not expected or required to perform some of the tasks on the list. Because I did not perform these tasks, I was rated low on them which also lowered my total score and my next increase. To this day I still feel I was unfairly treated." Jeanne states further, "This example points out how important it is to make sure you establish goals, expectations and assignment of duties and measure against these. Make sure your appraisal process never measures employees against duties or assignments that you do not require them to perform. This of course does not mean you shouldn't take into account duties that the employee is not performing if it is part of their assigned job."

We are sure that many of your professors have already cautioned you against the dangers of making personal friends with your subordinates. We point it out here because it will directly affect your ability to objectively and fairly evaluate your employees. If your employee/friend is not doing a good job, will you be able to tell the person so?

Other problems with evaluating performance are:

- Insufficient time to properly review materials and documentation.
- The appraiser's inability to rate people as outstanding or poor, but rather evaluating all employees as average. This is sometimes called nondifferentiation, where the rater only uses a portion of the rating scale.
- Performance goals that are either vague or conflict with one another.
- Performance appraisals that are used only as a control mechanism rather than also as a development tool as well.
- An organizational structure that does not reward management for the development of their people.

INCREASING THE EFFECTIVENESS OF YOUR PERFORMANCE APPRAISAL PROCESS

We want to take this opportunity to summarize what you, as the human resources manager, can do to assure that your hospitality organization has an effective performance appraisal process:

- Performance expectations must be clearly identified and communicated to all individuals involved in the process.
- Although the appraisal process is ongoing with continuous feedback, periodic system-

atic performance evaluations are held with each employee.

- There is a method by which the employee can respond to his or her performance evaluation as well as a formal system of appeals.
- Performance appraisals evaluate the individual's behavior, not the person.
- The hospitality enterprise provides a supportive organizational structure.
- Performance evaluations are candid and specific.
- Appraisers have the training necessary to conduct appraisal interviews. This is a skill and can be taught and learned.
- The performance appraisal process provides for both individual development and sound human resources management decision making.
- Your employees should know specifically what the consequences are of a poor performance evaluation.
- Use the appraisal session as a tool to find out how well you are doing your job.

INDUSTRY EXPERTS SPEAK

According to Dr. Michalski, "One thing I always do as a part of the appraisal process is to ask my employees to tell me one or two things I can do to help them be more effective on the job. Usually I will ask them to think about the following:

things I should do more of
things I should do less of and
things I should continue to do the same

This helps the dialog and discussions so that the employee and I can focus on how to improve his or her performance even if that means changing *my* behavior."

RETENTION

The word "retention" has been brought up repeatedly throughout this text because every human resources function that we have discussed so far impacts upon the retention of your employees. We define **retention** as the maintenance of a high-quality work force through programs that seek to decrease turnover and thereby maximize the longevity of the hospitality organization's people. Our ability, or lack of it, to retain our emloyees has a direct impact on human resources planning and recruitment. Labor shortages and the current low rate of unemployment have changed the nature of human resources management and the face of hospitality organizations. For the past decade, hospitality managers have identified retention and recruitment as the two most important resources activities. As early as the late 1980s managers were identifying retaining key people as their priority.[2]

Turnover rates in the hospitality industry have always been notoriously high, with some segments and geographic regions of the country reporting as high as 200–300 percent! By this time, you have a full understanding of the labor market and demographic changes that make the continuation of these percent figures not just unacceptable, but impossible, if you hope to have people to staff your hospitality operation when you graduate. What can you, as future hospitality human resources managers, do when you are out in industry?

To begin with, you will have to be receptive to innovative and nontraditional approaches to human resources management in the hospitality industry. Too frequently we hear students, upon learning about new human resources management methods, say that it won't work; the industry just isn't set up to work that way; "You wouldn't get management to buy into that where I work"; and endless other reasons why the new method will fail. Creativity and adaptability have to become part of your management style if you are to be successful in facing the challenges "the next chapter" will be bringing to you. So keep your minds open while we present some of the innovative approaches planned with retention as their goal that are working in the hospitality industry today!

Turnover

It is true that turnover is inevitable. Employees come and leave organizations for a variety of reasons. People move away, they retire. **Turnover** is the movement of your employees out of the hospitality organization. As such, it is one of the major factors in determining your labor supply. When turnover is effectively managed, it can be positive as it allows for new people with fresh ideas and energy to join your company. With unemployment rates at a twenty-four-year low as we enter the new millennium, the balance of power has shifted from employer to employee. In the 1980s no one in our industry was too concerned when annual turnover rates were calculated at 60 percent or more. Turnover rates of 100 percent and higher were almost routinely accepted.[3] By the late 1990s the National Restaurant Association in its 1996 Restaurant Operations Report stated the turnover rate for salaried employees of full-service operations with a check average under $10 to be 50 percent and hourly workers in full-service operations to be an alarming 100 percent![4] In the food service industry alone, it is predicted that 1.3 million new jobs will be created by the year 2005. When adding in managed turnover figures for retiring employees, it is estimated that 3.9 million job openings will occur between 1996 and 2005. These figures do *not* take into account unmanaged turnover.[5] It is this unmanaged turnover that bleeds a hospitality organization of its talent, its knowledge base, and its positive customer relations along with profits and its competitive edge in the marketplace.

A good place to begin discussing how to improve retention is to examine some of the reasons that high turnover exists in the hospitality industry. One of the realities in our industry is that it is not always seen as an attractive place to work. Let's face it, the work is physical, the hours long, the working conditions are not always the best, the times we're busiest are weekends and holidays when the rest of the world is off, and our pay scales stay pretty close to minimum wage (Figure 8-7). Sometimes it seems as if we are almost boastful of the sacrifices it takes to work in a food service operation or lodging property. How many times have you heard it said that everyone must "pay their dues" in hospitality? At this point, you are probably wondering what you are doing working on a degree in hospitality administration! The point we are trying to make is that this thinking is very outdated. Working within a sector of the hospitality industry does not have to be, and should not be, like the scenario we just described.

Cost of Turnover

Employee turnover is a direct drain on the bottom line. The U.S. Department of Labor estimates that it costs a company about 33 percent of a new hire's annual salary to replace a lost employee.[6] This includes the direct costs of replacement such as recruitment and advertising, clerical time to process paperwork, managerial time to oversee the employment process, orientation and training, possible overtime for other employees, along with uniform supply. You also have to take into account the indirect costs associated with employee turnover such as reduced productivity, lower employee morale, loss of customer goodwill and possible loss of sales. It is hard to come up with an exact dollar figure for some of these costs, yet we know that they exist. So much of our reputa-

FIGURE 8-7 Work in many industries is often physical with difficult working conditions. *(Courtesy of Burlington Northern Santa Fe Railway Company)*

tion in the *hospitality* industry is based upon the relationships our employees develop with our customers. How can we accurately place a dollar figure on those precious relationships?

Retention Methods and Programs

The number of hours worked, wages, the scheduling of work hours, training, promotions, physical job demands, benefits package, treatment by management, job challenge, work environment: each of these job-related concerns can be the reason our human resources stay with our hospitality operation, or it can be the reason they leave. A human resources tool frequently used to determine the reasons why people leave our organizations is the exit interview. Upon termination, either voluntary or involuntarily, an interview is conducted to determine the specific causes that resulted in losing an employee. A turnover report is then compiled with this information, and management then seeks to eliminate the reasons why these individuals left.

The problem with this logic is twofold: First, it assumes that the reasons people stay are the opposite of why people leave, and second, it assumes that the people who stay do so because there is a high degree of job satisfaction.[7] In either case, the assumption is likely to be invalid. A more innovative approach would be to study why the employees in your hospitality organization are staying, and if they are happy working in your operation or if they remain because there is no opportunity for them elsewhere.

Turnover is not a problem unique to the hospitality industry. Companies in many industries have needed to become more creative when looking at retention tools and methods. The following is a list of just some of the things you can do, as a manager with human resources responsibilities, to improve the retention rate at your company:

- Hire only the best people. Resist the urge to simply fill the vacancy. Look for the people who fit in with your company's philosophy about work. Everyone needs to be able to work together in the same direction.
- Make sure that the job fits the job description and job specification that the employee was hired to perform. Are the job duties and responsibilities realistic in the course of a work shift?
- Meaningful new hire orientation can help create loyalty. Have new employees spend ten minutes with the General Manager, company President, or even CEO if possible.
- Provide effective training. Follow up and evaluate the effectiveness of your standard training programs. Make sure that you are training for both horizontal and vertical growth.
- Be known as a people-oriented company whose managers set clear expectations for their employees. Give lots of praise and recognition when your people excel, correct them immediately when they do not.
- Treat your people with dignity and respect. Don't forget the Golden Rule—treat others as you would like to be treated. After all, isn't that how we want our employees to treat our guests?
- Review your compensation and benefits packages to ensure that your employees' needs are being met. Remember that what your employees need in the year 2000 is a lot different than in the 1980s, 1970s, or even 1990s. As a general rule, people do not leave just because of money issues unless they feel they are being underpaid and that the company is taking advantage of them. We discuss this is greater detail in Chapters 10 and 11.
- Improved quality of work life. Sure our employees must work when others are playing, but this does not have to mean *all the time*. Be flexible with your scheduling and sensitive to your employees' needs for their "special" times off.
- Make work fun! Develop a sense of community and a place where your employees want to be.

Recall that our definition of retention includes "a high-quality work force." This means that your people are with you for a long period of time because that is where they want to be. Your job, as human resources manager, is to find out what causes people to want to stay with your hospitality organization and then institute retention programs that reinforce those reasons.

Job Previews

Job previews are a procedure in which new employees are told about all aspects of the job, including the undesirable, before they are made a job offer. The preview is given to the new employee before he or she actually begins working in the job position. The logic behind job previews is that turnover will be reduced if employees are given a realistic picture of all aspects of their job, both the positive and the negative.

They can be used either at the time of recruitment or at the time of orientation when employees are gaining familiarity with the hospitality organization and specific operation that they will be working in. As you might note, job previews represent a very different approach from traditional recruitment and orientation methods. Why do they work in reducing turnover? Research provides us with a number of reasons.[8]

Haven't you dreaded going someplace or doing some activity (maybe giving a presentation in front of the class) only to discover that once you were doing it, it wasn't nearly as bad as you had thought it was going to be? The same psychology plays in presenting employees with a realistic job preview. Once they are actually performing the job tasks, they find that they aren't really as bad as they had imagined.

Another reason job previews reduce turnover is that some people leave the job position at the recruitment or orientation stage when they hear the negatives. Others who stay and experience the negative aspects of the job are more comfortable with them because they knew what to expect ahead of time. They did not feel that management deceived them just so that they would accept the job.

All these reasons for the success of realistic job previews make a lot of sense, so why are they not used more frequently? Sometimes job previews can increase turnover rather than reduce it. Particularly in industries such as hospitality where some entry-level job positions pay minimum wage, there is a tight labor market, and the industry is perceived negatively as a place to work.

Research shows that a critical factor in the successful use of job previews is to ensure that a strong binding occurs between the individual and the organization.[9] We talked about the importance of socializing when we discussed orientation procedures in Chapter 6. The more loyalty you can create in the individual, the more likely the success of job previews as a retention tool.

INDUSTRY EXPERTS SPEAK

Jeanne Michalski states, "We routinely conduct realistic job previews for our hourly positions. Our operation runs 24-hours-a-day, seven-days-a-week. We also have many employees who routinely work on-call. This means they may not know that they need to be on duty until a half hour before they must report. In addition, some of our jobs require extensive manual labor, operating heavy equipment and working outdoors in all types of weather.

"We often hire fifteen or more employees at one time to fill up training classes so we hold large "employment:"sessions. We begin each session (40–100 applicants) with a briefing where we share information on the company and most importantly on the realities of the job duties, schedule and working conditions. Invariably a number of applicants leave before the interview process begins and that is good. We want people who understand and will accept the conditions of the job. If they do not we will only be hiring more people the next month. Of course, we also communicate the benefits of our company during that information session!"

Employee Incentives

Many hospitality organizations are using **incentive programs** with great success as both retention tools and as performance motivators. Actually, high motivation levels in your human resources staff will translate into strong retention and reduced turnover.

What kinds of incentives could you use in your operation? Cash awards, trips, small gifts (such as watches), seminars for which expenses and wages are compensated, and company outings. The key to using incentives as retention tools is that they need to be tied to longevity. The longer a human resource is with your organization, the more the individual stands to lose by leaving your organization. Many companies have done a good job of rewarding service and creating loyalty in their staff.

CONCLUSION

The process of evaluation is summarized for you in Figure 8-8. After you identify which people are to be evaluated, the process begins by formulating achievable goals and determining the appropriate behaviors based on job competencies to observe to effectively measure job performance levels. It is critical that each stage in this process is communicated to all involved. Information then needs to be collected on the appropriate employee behaviors and competencies. During the appraisal session the extent to which the goals have been attained are mutually agreed upon by the employee being evaluated and the appraiser. The decisions made in the interview are implemented, and feedback is supplied to the employee on his or her job performance. The cycle then begins again with the feedback assisting in the formulation of achievable goals.

At its best, the performance appraisal is a difficult process. Some human resources managers are never completely comfortable with discussing negative and positive aspects of performance with the employee on a one-on-one basis. Remember, however, that people do respond to constructive criticism, just as you as a student perform better when you receive feedback as to your progress in the classroom before you receive your final grade! One of the most important aspects of the performance appraisal is that it shows your people that you care about them. What an effective motivator this can be!

Performance appraisals can be one of your most valuable tools in the management of your employees. They tie many of our human resources functions together with the mission statement and goals of the hospitality organization. As we continue to reduce turnover and improve the longevity of our work force, the benefits of a good performance appraisal

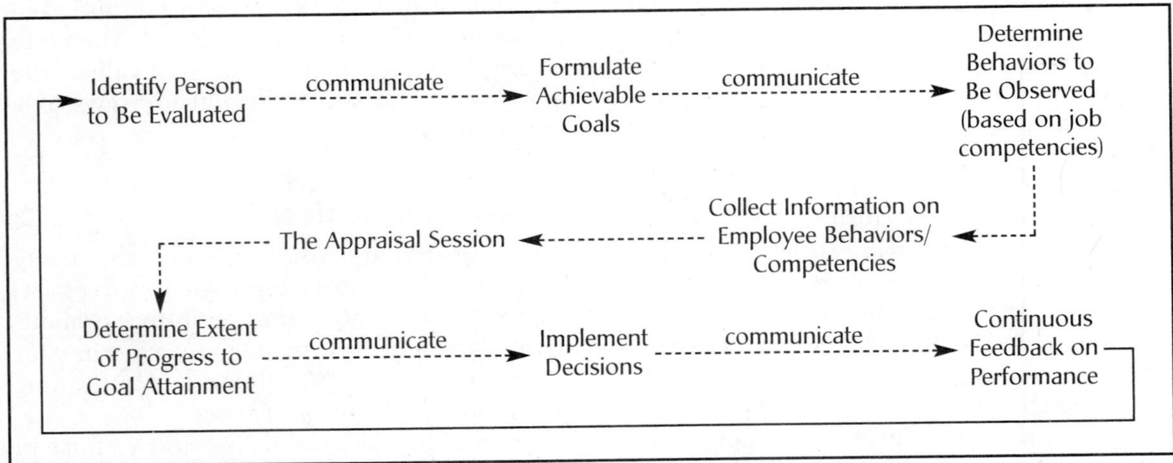

FIGURE 8-8 The process of evaluation.

process will allow both management and its employees to spend their time working together in improving both themselves and the hospitality organization.

If properly implemented, performance appraisals lead to increased productivity, higher job satisfaction, and an improved work environment. All activities, plans, and programs associated with the performance appraisal process must be directed towards operational needs. The dollars spent on these programs must make a visible difference in the operation of the hospitality property, be it in the lodging or food service sector of the industry.

CASE PROBLEM 8-1

You have been the Human Resources Manager of an all-suite, independent hotel located on the outskirts of Nashville for the past year. You have not been happy with the performance appraisal system at this property since you arrived. Employees seem intimidated by upcoming reviews, and managers seem unsure of their role in the process and uneasy about conducting the reviews. You are determined to devote your energies to improving this critical and valuable human resources tool.

Identify what specific steps you will take to improve the performance appraisal system. What items do you feel are important to include in the review form for all hourly employees? Why are these important to you and your management style? What bothers you the most about the way the performance appraisals are currently being conducted? How will you ensure that these things do not happen in the future?

CASE PROBLEM 8-2

In reviewing the current performance appraisal system at your property you decided to interview the hourly employees and get their feedback. These are some of their comments:

> "My managers do not know what I do. They have no basis on which to evaluate me. They couldn't do my job if they had to."
>
> "If there was a problem with the way I do my job, why wasn't I told right away? Why do I have to wait for some crazy performance review to find out I am doing something wrong?"
>
> "The ratings on these forms don't make any sense to my particular job. I don't even understand what they mean."
>
> "If the manager likes you, you know you are going to get a good review. If the manager doesn't like you it doesn't matter how good you do your job, your evaluation is going to be bad!"
>
> "My manager is the one who needs to be evaluated . . . by his staff."

Take each of these statements and write a plan for overcoming these criticisms in the new performance appraisal system you are developing. How will your performance appraisal system guarantee that employees will not be making these same comments?

Case Problem 8-3

Your location, right outside of Nashville, means that retaining your employees is critical for success. There is virtually no unemployment in this area and heavy competition for a quality hospitality work force. Though some turnover is inevitable, as the Human Resources Manager you recognize that it is in everyone's best interest to minimize turnover and improve retention rates.

Prepare a three-page plan of what you intend to do to improve your retention rates. Be specific. Remember that by definition retention calls for a "high-quality work force." How do job previews fit into your plan?

Key Words

appraisal instrument
appraisal session
Behaviorally Anchored Rating Scales (BARS)
competency assessment
critical incident files
critical incident method
development appraisal
goal setting
halo effect
horn error
incentive programs
job previews
management by objectives
performance appraisal process
performance evaluation
performance planning guide
primary bias
recent behavior bias
retention
360-degree appraisals
turnover

Recommended Reading

Bailey, D. 1992. "Coping with Employee Turnover." *Restaurant USA* 12(5): 18–20.

Branch, S. 1998. "You Hired 'Em. But Can You Keep 'Em?" *Fortune*, November 9, p. 247.

Dienhart, J. 1993. "Retention of Fast-Food Restaurant Employees." *Hospitality & Tourism Educator* 5(3): 31–35.

Gilbert, R. A. "When Business is Good, It's Because of the Economy." *Lodging Magazine*, 1997. www.ei-ahma.org/webs/lodging/1197/marketing1197.htm (13 July 1998).

Losyk, B. 1995. "How To Improve Employee Work Performance." *Restaurant USA* 15(2): 12–14.

———. 1995. "Turning Around Turnover: How to Keep the Best Employees." *Restaurant USA* 15(5): 34–35.

———. 1995. "Weighing Employee Performance: How to Conduct an Appraisal." *Restaurant USA* 15(9): 23–25.

Meyer, H. H., E. Kay, and J. R. P. French. 1965. "Split Roles in Performance Appraisal." *Harvard Business Review* (Jan.–Feb.): 123.

Morey, R. C. and D. A. Dittman. "Evaluating a Hotel GM's Performance: A Case Study in Benchmarking." *The Cornell Quarterly* 36(5): 30–35.

Stone, A. 1997. "Retention Span." *Restaurant & Institutions*, August 1.

Recommended Web Sites

1. Software-Aided Performance Management: www.knowledgepoint.com/hr/lbwhite.html
2. HRTools.com: www.knowledgepoint.com/hr/tool-home.html
3. PerformanceReview.com: www.performancereview.com/pfhtm/2body.htm
4. PerformanZone Navigator: www.reinforce.com/navigator.htm
5. The Common-Metric System: Performance Appraisal: www.pstc.com/brochures/Perform.html

Endnotes

1. See H. H. Meyer, E. Kay, and J. R. P. French, "Split Roles in Performance Appraisal," *Harvard Business Review* (Jan.–Feb. 1965): 123, for this classic article.
2. Hay Group, "Facts and Figures," *Human Resource Executive* 2, no. 8 (1988): 58.
3. Robert H. Woods and James F. Macaulay, "Rx for Turnover: Retention Programs that Work," *The Cornell H.R.A. Quarterly* 30, no. 1 (1989): 79.
4. Nicole G. Castagna, "Help Wanted," *Restaurants and Institutions*. May 1, 1997. www.rimag.com/09/help.htm (10 April 1998).
5. Ibid.
6. Linda Micco, "Retaining Core Workers Challenges Many U.S. Employers," *HR News Online*. June 19, 1998. www.shrm.org/hrnews/articles/061998.htm (23 June 1998).
7. C. L. Hughes, "Why Employees Stay Is More Critical Than Why They Leave," *Personnel Journal* 66, no. 10 (1987): 19, 22, 24, 28.
8. B. M. Meglino and A. S. DeNisi, "Realistic Job Previews: Some Thoughts on Their More Effective Use in Managing the Flow of Human Resources," *Human Resource Planning* 10, no. 3 (1987): 157–166.
9. Ibid.

Discussion Questions

1. What are some of the reasons why many human resources managers dislike performance appraisals?
2. Explain the differences between the development appraisal and the performance appraisal.
3. How much impact should the employee have in setting his or her performance goals? Discuss the reasons why.
4. Discuss what activities need to take place and what information you need to collect to prepare for the appraisal session.
5. What information should be on the performance planning guide?
6. Identify the steps in the appraisal session.
7. Describe three different methods of performance appraisals. Which do you prefer? Explain why, and be specific.
8. Explain the benefits of a 360-degree performance appraisal when used in the hospitality industry.

9. Discuss three mistakes that you might make in conducting performance appraisals and how each could be avoided.
10. Explain how job previews might be used as a retention tool. What are their advantages and disadvantages?
11. Think of eight different incentive programs you might use in the hospitality operation you are managing. List them and tell why each would help increase the longevity of your work force.

Chapter 9

Discipline, Counseling, and Exiting the Organization

 **Industry Advisor**

Ron Meliker, *Vice President of Human Resources, Sunbelt Beverage Corporation*

"Anyone can hold the helm when the sea is calm."

—Pubilius

"When dealing with people, remember you are not dealing with creatures of logic, but with creatures of emotion."

—Dale Carnegie

INTRODUCTION

How many of you have had the unpleasant task of disciplining or terminating an employee who worked for you? Do you remember how you felt the first time you fired someone? We do. And we imagine every hospitality manager remembers the feelings of anxiety he or she felt before that termination meeting. We have had to discipline our employees for being late, for not showing up for their shift, for poor performance, for being rude to the guests in our operations, and even for not using proper hygiene before they came to work. The emotions that build up inside you are dreadful; you find yourself filled with anxiety, uneasiness, and concern. Although you will never look forward to disciplinary and termination actions, we hope that in this chapter we provide some insight into transforming discipline from punishment to constructive criticism—constructive for both the people we manage and the hospitality operations we have a responsibility towards.

At the conclusion of this chapter you will be able to:

1. Describe the rights of both management and employees in a hospitality organization.
2. Identify the purpose of a code of conduct and a fair treatment policy for a hospitality organization.
3. Understand what constitutes sexual harassment.
4. Discuss the importance of protecting your employees and customers from workplace violence.
5. Implement the steps in the corrective action process.
6. Discuss the purpose of a discipline policy for a hospitality organization.
7. Explain the benefits of corrective action for hospitality organizations in the new century.
8. Describe the roles of performance counseling in the discipline process.

9. Implement termination procedures.
10. Explain the legal implications included in wrongful discharge lawsuits.
11. Describe the importance and understand the value of the exit interview.

CORRECTIVE ACTION

Because our employees are human, procedures for taking **corrective action** need to be part of our employment policies of our hospitality organizations. If our people always abided by the rules we developed for the operation of our properties, and if they never performed below the established performance standards, there would be no need for corrective actions. But unfortunately, until that day, a sound human resources textbook must include this chapter.

The purpose of the information in this section is to provide you, the manager with human resources responsibilities, with general guidelines for the establishment and implementation of corrective actions. In "the next chapter" we are focusing our attention on employee behaviors. When employee behavior is not what we need it to be, we seek to correct that behavior as opposed to disciplining the person who exhibited the behavior.

It would be impossible to include all of the situations in which you will find yourself, in the hospitality workplace. Everything we discuss in this section needs to be tempered with your discretion as manager. There are few disciplinary situations that are either black or white. In most situations, you will need to carefully weigh all the facts before reaching any conclusions that might have an adverse effect on both the individual(s) involved and your credibility as a fair, impartial human resources manager.

> **INDUSTRY EXPERTS SPEAK**
>
> Ron Meliker explains that since the mid-1990s the focus has changed from the concept of "discipline" to the concept of "corrective action." Discipline carries with it the feeling of punishment, it is negative in focus. Think of a child who does something inappropriate. Do we punish that child by putting him or her in "time out" or possibly spanking? What we really want to achieve (with children and our employees) is behavior modification. When they do something incorrect or inappropriate, our job as managers is to take corrective action so that the behavior does not reoccur. We seek to change negative behaviors to positive behaviors. Corrective action is improving upon a person's behavior, modifying negative behavior. It is viewed by employees as a positive action.

MANAGEMENT RIGHTS AND THE RIGHTS OF OUR EMPLOYEES

Management has the right to expect employees to abide by the workplace **code of conduct** and to meet the hospitality organization's performance standards. We would like our people to be conscientious and cooperative at all times when in our employ. However, it is necessary to develop a code of conduct, such as the example found in Table 9-1. These rules guide our employees in maintaining positive relationships with our guests, with the management team, and with each other. These rules also help to ensure a safe work environment for all concerned.

The consequences of infraction vary with each rule, as some are more critical to the safety of persons in the hospitality operation than others. Possession of a weapon; fighting; possession, use, or sale of an illegal substance; and failure to follow safety procedures—all are vio-

TABLE 9-1 Code of Conduct

The intent of this policy is to openly communicate to all employees Premier Beverage standards of conduct as a means of avoiding the occurrence of undesired conduct. Such policies and procedures are necessary for the orderly operation of our business, and for the protection and proper treatment of all employees. Employees are therefore urged to use reasonable judgment at all times and to seek supervisory advice in any doubtful situation.

The Company does not necessarily follow a "progressive discipline" system where a less severe type of discipline must be imposed before more serious disciplinary procedures are used. Instead, employment with the Company is at-will and can be terminated at any time with or without cause and with or without notice. The types of discipline listed below may be imposed in any order, at Company discretion, based on the facts and circumstances existing in each case. Supervisors should strive for consistency in disciplinary matters, and when a new, uncertain, or unusual situation occurs, the human resources department should be consulted.

To insure the consistent processing of disciplinary actions, the human resources department along with senior management will be responsible for the proper handling of such matters, including the assurance that employee rights are protected and that appropriate action is taken when circumstances warrant. Supervisory personnel should therefore consult with the human resources department and/or senior management prior to the implementation of disciplinary procedures whenever there is any question or doubt as to the proper action.

The illustrations of unacceptable conduct cited below are to provide specific and exemplary reasons for initiating disciplinary action, and to alert employees to the more common types of employment conduct violations. However, because human conduct is unpredictable, no attempt has been made here to establish a complete and comprehensive list of such conduct violations. Should there arise instances of unacceptable conduct not included in the following list, the Company may likewise find it necessary and appropriate to initiate disciplinary action.

Theft or inappropriate removal or possession of property

Falsification of timekeeping records or falsification or misrepresentation of other company records, reports, or documents

Violation of Company Drug or Alcohol Policies, including any Second Chance Agreements as adopted at the sole discretion of the Company

Fighting or threatening violence in the workplace

Boisterous or disruptive activity in the workplace

Negligence or improper conduct leading to damage to property

Insubordination or other disrespectful conduct

Violation of safety or health rules

Smoking in prohibited areas

Sexual or other unlawful harassment

Possession of dangerous or unauthorized materials, such as explosives or firearms, in the workplace or in Company vehicles or personal vehicles during working hours

Excessive absenteeism or a pattern of absenteeism or any absence without notice

Excessive tardiness or a pattern of excessive tardiness

Unauthorized absence from workstation during the workday

Sleeping on the job during working hours

Unauthorized use of telephones, mail system, or other company-owned equipment, including personal computers or Company vehicles

Unauthorized disclosure of business "secrets" or confidential information

Violation of personnel policies or work rules

Violation of Company Ethic Policies

Violation of Company computer usage and security policy

Unsatisfactory performance or conduct

Permitting the unauthorized use of a Company vehicle or allowing unauthorized passengers in a Company vehicle without prior approval

Making false or misrepresented claims for benefits provided by the Company

Fraudulently using the SUNBELT Benefit Programs for the benefit of individuals not eligible or not covered under the plans.

(Courtesy of Premier Beverage Company of Florida; SUNBELT Beverage Corporation)

lations that could result in personal harm or injury to either other employees or guests. The consequences of these violations might include **suspension** pending investigation, possible **termination**, and, in the case of illegal substances, prosecution.

Insubordination, tardiness, no-shows, and violation of some property rules (such as smoking in nondesignated areas [Figure 9-1]) could carry less-severe consequences. Some of the **employment-at-will** litigations, however, have found otherwise. Tardiness and absences are usually covered in a separate company policy statement. For other rule infractions, the severity of the violation is taken into account, and normal corrective action procedures established for your hospitality organization would be put into effect.

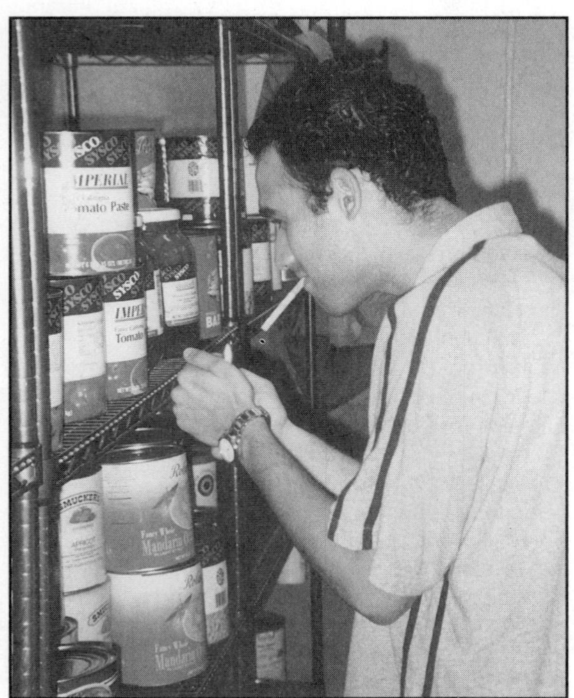

FIGURE 9-1 Smoking in prohibited areas would be a violation of the code of conduct.

Before a hospitality organization can expect its employees to obey the code of conduct that governs their behavior, the rules must be characterized by the following:

- They must be developed in a consistent manner.
- They must be written clearly.
- They must make sense; be valid.
- They must be communicated clearly to all employees.
- Middle management must be trained to understand the disciplinary procedures for each rule infraction and administer them consistently.
- Acknowledgment of receipt must be made in writing by each employee.

Consistency and communication are required if you are to successfully implement any corrective action for rule infractions. Without these two elements, disciplinary procedures that lead to termination could easily result in a **wrongful discharge** suit being filed against your hospitality organization by the disgruntled employee.

Hospitality management also has the right to expect job efficiency from each employee. Here is where the rights of our employees and several other human resources functions come into play. The employee needs to be placed in a job that is compatible with his or her abilities and skills. In addition, each employee should have been adequately oriented and trained for his or her job tasks. Your employees also are entitled to a fair and timely appraisal of their performance. When these systems are in place, the need to discipline for poor performance levels is greatly reduced. At times, however, failure to meet performance standards will result in corrective actions.

What else do our people have a right to expect from us, their managers and employers? They have a right to have any complaints and problems listened to in an impartial manner, and to have these complaints and problems promptly resolved. If employees do not feel that the matter has been satisfactorily resolved by the immediate supervisor, then the employees have a right to express their concern to a higher management level while simultaneously following the appropriate chain of command.

SEXUAL HARASSMENT

Sexual harassment can be defined as unwelcome conduct of a sexual nature that is perceived by the recipient to be offensive. It is one form of workplace harassment and sex discrimination that is in violation of Title VII of the Civil Rights Act of 1964. Section 1604.11 Sexual Harassment reads:

> "Harassment on the basis of sex is a violation of Sec. 703 of Title VII. Unwelcome sexual advances, requests for sexual favors, and other verbal or physical conduct of a sexual nature constitute sexual harassment when (1) submission to such conduct is made either explicitly or implicitly a term or condition of an individual's employment, (2) submission to or rejection of such conduct by an individual is used as the basis for employment decisions affecting such individual, or (3) such conduct has the purpose or effect of unreasonable interfering with an individual's work performance or creating an intimidating, hostile, or offensive working environment."

Sexual harassment then is discrimination and is illegal under not only federal, but state and local laws.

Sexual harassment may include a wide range of subtle and not-so-subtle behaviors, such as

- sexual jokes and innuendo
- leering, whistling, or touching
- unwanted sexual advances
- display, in the workplace, of sexually suggestive objects or pictures
- verbal abuse of a sexual nature
- requests for sexual favors
- commentary about an individual's body
- insulting comments or gestures
- asking a coworker for a date

In other words, your workplace should be free of any sexual connotations or overtones. It should be sexually secure. You and your employees must become sensitive to your own behaviors and how your behavior is received by other individuals in the hospitality organization.

There are two forms of sexual harassment and any lawsuit filed must be recognized as either/or. One is **quid pro quo** and the other is **hostile environment**. *Quid pro quo* is a Latin term that means "something for something." Employer demands that an employee must have sexual relations with him or her to get a promotion would be an example of quid pro quo. But so would an employer's demand that an employee dress a certain way in order to maintain job benefits, such as evenings off, be considered quid pro quo harassment. It is also illegal to retaliate against an employee who has filed a sexual harassment complaint.

Hostile work environment is one where an employee's work performance is inhibited by verbal or physical conduct of a sexual nature. This might include such things as sexual language, sexual jokes, unwanted touching, and/or suggestive comments. This environment is more difficult to define as there are no specific set standards for what constitutes hostile working environment. If sexually offensive behaviors in the workplace make it difficult or unpleasant for an employee to perform his or her job, then the environment is hostile. The EEOC will look at the following factors in making their determination of hostile working environment:

1. Whether the conduct was verbal or physical or both
2. How frequently it was repeated
3. Whether the conduct was hostile or patently offensive
4. Whether the alleged harasser was a co-worker or supervisor
5. Whether others joined in perpetrating the harassment
6. Whether the harassment was directed at more than one individual[1]

A victim of sexual harassment could be an applicant, employee, outside vendor, consultant, or customer. A victim may be a woman or a man. In March of 1998 the U.S. Supreme Court ruled that employers may be held liable for same-sex harassment under Title VII. The types of unacceptable conduct that we just discussed apply not only to the workplace but to conduct during business meetings, on business trips, and even at business-related social events such as company picnics. A victim of sexual harassment does not necessarily have to be the person harassed. It could be a third party who was offended by the behavior of two other individuals. For sexual harassment to have occurred, the conduct has to be unwelcome. Unwelcome means that the victim neither initiated nor solicited the conduct. Sexual harassment is illegal if:

- in order to keep your job, you feel you have to go along with it.
- in order to influence job-related decisions, such as promotions, good performance reviews, career development opportunities, and/or pay raises, you feel you have to go along with it.
- you are having difficulty focusing on your work.

Sexual harassment is illegal even if no one else sees the harassment occurring. It is illegal even if your job was not terminated. It is illegal even if you went along with it for awhile but clearly did not want to. It is illegal even if it happened only once, but it was serious (the unwanted touching of body parts). Sexual harassment is illegal, and the law still protects you in all of the situations identified here.

In June of 1998 the U.S. Supreme Court reached two landmark decisions in the area of sexual harassment. In *Faragher v. City of Boca Raton (97-282)* the Court stated that employers are always potentially liable for a supervisor's sexual misconduct toward an employee. In *Burlington Industries v. Ellerth (97-569)* the Court said that an employer can be sued even if the worker did not suffer an adverse employment impact. For an employer to succeed in litigation, they would have to prove that they "exercised reasonable care to prevent or correct promptly any sexually harassing behavior" and that "the employee unreasonably failed to take advantage of any preventive or corrective opportunities provided by the employer or to avoid harm otherwise."[2]

INDUSTRY EXPERTS SPEAK

Ron Meliker believes that these two rulings will have serious effects on how employers go about educating their work force on sexual harassment issues and company policy.
"The focus is going to be on your complaint procedures and awareness training for not only supervisors, but all employees with special emphasis on the companys formal complaint procedure. I see companies tightening up on their sexual harassment procedures. Conducting mass education of the work force to reinforce the companies anti-harassment

policy. Training managers to ensure that complaints are followed up in a timely manner which conforms to company procedure. Training employees so that they are educated in this area and clearly understand their rights and how to file a complaint should it become necessary. Furthermore, we will need to do a better job of keeping records and documentation of employees who have used our complaint process effectively thereby maintaining evidence that our companies policy on sexual harassment is clear and known by all employees. I believe this will become the new focus in the area of sexual harassment . . . NOT what sexual harassment is . . . but, how do we manage it professionally and legally."

Sexual Harassment Policies

All hospitality organizations should have a well-written policy on sexual harassment such as the one found in Table 9-2. State clearly the hospitality organization's intention to eliminate any form of harassment. It is best when the policy includes a very broad definition of the type of conduct that your company considers sexual harassment. Every employee should be reminded to refrain from sexual harassment and to immediately make management aware of any incidence. Managers should be held responsible for taking immediate corrective action in dealing with any incidence of sexual harassment brought to their attention.

The policy should clearly identify the **disciplinary actions**, up to termination, to which

TABLE 9-2 Policy Prohibiting Harassment

Premier Beverage is committed to maintaining a work environment that is free of discrimination. In keeping with this commitment, we will not tolerate unlawful harassment of our employees by anyone, including any supervisor, co-worker, or third party. Harassment consists of unwelcome conduct, whether verbal, physical or visual, that is based on a person's race, color, national origin, religion, age, sex, gender or disability. Harassment which affects job benefits, interferes with an individual's work performance, or creates an intimidating, hostile or offensive work environment will not be tolerated.

Harassment may include derogatory remarks, epithets, offensive jokes, the display or circulation of offensive printed or visual material, or offensive physical actions. Sexual harassment deserves special mention. Unwelcome sexual advances, requests of sexual favors, or other physical, verbal or visual conduct based on sex constitutes harassment when (1) submission to the conduct is required as a term or condition of employment or is the basis for employment action, or (2) the conduct unreasonably interferes with an individual's work performance or creates an intimidating, hostile or offensive workplace. Sexual harassment may include sexual propositions, innuendo, suggestive comments, sexually oriented jokes or teasing, or unwelcome physical contact such as patting, pinching, or brushing against another.

All Company employees are responsible for helping to enforce this policy against harassment. Any employee who has been the victim of prohibited harassment or who has witnessed such harassment must immediately notify their supervisor so the situation can be promptly investigated and remedied. If it is the supervisor who is responsible for the harassment or reporting the situation to the supervisor fails to remedy the situation, complaints of harassment must immediately be reported to a member of senior management or the human resources department. It is the Company's policy to investigate all harassment complaints thoroughly and promptly. To the fullest extent practicable, the Company will maintain the confidentiality of those involved. If an investigation confirms that harassment has occurred, the Company will take corrective action, which may include discipline up to and including immediate termination of employment. The Company also forbids retaliation against anyone who has reported harassment or who has cooperated in the investigation of harassment complaints.

(Courtesy of Premier Beverage Company of Florida; SUNBELT Beverage Corporation)

offenders will be subjected. It should also contain clearly written guidelines for what steps to follow if an employee feels that he or she is a victim of sexual harassment. Employees need to be reassured that there will be no retaliation against them for reporting harassment in the workplace. Procedures for investigating sexual harassment claims need to be clearly defined, identified, and disseminated to your work force (Table 9-3). Training and awareness programs need to be conducted on a frequent basis.

As a manager with human resources responsibilities in the hospitality industry it will be up to you to ensure that this policy is adhered to consistently and fairly. The best program for sexual harassment is prevention. There is a wide variety of training tools and materials available on this subject that are readily available and cost-effective. Make it clear to your employees that sexual harassment *will not be tolerated*. Implementation of programs to prevent sexual harassment requires time, effort, and financial resources. Commitment must come from the highest levels of management. Only through an aggressive proactive approach can sexual harassment in the hospitality workplace be eliminated and prevented.

TABLE 9-3 Sexual Harassment Complaint Procedure

1. Where any such verbal or physical conduct interferes with any employee's work performance or creates an intimidating, hostile or offensive work environment, the offended employee is urged to promptly report the incident to his or her department supervisor, department manager, or human resources department, or the State President. If you are not comfortable making the complaint to any of the above, you can report to Sunbelt's Vice President of Human Resources, or to any other member of senior management.
2. If a complaint involves a manager or supervisor, the complaint shall be filed directly with the next higher level in the company.
3. All complaints will be handled in a timely and confidential manner. In no event will information concerning a complaint be released by the Company to anyone within the Company who is not involved with the investigation. Nor will anyone involved be permitted to discuss the subject outside the investigation. The purpose of this provision is to protect the confidentiality of the employee who files a complaint, to encourage the reporting of any incidents of sexual harassment, and to protect the reputation of any employee wrongfully charged with sexual harassment.
4. Investigation of a complaint will normally include meeting with the parties involved and any named or apparent witnesses. Employees shall be given an impartial and fair hearing. All employees shall be protected from coercion, intimidation, retaliation, interference or discrimination for filing a complaint or assisting in an investigation.
5. If the investigation reveals that the complaint is valid, prompt attention and disciplinary action designed to stop the harassment immediately and to prevent its recurrence will be taken.

The Company recognizes that the question of whether a particular action or incident is sexual harassment requires a factual determination based on all facts in the matter. Because of the nature of this type of discrimination, the Company recognizes also that false accusations of sexual harassment can have serious effects on innocent individuals. We trust that all employees of the Company will continue to act responsibly to establish and maintain a pleasant working environment, free of discrimination, for all.

(Courtesy of Premier Beverage Company of Florida; SUNBELT Beverage Corporation)

Claims of workplace harassment are not always based on sexual harassment. Under the law all protected groups, such as age groups, religious groups, racial groups, could bring a similar claim against your hospitality organization. Work environments may not be racially hostile, religiously hostile, or age hostile any more than they can be sexually hostile. Make sure that all your employees understand this as well as the seriousness of any type of harassment claim.

WORKPLACE VIOLENCE

Our employees have a right to expect a safe working environment, safe from violence committed by nonstrangers. **Workplace violence** is defined as an intentional use of physical force against another person or oneself that occurs in the workplace and either results in or has a high possibility of resulting in injury or death. By 1995, workplace violence had become the second major cause of death on the job, surpassed only by automobile accidents. It is estimated that more than one million employees are assaulted and more than one thousand are murdered each year in acts of workplace violence.[3] Even so, relatively few employers have established effective programs to deal with this problem.

Some hospitality managers have yet to recognize that workplace violence is their problem. "Question: What do a pawnshop owner, convenience store clerk, psychologist, two sanitation managers, tavern owner, fisherman, cook, two cab drivers, furniture store owner, restaurant manager, maintenance supervisor, videostore owner and postal carrier all have in common? Answer: According to the Centers for Disease Control (CDC), all were murdered at work in the same week."[4] There are a number of reasons why it is important to institute programs and policies that seek to protect your employees.

- Under federal and state OSHA regulations employers have a general duty to "furnish to each employee, employment and a place of employment which is free from recognized hazards that are causing, or likely to cause, death or serious harm to the employee."
- Just one violent incident can create high costs for the employer in medical and psychiatric care, lost business and productivity, higher insurance rates, as well as the potential liability suits.
- Employers may be held liable on the grounds of negligent hiring or negligent retention of an employee who has a known background or tendency towards violence.
- Threats and other abusive behaviors are no longer being tolerated in the workplace.
- It is the right thing to do. As a manager with human resources responsibilities in the hospitality industry you have a moral obligation to provide a safe workplace for both your employees and your customers.

We have already discussed the importance of careful preemployment screening in Chapter 5. While you are checking references, be sure to inquire about any prior acts of violence or temperament. It is always better to screen out potential problems than to have to deal with them once hired. In addition you should utilize your community resources for programs that already exist to help you develop your workplace violence plans. Invite local police to your place of business so that they get to know who you are and become familiar with your property or operation. Frequently law enforcement experts will provide crime prevention programs and can teach your employees how to avoid being a victim.

Institute and review security procedures (Figure 9-2) for prevention of workplace vio-

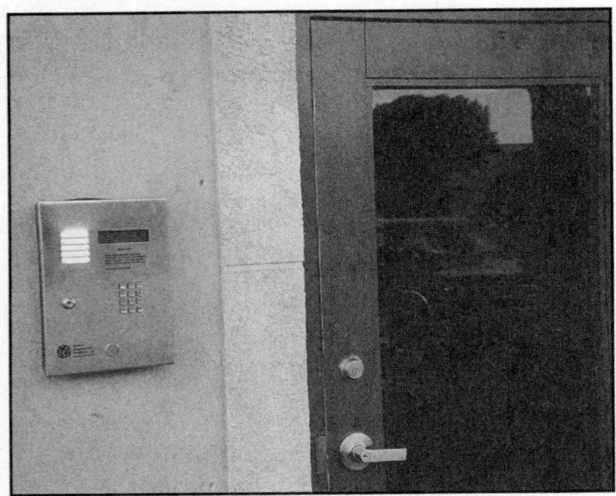

FIGURE 9-2 Securing receiving entrances is a security measure that you could implement in your hospitality organization.

lence as well as other crimes. Provide appropriate training to floor supervisors and line managers on appropriate ways to handle employee discipline, counseling, and termination. Train them how to recognize early warnings signs of a troubled employee. Adopt a zero tolerance policy toward unacceptable behavior. Threats about violence are not to be taken lightly or as something to joke about. Make sure that everyone is clear as to what your hospitality organization considers workplace violence. Make sure that management understands what zero tolerance really means.

It is unfortunate that workplace violence is a significant enough issue in society today that it has to be included within the context of this text. As a manager with human resources responsibilities it is important that you are aware that the potential for workplace violence is real. It is equally important that all employees know how and where to report acts of violence. Prepare some type of a threat-management plan so that if a threat ever does occur in your hospitality organization, you are well prepared to handle the situation.

THE DISCIPLINE PROCESS APPLIED

One key to successful implementation lies with a well-written **discipline policy**. This written policy will be located in the human resources policy manual. Each employee at time of hire should receive and sign for a copy of your company's policy for discipline. A second key aspect, and one over which you, the manager with human resources responsibilities has control, is to handle all potential disciplinary problems as soon as they occur. Because the discipline function is so distasteful, some managers have a tendency to put off these activities. Frequently, we recognize that a problem exits, but we fail to act upon it quickly. Delaying disciplinary actions can only magnify a problem situation and make it worse.

Perhaps we notice that Jennifer in the salad department has been late in preparing for dinner, or that Tony did not show for his job at the front desk. Instead of asking Jennifer what the problem is the first time she is late, we might wait, thinking that the problem will not reoccur. And we fail to ask Tony the next day if everything is all right and tell him how much we missed having him at his post. Before too long, Jennifer is never on time preparing for dinner, and when you do confront her she is angry and upset. "Why haven't you said something sooner? I didn't think it was creating a problem for the waitstaff, or you would have told me." And Tony, thinking no one notices—or even worse, cares—when he calls in sick, starts missing one day a week. By the time we call him in, we are upset and frustrated because of the extra work load it has placed upon the rest of the front desk staff. We now have to justify the overtime on everyone's time cards and are angry because this might reflect on our personal evaluations.

We can only blame ourselves. We must be timely and efficient in our human resources

FIGURE 9-3 Don't delay taking corrective action. Take action immediately. *(Courtesy of Strongbow Inn, Valparaiso, IN)*

management responsibilities (Figure 9-3). You can't ignore a problem and expect that it will go away. It won't! Good communication skills and practices implemented in a timely manner go a long way in reducing the need for implementing disciplinary policies. Another good method for avoiding the need for discipline is employee meetings. At these sessions, the concerns of our employees can be voiced. Frequently, we are unaware of some of the problems that can exist. These meetings also provide us with a forum for explaining new procedures and policies as well as soliciting suggestions from our people.

Remember that the purpose of the discipline policy for your hospitality organization is to provide the management with guidelines when communicating with an employee who fails to meet your organization's standards of conduct or performance. These guidelines provide a means for consistently applying and enforcing the established code of conduct and performance standards.

The Steps to Implementation

When an employee violates the organization's code of conduct or performs at a substandard level, there is a series of corrective actions that might take place. It is important that these actions occur in a fair and consistent manner. As noted earlier, there are certain, serious violations that could result in immediate suspension or termination.

Any action to discipline is a serious management decision and should be preceded by a careful, thorough investigation. As the manager with human resources responsibilities, you must be careful not to make a decision regarding either the incident or possible disciplinary action until you have gathered *all* the facts. Acting without full knowledge of the conditions surrounding the incident may result in the disciplinary action being overturned by arbitration (if your organization is unionized) or in a court of law. Another option would be to use an Alternative Dispute Resolution (ADR), which we discuss later in this chapter. If the incident requires the employee to be removed from his or her job, the employee should be suspended, pending the investigation. However, if the employee is exempt under the Fair Labor Standard Act (FLSA), suspension may not be the appropriate course of action. Rarely should an employee be terminated immediately. Oftentimes, situations are not as they really appear at first. Immediate termination puts your hospitality organization at risk for a wrongful discharge suit.

Part of your investigation will include the identification of any other employees or other persons involved. Each of these individuals should be questioned in the presence of another management person in addition to yourself. The person being questioned should also be permitted to have someone else present with him or her. If the investigation includes a guest or guests, it is useful to obtain a written report of the incident directly, including an identificacation of the employee(s) involved. If a police investigation is called for (theft or illegal substance), you will need to provide space for them to conduct their interviews. A thorough investigation and questioning of persons involved is needed for both performance and code of conduct violations.

Next, a meeting is called with the employee to present the results of your investigation. Again, it is important that a second member of management attend this meeting who will separately document the proceedings. The names of other employees whom you questioned are never revealed. The focus of this meeting is to be on the problem, not on the person. The meeting should be conducted in a quiet location with no interruptions. The following events occur during the meeting:

- ***Identification of problem.***
- ***Identification of specific rule or performance standard that was violated.*** It may be that the employee did not know or understand the rule or standard. Remember that it is management's responsibility to present the code of conduct and performance standards in a clear manner and to ensure that they are both communicated and consistently enforced throughout the hospitality organization. Your people should not only understand what your expectations of them are, but what the consequences are of not meeting those expectations.
- ***Listening to the employee.*** Remember that the goal of this session is to correct the problem, not humiliate or punish the employee. Even though you have facts obtained from other individuals, you still need to hear from that employee the reasons for consistently being late for work, or why the individual was rude to a guest the evening before. At this time you can also make sure that the employee understands the importance of being on time, or what constitutes unacceptable behavior with the guests in the hospitality operation.
- ***Reaching a mutual agreement or solution.*** Here the alternatives are explored for resolving the problem. The focus should be on getting the employee to modify his or her behavior so that it meets management's expectations. Be sure to include a timeline. For example, "the performance needs to be corrected in the next 30 days" or "the performance needs to be corrected immediately." A plan of action should be developed that would result in a solution to the problem. Once this has been accomplished, you ask the employee to:

  —***Summarize*** both the problem and the mutually agreed upon solution. By requesting that the employee summarize what just occurred, you have an opportunity to confirm that he or she has a clear understanding of the events of the disciplinary meeting. A time should be established when the two of you will get together to evaluate the progress of the action plan. Always stick to the agreed upon time schedule. If you don't the employee may get the impression that you don't view this as an important issue; or that performance has improved to an acceptable level, which may or may not be the case.

- ***Notification to employee of necessary formal actions that need to occur.*** Even if this is the employee's first violation, documentation still needs to be made of your corrective action meeting. The extent of the documentation depends upon the severity of the violation. If the violation is minor and a first time occurrence, a handwritten note in the employee's file stating the date, incident, and action plan established is sufficient. This information can serve as a reminder of what was agreed upon by both parties when the evaluatory meeting is held to review action plan progress.

INDUSTRY EXPERTS SPEAK

"It is important, from a human resources perspective, that managers adhere to policy when taking corrective actions with employees," points out Ron Meliker. "The first time the employee and supervisor have a meeting regarding a corrective action, documentation is a must. Sometimes it is the tendency of the supervisor to say, 'I need to make sure you correct your behavior on this incident and that it doesn't happen again. However, I won't put anything in your file about this incident this time. We will keep this just between us.'

"We use a 60-day probationary period for many of our corrective actions. It is up to the employee's supervisor to record the initial conversation and keep track of the employee's behavior (either improved or not improved) throughout the 60 day period. At the end of 60 days the employee should have come up to standards. Either way the supervisor must sit down with the employee, again documenting the discussion and actions taken. If a supervisor comes to me, say 30 days after the probationary period ends and says that the employee should be terminated, I will ask for the recorded documentation. If the supervisor has failed to document the employee's performance at the end of the 60 day period I have to assume that the employee ***has*** come up to standards and the employee stays. This procedure mandates that the supervisors bring closure, in written fashion, at the end of the 60 day probationary period. It is also important to note that coming up to standards by the end of the probationary period isn't enough. The employee must then maintain this acceptable level of performance if they are to avoid termination."

Follow-up and reinforcement of the action plan should take place after the corrective action meeting takes place. The role you assume is now one of performance counselor. The action plan has been developed, but you must assist the employee through counseling activities in guiding the individual's behavior toward acceptable standards.

Too frequently, in day-to-day operations, we forget to acknowledge acceptable behavior (Figure 9-4). If we see that the employee is back on target and successfully fulfilling the requirements of the action plan, we fail to communicate that message. It is no wonder then that our employees perceive discipline and corrective actions as punishment. Acknowledging desired performance and behavior would go a long way in changing that perception. Table 9-4 identifies the components of an effective corrective action meeting.

The Corrective Actions

The specific actions that you design into the disciplinary policy of your hospitality organiza-

FIGURE 9-4 Be sure to acknowledge acceptable behavior. *(Courtesy of Chili's Grill & Bar, Brinker International)*

TABLE 9-4 Requirements for Effective Corrective Action Meeting

Timeliness: Meet as soon as possible following the alleged infraction. Have another management witness.

Objectivity: Focus the meeting on the behavior and not on the individual.

Investigation: Be certain to interview witnesses and obtain ***all*** the facts.

Discipline: Be sure that corrective actions taken are consistent with prior incidents.

Document: Make accurate notes defining the infraction and action(s) taken.

tion should be carefully selected in view of the mission statement, goals, and objectives that guide the decision-making process for policy determination. The procedures used vary from hospitality organization to hospitality organization. Table 9-5 contains an example of this type of policy.

Corrective action steps typically number between three and five ranging from a series of verbal warning(s) to a series of written warnings. Your company might consider including probation as an additional step in this process. Termination should only be taken as a last resort after all other alternatives have been exhausted, or when the violation is too serious for other options to be considered. Written warnings are issued after a verbal warning has been documented and the behavior or performance does not improve. The written warning is prepared using a format similar to the one shown in Table 9-6. The policy for disciplinary actions provides management with guidelines for the implementation of actions.

THE PURPOSE OF DISCIPLINE

The intent of disciplinary actions has changed along with the increasing labor shortages and our ever-increasing need to retain, not dismiss, our employees. Twenty years ago our disciplinary actions were seen merely a way to document "bad" employees and to prevent a lawsuit. It was not uncommon for managers, wanting to rid themselves of an employee, to initiate disciplinary actions to justify the intended termination of that employee. Though this was never viewed as cost-effective (recall from our discussion of training that even the short-term employee has a cost investment made in them), it was a simplified way of "cleaning house." Good human resources management? No. Not then and certainly not in "the next chapter."

Today, our disciplinary policies and procedures are designed to assist our employees in correcting unacceptable behavior or performance levels. A hospitality operation has to rely upon standards of conduct and performance to meet its organizational goals. Managers with human resources responsibilities must assume that an understanding of acceptable norms rest with them.

If one of our employees has violated a code of conduct by smoking in a nondesignated area, what is it that we, as managers, want to have occur? Do we want the person to be punished for his or her behavior? Or do we want the behavior to change to fit in with the accepted norms of the work environment? Similarly, if our bellperson can never be located when a guest is ready to be taken to his or her room, what do we want to have occur? Is it more important that the bellperson is verbally or more formally punished for his or her behavior, or that the next time a guest checks in that the bellperson is ready and waiting to show the guest to his or her room?

We think that most of you will agree that we want the deviant behavior to be altered so that it conforms with acceptable levels of conduct and performance. In order for that to occur, we need to obtain a commitment from

TABLE 9-5 Discipline Policy

TYPES OF DISCIPLINE

Typically, the first step before discipline begins is ordinarily Oral Counseling. After oral counseling, in those infrequent instances when an employee's job performance continues to be unsatisfactory, other forms of discipline described below are taken by the supervisor to assist the employee in improving his or her performance. These three types of discipline—written warning, final written warning, probation and termination—may occur in any order and at any time job performance or conduct is determined to be unsatisfactory. They do not necessarily coincide with the timing of the performance appraisal process.

ORAL COUNSELING

When an employee's job performance or behavior is considered unsatisfactory, the supervisor meets with the employee in one or more counseling sessions to:

- Identify areas in need of improvement.
- Encourage the employee to provide his or her perspective on the situation and to respond to the supervisor's comments.
- Communicate clearly to the employee what should be done to reach a satisfactory level of performance.
- Establish a reasonable period of time for improvement to occur and a date to review progress made by the employee.

The date of the oral counseling session will be recorded by the supervisor.

WRITTEN WARNING

The supervisor meets with the employee to:

- Review employee's overall performance.
- Identify areas in need of improvement.
- Review previous counseling concerning performance.
- Establish a reasonable period of time in which the employee will be allowed to improve performance.
- Make clear that failure to improve will result in placing the employee on final written warning, if not discharge, and the consequences of that step.

This warning step is also documented by the supervisor. A copy is provided to the employee and another is placed in the employee's personnel file.

FINAL WRITTEN WARNING or PERFORMANCE PROBATION

The supervisor meets with the employee to:

- Review the lack of progress against objectives outlined in prior written warnings, if any.
- Make clear the employee will be terminated for unsatisfactory performance if performance has not improved to a satisfactory level during or by the end of this written warning and/or probationary period.

If an employee's performance improves to a satisfactory level, he or she is removed from discipline status. The supervisor prepares a memo noting the performance improvement and the termination of counseling or written warning/probationary status. However, a recurrence of the same or a similar performance problem within twelve months of the expiration of a written warning and/or probationary period notice can be grounds for termination without another series of oral, written, and/or probationary warnings.

An employee on discipline status may consult with higher levels of supervision.

TERMINATION

In instances where job performance or behavior is unacceptable, the employee is terminated.

(Courtesy of Premier Beverage Company of Florida; SUNBELT Beverage Corporation)

TABLE 9-6 Notice of Disciplinary Action

Notice of Disciplinary Action
Sunbelt Beverage Corp.

Location:

Employee's Name: | Date:

Position: | Department:

THIS IS TO CONFIRM THE DISCIPLINARY ACTION AGAINST YOU FOR THE REASON BELOW:

Date of Occurrence(s):

Description of Circumstances:

Company's Standards (What is Expected of Employee):

Previous Action of Employee and/or Company:

Action Taken: Warning | | Suspension for Days | | Discharge | |

Future Action:

Witness' Signature: | Employee's Signature:

Remarks:

Department Head's Signature:

PER 12

Copies To:
- ☐ Employee
- ☐ Personnel Folder
- ☐ Director of Personnel

(Courtesy of Premier Beverage Company of Florida; SUNBELT Beverage Corporation)

the food preparer and the bellperson that a change in behavior will take place. Before they can make that commitment, an understanding needs to be made concerning both the problem and the action plan necessary to correct it.

INDUSTRY EXPERTS SPEAK

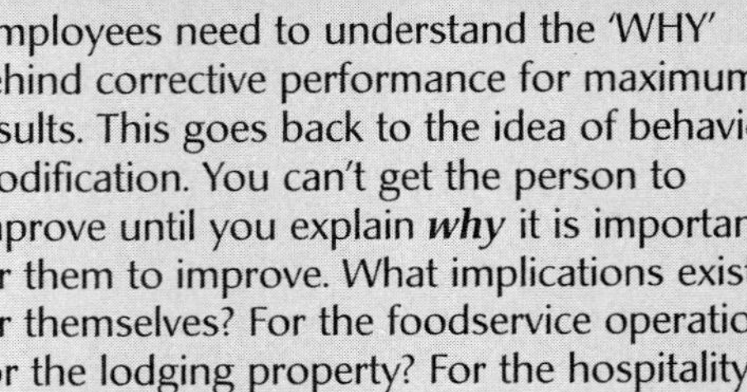

"Employees need to understand the 'WHY' behind corrective performance for maximum results. This goes back to the idea of behavior modification. You can't get the person to improve until you explain ***why*** it is important for them to improve. What implications exist for themselves? For the foodservice operation? For the lodging property? For the hospitality organization? If they don't modify their performance what effects will it have? Not just on themselves, but on all interested parties. Help put their behavior into perspective. Also have the employee suggest ways they think they can improve. Once you do this the employee is more likely to 'buy into' your suggestions, and also theirs, and make a greater personal commitment to improvement." —RON MELIKER

Progressive Discipline

The discussions in this chapter have been describing a corrective action approach to discipline that human resources professionals started using in the mid-1990s. Prior to that the concepts of **progressive discipline** or **positive discipline** were popular. These were terms for similar styles of discipline that emphasized constructive criticism and the return of the employee to the work environment as a productive member of the work force. They referred to a discipline approach that applied corrective measures by increasing degrees. They are designed to motivate an employee to correct their own behavior voluntarily without punitive measure. **Nonpunitive approaches** seek to avoid actions that could demoralize an employee and cause the work force to perceive management as cruel and unfair.

The concept of progressive discipline was first discussed in 1964.[5] Positive discipline is a three step progressive approach:

1. Verbal warning
2. Written planning
3. Decision-making leave (day off with pay)

Though a day off with pay sounds like an unusual disciplinary action, proponents believe in its effectiveness. During this day off, the employee is expected to decide whether to continue employment with the organization under the established rules and standards, or to terminate employment with the organization. If the employee decides to return and the behavior does not change, dismissal is the next action step.

It is these types of innovative approaches to human resources management that you, in "the next chapter," must be alert to. The problem with traditional, punitive approaches to discipline is that they fail to foster commitment to organizational goals. They are typically viewed as unfair by our employees and are often susceptible to union arbitration. It is hard for unions to argue against a system that provides the employee with a paid day off. In addition, traditional systems perpetuate managers' fear and distaste of the disciplinary process, which means that problem areas are not likely to be acted upon as quickly as they are brought to the attention of management. By using a more innovative approach to discipline, we can stop viewing the process as a way to document for eventual termination, but rather as a way to save valuable human resources for our hospitality organization.

CLASSIFICATION OF DISCIPLINE PROBLEMS

A word needs to be mentioned about the different types of discipline problems you will encounter. So far in our discussion we have treated problems in behavior or performance as though there existed a typical employee who acted and reacted to the work environment like all other typical employees. People are not alike (Figure 9-5), and thus the motivations for their behavior or performance problems vary. Thus, not only do you need to keep the severity of the violation in mind as you apply the corrective action process, but your investigation should also attempt to seek the reason the problem occurred. Problems occur within three frameworks:

- Employee knows what is required, but chooses to ignore the requirements.
- Employee breaks the rules, but does not understand the rules or have the training necessary to meet required standards.
- Employee tries or intends to meet requirements, but is incapable of doing so due to circumstances that he or she cannot control.

Employees in the third situation need our help and understanding so that they can return as functioning members of our work force again. Some of these individuals need to be referred to the **Employee Assistance Programs (EAPs)** that we discuss in Chapter 13. These programs are designed to assist employees with personal problems such as alcohol or drug dependency. The help required by these employees goes beyond what we are trained for as hospitality managers. The best help we can provide is our support and referral to professionals who can assist these individuals in overcoming their problems.

There are other reasons that might be responsible for employee misconduct that will require our careful attention. Is the employee late because the individual lost his or her driver's license and now has to rely on public transportation? Does the employee have a

FIGURE 9-5 People's motivations for their behaviors vary. *(Courtesy of Strongbow Inn, Valparaiso, IN)*

chronic illness such as asthma that is unsettled by the particular work location the person is in? Does the employee take longer-than-required breaks because he or she needs to take medication on a recurring basis? These are all situations that once understood by management can lead to productive employees who follow your hospitality organization's **rules of conduct** routinely.

ALTERNATIVES TO CORRECTIVE ACTION

Regardless of the cause of the problems, job performance is often negatively affected. Troubled employees affect both performance levels and the quality of service you offer in your hospitality operation. Problems can also account for increases in absenteeism, tardiness, job-related accidents, and sick leave, all of which result in rising costs for the hospitality enterprise.

So what can we do in the hospitality industry to help our people? Because very few of us are trained professionals in the area of counseling, we have to be careful not to get involved in situations that we are not trained to handle. If the hospitality organization where you work does not have an established Employee Assistance Program, then you should be aware of the public services available in your community. But before you can direct your problem employees to available help, you must first be astute enough to recognize that undesirable behaviors and performance levels are problem related. Although you might secretly wish for the behavior and performance to magically improve so that you won't have to deal with it, problems don't just disappear or resolve themselves. By constantly monitoring the performance of our employees, we are likely to capture any problems shortly after they occur.

Counseling as Part of Corrective Action

Corrective action attempts to modify the employees' performance or behavior so that they may retain their position in the work force. The method through which this is accomplished is **performance counseling**. The idea of counseling is a theme found throughout human resources management in "the next chapter" as we strive to find innovative ways to retain our valuable people.

Because these individuals are human, problems that affect job performance will occur while they are in our employ. When this happens, a disciplinary process that emphasizes counseling is an effort to get the employee back on the right track. Figure 9-6 shows you where counseling fits in the discipline process. Let's examine each of the steps in the process.

Problem Identification and Analysis

Problem identification should be initiated by the human resources manager as soon as signs of negative behavior or reduced performance levels are exhibited by the employee. The employee may easily be put on the defensive, so care must be taken in your initial approach. Open-ended questions, a comfortable atmosphere, an understanding that you are sincere in wanting to help the person, and active listening may help the employee feel as if he or she can confide in you (Figure 9-7). Active listening requires that you not make judgments about what the employee is telling you so that you really hear what the individual has to say.

It is not always easy to be a good listener. The problems you will identify will be either job related or personal. Again, if the problem is something that you are not trained to deal with, refer the employee to your EAP or to some other professional. Problem analysis requires empathy and an open mind. Some of the information the employee is sharing with

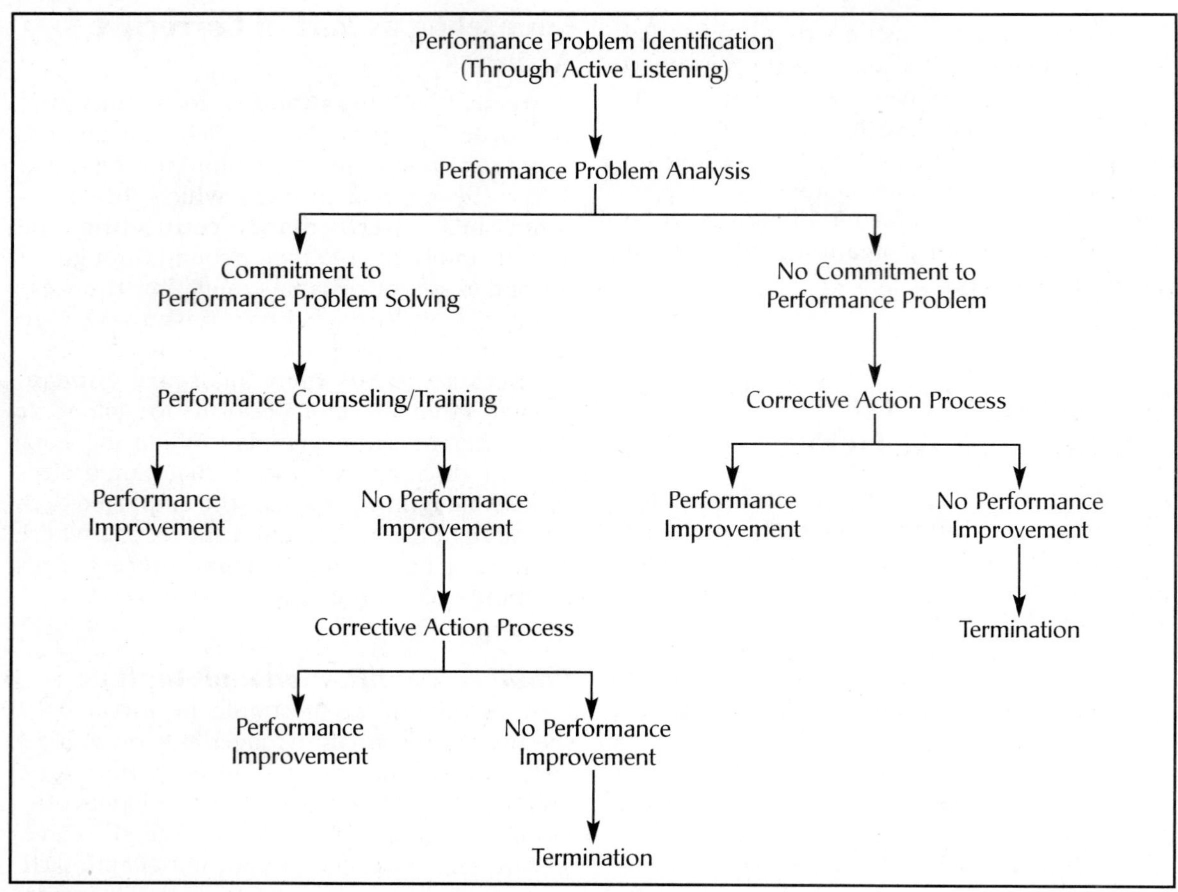

FIGURE 9-6 Where counseling fits in as part of the corrective action process.

you might very well be your responsibility to correct. What if the employee talks of inadequate equipment, facilities that are poorly designed, work group members who are uncooperative, a lack of skills training, nonexplicit instructions, or hazardous working conditions? Aren't these problems really management problems? Do not overlook the possibility that the low performance of your employee is the result of management failings.

Remember that the focus of performance counseling is on the job and improving job-related performance behaviors. When an employee is not meeting minimum standards, then job counseling is needed. The manager needs to be managing the employee's performance. When standards fall to an unacceptable level, then the manager really only has two choices to give the employee. You can either assist the employee in improving his or her performance to meet the required standards or terminate the employee when he or she does not.

Determining Commitment

The next step in the counseling process is to determine if the employee is committed to

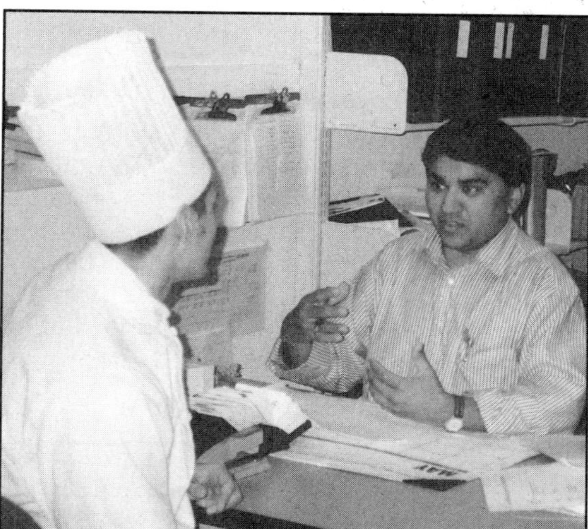

FIGURE 9-7 Counseling is a private matter between employee and employer.

improving performance so that it conforms with acceptable standards. Not all employees are going to recognize that a problem exists, or, even if they do, they might not be willing to make the effort to improve. In areas where labor is tight, this can be a particular problem if the employee believes that you simply cannot afford to suspend or terminate his or her employment. Not all employees are model citizens. They bring their anger, resentments, and grievances with them to the workplace. If these employees are not willing to work with you and make a commitment to improved performance, you have little choice but to continue the disciplinary process.

For employees who want to work with you toward solving the problem and improving their performance, counseling is initiated. Together, the two of you write an action plan that is geared toward performance improvement. The self-appraisal form found in Table 9-7 includes examples of some of the types of questions the problem employee might ask himself or herself during the counseling session. The answers to

TABLE 9-7 Self-Appraisal Form for Employees in Performance Counseling

Job Design and Satisfaction

Do you feel you are well placed in your present job assignment?

Do you have a clear understanding of the expectations your immediate supervisor has for you in your present job?

Do you have a clear understanding of the goals of the work unit to which you are assigned?

How do you feel about the kind of work you are doing in your present job?

How effectively do you feel you have met the responsibilities of your job position?

Performance Appraisal

How worthwhile was your last performance appraisal in helping you to improve your performance?

Summarize the overall strengths and weaknesses you have demonstrated in performing your present assignment.

Does your immediate supervisor give you the necessary information to enable you to know how you are getting on with your job?

Development

How do you feel about the progress you have made thus far in performing your job?

How confident are you that your career aspirations can be met by remaining in this hospitality organization?

Do you feel you have potential beyond your present job assignment? How have you demonstrated this potential?

How much assistance have you been given by your supervisor in planning your career development?

Do you feel that we have given you the proper training and resources to do your job successfully?

Communication

Do you receive enough information to perform your job effectively?

Do you receive enough information to understand the relationships among your job, the work unit to which you are assigned, and the mission of your hospitality organization?

these questions provide some direction for problem resolution. At each session, a performance review is made in writing by both you and the employee. An example of such a review is seen in Table 9-8. The review format should be modified to best meet the needs of the specific problem that the two of you are working on resolving.

Remember that the goal of the counseling process is to reverse the behavior or performance pattern into one that is in keeping with the goals of the hospitality organization. Feedback is an important element of this process. When the employee's performance improves, it is necessary to recognize it so that the employee better understands the type of behavior that is acceptable. Once the performance has improved, the counseling process continues to provide a monitoring mechanism of the employee's performance. Once the problem has been resolved to the satisfaction of both parties, the counseling period ends.

TABLE 9-8 Form for Review of Employee in Performance Counseling

Name of Employee ______________________ Work Unit ____________ Job ____________

Progress and Problems	Analysis by Manager	Analysis by Employee
What progress has been made by the employee during the review period in making the following adjustments:		
Job Adjustments?		
Behavior Adjustment?		
Work Unit Adjustment?		
What are the obstacles to achieving adjustment expectations in the areas listed above?		
What comments should be made on the *results* achieved for each of the adjustments listed above?		
In what areas has the employee made the MOST progress in adjustments? The LEAST progress?		
Do the adjustment expectations need to be revised?		
What are the plans and priorities for achieving adjustment expectations?		

Signature of Employee ____

Signature of Unit Manager ____

Date of Review______________________ Next Review Date ____________________

ALTERNATIVE DISPUTE RESOLUTION

Unionized workplaces have specific procedures for handling grievances in just about all union contracts. We discuss unions in Chapter 14. Historically, nonunion workplaces have not provided a systematic grievance procedure for their employees. This has resulted in expensive lawsuits for both employee and employer over discrimination and/or wrongful discharge claims. Today's worker is much more aware of his or her rights in the workplace and much more knowledgeable on issues involving employment law. What was needed by both employer and employee was a way to deal with workplace disputes before they reached the stage of litigation. **Alternative dispute resolutions (ADR)** are a relatively recent development that seek to meet that objective.

ADRs can be set up in a variety of different ways. Their objective is to provide procedures for employee complaints or dispute resolution. The intent is to keep the issue out of the judicial system by providing a procedure to resolve the issue equitably for all parties. Possible ways of establishing an ADR include:

- Complaint-resolution committees
- Complaint procedures specified in employee handbook
- Peer review panels
- Internal arbitration panels
- Internal mediation panels
- Pre-dispute employment agreements (clauses requiring binding arbitration)
- Settlement agreements (including a release and waiver of claims)

Both employees and employers have something to gain through the use of an alternative dispute resolution. For employees, the process provides them a means to be heard and to have a guarantee of due process when they have a grievance. Employers view ADR as a means to resolve minor issues before they become huge, unmanageable and possibly costly in the course of a discrimination or wrongful discharge claim. There were cases pending in the Supreme Court relative to ADR at the time this text was being written. For managers with human resources responsibilities in the hospitality industry alter-

INDUSTRY EXPERTS SPEAK

Ron Meliker states, "Alternative dispute resolution is one of the emerging trends in human resources management. More and more companies are moving towards this approach. To date, it has been used very effectively in bypassing the court system in numerous employment situations. General Electric (GE) started using ADR in the late seventies and since then, many mainstream American companies have instituted these programs. The issues I see with ADR implementation are twofold: the first is a heavy education piece for both managers and employees. Employees must understand that they give up their rights to legal recourse when they accept alternative dispute resolution. This requires them to sign a policy statement/waiver to that effect. This is relatively simple for new hires. They would be notified when the job offer was made that it was conditional upon them accepting and signing the policy terms your company has established for ADR. The second issue surrounds current employees and policy decisions that need to be made. For instance, if you decide to implement ADR in your organization what do you do about an employee who chooses not to sign a policy statement giving up their rights to legal recourse? Will your policy be to terminate them for failure to comply? Or do you let employees have the choice to sign or not sign recognizing that over time, normal attrition will remove these employees?"

native dispute resolution will need to be carefully watched in "the next chapter."

EXITING THE ORGANIZATION

So far in this chapter, numerous alternatives to the termination, dismissal, firing, or letting go of your employees have been presented. This is due to the fact that the hospitality industry continues to face a serious labor shortage, and that we have a serious investment in each of our people with respect to hiring, placement, orientation, and training expenditures. The last thing in the world that we want to do is to have all our efforts result in an unnecessary termination or in a **resignation**.

Despite all our retention efforts, sometimes we have to terminate an employee, or they need to resign from our employment. There is no list to show you that contains all the factors that need to be present before you decide whether to retain or terminate an employee. Each case must be judged on its own merits. This is when you, as the manager with human resources responsibilities, must use your own discretion, judgment, and company policy and procedures to guide you.

Termination

If you decide that termination is the last alternative available to you, then certain procedures must be followed, or you will quickly find your hospitality organization involved in a wrongful discharge lawsuit. Ask yourself the following questions:

- Was the employee informed of the rule violation or substandard performance levels?
- Was the employee given an opportunity to correct the behavior/performance?
- Did the employee understand the consequences of not correcting his or her behavior/performance?
- Has the rule/performance standard been consistently enforced?
- Has the rule/performance standard been applied in a nondiscriminatory manner?
- Has a thorough investigation of the situation been conducted?
- Has the investigation and disciplinary process been adequately documented?

Consistency, communication, and documentation appear to be the key words when faced with a decision to terminate. Improper terminations can result in lawsuits against the hospitality organization that destroy employee morale, motivation, and a sense of job security. All terminations should take into account the underlying reason(s) for the employee's behavior or substandard performance, and only take place after careful review of all facts and pertinent information. You should have a carefully outlined procedure for handling all terminations, as seen in Table 9-9. Ron Meliker states that a termination meeting should take no more than 10 minutes. You are simply announcing a decision you have already made and documented to the employee. Any longer than 10 minutes, good chances you are arguing over the merits of your decision. The termination meeting is to bring closure to the employment relationship.

The Exit Interview

The **exit interview** is used to provide the hospitality organization with information regarding attrition. For voluntary terminations, exit interviews can be particularly useful in determining why the employee is leaving your organization. Whenever an employee leaves your employ, there are a number of issues to resolve such as paycheck, benefits, rehiring privileges, and unemployment compensation. As managers, we hope to use the information from these interviews to uncover weak human

TABLE 9-9 Performance Management—Termination

- **Termination**
  - The last step in the corrective action process
  - Usually used when all prior steps fail
  - All termination require prior approval of State President/General Manager and Sunbelt's VP of Human Resources
- **Termination Meeting**
  - Have another management witness present
  - Prepare in advance
    - Identify facts and specific reasons
    - Anticipate questions/issues
  - Straight-forward and brief meeting
  - Advise employee immediately in meeting that they are being discharged (or terminated or "let go")
  - Keep the meeting brief – less than 10 minutes
  - Give specific reasons for termination
  - Respond to employee's questions factually and without emotion or argument
  - Detail and resolve all final matters (keys, monies, property, files, laptops, car, etc.)
  - Explain that HR will contact them within 14 days to explain their COBRA and PSP options
  - Both managers must document the meeting
- **Avoid Constructive Discharges**
  - When you ask an employee to resign rather than being terminated – the courts regard it as the same as being terminated
  - DO NOT ask employees to resign
  - If they voluntarily ask to resign instead of being terminated, then it is ok and have them do it in writing at that time
- **Remember**
  - By following Sunbelt's performance and appraisal programs and the company's policies and procedures . . .

    . . . you can avoid unnecessary problems, headaches and litigation from a former employee

(Courtesy of Premier Beverage Company of Florida; SUNBELT Beverage Corporation)

resources practices, to provide us with an evaluation of hiring practices, to discover a noncompetitive compensation plan, to locate specific sources of job dissatisfaction or supervisors who do not follow the policies and procedures of the hospitality organization (Figure 9-8). If we know why our employees are unhappy, we will be able to do a better job of reducing unwanted employee turnover.

Exit interview practices vary widely among hospitality organizations. Table 9-10 is an example of an exit interview form. The specific content of the questions should be modified to obtain the information that you feel is most useful for your hospitality organization. Why the employees are leaving, in the case of voluntary terminations, is of particular interest to us in our retention attempts. Sometimes, asking the employee what could be done to get him or her to stay yields a more productive response than merely asking the person why he or she is leaving. One of the biggest weaknesses of the exit interview is that the information obtained is only as valuable as the honesty of the employee responding. Sometimes the employee is reluctant to give completely honest answers.

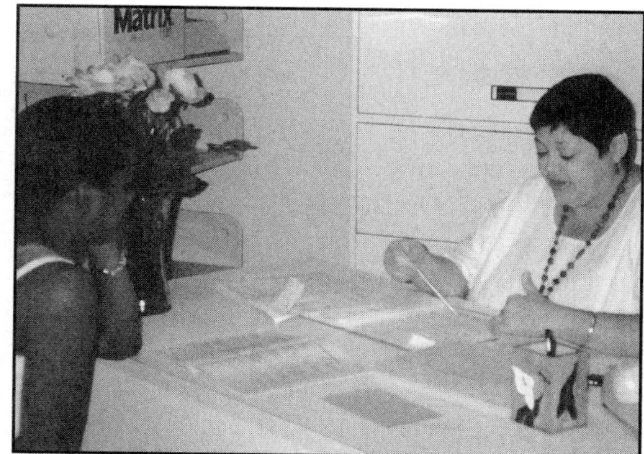

FIGURE 9-8 The exit interview can yield information that can lead to the improvement of your retention methods.

TABLE 9-10 Exit Interview Form

NAME: ______________________ LENGTH OF TIME EMPLOYED: ______________

POSITION: ______________________ DATE: ______________

A. THE COMPANY

1. Were the employee benefits adequate? ______________
2. Were the conditions of employment, salary, promotion/transfers, etc. adequate?______________
3. Was the pretraining you received adequate to perform a good job? If not, please explain how could it have been improved. ______________
4. Was the training and development after job placement adequate? Please explain how it could have been improved. ______________

B. SUPERVISION

1. Describe, briefly, the type of communications you had with your:
   a. General Manager(s) ______________
   b. District Manager(s) ______________
2. How could your supervision have been improved? ______________

C. EMPLOYEE RELATIONS

1. What did you like most about your job? ______________
2. What did you dislike about your job? ______________
3. Do you have any suggestions that would improve our employee relations and/or working conditions? Please explain. ______________
4. Would you ever consider working for ______________ again? __________
   Please explain. ______________
5. Have you accepted or been offered other employment? __________ If so, with what company or industry (i.e., restaurant, manufacturing, banking, etc.? ______________
6. Was your separation from ______________ handled to your satisfaction? __________
   Please explain. ______________
7. Please list in order of priority the reason(s) for your leaving.
   a. ______________
   b. ______________
   c. ______________
   d. ______________
8. How could we improve as a company? ______________
9. ANY ADDITIONAL COMMENTS? ______________

____
HUMAN RESOURCE SIGNATURE

Exit interviews should not be conducted on the last day of employment, as that can be a distractful day for the employee. On the last day, however, an **employee exit checklist** is completed, similar to the one shown in Table 9-11. This is a good policy to establish, particularly if the employee has keys, uniforms, or other property that belong to the hospitality organization.

If turnover is to be controlled, the real reasons why employees leave must be discovered and communicated to the management team. It simply does not make good human resources management sense not to conduct exit interviews.

INDUSTRY EXPERTS SPEAK

Ron Meliker finds that sometimes the more productive exit interviews are conducted after-the-fact (but no more than 4–6 weeks later). Sometimes if you wait awhile and the emotions are gone you get more useful information from the employee. "I will even meet them somewhere else and conduct the exit interview over a soda or cup of coffee. The more relaxed and non-threatening the atmosphere the more sincere information you can yield which will help the organization in the future. Oftentimes people are more comfortable and at ease outside of the work environment. I even had an employee who told me that upon reflection he had made a mistake and wanted me to tell him how he could get his job back! With both involuntary terminations and voluntary resignations exit interviews do allow you to learn things about your organization."

Wrongful Discharge

Throughout this chapter there has been a repeated emphasis on the importance of documentation. We cannot overstate this point. It is also important that certain pieces of this documentation have the signature of the terminated employee and manager. Counseling and disciplinary sessions should be documented with the employee's signature on the documentation. If an employee refuses to sign, ask another manager to witness and sign the document. Documentation must contain behavioral facts. Take care not to label employees ("John is a drug addict") or state your opinion regarding the behavior. If the termination is due to unacceptable behavior, which was seen by other employees, get a written notarized statement from the witnesses.

Due to recent legal rulings you should also review all human resources policies and procedures manuals for any statements that limit your right to discharge an employee-at-will. Courts have viewed human resources documents as implied employment contracts between the hospitality organization and the employee. The federal government and many states have altered the traditional employee-at-will concept, which states that the term of an individual's employment is discretionary or may be terminated at any time by either party.

With regulations imposed by the Family and Medial Leave Act (FMLA, covered in Chapter 11) and the Americans with Disabilities Act (ADA), along with the increase of AIDS and drug testing, more employees who have been terminated are filing for wrongful discharge. Some states have passed legislation requiring that certain notices be given employees who are about to be terminated; other states have said that terminations have violated an implied contract initiated at the time the individual was hired. Caution your staff not to make any oral or written statements in which a contract is implied. Otherwise, you are likely to find yourself on the losing side of a wrongful discharge suit filed for breach of contract. Not only are these employees winning reinstatement, but they are also entitled to back wages. Following the guidelines we have established throughout this chapter will help in keeping you out of the courtroom and in your hospitality operation where you belong.

TABLE 9-11 Employee Exit Checklist

Employee Name: ______________________________

SS# ______________________ Last Day Worked ______________________

W-2 Address (if different from present address):

Street: ______________________________

City, State, Zip: ______________________________

Employee Exit Checklist

______ Keys Returned—List: ______________________________

______ Uniform, Name Tag Returned—List: ______________________________

______ Other Items Returned—List: ______________________________

______ Exit Interview Completed (if applicable)

______ Outstanding Wage Advances, Loans, or Other Monies Reimbursed to the Company—List:

____

______ Other—List: ______________________________

____

____

To Be Completed by the Employee

Reason for Leaving: ______________________________

____

____

____

Signatures

______________	______	______________	______
Manager	Date	Employee	Date

Age discrimination suits have also come of age in the 1990s. Their frequency in the courts is likely to increase as the population ages. The **Age Discrimination in Employment Act** was passed in 1967 with the purpose of protecting employees in the 40–65 age group from bias in hiring or in firing. In 1978 the cap was raised to 70, and in 1986, the cap was eliminated in most occupations. In addition, many states have passed legislation prohibiting mandatory retirement.

Another interesting area of wrongful discharge relates to the subject of off-duty terminations. Can you terminate an employee for dating another employee? Can you terminate an employee for marrying another employee at one of your hospitality competitors? Can you terminate an employee for committing a crime? Can you terminate an employee for using drugs or getting drunk and obnoxious while not on your time and not in your operation? The answer to these questions used to be an absolute "yes." However, today the courts are less likely to view what employees do on their own time as any of your concern.

One of the major issues facing our industry (and others) is drug testing. Though the use of drugs is clearly illegal, the argument is that an employee's lifestyle outside the workplace has no relation to job performance or behavior on the job, and therefore cannot be viewed as grounds for termination. The individual's right to privacy is increasingly being supported by recent court rulings. Again, the legal concern is tied into the employment-at-will concept. Can employers fire employees without job-related cause? Is that an invasion of privacy or the employer's right to terminate at will?

Negligent Retention

There is a negative side with serious legal implications retaining an employee who should be terminated. The legal theory of **negligent retention** makes an employer liable for retaining an employee who is known to be unfit for his or her job position. Just as in negligent hiring, an employer must exercise reasonable care in the retention of an employee in light of the risk(s) created by the nature of that position. This means that not only is it necessary to screen prospective employees before they are hired, but that periodic screening of employees during the course of their employment might be necessary to reaffirm their suitability for the job.

A duty is placed on the employer to conduct an investigation of any information that might suggest that an employee is unfit to perform his or her job. For example, if an employer knew or should have known about rumors, allegations, or evidence of numerous speeding tickets by a delivery driver, that employer would have a duty to reasonably investigate the allegations an respond to the findings. To conduct such an investigation, the employer must have a reasonable suspicion that a problem exists. Once the investigation is completed, based upon the results the employer then has a duty to take reasonable intervention. As a result of the large number of claims being brought under negligent hiring and negligent retention, agencies abound that will conduct background research for you on both applicants and employees. Web sites are abundant for these companies. Just be sure to check references on them to make sure that they are legitimate themselves! We urge you to keep your eyes open on legislation in this area as it will require your close monitoring in "the next chapter."

The Effects of Exodus

There is no doubt that firing an employee is the most difficult and emotional job that hospitality managers have to face. But what about the employees being terminated? And what about remaining employees who are still at work in your hospitality operation? What can you do to assist them?

You have a responsibility to assist the employees left in your company in dealing with the loss. You are likely to be viewed as the "bad guy," especially by the terminated employee's friends and coworkers. They are likely to see that individual from a different perspective than you did as his or her supervisor. These employees will need you to provide them with an opportunity to vent their anger.

INDUSTRY EXPERTS SPEAK

A recent development that has prompted a new series of lawsuits is in the area of retaliation claims. These are claims made by current employees against their present employers. We are now seeing a higher proportion of lawsuits filed by current employees who say, "You didn't promote me because I am 'in some protected class.'" These are employees who while working for you are taking you to court. You have to be sure to train your managers that they ***can't*** treat this person differently—even if they will see them in the courtroom that afternoon. If managers treat these people differently, or they perceive they are being treated differently these employees may file a retaliation claim. A retaliation claim states that management is treating this employee differently and retaliating against them because they have filed a legal action against the company. Many legal experts see claims of this type as the next big employment law issue for the next decade. Some key questions for managers will be: How do you defend against it? How do you train managers to deal with it?

Oftentimes, your staff will simply need to be assured that their own jobs are safe, and that they are not in jeopardy of being terminated. Care must be taken not to "bad-mouth" or provide too many details about the terminated employee, or you might be subject to a defamation claim.

CONCLUSION

Corrective action is a disciplinary action taken against an employee for violating a standard of conduct or falling below the specified performance standards you have established. This is not a punitive action, but one taken to correct the behavior or performance problem. The counseling process is used for those employees who are willing to accept that a problem exists and want to make a commitment to self-improvement and problem resolution. Problem-solving sessions are held with the employee; action plans are developed and mutually agreed upon. When the performance or behavior improves, the employee is praised and the improvement is duly noted. Feedback is continuous until you both agree that the problem has been resolved.

When there is no other recourse to take, termination becomes the avenue you must choose, despite its unpleasantness. Care must be taken to temper the resentment and confusion that remaining employees may harbor. The key emphases throughout this chapter have been consistency, fairness, and documentation.

Let's turn our attention to a discussion of reward systems including compensation and benefits.

Case Problem 9-1

Benji and Stephanie had been coworkers for several months in a lodging property in Seattle. Both worked the front desk, each with a full-time schedule. Stephanie, in fact, enjoyed Benji's company so much that she asked her manager to make sure that they were scheduled for the same shifts. She would even ask the supervisor if they could take their breaks at the same time.

The other day as Benji was answering a call, Stephanie walked up behind him. As she was waiting for him to finish, she pulled out a balloon, proceeded to blow it up, aimed it just below Benji's belt and let it go. The balloon hit him just as he was finishing the phone call.

Was Benji sexually harassed? Would it have been sexual harassment if Benji had aimed the balloon at Stephanie's chest? Was there any behavior that management should have picked up on? The supervisor witnessed the entire event. Should any corrective action taken place? If not, why? If so, what corrective action should have occurred? How can management ensure that this behavior does not create a complaint of sexual harassment?

Case Problem 9-2

You have established the same rules of conduct for your hotel that are seen in Table 9-1. For each of the two corrective action situations presented here, describe how you will handle the situation.

- What corrective action will you take? Identify, for each, the steps in the corrective action process.
- Would you institute performance counseling in either of the situations? Why or why not?
- Would either of the situations require a probationary period? Which one(s)? Why or why not?
- For which situations do you feel it is necessary to implement termination procedures? Identify those procedures.

Corrective Action Situation A

January 2, 1999: Robert had been cleaning up the operation after the *very* hectic holiday season. This was the first day since prior to Thanksgiving that you were not operating at 100 percent. Robert was in a guest area (unoccupied at the time) when he decided to have a cigarette. Your assistant manager found him, cleaning the floors with a cigarette hanging out of his mouth as she brought a potential client into the area.

February 15, 1999: The assistant manager walked into a guest area that Robert had just finished cleaning. The room smelled of cigarette smoke, and she noticed a cigarette burn in the carpeting. The room was posted as a non-smoking area in accordance with recently passed state legislation.

Corrective Action Situation B

April 3, 2000: Susan was taking out trash to the dumpster when you walked by. You noticed that the bag seemed to be unusually heavy. You asked Susan to take the trash bag back inside and dump it out so that you could examine its contents. Upon doing so, you discovered eight dinner knives, six dinner forks, four spoons, a bottle of wine, and some canned goods.

May 1, 2000: Susan has gathered up all of the employee uniforms for pickup by the uniform company. This is a service that twice weekly picks up dirty uniforms and leaves a clean supply. You notice that there are clean bed linens and tablecloths mixed discreetly in with the dirty uniforms. Susan knows that the uniform company does not clean these items.

Case Problem 9-3

Kerri had worked for your hotel company for 12 years prior to her discharge. For the first 8 years, she was considered a model employee by supervisors and coworkers. Her performance appraisals were always marked "outstanding," and her personnel file contained numerous commendation letters from customer and supervisors.

Kerri's work problems began about four years ago when she went through a difficult divorce. The loss of her children was particularly upsetting to her sense of family. Kerri became withdrawn at work and often times argued with her supervisors. Absenteeism and tardiness became a chronic problem. Fifteen months prior to her termination she had been given a written warning that her attendance must improve or she could face possible discharge. Unfortunately, her attendance did not improve; however, she received no further corrective action until the day of her termination.

In addition to the absenteeism, Kerri's supervisors experienced other performance problems with her. The quality of her work had decreased to only an acceptable level of performance. Her supervisor had discussed this with her on three occasions, but no corrective action was ever initiated. It was a performance incident that occured on a Saturday night that caused her termination.

Kerri had been assigned to a VIP catering function off of the hotel premises at a location about 2 miles away. Two hours after Kerri had been sent over, a supervisor went to check on the set-up. When the supervisor arrived he noticed Kerri sitting in the back of the catering vehicle with her feet up reading a magazine. The supervisor decided to observe her from a distance. After about 20 minutes Kerri had not moved. The supervisor went back to the hotel property and reported this to the manager. Neither the supervisor nor manager confronted Kerri about the incident.

The next Monday morning, the supervisor and manager presented Kerri with a termination notice for "Poor work performance, excessive absenteeism, and loafing." She was handed a final paycheck that included eight hours of work for that day.

How do you think this case was handled? By the supervisor? By the manager? Were the concepts of corrective action applied? Do you think that there was just cause to terminate Kerri? Why or why not? If this case went to court for wrongful termination, how do you think the case would be decided? What arguments would you make? How, specifically, would you act differently if you were Kerri's supervisor?

Key Words

Age Discrimination in Employment Act
alternative dispute resolutions (ADR)
code of conduct
corrective action
disciplinary actions
discipline policy
Employee Assistance Program (EAP)
employment-at-will
employee exit checklist
exit interview
hostile environment
negligent retention
nonpunitive approaches
performance counseling
positive discipline
progressive discipline
quid pro quo
resignation
rules of conduct
sexual harassment
suspension
termination
workplace violence
wrongful discharge

Recommended Reading

Aalberts, R. J. and L. H. Seidman. 1996. "Sexual-Harassment Policies for the Workplace—A Tale of Two Companies." *The Cornell Quarterly* 37(3).

Aaron, T. and E. Dry. 1992. "Sexual Harassment in the Hospitality Industry." *The Cornell H.R.A. Quarterly* 33(2): 93–95.

Batty, J. 1993. "Preventing Sexual Harassment in the Restaurant." *Restaurants USA* 13(1): 30–34.

Bencivenga, D. 1999. "Dealing with The Dark Side: To Avoid Potential Violence." *HR Magazine* (January).

Caro, M. R. 1991. "The High Cost of Harassment." *Lodging* 16(10): 54–64.

Caudron, S. 1998. "Target: HR." *Workforce* 77(8): 44–52.

Denalli, J. 1990. "Exit Interviews." *Restaurants USA* 10(9): 33–34.

Godsey, K. D. 1995. "Battle of the Sexes." *Restaurant & Institutions* 105(6): 134–138.

Hamilton, A. J. and P. A. Veglahn. 1992. "Sexual Harassment: The Hostile Work Environment." *The Cornell H.R.A. Quarterly* 33(2): 88–92.

Jarin, K. "New Rules for Same Sex Harassment." *HR Magazine*. 1998. www.shrm.org.hrmagazine/articles/0698new.htm (4 October 1998).

Recommended Web Sites

1. "Workplace Violence: Nature of the Problem." *USA Today Magazine*. January 1997: www.wps.orgs/pubs/nature-of-the-problem.html
2. Preventing Workplace Violence: www.afscme.org/wrkplace/violtc.htm
3. Site of the Day: Workplace Violence: Awareness and Prevention: www.ifebp.org/resitbk.html
4. Legal Information Institute (Alternative Dispute Resolution Statutes): www.law.cornell.edu/topics/state_statues.html
5. Dealing with Workplace Violence: A Guide for Agency Planners (U. S. Office of Personnel Management): www.opm.gov/workplac/index.htm
6. Minnesota Center against Violence and Abuse: www.mincava.umn.edu/gbib.asp
7. Facts about Sexual Harassment (U.S. EEOC): www.eeoc.gov/facts/fs-sex.html
8. Charts & Graphs: Harassment on the Rise? www.intellectualcapital.com/issues/98/0312/icchart.htm
9. Questions and Answers about Sexual Harassment: www.qsa.gov/eeo/dis6.htm

Endnotes

1. Equal Employment Opportunity, *Questions and Answers about Sexual Harassment*, www.gsa.gov/eeo/dis6.htm (20 April 1998).
2. Robert LaGow, "Court Rulings Expand Definitions of Sexual Harassment." *HR News Online*, www.shrm.org/hrnews/articles/062698.htm (27 June 1998).
3. "Violence: No. 2 Cause of Workplace Death," *Occupational Hazards* 58, no. 9 (1996): 15.

4. Ronald W. Taylor, "The Rockem-Sockem Workplace." venable.com/wlu/rockem.htm (12 August 1998).
5. John Huberman, "Discipline without Punishment," *Harvard Business Review* 42, no. 4 (1964): 62.

Discussion Questions

1. Distinguish between the rights of management and the rights of employees in hospitality organizations.
2. List 20 possible codes of conduct for a food service operation.
3. Define the purpose of a fair policy statement.
4. Identify and describe the two forms of sexual harassment.
5. Describe several actions you can take as a manager with human resources responsibilities to prevent sexual harassment in your organization.
6. Discuss workplace violence and its implications in the hospitality workplace.
7. What are the critical factors for the successful implementation of a discipline policy?
8. List the steps in the implementation of the corrective action process. In your own words, briefly explain what each step accomplishes.
9. What is the purpose of corrective actions in a hospitality organization?
10. Identify the problems of traditional discipline approaches.
11. Describe the use of performance counseling as an alternate route in the discipline process. What is the goal of performance counseling?
12. Explain how alternative dispute resolution works in a nonunion workplace.
13. When do you use termination procedures in a hospitality organization?
14. Describe how an exit interview can be beneficial to your company.
15. Discuss two different ways you could be brought up in a wrongful discharge suit by one of your terminated employees.
16. What are the most important items to remember when implementing corrective action, counseling, and/or termination procedures?

SECTION 4

Reward Systems

CHAPTER 10
Compensation

"Wealth is the product of man's capacity to think."

—AYN RAND

"It is not the employer who pays the WAGES—he only handles the money. It is the PRODUCT (CUSTOMER) that pays the wages."

—HENRY FORD

INTRODUCTION

A major component of the reward systems designed for your hospitality enterprise will include the plans for compensation for both hourly and management employees. As was true for each of the human resources functional areas discussed previously, it is important that the compensation plan be linked to the mission statement and organization goals. The specifics of your compensation plan will vary based upon such considerations as the types of products and services offered and whether your hospitality organization operates on a profit or not-for-profit basis.

At the same time, compensation plans must be linked together with your organization's benefit program to ensure a harmonious relationship between the two. The variety and complexity of benefit programs offered by hospitality organizations continue to expand. With increasing frequency prospective job candidates are choosing the particular hospitality company they wish to work for on the basis of benefit offerings as opposed to the specific compensation. In "the next chapter" this trend is likely to continue.

As all service industries are competing for the same pool of unskilled and semiskilled employees, compensation structures are becoming more innovative and competitive in their approaches. Keeping abreast of the changes and innovations in the administration of these programs is increasingly important to your personal success as a manager with human resources responsibilities.

At the conclusion of this chapter you will be able to:

1. Understand the importance of compensation planning to sound human resources practices.
2. Distinguish between exempt and nonexempt personnel.
3. Develop a compensation plan for a hospitality organization.
4. Plan a job evaluation for a hospitality organization.
5. Plan an external compensation survey.
6. Identify the effects of a collective bargaining agreement on your compensation plan.
7. Explain the philosophies behind the tipping versus service charge debate.
8. Describe the role of compensation as a motivator in the service sector.
9. Discuss the advantages and disadvantages of a pay-for-performance compensation plan.

10. Distinguish between the various types of incentive programs.
11. Maintain an awareness of the legal issues pertaining to compensation in a service enterprise.
12. Identify the trends and changes in compensation planning.

MANAGEMENT PHILOSOPHY OF WORK AND COMPENSATION PLANNING IN THE HOSPITALITY INDUSTRY

The development of a sound compensation plan is critical to the credibility of your hospitality management team. The compensation plan translates into the policies and procedures that are used to implement and administer the compensation component of your total reward system. It is imperative that a great deal of care and thought go into **compensation planning**, as no other plan in your organization will be examined as closely for inequities in the structure.

The compensation policies that you initially develop set the precedent for all actions taken with respect to wages and salaries. These policies and procedures serve as a decision-making guideline for the operational managers. In large hospitality organizations, where compensation decision making occurs at a multitude of levels, it is these policies and procedures that help to ensure consistency in implementation.

Additionally, compensation planning involves a large portion of your hospitality operations budget. Labor costs continue to increase along with legislation raising minimum-wage levels. So for management credibility, improved decision making, and sound budgetary considerations your compensation plan (i.e., policies and procedures) must be carefully coordinated, communicated, integrated, and administered to ensure consistency.

This chapter discusses practices and policies commonly used in the hospitality industry today in the establishment of equitable compensation plans. It is important for you to remember that wage and salary policies are individually based upon your company's own needs and operational objectives. For a hospitality enterprise, however, to be successful in compensation planning, it is critical that all compensation policies and procedures are well planned, fully developed, and carefully articulated to the people within your operation.

EXEMPT VERSUS NONEXEMPT PERSONNEL

A mutual understanding of the terminology as we use it in the remainder of this chapter must be reached. Please note that this terminology is used for the purpose of explaining the different pay structures that exist in the hospitality industry. In the context of this chapter **wage** is money that is paid to your hourly employees regardless of whether their skill level is unskilled, semiskilled, or skilled. **Salary** is paid to those employees who work for a weekly, monthly, or annual rate of pay. While you probably think of salaried employees as management, in the hospitality industry our skilled personnel (such as chefs) are also frequently compensated on a base salary. And in other, less frequent situations, you will find management who are compensated on a hourly basis.

The terms *compensation* and *pay* will be used generically to include people employed by our organization. We define **compensation** as the rate of pay (or award) given to employees in the hospitality industry for the performance of work or the provision of services. In previous chapters we have used the terms hourly and salaried to make distinction between management and nonmanagement resources. Though that distinction was sufficient for previous and future discussions, the topic of compensation requires specific terminology.

When establishing a compensation plan for your people it becomes important, for **Fair Labor Standards Act (FLSA)** classification, to distinguish not between management and nonmanagement, but rather between exempt and nonexempt personnel. These terms stem from federal and state minimum wage and overtime regulations that specifically define the legal requirements that must be adhered to if you wish to exclude a category of employees from overtime pay.

Exempt personnel are those employees to whom, under Section 13(a)(1) of the federal minimum wage law, you are not required to pay overtime. According to the law, any employee employed in a bona fide executive, administrative, or professional capacity is considered exempt from both minimum wage and the overtime provisions of the law. We therefore say that these employees are exempt from overtime pay. Employees must meet several requirements or tests for exemption that are outlined in the law before exemption is presumed. Modifications are periodically made in the specific terms and conditions for exempt status. We suggest, therefore, that you check with the nearest Office of the Wage Hour Division for the most current information on specific exemptions. **Nonexempt personnel** are those employees who must be paid overtime according to the overtime provisions of the Fair Labor Standards Act. We say then that these employees are nonexempt from overtime pay.

Overtime Liability

The government agency responsible for the regulations regarding overtime is the Department of Labor. Hospitality organizations, as well as others, sometimes have difficulty making the distinction between exempt and nonexempt employees due to the complexity of the overtime regulations. This can lead to violations in the law, oftentimes, unknowingly. In 1998 alone, the United States Department of Labor investigations show, business paid $120 million in back wages and penalties for overtime violations. These violations involved more than 173,000 employees.[1]

In 1995 the Employment Policy Foundation estimated that the liability for back pay for each 1 percent of the white-collar work force that was found to be incorrectly classified as nonexempt rather than exempt would be $1.9 billion![2] Table 10-1 identifies the breakdown, by industry, of the percentage of employees who work overtime.

As you can see in Table 10-1, the services industry has the second largest percentage of overtime workers. If employees are eligible for overtime pay and they are incorrectly categorized as exempt, those employees are liable for back pay, overtime pay, and in some cases, punitive damages. It is important that you, as

TABLE 10-1 Overtime Percentages by Industry

	Percent of all OT workers who are		Percent share of all OT workers by Industry
Industry	**Male**	**Female**	
Agriculture	66.7%	33.3%	1.5%
Mining/Construction	94.7%	05.3%	8.4%
Manufacturing	73.3%	26.7%	30.4%
Transportation	87.5%	12.5%	5.6%
Communications/Utilities	83.3%	16.7%	2.7%
Trade	67.8%	32.2%	19.1%
Bank, Finance, Real Estate	51.2%	48.8%	2.7%
Services	39.3%	60.7%	24.5%
Public Administration	71.6%	28.4%	5.1%

(*Source:* Employment Policy Foundation: Washington, DC)

the manager with human resources responsibilities, understand the definitions for exempt employees and how those definitions apply specifically to your situation. It is up to you to contact the Wage and Hour Division of the Employment Standards Administration of the U.S. Department of Labor. A list of district offices, phone and fax numbers can be found at: www.dol.gov/dol/esa/public/contacts/whd/american2.htm.

INDUSTRY EXPERTS SPEAK

"The terms ***wage*** and ***salary*** are not used operatively in the industry. Rather, the term ***salary*** is used to cover all compensation plans. Most companies do not like to make an obvious distinction between wage and salaried employees. Only in salary or wage structure and how they are paid (i.e., hourly, semiweekly, weekly) is this distinction used. Operationally, wages and salaries are the same and mean the same," according to Richard Ysmael, Foodworks Management Services, Motorola Inc.

CONSIDERATIONS IN DEVELOPING A COMPENSATION PLAN

The compensation plan for your hospitality organization must fit into the overall human resources business plan. As is true in the development of any human resources plan, the place to begin is with the objectives. What are the objectives of your compensation plan? These stem directly from the mission statement of the hospitality enterprise and the organization's or unit's business and financial goals. You also need to take into consideration the role that compensation plays in your total rewards system (Figure 10-1).

Think for a moment about what you feel might be some possible objectives for a good compensation plan. Job satisfaction on the part of your employees would be one objective, as would a reduction in grievances, a fair pay structure, a system rewarding seniority, and a plan that will attract job candidates to your hospitality organization. Each of these objectives could be the basis of a compensation policy or procedure. The point we are trying to make is that the objectives of your compensation plan are unique to the mission and goals of your operation.

Now answer another question. From management's viewpoint, what do you feel is the most important consideration in the internal pay structure of your hospitality company? As a manager with human resources responsibilities you will be expected to assist in the control of labor costs. Sound management practices require that you pay competitively, but not excessively. If you pay excessive wages and salaries, you may be assured of enough labor, but your labor costs would skyrocket. The amount of discretion you will have in determining the compensation plan for your particular hospitality operation will be determined not only by external job factors, but internal factors as well.

What do you think your employees will feel is the most important characteristic of the compensation plan you develop? If your answer is that it be equitable or fair, you are absolutely correct! There is no way you can prevent your employees from comparing the compensation they earn with that of others. And not only will this comparison be among employees in your operation, but with other operations as well (Figure 10-2). Think for a moment about the period of time when you will be interviewing on your campus for your first postgraduation job. We guarantee that you will know the starting salaries for most of the companies interviewing on campus whether

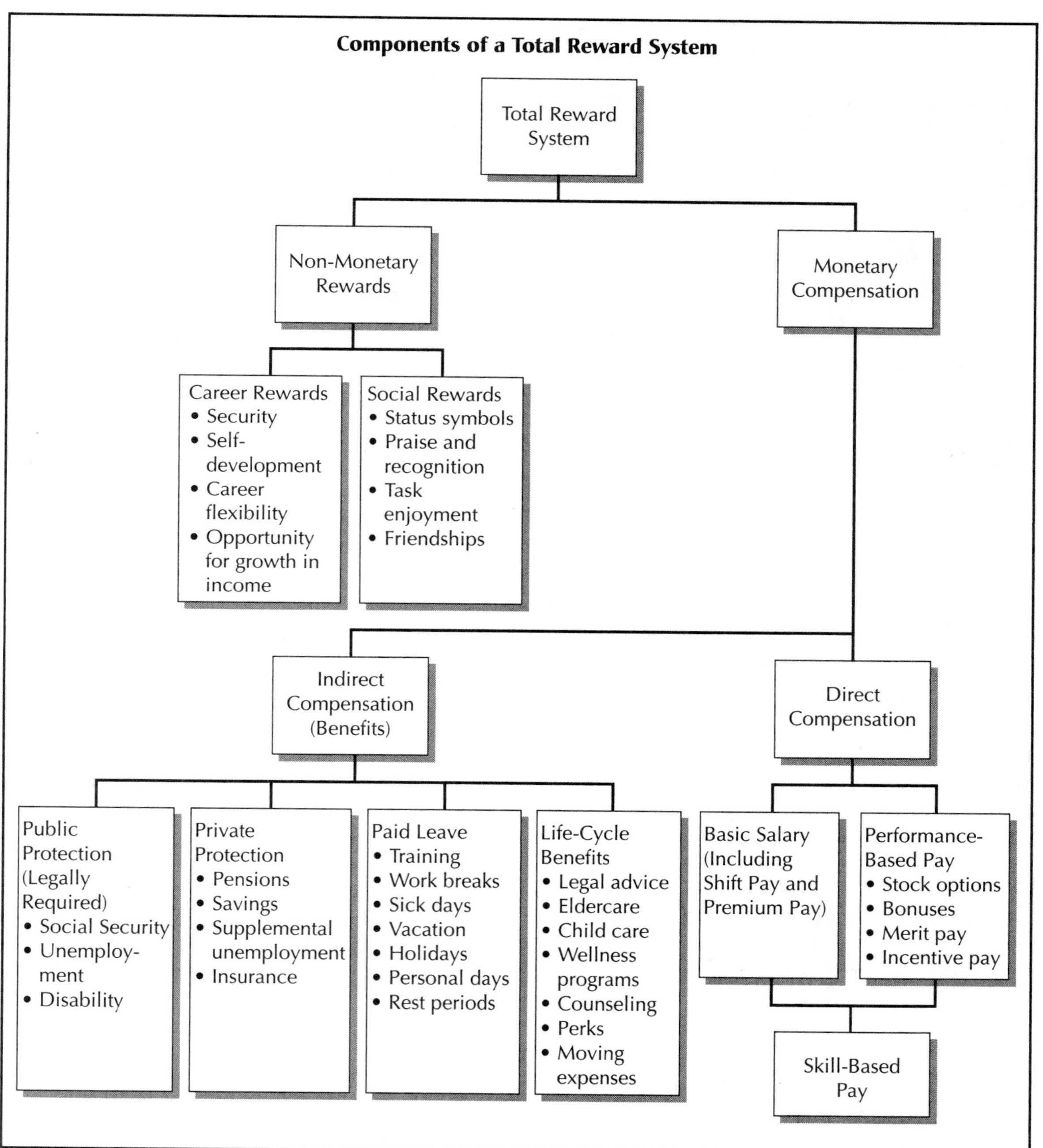

FIGURE 10-1 Components of a total reward system. *(Courtesy of Schuler, Randall S.,* Managing Human Resources, *6th ed., South-Western College Publishing (ITP), 1998, page 487, Exhibit 14.1)*

FIGURE 10-2 The ability to recruit and retain competent employees can be directly affected by the perceived fairness of your compensation plan. *(Courtesy of Chili's Grill & Bar, Brinker International)*

you personally interviewed with them or not. And part of the decision-making process that each of you will use in determining which job to accept will include a comparison, and ultimately a determination, of whether the salary being offered to you is equitable. If you do not feel an offer is fair, you will not accept that offer.

There is nothing that can destroy the morale of a group of employees faster than the belief that the pay structure is inequitable. That belief will occur if your employees feel that they are doing the same work (or more) as another who is getting paid more money. Skilled employees may feel that the quality of their work is higher than that of another worker, and that the pay structure has not taken their talents and experience into consideration. If this attitude of inequity persists, it will permeate your operation, and low morale along with higher turnover may be the result. Table 10-2 identifies the outcomes of a sound compensation plan in the hospitality industry.

TABLE 10-2 Outcomes of a Compensation Plan in the Hospitality Industry

The Goal:

To reduce the inequities among wages and salaries

Intended Outcomes:

Increased Motivation
Improved Job Performance
Advancement Opportunities
Reduced Absenteeism
Employee Retention
Employee Job Satisfaction
Attract Best Employees
Career Development
Competitive Advantage

One of the considerations that you need to take into account in the development of a compensation plan is that of equity. An external consideration that you must take into account involves the pool of available labor for each skill level that your hospitality enterprise requires. How much competition is there for the available labor supply? The low levels of unemployment in some market areas means that established pay rates must be competitive for recruitment and selection procedures to be effective. How attractive are your job openings as compared to the restaurant, hotel, or catering operation down the street from your property?

A related external consideration is how your hospitality company or organization is viewed as an employer. Do you have a reputation as a low-wage company? Pay must be set high enough to attract the people you need and still allow the company an opportunity to meet its labor expense budgets. Although the rate of pay is very important in attracting and retaining employees, do not forget that it must be considered as part of the total reward system, which also includes benefits, ability for advancement, and quality of the work environment. A planned process for individual growth and career development through promotions becomes an integrated component of a sound rewards system.

Internal considerations in the development of an equitable compensation plan include any collective bargaining agreements that might be in existence, whether you establish a single rate of pay or a range of rates for each job, if and how cost of living adjustments (COLA) will be maintained, and if and how seniority will be rewarded. The needs and expectations of your employees in "the next chapter" will be dynamic rather than static. A compensation plan should stimulate your people to work for pay increases through improved performance. Later in this chapter we further discuss the pay-for-performance compensation strategy.

In the hospitality industry, the largest single cost factor is that of wages and salaries. Both management and nonmanagement employees have a vested interest in assuring equitable compensation policies and procedures. To have a uniform centralized compensation plan is simply good human resources management.

JOB EVALUATION

There is no single approach to determining appropriate wages and salaries. Decisions now need to be made regarding how much you are going to pay your employees. These decisions must take into account both your management philosophy of compensation and the internal and external considerations discussed previously. What other factors are important in wage and salary determination for the hospitality industry? How do you decide how much to pay? For those of you who will be entering existing hospitality operations, how will you find out whether you are paying appropriate wages? Why is it necessary to establish a wage and salary scale?

An established wage and salary structure will assist you with labor cost containment and the administration of the compensation plan. Actually, you have already collected the information you need to begin the process of wage and salary determination. The job analysis provided us with information concerning job content that we then used to write job descriptions and job specifications. In a job evaluation this information is used to categorize the jobs and establish a job hierarchy.

The process of job evaluation examines the internal pay relationship within an organization. We define **job evaluation** as a systematic process that assesses the relationships that exist among job positions within a hospitality organization to provide a set of criteria for differentiating jobs for the purpose of wage determination. It helps establish which jobs should be paid more within the hospitality organization. Job evaluation assists you in maintaining internal equity in the pay rates among jobs.

In the job analysis process, we did not analyze the employee's performance level, but rather the duties and responsibilities associated with each job in your hospitality operation. So it is with job evaluation, the job analysis information assists you, the manager with human resources responsibilities, in grading the jobs by job families so that a pay rate can be assigned to each job grade level. In some hospitality organizations wage or salary ranges are used instead of one rate per job grade. At this stage, however, we are not attempting to determine what an employee's actual amount of pay should be within that range.

Compensation Surveys

The amount of money, before deductions, which is paid to an employee to perform a specific job is known as the **base pay** of that job. Earlier, we discussed one of the external considerations in developing a compensation plan, your competition. To ensure the competitiveness of your compensation structure, external surveys are conducted. Local area compensation surveys provide you with information concerning pay rates for the specific segment of the hospitality industry that is of concern to you. These data give you the ability to determine the competitive position of your pay rates in comparison to the level of compensation provided by other companies for comparable jobs.

In order to attract and retain the people your operation needs, it is important to know what other companies pay for comparable jobs. If your pay structure is too low, employee dissatisfaction may result in high turnover, excessive recruitment efforts, and high orientation and training costs. To maximize the benefits from a compensation survey, you must determine first if your operations are really comparable to the operation in the survey. This includes an examination of the duties the employees perform. If dishwashers are being paid $8.00/hour, you need to find out what their job descriptions require. A second consideration is an evaluation of the total reward system, including the benefit packages of your competitors. Your hospitality operation might be effective in attracting and retaining employees as a result of the benefits package you offer, even though your wage and salary levels are somewhat lower.

Hospitality operations should be viewed by you as competitive if:

- They are geographically close (although management jobs are competitive on a national basis)
- They provide similar products and/or services
- They draw employees away from your operation

Job Grading

The first step toward determining the value of each job is job grading. Once the job descriptions have been written, the jobs can be compared and evaluated against each other. **Job grading** can be defined as a method of establishing a job hierarchy through a comparison of job content. To do this, the jobs are categorized in terms of compensable factors obtained from the job analysis: the skill level required, job responsibilities, efforts, working conditions, and job requirements such as educational background and prior work experience. These compensable factors enable you to rank jobs by placing one job at a higher level or grade than another job in the hierarchy.

The judgments made by you and your management team determine which compensable factor(s) place a job at a higher point on the hierarchy scale (Figure 10-3). The philoso-

FIGURE 10-3 Job grading takes into consideration an organization's philosophy, mission statement, and goals. *(Courtesy of Left At Albuquerque, Palo Alto, CA)*

phy, mission statement, and organizational goals also influence which factors are weighted more than others. It is important to recognize that there is no one set of factors, but rather a group of factors that vary in their individual importance relative to their contribution to the overall success of your particular operation. As the mission statements of each hospitality enterprise vary, so does the importance of the various compensable factors that are used to rank the jobs within the enterprise. If you can distinguish between the important and unimportant aspects of a job, the result is a means by which jobs within your hospitality organization can be compared.

Let's use a job description for a line server and identify what the relevant compensable factors would be for a food service operation. We believe that those would be:

Skill Level/Job Requirements

—Education
—Experience
—Training required
—Knowledge of materials and processes
—Judgment and initiative
—Time required to learn the job

Effort

—Concentration
—Physical demand
—Physical fatigue

Job Responsibility

—Monetary
—Methods and procedures
—Contact with guests
—Public relations
—Cooperation
—Safety
—Supervision of others
—Dependability
—Coordination
—System to master

Working Conditions

—Danger from equipment
—Heat
—Shift hours

Remember, our evaluation process involves the job of a food service worker, not any one particular individual that is performing that job. For each of our compensable factors we need to determine a standard scale. Let's look at two of the compensation factors under skill level and see how this would be applied.

Education:

No high school diploma	5 points
High school diploma	15 points
Some college education	20 points
Bachelor's degree	25 points
Master's degree	30 points

Time required to learn the job:

0–1 week	5 points
2–3 weeks	10 points
4–8 weeks	15 points
9–26 weeks	20 points
27–52 weeks	25 points
1–2 years	30 points

Our job of food service worker requires a high school diploma, equal to 15 points, and 2–3 weeks to learn the job, which equals 10 points. This accumulation of points needs to be done for each of the other compensable factors so that we have a total number of points for the food service worker job in our food service operation.

Hospitality organizations frequently use the job-classification method of job evaluation that classifies jobs into a number of grades. These grades then become the basis of compensation administration. After the jobs are quantified according to the compensable factors we just discussed, each job in the organization is classified into a grade level. The result is job clusters or families, each with its own grade level number that remains consistent throughout the organization.

Statistical analysis procedures can be used for the purpose of job grading. Once a system is established, historical data from your hospitality operation can be used to update your job grades as operational changes cause job descriptions to be modified. With the aid of a computer, statistical techniques remove some of the subjectivity associated with traditional job grading methods and, hence, better assure equitable internal pay relationships among jobs. And as we discuss later, equity is critical in improving human relations and for using compensation as a motivational tool in human resources management.

Job Pricing

The next step in job evaluation (after job grading) is job pricing. We define **job pricing** as a method of setting the range of pay or rate of pay for each job grade. Decisions now need to be made to determine what your organization is willing to pay for each grade level. How much a job is worth is determined by several variables. These include the job information you have gathered through your job grading process, the external labor market data collected in your local compensation surveys, and any collective bargaining agreements that your hospitality organization may be guided by. You are now faced with the task of establishing wages and salaries alluring enough to attract quality people and simultaneously assuring them of a fair internal pay structure in order to maximize retention.

What do you need to take into consideration when you determine the pay differences within your hospitality operation? What considerations are those based upon? The determination of pay differences is a human resources management decision. One of your decisions includes where you want to be with respect to your local pay structure. Do you want to pay wages and salaries that are higher than your competition to attract employees away from your competitors? What type of a public relations image do you want to portray with respect to compensation? The competitiveness of the market, the quality of the employees available, and what your need is for quality people in your hospitality operation form the basis for determining starting wage and salary rates (Figure 10-4). These decisions all must take into account the effect of any collective bargaining agreements, along with a thorough understanding of the legal issues and laws pertaining to compensation administration.

In the hospitality industry the type of people we hire is as important to the success of our operation as the work that they perform. Table 10-3 identifies some of the people characteristics that may affect the level or amount of wages you decide to pay particular individuals. In particular, our industry has recognized the commitment of its people to the organization and hospitality industry at large. This is reflected in compensation plans that reward previous industry experience and length of service. Hospitality has been an industry proud to take

FIGURE 10-4 Conditions of the labor market—supply versus demand—largely influence the wage rates companies must pay their employees. *(Courtesy of Left At Albuquerque, Palo Alto, CA)*

TABLE 10-3 Characteristics of the Individuals You Hire That May Affect the Level of Compensation

- Skill level
- Education
- Length of service or seniority (industry and organizational commitment)
- Experience

care of its own and provide opportunities for advancement and career growth.

As job applicants continue to be scarce, your compensation plans will need to be innovative in providing for the long-term needs of your people. In the hospitality industry, the pay structures reflect the organization's belief that when an individual is hired, consideration should be given to what the long-term abilities and contributions of that individual will be to the operation, rather than what he or she can actually do on the day that the individual is hired.

What other traditions exist in the hospitality industry with respect to wage and salary differences? One factor may be the particular segment of the hospitality industry you will be working in. Another difference relates to the specific department your employees are in. And within departments there are the differences that we have already discussed that exist among the jobs themselves. And even among the employees working in the same job, pay differences exist based upon the individual's length of service with the industry, with the company, the employee's personal performance record, working conditions, and whether the company is unionized. Perhaps the "graveyard" front desk shift is paid higher than the more desirable daytime shifts. Or the night server in a 24-hour restaurant might be paid higher wages to compensate for fewer tips and a less desirable working environment.

As you have learned in this discussion, compensation plans and policies are heavily dependent upon the job analysis and job descriptions developed in Chapter 3. Providing both external and internal equity in your wage and salary structure is a vital component of your job as human resources manager. If your wage and salary structure is to be accepted, the results of your job evaluation process must be clearly communicated to employees at all levels of your hospitality enterprise. Equally important is the fair administration of the compensation program.

EFFECTS OF COLLECTIVE BARGAINING

A trade union operation requires that you, as the human resources manager, be fully aware of all collective bargaining agreements. The conditions pertaining to wage determination, increases, and incentive-type programs are as a general rule very specific. It is your responsibility to conduct all compensation planning within the framework that is established by those agreements.

Because one of the union's major concerns is with the equity of your pay structure, representatives will sometimes be willing to assist in the job evaluation process. Several conditions that might encourage employee interest in unions are tied to compensation. These include unequitable wages, wages that are inappropriate for the work performed, employees feeling that there is no flexibility or incentives in their wage earning capabilities, inadequate benefits, and employees who feel that they are not recognized for their performance on the job. This profile of compensation-related conditions shows again the importance and value of sound compensation decision making.

TIPPING OR SERVICE CHARGES?

The compensation our staff receives from tips is a long-standing tradition in our industry in the United States. Servers are paid less than the minimum wage standards required by the Fair Labor Standards Act (FLSA) because the difference is compensated by tips received. A **tip** is a gratuity given by a customer to an employee. This is quite different from the hospitality industry in many European countries where it is not unusual for an automatic service charge to be added to your bill. A **service charge** is an amount added to a customer's check by the employer. The amount is usually a fixed percentage of the check total.

Proponents of the service charge system argue that for too long our industry has permitted our customers to compensate the waitstaff instead of paying them their fair wages (Figure 10-5). It is true that no other service industry historically has relied on tipping to compensate its employees. While the theory of tips is that they are to serve as a reward for good service, they have long lost this attribute as customers routinely leave tips with little or no regard to the quality of the service received.

FIGURE 10-5 Customers are sometimes more comfortable adding a service charge to the bill as opposed to tipping the employee.

According to the law, when hospitality organizations institute a service charge system into their hospitality operations, that money is considered part of the operation's gross receipts. As such, it can be used by the employer to pay any business expense, including paying waitstaff the full minimum wage. The argument in favor of the service charge system states that if we want to treat our employees as professionals, then it is time we start compensating them professional wages.

A tip, according to the 1959 definition provided by the Internal Revenue Service, must be solely at the discretion of the customer. Furthermore, the customer must have the right to determine the amount of the tip and to whom the tip shall go. None of these factors can be determined by company policy. Those in favor of retaining the tipping system believe that the system does reward, with the highest gratuities, those employees who provide the best service. As such, the system of tipping serves to motivate the staff to sell more products and provide better service.

In hospitality operations using the tipping system, the division of gratuities among employees varies from company to company and from operation to operation. Some properties permit the employees who received the gratuity to keep all of it; some company policies require a pooling and division of all gratuities at the end of a designated shift. Even the procedures for dividing the gratuities vary. These policies are legal, provided that the tipped employee is not required to share tips with employees who do not regularly and customarily participate in tip-pooling arrangements such as chefs and dishwashers.

The decisions that you make with regard to the policies and procedures for handling gratuities in your hospitality operation reflect your own philosophy as a manager with human resources responsibilities. It is important for you to recognize that the policies you establish will become an integral part of your overall compensation plan.

The hospitality industry has historically not been known for its high rates of pay. Some of that reputation stems from undesirable working conditions in the form of late hours, weekends, and holidays. Let's face it, we have each selected a career in an industry that works its hardest when others are at play. To maintain a competitive edge with other service industries that are competing for the same people, your compensation rates must be periodically reviewed. Does the company you work for, or own, want to be viewed as a good employer? The community's perception of your operation and the hospitality industry as an employer is largely reflected in the compensation policies and procedures you develop.

COMPENSATION AS A MOTIVATIONAL TOOL?

Do you believe that money is a motivator for the people who report to you? Can wages be effective as motivational tools? Would you still work if you did not need the monetary rewards? In the United States, historically, most individuals would answer yes to that question.[3] So, if money is not the main reason you go to work, what does motivate you? Each of you undoubtedly came up with a somewhat different answer to that question, which is why a discussion on theory of pay as a motivational tool can become so complex. Once the basic individual needs in each of us is met, there is no single source of satisfaction that will motivate all of us.

The ability to understand why people behave as they do and the ability to motivate them to behave in a specific manner are two interrelated managerial qualities that are essential for effective human resources management. The process of goal setting can be directly related to motivational theories. Goal setting emphasizes the importance of investing an individual's mental and physical resources in the areas that have the highest potential for payoff. Therefore, the more clearly a goal and its rewards are visualized, the greater its motivational pull. This is equally true for all employees, regardless of where they fall in the job hierarchy.

The basic premise in our discussion of pay as a motivator is that your compensation plan does satisfy the employee's basic needs of food, shelter, and clothing that Maslow identifies in his Needs Hierarchy. When those needs are not met, pay becomes, according to Hertzberg, a dissatisfier in the workplace. Hertzberg's theory states that pay is not a motivational factor, but rather a hygiene or maintenance factor. According to these theories on motivation and others found in literature, the motivational value of money may change after a person's basic needs have been satisfied. Because human beings have a way of continually redefining their needs, whether money will motivate is to some degree a matter of the amount of pay involved and the amount of pay the employee is already earning. Therefore, whereas some people will be highly motivated to work for money, other compensatory factors, such as recognition for seniority, might be more motivational for other employees in our hospitality operations.

In traditional compensation plans, using the job evaluation technique discussed previously, equal job positions are usually slotted in the same pay range or grade. In such systems, job grade level and the assignment of an employee to that job are the basis for pay determination. The determinant of pay was established by the labor market and what the job was worth compared to all other jobs in the hospitality enterprise. In "the next chapter" you will be faced with a number of alternatives to this traditional way of thinking about compensation planning. The concept of **pay-for-performance** includes a variety of individual and group incentive plans such as gain sharing, commissions, bonuses, profit sharing, and employee stock ownership plans, which are some innovative compensation plans being used by other industries. The hospitality industry is now turning towards some of these ideas. Let's examine some of the key elements in each of these concepts.

PAY-FOR-PERFORMANCE

Some of the long-standing customs regarding pay structures in the hospitality industry will be changing as employees continue to become increasingly scarce. Historically, wage rates were structured to reward the employees with the highest skill levels with the higher wages. Oftentimes, the level of skill required by the job was determined to be more important (i.e., higher wage) than the contribution of the particular job to the achievement of the operation's objectives. In "the next chapter," there will be less disparity in compensation among unskilled, semiskilled, and skilled employees. More important than level of skill will be the level of the performance.

To motivate and retain our valuable employees, hospitality organizations are trying to develop methods of determining who should be and who should not be rewarded. Many of these programs are founded upon the idea of basing rewards on the level of performance each person obtains along with the value of that performance level to the overall success of the hospitality enterprise. Those that contribute the most to the achievement of the organizational goals and operational objectives are compensated with the largest reward (Figure 10-6). Those who do not make a significant contribution to the organization's success receive a proportionately lesser reward.

It is in pay-for-performance compensation plans that pay has its greatest influence as a motivator. People usually like to know what they can expect in return for their level of performance. In such a system, the staff knows what to expect regarding the level of effort that they must achieve in order to receive a desired outcome or reward. Rewards serve to motivate performance by satisfying the needs of our employee's that relate to work.

For compensation to be effective as a motivator, your employees must believe that good performance will lead to greater pay, and at the same time, that minimal performance levels will not be rewarded. Too often in traditional compensation plans, the employees perceive that no one recognizes extra effort and that even marginal performance levels will receive the same percentage pay increases each year. This will depend upon your merit budget and

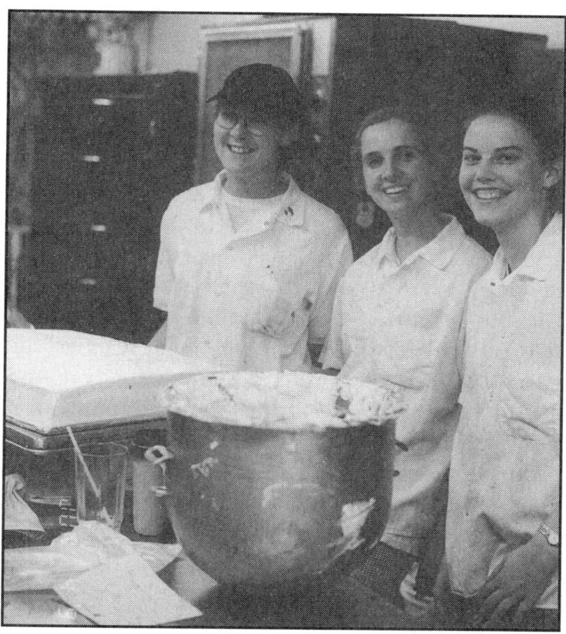

FIGURE 10-6 In pay-for-performance compensation plans employees are motivated to achieve company goals. *(Courtesy of Strongbow Inn, Valparaiso, IN)*

whether or not management can distinguish between good and bad performance and reward as such.

A pay-for-performance system is based upon established performance goals that are designed to be challenging, but obtainable. Here, risk taking is encouraged through a non-punitive appraisal process that is based upon both quantitative and qualitative performance measures. This approach tends to foster both creativity and team spirit among your people. In addition, such programs have been found to increase productivity levels. Although it is appealing to most people to believe that their pay is tied directly to their performance, there can be problems in implementing pay-for-performance plans. The major obstacle for most hospitality organizations, especially those with several decentralized levels of management, is the difficulty in accurately and objectively linking pay levels to performance. In addition, pay-for-performance plans must be clearly communicated to your employees, or those plans lose their effectiveness.

Let's now look at a few of the compensation plans that take into account job performance and see how each of them differs in its approach to basing pay on the measurable achievements of employees.

Individual and Group Incentive Pay Programs

Incentive plans relate increases in compensation to increases in performance based upon a set of established performance criteria or standards in an endeavor to directly reward above-average performance. Standards might be based upon amount of time saved, sales volume generated, breakage reduction in glassware and china, improved customer service, or improved safety records. In hospitality production operations, such as in-flight feeding kitchens, a piece-rate plan can be established.

For an incentive program to be effective, it must be based on performance only, and there must be a clear relationship between what your employees do and what they receive for doing it. Everyone likes to get rewarded for a job well done. This behavior pattern begins when you are a small child. You quickly learned that when you did something right, you received a reward in the form of a cookie, hug, or praise. The reward followed the performance immediately.

A growing number of hospitality companies are taking a new look at their compensation programs to see how they can better utilize incentive plans in their total rewards system. In a study conducted in the late 1990s it was found that between 40 and 70 percent of major corporations had some type of incentive plan in place as part of their compensation program.[4] These plans need to be clearly thought out. The basic idea behind incentives is that people will perform in ways that get rewarded and will not perform in ways that will not get rewarded. It is important, therefore, to make sure that the incentives you develop tie back into your strategic human resources plans and business results.

Individual incentive programs have been found to have a greater motivational effect on performance than do group incentive programs. This is due to the fact that in group incentive programs the reward is tied to the performance of the group rather than individual efforts. The larger the group, the less motivational the incentive program becomes. Group incentive programs aid in the development of cooperation and teamwork within your hospitality organization. The pros and cons of individual versus group incentive programs will need to be carefully weighed in light of your organization's goals.

There are a great variety of incentive plans that you might want to consider implementing in your hospitality organization. These might include contests, achievement/recognition awards (good safety records), gifts, prizes, merchandise, travel incentives (least glassware broken over a specified period of time), earned time off, commissions or bonuses, profit sharing, gain sharing, and employee stock ownership plans. We now briefly discuss a few of these options with which you may not be familiar.

Commission Plans

Commission plans relate pay directly to the amount of sales generated. On a straight commission plan, your employees must sell or they will receive no compensation. In the hospitality industry, a modification of the traditional commission plan can be used to relate rewards to performance. For example, your waitstaff could receive a percentage of the total wine sales or dessert sales they generate over a specified period of time. We just need to expand our thinking to include a greater number of employees who can be called sales persons.

Bonus Plans

Bonus plans or lump sums are offered on a periodic basis to employees who achieve a high level of performance. It is important that this level of performance is measurable and that the performance goal is agreed upon by both the employer and employee. These may be used in the hospitality industry instead of the annual raise used in traditional compensation planning. The message given by awarding bonuses is much different from the message given by annual pay raises. Pay raises are expected by each of your employees, independent of the level of performance they have maintained throughout the year. Bonuses, given for the achievement of specific performance levels, indicate to your people that mediocrity will not be accepted in your hosptiality organization. This has the effect of reducing the friction that is created by across-the-board increases. These increases actually penalize your high performers and create burnout and frustration when their contributions to the organization's success go unnoticed. Bonuses allow the outstanding employee to maximize his or her earnings, while the earnings of nonperformers are static.

Profit Sharing

Profit sharing is a program in which employees receive a portion of the hospitality company's profit at the end of the year. If profits are raised through the contributions of all employees, then all share in the rewards. The distribution of these profits may be deferred until the employee retires, or they may be distributed annually. The motivational factor behind profit sharing is that the employees will become more conscious of the effect their performance has on the bottom line, and, therefore, will be motivated to work toward the success of the hospitality organization. For this to occur, your people need to be made aware of how their individual performance can affect profits.

Gain Sharing

Gain sharing is a more sophisticated approach to profit sharing that is used as a group rather than as an individual incentive plan. Gain sharing distributes a portion of the company's profit based upon the contributions of specific employee groups to specific stated objectives. The implementation of gain sharing can contribute to a team-building atmosphere within the hospitality organization.

Employee Stock Ownership Plans

Employee stock ownership plans (ESOP) are offered to employees by a number of corporations such as Marriott and Motorola. An employee stock ownership plan gives employees the option to buy stock in the company that they work for. The specific guidelines for stock purchase vary from company to company. The idea behind ESOP is that they give your employees a chance for ownership in the company, thereby improving performance levels, increasing loyalty, and assisting in the development of a sense of teamwork.

Summary

The idea of paying for an individual's contribution to the hospitality organization rather than merely for his or her length of service is the heart of the pay-for-performance compensation system. This system is most effective when improved efforts can be related directly to improved performance. Although care must be taken in developing objective performance standards, the hospitality work environment provides numerous occasions for this system to be successfully applied. The motivational effects of these plans—improved morale and better communications—are all advantages in a well-administered and well-implemented system. They also become important tools in our continuing efforts to attract and retain our people.

Incentive programs have been created in an effort to motivate our people to reach new heights in production and efficiency in service. Incentive programs alone, however, do not make our people high achievers. In order to be effective, these programs have to be clearly communicated so that all people affected understand the opportunities the programs provide for their financial advancement (Figure 10-7). Do your employees know what performance is rewarded by additional pay? Incentive programs are most successful when the employee can readily see the relationship between what he or she does and the reward he or she receives. Whatever incentive program you select to implement, it must be administered accurately, with the performance levels being measured objectively to maintain the equity of your compensation plan.

FIGURE 10-7 Incentive programs must be effectively communicated to your employees so that each understands the potential for financial advancement. *(Courtesy of Strongbow Inn, Valparaiso, IN)*

LEGAL ISSUES IN COMPENSATION ADMINISTRATION

The decision-making process you use in compensation planning is closely governed by federal and state regulations. It is up to you to investigate the appropriate state laws that apply where your hospitality operation(s) is or are located; here we discuss the federal legislation that affects compensation decision-making.

Fair Labor Standards Act

The Fair Labor Standards Act (FLSA) is a broad federal statute that includes information and regulations on the following compensatory areas:

- Federal minimum wage law
- Employee meals and meals credit
- Equal pay
- Child labor
- Overtime
- Tip, tip credits, and tip-pooling procedures
- Uniform and uniform maintenance
- Recordkeeping
- Exempt versus nonexempt employees

This act was first passed in 1938 and has been amended several times for the purpose of raising the minimum wage rates and expanding the groups of employees covered under the act. As of this writing, employees covered by this act are entitled to receive a minimum wage of $5.15 per hour and overtime pay at a rate that is not less than one and one-half times the regular rate of pay for any hours worked over 40 in a workweek. Minimum wage exceptions are granted in a variety of specific situations, including circumstances relating to tipped employees. The act is enforced by the Department of Labor, which maintains regional offices of the Wage and Hour Division throughout the country. It is our recommendation that any specific questions you may have concerning your hospitality operations' compensation plans be addressed directly to their closest office.

Compensatory time is a spin-off of the FLSA provision regarding overtime. The use of compensatory time practices has been common in the hospitality industry, where the nature of the business requires shifts longer than 8 hours and some weeks longer than 40 hours. "Comp time" is then given to these employees instead of overtime pay. Generally, this is practiced on a voluntary basis. For example, the food service operation you are working in is busier than usual on a Saturday afternoon, and you ask one of your waitstaff to work a double shift. If the person agrees to work the double shift, you promise him or her an extra day off next week. Even though the double shift will put that employee over a 40-hour work week, you compensate by giving the individual an extra day off the following week.

The problem with this situation is that according to the Fair Labor Standards Act, you are in violation of not paying overtime. The extra hours your waitstaff employee worked in the first week cannot be offset by reduced work hours in the second week. Doing so is a dangerous practice. If an employee reports such policies to the Wage and Hour Division of the Department of Labor, you will be required to pay overtime rates (1.5 times the hourly rate of pay) for all hours worked over 40 in one week. (These regulations are different in California.) Overtime, however, is not paid on hours worked over eight in a given day.

The FLSA rules regarding compensatory time off are very specific. You must be sure to check with a legal advisor to make sure that your policies are in keeping with the requirements of the law.

Equal Pay Act of 1963

The **Equal Pay Act** was passed to prohibit companies from paying wage and salary differentials on the basis of sex. Jobs that require the same skill level, effort, responsibility, and working conditions must be paid at the same rate of compensation.[5] Seniority systems and merit or pay-for-performance systems can legally result in differentiated pay scales even though skills and responsibilities are the same. All employers who are governed by the FLSA are also covered by the provisions in the Equal Pay Act (EPA). The EPA is enforced by the Equal Employment Opportunity Commission (EEOC) (Table 10-4). Even though the EPA stipulates that pay rates must not discriminate between sexes, a pay differential still exists between the sexes.

Comparable Worth

In the early 1960s, the cry was one of "equal pay for equal work." The passing of the Equal Pay Act in 1963 and a year later of the Civil Rights Act was a response to the discriminatory practices that existed at that time in the United Sates. The hospitality industry, which historically has been dominated by white male employees, was no exception. During the 1980s, the slogan changed to "equal pay for comparable worth" and while still not covered by any laws, it continues to be a hotly debated issue. The proponents of **comparable worth** feel that jobs should receive the same rate of pay if they contribute equally to the success of the organization. Jobs of equal value are said to be of comparable worth to the organization.

The Civil Rights Act of 1964

The **Civil Rights Act of 1964** contains Titles I through VII. Title VII, which established the Equal Employment Opportunity Commission (EEOC), deals with a number of compensation-related elements. Title VII makes it unlawful for an employer to discriminate with respect to hiring, compensation, conditions, privileges, or terms of employment "on the basis of race, color, creed, sex, or national origin."

Executive Order 11246

Although **Executive Order 11246** is not a piece of legislation, it is an order issued in 1965 under President Lyndon Johnson. This order established affirmative action programs for all employers covered by the order (government contractors and subcontractors with ten or more employees and $10,000 in contracts). Employers who meet these criteria are subject to review by the Office of Federal Contract Compliance Programs (OFCCP), and, if found guilty of compensation discrimination, are subject to paying back wages with interest.

TABLE 10-4 Equal Pay Act Charges: 1992–1998 (Filed and Resolved)

	Fiscal Year						
	1992	1993	1994	1995	1996	1997	1998
Receipts	1,294	1,328	1,381	1,275	969	1,134	1,071
Resolutions	1,185	1,120	1,171	1,249	1,235	1,172	1,134
Monetary Benefits (Millions)*	$2.2	$2.4	$2.8	$2.8	$1.9	$2.4	$2.7

(*Source:* The U.S. Equal Employment Opportunity Commission, Washington, DC)

Age Discrimination Act of 1967

Just as Title VII prohibits discrimination on the basis of race, color, creed, sex, or national origin, the **Age Discrimination Act of 1967** prohibits discriminatory employment practices on the basis of age for those individuals between the ages of 40 and 69. The EEOC is the agency that administers this act. An amendment to this act in 1978 raised the age limit of mandatory retirement programs from 65 to 70. For hospitality organizations with a senior and, therefore, more highly compensated group of human resources, labor costs will be impacted.

Legal Miscellaneous

There are many legal constraints imposed upon hospitality companies by the legislation already discussed. In addition is the Social Security Act of 1935 that requires employers' as well as employee contributions to the plan. Typically these funds must be paid at least quarterly.

State legislation should be thoroughly investigated for all states where you have a responsibility toward a hospitality operation. Worker compensation, unemployment insurance laws, discrimination laws, and even minimum wage standards could differ significantly from what federal legislation requires.

TRENDS IN COMPENSATION PLANNING

Compensation planning has become one of the key human resources functions (Figure 10-8). Approaches and methods are becoming innovative tools to assist you in attracting and then retaining the people you need at all levels in your hospitality organization. We have identified five of the trends that you should keep informed of as you enter the hospitality industry.

FIGURE 10-8 Compensation planning sessions are a necessary component of sound human resources management. *(Courtesy of Motorola, Inc.)*

1. Your employees are no longer willing to sacrifice leisure time for extensive overtime hours. This relates directly to the issue of work-family, which we discuss at length in Chapter 11.
2. To accommodate the changes in attitude and demographics, your compensation plan will need to be flexible as opposed to rigid.
3. As pay becomes more closely related to an individual's performance level and/or contribution to the hospitality enterprise, tools to measure performance standards and contribution levels will become more reliable and more widely available. The increasing use of computers in the workplace, to handle data, will assist in the progression.
4. As the hospitality industry becomes more global and as individual companies expand their markets across the United States, compensation plans will need to become more considerate of the global, as opposed to the national, rate of pay.
5. The changes in compensation programs will increase the likelihood of hourly employees making more money than their supervisors. A watchful eye will need to be kept on the effect this occurrence will have on the traditional subordinate-supervisor relationships as the number of pay levels included in the compensation plan are reduced.

COMPENSATION ADMINISTRATION IN THE HOSPITALITY INDUSTRY

The success of a compensation plan lies in its credibility and how well it is maintained as both the hospitality enterprise and hospitality industry changes and grows. So far in this chapter, you have succeeded in developing an equitable plan, one that is based upon well-written job descriptions. All your compensation policies should be formalized into a written manual and made available to all employees. Once, however, this has been accomplished, it does not mean that you can forget about the compensation component of your total reward system. On the contrary, all elements of your reward system need constant attention in order to maintain their effectiveness in attracting and retaining the best people available.

If your compensation plan, along with the bonus, merit pay, and other incentive programs you have established in your hospitality operation are to be effective as motivational devices, they must be constantly communicated as such to your employees. Once your employees have been hired and have fallen into the job routine, they will need to be reminded of the opportunities that your compensation package provides for them. Promote the rewards that are offered and give your employees time to think about the incentives they are working toward.

Once an employee has earned a reward, take an opportunity to issue the reward where other employees can honor the recipient. Not only does this give the employee receiving the reward a chance to be recognized for his or her contribution, but it also allows the other workers to be reminded that rewards are obtainable for them as well.

The degree of autonomy you will have in compensation decision making will depend on the size of the hospitality organization you are working in. In large organizations, there will be a compensation department with staff personnel whose job is to administer the compensation plan. In very large organizations, these departments will include individuals who are experts in compensation. These compensation professionals may or may not have worked in a hospitality enterprise previously, but rather have developed competencies in the areas of compensation, benefits, pension plans, job analysis, and incentive pay systems. In these large hospitality companies the compensation professionals work with the line managers to obtain the compensation objectives of the hospitality enterprise.

In smaller hospitality organizations, compensation administration and decision making rests with the general manager of the food service or lodging operation. This would include decisions in the job evaluation process that we discussed earlier in this chapter, as well as decisions regarding changes in any of the established pricing structures. Compensation surveys should be conducted periodically (we suggest no less frequently than once a year, although significant changes in the local labor market may require more frequent review) to ensure that your hospitality organization's pay structure remains competitive. If it does not, you will find yourself losing some of your most valuable employees over pay differentials to neighboring hospitality operations. COLA, or cost of living adjustments, are provided for by some hospitality organizations to counter the effects of inflation in our economy.

As your hospitality organization is dynamic, not static, it grows larger, or perhaps even smaller in size. The jobs within your operation are similarly altered. Job re-evaluation must be conducted to take into consideration the changes that will be reflected in the job descriptions. None of the human resources management tools that we have described to you is firmly fixed in cement, never to be changed.

Maintaining the accuracy of the job descriptions is one of the most useful functions performed by a human resources manager. New jobs are likely to be created that will require evaluation, and efforts will need to be made to ensure the continued equity of your compensation plan.

As changes in the wage and salary structure influence both human resources development and recruitment, the administration of compensation is a vital human resources activity. As employees become scarce commodities in the service sector, keeping pay levels competitive will be a major challenge you face in "the next chapter."

CONCLUSION

Compensation development, implementation, and administration in hospitality organizations are vital human resources management activities. The satisfaction of your work force and, in essence, the success or failure of the operation, is heavily dependent upon an equitable compensation plan that both attracts and retains the caliber of people required by the mission statement of the hospitality enterprise. In "the next chapter," the continuing changes in the labor market will play a large role in determining the relationship between job hierarchy and pay structure. Pay is still used to satisfy our basic physical needs, but also assists us in recognizing our star performers and permits us the ability to give our employees a sense of accomplishment, no matter what job they perform for us in the hospitality operation. It is very difficult for a hospitality organization to keep all of its employees happy and satisfied, which is why it is so important that your selection of rewards is targeted at satisfying the needs of your employees. Of all the rewards an organization can offer to its employees, the wages and salaries are the most visible.

If you were to develop the ideal compensation plan for your hospitality organization, what would you want to provide?

- Competitive pay rates that would attract qualified, competent people.
- A reward for longevity with your company that would encourage retention among the employees.

- A promotional incentive that would motivate your people to seek the opportunities your hospitality organization has to offer.
- A reward for quality work to show all employees that your organization strives for excellence in the goods and services it provides.
- An equitable system that all employees view as fair.
- Procedures that permit a uniform approach to compensation changes that seek to maintain the integrity of the reward system.
- An effective method for controlling compensation costs. This, in effect, is based upon your organization's ability to pay.

Let's now turn our attention to compensation's partner in the reward system: benefits.

CASE PROBLEM 10-1

You are the human resources manager of a 90-room, nonunionized hotel located in South Carolina. The property has a limited-menu, coffee-shop–type restaurant with no alcoholic beverage service. There is one other hotel property in your geographic area that is close enough to compete with you for both guests and employees. The labor market in the area is very tight, with unemployment at a low 5.7 percent. The lowest wage you pay to your hourly employees is $7.70 per hour. No one in the area will work for any less.

Historically, you have never linked compensation directly to performance appraisals or productivity levels. You believe with the current labor market situation that a pay-for-performance compensation plan (for nonexempt employees) would be beneficial. The general manager, however, is less than enthusiastic. She feels that you will encounter a number of difficulties in switching to a pay-for-performance plan and that the problems will outweigh the benefits.

How will you convince the general manager that a pay-for-performance plan will be of benefit? Anticipate what concerns she may have, identify them, and develop solutions for each of them. Prepare a two-page transition plan to present to the general manager for the short-term implementation of a pay-for-performance system. Make sure that your plan addresses any potential concerns your employees may have.

Case Problem 10-2

You are a strong advocate of adding a service charge to every guest check. You feel that tipping is not an effective method of compensation for service employees. You are the food-and-beverage manager of a 300-seat dinner house. This is a chain with ten properties located throughout the eastern seaboard. The two individuals who own the chain of dinner houses strongly resist the idea of implementing a service-charge system. They believe that tipping is a preferred system. The chain is six years old and presently uses a tipping system. The only exception is that a 20% service charge is added to parties of twenty or more. These parties are notified of this policy at the time they make their reservations.

How will you convince the two owners that a service-charge system is the wave of the future? Prepare a three-page written report that you will present to them to convince them to switch from the current system of tipping. Be logical and thorough in your ideas.

OR, take the position of the owners and prepare a written report that will convince the manager of this operation that the tipping system should prevail. Be logical and thorough in your ideas. (Just because they own the operation does not mean they are dictators when it comes to establishing operational policies.)

Case Problem 10-3

Using the hospitality operation you prepared for Case 1, develop a three-page report arguing either for or against compensation as a motivational tool. Make sure that you are specific, using several different types of individual and group incentive pay plans as examples.

Key Words

Age Discrimination Act of 1967
base pay
bonus plan
Civil Rights Act of 1964
commission plan
comparable worth
compensation
compensation planning
compensatory time
employee stock ownership plans (ESOP)
Equal Pay Act
Executive Order 11246
exempt personnel
Fair Labor Standards Act (FLSA)
gain sharing
incentive plan
job evaluation
job grading
job pricing
nonexempt personnel
pay-for-performance
profit sharing
salary
service charge
tip
wage

Recommended Reading

Avery, M. "HR Pay Growth Accelerates." *HR Magazine* 1998. www.shrm.org/hrmagazine/articles/1198avery.htm

Bortolus, D. 1999. "HR Systems: A Bridge for Linking Payroll Data to the General Ledger." *HR Magazine* (January).

Dingman, H. B. and D. R. Dingman. "Compensation Survey: GMs Make Little Progress in Base Pay." *The Cornell Quarterly* 36(5): 27–29.

Fox, F. J. "Do-It-Yourself HRMS Evaluations." *HR Magazine*. 1998. wwwshrm.org/hrmagazine/articles/0898hrm.htm

Frazee, V. 1998. "Is the Balance Sheet Right for Your Expats?" *Global Workforce* 3(5): 19–26.

Gould, C. 1997. "What's the Latest in Global Compensation?" *Global Workforce* 2(3): 17–21.

Harlan, S. L. and C. W. Berheide. 1994. *Barriers to Workplace Advancement Experienced by Women in Low-Paying Occupations.* Albany, NY: Center for Women in Government.

Hawk, E. J. 1995. "Culture and Rewards: A Balancing Act." *Personnel Journal* 74(4): 30–37.

Hays, S. 1999. "Pros & Cons of Pay for Performance." *Workforce* 78(2): 68–73.

Laabs, J. 1998. "What Goes Down When Minimum Wages Go Up?" *Workforce* 77(8): 54–59.

Loysk, B. 1997. "Rewarding Work." *Restaurants USA* 17(9): 9–12.

Marcus, S. H. and A. H. Szpekman. "Compensation Strategies That Improve Employee Morale." *Solutions.* www.bcsolutionsmag.com/online/compensation_employee_morale.htm

Sunoo, B. P. 1999. "Overtime Abuse: You Could Be Guilty." *Workforce* 78(2): 40–51.

Wagner, K. 1998. "Gratuitous Behavior; Here's a Tip for Restauranteurs: Before You Cut into Your Waitstaff's Wages, Check State Regulations." *Denver Westword* (June 4).

Wamser, P. 1996. "Pay Growth Reflects HR's Shift to a Strategic Roll." *HR Magazine* (November).

Recommended Web Sites

1. The Basics of Overtime: ahlberg-cpa.com/basovrt.htm
2. Average Annual Pay by State and Industry: stats.bls.gov/news.release/annpay.nws.htm
3. American Compensation Association: www.acaonline.org
4. Fair Labor Standards Act Advisor—Wage and Hour Division: www.dol.gov/elaws/flsa.htm
5. Wynford Group—Calgary Canada, Compensation Surveys: www.wynford.ab.ca
6. Minimum Wage Hike: Fact; Fallacy: www.epf.org
7. Foodservice: Employment Mistakes (Minimum Wage): www.txrestaurant.org

Endnotes

1. B. P. Sunoo, "Overtime Abuse: You Could Be Guilty," *Workforce* 78 (February 1999): 40–51.
2. Ibid.
3. David W. Belcher, "Toward a Behavioral Science Theory of Wages," in M. S. Wortman (ed.), *Creative Personnel Management: Readings in Industrial Relations* (Boston: Allyn and Bacon, Inc., 1969): p. 202–218.
4. Jennifer Laabs, "Line Managers Can Make (or Break) Incentives Programs," *Workforce* 78 (February 1999): 80–83.
5. U.S. Department of Labor, "Equal Pay," *WHD Publication 1320* (Washington, DC: Government Printing Office, 1974).

Discussion Questions

1. Describe the process involved in compensation planning.
2. What is the one most important characteristic of a compensation plan?
3. Explain the concepts of external and internal pay equity.
4. List the intended outcomes of a sound compensation plan.
5. Describe the job evaluation process. List several examples of compensable factors important in the grading of jobs in your hospitality organization.
6. Present a brief argument for both tipping and a service-charge system.
7. Describe how a hospitality organization can develop a pay-for-performance compensation plan. How does this differ from traditional compensation plans?
8. Do you believe that pay can motivate performance in the hospitality industry? Why or why not? Identify some of the compensatory incentives an employer in the hospitality industry could offer to you that would personally motivate you to perform at a high level.
9. Differentiate among the following incentive programs: bonus plans, profit sharing, and gain sharing. Why might each of these programs fail to motivate improved performance?
10. What is the key focus of the FLSA? Discuss the legalities of compensatory time.
11. Identify potential problems in compensation administration in hospitality organizations.

CHAPTER 11
Benefits

INDUSTRY ADVISOR

KATHY ROADARMEL, *Vice President of Human Resources, Opryland Hotels & Attractions*

"The quality of employees will be directly proportional to the quality of life you maintain for them."

—CHARLES E. BRYAN

"Hold yourself responsible for a higher standard than anybody else expects of you."

—HENRY WARD BEECHER

"Waiter, there's no fly in my soup!"

—KERMIT THE FROG

INTRODUCTION

Benefits are compensation's partner in the achievement of an equitable, attractive, competitive reward system. As with all of the human resources functions we have discussed thus far, the topic of benefits is changing rapidly. The challenge in **benefit planning** is to design a program that can meet the needs and desires of the new work force. And like Kermit the Frog, those needs and desires might be quite unique based upon each employee's own personal life circumstances. This is an area where you are limited only by your creativity and resources in the types of programs you can develop to satisfy the needs of the people in your particular hospitality organization. The price tag associated with the various types of benefits programs you may select ranges from the very inexpensive to the high priced. Regardless of how small or large the operation you are responsible for, you will have an abundance of benefit options from which to select that will not be beyond your organization's means.

A continuing trend in benefits planning is the concept of **flexible benefits** or **cafeteria benefits programs**. In these programs your job as the human resources manager will be to select a **benefits menu**, a variety of benefit plans from which your employees can select what best suits their personal needs.

At the conclusion of this chapter you will be able to:

1. Describe the contribution that the benefits program will make to the total reward system in your hospitality organization.
2. Understand the importance of work-family issues on benefits planning.
3. Differentiate among the benefits, incentives, pay, and employee assistance programs.
4. Understand the continuing effects of changing social demographics on benefits planning.
5. Distinguish among the different types of benefits plan offerings.
6. Describe the provisions of the Family and Medical Leave Act (FMLA) and how they

impact an employee's request for a leave of absence.

7. Select among a vast array of different types of benefits for a program in a hospitality organization.
8. Understand how to plan a benefits program for a hospitality organization.
9. Maintain an awareness of legislation affecting benefits planning.
10. Describe the concept of a flexible benefits program including its advantages and disadvantages.

THE ROLE OF BENEFITS

Benefits are a complementary and complimentary component of the total reward system you develop for your hospitality organization. In most cases, the reward system will already be in place when you join an organization, and your task as manager with human resources responsibilities will be to effectively communicate, monitor, and administer the program. If, however, you find yourself in a position of designing a benefits program, you will also need some information on its planning and implementation.

In this chapter, you will need to view yourself as a benefits manager. As you will see, the scope of benefits planning is continually expanding and changing to meet the needs of a new American work force. As the American work force becomes more culturally diverse and as we hire job applicants from new labor pools, the benefits we offer will continue to grow more complex. Single parents and dual income families have different needs in their benefits package; older and younger employees want different things from their job; women and men oftentimes view work differently.

Much of the volatility in the benefits area is due to the government's ever-changing position on benefits, which is reflected in the variety of laws and regulations being proposed and approved. A simple leave of absence request from an employee may have implications under the Americans with Disabilities Act (ADA), the **Family and Medical Leave Act (FMLA)**, and/or **Worker's Compensation** laws. And if the hospitality organization is governed by a union's collective bargaining agreement, the request for a leave of absence may be further complicated. All of this is in addition to your company's own sickness and accident policies. Overlap in the laws in this area as well as other benefit offerings means that someone in the organization needs to be current and knowledgeable about the statutes and laws governing benefits. Many hospitality corporations find that benefits experts are crucial to understanding this complex arena.

Benefits differ from incentives and pay in that they are not tied to an employee's performance. At one time, benefits were referred to as *fringe benefits,* but that term is no longer appropriate as benefits are no longer a negligible component in your reward system. There is nothing fringe about employee benefits packages these days. Thousands of dollars are at stake as employees make choices for life insurance, health care coverage, retirement packages, disability insurance, and other benefit offerings. In hospitality organizations today, benefits can make up a serious 40 percent of payroll expenditures, according to Kathy Roadarmel at Opryland Hotels & Attractions, if you exclude FICA, unemployment, and disability. We define **benefits** as a favorable allowance provided by the employer for the employee in addition to wages and/or salary that subsidize auxiliary employee needs and services.

Benefits programs are used by hospitality organizations as recruitment, motivational, and retention tools. In today's labor market attractive benefits packages along with an appealing work environment can be used to attract and retain.[1] If benefit packages are to be

INDUSTRY EXPERTS SPEAK

Shelia Darden is the Manager of Compensation and Benefits at Opryland Hotel, and she states, "In today's rapidly changing work force and tight labor market, employers are challenged, more than ever, to create and provide competitive benefits in order to attract and retain their employees, while keeping the cost of benefits under control. Benefits was ranked as one of the top two most important factors in attracting and keeping employees, according to a recent survey.

"What many employers fail to do, however, is to effectively communicate the benefits that they already have. Many times employees are unaware of all the benefits that are being offered to them.

"To better communicate employee benefits and increase the effectiveness, Opryland Hotel created an Employee Benefits Communication Committee (Figure 11-1). This committee is charged with implementing a comprehensive Benefits Communication Program. The committee is made up of representatives of different departments, including Benefits, QA/Training, and Employee Events and Programs."

Through the program several ideas have been implemented including:

- Employee News Network—an ongoing video from ENN that runs on televisions located in various employee areas.
- Promotional Posters—for Personal Wellness, Parties and Fun, 401(k) enrollment, Open Enrollment for welfare benefits, and the like.
- Bulletin Board—located in Employee Services Center and features various benefits and photos of employees in their workplace.
- Newspaper Advertisements—to promote benefits while advertising for current job opportunities.

effectively used as such, it is important that your people view the benefits you offer as part of their overall reward for being members of your hospitality organization. You need to find ways to make the most of the employee benefits that you offer.

The role of benefits has changed largely due to a shift in employee demographics, expectations, and costs to both employer and employee. In the 1970s, traditional benefits programs were developed based on the structure of the family unit. At that time, most families were supported by a single wage earner, the male, who supported a nonworking spouse and dependent children. Benefits needs focused on medical insurance for the employee's dependents and himself or herself. Benefits were truly fringe rewards, initially only offered by the most-innovative organizations. In the 1980s, not only did the structure of the family

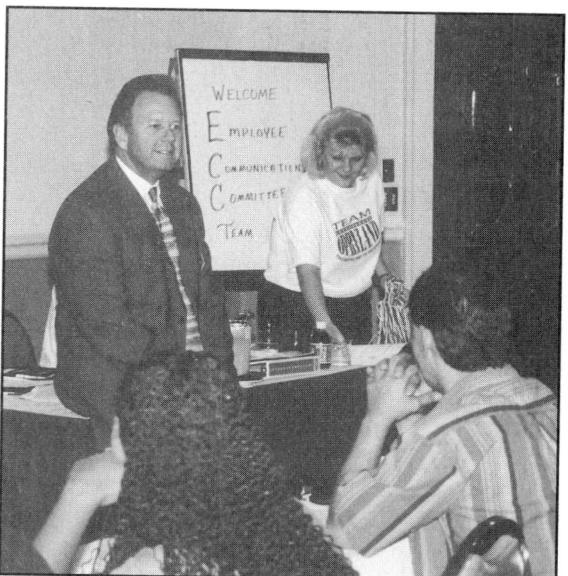

FIGURE 11-1 Opryland Hotels created an Employee Benefits Communications Committee to better communicate employee benefit offerings. *(Courtesy of Opryland Hotels & Attractions)*

unit change, but employees expected benefits to be part of their rewards package. The organization they worked for now owed these benefits to them. The family structure of the 1980s was composed of two incomes, with more women in the work force, and benefits shifted to accommodate these changes. Cafeteria plans emerged to address the changing demographics and the new needs of employees. The 1990s saw the social structure of world change, and with it came significant changes in the types of benefits employees—now both men and women—were offered. Benefits were viewed as the new way to increase an employee's pay.[2] The different types of benefits increased in number as did the variety within each type of benefit. Employees were given the ability to make profound decisions regarding how they spent their benefit dollars. In "the next chapter" this trend will continue. The work-family initiatives started in the 1990s will continue to impact us for years to come. Understanding our employees' diverse needs and wants will be crucial to the management of a successful benefits plan.

Work-Family Issues

Work-family (sometimes referred to as work-life) issues became a predominant workplace issue for managers with human resources responsibilities in the 1990s. The traditional workplace is vanishing as it is being replaced with company offerings of programs and benefits that better help the employee balance their work and personal lives. A 1995 study by DuPont revealed a correlation between employee commitment to business success and the effort the company made in helping their employees balance work and family responsibilities.[3] More recently a study was conducted by the Families and Work Institute, a nonprofit organization devoted specifically to issues involving the changing nature of work and family life (www.familiesandworkinsti.org). This study found specifically that:

- The vast majority (85 percent) of workers have day-to-day family responsibilities at home; 78 percent of married workers have partners who are also employed (compared to 66 percent in 1977).
- Roles of married women and men are changing. Employed married men are spending more hours per day (2.1 hours) on household chores than in the past.
- Two thirds of all employed parents with pre-kindergarten children rely on partners and relatives as the primary source of assistance with child-care responsibilities.
- The time employed fathers spend with their children (2.3 hours each workday) has increased significantly.
- The majority of parents (70 percent) feel that they do not spend enough time with their children and that they have less time for personal activities.[4]

Our people want more time for work, families, friends, and themselves. As both men and women juggle the roles of employee, partner, housekeeper, and sometimes parent and/or caregiver, they are looking to their employer for some type of relief, assistance, and understanding. More often than not, the benefits we offer can be of great assistance to our employees as they seek to balance their work and personal lives. The fact that management recognizes the importance of an employee's personal and family life is a significant factor in employee retention. Flexibility is key to managing today's work force.

Work-family issues will continue to increase in importance for both the employee and the manager with human resources responsibilities looking for employee commitment and loyalty. Family-friendly benefits not only lead to improved productivity but additionally are great recruitment and retention tools.

INDUSTRY EXPERTS SPEAK

Kathy Roadarmel, Vice President of Human Resources at Opryland Hotels & Attractions says, "It is no longer acceptable to provide ***basic*** benefits for employees. The competition for a bigger, better benefit package continues to heat up. Employees expect much more than medical/dental insurance. They expect a substantial discount program, free family counseling services, fitness facilities, child care, flexible scheduling, job sharing, and many other programs that used to be considered extraordinary. These benefits and other family-friendly programs will become standard offerings in the new century."

TRENDS AND INNOVATIVE APPROACHES IN BENEFITS PROGRAMS

Few organizations offer all the benefits identified here to all of their people. Each organization must carefully plan its benefits program so that it meets the goals of the organization while at the same time maintaining a competitiveness with other organizations vying for the same job candidates. Additional differences exist between the benefits offered to hourly or salaried employees. Sometimes low-paid service workers expect high benefits because tips vary greatly with business demand.

Knowing which benefits are right to select, implement, and administer in your organization depends upon a thorough understanding of benefit offerings that you *might* offer your employees. Table 11-1 identifies some of the possibilities available as benefit choices. A discussion on some of the most commonly found benefit offerings in the hospitality industry follows, in alphabetical order.

TABLE 11-1 Possible Benefit Choices

- Insurance
  - Medical and dental
  - Life
  - Disability, short term and long term
  - Accidental death and dismemberment
- Sick Pay
- Dependent Care, Child and Elder
  - Day care reimbursement account
  - Dependent care flexible spending account
- Paid Time Off, Vacation, and Holidays
- Family and Medical Leave
- Employee Savings Plan
- Retirement Plans
  - 401(k) plan
  - Profit sharing
  - Stock purchase plan
  - Employee stock ownership plan
  - IRA program
- Health Care and Dependent Care Spending Accounts
- Wellness Program
- Employee Assistance Program
- Educational Assistance Program
  - Student loan program
  - Parent loan program (for education of a dependent child)
- Discounted Banking Service
- Flexible Work Scheduling
- Credit Union Membership
- Health Care Membership
- Complimentary or Discounted Food/Beverage/Rooms

Child Care

Child care could be provided as a benefit for either hourly or salaried employees. The increasing need for quality child care is a direct result of dual income families and more single parents in the work force resulting in a change in the traditional child-rearing pattern (Figure 11-2). The lack of quality child-care facilities in the communities has prompted employer-sponsored child-care programs. And the

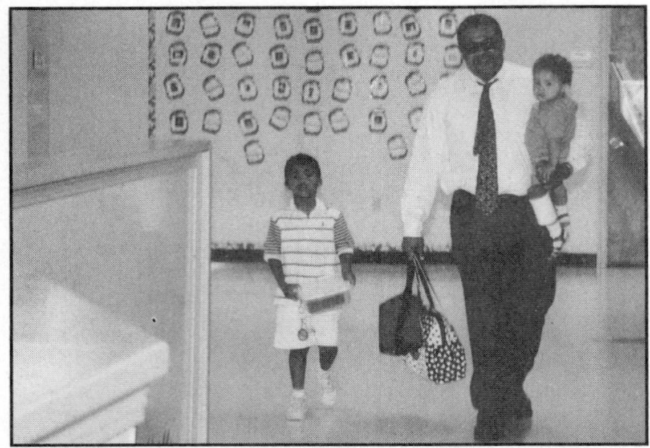

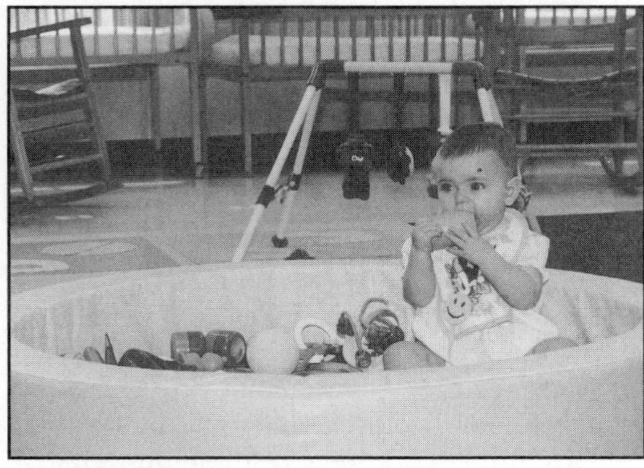

FIGURE 11-2 Employer-sponsored day care is an important benefit for the working parent(s). *(Courtesy of Opryland Child Development Center, Managed by LaPetite Academy Inc.)*

demand for these programs is growing. You will see an increasing number of job applicants making employment decisions based upon whether such programs are available or if benefit options include assistance with child-care expenses.

Table 11-2 is a breakdown of the types of child-care benefits offered by medium and large private establishments for their full-time employees in the "professional, technical, and related employees" and "blue-collar and service employee" employment sectors. Note that very few service employees are even eligible for child-care benefits. Though some hospitality organizations, such as Opryland, offer this much needed benefit, this is an area that will need improvement in "the next chapter" if hospitality is to continue to attract and retain great people.

The need for child care is not only important for dual income families, but it is critical to single-parent households. Increasingly, men are active participants with child-care responsibilities. As we have seen, it is both men and

TABLE 11-2 Child-Care Benefit Offering

Eligibility for child-care benefits, full-time employees, medium and large private establishments, 1995 (in percent).

	Professional, Technical, and Related Employees	Blue-Collar and Service Employees
Employer assistance for child care	15	3
Employer provided funds	7	2
On-site child care	8	1
Off-site child care	2	less than 0.5%

(*Source:* Bureau of Labor Statistics 1997)

women who experience the stress of trying to balance both career and family life. In the absence of quality child care, both parents may miss work due to their child-care responsibilities.

Benefits that can reduce the stress levels experienced by both men and women in the care of their children can make your employees more satisfied with their jobs as well as reduce the amount of absenteeism in your hospitality organization. Such programs include:

- Company child-care facilities
- Parental leave, unpaid or paid
- Financial assistance with child care
- Babysitting allowance
- Parenting seminars
- After-school programs
- Summer camps
- Sick-child centers
- Vacation care
- Time off to attend school events
- Flexible scheduling

The lodging segment of the hospitality industry has a great opportunity to provide company child-care facilities on property. The rooms needed to provide such a benefit to their employees already exist, and with moderate renovations, lodging facilities could readily become child-care facilities. Kathy Roadarmel points out that because employees in the hospitality industry typically work nontraditional hours, an on-site facility can be a true advantage as it will have more flexibility in its hours of operation. According to the Women's Bureau of the U.S. Labor Department, there were more than 14 million Americans (almost 20 percent of full-time workers) who were employed in nontraditional hours in 1991.[5] Employees at companies that provide on-site day care as an employee benefit state that it improves morale, gives them peace of mind, and breeds loyalty to the company.[6] As the need for such facilities increases, watch for more lodging operations to turn their company-provided facilities into revenue producers for other companies in the community, as well as for hotel guests traveling with children. Child-care centers are more difficult to implement for the restaurant operator given the geographic dispersion of work locations. Contracting with existing child-care facilities to negotiate a more favorable group rate for your employees is a viable solution.[7] Be sure to check into the costs, especially that of the additional insurance coverage for liability that you will need to carry.

The Americans with Disabilities Act (ADA), which we discussed in Chapter 4, also has implications for child-care settings. By definition an individual with a disability under the ADA can be an adult or a child. The ADA states that children with mental or physical disabilities be given the opportunity to participate in all activities and opportunities that are part of community life. Because the opportunity to benefit from being in a child-care setting is part of community life, children can no longer be excluded from a child-care facility on the basis of a disability.

Disabilities: Long Term and Short Term

Most of the employees we have working with us in the hospitality industry depend upon their jobs as their primary means of financial support. An injury or illness that disables an employee from working temporarily or permanently could destroy his or her ability to earn a living. Disability benefits are offered to protect our employees' earning power by making them eligible for all, or a portion, of their pay should they become sick or disabled and unable to work. Disability periods may be temporary or permanent and may result from a work-related accident or illness or be totally unrelated to work. In addition to paid sick leave benefits some hospitality organizations also offer **long-term disability** insurance and **short-term disability** insurance to their employees. Pay continuance plans such as these are usually offset or reduced due to Worker's Compensation or other benefits.

Worker's Compensation provides disability benefits due to a work-related injury or illness. These benefits vary from state to state. **Social security** disability benefits are paid when an employee is not able to perform any work that is available and reasonable, given the individual's work experience and education level. Social security typically does not begin paying until the sixth month of disability. That's why there are advantages in offering an income protection plan to your employees.

Short-Term Disability (STD) insurance plans are designed to provide income to an employee who becomes disabled and is unable to work after an initial waiting period, typically of one to seven days. Opryland Hotel, for example, defines disability under their short-term disability benefits as "being physically unable to perform any of your job functions for a period of six (6) or more consecutive work days. The illness or injury does not have to require hospitalization to qualify as a disability." Typically, the length of coverage for benefits payment is expressed in terms of a maximum number of weeks of benefits for a single period of disability.

For disabilities that last an extended length, group Long-Term Disability (LTD) plans are offered. LTD and STD plans are typically elective benefit options. That is, the employee must elect to participate in the plan and also support the premiums. The advantage of this option is that the group plans are much less expensive than the individual disability plans. LTD plans cover all forms of disability with an offset for benefits provided under Worker's Compensation, social security, or the Railroad Retirement Act.

Educational Assistance

Benefits plans that provide financial educational assistance for our employees in the hospitality industry are certainly not new, although their availability is increasing. The offerings of **educational assistance plans** vary from company to company. The most common is to provide tuition paybacks to employees who have satisfactorily completed course work. These plans typically require that an employee work a specific number of hours and maintain a designated grade-point average in order to be eligible for the assistance. Opryland Hotel offers 100 percent tuition reimbursement if the courses taken are industry or job related and approved by the employee's Department Head.

Some of the more innovative forms of educational assistance include providing low-cost educational loans for the children of your employees. In some organizations, consideration is being given to offering college tuition subsidies for employees' children as a benefit option. Retraining programs are also being offered in an effort to combat the increasing labor shortages. People who want to move to another department or division within the hospitality company are being retrained at the organization's expense. Seminars are no longer being restricted to management, but include the hourly unskilled and semiskilled work force in an effort to prepare them for job openings within the company.

Educational assistance benefits are costly, but are based on the theory that the hospitality organization will receive a return on its investment. To prevent employees from accepting these benefits in order to obtain a better job at another organization, some companies have required their employees to sign a promissory note agreeing to pay back the costs if they leave.

Elder Care

As our society is aging, new concerns regarding the care of our elderly parents and other dependents come into play. Whereas acceptability is increasing for men and women who need leave time to care for children, acceptance of the need to care for our senior citizens has been slow. The concept of **elder care** can become an important benefit to both hourly and management employees who are faced with the care of an elderly relative.

Elder care is the care of aging parents by their offspring. As "baby boomers" continue to age into their 50s, they remain caught between caring for children and caring for parents. While the responsibilities of child care decrease as time goes on, the responsibilities of elder care often increase with time as the parent(s) become increasingly dependent upon their children as caregivers. As the number of employees caring for elderly relatives in the hospitality industry increases, many companies are finding that benefits in this area are much needed and appreciated.

Employee Assistance Programs

Employee assistance programs (EAPs) are designed to assist employees with personal problems they may have in their lives that could potentially affect their job performance. These programs are covered in depth in Chapter 13.

The Family and Medical Leave Act (FMLA)

The Family and Medical Leave Act (FMLA) was signed into law on February 5, 1993, by President Bill Clinton. FMLA covers all private employees, state employees, and federal employees who work for an employer with 50 or more employees within 75 miles of a given workplace. FMLA entitles all eligible employees to a total of 12 weeks of leave during any 12-month period for one or more of the following:

- Birth of a child
- Placement (by the state) of a child for adoption or foster care
- Caring for a spouse, child, or parent with a serious health condition
- The serious health condition of the employee

An eligible employee is one who has worked at least 12 months for the employer and 1,250 hours in the past year. A serious health condition is defined as inpatient care at a hospital, hospice, or residential medical care facility, or continuing care by a doctor of medicine or osteopathy. The employer can require an employee to provide a doctor's certification of the serious health condition (see Table 11-3 for Opryland's requirement).

The Act specifies that leave can be on an unpaid basis, but an employer is allowed to substitute accrued paid leave (such as vacation, holiday, or sick pay) if the employee is eligible. Likewise, the employee may elect to substitute paid leave if eligible. The employer *is* required to continue coverage under any group health plan for the duration of the employee's FMLA leave at the level and under the conditions coverage would have been provided if the employee had remained working. If the employee chooses not return to work for reasons other than the health condition, the employer is entitled to recover from the employee the premium that was paid for health coverage on the employee's behalf.

The Family and Medical Leave Act requires that an employee who takes leave under the law be able to return to the same job or a job with equivalent status and pay unless that employee is among the 10 percent of highest paid employees in the company (Table 11-4).

Under this Act the employee is required to give the employer 30 days notice of the need

TABLE 11-3 Certification of Physician or Practitioner, Opryland Hotel

The employee is required to provide certification of need for leave to care for the employee's illness or injury or that of a family member. The certification must be provided within 15 days of the date it is requested by the company. Failure to do so can resulting the denial of leave.

A new statement will be required monthly or as needed to determine the continuation of disability. If there is a dispute about the medical opinion provided by the employee's physician/practitioner, the company may require a second opinion by a physician/practitioner of its choice, at the company's expense. If a third opinion is necessary, a third physician/practitioner may be selected, also at the company's expense. When the company requires a second or third opinion,

- The physician/practitioner must be agreed upon by both the employee and the company, and
- The physician/practitioner may not be employed on a regular basis by the company.

(Courtesy of Gaylord Entertainment Company)

TABLE 11-4 Job Restoration, Gaylord Entertainment Company

Most employees granted leave will be returned to the same position held prior to the leave, or one that is equivalent in pay, benefits, and other terms and conditions of employment.

Highly compensated employees are not excluded from coverage under the FMLA, although the employer is allowed to deny them restoration in certain situations. Highly compensated employees are defined by FMLA as salaried eligible employees who are among the highest paid 10 percent of employees of the employer within 75 miles of the facility where the employee works. These employees may be denied restoration under the following conditions:

- If the denial of restoration is necessary to prevent substantial and grievous economic injury to the operations of the company.
- If the employer notifies the employee of its intent to deny restoration as soon as the employer determines that substantial and grievous economic injury would occur.
- In any case where after leave has already commenced, the employee elects not to return to employment after receiving such notice.

(Courtesy of Gaylord Entertainment Company)

for such leave when possible. In emergency situations, as much notice as is practical. When an employee is taking leave due to a serious health condition, the employer can require a release from a physician/practitioner stating that it is all right for the employee to return to work.

Always be sure and check to determine state law regarding family-leave issues. As a manager with human resources responsibilities, you may find that you are required to adhere to higher legal standards than those outlined here. Oregon's family leave law, for example, applies to employers that employ 25 or more persons in the state; Vermont's parental leave law covers employers of 10. You also have an obligation to ensure that all employees are aware of the coverage provided under the Family and Medical Leave Act. Many hospitality organizations such as Opryland detail such coverage in their written benefit materials as well as during employee orientation (Figure 11-3).

The purpose of the Family and Medical Leave Act as stated by the 103d Congress of the United States in Public Law 103-3 of the United States Statutes at Large is to "balance the demands of the workplace with the needs of families, to promote the stability and economic security of families, and to promote national interests in preserving family integrity." A bipartisan commission found in 1995 (two years after the law was enacted) that workers with family incomes of $20,000–$30,000 were

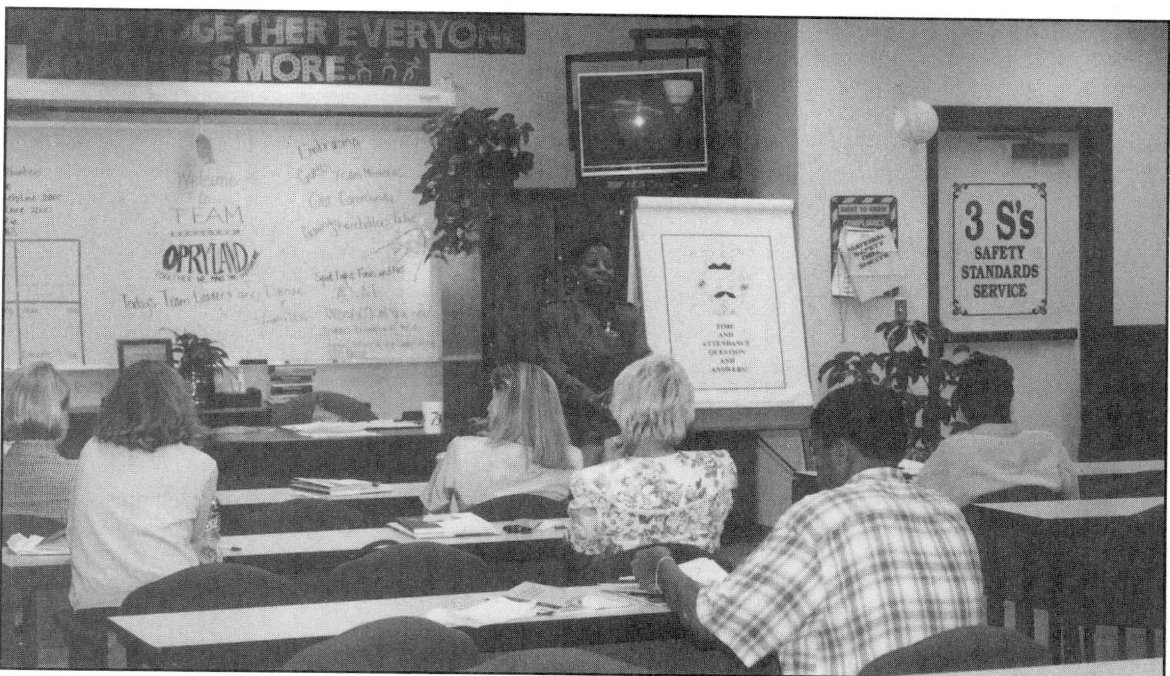

FIGURE 11-3 Employee orientation is a good place to explain to your employees their rights under the Family and Medical Leave Act. *(Courtesy of Opryland Hotels & Attractions)*

more likely to take unpaid leave under the FMLA than were employees with higher family incomes.[8] On the fifth anniversary of the Act, in 1998, the Department of Labor (responsible for enforcing the law) investigated 6,000 FMLA complaints. About 90 percent of those were resolved after compliance explanations were provided. The median length of time employees took off under the law was 10 days with only about 3.6 percent of all employees actually taking leave under the law.[9] It appears that because the leave is still unpaid, there are many employees who can't afford to take advantage of it. Clearly, the FMLA is a steppingstone to assisting with work-family issues for the people in our hospitality organizations. Many people feel that the law did not go far enough in helping working families; others believe the law is too complicated and is an unnecessary burden to businesses. This debate continues as we enter the new millennium.[10] There is still much that can be done in "the next chapter" to improve upon family-friendly policies in the hospitality industry.

Financial Planning Service

As the complexities of benefits planning and possible options increase, our entire staff could use some assistance in managing the benefits they receive. Research studies have shown that many employees bring their financial worries with them to the workplace and this affects job performance.[11] Financial planning assistance will gain popularity as a benefit offering in hospitality organizations as we approach "the next chapter." Some hospitality organizations may even find themselves providing on-

FIGURE 11-4 Large hospitality companies can even provide on-premise banking facilities as a benefit for their employees. *(Courtesy of Opryland Hotel on-site Branch of Nations Bank Exclusively for Employees)*

premise banking facilities as a benefit to their employees (Figure 11-4).

Flextime

Flextime allows our employees to vary their work hours to better accommodate their personal lives. Flextime is also known by a variety of other terms, such as flexitime, moving schedules, gliding time, dynamic schedules, and flexible working hours. This benefit has an enormous potential in the hospitality industry. For decades we have promoted the idea of split shifts. Flextime conforms to the peaks and valleys that typify our business patterns. After we define critical work hours, our people are then given the opportunity to determine which hours will complete the remainder of their workweek. Within these programs there are varying degrees of flexibility that the employees are permitted. Some flextime programs allow the employees to vary their schedule from day to day; others require the employees to stay on the schedule they select for a set period of time such as six months. Some programs require the same number of hours worked every day; others allow employees to balance shorter days with longer days. The range of time during which employees may start and finish their work may be from as little as 15 minutes up to 2 hours or more. The most typical flextime option lets employees set alternative work hours, such as 7 a.m. to 3 p.m. instead of 9 a.m. to 5 p.m. Compressed workweeks in which employees work longer hours on fewer days can also be part of the flextime option.[12]

Flextime as a benefit option is simply one more way to attract and retain your key people. Flexibility and accomodating your employees' needs will be the buzzwords in "the next chapter." The more-innovative applications of flextime permit job sharing, with two part-time employees sharing one job. This opportunity also accommodates the employee who has child-care or elder-care responsibilities as well as the employee who simply seeks more leisure time.

Language Assistance

As ethnic diversity increases in the hospitality workplace, so does the number of people for whom English is a second language. Increasingly, employers find themselves with willing, qualified employees who are not fluent enough in English to understand the various benefits offered to them. One of the benefits that some hospitality companies are offering is special classes for employees who speak English as a second language to assist them in benefits selection (Figure 11-5).

INDUSTRY EXPERTS SPEAK

Titus Seibold, Benefits Specialist for Opryland Hotel Convention Center, points out, "As the ever-growing global economy continues to expand and the workforce becomes more diversified, the language barrier between employer and employees also continues to grow. Because of the differences in both language and culture, it is important to develop new methods to ensure that all employees have a thorough understanding of the benefits package offered to them and what their responsibilities are concerning those benefits. For instance, differences in medical options must be adequately explained as well as procedures such as how to submit a claim. In many instances, those employees without an adequate grasp of the English language will select those options which they perceive as the simplest without understanding the details of the plan they have chosen."

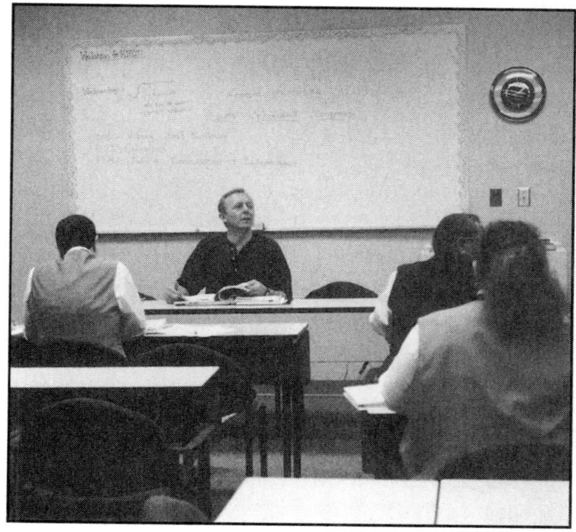

FIGURE 11-5 Benefits being explained to a group of employees for whom English is a second language. *(Courtesy of Opryland Hotels & Attractions)*

Medical Plans

The rapid escalation of health care costs has placed medical care beyond the ability of most of us to pay for a serious illness or injury, especially if hospitalization is required. Medical plans, one of the oldest benefits employers have offered to their employees, are designed to protect employees from financial disaster due to their own expensive medical needs or those of their family members. Comprehensive coverage of medical expenses resulting from an injury or illness is handled by the medical plans offered by your hospitality organization.

The costs of health care have risen steadily since the late 1970s. For hospitality organizations that provide health care for their staff this has translated into double-digit increases in insurance premiums. It was predicted that large employers' health plans would go up, on average, 7 percent in 1999. That was up from the 4-percent increase reported in 1998. The increase in health plan costs generally means that employees will pay more along with employers.[13] Much of the increased expense is due to the price inflation of the services covered by the typical health care plan. Price inflation is due to a number of factors, including malpractice suits, reduction in payments from Medicare, a reduction of in-patient care stimulated by the increase of **Health Maintenance Organizations (HMOs)**, consolidation of HMO's more expensive technology and medical procedures such as transplants, and a rise in catastrophic cases due in part to the AIDS epidemic.

HMOs provide a fixed set of medical services for a prepaid fee. Coverage is usually paid in full; however, some minimal copayment for certain services may be required. For example, the plan participant (the employee) might be required to pay a $5.00 copayment for prescriptions. According to the Bureau of Labor Statistics, 27 percent of full-time employees with medical care coverage were enrolled in health maintenance organizations. This figure had risen from 23 percent in 1993 and 17 percent in 1991.

Preferred Provider Organizations (PPOs) are another type of managed-care program. These are fee-for-service providers in that the service provider receives no payment unless covered employee is treated. These differ from the traditional fee-for-service in that benefits are more generous if the covered employee uses a provider within the chosen network (preferred) than if they choose a provider outside the network. In a traditional fee-for-service, the participants select a provider of their choice for their medical care. The plan then reimburses either the participant or the provider for all or some of the costs. For PPO plans to be effective, the employee must have some incentive for selecting the preferred provider over a provider of their choice. The Bureau of Labor Statistics reports that in 1995, 24 percent of full-time employees with medical care coverage were enrolled in a PPO. This is up from 26 percent in 1993 and 16 percent in 1991.

The 1980s found benefits managers experimenting with **cost containment** measures to control the rising premium costs. Unfortunately, some of the measures contributed to the inflation in prices. These include the shift from inpatient care services to outpatient care, and a steady rise in state-mandated benefits.

One approach to cost containment that has been proven to be effective for hospitality organizations is that of cost sharing. **Cost sharing** refers to a plan that requests a larger employee contribution to the health care benefit expenses. Though it is unreasonable to expect our employees to shoulder the entire burden of health care increases, there will be an increase over the copayments seen in the 1990s.

Cost sharing also has proven to make employees more cautious when visiting medical facilities. If their share of copayment is negligible, there is likely to be a higher abuse of services than if they had to pay $15–$30 for each visit. In line with cost sharing are incentive programs for those employees with limited utilization of their health care benefits in a given year. By rewarding these people with smaller copayments, the abusers of medical benefits would hence be penalized.

Just what type of provisions are contained in health care packages? The following is a list of some of the options that you might want to consider including in a plan for your hospitality organization. Just remember that for every option your package provides there is a corresponding cost:

- Major medical and hospital
- Psychiatric
- Stress-related care
- Alcohol and drug abuse treatment
- Maternity

- Outpatient services
- Home health care
- Newborn child care
- Vision plans
- Prescription drugs

Each of these options will contain varying conditions of eligibility, costs, and benefits provided. It is up to you, the manager with human resources responsibilities, to keep current with the latest trends in health care benefit management as cost containment continues to be the buzzword throughout "the next chapter."

Paid Time Off

Time-off policies vary widely from operation to operation based upon the different business needs of each. Vacation time is accrued based upon the length of service of each employee with your hospitality company. Some policies permit employees to carry over vacation time from year to year; other policies allow a portion of earned time to be held over; still other organizations believe that their people need to use the time off during the year it is earned. Which policy your organization has or will establish is dependent upon the hospitality enterprise's mission statement, goals, and operational objectives.

Paid time off policies were greatly extended in the 1990s to accommodate the changing social needs of the work force. With work-family issues rising to the top of management concerns in dealing with the new work force, the need for additional paid time off policies increased. Holiday pay, personal leave, funeral leave, jury duty leave, military leave, sick leave, and family leave are just some of the policies that exist in today's workplace. In addition, many employers in the hospitality industry are finding that their employees would like additional time off without pay so that they can spend more time with family and personal interests. We predict that this trend will continue long into "the next chapter."

Retirement Plans

Health care benefits are not the sole contributor to escalating benefit costs. As our population ages, the hospitality organization's expenditures for **retirement plans** increases. This situation is further impacted by a reduction in the number of the work force who contribute their earnings to these programs. An increase in withdrawals and a decrease in contributions result in the need to carefully manage your organization's retirement plans.

Retirement plans come in a variety of forms, but the basic purpose of these plans remains the same: to provide retirees with a proportion of their income. These programs are a supplement to social security and other savings plans to which your employees may have contributed.

An accompanying service provided in connection with retirement plans is preretirement planning programs. Typically, these programs are offered in the form of seminars, meetings, or carefully prepared written materials explaining the retirement plans offered by your hospitality company and postretirement financial planning. As plans for retirement become more complex, and the retirement age declines, this is an important auxiliary service that your company can provide at a relatively low cost to employees at all age levels.

The trend in retirement planning is toward less reliance on government (as viewed in the tightening of social security restrictions) and a shifting of responsibility to the individual worker. Let's explore some of the retirement programs available for our employees.

Defined Benefit Plans

This traditional type of retirement plan was at one time better known as a pension plan and made up the majority of all types of retirement programs. Based upon a formula, the employer agrees to pay the employee a specific amount of income upon retirement age. This money is contributed by the employer as tax-deferred income. Upon retirement, the employee can elect to withdraw the pension in monthly payments or as a single lump sum. The amount of contribution made to the **defined benefit plan** by the employer is typically based upon length of service and an average income during the last few years of service to the hospitality organization. These are known as terminal earnings-based programs.

The Tax Reform Act of 1986 negatively affected the attractiveness of this type of retirement plan by reducing the tax advantages. Most hospitality companies and a large number of other employers have moved away from defined benefit plans to defined contribution plans. Defined benefit plans have declined from 63 percent of all full-time employees in 1988 to 52 percent covered in 1995, according to the Bureau of Labor Statistics, whereas defined contribution plan participation increased from 45 percent in 1988 to 55 percent in 1995. The advantage of these programs is their ability to calculate more closely what your employees will actually be receiving for their retirement income.

Defined Contribution Plans

Defined contribution plans are established so that both employer and employee may make contributions to an established account. Some of these plans are only employee supported, whereas profit sharing plans are typically only employer supported. Generally, however, both the employer and the employee make a predetermined (defined) contribution to a tax-deferred account. These plans work well for low-wage earners as well as higher-paid management personnel. They are readily acceptable as they are easy for your employees to understand. Typically, annual statements are mailed so that the employees can see exactly how much of their contribution is in the plan.

401(k) Plans

401(k) plans are specific types of defined contribution plans where the employer guarantees to match a percentage of the employee's contribution to the plan. These act as a retirement savings account and are based upon an employee's voluntary contribution to the plan. The benefit of these plans is a tax advantage known as income deferral. **Income deferral** allows your employees to reduce their current income tax liability by setting aside a portion before it is taxed. Their gross income is reduced by the amount of their income deferral so that less tax is paid. Payment of this tax is made when distribution from the accounts is received by the employee upon retirement. Most organizations provide payroll deductions so that it is quite easy for your employees to make contributions to 401(k) plans. Generally, a number of investment options are provided to those participating in these plans. These investment options include:

- Equity funds. Assets invested in stock and securities; high return, risk may be high or low depending on the portfolio mix.
- Money market funds. Assets invested in short-term instruments such as treasury bills; earnings should approximate rate of inflation.
- Balanced fund. Assets invested in both equity and fixed-income investments; fixed-income portion is directed to guaranteed investment opportunities such as bonds; minimizes risk over straight equity fund arrangements.
- Company stock fund. Assets invested entirely in the employer's common stock; perhaps high risk.

Profit Sharing

Profit sharing is another type of defined contribution plan that permits the employee to share in a portion of the hospitality company's profit. These are defined contribution plans where the employer's contribution is determined by the company's profitability. Thus, the contribution will vary from year to year.

The formula developed to calculate an individual employee's earnings generally determines the amount of total contribution that is distributed to individual employee accounts based on annual earnings. An employee's right to his account typically vests over a period of time, which builds loyalty. Most defined contribution plans have a vesting schedule.

Employee Stock Ownership Plan

Employee stock ownership plan (ESOP) also operates as a defined contribution plan. In these plans, the hospitality company makes contributions to its employees in the form of company stock. The maximum annual company contribution is determined by federal law and divided among eligible employees in proportion to their annual compensation. These plans may be used for both hourly and management employees. Table 11-5 shows the breakdown of full-time employee participation among the various types of retirement programs.

TABLE 11-5 Participation in Retirement Programs: 1995

	Percent of Participation
All Retirement	80
Defined Benefit	52
Defined Contribution	55
Types of Plans:	
Savings and Thrift	41
Deferred Profit Sharing	13
Employee Stock Ownership	5
Money Purchase Pension	7
401(k) Plans:	
With Employer Contribution	45
Without Employer Contribution	9

(*Source:* U.S. Bureau of Labor Statistics)

Unique Benefit Offerings

The types of benefits that you, as the manager with human resources responsibilities, may select for your hospitality organization's benefit plan can be placed in six categories:

- Retirement Related
  - —Pensions
  - —Preretirement counseling
  - —401(k)
  - —Cash deferred
  - —Profit sharing
- Insurance Related
  - —Health related
    - Medical
    - Dental
    - Prescription drugs
    - Vision
    - Mental and psychological
  - —Disability income
  - —Life insurance
    - Group
    - Survivor security
    - Employees over 65
    - Retirees
- Time not Worked
  - —Holiday
  - —Vacation
  - —Leaves of absence
    - Parental
    - Sick
    - Personal
  - —Meal periods
  - —Days off

- Financially Related
  - —Educational assistance
  - —Child care
  - —Financial counseling
  - —Social and recreational
  - —Credit unions
  - —Employee meals (Figure 11-6)
  - —Uniforms/drycleaning
  - —Parking assistance
  - —Legal counseling
  - —Service awards
  - —Discount programs
- Health and Wellness Related
  - —Fitness center
  - —Day care subsidy
  - —Eldercare benefit
  - —Employee Assistance Program
  - —Wellness program (Figure 11-7)
- Legally Required
  - —The Family and Medical Leave Act
  - —Worker's Compensation
  - —Social security
  - —Unemployment insurance
  - —State mandated

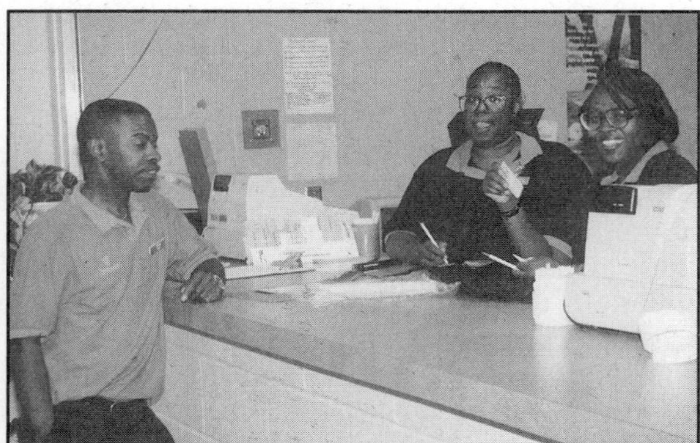

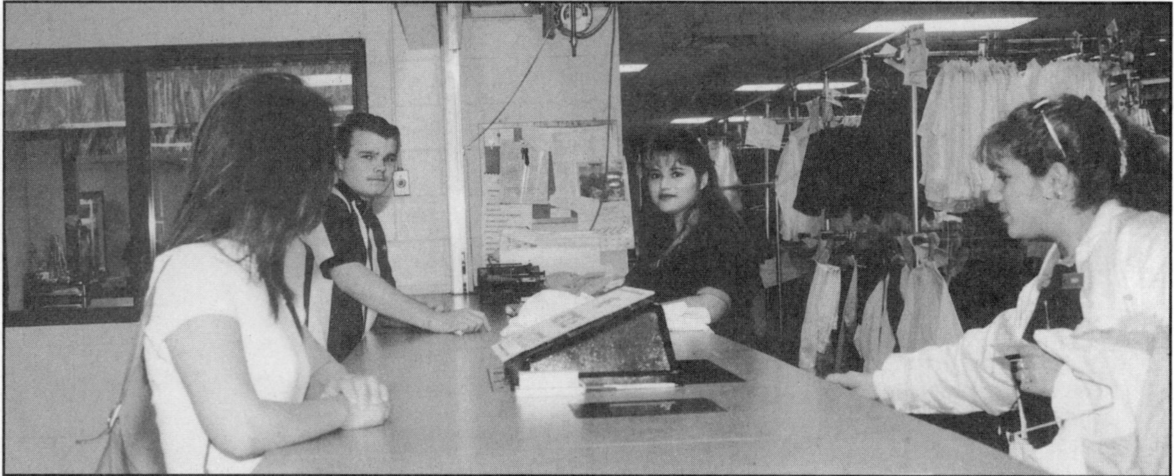

FIGURE 11-6 Financially related benefits such as an employee cafeteria, on-premise dry-cleaning, and uniform (wardrobe) distribution center are viewed as great benefits by employees. *(Courtesy of Opryland Hotels & Attractions)*

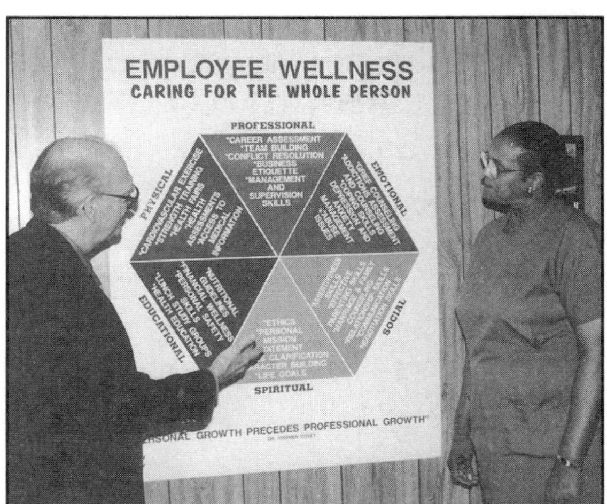

FIGURE 11-7 Wellness programs are being offered as a benefit that serves both employee and employer. *(Courtesy of Gaylord Entertainment Company)*

One of the benefits-planning decisions that will need to be made is the determination of what benefits will be company sponsored and which will require a contribution from your employees, if they wish to participate. Some benefits (health plans) can be funded with pretax contributions of employee money, thus saving taxes for both the employee and employer on amounts contributed. Generally, for our employees' convenience, these contributions are deducted automatically from their paycheck by the payroll department. Figure 11-8 shows an example of the benefit package offered by Gaylord Entertainment.

SPECIAL CONCERNS OF BENEFITS PLAN DESIGN

As you have already seen, rewards to your employees are not always received in the form of pay. As you choose from the multitude of benefit offerings you must take care to provide a balanced program for your employees. Part of your human resources responsibility is to be on the lookout for ways to improve the plans already established. Benefit plans might be improved by suggesting changes that would make them more cost-effective. Improvements might be suggested that would make the existing benefits plan better understood by the employees who participate in them. Don't feel as though your hospitality organization doesn't need your ideas regarding benefits planning simply because they already exist. Benefits plan design will continue to be one of the most proactive, evolving, and expensive human resources functions in "the next chapter."

Benefits Planning

Because benefits have become such an integral part of your total reward system, care must be taken so that your benefits plan fits into the organizational goals of the hospitality enterprise. One way to ensure this is to prepare operational objectives for your benefits plan, and then design the plan so that it will meet those objectives. Table 11-6 identifies some of the considerations in benefits planning.

TABLE 11-6 Considerations in Benefits Planning

- Availability of labor
- Corporate mission statement
- Demographics and needs of your employees
- Different groups have different plans (full-time vs. part-time, hourly vs. salaried)
- How much the hospitality organization can afford to pay
- Number of part-time employees
- Organizational goals
- Potential short- and long-term costs
- What the competition is doing
- Who should participate (eligibility)
- Whether employees will have a choice in benefit selection

OPRYLAND HOTEL
CONVENTION CENTER

A Summary of Gaylord Entertainment's
Benefit Package

CHOICES Benefits Program (full-time employees):

- Medical / Dental Coverage
  Employees are given choices of three medical/dental plans (2 PPO and 1 HMO) which provide comprehensive medical and dental coverage.
- Supplemental Life Insurance
  Provides life insurance in amounts up to 3 times annual salary.
- Supplemental Accidental Death and Dismemberment Insurance
  Provides accidental death and dismemberment insurance in amounts up to 10 times annual salary for the employee and their qualified dependents.
- Dependent Life Insurance
  Provides life insurance in amounts up to $10,000 for the qualified dependents of each full-time employee.
- Health Care Spending Account
  Provides full-time employees the opportunity to put up to $3,000 tax-free in an account to pay for medical expenses not covered by insurance.
- Dependent/Child Care Spending Account
  Provides full-time employees the opportunity to put up to $5,000 tax-free in an account to pay for child care and dependent care expenses.

Company Provided Benefits:

- Paid time off for Vacations and Holidays
  Provides for 6½ paid holidays, plus a floating holiday after 1 year full-time service and up to 4 weeks vacation based on length of service.
- Basic Life Insurance
  Provides life insurance in the amount of 1 times annual salary for each full-time employee.
- Basic Accidental Death and Dismemberment Insurance
  Provides accidental death and dismemberment insurance in the amount of 1 times annual salary for each full-time employee.

2800 Opryland Drive
Nashville, Tennessee 37214-1297
Telephone 615-889-1000
Facsimile 615-871-6942

A GAYLORD ENTERTAINMENT COMPANY

FIGURE 11-8 A Summary of Gaylord Entertainment's Benefit Package. *(Courtesy of Gaylord Entertainment Company)*

- Short-Term Disability
  Provides for paid time off for extended illnesses and injuries that are not work-related.

- Long-Term Disability
  Provides for paid time off for illnesses and injuries that are not work-related that result in being off work for more than 6 months.

- Retirement Plan
  After 1 year of full-time service, employees are eligible for company-funded retirement plan.

Other Available Benefits:

- 401(k) Retirement Savings Plan
  Qualified employees can contribute up to 20% of salary into a retirement fund; the company matches the first 6% with 50 cents for each dollar contributed.

- Employee Stock Purchase Plan
  Qualified employees can purchase stock in Gaylord Entertainment Company through payroll deductions.

- Free Employee Meals / Paid Breaks
  Employees are given $3.00 daily meal credit in employee cafeteria and receive regular paid breaks.

- Discounted On-Site Child Care
  Employees receive discounted child care at on-site child development center which is available 7 days a week.

- Employee Discount Programs
  Discounts available to all employees including discounted dry-cleaning service, 40% discount in on-property retail outlets, varying discounts from local merchants, and discounted vision care.

- Employee Fitness Center
  Fitness center available to all full-time employees 24 hours a day, 7 days a week for $15 monthly fee.

- Employee Assistance & Wellness Program
  Employee wellness program available to employees and their family members providing various group seminars as well as individual counseling.

FIGURE 11-8 *(concluded)*

Communication becomes a critical component of benefits planning. The more alternatives your plan provides for your employees, the better your communciation system has to be. Many people have a difficult time understanding the financial planning provisions and variety of medical insurance options. The rapid changes in legislation tend to perpetuate this confusion. In addition, your plan has to be flexible enough to accommodate changes based upon employee needs. Getting your employees involved in the design or redesign phases of benefits planning can lend valuable insight into their needs.

Issues for Beyond the Year 2000

Health care insurance has been offered by hospitality organizations for decades in an effort to attract and retain quality employees. Once our people wish to retire, retiree health care benefits are sometimes provided. No one anticipated the increasing expense of maintaining these benefit offerings. With medical costs increasing and our populace of employees aging and retiring earlier (more retirees to provide for), the future of this benefit is unsure. A number of measures are being taken in an attempt to make costs more manageable. Serious questions remain about the medical care of our aging society and who will maintain financial responsibility for their care.

The AIDS issue continued to gain attention throughout the 1990s as medical expenses for patients can be enormous. The burden of expense has been on insurance companies and have meant financial ruin for smaller insurance companies or employers who self-funded their medical benefits. An increasing concern is AIDS-infected mothers and children. Although now covered under the Americans with Disabilities Act (ADA), the AIDS issue will be one that employers continue to struggle with in the future. Again, the question is raised: Who will take the financial responsibility for their care?

Rising expenditures for benefit plans make cost containment the issue in "the next chapter." To assist with this and other benefit issues, consulting companies have emerged that specialize in benefits. These firms have the knowledge and information regarding various insurance companies, legislative changes and interpretations, as well as the skills to negotiate with pharmaceutical companies, all in an effort to reduce the costs in providing these benefits to the employee. As the benefits arena continues in its complexity, more hospitality organizations may find themselves relying on benefits specialists.

Effects of Legislation

Throughout our discussion, we have referred to the legislative environment that surrounds benefits planning. Much of this legislation is sending mixed signals to both employers and employees. The federal government historically (particularly the Reagan administration) has called for a self-reliance position for the American people. This posture was taken largely as a result of the weakening social security system established by the Social Security Act of 1935. For a large portion of participants, these retirement benefits are no longer completely tax free. Though the government would like to see a lesser dependence on social security, it has simultaneously reduced the tax incentives for doing so.

In the past 35 years much legislation has been approved that imposes restrictions and/or administrative policies in the benefits arena. The **Employee Retirement Income Security Act (ERISA)** of 1974 was established to protect employees from failing **pension plans** that are maintained and operated by companies, including hospitality organizations. Standards have been established in this act that must be met for the company to be eligible for tax deductions for contributions made to the pension plan. The Internal Revenue Service and the Department of Labor can provide you with the additional information you need to assure that your hospitality company is meeting the requirements of ERISA. The passing of ERISA was a response to move away from government supported retirement plans, such as social security.

Both employees and employers must contribute to the social security funds, making this a mandatory benefit program. This tax was established by the Federal Insurance Contribution Act (FICA). As of 1998, the amount required by the employer is 7.65 percent that matches the employee's contribution of 7.65 percent of the first $76,200 in pay. Frequent amendments to this act result in the increase of contributions, by both employer and employee.

Some of the legislation that has passed is aimed at reducing the disparity in benefits between highly paid executives and hourly wage earners. The Tax Equity Fiscal Responsibility Act of 1982 (TEFRA) limits the amount of pension benefits that executives can receive with tax advantages.

In 1986, the **Consolidated Omnibus Budget Reconcilaition Act (COBRA)** was passed that required employers to meet certain conditions to provide extended health care benefits to retirees, employees who voluntarily or involuntarily quit, and divorced or widowed spouses and dependent children of present employees.

After COBRA, employers were faced with the famous Tax Reform Act of 1986 that imposed numerous significant changes in the tax laws effecting a number of employee benefits. Effective January 1, 1989, provisions were added to the act in section 89 that attempted to further restrict executive benefits at the expense of the employer. Equal benefits for all employees is the main purpose of the additional restrictions.

The **Older Workers Benefit Protection Act** was passed in October of 1990. It is also known as the Betts Bill because it was passed to overturn the U.S. Supreme Court's decision in the *Betts* case. The law has specific requirements that substantially modify the Age Discrimination in Employment Act (ADEA) to ensure equality of treatment between older and younger employees under employee benefit plans. These requirements are quite complex. Managers with human resources responsibilities in the hospitality industry would be well advised to seek the advice of a benefits expert or attorney for clear interpretation of this and other laws described in this chapter.

In August of 1996 the **Health Insurance Portability and Accountability Act (HIPAA)** was signed into law. This law amends COBRA to clarify that the extended maximum coverage of 29 months, under COBRA, for qualifying disabilities applies not just to the covered employee but to any qualified beneficiary. It also expands ERISA's disclosure requirements by requiring that group health plans provide a summary description of any modification or change that significantly reduces covered services or benefits to participants and beneficiaries no later than 60 days after the modification or change was made. Additionally, HIPAA forbids health insurance exclusions based upon health statutes and limits the imposition of preexisting condition exclusions, it requires that group health plans issue "certificates of coverage" to employees and dependents when they are no longer covered by the plan or after their COBRA coverage ends, and it requires group health plans to allow special enrollment periods for employees and dependents who previously declined coverage under the plan because of other coverage.

What all this means for you, the manager with human resources resopnsibilities, is more paperwork and more complexity in understanding what your legal responsibilities are surrounding benefit programs.

FLEXIBLE BENEFITS PROGRAMS

The concept of flexible or cafeteria benefits programs grew in popularity throughout the 1980s and 1990s. As the name implies, these programs identify a list or "menu" of benefits options that the employees in your hospitality organization may choose from. This has the advantage of allowing the employees to select the benefits that they need the most and eliminates the expense of employer-supported benefits that are not used.

Again, it is changing social demographics that are largely responsible for the increasing popularity of these plans. Two-income families in traditional benefit programs typically end up with dual coverage for the same benefits plans. Single people with no dependents end up subsidizing their coworkers with families. Younger employees have different needs than do those nearing retirement. Single parents have needs revolving around their children. Lifestyles have changed, and the baby boomers are enjoying their leisure time, the time off from their job duties and responsibilities. Whereas some of our older workers wish to retire later in life, many are opting for earlier retirement and time to enjoy life. There no longer exists the average American worker. The diversity in our work force will continue to increase along with the diversity of needs.

Flexible benefits programs began in the 1970s. They were first introduced by the Educational Testing Services (ETS). These progressive programs have grown in number since then. The Internal Revenue defines a cafeteria plan as "a written plan under which all participants could choose among two or more benefits or cash, property, or other taxable benefits." In 1986, the Tax Reform Act eliminated those plans with cash options.

A flexible benefits plan may consist of a core of key benefits that are provided for all employees and a menu or a listing of alternative benefits plans from which the employee may select. Many recent plans do not have a core, and participants may elect freely among benefits offered. An important part of designing these programs is careful determination of the benefits to be included in the plan. Consideration, therefore, must be given to the characteristics of your work force so that the benefits you select meet the needs of your employees. Getting the input of your employees can be a valuable approach when designing such a program. Table 11-7 is an example of Gaylord Entertainment's flexible benefits program called CHOICES. Once the benefits list has been developed, a determination must be made as to how much, or what part of, the plan will be funded by the hospitality organization, and how much by the employees themselves.

The operation of the flexible benefits plan is simple; however, the administration can be a nightmare requiring added communication. Each employee is allocated "benefit dollars" that may be based upon pay level, hourly versus salaried, and/or length of service. The most common arrangement is to differentiate hourly and salaried. Your employees may then take these "dollars" and use them to select benefits from the menu you offer them. In some plans, employees may take a salary reduction and "buy" more benefits, if they feel they need the coverage. Some hospitality companies require that a minimum amount of health care, life, and/or disability insurance be purchased. In other plans, choices are completely unrestricted. That means that care must be taken to make sure that your employees understand the benefits: what is good for them and what is not.

What are some of the advantages that hospitality organizations have discovered through offering flexible benefits plans? Recent studies and experience indicate that cost containment is not achieved. Because, however, a flexible benefits plan meets the specific needs of your

TABLE 11-7 CHOICES Benefit Program, Gaylord Entertainment

The company maintains a comprehensive program (**CHOICES**) of employee benefits designed to help protect you and your dependents against the financial uncertainties that may accompany sickness, accidental injury or death. These benefits are provided through a flexible benefits program and defined under Section 125 of the Internal Revenue Code.

The purpose of the **CHOICES** program is to recognize the fact that different people have different wants and needs. So, instead of buying the same level of benefits for everyone, each year the company will deposit an allowance–called **CHOICE**dollars–to your **CHOICES** account. The amount of this allowance is determined by dependent eligibility. You will use your **CHOICE**dollars to buy the benefits you want.

If you buy benefits that add up to the total amount of your allowance, there is no effect on your pay. If you buy benefits that cost more than your allowance, you pay the difference in pretax dollars from your pay in most cases. If you buy benefits that cost less than your benefit allowance, you would then receive the difference in cash as regular taxable income.

You must determine the amount of your pre-tax premium at the beginning of each plan year (or upon entry into the plan) as the government applies certain rules in exchange for the tax advantage. After your benefit elections have been made for the plan year, you can only change your elections if you have a qualifying change in your family status (Refer to "Changing Your Benefit Election" section in each applicable booklet).

(Courtesy of Gaylord Entertainment Company)

employees, greater employee satisfaction is produced. In a review of the top 100 family-friendly companies made in 1997, the majority of the 57 companies ranked as family-friendly offered flexible benefit options.[14] Because of these advantages, employers also see greater company loyalty, improved retention, and an attractive recruitment tool. Typically, employees like the plan because it gives them a sense of control over their lives.

Flexible benefits plans are not without disadvantages. Foremost is the initial expense to convert from a traditional benefits program. The design and implementation of flex plans require much time and energy. The transition phase must be carefully planned with open communication between employer and employee. If your employees do not fully understand the new program, they are likely to perceive that you are taking away something that is rightfully theirs. Remember that today benefits are expected as part of the reward system you offer.

Other problems with these programs stem from unions that are generally not supportive, and with small companies who can't afford the extended bookkeeping that is required to keep track of who receives which benefits, although software programs are becoming both available and cost-effective to help manage these programs. Though tax laws have so far been favorable to these types of plans, changes in legislation may make them less attractive in the future. A potential problem is that an employee could choose a totally inappropriate package resulting in a serious financial loss.

Despite the disadvantages, the increasing popularity of flexible benefits plans is expected to keep growing in the upcoming years. The hospitality companies that have adopted these plans find high employee acceptance. Although they represent greater administrative challenges and require closer communication efforts, flexible benefits plans also offer a more productive, happy work force.

CONCLUSION

Benefits programs are the second component in the reward systems that you design, implement, and administer in your hospitality operation. They have become an important component in the attraction and retention of quality employees for human resources managers. As we proceed through the beginning of the new century, this role is not likely to lessen in its importance in the operation of hospitality establishments.

Twenty years ago, profit sharing was the most important element in a progressive benefits program. Since then, benefits programs have expanded to include provisions for dental care, preventative care, paid vacations, pension portability, in-house employee stores (Figure 11-9), child care, family counseling, elder care, and fitness centers. The changes in benefits planning stem from changing demographics in American society, the rising costs of providing retirement and health care coverage, as well as the effects of legislation and mandated benefits.

Though no longer a supplementary component of compensation, the goals of benefits programs have remained consistent. They remain:

INDUSTRY EXPERTS SPEAK

According to Kathy Roadarmel, "Regardless of the size and demographics of the hospitality organization every employee wants everything when it comes to benefits offerings. At the same time all employers want to be more family friendly. What ends up happening is that companies keep building and building on benefit plans. The plans keep getting bigger and bigger. One of the problems an employer faces is that once a benefit has been offered it is ***very*** difficult for it to be taken away, regardless of cost ineffectiveness of the particular benefit. Even if less than 1 percent of your workforce is using a benefit you can guarantee that 1 percent will be very vocal the moment it is no longer offered. Remember that while employee incentive programs can go away if they are not working, you can't take away benefits no matter how cost ineffective they become."

FIGURE 11-9 Large hospitality properties can offer on-premise company stores for their employees. *(Courtesy of Opryland Hotels & Attractions)*

- To create a climate for improved human relations.
- To attract and retain employees.
- To provide an incentive for increased performance through job satisfaction.
- To install a sense of partnership between employee and the hospitality organization.
- To protect the financial resources of employees.
- To provide security.
- To reward loyal service.
- To improve general morale.

To be effective in meeting these goals the benefit programs require periodic review and modification. They require an understanding of existing legislation and awareness of new legislation. They need to be employee driven and well communicated.

Case Problem 11-1

As the human resources manager for a 1,000-room hotel property located in the Midwest you are responsible for benefits design and administration. You are in the process of reevaluating your hospitality company's benefit offerings. Benefits are expensive for the company to offer, but they are also a great way to recruit and retain quality employees.

You have a decision to make. This is your only choice: you can offer outstanding benefits for a limited number of employees, *or* you can offer middle-of-the-road or average benefits for a large number of employees. (One way you can afford to offer outstanding benefits by hiring more part-time employees because the number of full-time employees eligible for benefits would be reduced.) What decision will you make? In a three-page report justify your decision. Be sure to include at least four advantages of the plan you selected and four disadvantages of the plan you did not choose. Be narrative in your explanations.

Case Problem 11-2

No longer does rising to the top mean that men and women must sacrifice their health, family, and well-being. In the new millennium, business success is defined on employees' own terms. In a three-page report, design a benefits plan that emphasizes work-family issues yet is still affordable to the hospitality organization described in Case Problem 11-1. Include your plans for internally marketing, or selling, this plan to all your employees.

Case Problem 11-3

You are the General Manager of the hospitality organization described in Case Problem 11-1. Your property remains nonunion, even though the geographic area is heavily unionized. You have recently been analyzing the costs of your compensation benefits. Eighteen years ago when you first opened, the average employee earned about $6,500, and the average cost of benefits was about $1,000 per employee. Today, your analysis indicates, that the average pay has increased to about $16,000 (or about two and a half times). The benefit costs have increased to $5,000 per employee (or about five times). Prepare a three-page analysis of these figures. Be sure to include answers to the following questions: How concerned are you about these figures? What might explain the increase? What, if any, benefits do you see as a result of these increases?

Key Words

benefits
benefits menu
benefits planning
cafeteria benefits program
child care
Consolidated Omnibus Budget Reconciliation Act (COBRA)
cost containment
cost sharing
defined benefits plan
defined contribution plan
educational assistance plan
elder care
Employee Retirement Income Security Act, 1974 (ERISA)
Employee Stock Ownership Plan (ESOP)
Family and Medical Leave Act (FLMA)
flexible benefits programs
flextime
Health Insurance Portability and Accountability Act (HIPAA)
Health Maintenance Organizations (HMOs)
income deferral
long-term disability
Older Workers Benefit Protection Act
pension plans
Preferred Provider Organizations (PPOs)
profit sharing
retirement plans
short-term disability
social security
work-family
Worker's Compensation
401(k) plan

Recommended Reading

Boise, L. 1996. "Family Responsibilities and Absenteeism: Employees Caring for Parents versus Employees Caring for Children." *Journal of Managerial Issues* 8(2): 218–239.

Bond, J. T., E. Galinsky, and J. E. Swanberg. 1998. *The 1997 National Study of the Changing Workforce*. Families and Work Institute.

DeGroot, J. 1998. "Work and Life: The End of the Zero-sum Game." *Harvard Business Review* (November/December): 119. web.lexis-nexis.com/more/shrm/19213/4009918/5 (4 December 1998).

Hunt, A. R. 1998. "Healthcare Is Issue of the Decade: Politicians Voter Backlash This Autumn If They Ignore Call for Action." *The Wall Street Journal* 231(123): A9.

London, S. I. 1998. *How to Comply with Federal Employee Laws*. International Personnel Management Association.

Micco, L. 1998. "Health Care Watchdog Unveils New Report Cards for HMOs." *HR News Online*. www.shrm.org/hrnews/articles/072898.htm (8 August 1998).

Perry, P. M. 1996. "Easing the Pain of Health Insurance Costs." *Restaurants USA* 16(5): 32–36.

Purcell, G. "A Guide to Cost-Effective Pharmacy Benefits." *BCSolutions Magazine*. www.bcsolutionsmag.com/Archives/may98/Phamr.htm (10 August 1998).

Roach, D. and A. McLauchin. 1993. "New Family and Medical Leave Is in Effect." *Restaurants USA* 13(8): 8–9.

Rutherford, E. A. 1995. "Employee Benefits under Mandatory Leave Laws: What Is Your Policy?" *Benefits Law Journal* 8(3): 91.

Sheley, Elizabeth. 1996. "Flexible Work Options: Factors That Make Them Work." *HR Magazine* (February). www.shrm.org/hrmagazine/articles/0296cover.html (4 October 1998).

Simmons, J. 1998. "Kid Friendly; Advocate for Child-Care Reform Out to Make It Everyone's Cause." *The Rocky Mountain News*, February 2, p. 3D.

Wyld, D. C. 1995. "The Family and Medical Leave Act: What Hospitality Managers Need to Know." *The Cornell Quarterly* 36(4): 54–63.

Recommended Web Sites

1. Benefits Interface: benefits.org/trivia/index-body.htm
2. Employee Benefits News: data.thirdcoast.net/ebn/sbsearch.cfm
3. HR Bene-Caster: hrsys.com
4. Benefits & Compensation Solutions Magazine: www.bcsolutionsmag.com
5. BenefitsLink™: www.benefitslink.com/index.shtml
6. Employee Benefits News: www.benefitsnews.com/guide.html
7. International Foundation of Employee Benefit Plans: www.ifebp.org
8. Family and Medical Leave Act Information: www.dol.gov/dol/esa/fmla.htm
9. Families and Work Institute: www.familiesandworkinst.org

Endnotes

1. C. Mason-Draffen, "Solutions/Practical Answers to Business Problems/Keeping Good Workers Is All Part of the Benefits Package," *Newsday*, 1998. web.lexis-nexis.com/more/shrm/19218/3895114/4 (26 October 1998).
2. Unknown. "Benefits: The New Way To Raise Pay?" *Investor's Business Daily*, 1998. web.lexis-nexis.com/more/shrm/19216/3798087/1 (3 October 1998).
3. Ann Vincola, "New Strategies For Work/Life Initiatives," *Business Solutions Magazine*. www.bcsolutionsmag.com/Archives/special_sections/WORK_LIF.html (10 August 1998).
4. Families and Work Institute, "New Study Shows How Today's Jobs Affect Productivity and Life at Home," *The 1997 National Study of the Changing Workforce*, April 15, 1998. www.familiesandworkinsti.org/pl.html (9 June 1998).
5. Unknown, "Moonlight and Child Care," *American Demographics* 18, no. 8 (1996): 20.
6. M. Nothaft, "More Companies Begin Providing On-site Day Care as Employee Perk," *The Arizona Republic*, 1998. web.lexis-nexis.com/more/shrm/19215/3875955/5 (15 October 1998).
7. Unknown, "Construction Begins on 'Inn for Children,'" *Hotel & Motel Management* 211, no. 16 (1996): 58.
8. Glenn Burkins, "The Checkoff," *The Wall Street Journal*, 227, no. 90 (1995): 1.
9. Barbara Kate Repa, "The Family and Medical Leave Act: Is It Lip Service Leave?" *Your Rights in the Workplace*, 1998. www.nolo.com/ChunkEMP/familyleave.html (23 August 1998).
10. K. Wright, "The Cost of Family Leave: Opinions Differ on Whether the Federal Law Should Be Broadened in Scope or Whether It Already Burdens Businesses Too Heavily," *Omaha World-Herald*, June 22, 1999. web.lexis-nexis.com/more/shrm/19215/4736738/2 (1 July 1999).

11. Norma R. Fritz, "Helping Employees Manage Their Finances," *Personnel* 65, no. 2 (1988): 6–9.
12. L. Koss-Feder, "Solutions/Flextime Option Helps Keep the Best Workers in Your Employ," *Newsday,* February 1, 1999. web.lexis-nexis.com/more/shrm/19215/4241033/5 (4 February 1999).
13. S. Armour, "Health-Plan Costs to Soar This Year," *USA Today,* January 6, 1999. web.lexis-nexis.com/more/shrm/19215/4144819/3 (8 January 1999).
14. The Institute of Management and Administration, "Eight Ways to Stop Selling Your Cafeteria Plan Short," *Managing Flexible Benefits Plans,* 1998. www.ioma.com/newsletters/mfbp/articles/0198.shtml (10 August 1998).

DISCUSSION QUESTIONS

1. Briefly discuss the role of benefits in the development of a total reward system in the hospitality industry.
2. Explain the difference between benefits and incentives.
3. Describe how the changes in family structure and the importance of work-family issues have affected the selection of benefits offerings in the hospitality industry.
4. Describe The Family and Medical Leave Act and its impact on the hospitality workplace.
5. Briefly define the following benefits options: child care, elder care, educational assistance, language assistance, long-term care, and retirement planning.
6. Explain the use of flextime in a hospitality operation.
7. Identify and describe two cost-containment measures aimed specifically at the rising cost of health care.
8. Describe legally required benefits.
9. Explain the difference between defined benefit plans and defined contribution plans.
10. How can hospitality managers better communicate to their employees about benefits programs?
11. What are the most significant effects of the legislation surrounding benefits?
12. Select five benefits options that you strongly feel should be part of a benefits plan (other than legally required). Defend why you feel so strongly about these choices.
13. Would you support letting all employees determine their own benefits package? Why or why not?
14. What are the values and problems in establishing a flexible benefits plan?
15. What are the objectives of a benefits program in the hospitality industry?

Section 5

Positive Employee Relations: Meeting the Needs of a New Work Force

CHAPTER 12

Multiculturalism in the Hospitality Workplace

"People have one thing in common: they are all different."

—ROBERT ZEND

"Emancipate yourselves from mental slavery. None but ourselves can free our minds."

—BOB MARLEY

INTRODUCTION

Regardless of which part of the United States, or world, that you come from, the cultural diversity that surrounds you in your daily life is probably more prevalent than it has been in the past. The focus in the chapter you are about to read is on the cultural diversity that is found today in the United States, and how that diversity affects your job as a hospitality manager with human resources responsibilities. We do not discuss international management techniques that are important when American businesspeople travel to work abroad. Rather we examine the vast diversity of cultures, and their influences, on businesses in the hospitality industry in North America. Learning how to negotiate contracts, motivate employees, communicate, train, maximize profit margins, and learning appropriate interpersonal etiquette in relating to culturally different personnel and customers can be crucial to your business effectiveness. This is true whenever you are working within the framework of one cultural orientation and attempt to manage people who represent a variety, or diversity, of other cultural orientations.

Our discussion revolves around the concept of **multicultural management** and its related techniques. This is a relatively new focus in human resources management in the hospitality industry, but one that is essential to your managerial effectiveness, given the increasing cultural diversity of the industry with respect to management, employees, and guests.

At the conclusion of this chapter you will be able to:

1. Define multicultural management.
2. Understand various concepts related to multicultural management such as ethnicity, culture, and ethnic pluralism.
3. Explain the importance of cultural awareness to effective human resources management practices in the hospitality industry.
4. Determine how basic human resources functions may be impacted by cultural diversity in the hospitality workplace.
5. Explain how cultural differences affect your ability to function effectively with employees and customers.

6. Define conflict management and determine its effect in managing cultural diversity.

BASIC CONCEPTS OF MULTICULTURAL MANAGEMENT

American culture is ethnically diverse. Think for a moment about your own ethnicity. What is your ethnic makeup? Asian? Italian? Cuban? German? Polish? Chicano? French? African? Spanish? Jewish? Russian? Swiss? Indian? If Indian, native or eastern? If native Indian, are you Cherokee-speaking Iroquoian, Seminole from Florida, Apache from the southwestern parts of the United States, or Cheyenne originally from Minnesota or the Dakotas? When we asked you what your ethnic makeup was did you respond, "American"? Unless you are native or American Indian or perhaps North American Eskimo, your answer of "American" was incorrect. Are you surprised? Curious? Offended?

Ethnic group, as we define it, relates to a group of people who share common origins, experiences, and cultural characteristics. This may include such elements as a point of origin, a common belief system, and/or a common system of communication. Your **ethnic makeup** refers to your background, origins, or heritage. The common characteristics shared by members of an ethnic group that distinguish them from other groups are part of that group's culture. **Culture** refers to customs, beliefs, practices, traditions, values, ideologies, and lifestyles of a particular ethnic group.

What was your reaction when we told you that unless your heritage was native Indian or Eskimo that your ethnic makeup was *not* American? Were you surprised, curious, or offended? Your reaction will give you an indication of your acceptance of the principles of multicultural management as they pertain to ethnic differences. Most of you reading this material think of yourselves as Americans, and you are. Multicultural management does not imply that you are not American, but it does emphasize that in addition to being American, our ethnic makeup contains other components. Therefore, some people are bi-ethnic or perhaps even tri-ethnic. Some are biracial and bilingual, too. Thus, American society is ethnically pluralistic.

You have probably already heard references to African American, Chinese American (or sometimes Chinese-born Americans), Cuban American, Italian American, and many others. Members of these ethnic groups, with their strong sense of ethnicity, recognize (and want to have recognized) their dual heritage. Your **ethnicity** is your sense of belonging to a particular ethnic group, a self identity. **Ethnic pluralism** defines a state of coexistence of ethnic groups, an existence that is separate, but equal. For example, it's okay to be both Cuban and American. When ethnic pluralism exists within an organization, individuals do not have to shun or deny their Cubanness to be American or their Americanness to be Cuban. They have dual ethnic identities and are recognized as such.

Well, you might be thinking, how can one individual be *both* Cuban and American. How does ethnic pluralism operate? We said earlier that members of ethnic groups share a commonality of culture. For individuals with two or more ethnic backgrounds this means an integration of two or more cultures forming their own, oftentimes unique, ethnic makeup. When ethnic and **cultural pluralism** are accepted and understood, individuals can harmoniously go about their daily life. When there is a struggle and tension, either between ethnic groups within a particular society or within the psychological state of individuals over diverse beliefs, practices, values, or ideologies, ethnic conflict is occurring.

Our focus of attention in multicultural management is on the potential conflict that can result when cultural differences such as ethnicity and race, come together in the hospitality work environment without mutual knowledge, understanding, and respect (Figure 12-1). We are particularly concerned about the cultural tensions that may result between managers from one ethnic group and employees from other ethnic groups, and how these tensions may negatively affect work quality and the principles of human resources management. We are equally concerned about the cultural tensions that may result between employees from one ethnic group and customers from other ethnic groups, and how these tensions may negatively affect service. These concerns give rise to the idea of multicultural management.

Multicultural management is the application of general human resources management principles and strategies within the context of the cultural diversity found in your hospitality operation. This approach to human resources management operates on the premise that both the managers' and employees' cultural orientations, backgrounds, and experiences—including their respective ethnic identities—are important influences that affect how both behave

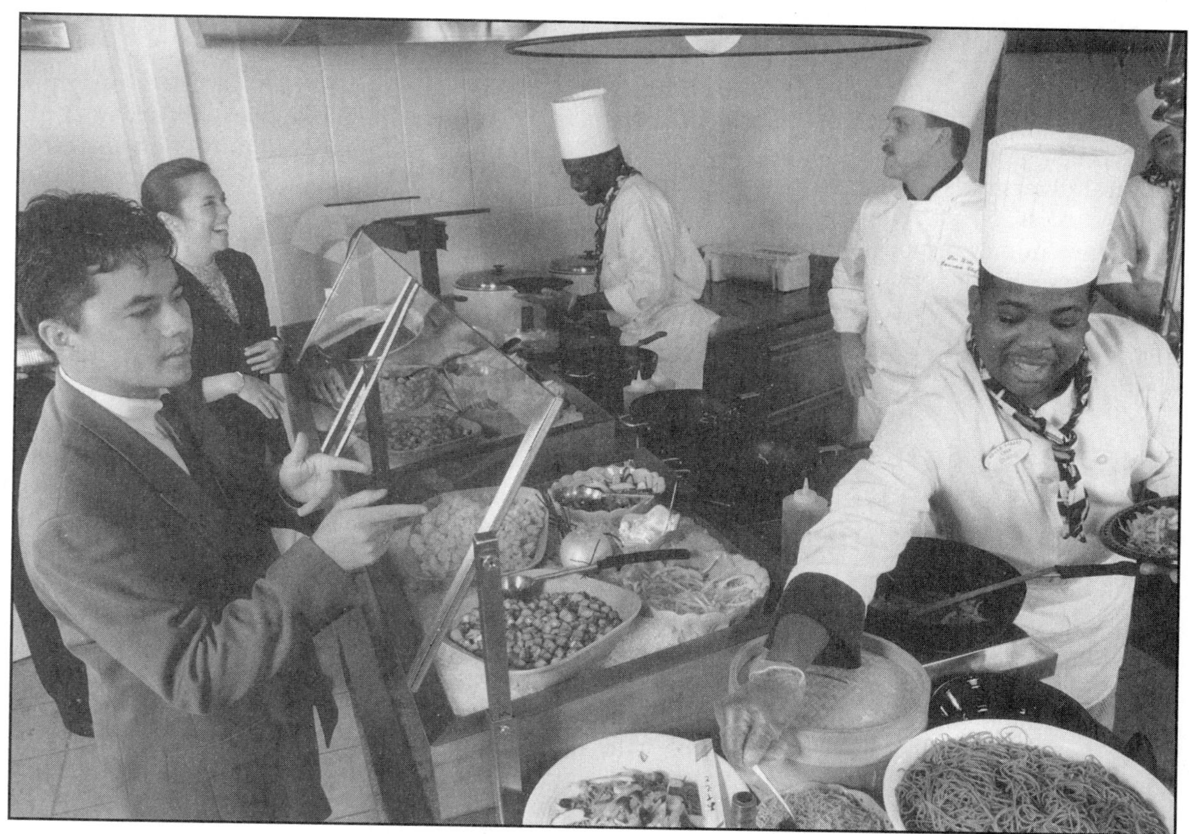

FIGURE 12-1 Multicultural management strives for cultural understanding and respect. *(Courtesy of ARAMARK Corporation)*

in the workplace. Multicultural Management also assumes that work habits and attitudes are influenced by culture. Thus, culture matters when managing a work populace that is ethnically and culturally pluralistic. Today's hospitality managers are expected to effectively manage cultural diversity. It is a part of the daily life of both their role functions in their job assignments and in the hospitality industry itself.

Multicultural management is *not* a separate human resources function. Rather it is an integral part of all the human resources policies, practices, principles, and procedures that we have been discussing in previous chapters. It is not something separate and distinct. Rather it permeates all the activities that you as a hospitality manager will have to do each day such as motivating, training, disciplining, assessing the quality of job performance, and guaranteeing customer satisfaction. Managing cultural diversity is a fundamental element of your success as an effective manager with human resources responsibilities in the culturally diverse hospitality environment and the culturally pluralistic consumer marketplace that the industry serves.

THE IMPACT OF CULTURAL DIVERSITY IN THE HOSPITALITY WORK FORCE

Several realities about American society and the hospitality industry indicate that the principles of multicultural management will become increasingly significant in "the next chapter." Demographers are already analyzing what the populace of the United States will look like in the year 2010 based on the data collected during Census 2000. What we have already seen is that the face of the work force today is very different than the face of the work force yesterday.

Demographics

Most immigrants entering the United States now come from parts of the world such as Southeast Asia, the Middle East, the Pacific Islands, the Caribbeans, and South Africa, where people and cultures are significantly different from earlier generations of immigrants (Tables 12-1 and 12-2). Even though legal immigration has been regulated, illegal immigration continues to increase. Many of the new immigrants are entering the work force in unskilled or semiskilled positions and in service industries like hospitality (Figure 12-2).

Whereas 47 percent of the work force in the late 1980s was native white males, by the year 2000 that figure dropped significantly. This means that the workplace is increasingly comprised of people from a variety of ethnic groups and women. **Gender diversity** issues are found in companies that traditionally hired males to fill their professional and managerial ranks. In the late 1950s this was the labor pool with 95 percent of the awarded MBAs going to men, along with 90 percent of the BBAs.[1] This is not, however, the gender labor pool in "the next chapter."

In addition to the human resources management challenges surrounding ethnic and gender diversity are the additional challenges of **age diversity**. The median age population in the United States has been steadily increasing. As the baby boomer population continues to age, so will the population of our elderly grow.

Different age groups hold different values and have different lifestyles, just as different ethnic groups have different values, lifestyles, and customs. Part of the challenge of multicultural management is the ability to recognize these differences and use them to your advantage as part of your human resources management strategies. Oftentimes, both generations find it uncomfortable when the roles are reversed and the younger manager is supervising the older hourly employee. It can be tough

TABLE 12-1 Country of Origin of the Foreign Born by Citizenship Status

(Numbers in thousands)

	Total Foreign Born		Naturalized Citizen		Not U.S. Citizen	
Country of Origin	**Number**	**Percent**	**Number**	**Percent**	**Number**	**Percent**
All Countries	25,779	100.0	9,043	100.0	16,736	100.0
Mexico	7,017	27.2	1,044	11.5	5,973	35.7
Cuba	913	3.5	474	5.2	440	2.6
Dominican Republic	632	2.5	195	5.2	437	2.6
El Salvador	607	2.4	110	1.2	497	3.0
Great Britain	606	2.4	237	2.6	369	2.2
China and Hong Kong	1,107	4.3	536	5.9	570	3.4
India	748	2.9	263	2.9	485	2.9
Korea	591	2.3	220	2.4	372	2.2
Phillipines	1,132	4.0	657	7.3	475	2.8
Vietnam	770	3.0	385	4.3	385	2.3
Elsewhere	11,655	45.2	4,921	54.4	6,734	40.2

(*Source:* U.S. Census Bureau, *Current Population Survey,* March 1997 (Washington, DC))

TABLE 12-2 Year of Entry into the United States of the Foreign Born by Citizenship Status

(Numbers in thousands)

	Total Foreign Born		Naturalized Citizen		Not U.S. Citizen	
Came to the United States	**Number**	**Percent**	**Number**	**Percent**	**Number**	**Percent**
All Years of Entry	25,779	100.0	9,043	100.0	16,736	100.0
Before 1970	4,749	18.4	3,523	39	1,226	7.3
1970 to 1979	4,935	19.1	2,580	28.5	2,356	14.1
1980 to 1989	8,555	33.2	2,414	26.7	6,141	36.7
Since 1990	7,539	29.2	526	5.8	7,013	41.9

(*Source:* U.S. Census Bureau, *Current Population Survey,* March 1997 (Washington, DC))

for both individuals when the young manager has to direct the older employee to clean tables or to mop the floor. The generation gap is really nothing more than a difference in values and attitudes. The **multicultural manager** who understands this and is sensitized to these differences will see the value in all his or her employees regardless of ethnicity, gender, or age.

Our Consumers

On the other side of the coin is the growing cultural diversity of hospitality consumers.

FIGURE 12-2 Ethnic and gender diversity is improving in all job positions in the hospitality industry. *(Courtesy of ARAMARK Corporation)*

More people of a wider variety of ethnic, social, and cultural backgrounds are traveling, eating out, and engaging in other leisure activities serviced by the hospitality industry. These multicultural consumers will demand some adjustments in service styles and qualities, just as the cultural diversity of hospitality employees will require some alterations in traditional human resources management principles to maximize job performance. We cannot forget or ignore the importance of the changing demographics of our guests. In a study on consumer spending, expenditures from multicultural homes exceeded expenditures in white households in five categories studied, including that of entertainment. It forecast that multicultural household spending in the areas of health care and entertainment would grow nearly three to three-and-a-half times faster than in white homes.[2] No matter where we find ourselves employed, we must take it upon ourselves to understand the marketplace form a cultural perspective, including the impact of ethnicity, gender, and age.

Recruitment and Retention

The biggest challenge each of you will face as managers in "the next chapter" in the hospitality industry is attracting and retaining a qualified work force. Hospitality has historically depended on the 16- to 24-year-old white males and females to fill its vacant job positions. This age group among Anglos has declined in size. Service industries are expanding, making competition for a limited supply of qualified workers even tougher. Gone are the days of applicants with a work ethic and cultural orientation similar to yours knocking your door down to wait tables in your restaurant, manage the cocktail lounge, work at your front desk, train your bellhops, clean your property's rooms, supervise your banquets and catering functions, and wash your restaurant's dishes.

The current immigration and work-force patterns present some very different challenges to managers with human resources responsibilities in the hospitality industry. Many managers can trace their ancestry and cultural origins back to the Ellis Island immigrants who came to America from Western European countries. The geographic locations, ethnic heritages, and cultural traditions of today's immigrants are quite different, as we saw in Tables 12-1 and 12-2. The reasons for entering the United States are often quite different as well. In the 1920s immigrants entered our shores willingly, freely leaving their homelands in search of opportunities and a better way of life. Starting in the 1980s many immigrants came to the United States because of political or economic oppression. They often left their homeland because it was not safe to stay. These immigrants have looked to the United States for safe harbor and in many cases view their stay here as temporary. When people view their immigration as temporary, they are less likely to adapt to the customs and culture of the host country. This situation is not unique to the United States. Many other countries are also finding that their immigration patterns are being altered.

For many immigrants English is a second language, or a language that they cannot speak at all. Many struggle with the idea of assimilation as they hope to return home when things are better in their country of origin. The new immigrant challenge you will face as a manager with human resources responsibilities in the hospitality industry will vary depending on which state and metropolitan area you reside in. See Table 12-3 for the top ten states of residence for immigrants.

TABLE 12-3 Top Ten Metropolitan Statistical Areas of Residence for Immigrants

1. Los Angeles-Long Beach, CA
2. New York, NY
3. Miami, FL
4. Chicago, IL
5. Orange County, CA
6. San Francisco, CA
7. San Diego, CA
8. Oakland, CA
9. Houston, TX
10. San Jose, CA

(*Source:* United States Immigration & Naturalization Service, June 22, 1998 (Washington, DC))

Some Americans feel threatened by the new wave of immigrants, not unlike their ancestors who feared that jobs would be taken away from them. Racism and ethnic prejudice are still prevalent in the workplace at the turn of the twenty-first century, although somewhat more subtle, as it was at the turn of the twentieth century. As hospitality managers, part of your human resources responsibilities will be to deal with these fears and injustices. Teams of workers still need to be developed so that they are able to operate in a manner that is competent and efficient in their task performances. Management needs to ensure that all employees are treated fairly with regards to their labor rights. In a real sense, your success as hospitality manager with human resources responsibilities will depend largely upon how well you respond to the challenges of ethnic and cultural diversity among your employees and consumers (Figure 12-3).

Sexual Orientation in the Workplace

Lifestyle diversity is another area of cultural pluralism that requires the awareness and sensitivity of the manager with human resources responsibilities. In today's workplace we find

FIGURE 12-3 Hospitality managers across the United States must accept changes in the demographics of their labor pool and customer base. *(Courtesy of ARAMARK Corporation)*

many employees who are lesbian and gay. Sexual orientation becomes an increasingly important aspect of diversity and multiculturalism as greater numbers of lesbian and gay employees reveal their sexual orientation. There are several organizations, such as The Human Rights Campaign (the largest national lesbian and gay political organization in the United States), who argue for equal status in the workplace of lesbians and gays. Workplace issues to which they give attention include:

- adopting domestic partner benefits
- adding the words "sexual orientation" to nondiscrimination policies and codes of conduct
- the formation of employer-sanctioned lesbian and gay employee groups

Currently, there is no federal law against discrimination based on sexual orientation. State laws vary widely, and as a manager with human resources responsibilities you will need to be sure of the specific laws that affect your workplace. Eight states—Colorado, Louisiana, Maryland, New Mexico, New York, Ohio, Pennsylvania, and Washington—have executive orders banning discrimination in public employment based on sexual orientation. Nine states—California, Connecticut, Hawaii, Massachusetts, Minnesota, New Jersey, Rhode Island, Wisconsin, and Vermont—and the District of Columbia have comprehensive legislation that bans discrimination based on sexual orientation that protects lesbian and gay applicants and employees.

Many employers and organizations have voluntarily implemented nondiscriminatory policies and procedures. Some have even issued statements concerning the organization's policy of nondiscrimination based on sexual orientation.

THE DYNAMICS OF CULTURAL DIVERSITY AND HUMAN RESOURCES MANAGEMENT

Because the hospitality industry is labor-intensive and service centered, it is a people enterprise. Both the industry's power and potential are nested in the extent to which its multicultural human resources are effectively managed to maximize their productivity. To realize this potential, you as a hospitality manager with human resources responsibilities need to understand how cultural pluralism affects human behavior in general, and in the workplace in particular, along with its influences upon work incentives, work habits, job performance, expectations, satisfaction, and motivation. You need to realize the enormous stress cultural and ethnic differences can impose upon efforts to communicate with and manage culturally diverse employees when these differences are not addressed deliberately in the interpersonal relations. Diversity is about empowering people to understand, value, and use the differences in every person in the hospitality organization (Figure 12-4). You also need to develop skills in how to apply principles and strategies of human resources development within the context of ethnic and cultural diversity.

Unless you understand the behaviors, values, beliefs, ideologies, customs, and traditions of your culturally diverse employees, and are able to use these to your benefit in your management style, you will be at a decided disadvantage in providing the leadership required to achieve maximum success in the industry. Of necessity you must learn how to manage culturally diverse people to service a culturally pluralistic industry and consumer marketplace. Your preparation for this task begins with developing an awareness of and sensitivity to differences in the work values, beliefs, and behaviors of your employees from various cultural orientations. Increasingly, a hospitality organization's success or failure is determined upon its ability to understand the dynamics of cultural pluralism and fully utilize and fully value the culturally diverse workplace (Figure 12-5).

FIGURE 12-4 Employees are more likely to help make your business a success when they are treated with respect and valued for their cultural differences. *(Courtesy of Chili's Grill & Bar, Brinker International)*

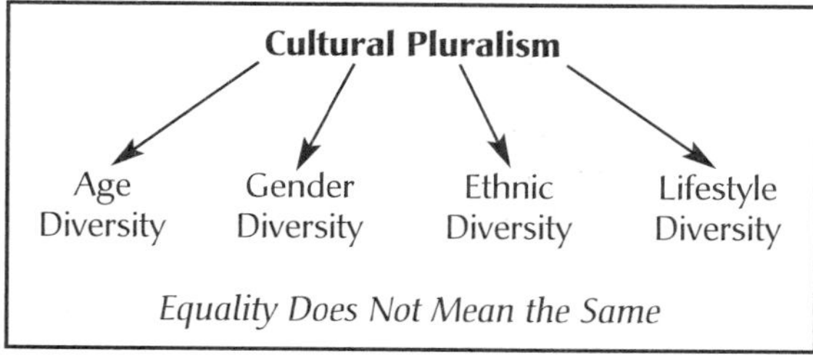

FIGURE 12-5 The dynamics of cultural pluralism.

The Human Resources Functions

This discussion of cultural diversity will allow you to incorporate your understanding of and sensitivity to ethnic, racial, and cultural differences into each of the human resources functions routinely performed by hospitality managers. A further study of the diversity of cultures found in your hospitality organization will provide you with specific information that will assist you in understanding how multiculturalism affects human behavior. The depth of your knowledge will affect your ability or inability to successfully manage the culturally diverse employees in your operation.

Culture is a complex multidimensional phenomenon. It is manifested in numerous ways, some of which are very explicit, others more subtle. Some cultural expressions surface in the workplace, whereas others do not. Examples of situations where culture can influence your behavior and that of culturally diverse employees in the workplace are:

- Communication problem in recruitment
- Policies and procedures such as:
  - —Interviewing
  - —Disciplinary actions
  - —Rules of conduct
  - —Dress codes
  - —Perceptions of time
  - —Service procedures
- Motivation for professional development
- Employee counseling
- Work schedule
- Role of women in the operation

The cultural influences that affect your role as trainer will stem from differences in values, beliefs, work ethic, roles of social decorum, interpersonal relations, and patterns of learning, as exhibited by the various ethnic groups. A culturally sensitive hospitality manager knows how to recognize these differences among his or her employees and understand how they affect job-related performance and personal behaviors. They can then be used advantageously in the human resources training and development processes. With respect to employee development, the multicultural manager has the ability to determine performance levels and assess training needs from a cross-cultural perspective.

The relationships affected by cultural diversity and the barriers cultural differences may generate are not limited to the interactions between management and employees. Our guests, clients, and consumers in the hospitality industry also represent a distinct pool of ethnic, cultural, social, racial, and national differences. Any time interactions occur, either *within* or *among* any of these three pools of people, misunderstandings and conflict due to differences in cultural values, beliefs, experiences, and behaviors can, will, and do occur. The extent to which you, as a manager with human resources responsibilities, understand these differences and use them to form your leadership style, has a direct effect upon the ultimate success of your organization with respect to the effectiveness of operations, quality of service, and profit margin.

In today's workplace it is important that everyone understand your commitment to managing cultural diversity. "Diversity" is a key business initiative.

Personal Cultural Barriers

Our own sense of cultural identity can become a personal barrier, and in so doing it can affect our effectiveness. Have you ever heard a manager say, "I'll never hire another (you fill in your choice of ethnic group). They are always late, or lazy, or sloppy, or unclean, or slow, or undependable!" Too often an isolated unpleasant experience with one member of an ethnic group leads us to generalize that negative encounter and its related characteristics to *all* members of that ethnic group. This is **stereotyping**.

Sometimes negative attitudes toward ethnic group members exist even though we have had no direct experience or personal contact with that group. This is **prejudice**. How ridiculous it would sound if we said, "I'll never hire another Anglo because they are too ambitious and hardworking." Regardless of your ethnic makeup, we are sure that you know of at least one Anglo who is not always ambitious or hardworking. You probably even know African Americans and Hispanics who are even more ambitious than Anglos and some Anglos who are lazy, unclean, sloppy, and slow.

Ambition, work ethic, time usage, space, cleanliness, and methods of conducting business are all affected by cultural values and ethnic backgrounds. When they are defined by standards from our own personal cultural orientation, we tend to view them as "good," "proper," "right," and "positive." When they are shaped, however, by another ethnic group's culture, the same values and behavior can become "bad," "inappropriate," and "negative." Perhaps you have seen the cartoon that describes similar characteristics in both a male and female. Whereas the man is ambitious and a disciplinarian, the woman who acts in the same way is pushy and inflexible! This is gender prejudice that is preferential to males.

A major factor in the management of ethnic and cultural diversity lies in overcoming your own misconceptions, prejudices, and biases about ethnic and cultural differences. **Cultural awareness** assists in this process by moving you out of your own cultural orientation and helping you develop a sensitivity to different styles of operation. Instead of viewing the actions of an ethnic employee from your personal cultural perspective, multicultural management creates a culturally pluralistic knowledge base to view the values, beliefs, and behaviors in the cultural context in which they were intended. Each culture differs from the dominant Anglo culture and, hence, deserves to be understood and appreciated for its own value system. Diversity does not interfere with the effective operations of the hospitality industry. Rather it enriches and enlivens it when hospitality managers know how to use cultural diversity as an asset to the business and their personal management style.

CONFLICT MANAGEMENT

The primary ethnic groups in the hospitality industry today are African American, Americans from Asian ethnic groups, and Americans from Hispanic ethnic groups. Great care, however, must be taken whenever you attempt to make generalizations about all ethnic groups because of the differences within the group. For example, among Hispanics there are subgroups whose origins are Puerto Rican, Cuban, Mexican, Spanish, and South American. Depending upon the location of your hospitality operation, other ethnic groups may also be prominent in the workplace. An examination of some of the core values, attitudes, behaviors, and traditions of these ethnic groups explains how these differences may affect the behaviors and performance of individuals from those ethnic groups as they interact in the hospitality industry. Such a study will also indicate potential conflict areas with respect to beliefs, values, practices, and ideologies. This same approach may be used to study differences among any of the cultural groups we have discussed.

Whenever you have people interacting in a work environment, the potential for conflict exists. Some people suggest that when individuals merely interact among themselves, conflict is inevitable because of differences in perspectives, experiences, and values. Others believe that conflict stimulates creativity, and that an environment needs conflict in order to be healthy. Whatever your views on conflict are, one thing is certain: When conflict exists, it must be properly managed. Oftentimes your success as a manager will be judged by how well you are able to manage conflict and turn it into a positive resource and productive energy.

When managing a work environment filled with cultural diversity, the potential exists for the conflict to be the result of cultural differences, misconceptions, or stereotypes by management and coworkers about the ethnic or cultural group, language or cultural barriers. As a result of the differences that exist, each side misinterprets or dismisses the viewpoint of the other by failing to understand the cultural framework in which the other operates. When these differences, misconceptions, and barriers affect the hospitality organization's ability to provide effective and efficient services to its guests, someone has to have the skills and ability to act as mediator to resolve the conflict. As the hospitality manager who deals with the organization's human resources, **conflict management** becomes your responsibility.

As a mediator, your job is to represent both sides of the conflict fairly so that the differences or tension can be resolved in the best interests of all concerned (Figure 12-6). As we have already mentioned, it is impossible to represent a group fairly unless you have an understanding of that group's cultural orientation. In this role of mediator, the principles of multicultural management become closely tied to employee relations.

As a manager, you can perform more effectively by expanding your understanding of interpersonal and intergroup relations. Accepting the importance of cultural understanding and fair treatment in the workplace is one thing, but assuring it is quite another. Let's take a moment to examine the principles behind managing employee conflict as they relate to cultural diversity.

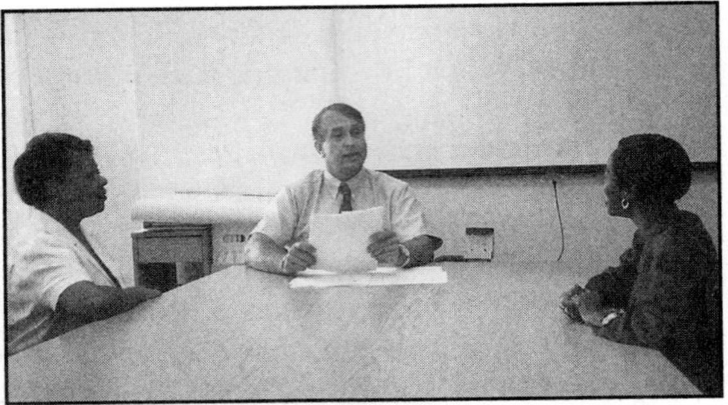

FIGURE 12-6 Conflict resolution requires a mediator who can represent both sides of the issue fairly.

Resolutions to Conflicts

Conflicts occur in hospitality organizations for a variety of reasons in addition to the cultural diversity factor. Conflicts have historically occurred between the front of the house staff and the back of the house, whether it is the front desk versus housekeeping or the waitstaff versus the cooks. The temperamental chef is still a common stereotype even today. The last thing that a hospitality manager needs on a busy day or evening is an open confrontation between two of the operation's employees.

Throughout this text we have pointed out the importance of open channels of communication. Nowhere is this more important than in the prevention of conflict in the workplace. Getting people to know and understand each other before conflict occurs is the optimum solution. The more people understand about other ethnic groups, cultures, and behavioral styles, the more likely they are to reach a compromise. Employee communication is part of a sound human resources management plan, not an afterthought.

Unfortunately, a typical management approach to conflict is to ignore the situation, taking the attitude that the parties involved will be able to work out the differences on their own. Ill-managed or ignored conflicts will only fester, and in the long term, lower staff morale and job productivity will be the end result. In an era when reducing turnover will become an increasingly critical goal, conflict situations simply cannot be permitted to linger.

Another resolution to conflicts in the workplace is to change the structure of the interpersonal relationships by moving your employees around. The logic is that by changing the environmental conditions that created the conflict to begin with, you will diffuse the tensions, and the conflict will be resolved. For those of you with work experience in the hospitality industry, you can see the difficulty in changing employees from one department to another. Skill levels and abilities are seldom identical from job position to job position. And even if moving people around could easily be accomplished, aren't you just setting the stage for another conflict, only with different players? The conflict has not been resolved; the interpersonal relationships involved have merely been shifted from one context or location to another.

For the multicultural manager, there is another option available when dealing with conflict that is created by the cultural diversity in the work environment. You act as a culturally sensitized mediator, one who is aware of the conflict points in the routine ways of functioning among individuals from different cultural backgrounds. You can ease tensions and help employees in conflict understand each others' points of view, thereby facilitating conflict resolution. It is always easier to change a person's behavior than to attempt to change the person. Cultural awareness and sensitivity of the ethnic and other culture groups that work in your hospitality operation combined with knowledge of the causes of individual differences can assist you in getting both parties to modify their negative behavior.

Many hospitality organizations conduct diversity training on an ongoing basis (Figure 12-7). These training sessions focus on developing cultural awareness and assist employees in developing the skills they need to work with

FIGURE 12-7 Cultural sensitivity training is geared toward improving employee work relations. *(Courtesy of Left At Albuquerque, Palo Alto, CA)*

people from a diversity of backgrounds. It is important to correct misconceptions, misunderstandings, biases, and stereotypes about ethnic and cultural group members by individuals outside the groups. This requires that you have a knowledge base of the ethnicity and culture that surrounds you in the workplace before you can sufficiently help your multicultural employees to understand and respect their own and each other's cultures, as well as work better with each other. Knowledge of ethnicity, gender differences, age influences, and sexual orientation are also fundamental to your overall effectiveness as a multicultural manager.

Even the most conflict-free multicultural work environments require a system of accommodation and compromise to maintain organizational stability and maximize productivity. The needs of each individual employee can only be met if the manager with human resources responsibilities has the appropriate knowledge base, understanding, and sensitivity to break down the ethnic and cultural barriers that may exist.

CONCLUSION

The continued existence of a multicultural environment and an ethnically pluralistic work force in the hospitality workplace is a reality each of you faces in "the next chapter." Understanding cultural and ethnic pluralism and accepting cultural diversity must be seen not merely as a necessity but as a creative potential and positive resource for enriching the hospitality industry's quality and productivity. If you are going to make appropriate decisions as managers, you have to have an understanding of how the value systems of different cultures operate, and how these affect job-related attitudes, values, and behaviors. This understanding increases the likelihood of your effectiveness as a human resources developer.

The service industry has historically obtained a significant proportion of its work force from the 16- to 24-year-old age group. Taking into consideration the continued reduction of this age group among Anglos of the mainstream culture, hospitality operations will be forced to seek out some other sources of labor supply to meet their human resources requirements. Increasingly, this resource will be from among groups who are racially, culturally, and socially different from the middle-class mainstream of society. It will also include more women and recent immigrants.

The United States is becoming increasingly culturally and ethnically diverse, as is the labor force that supplies the service industries. The populace of immigrants will be, and to a great extent already is, able to assist the hospitality industry in meeting its labor needs, as are the other alternative sources of labor.

The increasing diversity of the hospitality work force places a special demand upon managers with human resources responsibilities to communicate with, motivate, attract, and retain employees from a culturally different background. Cultural awareness, knowledge, and sensitivity are necessary to meet these demands. Becoming a multicultural manager requires understanding both yourself and the diverse cultural groups you are expected to manage. Knowing what cultural factors (values, beliefs, experiences, and backgrounds) affect your everyday life can help you understand how ethnicity and culture shape the lives of the human resources in your operation. A study of ethnic groups and their cultures is really a study of people and learning how their values affect the way they interrelate in a variety of social and interpersonal contexts, including the workplace.

Multicultural management must be an ongoing, integral part of hospitality industry operations. It is a process that occurs simultaneously as you go about fulfilling your routine responsibilities as a human resources manager within the context of the cultural and ethnic diversity that characterizes the hospitality industry's settings, purposes, employees, and consumers. The diversity of cultures can be an asset, not a detriment, to your hospitality organization. Your ability to manage that diversity is fundamental in your personal success and in your organization's effectiveness.

Case Problem 12-1

You have been the front office manager of a 300-room property for the past 12 months. The property is located on the outskirts of a large metropolitan area. A job vacancy for executive housekeeper has been posted and has attracted your interest. In this position you would be responsible for a staff of 50 full-time employees and 15–25 part-time employees.

During your tenure at the front desk you have noticed that there seems to be more conflict among the housekeeping employees as well as between the housekeeping department and other departments. You suspect that some of this conflict might be due to the vast array of cultural differences found within the housekeeping department. You feel that you are ready to accept this challenge.

What city is your hotel property in? This will affect the specific types of cultural diversity you find within the hotel. What do these cultural differences look like? Be specific. Why do your think that the cultural factors will be a greater challenge in housekeeping than they are at the front desk? Based upon the specific types of cultural and ethnic diversity that you identified, what do you believe are some of the causes of the existing conflicts within and between the housekeeping department? Identify two solutions for resolving the existing conflict. Be specific to the cultural and ethnic differences you identified.

Case Problem 12-2

Shortly after you were hired as the Human Resources Manager for a small quick-service chain in Texas, you faced a problem. Kim is one of your store managers with a slight hearing impairment. She has brought it to your attention that she feels that your company is underutilizing qualified disabled employees.

Help Kim develop a three-page plan to employ more qualified disabled persons in jobs they could handle successfully. Identify what types of jobs in your company might successfully accommodate qualified disabled persons. How would you handle any unique training needs? What about the attitudes and potential misconceptions other employees might hold about working with disabled persons? How do you think employing qualified disabled persons will affect turnover?

Case Problem 12-3

After Kim came to you with her request in Case Problem 12-2, you started thinking about the cultural sensitivity (or lack thereof) of the employees who work in your quick-service company. You decide to prepare a three-page report to the president of the company that would outline and describe the key elements of a successful cultural diversity training program. Identify what you will need from the president to get such a program started. Discuss both short-term and long-term implementation and implications of your program. The goal of this program would be to provide the same opportunities for all employees while allowing for individual differences at the same time.

Key Words

age diversity
conflict management
cultural awareness
cultural pluralism
culture
ethnic group
ethnicity
ethnic makeup
ethnic pluralism
gender diversity
lifestyle diversity
multicultural manager
multicultural management
prejudice
stereotyping

Recommended Reading

Bowen, W., Bok, D., and Burkhart, G. 1999. "Report Card on Diversity: Lessons for Business from Higher Education." *Harvard Business Review* (January/February): 140–147.

Faircloth, A. 1998. "Guess Who's Coming to Denny's: And Shoneys . . . " *Fortune,* August 3. web.lexis-nexis.com/more/shrm/19215/3561964/1 (10 August 1998).

Flynn, G. 1995. "Do You Have the Right Approach to Diversity?" *Personnel Journal* 74(10): 68–75.

———. 1998. "The Harsh Reality of Diversity Programs." *Personnel Journal* 77(12): 26–35.

Laabs, J. 1994. "Individuals with Disabilities Augment Marriott's Work Force." *Personnel Journal* 73(9): 46–53.

Miller, C. W. 1998. "Research Shows Businesses Benefit from Diversity." *Roanoke Times & World News,* July 19, p. 1.

Powers, B. and A. Ellis. 1995. *A Manager's Guide to Sexual Orientation in the Workplace.* Routledge Publishers.

Simons, T. 1996. "Executive Conflict Management." *Cornell Hotel and Restaurant Administration Quarterly* (4): 2–9.

Solomon, C. M. 1993. "Managing Today's Immigrants." *Personnel Journal* 72(2): 56–65.

Thompson, R. W. 1998. "Holocaust Survivor Urges HR Professionals to Remember the Less Fortunate." www.shrm.org/hrnews/articles/102798.htm (2 November 1998).

Recommended Web Sites

1. Sexual Orientation in the Workplace: alexia.lis.uiuc.edu/~.is405/diversity/sexualo.htm
2. Domestic Patnership Plans: qrd.tcp.com/qrd/browse/dp.benefits.orgs.list
3. Organizations with "Sexual Orientation" in their Policies: qrd.tcp.com/qrd/browse/sexual.orientation.nondiscrimination.list
4. CorVision Diversity Training Materials: www.corvision.com/htmldox/corvpgl/dox/b&idiver.htm
5. Workplace Diversity Initiative: www.hrc.org/issues/workplac/nd/ndlist.html
6. Immigration and Naturalization Statistics: www.ins.usdoj.gov/stats/index.html
7. Disability Resources: disability.com/index.html
8. Diversity Reading List: www.berkshire-aap.com/d_read.html

Endnotes

1. S. G. Butruille, "Corporate Caretaking," *Training and Development Journal* (April 1990): 49–55.
2. Tom Maguire, "Ethnics Outspend in Areas." *American Demographics* (December 1998). www.demographics.com/publications/ad/98_ad/9812_ad/ad981205a.htm (5 February 1999).

Discussion Questions

1. Define and distinguish the four fundamental concepts of multicultural management.
2. Explain why cultural pluralism is becoming such a strong presence and force in the hospitality industry.
3. Explain some reasons why multicultural management is essential to the effective functioning of the hospitality industry.
4. Explain how culture and ethnicity influence attitudes and behaviors of managers and employees in the workplace.
5. Describe and discuss a scenario involving ethnic conflict in the workplace that you have experienced, witnessed, or heard about. Explain how it amplifies the needs for and principles of multicultural management.
6. Explain the relationship between human resources development and multicultural management in the hospitality industry.
7. What are potential conflict points created by cultural pluralism in the hospitality industry?
8. What skills and competencies are necessary to be an effective multicultural manager?

CHAPTER 13

Employee Assistance Programs

"Understanding of our fellow human beings becomes fruitful only when it is sustained by sympathetic feelings in joy and sorrow."

—ALBERT EINSTEIN

"Seek first to understand, then to be understood."

—STEPHEN COVEY

"Houston, we have a problem."

—JAMES LOVEL

At the conclusion of this chapter you will be able to:

1. Define an Employee Assistance Program and its role in employee retention.
2. Identify problems that you think could be handled by an EAP.
3. Describe the differences between in-house and contracted-out EAPs.
4. Describe the development and implementation of an EAP in a hospitality organization.
5. Identify the evaluation methods used to determine the cost effectiveness of an EAP.
6. Explain the role of employee assistance programs in the strategic human resources management plan for a hospitality organization.
7. Understand the effects of AIDS in the hospitality workplace.

INTRODUCTION

Employee Assistance Programs (EAPs) have rapidly become a valuable management tool in the hospitality industry in our quest to retain our valued employees. Employee assistance programs work in tandem with the corrective action and counseling programs we discussed in Chapter 9. Together, these programs help in the retention of the "troubled" employee as well as any employee who must deal with a variety of personal problems outside the immediate work environment. As you will soon see, the problems EAPs assist with are very diversified.

THE PHILOSOPHY OF EMPLOYEE ASSISTANCE PROGRAMS

Jeffery has been with your hospitality organization for over ten years, and you have come to know him as an employee who is both reliable and trustworthy. Though Jeffery's job position is storeroom clerk, the responsibilities he has gained throughout the years include receiving and inventory. Recently, you have heard your other employees complaining that supplies are not being maintained as they should be. Frequently, the other employees tell you they do not have the supplies to perform their job duties, and this is beginning to reflect upon their own job performance. Checking the inventory sheets, you find that supplies are up to par and that there is no indication of ever running out of any supplies. You suspect that Jeffery has been stealing. What do you do?

If your hospitality organization has an established employee assistance program and you have had training in dealing with employee problems, your approach with Jeffery is likely to be one of **intervention** as opposed to the all too frequent confrontation approach. What if Jeffery has a substance dependency? What if Jeffery's wife left him with three children to feed and clothe? What if Jeffery's mother is a victim of cancer or if he has a friend in his care with AIDS? Do any of these situations condone Jeffery stealing from your storeroom? Would you have more compassion for Jeffery if his wife had left him than if he had a substance dependency or was caring for an AIDS victim?

None of these situations, which are just a sample of the type of personal problems your employees might bring with them to the workplace, is a justification for stealing. On the other hand, Jeffery has been a valued employee; all of his performance appraisals for the past ten years reflect that. When you intervene in the situation, you find out that, indeed, Jeffery has a chemical dependency. That afternoon he enters into a twenty-eight-day treatment center for addicts.

What we have just presented to you is an oversimplification of how having an EAP in your organization can assist you in retaining your valued employees, and help another human being get his life back on the right track

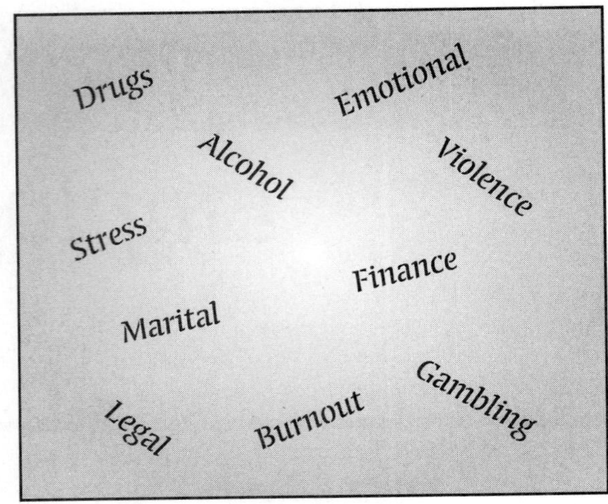

FIGURE 13-1 EAPs provide assistance for a variety of personal problems.

(Figure 13-1). Companies throughout the United States have discovered that Employee Assistance Programs are not only effective in reclaiming "lost" employees and lost productivity, but that they also provide positive reinforcement to already productive employees to enable them to do their best work. Assisting employees, regardless of the personal issue or motivation, is beneficial to both the long-term interests of the hospitality organization *and* society.

A Historical Perspective

In the 1920s, occupational counseling programs were established in companies to help employees deal with personal problems that were causing deficient performance in the workplace. **Substance abuse** programs, in particular those dealing with alcoholism, can be found at Dupont in the 1940s. The establishment of Alcoholics Anonymous (AA), the promotion of using performance evaluations to discover alcoholics at an early stage, and the recognition by the American Medical Association (AMA) of alcoholism as a disease in the late 1960s all helped to support the need for employers to assist the alcoholic employee with recovery.

The drug-abuse crisis of the 1960s and 1970s brought drug- and alcohol-abuse programs together under the auspices of "substance" abuse. During the same time period, the changing demographics in the United States saw a weakening of the family structure and more single-parent households resulting in family, child, legal, and financial personal problems for many of the nation's employees. Mental and emotional problems were seen as illnesses, not as a social stigma. Basically, any personal problems that could adversely affect work performance are candidates for coverage under employee assistance programs. If your people are not able to function well in their personal lives, it is unlikely that they will be able to function effectively when they enter the hospitality workplace.

As demographics change, the problems covered by EAPs must evolve in response to the needs of the employees. Relating to family issues, the 1970s and 1980s saw child care at the forefront; in the 1990s the concerns expanded to parenting young children or teenagers. One of the most recent areas of concern is that of elder care and its obligations on employees in the workplace. In a survey of 1,050 major U.S. employers, 26 percent offered elder care benefits. Of those offering these benefits, 77 percent offered resource and referral services and 19 percent offered counseling services.[1]

Employee Assistance Programs have broadened in scope way beyond the original employer's involvement in programs dealing specifically with alcoholism. In the hospitality industry ITT Sheraton was one of the first hotel chains to offer EAP services in each of its 400 hotel properties.[2] Today numerous other companies such as Marriott, Opryland Hotel, Red Lobster, Walt Disney World, ARAMARK, Brinker International, Bristol Hotels & Resorts, and Burger King Corporation—to name just a few—have invested in Employee Assistance Programs for their people.

Any one of these problems can, and does, cause impaired job performance in the hospitality industry, as well as every other industry in the United States today. The term Employee Assistance Program, first used in the 1970s, broadened the scope of problems covered. Table 13-1 identifies some of the problems that can be included in an EAP.

The Americans with Disabilities Act of 1990 (ADA) has had a direct effect on the expansion of services provided for under EAPs. The ADA considers an individual to have a "disability" if he or she has a physical or mental impairment

TABLE 13-1 Problems Covered by an EAP

- Alcohol abuse
- Alcohol dependency
- Career development difficulties
- Children/adolescent
- Depression/burnout
- Domestic violence
- Drug abuse
- Elder-care issues
- Emotional difficulties
- English as a second language
- Family issues
- Gambling, compulsive
- HIV/AIDS
- Legal problems
- Life transition
- Literacy
- Marital difficulties
- Mental health
- Personal financial problems
- Psychological
- Single parenting
- Stress-related problems

that substantially limits one or more major life activities, has a record of such an impairment, or is regarded as having such an impairment. Because persons with HIV have physical impairments that substantially limit one or more major life activities, they are a protected class under this legislation. In June 1998 the U.S. Supreme Court passed down its first AIDS-related ruling, and found that a Maine woman infected with the virus that causes AIDS *is* protected from discrimination under the American with Disabilities Act. Employers can no longer discriminate against persons with HIV or AIDS in any of their employment practices, including but not limited to, recruitment, application procedures, hiring, placement, training and development, promotions, discipline, and performance appraisals. Employee Assistance Programs can greatly help in supporting ADA legislation.

What Is an Employee Assistance Program?

We define an **Employee Assistance Program (EAP)** in the hospitality industry as an employer-provided program that is used as a management tool to assist employees in dealing with personal problems before they seriously impair job performance. Employee assistance programs do not claim to be a panacea for performance deficiencies, nor do they claim to turn every employee with personal problems into a full-fledged contributing member of your work team. However, as company-sponsored programs they are designed to alleviate problems that employees face that hinder their effectiveness in the hospitality workplace.

For the employee who is willing to admit his or her problems and seek assistance in their resolution, EAPs provide a means by which the employee can do so, and still keep working. For the employee who is at the early stages of a potential problematic situation, EAPs offer a place the employee can turn to for advice and counseling without fear that doing so will result in the loss of his or her job. For the employer, EAPs provide a course of corrective action and disciplinary procedures that can protect the employer from a lawsuit if the situation results in a termination (Figure 13-2). It also becomes another retention tool in a period when losing an employee with personal problems can create operational problems.

The skyrocketing costs of health care make EAPs a complementary component of the entire benefits package. A strong emphasis is placed on the preventive aspects of the EAP. By creating an attitude in the workplace environment that says, "everyone has personal problems, and we realize that those problems will affect your job performance if you don't seek help as quickly as possible; here is a program that is designed to do that for you," your employees are more likely to seek help before they reach a crisis stage with their problem.

FIGURE 13-2 EAPs provide a course of corrective action that benefits both employee and employer. *(Courtesy of Opryland Hotels & Attractions)*

INDUSTRY EXPERTS SPEAK

Jim Tye, former Director of Employment for Furr's/Bishop's Cafeterias, L.P., was involved with his company's EAP and offers the following thoughts: "Anyone who has been in the hospitality industry for any length of time will tell you that one of the greatest satisfactions comes from seeing the growth and development of others. At the same time, the very nature of our business affords us an incredible opportunity to help others. Employee Assistance Programs carry that mission a step further: the commitment by a corporation to formally and systematically assist employees with specific problems becomes a very human statement, as well as having long-term effects on productivity and profitability for the company. One need only witness families reunited; troubled children returned to healthful, productive activities from a bout with drugs or alcohol; or financial counseling aid a family deeply in debt to really appreciate the human side of what we can do."

WHY SHOULD I PROVIDE AN EAP?

Clearly, EAPs convey an "I care" message to the people working in your hospitality organization. They are humanistic and serve to exemplify sound human resources management practices. In addition, they encourage your employees to improve their lifestyles by confronting their problems early on. For employees whose **personal problems** have already reached crisis proportions, the EAP provides them with an opportunity to get their lives back on the right track, while it allows them to remain employed.

Perhaps some of you are thinking, "This all sounds nice, but let's get real. Who has the time and money to fool with a goody-goody program like an EAP? Besides, the chances of an employee having a personal problem so bad that it affects his or her productivity is slim. Furthermore, if an employee has a problem it's the employee's problem, not mine. I get paid to manage this operation, not hold someone's hand!" To address some of these issues that you might be raising let's first look at how extensive the problems are, and then examine what the **"troubled" employee** costs U.S. businesses each year.

The Scope of the Problem

The United States Department of Labor estimates that 71 percent of illegal drug users are employed. This translates into over 10 million employed people who are current users of illicit drugs. Of those individuals that called the cocaine helpline, 75 percent reported using drugs on the job, 64 percent admitted that their use of drugs adversely affected their job performance, 44 percent admitted selling drugs to other employees, and 18 percent had stolen from their coworkers to support their drug habit.

The combined studies by a number of different workplace drug agencies and institutes indicates the following:

- Marijuana use is increasing.
- Abuse of prescription drugs is on the rise.
- Low unemployment rates makes it harder to eliminate all drug users from the workplace.
- Drug users are moving to small businesses. (Less likely chance of a small to mid-size operation conducting drug screening.)
- Drug sales have moved from the street to the workplace.
- Substance abuse by women is on the increase.
- Young employees tend to be more comfortable with drug use.[3]

Drug abuse includes both illegal and legal drugs.

See Table 13-2 for a list of indicators of chemical dependency in the workplace.

TABLE 13-2 Indicators of Chemical Dependency in the Workplace

Place an "X" next to behaviors exhibited by employee, or reported to you by others. More than four "Xs" should alert you that some problem exists.

JOB PERFORMANCE

[ ] Frequent Monday or Friday absences.
[ ] Longer or more frequent absences.
[ ] Multiple instances of unauthorized leaving work site.
[ ] Excessive morning or noontime tardiness.
[ ] Increased number of "cuts" during work day.
[ ] Difficulty in concentrating.
[ ] Difficulty in recalling simple instructions.
[ ] Increased inability to learn from or recall previous mistakes.
[ ] Alternating periods of high and low work performance.
[ ] Marked inattention to detail.
[ ] Increased overt boredom, tiredness, or disruptive behavior.
[ ] Marked decline in productivity.
[ ] Missed deadlines.
[ ] Increased excuses for incomplete, missing, or unacceptable work.
[ ] Increased signs of disorientation; frequent instances of loss of train of thought.
[ ] Sleeping on the job.
[ ] Less responsible about doing assignments.

SOCIAL

[ ] Decreased interaction with peers and family.
[ ] Change in peer groups.
[ ] Hypersensitivity to perceived or actual criticism.
[ ] Withdrawal from previous friends.
[ ] Drastic changes in personality.
[ ] Coworkers or friends talking to you about employee's behavior or attitude changes.
[ ] Drastic change in taste of music.
[ ] Defending the right to drink or to smoke marijuana.
[ ] Irritability or lack of emotion.
[ ] Extreme, rapid mood swings without apparent reason.
[ ] Inappropriate emotional responses.
[ ] Loss of previous goals.
[ ] Consistent reports of lost, borrowed, or stolen belongings.

PERSONAL GROOMING AND HEALTH

[ ] Change in eating or sleeping habits.
[ ] Decreased attention to personal hygiene.
[ ] Appearance of rash around mouth or nose.
[ ] Inappropriate clothing (long sleeves or jackets on warm days, lightweight attire in cold weather).
[ ] Frequent instance of stiff or painful arms.
[ ] Inappropriate, sudden, and unprecipitated sweats.
[ ] Increased coughing, post-nasal drip, or sore throats.
[ ] Continual symptoms of flu or gastrointestinal upset.
[ ] "Needle tattoos" caused by carbon residue from heated syringe or substances.
[ ] Selling of personal belongings, with no evidence or proceeds.
[ ] Dark glasses often and inappropriately worn indoors.
[ ] Nicotine spots on thumb and index finger, particular to pot smoker.
[ ] Change in taste of dress or clothing.

FAMILY

[ ] Are you missing money or other valuables from your home?
[ ] Is child less responsible about doing chores?
[ ] Do you catch your child in lies?
[ ] Is there an increase in family arguments?
[ ] Do you disapprove of your child's choice of friends?
[ ] Does your child become unresponsive to discussions about drugs and alcohol?
[ ] Is there open defiance regarding family rules?
[ ] Has your child ever run away from home?
[ ] Has there been violence or hostility toward family members?

(*Source:* Glenbeigh Hospital of Miami)

Alcohol abuse is another work-related problem. Documentation from the hospitality industry suggests that usage might be higher for our employees. Some reasons for this include the consistent availability of alcohol, working conditions that include exposure to high temperatures, the different working hours our employees work, and an all too frequent acceptance of drinking by management.[4]

What is even more shocking is that a government survey that looked at substance abuse by industry found that employees in eating and drinking establishments had the highest rate of illicit drug use, and the second highest rate of heavy drinking of all U.S. occupations surveyed. In a survey of full-time workers from 1991 to 1993, 16.3 percent of workers at eating and drinking establishments said that they currently used illicit drugs. This was more than any other industry in the survey. Additionally, 15.4 percent of the full-time employees stated that they drank heavily (defined as five or more drinks on five or more occasions within the past thirty days).[5] The U.S. Department of Labor estimates that one in every ten people in this country has an alcohol problem.

The National Mental Health Association (NMHA) states that more than 51 million Americans have a mental disorder, yet only about 16 percent seek treatment. It is believed that a majority of the Americans who commit suicide each year have a mental disorder. Suicide is the eighth leading cause of death in the United States.[6] Clinical depression is experienced by 17.6 million adult Americans each year with only one third seeking treatment. It is estimated that depression costs $43.7 billion annually to the U.S. economy, including a $23.8 billion loss in absenteeism and lost productivity to American businesses according to the National Mental Health Association's National Public Education Campaign on Clinical Depression. On January 1, 1998, the **Mental Health Parity Act of 1996** went into effect. This Act requires all employers with fifty or more employees that offer a group health plan to ensure the equal existence of benefits for mental conditions as compared to physical conditions.

Mental wellness has become an important goal of industry.

Costs of the "Troubled" Employee

Why does this matter to you, the manager with human resources responsibilities? Employees working under the influence of drugs or alcohol function at approximately two thirds of their potential. Substance-abusing employees are three times as likely to use sick leave benefits, three times as likely to have accidents on the job, use their health benefits four times more often then other employees, miss work five times more frequently, and lower the overall productivity of the work force.

It is estimated that each year alcohol abuse and alcoholism cost the U.S. economy $148 billion; drug abuse and dependence cost an estimated $98 billion annually.[7] It is believed that alcoholism alone causes 500 million lost workdays each year. The National Mental Health Organization estimates economic costs of mental illness at $147.8 billion each year. A byproduct of drug- and alcohol-related problems is in the area of workplace violence. One of the four top reasons for the rise in workplace violence is drug- and alcohol-related problems. Domestic violence is on the rise and with it the spillover effect into the workplace. It is estimated that domestic violence costs anywhere from $3 to $10 billion annually in loss productivity due to absenteeism, employee turnover, and health-care expenses.[8]

In addition to the personal problems already identified is the nation's AIDS crisis and the effect it is having on the hospitality industry. The impact of this disease continues to be devastating and will continue to be so until a cure is found. Indirect costs include lost productivity while health care expenses are escalating due to intensive care needs and premature mortality.

Attendance, productivity, use of health care benefits, safety, behavior, and work quality are all affected by the personal problems our employees bring with them to the hospitality workplace. We hope that you now are in agreement that the development of an employee assistance program can benefit your hospitality organization.

These programs can assist employees with a wide range of problems that they may be encountering in their personal lives. Having an employee assistance program available to your employees can help prevent these problems from escalating, leading to a happier and healthier work force (Figure 13-3). Let's now look at the types of EAPs most commonly found, and then discuss how to develop and implement a program.

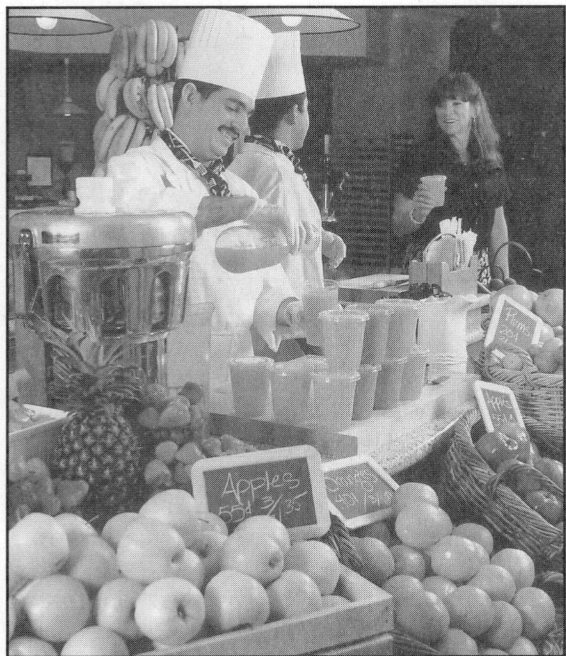

FIGURE 13-3 A successful EAP assists in maintaining a happy and healthy work force. *(Courtesy of ARAMARK Corporation)*

IN-HOUSE VERSUS CONTRACTED-OUT EAPs

Employee Assistance Programs vary in their approach among hospitality organizations. Despite this diversity, they all maintain the same goals of identifying employees with personal problems that may be affecting their job performance, providing an avenue for those employees to seek counseling and help, and maintaining the confidentiality of the employee(s) participating in the program.

Even the smallest hospitality company can implement an EAP. The most popular method for companies that can't afford to operate their own program and are too small to have a contractor, or third-party provider, come in and provide one for them is the consortium. In a consortium, several small hospitality companies or operations would band together, possibly structuring themselves as a private, nonprofit corporation. Each of the member companies would pay a flat rate based upon its average use of the EAP per employee.

In-House EAPs

Hospitality organizations that provide **in-house EAPs** have to be large enough to support a professional EAP Director and, if necessary, a counseling staff. The remainder of the human resources management staff will also require some training and education as to the use of the EAP in established human resources practices, such as corrective action procedures.

One of the greatest disadvantages of operating an in-house EAP is the potential lack of confidentiality. For the EAP to be successful, the confidentiality of the employee using the services has to be guaranteed. Information from any part of the EAP, including the counseling sessions, never becomes part of the employee's personnel file. If your people do not believe that confidentiality will be maintained, they will not fully use the services the program offers to them.

The advantage of operating an in-house program is that you have greater management control over the program itself. Your company will hire the counseling staff, and they will become members of your hospitality organization.

Contracted-Out EAPs

Just as with any contracted service, the EAP provider offers assessment and counseling services for a fee. These services are offered in a location outside of the work site, assuring confidentiality. To be of maximum benefit, however, the off-site location of the **contracted-out EAP** must be accessible to your work force.

Usually, the service will also include telephone counseling that is aimed at crisis intervention. This crisis intervention uses a hot-line style, and it offers complete anonymity to the troubled employee. Counselors discuss the problem with the employee, and if they feel therapy is needed, the employee is referred to an outside resource. The costs of these programs vary depending on the number of employees using the program and the types of services the contractor provides.

Caution must be exercised when selecting a third-party provider to provide EAP services for your employees. It is important that the provider understand the hospitality industry and its unique pressures and stresses. The hours our employees work can oftentimes be straight around-the-clock with no days off. The contractor you select must be willing to meet the needs and schedules of your staff. EAP specialists and professional counselors should be licensed or certified. You do not want amateurs counseling your valued employees. Most employee assistance programs today are contracted-out. Use the same care and consideration you would use before entering into any type of contractual arrangement with a service provider.

SETTING UP AN EAP

An effective EAP provides a system of education for all employees in the hospitality organization. This serves to explain how the EAP works and stresses its confidentiality. Supervisors are taught how to identify performance deficiencies that may be due to personal problems. An emphasis is placed on not diagnosing or judging the employee. Rather, the supervisors are taught to refer the troubled employee to the appropriate resource.

Development

Development begins with an assessment of the needs of your organization and takes into consideration the following elements:

- Review of organizational profile.
- Review of current benefits program. (After all, an EAP should be a new benefit).
- Review of employee policies and procedures.
- Determine extent of start-up program, what type(s) of assistance will be provided.
- Determine test market. Ideally, you would identify test units (in each region/division) to determine employee acceptance and to work out any problems before implementing companywide.
- Determine resource requirements. Will extra staff be needed? What role will operations play? What is the approximate cost?

Once your hospitality organization has determined its needs and the extent of the EAP, an action plan must be initiated. The action plan will:

- Schedule activities.
- Assign responsibilities.
- Update administration.
- Reinforce management commitment and support.

Implementation

The core of the implementation process is the establishment of a policy statement on the EAP and how it will operate. This policy must be written, published, and distributed to all employees. This communication is critical to the acceptance and success of the program. Employees must view the EAP as a benefit, not as an invasion of privacy.

Specific procedures need to be developed with respect to:

- Supervisory referral.
- Self-referral.
- Confidentiality.

A choice needs to be made based upon your company's needs and objectives as to whether you are going to select an in-house or contracted-out type of program. Supervisory training and employee orientation then follow.

DETERMINING THE COST-EFFECTIVENESS OF YOUR EAP

Compared to the costs of other benefits, EAPs are relatively inexpensive. This is largely due to the small proportion of employees who use the program. You should check into your health insurance plans to make sure that they will accommodate the occasional employee who needs extensive treatment and hospitalization.

The literature contains much information on the effectiveness of EAPs. This effectiveness ranges from reduced absenteeism to improved retention to literally saving lives. What hospitality operator wouldn't enjoy knowing that there will be fewer employees calling in sick, quitting, or coming to work late?

Employee assistance programs can also serve to reduce the rising cost of health care and Worker's Compensation claims. Better job performance is frequently the end result. Compared to the high cost of termination, EAP expenses are nominal (Figure 13-4).

FIGURE 13-4 Employee assistance programs result in lower turnover, high productivity, and improved safety records. *(Courtesy of Strongbow Inn, Valparaiso, IN)*

The following are some ways you might measure or evaluate the effectiveness of your EAP:

- Usage
- Direct feedback
- Comparative costs/cost containment
  —Turnover/retention
  —Health benefits
  —Absenteeism
  —Safety
  —Worker's Compensation

Historical data are a necessity in order to make a significant comparative cost-savings analysis.

USE OF AN EAP

Once your EAP is firmly in place and clearly communicated to all employees, and training has been conducted for all persons involved, how does a troubled employee take advantage of the program? There are basically two paths. In the first—80 percent of all cases—the employees contact the program directly. The remainder of the cases are referrals by supervisors who notice a decline in performance levels.

On-line supervisors are the best persons to notice a change in performance or personal behavior, because they observe employees on a daily basis. When a decline in performance or behavior occurs, the supervisor confronts the employee in an attempt to determine the cause. This intervention is an important component of the EAP, as it frequently works to break the pattern of denial in which many troubled employees are trapped. As we noted in the previous chapter, performance decline can be caused by factors other than personal problems. If the condition appears to be related to personal problems, the employee is referred to the EAP staff.

Once you have attempted to assist the employee through the corrective interview, it is your responsibility to continue monitoring performance. The employee can take one of two paths: seek help and improve performance, or refuse assistance, in which case standard corrective action practices are implemented. At each stage of the corrective action process, EAP participation is offered, again in an attempt to break the denial pattern. Participation in the EAP is not a substitute for maintaining acceptable job performance standards.

AIDS IN THE WORKPLACE

The AIDS epidemic affects us all. For the hospitality manager, as with managers in all types of businesses throughout this country, knowledge and understanding of AIDS are critical for your success. What will you tell the housekeeper who won't clean a room because he or she fears the person(s) staying there might have AIDS? What do you tell your server who refuses to wait on a table for the same reason? What do you say to the guest who asks if any of your cooks has AIDS? What if an employee cuts himself in the kitchen, and the other workers are afraid of contracting AIDS? What do you tell an employee who comes to you in fear that he may have AIDS or be HIV positive? AIDS is and will be one of the personal problems your employees may seek help with through your employee assistance program. The confidential nature of the EAP provides a natural setting and a valuable counseling tool in dealing with the depression employees face that receive a positive antibody test, the loss of a friend or family member, or an AIDS diagnosis themselves (Figure 13-5). It is for these reasons and because of the many misconceptions about AIDS that we include this section.

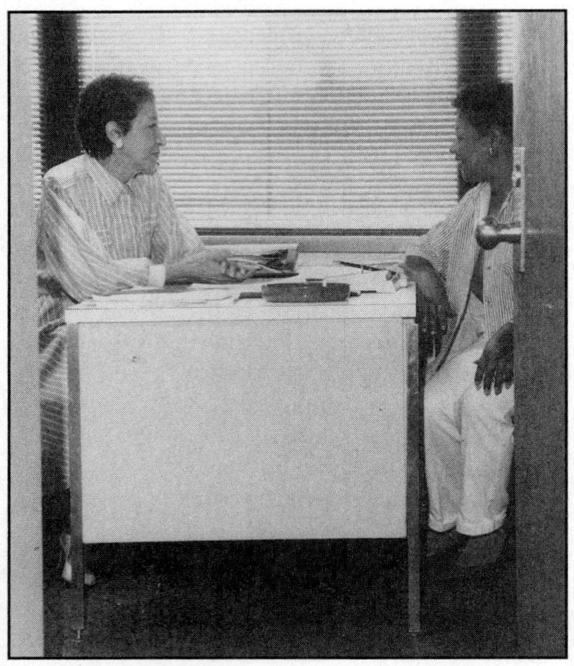

FIGURE 13-5 EAP counselors ensure that total confidentiality is maintained. *(Photo by Michael Upright)*

The Facts

Human Immunodeficiency Virus (HIV) was discovered in 1983. It is the virus that causes AIDS. HIV is a virus that, when active, destroys the body's defense system against disease and infection. It is transmitted through sexual contact, an injection with infected blood, shared needles (commonly associated with drug addiction), or passed by infected mothers to their newborn babies through birth or breast feeding. HIV can disable the body's immune system and destroy it's ability to fight diseases. These are the only documented methods by which HIV has been contracted/transmitted.

The term **AIDS** stands for **Acquired Immune Deficiency Syndrome**. Before researchers discovered HIV, they referred to the set of symptoms and diseases characterized by a total breakdown of the immune system as "AIDS." This definition was later changed to include any person who was infected with HIV or who had an advanced breakdown of the immune system. When a person is given an AIDS diagnosis by a doctor, it means that they are infected with HIV or that they have one of a number of diseases or cancers. Once a person is given an AIDS diagnosis, he or she is always considered to have AIDS even if he or she recovers from the disease that diagnosed them.

HIV cannot be spread by casual contact. Although there is much that is not known about HIV, it is known how HIV is and *is not* transmitted. To become infected with HIV, it must get into your blood. Did you know that according to federal food safety officials, HIV cannot be transmitted through the preparation or service of food? Food simply cannot be contaminated with HIV. HIV is not transmitted through kissing, hugging, shaking hands, or insect bites. According to C. Everett Koop, former Surgeon General of the U.S. Public Health Service, no AIDS cases have occurred from using swimming pools or hot tubs, sharing linen, or touching toilets or telephones.

If this is true, then where has all the hysteria come from surrounding the AIDS epidemic? The fact that, to date, there is no known cure is part of the reason. The other scary aspect of AIDS is that HIV is a "sleeper." That means that the virus can lay dormant inside a human carrier for years before it begins to attack the nervous system. Carriers can pass HIV for years before they know they have it, unless they seek a specific blood test to determine if HIV antibodies are present. It also means that the exact scope of the AIDS epidemic is, at present, still unknown. In 1998 it was estimated that over 30 million people were living with HIV worldwide, that an estimated 800,000 Americans were living with HIV, and that at least 40,000 new infections were occurring each year in the United States. Worldwide, the rate of new infections in developing countries was perceived as out of control with twenty-seven countries seeing their HIV infection rates more than doubling. AIDS killed as many people as malaria in 1997.[9] Of the 40,000 new infections that occurred in the United States, half will be under the age of 25. Women, young people, and minorities are the most likely to contract HIV. As a manager with human resources responsibilities in the hospitality industry, AIDS will continue to make a business impact. Hospitality organizations have lost talent while coworkers have grieved colleagues, friends, and family members. We must continue to be aware of HIV/AIDS in the hospitality workplace.

The Hospitality Manager and AIDS

How specifically does this impact you, the manager with human resources responsibilities, in a hospitality operation? Only through education can you intelligently and accurately answer the types of questions your employees might ask you, questions similar to those we asked you at the beginning of this section.

The education, however, does not stop with you. Part of your responsibility will also be to educate the people working for you, and in some cases the educational process will extend to the public that enters your establishment with its own fears and concerns. The workplace provides an excellent setting for this type of education. The National Restaurant Association and the American Hotel and Motel Association have both responded to the need for information. Each organization has produced educational materials for both you and your employees.

One of the key points that both associations make is that there is nothing unique about AIDS in the hospitality industry. Hospitality is facing this crisis along with all other industries. Educational programs and operating procedures cover all communicable diseases. Current disinfecting methods and sanitary food-handling procedures already in effect in the hospitality industry guard against all forms of communicable diseases, including AIDS.[10]

The other arena in which AIDS affects all businesses is in benefits planning and design. For AIDS victims, medical coverage becomes a number one concern. Although victims cannot be fired under the law, they still require medical coverage when the disease leaves them physically unable to work. Laws such as the 1986 Budget Reconciliation Act require that companies with over twenty employees that offer group insurance rates continue coverage for up to eighteen months after the employee leaves the company.

Education is our most effective weapon in reducing the potential hysteria that can be created. The National Restaurant Association has outlined the following four steps in a crisis program:

1. Assemble a crisis team. This is done before a crisis strikes. The team is trained to handle any crisis that the operation may face, be it a fire or AIDS.
2. Develop an AIDS policy statement that explains the company's position for both employees and guests.
3. Educate your employees.
4. Develop an AIDS communication strategy.

There are many problems relating to HIV/AIDS that you will have to deal with in the workplace. These range from rising health benefits costs to emotional distress to possible discrimination suits to guest hysteria. The more you read and learn about AIDS, the better prepared you will be to handle these situations.

INDUSTRY EXPERTS SPEAK

According to Jim Tye, "As the hospitality industry continues to grow amid what will surely be a shrinking labor pool, the role of a basic Employee Assistance Program will become increasingly important. Employee Assistance Programs, when properly developed, implemented, and evaluated have shown the potential for dramatic impact on a company's financial position when considered only in the areas of employee retention, safety, and productivity. Of course, there is the very important benefit, almost an intangible, of knowing that the company is genuinely interested in helping others."

CONCLUSION

To management, and in particular to human resources management, the dollars and cents logic in support of EAPs clearly speaks for itself. Conservative estimates place the cost to industry from personal, employee-related problems to be in excess of $50 billion per year with, in addition, as much as 25 percent productivity lost at all levels. One major corporation with a well-established assistance program has seen a five to one return on its investment, a 49 percent decrease in the use of health benefits, and a 61 percent decrease in on-the-job accidents. In today's competitive, cost-conscious business environment, figures such as these indeed become very significant. With the impending impact of AIDs yet to have reached its full potential, future human resources professionals in our industry must be ready to assume these responsibilities.

The goal of any EAP is to return the employee to full productivity, whenever possible. An effective EAP catches the personal problems at a very early stage and, in many cases, prevents more serious concerns from occurring. Your employees are your most valuable asset. Employee Assistance Programs convey that message.

CASE PROBLEM 13-1

As a manager of a medium-size resort property located in a secluded geographical area, you are in the middle of a very busy season, having been able to attract several small conference groups.

One morning after a particularly busy weekend, your executive housekeeper comes to you with a problem. Her housekeepers have told her that they will not clean several of their assigned rooms, as they strongly believe that the guests staying in those rooms could have AIDS. Your executive housekeeper is not sure what to do. Getting employees to work at your location is very difficult, and the housekeeping department is filled with good, reliable staff. The executive housekeeper tells you that she would clean the rooms herself, but she is not entirely sure that she might not be putting herself at risk.

There are several options that you as the manager with human resources responsibilities have available to you. Identify each of them and then discuss which of the alternative courses of action you would choose. (***Hint:*** You have two issues that you are dealing with in this case problem. The first is the immediate concern of getting the rooms cleaned. You have all rooms reserved for this evening. The second issue revolves around the lack of information and misconceptions your staff has about AIDS and its transmission from person to person.)

Case Problem 13-2

You are the district human resources manager of a regional chain of cafeteria food-service operations. Many of the operational managers have indicated over a period of time that no-shows and absentee turnover ratios have been gradually increasing. The president of the company has asked you to investigate the possibility of establishing an employee assistance program in an effort to curb this trend. She has asked you to prepare an initial three-page report that will provide her with the following information:

- A goal statement for the EAP
- An itemized list of the personal problem areas that this EAP would cover
- Whether you would recommend an in-house or contracted-out EAP
- A defense for the role an EAP would have in the human resources management plan for your hospitality organization
- Your personal view of EAPs

Key Words

Acquired Immune Deficiency Syndrome (AIDS)
contracted-out EAP
Employee Assistance Program (EAP)
Human Immunodeficiency Virus (HIV)
in-house EAP
intervention
Mental Health Parity Act of 1996
personal problems
substance abuse
"troubled" employee

Recommended Reading

American Red Cross. 1998. *Basic HIV/AIDS Program Facts Book.* The American National Red Cross.

Bahls, J. E. 1998. "Dealing With Drugs Keep It Legal." *HR Magazine.* www.shrm.org/hrmagazine/articles.0398drug.htm (4 October 1998).

Beller, L. 1995. "Elder Care's Growing Presence as an HR Matter." *Benefits & Compensation Solution* 17(October): 20–21.

Berridge, J., C. Highley-Marchington, C. L. Cooper, and J. C. Highley. 1997. *Employee Assistance Programmes and Workplace Counselling.* New York: John Wiley & Sons.

Canoni, J. D. 1998. *How the Supreme Court's HIV-Infection and Sexual Harassment Decisions Affect Employers.* www.nhdd.com/hot/wh50.htm (3 October 1998).

Dulen, J. 1997. "Fixed Media." *Restaurants & Institutions,* February 15.

Flynn, G. 1996. "Get the Best from Employees with Learning Disabilities." *Personnel Journal* 75(1): 76–84.

———. 1998. "Why Employees Are So Angry." *Personnel Journal* 77(9): 26–32.

Guhr, L. 1997. "Hidden Costs Involved with an On-the-Job Alcoholic." *Wichita Business Journal,* November 10.

Pincus, L. B. and S. M. Trivedi. 1994. "A Time for Action: Responding to AIDS." *Training & Development* 48(1): 45–51.

President's Drug Advisory Council. *Drugs Don't Work in Your Workplace.* Washington, DC: President's Drug Advisory Council, Executive Office of the President.

Rager, R., L. Lamson, and L. Castner. 1990. "Employee Wellness Programs for the Hospitality Industry: Some Promising New Approaches for Human Resource Development." *Hospitality Research Journal* 14(2): 643–645.

Recommended Web Sites

1. American Counseling Association: www.counseling.org
2. American Red Cross—HIV/AIDS: www.redcross.org/hss/HIVAIDS/index.html
3. National AIDS Fund: www.aidsfund.org
4. Business Responds to AIDS and Labor Responds to AIDS Resource Service: www.brta-lrta.org/blrs.htm
5. HIV/AIDS Workplace Toolkit: www.shrm.org/diversity/AIDSguide
6. National Clearinghouse for Alcohol and Drug Information: www.health.org/makelink.htm
7. The National Mental Health Association: www.nmha.org
8. Employee Assistance Professionals Association: www.eap-association.com
9. Establish a Workplace Program: www.dol.gov/dol/asp/public/programs/drugs/howto.htm

Endnotes

1. Kate Walter, "Elder Care Obligations," *HR Magazine,* 1996. www.shrm.org/hrmagazine/articles/0796eld.htm (6 June 1996).
2. Leslee Jacquette, "Delta Will Help Employees Solve Problems," *Hotel & Motel Managment* 207, no. 17 (1992): p. 34.
3. Jane Ester Bahls, "Drugs in the Workplace," *HR Magazine*. 1998. www.shrm.org/hrmagazine/articles/0298cov.htm (4 October 1998).
4. Jim Peters, "How to Set Up an Employee Assistance Program," *Restaurant Business* 87, no. 15 (1988): pp. 81–83, 90, 99.
5. Lisa Jennings, "From the Frying Pan . . . into the Bottle; Food-Service Workers Run High Risk of Substance Abuse." *The Commercial Appeal.* November 11, 1998. web.lexis-nexis.com/more/shrm/19213/3976298/4 (15 November 1998).
6. National Mental Health Association, "MHIC: Mental Illness and the Family: Mental Health Statistics." *MHIC Factsheet.* 1997. www.nmha.org/infoctr/factsheets/15.cfm (15 March 1999).
7. National Institute on Drug Abuse and The National Institute on Alcohol Abuse and Alcoholism, "The Economic Costs of Alcohol and Drug Abuse in the United States—1992." *Executive Summary.* 1998. www.health.org/pressrel/sept98/csat-study.html (15 March 1999).
8. Stephenie Overman, "Preventing Domestic Violence from Spilling Over into the Workplace," *Restaurants USA* 17, no. 7 (1997): p. 36.
9. HIVInSite, "How Many People have HIV?" *Back to Basics.* 1998. hivinsite.ucsf.edu/topics/basics/2098.3e7f.html (15 March 1999).
10. Doreen Bell, "AIDS Prevention Practices," *Lodging Hospitality* 44, no. 2 (1988): p. 92.

Discussion Questions

1. What is an Employee Assistance Program?
2. Identify several personal problems that you think could be handled by an Employee Assistance Program.
3. How do EAPs fit into the corrective action process?
4. Describe the differences between an in-house and a contracted-out EAP.
5. Describe the development and implementation process for an Employee Assistance Program in the segment of the hospitality industry you hope to work in.
6. Are EAPs cost-effective? Explain your answer.
7. What is the effect of HIV/AIDS in the workplace? What is the best tool against HIV/AIDS?
8. Would you implement an EAP where you work? Why or why not?

CHAPTER 14

Labor Relations in the Hospitality Industry

 **INDUSTRY ADVISOR**

REGYNALD G. WASHINGTON, *President and CEO, Washington Enterprises, Inc.*

"Join the union, girls, and together say Equal Pay for Equal Work."

—SUSAN B. ANTHONY, *The Revolution* (Woman Suffrage newspaper), March 18, 1869

"Now is no time to think of what you do not have; think of what you can do with what there is."

—ERNEST HEMINGWAY

INTRODUCTION

Unions, negotiators, grievances, mediation, arbitration, labor law, and collective bargaining: How do all these organizations, people, and processes that we call **labor relations** affect you in your role as a manager with human resources responsibilities? Based upon your current knowledge of labor relations, what are your feelings about unions? Do you think that they are only for the benefit of the worker and are a detriment to the hospitality organization? Do you think that they protect incompetent workers and make it almost impossible to fire anyone? Do you believe that unions are filled with corruption, that negotiators are unfair and inflexible, that union contracts prevent you from really doing your job as manager, and that strikes have unnecessarily hurt a lot of companies? Have unions outlived their usefulness? Are they historic dinosaurs that should be put to bed?

Many of you will, at some time in your careers, have managerial responsibilities in a hospitality organization that is a **union shop**. Your success will come largely from how well you understand what unions are, the strategies used by union negotiators, the processes of mediation and arbitration, how union organizers can enter your nonunion shop, and what your rights and obligations are in dealing with the organizers. Although you could take several courses in unions and their management, we have compiled for you the most-critical information to assist you in becoming a successful hospitality manager.

At the conclusion of this chapter you will be able to:

1. Describe what a union is.
2. Discuss the major historical developments that have influenced unions.

3. Maintain an awareness of the laws regulating labor relations and union activities.
4. Identify the reasons why people join unions in the hospitality industry.
5. Explain the importance of positive union relations as it relates to the impact of human resources management.
6. Describe how unions organize employees so that you can prevent unionization in a nonunion hospitality organization.
7. Identify negotiable demands that either union or management could request during the process of collective bargaining.
8. Describe the grievance procedure.
9. Explain the processes of arbitration and mediation.

THE CHANGING FACE OF UNIONS

A **union** is nothing more than a group of employees who feel that they can obtain, from management, what they want more effectively as a group than as individuals. By bargaining as a group, they feel they have more power and that management is more likely to listen to them. Throughout history, in the form of federal and state legislation, employees have been given certain rights that permit them to bargain collectively, that is, bargain as a group as opposed to each individual bargaining separately with his or her supervisor.

Whether you are pro-union, anti-union, or neutral; whether you believe that unions have outlived their usefulness or that they are facing a new revitalization, one fact that cannot be challenged is the numerous changes that unions have undergone in the past several years. American organized labor, in the hospitality industry as well as all others, will face many challenges in "the next chapter" as it tries to find its place in a changing society. Before we look at where organized labor is heading, the factors behind the changes in union efforts and the union's role in the workplace, let's take a brief historical journey into unions.

To understand the union of today, you must understand the reasons for its inception and the legislation protecting and governing union activities. Many of the historical events serve as precedents for the types of actions you should take when assuming human resources responsibilities. As we discussed in the first chapter, the climate is such that both our guests and our employees are more knowledgeable about the service sector. Not only will our guests be demanding improved service, our employees will be demanding a work environment, compensation, and benefits that are comparable to the improved level of service. Employee concerns regarding work-family issues, pay inequities between men and women, along with job security are work issues that the unions of today take very seriously. As you are about to read, it was poor working conditions, low compensation, and nonexistent benefits that provided unions the impetus for their inception. The desire for better working conditions can be traced back to the beginnings of the labor movement.

Union Beginnings

The efforts to organize unions in the United States began with the journeymen, who were tired of harsh treatment, poor working conditions, and no say in decisions made by their trade masters. Once a young man was accepted by a master craftsman, he lived with the family for several years in exchange for learning a trade (Figure 14-1). After a designated period of time the apprentice became a journeyman, who was then paid wages. If a journeyman was able to save enough money to open his own business, then he, too, could become a trade master. However, if one wanted to learn a specific trade, both apprentices

FIGURE 14-1 Master craftsmen, such as bakers, taught their craft to apprentices and journeymen. *(Courtesy of Strongbow Inn, Valparaiso, IN)*

and journeymen were completely at the mercy of their masters.

The first unions formed were local **trade unions** representing the shoemakers, printers, and carpenters. Bargaining, as we know it today, did not exist, although the unions did strike. Their primary complaints revolved around wages, the number of work hours, and how many apprentices were permitted into a specific trade.

In 1886, the formation of the **American Federation of Labor (AFL)**, under the leadership of its first president Samuel Gompers, sought the eight-hour workday. The AFL had a unique strategy for organizing. Instead of organizing based on specific trades, the AFL sought to form **craft unions** that were made up of people performing similar tasks, such as bakers.

The power of unions was increased by the **Clayton Act (1914)**, the first of many federal labor laws (Table 14-1), which both enabled employees to **strike** legally and made it easier for employers to obtain an **injunction** (a law stopping anyone from doing something such as strike). The period of the 1920s represented an intensive campaign by management to discourage the growth of the labor unions. Benefit and recreational (social) programs were established by companies. Welfare programs for employees were considered good management practice. Yellow-dog contracts were common. In these contracts, the employee agreed, at the time of hire, not to join a union.

The **Norris-LaGuardia Act of 1932** drastically reduced the conditions under which an injunction in a labor dispute could be issued by specifying the following five conditions that must prevail:

- Unlawful acts must have been threatened or occurring.
- Substantial damage to property must be seen as likely.

- The damage or injury must be greater if the injunction is denied.
- No adequate remedies in damages.
- Local police are unable or unwilling to provide protection.
- Norris-LaGuardia also made yellow-dog contracts unenforceable.

TABLE 14-1 Federal Labor Laws

The Clayton Act (passed 1914)
Clarified labor's position under antitrust laws.

Davis-Bacon Act (passed 1931)
Required minimum wage to be specified for construction contracts entered into by the federal government.

Norris-LaGuardia Act (passed 1932)
Prohibited Federal courts from enforcing "yellow dog" contracts. (Under these agreements employees promised not to join a union or promised to discontinue membership in one.)

The Wagner Act (passed 1935)
Known as **The National Labor Relations Act (NLRA)**, this act applied to all companies and employees engaged in interstate commerce (with some exceptions). The rights to organize and join labor movements, to choose representation, to bargain collectively, and to strike were provided.

Fair Labor Standards Act (passed in 1938)
Established minimum wage and maximum hours worked for all employees engaged in interstate commerce.

Taft-Hartly Act (passed 1947)
First major modification of the National Labor Relations Act. Included numerous provisions.

Landrum-Griffin Act (passed in 1959)
Made major additions to the Taft-Hartley Act, including the definition of additional unfair labor practices.

Civil Service Reform Act (passed in 1978)
Passed to protect all nonuniformed, nonmanagerial federal service employees.

Labor Laws That Continue to Affect Us Today

There are three federal laws that will affect you today in your labor relations in the hospitality industry. The **National Labor Relations Act of 1935 (NLRA)** is also called the **Wagner Act**. This was a pro-union act that established the **National Labor Relations Board (NLRB)**. The act sets forth "unfair labor practices" governing the conduct of employees, unions, and their agents.

The simplest explanation of the Wagner Act is that it describes the conditions under which collective bargaining may take place and guarantees employees the right to act together, as a group, rather than as individuals. This act had a significant impact on increasing union membership.

The National Labor Relations Board administers this act. It conducts union elections, certifies the results, and prevents both management and workers from committing unfair labor practices. An **unfair labor practice** is a violation of the law by either a union promoting unionization or an employer opposing unionization. Interrogation, threats, spying, or firing an employee for union activities would be considered unfair labor practices as would any practice that interferes with the right of the employee to organize or disciminates against your employees for participating in union activities. Table 14-2 gives you some additional examples of unfair labor practices that you might encounter in the hospitality industry.

By 1941, there were two major national labor federations: the AFL, which as we stated previously was made up of craft workers, and the **Congress of Industrial Organizations (CIO)**, which was composed of a group of industrial unions. **Industrial unions** were made up of workers from an entire industry, regardless of their occupation. A good example is the **Hotel and Restaurant Workers and Bartenders International (HRWBI)**, which

TABLE 14-2 Examples of Unfair Labor Practices by Union and by Management

Management cannot:

- offer a promotion or salary increase to an employee if he or she stays out of a union.
- discriminate against an employee in any manner for joining a union.
- refuse to hire a person because he or she belongs to a union.
- not bargain in good faith over union demands.
- harass an employee who files a grievance with the union.
- give wage increases to employees who are considering a union.

Union cannot:

- make harmful threats to a nonstriking worker.
- fire union members for crossing a picket line in an unlawful strike.
- cause an employer to discriminate against an employee.
- make acts of force, violence, or threats.
- coerce an employer on his or her choice of representation.
- charge excessive or discriminatory dues as a condition of union membership.

is a major union for the food service industry. Industrial unions are vertical unions as they cover all skill levels from the top to the lowest. As you recall, craft unions were made up of people that shared a common craft, regardless of the particular industry. An example might be all bakers: It would not matter if they worked in a restaurant or in a local bakery or for a large manufacturer of baked-good products.

The **Labor-Management Relations Act** or **Taft-Hartley Act** was passed in 1947 as an amendment to the Wagner Act. This amendment was considered to be mostly pro-management as it extended governmental intervention into labor relations.[1] The Taft-Hartley Act also made closed shop agreements illegal, although it permitted union shops, except where prohibited by state laws. This resulted in a number of the right-to-work laws that many states still maintain today. A closed shop was an organization that stipulated that a person must join the union prior to being hired. Union shops require that a person must join the union within a specified period of time after being hired, typically after a thirty- or sixty-day probationary period.

The second amendment to the Wagner Act was the **Labor-Management Reporting and Disclosure Act of 1959**, Public Law 86-257 (more commonly known as the **Landrum-Griffin Act**). This amendment is considered to be a union Bill of Rights as it sought to protect the rights of union members. The act defined specific ethical standards and codes of conduct that all labor organizations are to adhere to. This act helped to alleviate some of the abuses towards employees by both union officials and management. Essentially, power was taken away from the unions and given back to the employees, whose interests the unions were supposed to be looking out for.

The three basic purposes of the Landrum-Griffin amendment are:

- To regulate the internal affairs of the unions and reduce the possibility of labor racketeering.
- To ensure union democracy by preventing unethical collusion between the company and the union.
- To protect union funds and prevent misuse by union leaders.

The power of the unions increased rapidly after World War II with union membership soaring. Union demands for welfare and benefit programs were aggressive, and strikes were bitter. The Taft-Hartley Act was, in large, a public response to the unions' growing power and influence. Even with the passage of the Taft-Hartley Act, union membership grew and in 1955 the two major labor federations, the AFL and CIO merged.[2]

State Labor Laws

State labor laws vary widely, so it is always best that you check with your regional labor offices to make sure that you are in compliance with the law when dealing with labor relations matters in your hospitality organization. State right-to-work laws are just one example.

Right-to-work laws are not highly thought of by unions, as they forbid contracts that require workers to join unions when they are hired. Because unions must, by law, represent all employees in an organization that is unionized, the right-to-work law prohibits them from collecting dues from all people in the bargaining unit. Unions rely upon their dues to meet operating expenses. If an operation has a large number of nonunion members in a bargaining unit, the union's effectiveness can be hindered. In a democratic society most people believe it is wrong to require union membership of employees. The nonunion and union employees both benefit equally from union negotiations for pay increases and better benefits packages. What do you think? Should employees be required to join a union that represents them and pay dues as a requirement of employment?

Labor laws, both state and federal, are subject to change. Those of you who will be employed by a large hospitality organization will find that you are likely to have a labor-relations consultant or attorney working for your company. If you work for a smaller organization, these experts are still available to you, for a fee, to answer your questions. It is usually best to consult with them before you take any actions of which you are unsure.

LABOR UNIONS DURING THE LAST TEN DECADES

The 1960s saw the unionization of public, professional, and farm personnel with the issuance of Executive Order 10988. This changed the face of union membership. The traditional industrial and craft unions have since seen a decline in membership. The 1960s also saw **organized labor** maintaining a strong presence in the area of manufacturing. Employers began a greater acceptance of collective bargaining, and unions were able to negotiate substantial economic gains for their members.

The 1970s, however, were a period of higher inflation, growing unemployment, and a decline in some industrialized industries. Union workers were paid higher wages but were not able to increase productivity enough to offset this increase in wages. This resulted in a request for union concessions from employers. Union membership in the private sector began a steady decline, from 29.1 percent of the private labor market in 1970, to 25.1 percent in 1976 and to 17.8 percent in 1983.[3] In 1978 the AFL-CIO helped write legislation that would amend the NLRA to make it easier to organize. Business mobilized against this proposed legislation, which was defeated. This was a significant defeat to the labor movement. In the 1990s another attempt was made to strengthen the labor laws in favor of the unions revolving around the issue of strike replacement. These attempts were also defeated.

The hospitality industry has historically had only a small percentage of its workers join unions, with the early 1970s being the period of highest membership. In 1981, only 14 percent of hospitality workers were unionized, with the Hotel and Restaurant Workers and Bartenders International (HRWBI) ranking as the 14th largest union in the United States.[4] The **Hotel Employees & Restaurant Employees International (HERE)** is the major union in the hospitality industry. It has experienced a steady decline in membership, from a high of 507,000 members in 1970 to about 280,000 members in 1989.[5] On the HERE Web site in 1999 the union claimed to represent over 300,000 workers in North America.[6]

INDUSTRY EXPERTS SPEAK

When asked the question, "Will unions be around in the future?", Mr. Regynald G. Washington stated a resounding, "**Absolutely!!**".

Effects on Unions Today

Whether unions will prosper or decline in the new century is a matter of great debate. Many feel that unions have outlived their useful purpose and are dying. Other labor-relations experts believe that the union movement will be reborn in this country as unions rise to meet the needs of the new American worker. It is clear from reading these two diametrically opposed positions that union leaders are not presenting a united front.

Just what challenges does organized labor face in obtaining and retaining membership in its local and national organizations? Many of these challenges are the same as those that have been presented to you in previous chapters. For one, the composition of the work force. The first union members were primarily native white males, who worked full-time as the sole heads of households. More women, immigrants, and part-timers are in the labor force and have different needs from the white male in the workplace. Unions will need to meet the new needs of the new labor force if they hope to entice them into becoming dues-paying members.

Typically, women and minorities are found in the low-wage, low-status job positions. Unions are promoting upward mobility for minorities and women. The concerns that these new groups of workers have differ greatly from those of their native male counterparts. For many, English is a second language, or one that they don't speak at all. There can be no doubt that the changed work force has a direct effect on unions and their agendas. Employees today insist on having a more integral role in the structuring of their jobs, with or without union assistance. In a time of labor shortages employers cannot afford not to listen to employee demands (Figure 14-2). Will employers, or unions, be the ones to make jobs more secure?

With minimum wage increases being mandated by state and federal laws, the hourly employee's ability to pay union dues also increases. Which person you hire also becomes a more important decision, as you will be forced to pay higher rates of compensation. Teens and unskilled labor become less attractive when you have to pay them more. Teens are less likely to join unions because they view the jobs in hospitality as temporary. Hence, the increase in minimum wage could have the potential effect of increasing the type of individuals who would find joining unions attractive, if the union leaders seek them. It could take away the need for one of organized labor's basic bargaining items: higher wages. Unions

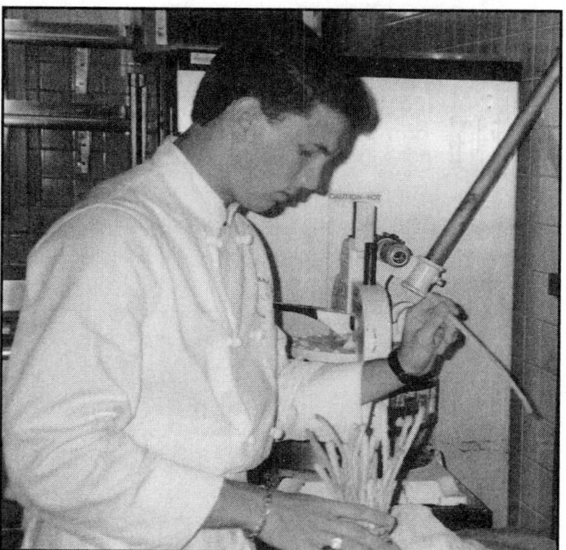

FIGURE 14-2 Employees are more likely to perceive a union as a positive force if they are dissatisfied on the job.

today are having to better accommodate a highly competitive labor market. Additional factors that affect the unions' ability to negotiate pay increases are the trend to merit pay, a greater use of temporary and part-time employees, the increasing importance of non-standard work arrangements, and globalization. As hospitality companies sell more services abroad, they will hire more foreign workers.

The change in the U.S. economy from an industrial society to a service society means that unions will try to attract hospitality employees more so in this century than ever before. The base has switched from manufacturing to service, and so, too, the unions must adjust their recruiting strategies as millions of new jobs are being created in the service sector. Look for unions to attempt to organize the virtually untapped and unorganized service workers.

INDUSTRY EXPERTS SPEAK

Mr. Washington says, "In order for unions to attract new members they will need to establish strong creditability with labor agreements already enforced. This will be accomplished through integrity with existing union members, in other words delivering on their promises as stated in the contract, as well as offering union membership, higher wages, and employee benefits."

Will unions be phased out by the year 2020? Will they become merely fraternal organizations as opposed to bargaining units? Will there be a rebirth of unions with service workers leading the way? Though we can't answer any of these questions for you today, all are worth taking note of. No matter what direction unions take, they will, more than likely, at some point in the future have some affect on your human resources responsibilities.

WHY DO PEOPLE JOIN UNIONS?

Perhaps by examining some of the reasons why workers join unions, you can be better prepared to keep your employees from feeling the need to join organized labor. You will recall that unions originated because of bad working conditions, low wages, and abusive treatment by management of its workers. Federal legislation has come a long way in assuring our people that we won't underpay them, that we will maintain a reasonable workweek length, and that we will provide a safe and healthful work environment for them in which to perform their job duties and responsibilities. For many of our employees, though, unions can provide job security, increases in compensation, extensions in benefit offerings, protection from arbitrary management decisions, reasonable work loads, and a process to grieve what they feel are unjust practices.

Think for a moment about our discussions on motivation, and how throughout each chapter the human resources functions you perform relate directly or indirectly to the retention efforts of your hospitality organization. The theme that all of the industry experts have stressed to you is protection of your valuable human assets. Unions seek to protect and promote the interests of their members. If you, in performing your human resources responsibilities, do not keep the interests of your people foremost in your mind, chances are good that a union will be able to easily unionize your hospitality organization. Table 14-3 identifies some conditions that could encourage employee interest in unions.

In some hospitality organizations, union membership is compulsory according to the union agreement. This means that a new hire must join the union and pay dues if he or she wants to obtain the job. Present employees must join the union and pay dues if they want

TABLE 14-3 Conditions Encouraging Employee Interest in Unions

- Wages inappropriate.
- People feel that there is no flexibility in their earning capabilities.
- Unpleasant working environment.
- Inadequate benefits.
- Job insecurity.
- Employees feel that management does not respect them.
- Discrimination.
- Favoritism.
- Inconsistent discipline.
- Employees do not feel that they are truly a part of the hospitality organization.
- Employees feel that management is taking advantage of them.
- Employees have no pride in their work.
- Failure to recognize individual efforts and performance.
- Poor communications.

to keep their jobs. Unionized organizations that do not have union agreements requiring compulsory membership permit employees who do not join the union to share in the benefits of the union-bargaining activities. Hence, some employees could get a "free ride."

INDUSTRY EXPERTS SPEAK

Regynald G. Washington points out the fact that "a union is a business operated for a profit and, therefore, unions are not particularly interested in mom-and-pop operations, but aggressively pursue large hospitality facilities with large numbers of employees. Additionally, union officials are elected by the members of the union, and popularity as well as response to employee complaints play a major role. Union officials usually handle employee complaints quickly and aggressively in order to maintain their popularity that will eventually end up as a vote."

EFFECTIVE COLLECTIVE BARGAINING MANAGEMENT

What are some of the things that you can do, as a human resources manager, to avoid the unionization of your hospitality organization? Let's walk through each of the human resources functions covered in this text.

- ***Hiring process.*** Always go for the absolute best person you can. In the hospitality industry, personality can often be the key to success.
- ***Orientation/training.*** Make sure that your people are comfortable and knowledgeable about their new work environment and company. Tell people your expectations.
- ***Performance appraisal.*** The system for appraisal must be clearly communicated, understood, and fair.
- ***Development.*** Your employees must see a way to move up and into other job positions.
- ***Positive counseling.*** Troubled employees have opportunities to resolve personal problems and turn their performance records around without fear of punishment.
- ***Compensation.*** Both current and future pay must be viewed as equitable.
- ***Open communications.*** You can't manage from behind your desk; you have to be available to your people. There are positive benefits to management and employee daily communications as they relate to the vehicle for positive labor-relations management.
- ***Consistency in management.*** This is the best policy for keeping you away from union activity. When you go into arbitration, unions will look for inconsistencies in management.

INDUSTRY EXPERTS SPEAK

Regynald G. Washington relates the following story: "A recent union case was lost by management due to inconsistency in management. A cocktail server was terminated for overcharging customers for drinks. Management learned of the problem from a coworker of the terminated cocktail worker. Management sent unannounced service shoppers into the bar and found that the overcharging problem was true. The beverage manager, however, of the operation had permitted special arrangements (requested days off) for the cocktail server that had tipped off management to the overcharging problem in the lounge. The cocktail server that tipped off management to the overcharging problem had many personal problems with her husband who battered her, sick kids who had too often to be taken to the doctors, etc. The beverage manager had received similar requests from other cocktail servers that worked the same shift in that same lounge and were denied schedule adjustments. Although service shoppers caught the cocktail server overcharging the guest, the arbitrator ruled in favor of the employee due to the favoritism shown to the terminated cocktail server's coworker. Several cocktail servers were subpoenaed to testify that they had been denied unusual schedules requested because of personal problems. Inconsistency in management was key to the loss of the arbitration."

Table 14-4 identifies some other ways for preventing unionization in the hospitality industry. Most of the suggestions relate to simply fair and sound good management practices. One of the major reasons that people join unions is for job security. If a hospitality organization does not provide security for its employees through the areas just identified, then unionization can more easily occur.

TABLE 14-4 Methods of Union Prevention

- Establish credibility between management and employees.
- Promote open door policies.
- Encourage employees to report problems.
- Take employee complaints seriously.
- Keep commitments to employees in a timely manner.
- Understand the need for appreciation.
- Know how to give positive feedback.
- Maintain high standards.
- Allow employee participation programs.
- Provide a positive work environment.
- Open channels of communication.
- Listen to employees.

In addition, many establishments maintain a "no solicitation" rule. This means that in addition to keeping unions from soliciting your employees, the rule must be enforced equitably for every group from the Girl Scouts to the United Way or it will be viewed as an unfair management labor practice.

THE UNION CAMPAIGN AND ELECTION

The union may approach your hospitality organization either internally or externally (Figure 14-3). Internally, one of your employees may be contacted to assist the union in organizing your employees. Table 14-5 shows some potential signs of union activity. Or, your employees might be angry with management and collectively (or as a select group) decide to call in the union for help. Externally, a union organizer might enter your operation and sit at the bar and talk to the bartender about how he or she likes working for you, or have lunch and talk to the server. Due to the nature of the hospitality business, it is quite easy for a union organizer to infiltrate your organization.

FIGURE 14-3 Small groups of employees discussing "secret" agendas is often a sign of union organization. *(Photo by Michael Upright)*

TABLE 14-5 Signs of Union Activity
• Presence of unfamiliar faces
• Anyone making a list of employee names
• Groups of employees who are deep in conversation until you approach
• New informal groups with emerging group leaders
• Business being conducted during breaks or lunch
• A sudden increase in questions about company policy, procedures and benefits
• Anticompany graffiti in employee rest rooms and break areas
• A number of small gatherings of employees
• Gossip among disgruntled employees

During the covert campaign, the union organizers will be attempting to win union recognition. Petitions and authorization cards will be passed among your employees (Figure 14-4). As a manager, you don't want to look at anything a union organizer has to give you, especially union authorization cards. Looking at them will oftentimes commit your company to that union's organization efforts.

Once you know that a union is attempting to organize your employees, get help! Hire a labor lawyer when dealing with unions if your hospitality organization does not have such a person already on staff. This area of law is a tough one, and you, as manager, are going to be limited in the actions that you can take. Your best approach is to listen and document everything that goes on, on a day-to-day basis. You need to be aware that the process of unionization can involve great conflict between employers and unions. This conflict might be used in attempts to gain employee support for the union.

The Election

To file for an election, 30 percent of your employees need to be organized. Once the union has filed an election petition, both employer and union will use campaign techniques (similar to those you are familiar with during election periods) to win the employees

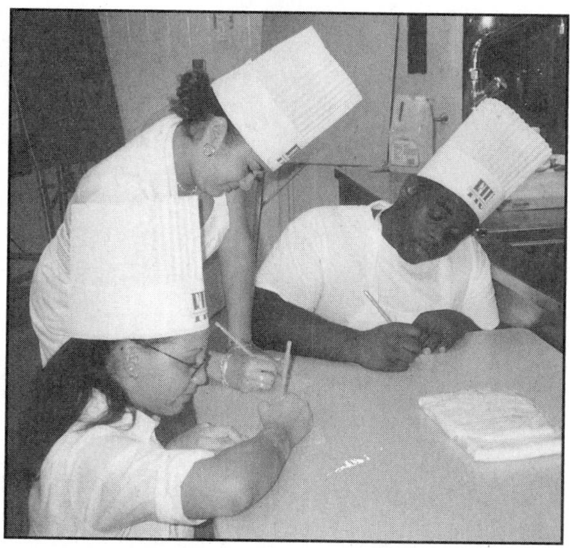

FIGURE 14-4 Employees interested in unionization sign authorization cards.

over to their point of view. Unions will be making campaign speeches to sway employees to join the union, and employers will be making campaign speeches to persuade the employees to keep the company union free. About two weeks after the petition is filed for an election, a hearing is held. A hearing is very much like a court proceeding, with each side, management and the union agent, testifying.

The election is usually held thirty days after the hearing. To win a union election, you need a 50 percent vote plus one of all voting employees. It is unlawful for an employer to recognize a union that does not represent a majority of the employees. Once the union becomes certified, you are legally bound to negotiate with that union. If the union loses the election, then no union can attempt to organize your employees for a period of one year.

THE COLLECTIVE BARGAINING AGREEMENT

After the union has won the recognition election and is legally recognized as your organization's bargaining unit, the collective-bargaining agreement is negotiated by representatives of both the union and management. The process through which this agreement is developed is called **collective bargaining** (Figure 14-5). Items that can be bargained for are guided by numerous labor laws, but generally include working conditions, pay, human resources management practices (such as hiring, promotions, sick leave, benefits, and disciplinary procedures), grievance procedures, and length of agreement. While the union attempts to bargain for its position, management must bargain in good faith, but management does not have

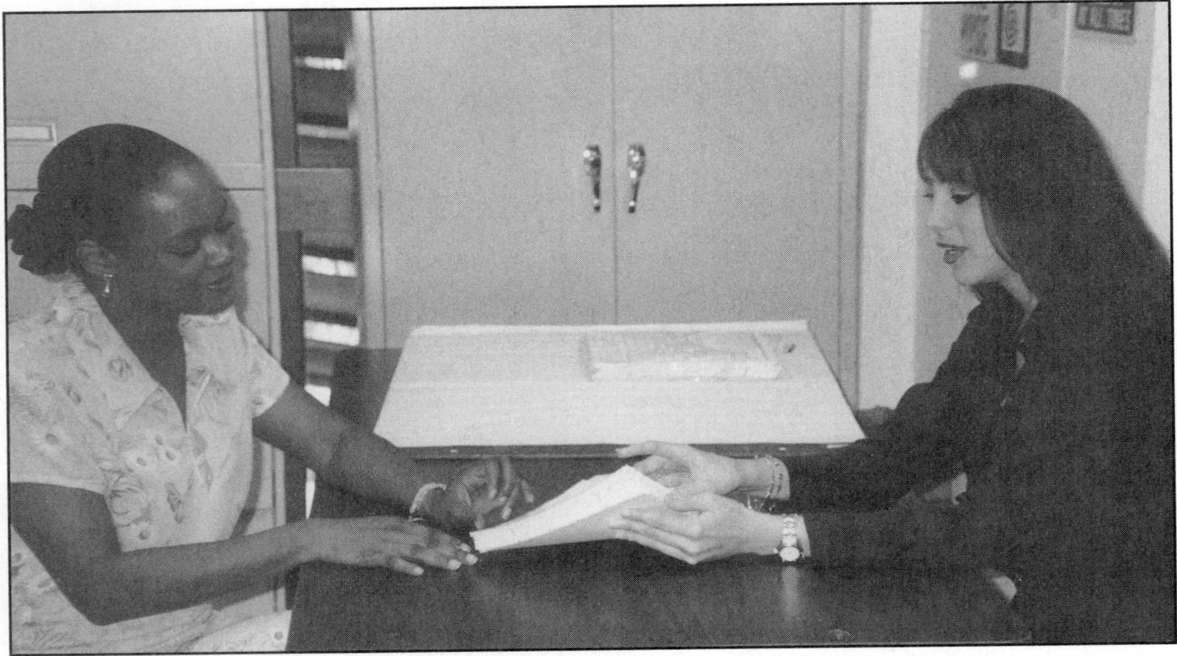

FIGURE 14-5 The process of negotiation is used to develop a collective bargaining agreement.

to accept the union's position. Each side has its own list of demands. The bargaining process is give-and-take on the part of both groups.

INDUSTRY EXPERTS SPEAK

Mr. Washington points out, "Unions usually discredit management and perform character assassinations on various members of the management staff. This is used as a weapon to positively influence an arbitrator to rule in favor of the union. Therefore, it is necessary to focus on how management develops credibility and respect with the union. This leads to effective labor-relations management. It is important that management have total involvement in labor contract-negotiations."

It is important for management to enter the bargaining process with a list of its own demands. Can you think of things, that if in a union shop, you would like the union to either give up or adopt? What about the following:

- Fewer vacation hours
- Fewer sick leave hours
- Fewer paid holidays
- A restriction on accrual of sick hours and vacation hours to be used during the current year
- Shorter breaks
- Restriction on personal calls made on the company phone
- Laundering of uniforms done by employees
- Increase in the probationary hire period
- Temp-help to eliminate overtime

These are just some items that you might want to demand from the union. Remember, the process of collective bargaining is one of **negotiation**. Neither party enters the negotiations expecting to receive its entire list of demands. Some items are even included as "throwaways," those items added strictly for the purpose of negotiating.

The point we would like you to remember is that you are always better off entering the negotiations with a demand list of your own. The alternative is simply to counter the union's demands, which does not permit you to bargain from a position of utmost strength. You should not view the negotiating process as merely a place to minimize your losses!

The Contract

At the end of collective bargaining, the union contract is signed by both management and the union. During the life of the contract, numerous interpretations will need to be made as incidents occur between employees and management. Effective labor relations stem from a willingness on the part of both the employees and management to make the union contract work. Large hospitality organizations, such as Walt Disney World, have a staff of employees whose job is to troubleshoot between the employees and management. In other companies, union officers or stewards are elected to assist in resolving problems between employees and their supervisors. Though it is the steward's job to protect the rights of the employees as specified in the union contract, stewards do not have managerial authority or responsibility (Figure 14-6).

It is critical that as a hospitality manager in a union shop, you learn the union contract! It is customary for union officials to hold union-contract educational seminars at the local union hall. These sessions usually are conducted by the union's attorney and union officials. Ongoing contract training is administered to all shop stewards. Management personnel cannot effectively manage union employees when the union employees are more informed regarding

FIGURE 14-6 A steward serves as the union representative at the workplace.

contract issues than management people. A labor-relations lawyer can assist you and other management team members. Typically, you would use the lawyer who negotiated the contract, because the contract is written in legal language.

Most union contracts specify a **grievance procedure**, which is used to resolve complaints and disputes between employees and management. This formalized procedure makes it easier for management to deal with the union in an open forum. It also makes it easier for employees who want to bring up complaints against management. When grievances cannot be resolved by this process, the grievance goes to arbitration.

INDUSTRY EXPERTS SPEAK

Mr. Regynald G. Washington has the following comments on the importance of union contracts: "The union contract sets the landscape for the professional relationship between management and the labor union. The contract is law and serves as a binding legal document between the two parties. Clarity of contract language will help minimize labor disputes and arbitrations. Loose contract language creates ambiguity and creates the necessity for a professional arbitrator to interpret the language. The labor contract will also drive what it will cost management to operate their organization, i.e., wages, benefits, frequency of increases, sick pay, line scheduling efficiencies, average hourly rate, productivity loads, etc. The labor contract serves as the flight plan required to successfully pilot the relationship between labor and management."

INDUSTRY EXPERTS SPEAK

According to Mr. Regynald G. Washington, the following is what management can and cannot do once employees have gained enough authorization cards for an election.

1. Organizer must have commitment of 30 percent of unit.
2. Organizer then files petition for election with the National Labor Relations Board.
3. National Labor Relations Board will notify employer that petition was filed requesting a response from employer.
4. Employer will have two options; to agree or not agree.
5. If management does not agree, a hearing will be scheduled to determine the appropriate unit.
6. If numbers are justified, the National Labor Relations Board will order an election requiring 50 + 1 to carry.
7. If it carries, the National Labor Relations Board will certify the union as the appropriate bargaining agent for that unit.
8. Management must then agree to come to the table to bargain.

ARBITRATION AND MEDIATION

Although it is always better for both parties to resolve conflicts in-house, a peaceful **arbitration** with a third party is still a better alternative than a strike or lockout. The arbitrator and mediator are neutral umpires selected by the mutual agreement of both union and management. An **arbitrator** is the final judge, his or her decision is final and binding. A **mediator** has no power other than the opportunity to use persuasion.

In the process of **mediation**, the mediator sits down with both parties and identifies the issues that are preventing agreement. It is the mediator's job to try to get each side to fully see the other side's position on a given issue. The mediator then attempts to get the two parties to agree to develop some alternative solutions to the problem that had not been thought of before. Finally, the mediator tries to get both parties to agree to a solution that is fair to everyone involved. If a solution is found to which both parties agree, the grievance is resolved, although nothing the mediator does or says is binding on either party. The two parties must mutually agree to a solution. If no solution can be agreed upon, the mediation fails.

Arbitration takes place only after mediation has been tried and has failed. Because the decision of the arbitrator is by law binding on both parties, the selection of this individual is of utmost importance. Sources for arbitrators include the **Federal Mediator Conciliation Service**, which maintains a panel of certified arbitrators, as does the **American Arbitration Association**. These arbitrators are paid daily fees that can be quite high. The cost is shared equally by both parties. Arbitration is an expensive process. In addition to the arbitrator, both sides will want to have legal counsel representing them during the proceedings. Therefore, issues do not go to arbitration routinely or unless the issue is an important one to the union.

At the end of the arbitration, one party will have won, and one party will have lost. Why then would either party want to go to arbitration? Remember, we said that arbitration takes place only after mediation has failed. Thus, only when an impasse is reached over a grievance or the contract. If this impasse is not resolved, then a strike or work slowdown is likely to be the result. It is best to avoid arbitration if you can. Very seldom does management win in cases that pair the big corporation against the little employee. Arbitration costs lots of money.

INDUSTRY EXPERTS SPEAK

Mr. Washington relates the following story: "A management person was overheard by a shop steward bad mouthing the union. The shop steward happened to be an employee who had no previous notations on their record card for performance. Management was reminded by the shop steward that bad mouthing the union was inappropriate.
On the following day, the manager who allegedly bad mouthed the union called the shop steward into his office and issued him a formal reprimand for job performance.
The union disputed the reprimand and threatened to file an unfair labor practice charge due to the union bashing and its close association in time to the formal reprimand. The formal reprimand was regarded by the union as retaliation against the shop steward for reminding the manager of his unprofessional conduct. Management is expected at all times to respect the labor agreement and to exemplify the highest level of professional conduct."

CONCLUSION

In the past several years, many companies have taken a union-avoidance posture. Management has done this by encouraging such practices as self-management, employee involvement, coparticipation with management, participative decision making, quality circles, team problem solving, better communication with employees (including keeping them informed about organizational changes), as well as instituting some of the retention methods we have been discussing throughout this text. This approach keeps management and employees talking to each other rather than establishing a "them" versus "us" type of mentality.

Although service industries have not historically been heavily unionized, there is a chance that this may change in "the next chapter." With demographic changes and economic shifts, unions will be looking at the labor force in the service industry as potential members. An additional human resources responsibility that you will need to assume is an awareness of union activities in the hospitality industry.

CASE PROBLEM 14-1

You are the manager with human resources responsibilities for an off-premise catering company located in New England. Your company presently has four separate locations and hopes to expand to other areas. You have been with the company for three years and really enjoy your work and responsibilities.

The National Labor Relations Board has just notified you that the ABC Union has filed a petition stating that they wish to represent your catering company's servers and bartenders. Your company has never had any of its employees represented by a union, and it is your preference to keep it your company nonunion. You have been asked by management to recommend a strategy. You have also been asked to outline the employer campaign against unionization. What tactics can you use? How effective do you think they will be? What actions can you, and can you not, take? You don't want any charges of unfair labor practices filed against you.

CASE PROBLEM 14-2

The union's organizational efforts identified in Case Problem 14-1 have paid off—for the union. One of your employees was contacted by the union to assist in organizing the other employees. Petitions and authorization cards were passed among your employees, and you were careful not to look at any of these materials. Why was this an important strategy on your part?

A petition was filed for an election and signed by 50 percent of your employees. A hearing was held two weeks later with both union and management testifying. The election was held thirty days after the hearing, carrying 85 percent of the employees who voted. The union is now certified, and you are legally bound to negotiate with that union.

You are now ready to negotiate the collective bargaining agreement. As part of the management team, it will be your responsibility to identify a list of items and conditions that are, and are not, acceptable. Prepare an outline of items that can be bargained for by your legal representative. Be sure to consider working conditions, compensation, and benefits packages. Which of these items are nonnegotiable?

Case Problem 14-3

You have noticed the following events occurring in the hospitality operation you have described in Case Problem 14-1:

- Gossip among disgruntled employees
- Business being conducted during lunch
- An employee making lists of employee names
- Unfamiliar faces around the premises
- Increased questions about company policies

Based upon these events, you suspect that an attempt at union organization may be occurring. Currently, you operate a nonunion operation.

As the manager with human resources responsibilities, discuss in three to four paragraphs your feelings about these suspected union organizational activities. Identify both short-term and long-term benefits of unionization. Identify steps that you can take to nullify these organizational efforts should management desire to do so. Identify eight conditions that could have prompted these organizational efforts in your hospitality operation. Be specific.

Key Words

American Arbitration Association
American Federation of Labor (AFL)
arbitration
arbitrator
Clayton Act (1914)
collective bargaining
Congress of Industrial Organizations (CIO)
craft unions
Federal Mediator Conciliation Service
grievance procedure
Hotel and Restaurant Workers and Bartenders International (HRWBI)
Hotel Employees & Restaurant Employees International (HERE)
industrial unions
injunction
labor relations
Labor-Management Relations Act (1947) or Taft-Hartley Act
Labor-Management Reporting and Disclosure Act of 1959 or Landrum-Griffin Act
mediation
mediator
National Labor Relations Act of 1935 (NLRA or Wagner Act)
National Labor Relations Board (NLRB)
negotiation
Norris-LaGuardia Act of 1932
organized labor
strike
trade unions
unfair labor practices
union
union shops

Recommended Reading

Allen, R. L. 1998. "Panel Warns Industry about Union Recruiting Tactics. *Nation's Restaurant News* 32(11): 100.

Ancel, J. "Right to Organize Gains More Attention from AFL-CIO." *Kansas City Business Journal.* 1999. www.amcity.com/kansascity/stories/1999/03/15/editorial3.html (21 March 1999).

Clay, J. M. and E. C. Stephens. 1995. "Union Organizers' Access to Hotels' Private Property." *Cornell Quarterly* 36(2): 20–28.

Heath, R. P. "The New Working Class." *American Demographics* (January, 1998). www.demographics.com/Publications/AD/98_ad9801_ad/ad980131.htm (10 May 1998).

Kimmeldorf, H. 1991. "Bringing Unions Back In (Or Why We Need a New Old Labor History)." *Labor History* 32(Winter): 91–129.

Krupin, J. P. "Confronting Unionization: Strategies to Keep Employees from Organizing." *Restaurants USA* 16(2): 8–9.

Lewis, D. E. 1999. "Labor Ranks Swelled by 101,000 Last Year; Despite Rise, Proportion of Union Members in Work Force Dropped in '98." *The Boston Globe*, January 26, p. D1.

Murrmann, S. K. and K. F. Murrmann. 1990. "Union Membership Trends and Organizing Activities in the Hotel and Restaurant Industries." *Hospitality Research Journal* 14(2): 491–496.

———. "Employee Attitudes toward a Nonunion Grievance Procedure and Their Influence on Unionization." *Hospitality Research Journal* 16(1): 41–49.

Weiler, P. C. 1990. *Governing the Workplace: The Future of Labor and Employment Law.* Cambridge: Harvard University Press.

Recommended Web Sites

1. Hotel Employees and Restaurant Employees (HERE): www.hereunion.org
2. Today's Unions — AFL-CIO: www.aflcio.org/home.htm
3. Food & Allied Service Trades: www.fastaflcio.org
4. International Union of Food, Agricultural, Hotel, Restaurant, Catering, Tobacco and Allied Workers' Associations — IUF: www.iuf.org
5. Internet Resources for Labor History: www.iupui.edu/it/imir/HIST/labor.htm
6. Guide to Labor Oriented Internet Resources: www.lib.berkeley.edu/IIRL/iirlnet.html
7. International Labour Organization: www.ilo.org
8. Institute of Collective Bargaining: ilr.cornell.edu/depts/ICB
9. National Labor Relations Board: www.nlrb.gov

Endnotes

1. Office of the General Counsel, National Labor Relations Board, "A Guide to Basic Law and Procedures under the National Labor Relations Act," (Washington, DC: U.S. Government Printing Office, 1978).
2. I. Bernstein, "The Growth of the American Unions," *American Economic Review* 44(1954): 303–304.
3. Leo Troy, "The Rise and Fall of American Trade Unions: The Labor Movement from FDR to RR," *Unions in Transition: Entering the Second Century,* ed. Seymour M. Lipset (San Francisco: Institute for Contemporary Studies, 1986), p. 82.
4. Carol Lynn Tiers, "Unions Gear-up Activity in Fast Food Industry," *Restaurant Business* (November 1, 1988): p. 68.
5. Suzanne K. Murrmann and Kent F. Murrmann, "Union Membership Trends and Organizing Activities in the Hotel and Restaurant Industries," *Hospitality Research Journal* 14, no. 2 (1991): p. 491.
6. Hotel Employees & Restaurant Employees International Union, "HERE," www.hereunion.org (21 March 1999).

Discussion Questions

1. What is a union? Are you pro-union, anti-union, or neutral? State the reasons why you took that position. Did you feel differently before reading this chapter?
2. Have you ever worked in a union shop? If so, describe how it was different from a nonunion shop. If not, describe how you believe it would be different based upon what you read in this chapter.
3. Describe the three major pieces of federal legislation that affect labor relations today and their impact on the union movement.
4. What are some of the reasons that people join unions? How, in the next decade, can human resources management affect unionization in a nonunion hospitality organization?
5. Describe some of the challenges facing organized labor in the next five years.
6. Describe the events that occur in a union campaign and election.
7. Explain the collective bargaining process and the union contract.
8. Discuss the differences between mediation and arbitration.
9. Describe the effect of alternative dispute resolutions on the arbitration process.

Approaching the Year 2010

CHAPTER 15

Computer Applications in Human Resources Management

INDUSTRY ADVISOR

ANDREW J. JUSKA, *Vice President of Operations, Signature Companies*

"Computers are useless; they can only give answers."

—PICASSO

"Man's mind, once stretched by a new idea, never regains its original dimensions."

—OLIVER WENDELL HOLMES

"I do not fear computers. I fear the lack of them."

—ISAAC ASIMOV

INTRODUCTION

The computerization of human resources management has extended into arenas only imagined two decades ago. The decrease in the cost of company computer networks and company extranets combined with the easy accessibility of the Internet and World Wide Web (WWW) means that with just a few keystrokes, or clicks on a mouse, your company can link instantly to sources of information that used to take weeks or months to access. Not only do today's computer networks allow your company access to this wealth of information, they also allow your employees accessibility to that same information, to each other, and to their customers. Today, few human resources departments are found without internal computer networks. This can be attributed, in part, to the rapid advancements in computer technology. Hardware, in particular desktop computers, have decreased in cost and that has made these small systems affordable for even the smallest hospitality operation.

The majority of hospitality companies that you will be working in will not only have computer workstations in the human resources department but will have all departments linked in an internal company network called an Intranet. The larger hospitality organizations will have direct links to multiple locations and many will have customized company web sites. In addition, there are numerous software programs to choose from for each application of human resources that you have read about in the preceding chapters. These programs can generate reports, perform various kinds of data analysis, and simulate a variety of "what if" scenarios.

For hospitality managers with human resources responsibilities in "the next chapter," an understanding of computer applications will be a job requirement. As you learn in this chapter, such an understanding will not only simplify your job but will assist in the organizational effectiveness and decision-making process of the hospitality enterprise. Top management is depending more and more on information provided by the human resources department.

At the conclusion of this chapter you will be able to:

1. Explain the applications and use of software within the human resources functions.
2. Understand the integration of Human Resource Information Systems (HRIS) with Information Systems (IS).
3. Understand the importance of conducting a needs-assessment prior to purchasing software.
4. Explain how to successfully introduce computers in your hospitality organization.
5. Describe the differences between vendor-selected software and designing your own software.
6. Identify the benefits of computer applications in hospitality human resources management.
7. Distinguish the difference between Intranet, Extranet and Internet.
8. Describe the appropriate uses of e-mail in the hospitality workplace.
9. Discuss what is meant by virtual-HR.

COMPUTERS AND HUMAN RESOURCES MANAGEMENT

In a people-oriented business such as hospitality, computers can allow managers to become more people oriented. Though guest service is something that only your people can do, **automation** gives you more time to focus on the heart of your business: the guest! Recall that in the first chapter we said that sound human resources skills and tools would allow you to maintain your commitment to high-quality products and excellent service. Computers should be thought of as simply another human resources management tool, like your development program, your placement process, or EAP, which when used properly, can help you maximize the quality of the products and services you offer.

The ultimate purpose of the computer for hospitality managers is to improve the quality of the service. It achieves its purpose by freeing you from time-consuming paperwork and giving you more time to interact with your guests. The speed at which information can be processed and reported expedites decision making. The advances in desktop publishing serve to improve communications throughout the hospitality organization. E-mail and improved accessibility to the **World Wide Web (WWW)** for information make the human resources arena function even more effectively. The "Information Age" surrounds us and in the twenty-first century is an integral part of our everyday lives as managers with human resources responsibilities in the hospitality industry.

With the use of multimedia PCs, many organizations have a structure that allows the employee the ability to handle many of the routine administrative tasks that were once handled by human resources. These self-service applications allow employees to conduct a wide range of human resources functions from a simple change of address to benefits enrollment to development through an online training program (Figure 15-1). When companies design information systems that allow employees to perform more HR functions for themselves, the managers with human re-

FIGURE 15-1 Employees today can turn on their PC and perform many HR applications for themselves. *(Courtesy of ARAMARK Corporation)*

sources responsibilities have more time to focus on the more strategic components of their jobs such as planning, coaching, and counseling, ultimately making them a more effective partner in management decision making.[1]

Computers, with their enormous capacity for storing, maintaining, and retrieving information in a usable format have helped human resources departments in becoming the information center for hospitality organizations. What could be more important to management decision making than information about the hospitality organization's most critical resource, its people? Which department is responsible for information on people? The human resource department, division, office, manager: wherever and whoever in your hospitality organization assumes the human resources responsibilities.

The computer is not a substitute for managerial expertise and experience, but it does have the capability of providing valuable analytical data and decision-support information to improve your effectiveness when carrying out human resources responsibilities.

What the Computer Can Do

Computers support you as a manager as you carry out your human resources responsibilities by performing a variety of time-consuming tasks. For example, much of the work in the human resources office is clerical in nature. Many of the routine tasks can be automated, reducing the number of individuals required for these tasks. Think back upon the human resources functions that we have discussed.

Select any one of those functions and think through the amount of information gathering and paperwork that goes into the successful completion of that particular human resources function. Perhaps, if your hospitality organization is very small, the amount of time spent in clerical tasks will not seem too overwhelming. The larger the hospitality organization, however, the greater the complexity of the data gathered and, more importantly, the greater the chance for error.

In large corporations, one of the biggest problems is the maintenance of a current data file on all of your people. If there is a backlog in information gathering, or even in the recording of the information, inappropriate decisions could be made. For example, budgeting and the control of expenses are vital to the financial success of each department within a hospitality operation. Though it is senior management's responsibility to prepare the departmental budgets, it is the manager with human resources responsibilities who should be preparing each department manager within the operation to control those budgets through the use of the computer.

The technology exists today to actually make an office paperless. That means no postnotes, no notepads, no phone rolodex, no day planner. Human resources functions such as recruitment, hiring, performance appraisals, compensation, and benefits administration and training can all be done without paper. Though no paper might sound somewhat intimidating at first, there are several benefits you might want to consider before rejecting this idea:

- Increased storage efficiency
- More cost-effective
- Saves time
- Improves the accuracy of data
- Maintains the security of data
- Improves workplace communication[2]

INDUSTRY EXPERTS SPEAK

Andrew Juska states, "The HR department of today will be as familiar with a computer and the WWW as their predecessors were with a fountain pen and a deskful of forms. From complex virtual human resources systems to a single workstation, the human resources department will be headed towards a tremendous reduction in the shuffling of papers. However, HR will always stand for ***HUMAN*** resources and our business will always be ***HOSPITALITY***. While we will use computer systems to train, recruit, process payroll and benefits and to store data, they will never smile at our guests and thank them for their business. We will remain a people industry. Success will still be generated by quality service."

In addition to automating clerical tasks, the computer can also be used in the development of standardized reports. Take out a piece of paper and identify the many reports the manager assuming human resources responsibilities must generate. Think through each of the human resources functions we have discussed and the federal legislation that governs each of them. Many of the standardized reports you will generate are required to show federal compliance.

Now compare your list with the following areas that require standardized reports, either for purposes of federal compliance or for management decision making:

- Attendance analysis (sick leave, vacation leave, etc.)
- Immigration tracking
- Training history (job safety and sanitation)
- Training, types (what crosstraining does each human resource have, which job positions are they qualified to fill from a training/job knowledge perspective)
- Retention/turnover analysis
- EEO, AA, and ADA compliance

- Job applicant tracking
- Payroll
- Career development/promotions
- Skills inventories
- Manpower analysis (how many human resources are in which departments)
- Educational assistance program utilization
- COBRA compliance
- Accident reporting
- Applicant search expenditures (cost per hire)

How many more examples of reports generated from human resources functions did you think of?

Computers can assist you, first, with routine clerical tasks and, second, in the generation of standardized reports (Figure 15-2). These two uses of computers are handled by routine data-processing systems, those that assist you in day-to-day operations. Computers give you the ability to streamline these routine, yet important, tasks. Just ask your employees how important it is to process their payroll checks! Or check with your lawyer about the fines for not maintaining federal reporting requirements!

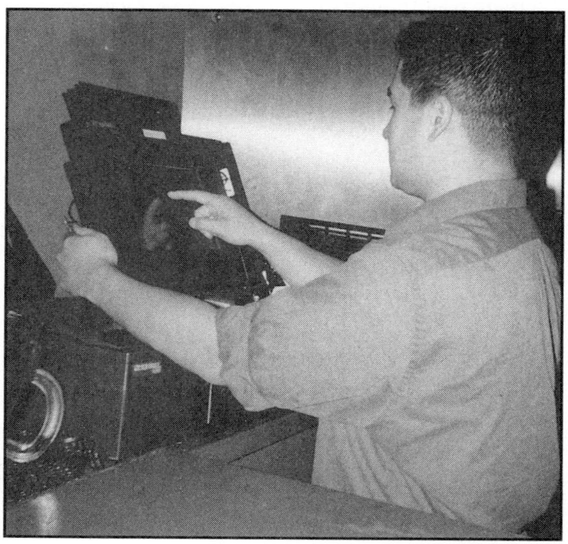

FIGURE 15-2 The use of computers can greatly reduce the amount of routine paperwork. *(Courtesy of Left At Albuquerque, Palo Alto, CA)*

TABLE 15-1 The Use of Computers in Human Resources Management: General Applications

- Clerical functions
- Budgeting
- Record keeping
- Federal and state compliance
- Desktop publishing
- Career pathing
- Skills inventories
- Compensation administration
- Benefits administration
- Short- and long-term planning
- Scheduling

A third general application of the computer is to provide management with the information it needs to make decisions. Better management decision making translates into improved organizational effectiveness for the hospitality enterprise. Because the computer can supply information more rapidly and with greater accuracy than manual procedures, feedback is provided on a more frequent basis. Table 15-1 provides you with a list of the more general applications of the computer in dealing with human resources responsibilities. Let us now look at some of the more specific applications within some of the human resources functions that have been discussed previously.

The Computerization of Human Resources Functions

Imagine for a moment that the hospitality organization you are working for has not incorporated any of its human resources functions into the existing automated information system. Suppose that you have been asked by your boss to identify areas, within the scope of your human resources responsibilities, that need to be automated. Which human resources functions do you feel would be among the first to be computerized?

How many of you answered payroll? There is no question that compensation plans, with their increasing complexity and federal regulations, can best be implemented and managed through a computerized system. The priority in which human resources functions are computerized for any one particular hospitality operation is hard to determine. A needs assessment and additional information about the size of the operation are required. For those hospitality operations that provide a variety of services and options for their human resources, the order in which the specific human resources functions are discussed in this chapter will typically make the most sense for purposes of implementation.

Compensation Administration

Compensation administration involves not only payroll record keeping and paycheck issuance, but the development of pay grades, ranges, and wage amounts. The effect of wage increases and the impact of merit increases can be pretested by asking the computer to answer a number of "what if" questions. Increases in compensation can have a far-reaching impact on the hospitality organization's future. Without computerization, it is almost impossible to determine the effects of such increases.

In addition to handling these needs, **Human Resource Information Systems (HRIS)** can be developed that can integrate performance evaluations with salary adjustments and/or career development progress. Compensation levels could be determined by bringing in appropriate data from the job evaluation process.

INDUSTRY EXPERTS SPEAK

Mr. Juska tells us that, "Computer payroll programs can now generate daily labor reports for each department. Most systems have the capabilities to deliver up to the minute payroll information. Labor costs traditionally have been a wait and see until the end of the month profit and loss statement. With today's systems labor costs can be checked daily by management. It will be HR's responsibility to make sure that computer training is included for the Executive Chef (Figure 15-3), Stewards, banquet managers, and others who have traditionally not used computers in their work.

"In addition, most computer payroll systems allow for advanced scheduling to be linked to your projected revenues. Now you can control your labor costs in advance with careful scheduling. You can also set limits, via the payroll system, on whether you will allow your employees to punch in early or punch out late. These computerized systems have taken the guesswork out of controlling labor costs. At any time I can generate reports such as employees who are approaching overtime, current employees on the clock, exact punch out times and up to the minute labor reports. I can do this from my laptop in the office . . . or even at home!"

FIGURE 15-3 Training on the use of computers needs to include chefs and other employees who have not traditionally used computers.

Combined or integrated human resources systems are oftentimes advantageous for a hospitality organization. Even though the functions of compensation, benefits, career development, and job evaluation are quite different, they use much of the same information. Instead of having each function entering the same data repeatedly, human resource information systems are designed so that the data needs to be entered only once, yet all functional areas have access to it when the data is needed. HRIS applications are discussed later in this chapter.

In pay-for-performance compensation plans, computerization becomes even more important. Before your people can be rewarded for their performance, accurate employee information is a must! Mistakes in rewarding performance due to inadequate or faulty information could be disastrous to the morale and motivation of your staff.

Benefits Administration

Much of benefits administration deals with maintenance decisions. The computer can save enormous amounts of time when dealing with the "paper trail" required to meet federal compliance and the support needed to offer flexible benefits. Think about the maintenance involved in a hospitality operation that has a flexible benefits plan that allows participants to select from four different health care plans, two different dental plans, and three different pension plans, in addition to day care, life insurance, elder care, and educational-assistance benefits offerings. How will you keep track of health insurance and pension accruals, tuition reimbursements, and day care contributions? How will you keep track of which employee has selected which health care, dental, and pension plan? How will you administrate who is entitled to what under which plan? Does all this seem a bit confusing and overwhelming? Without computerization, not only would it be an administrator's nightmare, but the potential for inaccuracies and mistakes is enormous!

As we pointed out in the chapter on benefits, there are many advantages for your employees when a hospitality organization offers a flexible benefits plan. The biggest disadvantage for the employer has been the record keeping that accompanies the implementation and administration of these types of benefits plans. The design of benefits **software** to maintain these records has virtually eliminated this prior disadvantage in offering a flexible benefits plan.

Software has been available for many years that can track the choices your employees make, make the appropriate payroll deductions, and provide you with a report of the costs.[3] Many companies today often start the automation of human resources functions with benefits enrollment. They have found that by automating that process and eliminating the manual tasks associated with benefits enrollment, the organization can achieve the quickest and most measurable return on investment.[4]

Even for hospitality organizations that choose not to offer flexible benefits, software is available to assist you in updating your personnel files. Benefits plans most typically operate based on information supplied by your employees when they are first hired. People's lives are seldom fixed; they get married or get divorced, they have children or their children grow up and leave their home, they move. All of this information must be modified in the employee's personnel files so that the company pays only for benefits that they actually should be providing.

Human Resources Planning

Effective human resources planning also requires an almost insatiable supply of information. Programs that can link employee supply-and-demand analysis with costs and benefits, programs that can assist in forecasting, and those that can generate decision-making information on alternatives to achieving strategic human resources plans are all ways that the computer can assist in human resources planning activities.

Succession planning can also make use of computer capabilities to identify progression paths that focus on key employees and their replacements. These systems can better track individuals in the succession plan to ensure continuity in vacated positions. Systems capable of coordinating skills-inventory data with succession planning are of great value to larger hospitality organizations. Typically, succession plans are developed only for top managerial positions. Expanded **data base** fields permit succession planning to be carried to lower position levels. Computers have the capacity to identify qualified internal candidates for vacant job positions: a great asset to a hospitality organization.

As the manager with human resources responsibilities in a hospitality organization seeks to become more of a strategic partner in the decision-making process, upgrading and enhancing your computer systems becomes critical. In a study conducted in 1997, 80 percent of the respondents indicated that human resources was responsible for its HR systems planning, budgeting, and implementation direction, while 72 percent stated that improvements in technology had enhanced their ability to interact with and serve the individual business units.[5] Since the late 1970s even more HR departments have recognized that their job is not just to service the employees, but that HR truly provides a service to the entire hospitality organization. Back-of-the-house managers are being moved to the front-of-the-house with the new technologies that are available. Technology has enabled human resources in the hospitality industry to become highly strategic jobs. Technology is being viewed as a way to add value, rather than to merely cut costs.[6]

Computer applications in manpower planning have barely touched the surface. As this function becomes of increasing importance to hospitality organizations in "the next chapter," watch for a greater sophistication in the use of computer systems to assist in human resources planning decisions.

Recruitment and Selection

Suppose that you have a job opening in your hospitality organization. You have been successful in your recruiting efforts and now, in front of you, is a pile of applications and résumés. Now, imagine that you can turn to your desktop computer. You enter the qualifications of all the applicants along with the job description and specification for the open position. Next, you request a list of the best candidates, and the computer generates one, prioritized, of course!

A computerized recruitment system could handle this selection task with ease, along with other elements of the recruitment process. For example, just with the applicant data that is already stored, your system has built up a pool of applicants that could be recalled at the touch of a fingertip any time a job opening occurs. The longer the selection capacities are used, the more data you will have to analyze the selection results. Is there a particular applicant profile that best fits a specific job position? What is the turnover rate of the applicants selected by the computer? What are the performance records of those individuals? Knowing the answers to questions such as these will enable you to further refine the selection system.

The selection procedure used by the computer also requires that you enter information about the vacant position. As you already know, the information necessary to make a valid selection decision is found in the job description and job specification. If this data is entered into the computer system for all job positions, you have the ability to recall, almost immediately, the job details for any vacant position. Reduced is the "paper trail" of required information that can sometimes delay the recruitment process.

Such an automated hiring system also gives you the capacity to track the applicants as they continue through the recruitment process. The applicant-tracking flow chart could be generated at any given moment and tell you exactly where the applicants stand in the process. Have they had their second interview? Are their letters of recommendation on file? Have the reference checks been completed? Is preemployment testing required and, if so, what is its status? If the automated hiring system is tied into a word processing system, offer and rejection letters could be generated to the appropriate applicants.

Once you automate the recruitment process, you will have a greater ability to keep track of the costs associated with obtaining a new hire. An analysis could be made to determine the most cost-effective advertising media. Monetary figures, such as cost per hire and cost per applicant, could easily be generated. All of this information translates into better administration of the entire recruitment process, from placing the first ad to selecting applicants to interviewing to making a job offer. Effectiveness in making the right applicant selection is also improved. Computer-assisted interviewing has been proven to shorten the hiring cycle. A computer-assisted interview can be programmed to look for key characteristics and experiences in a person's background. For example, if you are looking for someone in sales in your banquet department, you would want the computer to search out individuals who had been in customer service and sales environments, an individual who could assist clients with the details of planning their party or meeting. Companies who have used computer-assisted interviewing have found that their turnover rates are reduced, the cost per qualified job candidate is lowered, and they are able to generate a pool of qualified applicants in a shorter period of time.[7] All of these factors translate to a cost savings.

The technology exists, at present, to use computer information systems in all of the applications just discussed. Confidentiality can be protected by restricting levels of access into the system.

INDUSTRY EXPERTS SPEAK 

Andrew Juska says, "Who would have thought that next to the Chef's favorite cookbook would be manuals on computer programs! More and more department managers in hospitality organizations are using computers to make the clerical part of their duties faster, more efficient and more cost effective. Executive Chefs, purchasing directors and catering directors are just some of the department heads who are benefiting from computer use. Think of the tasks that traditionally were hand written and typed that can now be automated. It is the availability of inexpensive workstations along with the new advances in hospitality specific software programs which has made the transition to information technology both affordable and easy. However, the sometimes ignored management responsibility of training, training, training must not be forgotten. As information technology becomes more integrated into your entire organization, the need for training in these technologies will be paramount to success."

Training Management

There are a variety of uses for the human resource information system in training program management. Once you have a data base, the system can match the specific training requirements of various job positions with the training needs of your employees. The identification of training needs can be a time-consuming process when handled manually. Additional paperwork is involved in monitoring the progress of your employees as they participate in various training programs.

There is no doubt that computers can perform routine tasks, once done with pen and paper, more cheaply, more quickly, and usually with greater accuracy. A safety program is offered in many hospitality operations. Not only will automatization establish records for purposes of Occupational Safety and Health Administration documentation requirements, the system could be tied into your accident reports to troubleshoot problem areas. For example, your accident reports indicate an increase in the number of falls on wet floors. Your safety training program can then immediately be modified to emphasize the proper procedures and policies for mopping floors. The result could be a reduction in the number of accidents (Figure 15-4).

Training program management software systems can also be tied into development programs, performance appraisal systems, and succession planning. The information from each of these areas could be combined to ensure that the training needs of all your employees are met as the hospitality organization progresses towards the target goals and objectives identified in the strategic human resources plan. Career development plans can also be integrated so that the computer can identify weaknesses in an individual's profile that could be rectified through appropriate training or education. From the perspective of the hospitality organization, the computer can alert you to weaknesses in the company's current work force or even identify potential career paths for your employees. Because the computer operates with total objectivity, it can provide you with a better assessment of the talent that exists in your operation.

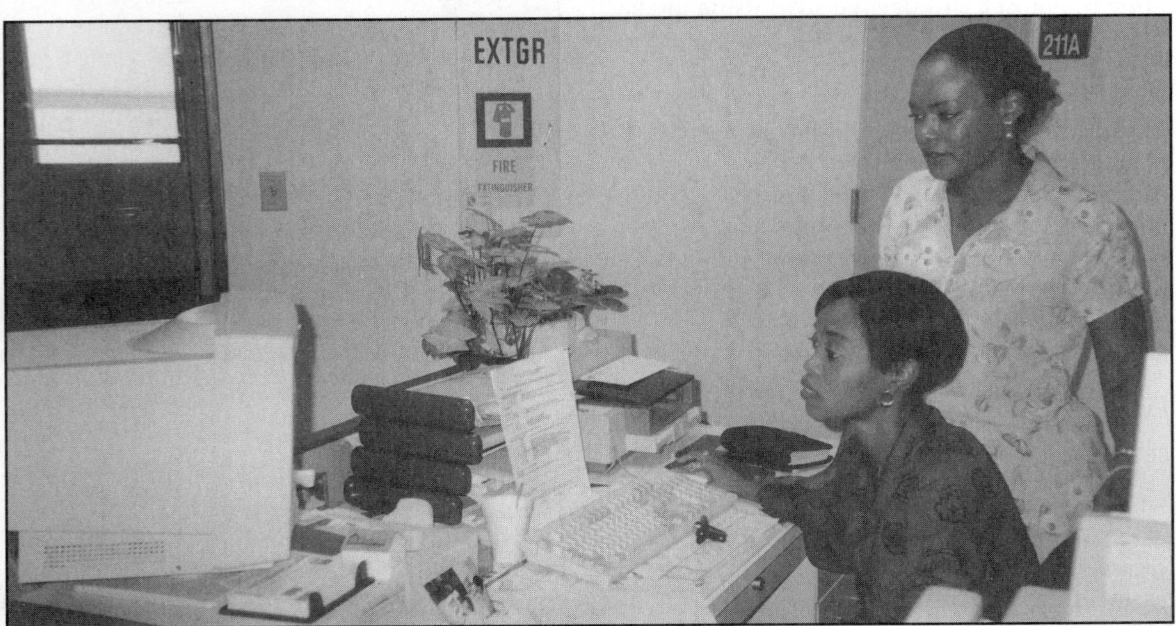

FIGURE 15-4 Safety training is just one of the many applications of advanced technology.

Other Human Resources Uses

The automation of human resources functions yields some additional capabilities. The record-keeping and reporting component of the Equal Employment Opportunity Act (EEOA) maintains strict requirements. With the data base you established during the recruitment and promotion process, accurate information can be readily provided on ethnic identities, race, religion, and sex.

Record keeping is also required to meet the regulations established in the Employee Retirement Income Security Act (ERISA) and the Consolidated Omnibus Budget Reconciliation Act (COBRA). Very specific timetables have been established by the federal government with stiff financial penalties for failure to comply.[8]

Computerization also allows for the analysis of data. Some examples of such usage in human resources management would include turnover, attendance, and patterns of sick leave. In addition, software is available that will produce organization charts and safety statistics, assist in negotiations planning, tie performance appraisals to merit payments, monitor management development, and conduct budgetary analysis.

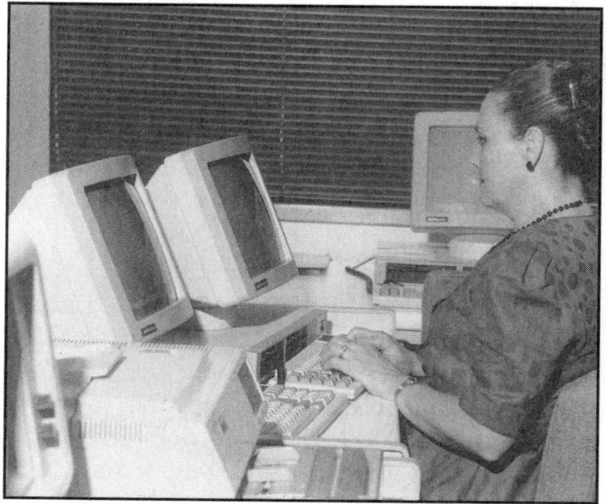

FIGURE 15-5 Information systems are a valuable asset to the hospitality manager with human resources responsibilities. *(Photo by Michael Upright)*

These applications have become an integral part of human resources management in the hospitality industry (Figure 15-5). Let's turn our attention to defining what a human resource information system is and how we might implement it, or other software packages, into our hospitality organization to assist us with our human resources management responsibilities.

HUMAN RESOURCE INFORMATION SYSTEMS VERSUS INFORMATION SYSTEMS

A computer is nothing more than an electronic device that can operate only under the control of a software program or programs. Software programs are written by people for the purpose of manipulating data in a specified manner. The data that is to be manipulated is gathered and entered into the computer by people. The accuracy of the program is only as accurate as the programmer and the data. The computer has no way of determining the accuracy of its output. In other words, it does not know the difference between "real" data and bad data, nor can it tell you whether the program it's operating under is "right" for the particular application you have in mind. GIGO spells garbage in-garbage out, which is exactly what will happen to you and your credibility if care is not taken in software selection, data gathering, and data entering.

There is no "typical" computer or software system for human resources functions in the hospitality industry. Actually one of the advantages of computer (hardware) and software systems is their flexibility and adaptability. You can select both the hardware and software that fit your specific purposes.

Management Information Systems (MIS) revolutionized personnel management in the 1960s. These large-scale management tools provided a wholelistic look at the hospitality business environment.[9] Today, these are referred to as simply **Information Systems (IS)**. An information system refers to information or data that is integrated for the purposes of decisionmaking. The logic is that the integrated data will serve to improve the decision-making process. An information system that is designed for the purpose of maximizing human resources decision-making is known as a *human resource information system* or *HRIS*. These systems can be centrally maintained to report on information related to all human resources in your organization. You have already read some of the ways in which HRIS can enhance human resources decisions.

INDUSTRY EXPERTS SPEAK

"Depending on the size and complexity of your hospitality company's computer system, the HR department may work side by side with the Information Systems Management (IS) department. The IS department traditionally handles the hardware and flow of information and may manage or supervise the company's web site. The HR department would be responsible for the training of all employees on the use of computers relative to their functions. These two departments must work very closely to keep the flow of information up and running and only available to those with the proper authority. In smaller hospitality operations the duties of these two departments are combined and fall under HR. This has created the need for managers with human resources responsibilities to learn network administration."

Human resource information systems have the capability to store vast amounts of data from a variety of input sources. The HRIS is designed to retrieve discrete pieces of data, about employees and jobs, and translate them into useful information rapidly and without error. These systems need to be thought of as a management tool that can be used to make a hospitality organization more efficient and productive. Most HRIS's are designed to be interactive. This means that they permit managers to view the output on their computer monitors as it is being manipulated. This permits the manager to make instant alterations, as they are required. Once the data and the format are satisfactory, the report can be printed into a "hard copy."

Integration of HRIS with IS

Most human resource information systems are implemented using the hospitality organization's **network** or Extranet. What if your company is small and does not have a network or Extranet? Many hospitality organizations use microcomputers, such as the IBM PC or Apple IIEs or any one of a number of such systems that are available on the market today. But wait, let's backtrack for a moment and see how the world of computers with human resources applications has evolved.

A Study of Past Events

As was the case in the development of a number of the human resources functions such as training and preemployment testing, the military and government were the first to apply computer technology to applications in human resources management.[10] It was actually the finance department that first computerized payroll systems in the early 1950s.[11] These systems ran on big mainframe systems, usually so large that entire rooms were devoted to them.

The systems were so complex that computer professionals, not human resources managers, operated them. Typically, requests from the human resources departments were given low-priority status.

It was during the late 1970s that computer technology began to be used to manage the challenges faced by human resources management. The revolution of the microcomputer increased the availability of hardware along with reducing the costs. The 80s brought with it the personal computer and an enormous reduction of cost. This triggered the avalanche of software programs, gradually improving in user friendliness. Computers were stored on desktops and no longer required computer specialists to operate them.

Today, numerous software systems include not only complete Human Resource Information Systems, but functionally specific programs as well. As the number of software vendors increases with each passing year, the manager with human resources responsibilities must be prepared to understand the proposed applications of the software he or she is choosing among (Figure 15-6).

THE PURPOSE OF A NEEDS ANALYSIS

The particular work environment of a hospitality organization determines the requirements of the automated human resource information system. No two human resource information systems are identical. Software designed for specific applications all have their limitations.

FIGURE 15-6 There is an avalanche of software programs available today with HRIS applications.

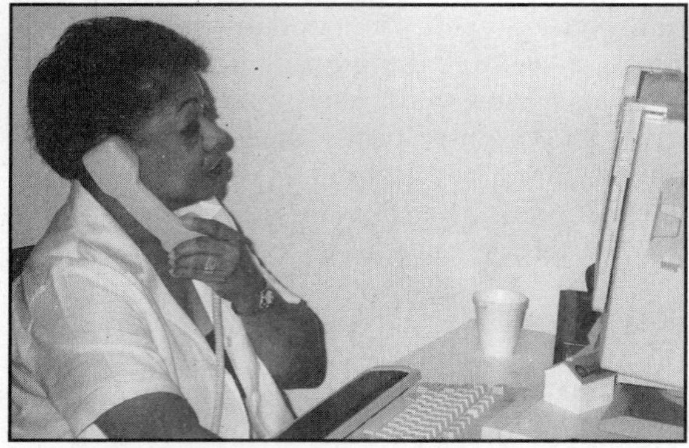

FIGURE 15-7 Software selections for human resource applications should be carefully made.

How do you know which software will perform optimally for your hospitality organization? Should you select a complete Human Resource Information System or several individual packages designed for specific applications?

The software or system that will work best is the one that is based upon the human resources information needs of your particular operation. We talked earlier in the text about the importance of establishing human resources goals and objectives. Your information needs should reflect those objectives. The software that you select should be designed to fulfill the hospitality organization's information needs. In other words, the human resources objectives determine the software applications you require (Figure 15-7). Don't let the software vendor convince you that your objectives should be modified to meet the capabilities of the software they are selling.

System and Software Decisions

Once your information needs have been identified, you need to determine whether you will need a complete HRIS or software with separate applications. This decision depends upon the size and computer capabilities of your operation. If your organization already has an HRIS running on a network or microcomputer, you will need to provide human resources information to supplement the data already contained on the system.

It is now time to make software decisions. Even though there is an abundance of software with human resources applications on the market, sometimes nothing less than custom-designed software will match your particular information needs. Making sure that you have the right software is critical! Designing software is not a skill mastered by most hospitality managers. It is well worth the money to hire a computer technician with programming capabilities to do the design and development. Make sure that all the "bugs" are worked out before the technician leaves.

Selecting special-application software already available on the market is probably the quickest, most inexpensive, and easiest alternative. Great care should be taken when reviewing all the products available on the market. The key objective is that the software matches the requirements of your hospitality organization. If you discover that the needs of your operation are unique and not met by any of the shelf software, you might be forced to develop (or have developed) a custom package.

As you select software, you might want to consider if the software has the capability to generate information in formats different from the standardized report form the software is programmed to generate. Some software packages permit you to generate ad hoc, or specialized reports, on an as-needed basis to fulfill a specific human resources function requirement. It is often quite useful to have the capability of building specialized reports from information in the data files. Another consideration might be the format in which reports are presented. Are they easy to read and interpret? Are they similar to what the staff is already used to seeing? Are they in a tabular or narrative format? How user friendly are the input and retrieval processes? What are the upgrade capabilities? What is functional today might be outdated tomorrow. These are just a few examples of considerations that need to be taken into account when selecting software.

After your software has been selected, and only after your software has been selected, can you shop for **hardware**. Some software can only run on specific hardware, so care must be taken in the selection process. Work with a knowledgeable individual whom you trust when making hardware selections.

INDUSTRY EXPERTS SPEAK

According to Andrew Juska there is little doubt that the majority of hospitality companies will have PC workstations in various departments, and most of these computers will be linked in a company network using systems such as Windows NT or Novell. These systems will allow employees (with proper login codes) access to company information that will greatly assist them in their duties. Popular contact managers such as ***Goldmine*** and ***Act*** will link customers and streamline the process of selling and keeping in contact with your customer.

Always remember that software and hardware selections must be based upon the human resources information needs of your particular hospitality operation. Define what specific applications your operation requires and make your selection decisions accordingly.

THE COMPUTER AND THE MANAGER WITH HUMAN RESOURCES RESPONSIBILITIES

Software with specific applications for human resources functions has been available on the market for a long time now, whereas the HRIS or integrated systems came onto the scene in the mid- to late-1980s. One of the advantages of a rapidly advancing technological society is that computer applications have long been cost-effective for even small hospitality operations.

Justifying the investment in an automated system requires that you evaluate both the tangible and intangible savings generated. Most companies realize a short payback period in their computer investment with savings in the future.

"Computerese" has evolved a long way in the hospitality industry, since point-of-sale cash registers (probably the first computer) were introduced. From large hospitality corporations to entrepreneurs, the personal computer has been an important ingredient for success. Listed here are some of the benefits of computerization:

- Gives management more control over their data
- Improves the accuracy of information
- Provides for timeliness of information
- Offers savings on reduced clerical efforts
- Provides new capabilities for record maintenance and reports
- Permits human resources applications in new areas that require detailed analysis
- Can manipulate numerous variables simultaneously
- Provides consistency in report formats
- Permits the human resources arena to provide greater service to operational management
- Allows savings over manual methods of collecting, maintaining, and reporting information
- Allows human resources to play a greater role in organizational strategic decision making
- Offers improved communications between human resources and operating divisions

Managers with human resources responsibilities are more stimulated as there is less busywork and more creative thinking involved in their jobs. If you still need a convincing selling point for automation, ask a manager with a computerized information system if he or she would switch back to the old methods. We predict that the answer will be a resounding "NO!"

TRENDS FOR 2000 AND BEYOND

It was not all that long ago that the hospitality industry was considered a low-tech industry. Technology came along, but most of us in hospitality believed that the technology belonged elsewhere. We were a service industry, a people business, and we would always need people not technology. Part of that statement is still true; we will always need people in the hospitality industry. However, the hospitality industry also needs technology. We have come to depend upon it, and our dependence will only increase, not decrease or diminish, in the "the next chapter."

Internet, Intranet, and Extranet

The **Internet** is a series of computers and modems that are connected together by wires in a way that allows them to communicate with each other. Internet addresses, such as www.delmar.com, are called the hostname. When you enter in a hostname, it gets looked up on a machine called a name server.

The use of the Internet exploded at the end of the century. As early as 1997, a study showed that approximately two out of five food service operators used the Internet.[12] The abundance of information available increases literally every day. From calculating per room building costs to recipe-costing techniques the Internet has it all. Our guests can check out our company's web site to check everything from room availability to what the menu is in each of our dining rooms.

The **Intranet** is an internal company-based network that allows management to control accessibility of data. For example, the chef in an on-premises catering facility could view menu files (and changes) for upcoming functions. An Intranet would also enable department managers access to payroll data, giving him or her better control over labor costs. You could combine your Intranet with a standard word processing program and publish an electronic version of your employee handbook. This makes updating the employee manual much easier and gives management the advantage of making sure that information the employees receive is current. More and more hospitality companies are establishing Intranets because they can offer better access to information for their employees.

The **Extranet** is a network that allows employees secure access to information and services outside of the hospitality company's own internal (Intranet) network. For example, let's say that your bartender wanted to make a change in her medical coverage from single coverage to family. Traditionally, she would have to go to the human resources department or benefits office and fill out some paperwork, which would then be mailed to the insurance provider. With an Extranet, she would simply go to a terminal and connect directly to the insurance provider, make the change in coverage, and be notified electronically when the change in coverage would be effective. The same type of procedure could be used to connect to the company retirement plans. This has some obvious advantages to both the manager with human resources responsibilities and the employee. Extranets can automate and simplify human resources functions that are already in place in addition to providing you with access to services that otherwise would have been unaffordable.

Internet and E-mail: Uses and Abuses

Along with the explosion of technology comes the potential for misuse and abuse of these valuable tools. From non–job-related net surfing at work to personal use of e-mail, all technology-supported hospitality workplaces are potentially vulnerable. The end of the century saw the start of numerous high-profile legal cases involving e-mail. Claims of discrimination, sexual harassment, wrongful termination, and fostering a hostile work environment have the potential of being documented by e-mail records and files. Because electronic mail correspondence is discoverable material, it must be turned over to the other side in a legal action against the company.

One of the challenges for management is how to regulate usage without making the technology useless. More and more companies are installing Internet access for their employees. This is great as it allows your managers to conduct research and communicate outside the internal electronic mail system. It also raises an issue of productivity. How much time during the day is spent surfing the Internet on non–work-related things? Is this an issue that should be dealt with by electronic monitoring and strict policies or is it a job performance matter when the person's work is left incomplete? There are no easy answers to these questions.

It is however important to develop rules and procedures for your interoffice e-mail. Often times employees will write things in e-mail that they would not write otherwise. Some companies have zero tolerance approaches to their e-mail policy. Others place a ban on certain types of e-mail such as chain letters or jokes. Table 15-2 is an example of a policy relating to several communication systems.

TABLE 15-2 Use of Telephone, Mail, and Computer Systems

Of all the communication tools we use at Premier Beverage, the telephone, mail and computer are some of the most important. Personal use of the mail, electronic mail, or telephone systems is not permitted. Likewise, the use of company-paid postage for personal correspondence is not permitted. Employees should practice discretion in using company telephones when making local personal calls and may be required to reimburse company for any charges resulting from their personal use of the telephone. Employees should contact their supervisor with any questions about telephone procedures and for departmental policy regarding personal outgoing calls during breaks, meal periods, or other times.

To assure effective telephone communications, employees should always use the approved greeting and speak in a courteous and professional manner. Please confirm information received from the caller, and hang up only after the caller has done so.

For employees with voice-mail, please maintain a current greeting for your callers.

Premier Beverage reserves the right to monitor incoming and outgoing telephone calls connected through the company's telephone system at any time and without notice. Also, voice mail messages stored within the telephone system are considered business communications and are subject to monitoring, review and retrieval by authorized Premier Beverage personnel.

All information stored on Premier Beverage computer and data processing equipment is considered company property. The electronic mail system is for business use only and any personal or unauthorized use of this system may lead to disciplinary action up to and including termination. Electronic mail messages created, received, sent or stored with the system are subject to monitoring, retrieval and review by authorized personnel at any time without notice.

(Courtesy Premier Beverage Company of Florida; SUN-BELT Beverage Corporation)

Clearly, issues involving the appropriate use of these technologies are going to continue to come up more and more. It is in your best interest as a manager with human resources responsibilities to remain well-informed on these issues so that you can be proactive in your approach.

Virtual HR

A vision for the future is virtual HR. **Virtual HR** is a reality-based concept that would enable a human resources department to be completely paperless. Virtual HR literally takes away every piece of paper from the manager with human resources responsibilities. Virtually every task and function is performed electronically. For example, the employee would be able to quickly access his or her own personnel information to check on everything from how many vacation days are left to making changes on W2 forms to reviewing disciplinary notices or letters of commendation.

The savings to the hospitality organization are time and cost reductions in paper and distribution. Even though there are no forms to fill out, these paperless systems are traceable and secure. Virtual HR has only recently begun to develop into more than eliminating routine administrative tasks. The future of integrating the human resources department with web-based technology will most certainly take place in "the next chapter."

CONCLUSION

Human resources applications using the computer go far beyond their origins in record keeping. Automation continues to find solutions to the daily problems encountered in human resources management. In recent years, great strides have been made in using computer potential for the accumulation, manipulation, and reporting of data relating to human resources management. Computers are no longer merely electronic filing cabinets. As human resources management continues to explore the opportunities in the technological age, human resources functions are given a new respect and place of importance in the hierarchy of the hospitality enterprise. One of the most significant developments for hospitality organizations has been the development of the desktop or personal computer.

The computer has become a multipurpose tool in the effective management of our valued employees. The manager with human resources responsibilities does not have to be a programmer but will need an awareness of how computer capabilities can make the manager more effective in his or her job. Changing managers' work habits has not been easy. Nor has it been easy for all seasoned managers to trust the strange, new machinery. Each of you has an enormous advantage upon entering the hospitality management work force upon graduation. Most, if not all, of you have been exposed to the computer at some point during your education. You will make use of the benefits of the computer with much greater ease than many managers who have been in the field for several years. As computer technology improves, and software becomes more friendly, computer fear will hopefully subside, and all managers with or without human resources responsibilities will take advantage of this incredible tool that is available to them.

There can be little doubt, after reading this chapter, that the computerization of human resources functions is an asset to any manager charged with human resources responsibilities. In "the next chapter" there will probably be a software package available for every human resources function that has been discussed. As the hospitality organization continues to rely on the human resources arena for more-accurate information, the need will increase for improved human resource information systems. As the information needs of the organization change, the systems that organize that data will grow and adapt to fit the needs. For many years, however, a great need will continue to exist for adequate training in both the use of computers and the software that runs them. The future of human resource information systems lies in the training of individuals who are knowledgeable about human resources to also become computer literate. At the present time, there are many who continue to resist the information society of the new century.

Remember that you don't work for the computer, it works for you to facilitate the storage, manipulation, and retrieval of large amounts of information on a multitude of people. If you become tied to your computer, instead of using it to free you from time spent in the office, you will be taken away from your guests. Used effectively, the computer can save you time in the performance of your human resources responsibilities, providing you with new ways to organize and execute your responsibilities, while at the same time saving your employer(s) money. If a manager systematizes the routine data-gathering tasks involved in human resources management, the manager assuming human resources responsibilities takes on an elevated position in the hospitality organization. Human resource information systems give hospitality managers better ways of managing human resources.

Top management increasingly looks toward the human resources arena for credible data that can assist in cost-containment measures, in minimizing legal risks, in dealing with the ever-changing government policies and regulations, and in improving retention. Unreliable, outdated, and inconsistent information can carry a high price for the hospitality enterprise of "the next chapter." Management decision making, where alternatives explored are based on sufficient and accurate data, can give hospitality organizations a competitive edge. Computer applications have traveled a long way from their origin in payroll record keeping!

CASE PROBLEM 15

Anytime a hospitality manager finds himself or herself in a new job position, challenges and opportunities abound. When that management position includes human resources responsibilities, both the opportunities and challenges increase. The changes in technology can be thought of as both a challenge and an opportunity.

The management position that you recently assumed can provide you with the opportunity to share your knowledge of computer applications in the hospitality industry with the existing management team. The job position might be the first one you assume after graduation, or it might be a job that you find yourself in later in your hospitality career.

Select the hospitality environment in which you see yourself in the future, or perhaps the hospitality management job that you have now. It does not matter whether the job is in the lodging, food service, or tourism sector of the hospitality industry. The common condition that exists is a lack of computer applications for human resources management functions. You are convinced, based upon your knowledge in this area, that the hospitality operation could benefit by the implementation of an HRIS.

While this is an opportunity for you to shine and become a valued member of the management team, your challenge is to convince the other members of the management team who have no

CASE PROBLEM 15 *(concluded)*

knowledge about HRIS. Develop a three-page plan that you will use in making an oral presentation to the management team. Discuss your ideas for an HRIS. At a minimum this plan should include a definition of what an HRIS is, along with any other definitions you feel the management team must understand in order to benefit from your presentation. An overview of the software applications for human resources functions, a needs assessment, and an identification of some of the benefits of computer applications in your hospitality operation should also be included. What policies will need to be initiated or developed?

Remember that you will need to be convincing in your presentation. In order to be competitive, computers are a necessity, not merely an amenity. You will need to present some specifics of the hospitality operation you are working in. You will also need a justification of the cost investment.

Key Words

automation
data base
Extranet
hardware
Human Resource Information System (HRIS)
Information Systems (IS)
Internet
Intranet
network
software
virtual HR
World Wide Web (WWW)

Recommended Reading

Bruns, R. "Know Thy Guest." *Lodging Magazine*. 1998. www.lodgingmagazine.com/9806/coverstory.htm (7 May 1999).

Greengard, S. 1994. "The Next Generation." *Personnel Journal* 73(3): 40–46.

———. 1994. "New Technology Is HR's Route to Reengineering." *Personnel Journal* 73(7): 32a–32o.

———. 1998. "Making Dollars and Sense Out of Employee Self-Service." *Personnel Journal* 77(7): 67–69.

Hamilton, M. "Catching Up with Technology." *Lodging Magazine*. 1999. www.lodgingmagazine.com/9905/technology.htm (23 May 1999).

Jones, J. W. 1998. *Virtual HR: Human Resources Management in the Information Age.* www.amazon.com

Meade, J. "International Intranets." *HR Magazine*. 1998. www.shrm.org/hrmagazine/articles/0598int.htm (4 October 1998).

Murphy, J., E. J. Forrest, C. E. Wotring, and R. Brymer. 1996. "Hotel Management and Marketing on the Internet: An Analysis of Sites and Features." *Cornell Quarterly* 77(3): 70–82.

O'Connell, S. "The Virtual Workplace Moves at Warp Speed." *HR Magazine*. 1996. www.shrm.org/hrmagazine/articles/0396cov.htm (4 October 1998).

Perry, P. P. 1997. "Honing Your Home Page." *Restaurants USA* 17(8): 21–25.

Shair, D. "HR Windows: Take a Seat with Top Management." *HR Magazine.* 1999. www.shrm.org/hrmagazine/articles/0599soft.htm (20 May 1999).

Sheley, E. "High-Tech Recruiting Methods." *HR Magazine.* 1995. www.shrm.org/hrmagazine/articles/09recruitment.html (4 October 1998).

Stone Gonzalez, J. 1998. *The 21st Century Intranet.* Prentice Hall Computer Books.

Van Hoof, H. B., R. C. Galen, T. E. Combrink, and M. J. Verbeeten. 1995. "Technology Needs and Perceptions—An Assessment of the U.S. Lodging Industry." *Cornell Quarterly* 36(5): 64–69.

Recommended Web Sites

1. Intranet Design Magazine: idm.internet.com/index.html
2. Internet Society (ISOC): www.isoc.org
3. CERT Coordination Center: www.cert.org
4. Intranet Research Center: www.cio.com/forums/intranet
5. International Association for Human Resource Information Managment: www.ihrim.org/welcome.html
6. The Internet2 Project: www.internet2.edu
7. Intranet Journal: www.intranetjournal.com
8. Next Generation Internet (NGI) Initiative: www.ngi.gov
9. Intranet Resources: www.strom.com/pubwork/intranet.html

Endnotes

1. Gillian Flynn, "HR Hears the Call of Technology," *Personnel Journal* 74, no. 5 (1995): 62–68.
2. Valerie Frazee, "Go Paperless One Sheet at a Time," *Personnel Journal* 75, no. 11 (1996): 68–76.
3. Alfred J. Walker, "New Technologies in Human Resources Planning," *Human Resources Planning* 9, no. 4 (1986): 149–159.
4. Jim LeTart, "Time for Strategy," *HR Magazine.* 1997. www.shrm.org/hrmagazine/articles/1297tech.htm (4 October 1998).
5. David Link, "The Use of Information Technology in HR," *BC Solutions Magazine.* 1997. www.bcsolutionsmag.com/Archives/Nov1997/TECH1.html (10 August 1998).
6. Mark Hamstra, "Operators Grapple with Technology at Work," *Nation's Restaurant News* 32, no. 40 (1998): 78.
7. Linda Thornburg, "Computer-Assisted Interviewing Shortens Hiring Cycle," *HR Magazine,* 1998. www.shrm.org/hrmagazine/articles/0298rec.htm (4 October 1998).
8. Lawrence R. Miller, "Law and Information Systems," *Journal of Systems Management* 28, no. 1 (1977): 21–30.
9. John F. Griffin, "Management Information Systems—A Challenge to Personnel," *Personnel Journal* 46, no. 6 (1967): 371–381.

10. Richard A. Kaumeyer, Jr., *Planning and Using Skills Inventory Systems* (New York: Van Nostrand Reinhold Company, 1979), p. 10.
11. Edward Blair, "Bootstrapping Your HRIS Capabilities," *Personnel Administrator* 33, no. 2 (1988): 68–72.
12. B. Grindy, "Restaurants Are Putting Technology to Work," *Restaurants USA* 17, no. 8 (1997): 11–12.

Discussion Questions

1. Rank in terms of priority of need, the major uses of a computer in a hospitality organization that has never been computerized. Limit your responses to human resources responsibilities.
2. Explain how Human Resources Information Systems (HRIS) are integrated with Information Systems (IS).
3. What is the role of the computer in decision making in a hospitality organization?
4. Discuss the importance of conducting a needs analysis prior to the implementation of a computer system.
5. Why would you want to design your own software as opposed to purchasing vendor supplied software?
6. Identify several benefits to the automation of human resources functions.
7. React to the following statement: "Using computers to monitor human resources responsibilities and functions reduces the need for direct personal contact between management and employees."

CHAPTER 16

The Next Chapter...

"The most exciting breakthroughs of the the 21st century will not occur because of technology but because of an expanding concept of what it means to be human."

—JOHN NAISBITT/PATRICIA ABURDENCE

"Who controls the past controls the future: who controls the present controls the past."

—GEORGE ORWELL

INTRODUCTION

Human resources management is no longer referred to as "personnel" in the twenty-first century. The change is more than merely one of nomenclature. It represents a change in attitude, a change in conception, a change in status.

Personnel functions were considered primarily related to record keeping and administration. Personnel offices were located in out-of-the way places in the hospitality operation, down by the employee lockers and "break" room. The human resources office is no longer hidden. With employees being viewed as a valuable asset with a direct impact on the bottom line, hospitality companies are recognizing that properly managed human resources can give them a competitive edge. Human resources professionals are seen at top-level strategic planning sessions, and more COOs and CEOs are using human resources positions as the avenue to the top.

At the conclusion of this chapter you will be able to:

1. Discuss how the human resources arena will be important to organizational effectiveness.
2. Explain the future role of the human resources manager in the hospitality industry.
3. Identify the most likely developments and trends in the hospitality work force in "the next chapter."
4. Identify three predictions regarding human resources management in the hospitality industry in the year 2010 provided by industry advisors.
5. Obtain advice (we hope you will use) from each of the industry advisors as you enter the hospitality work force.

THE INCREASING IMPORTANCE OF HUMAN RESOURCES MANAGEMENT

Change, globalization, increased competition for limited human resources, along with technological advancements are just some of the vast challenges facing hospitality managers with human resources responsibilities at the beginning of the twenty-first century. Who can imagine what additional challenges the next five or ten years will bring our way. The issues that you will be facing are much more complex than those of your predecessors. The impact that your role will make on the hospitality organization will be much more far-reaching in its implications. In a survey reported in 1987, it was found that CEOs expect the human resources division to:

- Understand and support the needs of the business
- Play a major role in the use and development of talent
- Formulate cost-containment measures
- Formulate productivity improvement measures
- Help both shape and communicate corporate values[1]

Those expectations indicated that human resources management was going to have a much greater impact on the hospitality organization's strategic plan. Every human resources function began to revolve around the mission statement, organizational goals, and operational objectives. Human resources programs were not developed in the early 1990s merely for the sake of the human resources division, rather managers with human resources responsibilities began serving as critical support for the operational managers. Strong support in areas of problem solving and decision making were given. Human resources managers became change agents as people skills were as important as financial skills to successful hospitality operations. Corporate cultures improved as managers became counselors and coaches and began to manage their people instead of the job tasks. The human resources arena became the information center for the organization's most valuable asset: its people (Figure 16-1).

FIGURE 16-1 Sound human resources management practices make the hospitality industry a great place to work for all employees. *(Photo A courtesy of Marriott Corporation; Photo B by Michael Upright)*

In 1991 the Educational Foundation of the National Restaurant Association conducted what was considered to be a "futuristic" study of the food service manager in the year 2000. Among other findings, this study identified the five *most likely* developments that food service managers would need to make by 2000. Managers will:

- need greater computer proficiency.
- supervise a more culturally diverse staff.
- find that service will become a more competitive point of difference.
- need better teaching and training skills.
- possess greater people-management skills.[2]

As we now know, the panel of industry experts who participated in this study were quite accurate with their predictions.

Even in the twenty-first century, a hospitality organization will still need its human resources policies and procedures to ensure consistency and continuity. This will still be an important role for human resources management in "the next chapter." Imagine if every operational manager and supervisor were permitted to set his or her own wages, discipline according to their own whims, run recruitment ads whenever the manager felt it was needed, and hire at random. The point we want to stress is that human resources responsibilities will continue to expand well beyond their more traditional boundaries. Human resources systems planning will continue to be part of a hospitality organization's business plan.

Looking through the literature, you can see that having human resources managers serve as advisors to the executive board is not a new idea.

> *If he is truly to function as an adviser to top management, the personnel executive will have to live down the stereotype of a hail-fellow-well-met trying to keep everybody happy by administering a variety of employee benefits and services. These may still be important, but they are not of first importance today.*[3]

Forgetting for the moment that Myers only talked about the "personnel man," it is clear that even forty years ago the insignificant role of personnel was being challenged.

> *The point of view expressed here is that people as an organizational resource, are at least equally important with the others, and that ignorance, neglect, waste, or poor handling of this resource has the same consequences as ignorance, neglect, waste, or poor handling of money, materials, or market.*[4]

Historically, part of the problem with human resources management is that it has always been difficult to fix a dollar amount on the return on investment from costly employee programs. Human resources has (and sometimes unfortunately is) often been viewed as an area of necessary expense to satisfy the lawyers and accountants while providing a general service to the employees. The challenge of the human resources professional has been to explain why his or her department is strategically necessary to the company's mission statement and organizational goals. A change in how personnel functions are viewed occurs when employees are thought of as an asset, rather than as an expense item. Human resources functions can then be recognized for their contribution to the bottom line. Human resources management can then be viewed as a profit center. Cost savings are not only tangible. What about the nontangible cost savings that occur when a union grievance does *not* occur? How much is saved when ERISA, OSHA, ADA, FMLA, EEO, or AA penalties do *not* have to be paid? What is it worth in dollars and public relations *not* to have a lawsuit filed against you by a disgruntled employee?

Criticisms of the personnel function have not always related to costs. Many have felt that personnel responsibilities were insignificant to the overall effectiveness of the organization. In the early 1970s, the following criticisms were pointed out:

- *"The personnel function is not management oriented.*

- *The personnel function is not adaptable to change.*
- *The personnel system is absorbed in relatively unimportant tasks like record keeping.*
- *In general, administrative offices function at low levels of productivity and are measured against inappropriate standards."*[5]

Human resources management has undergone and still is undergoing remarkable transformations. Human resources management in the twenty-first century has certainly come along way from the personnel management of the 1970s. Today HR is part of a team that helps to create an innovative work environment for all people in the hospitality organization (Figure 16-2). In many companies, they have taken the lead in helping their organizations break away from traditional models. Human resources management departments have done this by leading by example. Papa John's created their HR department in 1993, eight years after they began. Within two years the human resources department was able to standardize Papa John's culture, benefits, retention, and recruitment efforts, all of which are credited with giving the company their competitive edge in the marketplace. The mission statement of "exceeding the needs and expectations" of customers along with a commitment of rewarding contributions and performance set this company apart from the rest in the 1990s.[6]

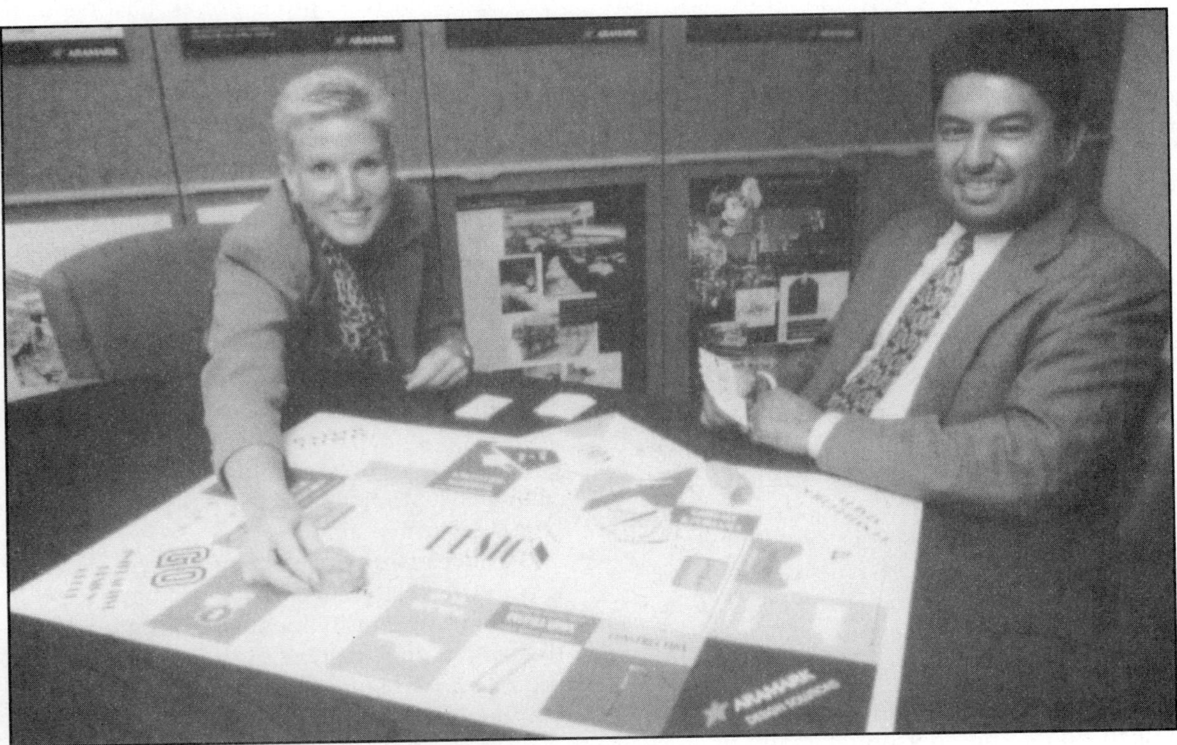

FIGURE 16-2 Human resources departments often take the lead in creating innovative work environments for employees. *(Courtesy of ARAMARK Corporation)*

If human resources management is no longer to be perceived as playing merely a mechanical, bookkeeping function, then the manager who assumes these responsibilities will need to adapt new strategies to meet the challenges of "the next chapter."

THE HUMAN RESOURCES PROFESSIONAL

As we pointed out in the first chapter, every hospitality manager has human resources responsibilities. The human resources professional has developed the general or specialized skills and knowledge to manage the functions in this arena. The importance of these skills is not only reflected in a review of the literature, but in the increase of course offerings related to human resources functions in colleges and universities. Regardless of the advancements made in computer technology, human resources management still requires the skills and labors of people! Not only have human resources departments and divisions within the hospitality organization taken on greater prominence, the human resources professional enjoys a much greater status. People will always need to be recruited, hired, trained, developed, motivated, counseled, disciplined, and possibly terminated. The ability, however, to understand the hospitality business outside of the human resources functions will also continue to be critical to the human resources professional in "the next chapter."

With no end in sight to the labor shortage, maximizing the productivity of the people already in your hospitality operation will continue to be important. Top management will be turning to the human resources professional to assist them in achieving this goal. In larger corporate organizations, human resources executives are reporting directly to the top levels of the corporate structure. Respect for the human resources professional continues to rise.

Opportunities for advancement for the human resources professional will be more prevalent in "the next chapter" for the right people. What skills do the right people possess? More management and finance oriented than human resources professionals in the past, they will understand a balance sheet and what affects it. These individuals understand the total business environment of the hospitality industry and their organization. They see the direct effect of human resources management on the bottom line. As human resource information systems become more integrated into the hospitality environment, the human resources professional will need to be proficient in computer skills, including Internet, Extranet, and Intranet capabilities (Figure 16-3).

In a study conducted by *Workforce* in the late 1990s to determine the direction of the human resources profession, the following are some of the predictions for the "Strategic Role of HR" for the year 2008:

- Focus will be on organizational performance.
- HR's value will be in having the right people ready at the right time.
- Role will evolve from strategic business partner to strategic business leader.
- Line managers will become more dependent upon the HR professional.
- Leading change will be HR's greatest corporate contribution.[7]

The human resources professional in "the next chapter" will be as comfortable discussing business strategy as he or she will be explaining the benefits package or in strategic human resources planning sessions. The ability to attract, develop, and retain a highly motivated work force will still be critical job responsibilities. A forward looking, strategic, and integrated approach to human resources issues will be

FIGURE 16-3 Human resources professionals will need to be proficient in computer skills.

of equal importance. With these skills and abilities, the human resources professional will find the potential high for career growth and mobility.

CHALLENGES OF THE FUTURE

What forces will be affecting you as you assume human resources responsibilities in "the next chapter"? We have already taken into consideration many of these forces as we discussed the various human resources functions. Many of these forces will challenge us, and many will make our jobs more exciting and rewarding. Let's take this opportunity to summarize some of the challenges and changes facing us in "the next chapter":

- Extensive planning to meet tomorrow's work force needs in light of a worker shortage
- Continued search for ways to use our human resources more effectively
- The integration of work with quality-of-life initiatives
- Accelerating demand for better trained human resources
- Increasing sophistication in technology leading to improved human resource information systems
- Employees given more choices about work arrangements/schedules
- Strategic human resources planning seeking input from the employees

- Better working relationships between unions and management
- Greater governmental influence and control through legislation
- Greater increase in the availability of human resources support services offered (EAPs, child care, work-family, elder care, etc.)
- Business-education partnerships (school-work programs)
- More creativity in attracting and retaining our human resources
- Greater increase in the cultural diversity of our work force (Figure 16-4)
- Innovative changes in compensation and benefits plans
- Communication becoming instantaneous through company Intranets
- Internet technology allowing more companies the opportunity to enter global markets
- Career paths running horizontal as well as vertical
- Health care costs continuing to rise
- Compensation plans becoming competitive and performance driven; closer link to business outcomes
- A constant need for training
- Education of the work force as important as training

ANALYSIS OF YEAR 2000 PREDICTIONS

In 1989 the Industry Experts who served as advisors to the first edition of this textbook

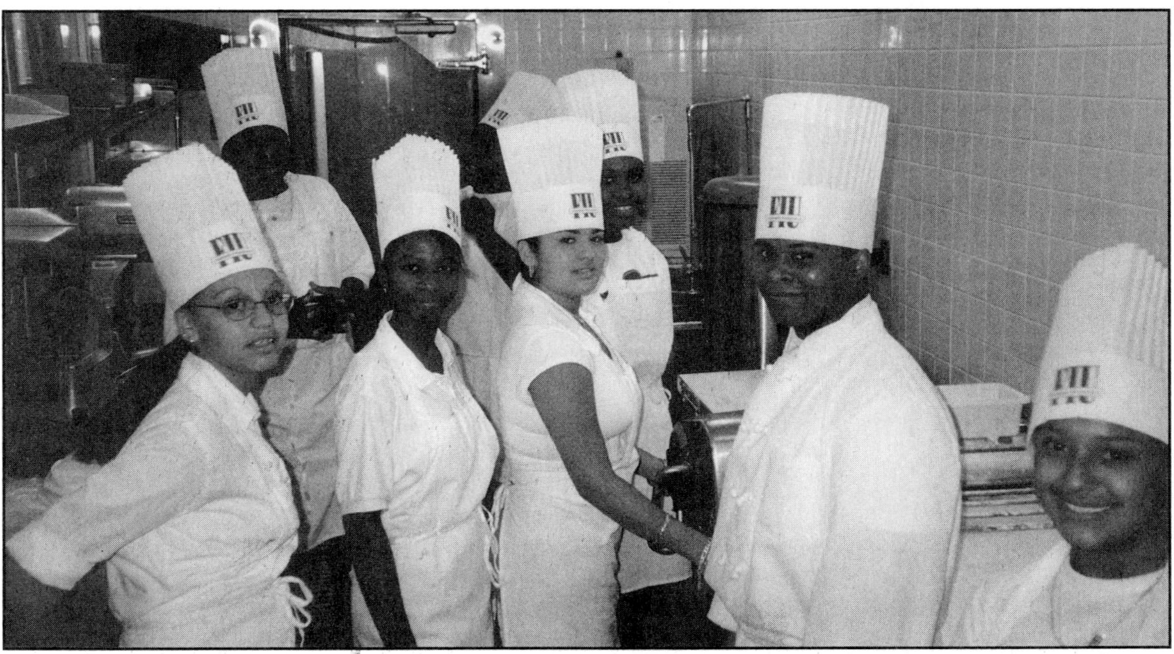

FIGURE 16-4 The diverse cultural environment of a hospitality company will continue to be a management challenge.

were asked to make three predictions about human resource management in the hospitality industry in the year 2000. Upon reviewing their responses ten years later, one can see that the reviewers were remarkably accurate with their predictions.

The following are some of the very accurate predictions that were made by one or more of our industry advisors in 1989 about the year 2000:

- The labor shortage will be a critical problem for our industry to solve.
- To insure the financial investment in a property, a formalized aggressive human resources development program will become important.
- Part-time employees will be even more important in the year 2000. We must appreciate that our work is secondary to their outside responsibilities.
- The expression "Our people are our most important asset" will become more than just rhetoric.
- In order to competitively attract quality managers, the hospitality industry will adjust the present excessive hours of work.
- A better quality of life will be even more of an issue than it is now. We'll probably see more flex time, four-day workweeks, and permanent or semipermanent schedules.
- The focus will be on training and retention of employees (Figure 16-5).
- Human resources managers will be stronger business partners with operations and marketing than currently perceived.
- The labor market will be a key determinant to a company's growth strategy.
- The skills required by the professional manager in the hospitality industry will be increased.

FIGURE 16-5 The focus will be on training and retention of employees. *(Courtesy of Strongbow Inn, Valparaiso, IN)*

- Fewer people in the labor pool with even basic reading, writing, and arithmetic (skills) will be available.
- Collective bargaining will continue to exist through the 1990s. Union business managers will be highly skilled and extremely competent regarding union affairs and contract negotiations.

PREDICTIONS FOR THE YEAR 2010

Having access again to our own panel of experts—the industry professionals who served as advisors to the chapters you have read—allowed me to once again ask them to make their own predictions. What follows is their response to this statement: "Make three predictions about human resources management in the year 2010."

Michael Hurst, ***Owner, 15th Street Fisheries:***

"1) Training will be viewed as a fixed cost and not a variable cost. From a service standpoint, as well as a safety standpoint, staff needs to be aware of current regulations, procedures, and new technologies.

"2) There will be more part-timers in the workplace. I strive to have 50 percent of my service staff work 3 days a week or less.

"3) Greater flexibility in scheduling. Scheduling will be done with the best interests of the employee in mind. Classically, the concept of management has been that the employee serves the interest of the workplace. In the next ten years, management must learn how to get the workplace to serve the best interests of the employee and still get the work done. We need to build in enough flexibility to adjust to employee needs. We need to make sure that we have enough staff so that our employees have a life as well as a job."

Ed Evans, ***Senior Vice President Human Resources, ARAMARK Uniform and Career Apparel:***

"1) Benefits will be 'transportable' making retention of employees a matter of not only compensation, but meaningful work and the opportunity to advance.

"2) Training will be accomplished and managed to a much greater extent through technology. Hospitality organizations will select based upon behavioral criteria and will technical skill them post hire.

"3) With the competition for labor, the generation "Xers" will be faced with incredible challenges looking after the needs of the baby boomers as they attempt to lure them back into the workplace on a full or part time basis.

"4) The gap between the skilled and the unskilled (formally trained and non-formally trained) employee will grow as will the presence of drugs and illiteracy in the workplace."

Jan Barr, ***SPHR, Human Resources Director, Chili's Grill & Bar, Brinker International:***

"1) The shortage of available workers for the hospitality industry will continue to be the major challenge for employers, both at the hourly level and for managers. To survive, companies must be able to evaluate 'the potential to lead' in management and must look to alternative sources for hourly employees. To prosper, companies must attract and develop leaders, not managers, and must become the employer of choice for hourly employees.

"2) Human Resources professionals must become a vital part of the planning of strategic business decisions. Constant change will be required for successful companies, and the Human Resources role as 'implementers of change' will be critical. In 10 years, change will be an accepted way of doing business, if Human Resources professionals are effective.

"3) Our industry must find alternatives for the lifestyle issues inherent in a 7-days-a-week/52-weeks-a-year business. Part time, flex time, more paid holidays, rotating weekends, child care, elderly care, cafeteria style benefits, etc., must become acceptable if we want to keep our winners. Overall, though, we must keep the unique, fun, exciting spirit alive in our industry. It's what keeps it special for all of us." (See Figure 16-6.)

Bob Morrison, ***Founder and Principal, Quetico Corporation:***

"1) Attracting and retaining employees will be the top priority for all hospitality businesses.

"2) Providing a flexible and challenging work environment will be paramount in your ability to keep top employees.

"3) Customers will demand increasingly higher standards from service and hospitality employees and this will mean that you must employ people with strong interpersonal and social skills."

Loret Carbone, ***Senior Vice President of Human Resources, Left At Albuquerque:***

"1) Everyone will realize that people are a business's most important asset. Companies will be more competitive in attracting and maintaining talented workers. Recruitment procedures, compensation, benefits, corporate culture, and leadership styles will reflect this.

"2) The federal and state labor laws will be more complicated and compliance will take much more time and energy.

"3) The human resources manager with the strongest interpersonal skills will be the most successful."

FIGURE 16-6 We must keep the unique, fun, exciting spirit alive in the hospitality industry. *(Photo A courtesy of Chili's Grill & Bar, Brinker International; Photo B courtesy of ARAMARK Corporation)*

Pam Farr, ***Senior Vice President, Marriott Lodging for Marriott International Corporation:***

"1) There will be a greater reliance on top human resources thought leaders to rise above the clutter of information spawned by the information age.

"2) Managers and executives will rely more heavily on personal coaches/advisors in all aspects of their lives, including health, fitness, spiritualism, professional effectiveness, and interpersonal relationships to survive the intensity of the world.

"3) 'Cottage industries' will emerge via the Internet, which will revolutionize how human resources services are provided to both large and entrepreneurial companies."

Jeanne Michalski, ***Assistant Vice President of Employee Development, Burlington Northern Santa Fe Railway:***

"1) The need to focus on reducing turnover and ensuring retention of good employees. This is a topic that will require more attention and innovative approaches in the coming years.

"2) Another area that will differentiate successful companies from their less successful competitors is customer/guest services. While this is already an important concept in the hospitality industry, I think those that carry it the furthest will be the most successful.

"3) With the use of the Internet there will be many changes. Employers and employees will need to look for ways to utilize that technology."

Ronald H. Meliker, ***Corporate Vice President Human Resources, Sunbelt Beverage Corporation:***

"1) Tightening labor market of less skilled workers requiring heavier emphasis and cost for training.

"2) More varied and flexible work schedules to meet the demands of fewer available qualified employees.

"3) More internal training for advancement up the organizational ladder."

Kathy Roadarmel, ***Vice President of Human Resources, Opryland Hotels & Attractions:***

"1) Workers will have completely shifted their focus away from 'finding balance' in their work and personal lives and will be more focused on family. They will demand more time-off benefits.

"2) Healthcare costs will have risen so sharply that most large companies will provide on-site medical care to employees and their families as a benefit. This will also serve to reduce insurance costs to employers.

"3) Wages will not be as important as benefits in the year 2010. In order to stay competitive, Human Resources managers will be seeking unique benefit offerings to lure potential employees. The company that offers educational assistance, couriers to run personal errands, housekeeping services, day care, on-site medical care, on-site family fitness facilities, etc., is the company that will have the most recruiting and retention success."

Regynald G. Washington, ***President and CEO, Washington Enterprises:***

"1) As our society becomes more litigious, human resource practices will be carefully designed and managed as to avoid potential litigation.

"2) Organized labor will experience a resurgence that will result in increased growth in organized labor activity across the country.

"3) New and sophisticated union leadership will direct strong financial and manpower resources towards the task of organizing."

Andrew J. Juska, ***Vice President of Operations, Signature Companies:***

"1) Computer technology and the use of web based systems for human resource departments will continue to increase. Employees accessing information through the company Intranet will continue to grow at an accelerated rate.

"2) Virtual Human Resources will become the accepted format for standard human resources functions and tasks.

"3) Computers and the World Wide Web are here to stay. Training employees to use these systems efficiently and effectively will be a major challenge."

ADVICE FROM THE INDUSTRY EXPERTS

The industry advisors were asked to provide you with some additional information. "What is one piece of advice you would give students who are about to graduate and enter the hospitality work force?" Their suggestions follow.

Michael Hurst: ***"Keep going to school even after you graduate.*** Take night courses in an area that relates to your job. The better jobs of tomorrow are going to go to those people who accelerate their growth into the jobs. In addition, you should get known outside of work. It could be church, school, or community service."

Ed Evans: ***"Enjoy what you do—have fun.*** The best way to achieve maximum success is to find a place you want to be—right industry, right company(ies), right job—BE YOURSELF.

"Leadership is not the same as management. Management is about taking care of things at the level they are—leadership is about taking people some place new; Unlike management, which is hierarchical, leadership is about people choosing to FOLLOW.

"Surround yourself with the best people. Nothing happens in this business without people—your only competitive advantage is the right people, with the right skills, tools, and direction, and everybody wants them.

"Never Stop Learning. The only thing that will not change in your lifetime is that everything will change. It will all change at an exponentially quicker pace. As you graduate, your training is complete, hopefully you take with you the desire ***and*** skills to learn."

Jan Barr: "In this crazy, unpredictable industry you chose, be careful to keep it all in perspective. Take being successful seriously, but don't take yourself too seriously. Work incredibly hard when you're at work, but find a balance in your life. That balance is what allows you to stay in this industry for the long run and still love it."

Bob Morrison: "Always make managing and motivating employees your top priority as they are the ones who most frequently deal with your customers, and this interaction will ultimately determine the success and/or failure of your hospitality business." (See Figure 16-7.)

Loret Carbone: ***"Be patient.*** It takes time to learn everything you will need to know to reach your goals. If you feel you are 'stuck,' find a mentor to inspire and guide you. But remember, this isn't a sprint. It's a marathon. And the winners will be the people who pace themselves and relish the little successes along the way."

Pam Farr: ***"Work hard, have fun, and follow your dream."***

Jeanne Michalski: "Take every opportunity to learn as much of your business as possible. You may think that you are interested in hotel management or food service, for example, but

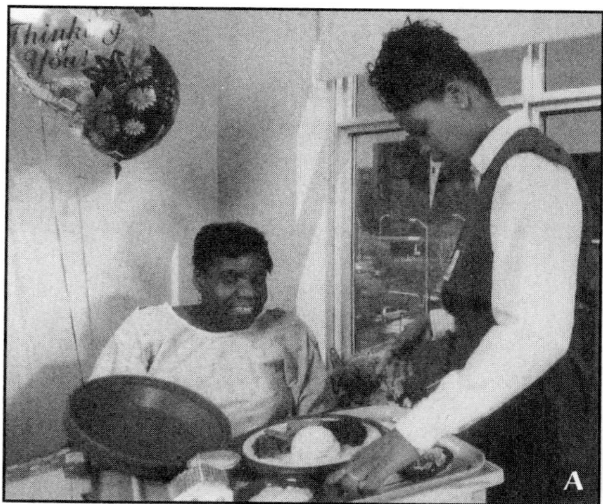

FIGURE 16-7 Understand that your job ***is*** customers. *(Photo A courtesy of ARAMARK Corporation; Photo B courtesy of Chili's Grill & Bar, Brinker International)*

don't let that stop you from learning as much about the total operations as possible. Many people focus their efforts on moving up as rapidly as possible, which often creates an individual who knows one topic well but does not have that breadth of experience that in the long run will lead to a top management position."

Ron Meliker: "The ability to adapt quickly to your organization's shift in strategic direction (which you helped shape) and to stay focused on your organization's goals and objectives and to ensure that your human resources goals and objectives parallel those of your organization."

Kathy Roadarmel: "As you develop benefits and programs to attract and retain employees in a competitive employment arena, remember that the goal is to provide a unique work environment that fosters creativity, recognizes people as individuals, and encourages them to be passionate about their work."

Regynald G. Washington: "It is important to know the difference between a leader and a manager. Managers do things right. Leaders do the right thing. Real leaders focus on guiding not ruling. In most cases, leaders who focus on ruling often find themselves in major conflict as it relates to the perceived interpretation of the negotiated labor agreement. An arrogant, insensitive connotation is associated with ruling."

Andrew J. Juska: "Make sure that you enjoy your work. Set goals. Understand that the companies you work for are in business to make money. Learn how much everything costs—from apples and chicken breasts to pencils and copy paper to light bulbs and mop heads. Learn how to manage your time. Develop interests outside the workplace. Train for and run a marathon."

CONCLUSION

Human resources management continues to assume a larger role in the organizational effectiveness of the hospitality enterprise. We can no longer afford to give lip service to the importance of our people. In "the next chapter" we must act upon our knowledge. Labor is our partner, not our enemy.

Your biggest challenge as you leave the classroom and assume human resources responsibilities will be the severe labor shortage. Each of the human resources functions discussed in this text plays a vital role in either attracting or retaining a motivated work force. We will continue to seek new and innovative approaches to the challenges we face in the management of our human resources. Solutions, instead of theories, will be needed if we are to succeed. It is our sincere hope that this text, with the input and advice of hundreds of years of hospitality experience, will provide you with at least some of those solutions. Despite the challenges, the rewards prevail!

"If you can dream it, you can do it."
—WALT DISNEY

Recommended Reading

Kemske, F. 1998. "HR 2008: A Forecast Based on Our Exclusive Study." *Workforce* 77(1): 46–60.

Laabs, J. 1996. "Charting the Top Ten Concerns of Today and Tomorrow." *Workforce* 75(1): 28–37.

Micco, L. "Workforce 2020 Requires Diversity, Increased Flexibility." *HR News Online.* 1997. www.shrm.org/hrnews/articles/042097a.htm (4 October 1998).

National Restaurant Association. *1999 Restaurant Industry Forecast Operational Trends.* www.restaurant.org/research/forecast/fc99-07.htm (7 May 1999).

Endnotes

1. Joan Frazee and Janet Harrington-Kuller, "Money Matters: Selling HRIS to Management," *Personnel Journal* 66, no. 8 (1987): 98–107.
2. Unknown, "The Foodservice Manager in the Year 2000," *Restaurants USA* 12, no. 2 (1992): 36–37.
3. Charles A. Myers, "New Frontiers for Personnel Management," *Personnel* 41, no. 3 (1964): 31–38.
4. E. Wright Bakke, "The Human Resources Function," in Bakke, E. Wright, Clark Kerr, and Charles W. Anrod (eds.), *Unions, Management, and the Public* (New York: Harcourt, Brace and World, Inc. (1960), p. 198.
5. Edward A. Tomeski and Harold Lazarus, "The Computer and the Personnel Department," *Business Horizons* 16, no. 3 (1973): 62.
6. Brenda Paik Sunoo, "Papa John's Rolls Out Hot HR Menu," *Personnel Journal* 74, no. 9 (1995): 38–47.
7. Floyd Kemske, "10 Predictions for the Strategic Role of HR," *Workforce* 77, no. 1 (1998): 46–60.

Index

D

E

F

G

H

I